The Global
#MeToo Movement

The Global
#MeToo Movement

Editors

Ann M. Noel
David B. Oppenheimer

Berkeley Center on Comparative Equality and
Anti-Discrimination Law

Cover design by Morgan Morrissette Wright and Sharon D. Ray

A Full Court Press, Fastcase, Inc., Publication.

Printed and bound in the United States of America.

10 9 8 7 6 5 4 3 2 1

ISBN (print): 978-1-949884-39-5
ISBN (online): 978-1-949884-38-8

While women (and men) have been sexually harassed from time immemorial, it wasn't until the 1970s that feminist legal activist scholars gave it a name and a legal theory, and not until 2006 that Tarana Burke gave the movement to express solidarity among survivors in the United States a hashtag—#MeToo. Meanwhile, across the globe, women have found solidarity in joining together to speak out against harassment and violence. In honor of Burke, and all those who have joined in speaking out, we dedicate this book to their activism and vision.

Contents

EUROPE

MIDDLE EAST/ASIA/OCEANIA

AFRICA

INTERNATIONAL LAW

INTERSECTIONAL ISSUES OF CLASS, GENDER, DISABILITY, AND CASTE

TECHNIQUES TO COMBAT HARASSMENT: A CRITICAL REVIEW

Acknowledgments

Our profound thanks, first, to Catharine MacKinnon, our visionary, who gave us a name and a legal claim for sexual harassment. Thanks to all our authors who wrote these brilliant chapters. Heartfelt thanks to Berkeley School of Law Dean Erwin Chemerinsky, who enthusiastically endorsed our ideas for a Berkeley conference on sexual harassment law back in fall 2017, and has supported the work of the Berkeley Center for Comparative Equality and Anti-Discrimination Law, to make our #MeToo conferences and this book a reality. Thanks to our French sisters at Foundation des Femmes for their generous support of this book project. Our gratitude and thanks to the Berkeley Center's incredible staff and interns, who all brought their talents and creativity to make this book work: Caroline Cheng, keeping the Center's many projects, including this one, going efficiently; Lily Yang, Claudia Alvarenga, Sara Imam, Jenny Jian Jang, and Charlie Tsunoda, who helped organize our two conferences leading to the book project; Nicole Mendoza, for her research and archiving; Talia Harris, who transcribed Saru Jayaraman's talk, kept track of documents and video editing; Nicole Khoury for creating a website for the book; Subaita Rahman, for social media marketing and video editing; and Sarah Gallo, for her terrific copy editing. Thanks also to Allison Mages, for her copy editing, especially impressive with chapters with foreign language complications. Our appreciation to our publisher Full Court Press, who shared our vision on making this book affordable for all, and were true partners in this process, giving us the talented copy editor Susan Jenkins, the marketing expertise of Hannah Holmes, the designer pro Sharon Ray, and the full backing and involvement of publishers Morgan Morrissette Wright and Steve Errick. Thanks to the Center's Co-Director for its Sexual Harassment/Violence Working Group, Amy Oppenheimer, a constant supporter of this book and a wonderful font of commonsense ideas and solutions. Our loving gratitude to our partners Izzy and Marcy, and our family and friends, who supported us throughout this process. And finally, we thank the courageous women (and men) around the world who stood up and said, #MeToo.

Contributing to the Global #MeToo Movement

Ann M. Noel[1]

In 2006, Tarana Burke, an African American activist working with victims of sexual harassment and assault, coined the phrase "MeToo" on social media to raise awareness of the pervasiveness of sexual abuse and assault in society.[2] In October 2017, after the *New York Times*[3] and *The New Yorker*[4] broke their stories about multiple accusations of sexual assault by Hollywood producer Harvey Weinstein, the actress Alyssa Milano encouraged women on Twitter to say "#MeToo"[5] if they too had experienced sexual harassment or assault.[6]

---

1. Co-Director, Sexual Harassment/Violence Working Group, Berkeley Center on Comparative Equality and Anti-Discrimination Law, former General Counsel, California Fair Employment and Housing Commission.

2. *#MeToo: A timeline of events*, CHI. TRIBUNE, Dec. 6, 2019, https://www.chicago tribune.com/lifestyles/ct-me-too-timeline-20171208-htmlstory.html; https://www.chicago tribune.com/lifestyles/ct-me-too-timeline-20171208-htmlstory.html; Sandra E. Garcia, *The Woman Who Created #MeToo Long Before Hashtags*, N.Y. TIMES, Oct. 20, 2017, https://www .nytimes.com/2017/10/20/us/me-too-movement-tarana-burke.html.

3. Jodi Kantor and Megan Twohey, *Harvey Weinstein Paid Off Sexual Harassment Accusers for Decades*, N.Y. TIMES, Oct. 5, 2017, https://www.nytimes.com/2017/10/05/us/ harvey-weinstein-harassment-allegations.html.

4. Ronan Farrow, *From Aggressive Overtures to Sexual Assault: Harvey Weinstein's Accusers Tell Their Stories*, NEW YORKER, Oct. 10, 2017, https://www.newyorker.com/news/news -desk/from-aggressive-overtures-to-sexual-assault-harvey-weinsteins-accusers-tell-their -stories?verso=true.

5. #MeToo, TWITTER, https://twitter.com/hashtag/metoo.

6. Samantha Smith, *#MeToo: Harvey Weinstein case moves thousands to tell their own stories of abuse, break silence*, WASH. POST, Oct. 16, 2017, https://www.washingtonpost.com /news/morning-mix/wp/2017/10/16/me-too-alyssa-milano-urged-assault-victims-to-tweet-in -solidarity-the-response-was-massive/.

If the phrase in 2006 had limited reach beyond Burke's 500 social media followers,[7] by 2017, with the widespread coverage of the Weinstein scandal, and widespread usage of social media worldwide, the hashtag went viral with 12 million posts, both in the United States and internationally.[8]

In many instances, the movement was producing remarkable changes in how accusations of sexual harassment were perceived and handled by employers, the news media, and society. For the first time, powerful men—producers, directors, news anchors, coaches, and employers—were losing their jobs because of their harassment of persons (usually, but not always, women) over whom they had wielded power.[9] As Catharine MacKinnon pointed out, "#MeToo was accomplishing changes that the law so far had not. Sexually assaulted women were being believed and valued who had been disbelieved and denigrated."[10]

The Berkeley Center on Comparative Equality and Anti-Discrimination Law ("Center") Proposes a Book on the Global #MeToo Movement

In October 2017, I was working with my co-editor, Berkeley Law Professor David Oppenheimer, on projects with the Berkeley Center on Comparative Equality and Anti-Discrimination Law, which David had founded in 2011. We were discussing what topics to feature at a conference for the next spring and we were both mesmerized, and more than a little obsessed, with the developments around sexual harassment. David started his career prosecuting, among other workplace misconduct, sexual harassment cases for California's Department of Fair Employment and Housing. I started mine at the California Fair Employment and Housing Commission working with legislators to write good state laws to hold to account sexual harassers and their employers, writing regulations to interpret those laws, and adjudicating as an administrative law judge sexual harassment cases that lawyers like David prosecuted before me.

---

7. Emma Brockes, *#MeToo founder Tarana Burke: "You have to use your privilege to serve other people,"* THE GUARDIAN, Jan. 15, 2018, https://www.theguardian.com/world/2018/jan/15/me-too-founder-tarana-burke-women-sexual-assault.

8. Garcia, *supra*, note 2.

9. Audrey Carlsen et al., *#MeToo Brought Down 201 Powerful Men. Nearly Half of Their Replacements Are Women,* N.Y. TIMES, Oct. 29, 2018, https://www.nytimes.com/interactive/2018/10/23/us/metoo-replacements.html.

10. Catharine MacKinnon, in *"This Moment Turned Out to Be Fleeting,"* N.Y. TIMES, Oct. 6, 2018, https://www.nytimes.com/2018/10/06/opinion/me-too-weinstein-one-year.html.

Work with the Center gave us a unique international vantage point to examine the problem of sexual harassment. The Center brings together legal scholars, activists, NGO workers, government anti-discrimination agency lawyers and officials, and legal practitioners from six continents to address the problems of systemic inequality and discrimination. Our principal mission is to expand our understanding of inequality and discrimination through the tools of comparative legal studies and to transfer that knowledge from those who study inequality to those who enforce anti-discrimination law (and vice versa).

Although we are a scholarly center, our objective is not simply to study the problem of inequality and discrimination, but to help activists/advocates use the work being done by scholars to bring positive change globally. And the #MeToo movement presented a challenge, a rebuke, and an opportunity for us to acknowledge how current laws had helped but also hindered sexual harassment victims, and to join with activists worldwide to advocate for necessary changes in the law to support victims and to promote gender equality.

Inspired by #MeToo, we formed our Sexual Harassment/Violence Working Group in the fall of 2017 to examine how the global #MeToo movement was affecting the legal and social movements against sexual harassment and violence. I co-direct this Working Group along with California practitioner Amy Oppenheimer,[11] who has pioneered professional standards for workplace investigations of harassment allegations. I had served as the former general counsel of California's Fair Employment and Housing Commission. Priding itself as the national leader in development of progressive laws on sexual harassment, the Commission worked with the California legislature to pass innovative laws over the past 30 years, to hold employers and sexual harassers accountable for harassment, and to support harassment victims. Yet with the revelations exploding about widespread sexual harassment affecting women worldwide, including California, it was clear that a complete rethinking about the problem was in order.

Responding to the MeToo movement, the Center held two conferences, in May 2018 and 2019, with thought leaders from universities, industry, NGOs, and government, and with participants from Africa, Asia, Australia, Europe, and North and South America. Our discussions focused on how the worldwide #MeToo movement was changing the public discussion of sexual harassment on every continent. After a series of fascinating reports about the progress the movement has driven, as well as the backlash against women reporting sexual harassment and violence, we decided to write this book on the global impact of

---

11. Amy is also David's sister. They grew up together in the Civil Rights movement, inspired by the civil rights lawyers of the 1960s, and their parents' activism.

the movement, utilizing many of our conference participants and Center members as our authors.

Assessing This Moment

For the 48 authors of this book—equality scholars, legal practitioners, and activists—the #MeToo movement was a moment of great reckoning. Many of the authors had written books, law review articles, and their PhD theses on the subject, had worked with their legislative bodies to pass laws about harassment, had litigated sexual harassment cases, and had supported activists and victims fighting harassment. Yet as Catharine MacKinnon, who coined the term "sexual harassment" and pioneered its legal claim, has noted, "#MeToo is cultural, driven principally by forces other than litigation, and is surpassing law in changing norms and providing relief for human rights violations that the law did not—in some ways in current form could not, although law is embedded in culture and can and will change with it."[12] The challenge now is to assess honestly where we've been and where we are now at this important moment in the struggle for gender equality. What has the #MeToo movement taught us, what has worked, what has not, and how can we support what needs to come next?

Catharine MacKinnon writes in our first chapter, "We are in the middle of the first mass movement against sexual abuse in the history of the world. Global #MeToo sprung from the law of sexual harassment, quickly overtook it, and is shifting law, cultures, and politics everywhere."[13]

#MeToo Everywhere—Country Chapters

We asked our extensive network of Center members to write chapters about the MeToo movements in their countries; 36 agreed to do so, writing about 27 countries. We have chapters covering the #MeToo movements in North and South America, Europe, the Middle East, Africa, Asia, and Australia.[14]

---

12. Catharine A. MacKinnon, *Global #MeToo, infra*, chapter 1.

13. *Ibid.*

14. Our coverage of the world's #MeToo movements is extensive, but certainly not encyclopedic. We have only two reports from African countries, Nigeria and South Africa, reflecting our limited contacts there at the time we recruited authors for the book. This is changing. We will hold our 2021 annual conference in Cape Town, South Africa, and we are working with the Africa-based End Sexual Harassment in Africa initiative to create model anti-harassment laws for equality advocates to use to change African countries' laws on harassment.

Our authors describe the state of equality in their country when the #MeToo movement began and describe how the movement has had an impact in their country. They describe their country's laws regarding sexual harassment (if any) and other laws protecting women against rape, sexual assault, and domestic violence. They describe the reality of the situation: whether these laws are enforced, what barriers there are to people filing complaints of harassment in the workplace or with law enforcement. They address any changes in their country stemming from #MeToo—changes in the law, in activism, in accusers being believed. Finally, they discuss what needs to be done going forward.

For many country chapter authors, their first reaction was to note that the struggle against sexual and other forms of harassment long preceded the #MeToo movement and focusing the story solely around #MeToo was a very U.S.-centric orientation, ignoring struggles for gender equality in all of their individual, country-specific iterations. What the #MeToo movement allowed in the age of social media, however, was for women to be able to share their stories with each other, often anonymously, and through that sharing realize that they were not alone—that on the contrary, the problem is global, and it is enormous.

The United Nations and International Law

Woven through many chapters' stories is how their countries' laws and practices conform to or deviate from international standards of equality, set by United Nations covenants and treaties. We have included a chapter on international United Nations treaties covering harassment, written by Purna Sen, the UN's Executive Coordinator and Spokesperson on Addressing Sexual Harassment and Other Forms of Discrimination.

Intersectionality

In addition to the country chapters, we address and discuss how intersectionality affects the different ways individuals experience harassment. "Intersectionality" is a term coined by University of California, Los Angeles law professor Kimberlé Crenshaw to examine how the interconnected nature of social categorizations such as race, class, and gender, which apply to a given individual or group, create overlapping and interdependent systems of discrimination or disadvantage.[15] So, for example, a woman may be targeted for harassment

---

15. Kimberlé Crenshaw, *Demarginalizing the Intersection of Race and Sex: A Black Feminist Critique of Antidiscrimination Doctrine, Feminist Theory and Antiracist Politics*, 1 U. CHIC. LEGAL F., art. 8 (1989), http://chicagounbound.uchicago.edu/uclf/vol1989/iss1/8.

because of her perceived or real vulnerabilities due to disability, caste, or religion in addition to her sex. She may be more likely to be believed or disbelieved because of her race or class. Her economic situation, for example being dependent on tips from male customers to survive, may make her especially vulnerable to sexual harassment. She may be unable to complain about the harassment due to her disability, gender identity, or sexual orientation. The book has chapters discussing intersectional issues with class, sexual orientation and gender, disability, caste, and race, with race discussed at length in the Brazil country chapter.

Techniques to Combat Harassment

MacKinnon writes: "In law, many crucial issues are being newly discussed, fresh and creative solutions proposed. These include consideration of the role and content of nondisclosure agreements, independence of investigation and adjudication, equitability in procedures at all stages, elimination of criminal law standards from civil and administrative adjudications, and—radiating out—equal hiring, equal numbers of women on boards, equal pay and many more women in politics. Anyone who doubted that sexual abuse was central to the second-class status of women might consider what taking it seriously for once on a systemic basis has set off. Outcomes in these cases, with many others, will provide some measures of the distance traveled and the distance yet to go."[16]

Our country chapter authors write about many of these subjects as they have developed in their own countries,[17] but they are discussed in depth in chapters on anti-harassment training and symbolic compliance, corporate governance, non-disclosure agreements, and effective workplace investigations.

Changing the Law on Defamation

At our 2019 conference on sexual harassment, a major topic of conversation for many international presenters was the way that their countries' strong laws on defamation were squelching any movement by women to come forward, except anonymously, to report harassment, for fear of being sued for defamation. This is a major problem worldwide except in the United States, thanks to a

---

16.   MacKinnon, *supra* note 12.

17.   See, for example, *Silent Women? Non-Disclosure Agreements and the #MeToo Movement in the United Kingdom*, Aileen McColgan's discussion of the role of non-disclosure agreements in the United Kingdom, chapter 12.

landmark U.S. Supreme Court case, *New York Times v. Sullivan*.[18] That decision, and the 1960s civil rights struggle that generated it, are discussed in our last chapter, by co-editor David Oppenheimer.

Common Themes

Although each country discussed in this book tells its own story of triumphs and challenges, common themes emerged across the globe. Harassment is pervasive everywhere. Good laws promoting equality, including international conventions and protocols, can make a positive difference to establish normative standards, but good laws are not enough. They must be enforced, and that takes cultural shifts that #MeToo is helping engender. The problem identified all over the world is that these triumphs that we celebrate—a Hollywood producer finally held to account, a prominent television anchor fired for sexual assault, a ride share app CEO removed from the company that he founded—have all benefited women with the luxury to complain and to seek redress. Denise Abade, the author of our chapter on Brazil, has described the problem and the challenge for #MeToo in her country, but she could have been describing any country, anywhere:

> We have to recognize that in Brazil empowerment against sexual harassment is a privilege of a minority armed with information, aware of their rights, who discovered how to arm themselves and know that they will have protection if they do not accept this type of violence. The question is how to get to the other end—where the most vulnerable, with less schooling, with little perception of the social role of women, those without access to the necessary channels to protect themselves. Those who are afraid of being judged, harassed, losing their job or reputation: the vast majority of Brazilians. It is promising what we see happening, but it gives us the misperception that change in society's behavior has come for all. It has not. There is still a gulf between the awareness of the minority and the reconstruction necessary to change the course of history.[19]

This is our challenge. We must share what has worked with each other— laws, social media campaigns, support for lawsuits, organizing tactics—and what has failed—inadequate or no laws, social media attacks, censorship and

---

18. New York Times Co. v. Sullivan [1964] 376 U.S, 254 (United States).
19. *Brazilian Sexual Harassment Law and the #MeToo Movement, infra*, chapter 7.

lies by governments and powerful interests, bigoted judges and indifferent law enforcement, and no access to justice. We hope that this book contributes to the conversation, and to meaningful solutions.

The Berkeley Center on Comparative Equality and Anti-Discrimination Law

The Berkeley Center on Comparative Equality and Anti-Discrimination Law brings together over 500 scholars, advocates and activists (including NGO workers, government anti-discrimination agency lawyers and officials, PhD candidates and other graduate students, and legal practitioners) from six continents, to address the problems of systemic inequality and discrimination. Our principal mission is to expand our understanding of inequality and discrimination and to transfer that knowledge between those who study inequality to those who enforce anti-discrimination law. Our objective is not simply to study the problems of inequality and discrimination, but to help meaningfully address inequality and discrimination globally.

To better understand world-wide comparative inequality, we:

- Convene Working Groups to address specific problems where we see opportunities for scholars and activists to work together, including sexual harassment and violence, disability rights, pay equity, and the equality rights of climate migrants/refugees;
- Hold small conferences of leading thinkers in advocacy, leadership, and scholarship to address inequality issues;
- Convene video-conference scholarly workshops, at which emerging scholars (including PhD candidates and early career academic instructors) present works in progress to experienced scholars from around the globe;
- Hold an annual scholarly conference at which emerging, experienced and senior scholars from six continents meet to present and discuss new work;
- Publish an electronic journal where abstracts of scholarly work by our members and other scholars are distributed to a broad community of academics, practitioners, and activists;
- Publish books on comparative equality and anti-discrimination law and circulate information about our members' new books in the field;

- Bring visiting scholars to Berkeley Law to conduct research and present their work; and
- Cooperate and partner with research centers and NGOs from around the globe.

Our Working Groups combine scholars, advocates, students, activists/practitioners, and industry leaders from around the globe, and meet regularly through video-conferencing, regional meetings, and international meetings. The object of the Working Groups is to move beyond an academic understanding of inequality and discrimination to articulate and disseminate practices that will have a meaningful impact. Although the groups operate in different "silos," they cross-pollinate their work, as many of the most serious problems in inequality law are intersectional.

Since its formation in 2017, our Sexual Harassment/Violence Working Group has sponsored three conferences in May 2018, May 2019, and February 2020 on sexual harassment and the worldwide #MeToo movement; our members have authored this book; and we are now working with UN Women and a consortium of African scholar/activists on model legislation on sexual harassment.

About Our Authors

Denise Neves Abade is a Brazilian Senior Federal Prosecutor since 1996 and also a Law Professor at Mackenzie Law University Law School, São Paulo, Brazil. She has a PhD in Constitutional and Procedural Law at Valladolid University, Spain, and a Master's degree in Procedural Law at the University of São Paulo, Brazil. She is the President of the Committee for Equality of Gender and Race/Southeast Region at the Federal Prosecution Service. Her entire career, she has focused on inequality and its impact on the integrity of the rule of law: her academic career on fundamental rights in proceedings and, as a Prosecutor, on gender equality, defense of the environment and international judicial cooperation. In Brazil, Prosecutors act not only in criminal proceedings, but also take action required to guarantee diffuse and collective rights.

Zuzana Andreska is a gender studies graduate and law student at the Charles University in Prague, Czech Republic. She has worked for the Department of Gender Equality of the Office of the Czech Government and currently works as a research assistant to Barbara Havelková doing research on feminist legal theory and a critique of androcentrism.

Shreya Atrey is an Associate Professor in International Human Rights Law at the Department for Continuing Education and the Faculty of Law, based at the Bonavero Human Rights Institute at the University of Oxford. Her research is on discrimination law, feminist theory, poverty and disability law. Her monograph, *Intersectional Discrimination* (OUP 2019), presents an account of intersectionality theory in comparative discrimination law. Previously, she was based at the University of Bristol Law School where she taught on Constitutional Rights, Public Law and International Human Rights Law courses. She has been a Max Weber Fellow at the European University Institute, Florence and a Hauser Postdoctoral Global Fellow at the NYU School of Law, New York. She completed BCL with distinction and DPhil in Law on the Rhodes Scholarship from Magdalen College, University of Oxford. She has served as the Chairperson of the Oxford Pro Bono Publico and is currently an associate member of the Oxford Human Rights Hub. Atrey is an Official Fellow of Kellogg College.

Zulaikha Aziz is a human rights attorney and international development specialist, focusing on rule of law, legal empowerment, women's rights and gender equality. She has more than 15 years of experience working in Asia, the Middle East and North Africa, Eastern Europe and the Americas on legal and economic initiatives to improve the lives and livelihoods of women and men around the world. Her work and scholarship focus specifically on the empowerment of the world's most vulnerable communities. She has worked with institutions including the UNDP, UN Women, the World Bank, and USAID as well as local NGOs and civil society organizations. Most recently, she served as the rule of law specialist for The Asia Foundation in Kabul, Afghanistan. Zulaikha has a B.A. in Economics from McGill University, a M.Sc. in International Development Studies from The London School of Economics and Political Science and a J.D. from the University of California, Berkeley School of law.

Ivana Bacik is a barrister and Reid Professor of Criminal Law, Criminology and Penology at Trinity College Dublin. She is a Senator in the Irish Parliament (Oireachtas) for Dublin University (elected 2007, re-elected 2011 and again 2016). Her research interests include feminist theory of law and equality law. She co-authored a major national study on gender in the legal professions (Bacik, Costello and Drew, Gender InJustice, 2003); her other publications include Legal Cases that Changed Ireland (co-edited with Mary Rogan, Clarus Press, 2016). She chaired the Oireachtas 'Vótáil100' Committee program in 2018 to mark the centenary of women's suffrage in Ireland, and co-chairs the Trinity College Law School Athena SWAN gender equality benchmarking application process.

Kadriye Bakirci is a Professor of Employment/Labour and Social Security Law at Hacettepe University, Ankara, Turkey. She completed her LLB, LLM, and PhD degrees at Istanbul University Faculty of Law. She attended the Institute of Advanced Legal Studies (London), the London School of Economics and Political Science (Law Department); Cambridge, Stockholm, Columbia Law Faculties; Lund University Business Law Department and the International Labour Organisation (Geneva) as a visiting scholar/fellow. She is the member of several international and national legal organizations and various non-governmental human and women's rights groups. She is the national expert for Turkey of the European Labour Law Network (ELLN); the national expert for Turkey of the European Network of Legal Experts in Gender Equality and Non-Discrimination (EELN); and a member of the Violence Against Women Europe Group. She has written eleven books and various national and international articles published. Her publications have been influential for law reform.

Daphne Barak-Erez is a Justice of the Supreme Court of Israel since 2012. Before her appointment to the court, Justice Barak-Erez was the Dean of the Faculty of Law at Tel-Aviv University and the Stewart and Judy Colton Professor in Law and Security. She also served as the Director of the Minerva Center for Human Rights and the Director of the Cegla Center for Interdisciplinary Research of Law at Tel Aviv University. She holds a JSD, LL.M, and LL. B. from Tel Aviv University. Justice Barak-Erez has taught as Visiting Professor at various universities, including the University of Toronto, Columbia Law School and Stanford Law School. She also has held various public positions, including as the chairperson of the Israeli Association of Public Law, a member of the Council of Higher Education in Israel, and the President of the Israeli Law and Society Association. She was awarded several prizes, including the Rector's Prize for Excellence in Teaching (three times), the Zeltner Prize, the Heshin Prize, the Woman of the City Award (by the City of Tel-Aviv) and the Women in Law Award (by the Israeli Bar). She is the author and editor of several books and of many articles in Israel, England, Canada and the United States.

Estefania Vela Barba is co-founder and Executive Director of Intersecta, a policy research and advocacy organization committed to ending gender discrimination in Mexico. She has a B.A. in Law from ITAM and an LL.M. from Yale Law School, where she is also developing her J.S.D. dissertation. She has published in English and in Spanish on issues related to gender, sexuality, reproduction, and the law, including a book on employment discrimination in Mexico. She's been invited to contribute in a variety of media, including *The New York Times* en Español, *The Washington Post*, and *Vice México*.

Nasrina Bargzie is an Afghan American attorney specializing in complex commercial litigation, national security, international human rights, and governance. She is a 2005 graduate of University California Berkeley School of Law. Bargzie was a law clerk at the Ninth Circuit Court of Appeals for Judge William Fletcher, a fellow at the national American Civil Liberties Union working on post-911 torture and speech issues, directed the National Security and Civil Rights Program at the Asian Law Caucus organizing and bringing litigation on behalf of Arab Middle Eastern Muslim and South Asian communities, was counsel for Fortune 500 companies at Boies Schiller and Flexner LLP, taught Global Litigation at Stanford University School of Law, and has worked on voting rights, war crimes and gender issues in Afghanistan.

Emmanuelle Bribosia is Professor of Law and Vice-President of the Institute for European Studies (Université Libre de Bruxelles, Belgium). Her research activities focus on international and European human rights protection as well as on the right to equality and non-discrimination, with an emphasis on the interdisciplinary approach of these research themes (more details on her web-page: http://cde.ulb.be/member/prof-emmanuelle-bribosia/). As the senior member of the European Network of Legal Experts in the Non-Discrimination Field and the governing board of the Berkeley Center on Comparative and Anti-Discrimination Law, Professor Bribosia pursues many of her research projects in an international setting. In 2014, she launched, jointly with professor Isabelle Rorive, the Equality Law Clinic (http://equalitylawclinic.ulb.be).

Marie Mercat-Bruns is an Affiliated Professor at Sciences Po Law School, a member of the Gender Program Presage. She is also a tenured Associate Law Professor at the Conservatoire National des Arts et Métiers, she copilots the Gender Program (LISE, CNRS) and the Master in Business Law. She was appointed in 2019 as an expert on gender equality in France for the EU Commission. She holds an LLM (University of Pennsylvania Law School) and a prize-winning comparative PhD on Law and Aging (University of Paris West Nanterre). She contributed to a report in 2018 for the Ministry of Justice to prepare the 2019 reform of guardianship law. Her publications include: *Systemic discrimination: rethinking the tools of gender equality*, EUROPEAN EQUALITY LAW REVIEW 2018/2, p. 1, and books: with D. OPPENHEIMER and C. SARTORIUS, ENFORCEMENT AND EFFECTIVENESS OF ANTIDISCRIMINATION LAW (Springer 2018); and DISCRIMINATION AT WORK: COMPARING EUROPEAN, FRENCH, AND AMERICAN LAW (UC Press, 2016).

Lucy-Ann Buckley is a Senior Lecturer in Law at the National University of Ireland Galway, where she is also affiliated with the Centre for Disability Law and Policy. She originally studied law at University College Cork, and later at the University of Oxford and Trinity College Dublin, where she obtained her PhD. Dr Buckley specializes in equality law and social justice. She has published widely regarding gender equality issues in family and labor law, including intersectional discrimination on the grounds of gender and disability in employment. She is also actively engaged in international policy development on equality matters, most recently in the States of Guernsey (Channel Islands), where she is an expert advisor on the development of a new anti-discrimination law on gender, disability and other grounds.

Laura Carlson is a professor of private law at Stockholm University. Carlson specializes in employment and labor law, gender, discrimination, academic freedom and critical legal theories. She has been the 2014/2015 Stockholm Centre Oxford Fellow, Faculty of Law, University of Oxford, and has received a Juris doctor from Stockholm University (2007), a Master of Laws from Uppsala University (2000), a Juris Doctor from University of Minnesota (1991) and a Bachelor of Arts, History from Carleton College (1983). Carlson is the Editor-in-Chief, Brill Research Perspectives in Comparative Discrimination Law and a board member of the Berkeley Center on Comparative Equality & Anti-Discrimination Law. Carlson's books include THE FUNDAMENTALS OF SWEDISH LAW (2019), WORKERS, COLLECTIVISM AND THE LAW: GRAPPLING WITH DEMOCRACY (2018), COMPARATIVE DISCRIMINATION LAW: HISTORICAL AND THEORETICAL FRAMEWORKS, Brill (2017) and SEARCHING FOR EQUALITY: SEX DISCRIMINATION, PARENTAL LEAVE AND THE SWEDISH MODEL WITH COMPARISONS TO EU, UK AND US LAW (2007).

Yukyong Choe is a Senior Research Fellow at the Korea Legislation Research Institute and Adjunct Professor at Ewha Womans University. After receiving both her LLM and JSD from U.C. Berkeley Law in 2011, Choe has taught Constitutional Law and Law and Society at Seoul National University and Yonsei Law School. She has done research and written about multi-culturalism, citizenship policy and legal reform, and her most recent research covers judicial politics, human rights focusing on gender equality, legislative evaluation and regulatory innovation under new technology. Choe won a Vice Prime Minister Prize in 2019 for her government research. From 2014-2015, she worked for the Judicial Policy Research Institute as a Senior Research Fellow.

Jessica Clarke is a Professor of Law and the Co-Director of the George Barrett Social Justice Program at Vanderbilt Law School in Nashville, Tennessee. Her research focuses on American equality law. Her work has been published in the Harvard Law Review, Yale Law Journal, and California Law Review, among other journals. After graduating from Yale Law School, Professor Clarke was a law clerk for Judge Shira Scheindlin of the U.S. District Court for the Southern District of New York and Judge Rosemary Pooler of the U.S. Court of Appeals for the Second Circuit. From 2009 to 2011, she taught at Columbia Law School in New York City as an associate-in-law, and from 2011 to 2018, she was an associate professor at the University of Minnesota Law School, in Minneapolis, Minnesota.

Debbie Collier is Head of Department and Associate Professor in the Department of Commercial Law at the University of Cape Town. She is involved in teaching and research supervision relating to various aspects of commercial and employment law. Her research interests are in the field of employment law and development, increasingly in the context of workplace discrimination and equality law. Debbie has published numerous articles and book chapters and is involved with the International Labour Organisation (ILO) on several labor law projects in the Southern African Development Community–SADC region."

Peter Dunne is a Senior Lecturer at the University of Bristol and an Associate Member of Garden Court Chambers. He is the Senior Expert for Sexual Orientation with the European Equality Law Network. From 2017-2018, Dr. Dunne undertook EU-funded research on trans and intersex non-discrimination protections in Europe. He regularly works with the European Commission and the UK government on LGBT+ rights, and his work has been cited by, among others, the English High Court, German Federal Court and Hong Kong Inter-Departmental Working Group on Gender Recognition. In 2015, Dr Dunne was an expert to the UK Parliamentary Inquiry on Transgender Equality, and he co-organized the first National Trans Youth Forum in Ireland. He holds degrees from Harvard Law School and the University of Cambridge.

Lauren B. Edelman is Agnes Roddy Robb Professor of Law and Professor of Sociology at the University of California, Berkeley. She previously taught at the University of Wisconsin Madison and has held fellowships at the Center for Advanced Studies in the Behavioral Sciences at Stanford and the Rockefeller Foundation Center in Bellagio, Italy as well as a Guggenheim Fellowship. Her research is on law and organizations, law and inequality, workplace discrimination and harassment, symbolic compliance, disputing and rights mobilization, empirical critical race theory, and most recently, disabilities in the workplace. Her recent book, WORKING LAW: COURTS, CORPORATIONS AND SYMBOLIC CIVIL RIGHTS (University of Chicago Press), won the 2018 Distinguished Scholarly Book Award from the American Sociological Association and the 2017 George R. Terry Book Award from the Academy of Management. She also recently received the Kalven Award for research in law and society.

Catherine L. Fisk is the Barbara Nachtrieb Armstrong Professor of Law at the University of California, Berkeley. She teaches courses on labor law, employment and employment discrimination law, civil procedure, and the legal profession. Professor Fisk is the author of scores of articles and half a dozen books on labor and employment law, legal history, and the legal profession.

Barbara Havelková is a Law Fellow at St Hilda's College and an Associate Professor at the Faculty of Law, University of Oxford. She holds degrees from Charles University in Prague (Mgr.—Master in Law; summa cum laude), Europa-Institut of Saarland University (LLM) and the University of Oxford (Mst in Legal Research, DPhil). Barbara's research and teaching interests include gender legal studies and feminist jurisprudence, equality and anti-discrimination law, constitutional law, EU law and law in post-socialist transitions. Her book, GENDER EQUALITY IN LAW: UNCOVERING THE LEGACIES OF CZECH STATE SOCIALISM, was published by Hart/Bloomsbury in 2017, and a volume on ANTI-DISCRIMINATION LAW IN CIVIL LAW JURISDICTIONS, she co-authored and co-edited, came out in 2019 with Oxford University Press.

Costanza Hermanin is Visiting Professor at the Department of Political Science and International Affairs of John Cabot University in Rome. She has been teaching for over ten years in universities across Europe: Sciences-Po Paris, the College of Europe in Bruges, and LUISS Rome. Professor Hermanin got her Ph.D. from the European University Institute in Florence and was awarded a Fulbright Postdoc Scholarship that she spent partly at Columbia Law School and partly at U.C. Berkeley. She has edited FIGHTING DISCRIMINATION IN EUROPE (Routledge, 2012) and is among the founding members of Berkeley's Center for Comparative Equality and Anti-Discrimination Law. Her research focuses on the European Union's decision-making and policy in the areas of justice and home affairs, on migration, gender politics and equality law. She worked in the cabinet of Italy's Minister of Justice (2016-2018). Previously, she was a Senior Analyst for the Open Society Foundation in Brussels.

Kazuko Ito is a Tokyo human rights lawyer and the Secretary General of Human Rights Now, a Tokyo-based human rights NGO with ECOSOC (UN Economic and Social Council) consultative status. Since 1994, Ito has worked as a practicing lawyer on various human rights issues including women's rights. As a visiting scholar at NYU School of Law in 2004-2005, she researched the comparative study of criminal justice systems as well as international human rights law. Since 2006, as the Secretary General of Human Rights Now, she has led various human rights campaigns in Japan and Asia, including on racial discrimination, sex trafficking, the #MeToo movement, and modern slavery in the global supply chain of Japanese industry. Ito served as the chief of the Gender Equality Committee of the Japan Federation of Bar Associations and serves as a board member of the International Human Rights Law Association and the Japan Association of Gender and Law. Her publications include: *Wrongful Convictions and Recent Criminal Justice Reform in Japan,* 80 Cin. L. Rev. 2013, HUMAN RIGHTS, BEYOND THE BORDER (Iwanami Shoten 2014), and WHY WAS HE ACQUITTED? JAPANESE JUSTICE SYSTEM DOES NOT TAKE SERIOUS CONSIDERATION OVER SEXUAL VIOLENCE (Discovery 21, 2019).

Jenny Jian Jang is an intern at the Berkeley Center on Comparative Equality and Anti-Discrimination Law and a fourth-year political science major and human rights minor at the University of California, Berkeley. Her work on this book combines her interest in resistance to inequality and sexual violence with her personal experience with South Korean culture and society. Her additional interests include organizing progressive issue-based campaigns and advocating for immigrant rights.

Saru Jayaraman is the President of One Fair Wage, Co-Founder of the Restaurant Opportunities Centers United (ROC United), and Director of the Food Labor Research Center at the University of California, Berkeley. Jayaraman is a graduate of Yale Law School and the Harvard Kennedy School of Government. She was recognized as a Champion of Change by the White House in 2014 and received a James Beard Foundation Leadership Award in 2015. Saru authored BEHIND THE KITCHEN DOOR (Cornell University Press, 2013), a national bestseller. Her most recent book is FORKED: A NEW STANDARD FOR AMERICAN DINING (Oxford University Press, 2016). She attended the Golden Globes in January 2018 with Amy Poehler as part of the Times Up action to address sexual harassment. In 2019, she was named the *San Francisco Chronicle* Visionary of the Year.

Kalpana Kannabiran, feminist sociologist, legal scholar, and rights advocate, is currently Professor and Director, Council for Social Development, Hyderabad, an ICSSR institute. She was part of the founding faculty of NALSAR University of Law where she taught sociology and law for a decade, 1999-2009, and is co-founder of Asmita Resource Centre for Women set up in 1991, where she has led the legal services and outreach program. Recipient of the Amartya Sen Award for Distinguished Social Scientists 2012 in the field of law, her work has focused on understanding the social foundations of non-discrimination, structural violence, and questions of constitutionalism and social justice in India— with a specific focus on gender, sexual minorities, caste, adivasi/indigenous rights and disability rights.

Puja Kapai is an Associate Professor and Convener of the Women's Studies Research Centre at the Faculty of Law of the University of Hong Kong. Her expertise lies in human rights law, equality and minority rights. Her teaching, research and advocacy focus on the rights of marginalized communities in relation to gender, race, religion, sexuality, citizenship, using an intersectional framework, especially on education, democratic participation, gender- and race-based violence. Her research reports have been presented to the Chief Executive of the HKSAR Administration, Mrs. Carrie Lam and Chief Secretary Matthew Cheung, Hong Kong's Legislative Council and United Nations treaty bodies. Professor Kapai received the International Women of Courage

Hong Kong Award 2015, HKU Faculty of Law's Outstanding Teaching Award 2016, its Knowledge Exchange Award 2017, and the American Chamber of Commerce's Women of Influence Professional Woman of the Year Award 2019, in recognition of her contribution to teaching, research, and the impact of her work in the community.

Ulrike Lembke is Professor for Public Law and Gender Studies at the Humboldt University in Berlin where she teaches Anti-Discrimination Law, Legal Politics and Law-Making, Fundamental & Human Rights, and transdisciplinary Legal Gender Studies. She is co-editor of the first textbook of feminist legal studies in Germany, currently revised for the third edition, and editor of volumes on sexuality and the law as well as on human rights and gender. Her research is on anti-discrimination law, human rights at home, legal theory and socio-legal studies, gender-based violence, reproductive rights, public intimacy, intersectionality, and translating legal discourse. After graduating from Greifswald University, her legal clerkship focused on public law and fundamental rights. She taught at the universities of Hamburg, Marburg, Bielefeld, and Hagen. Her legal activism unfolds, inter alia, as a board member of the German Women Lawyers' Association and the Feminist Law Institute, and as an expert in the European Equality Law Network.

Chloe Leroy studied law in Belgium at the ULB (Université Libre de Bruxelles—Free University of Brussels) and specialized in Gender Studies. She has been involved in the Equality Law Clinic since 2016. In 2019, she was a researcher at the Centre Perelman for Legal Philosophy where she worked on issues related to legal recognition of gender identities, sexual harassment and the rights of trans* people.

Catharine A. MacKinnon is the Elizabeth A. Long Professor of Law at Michigan Law and the James Barr Ames Visiting Professor of Law at Harvard Law School since 2009. She holds a BA from Smith College, a JD from Yale Law School, and a PhD in political science from Yale. She specializes in sex equality issues under international and domestic (including comparative, criminal, and constitutional) law and legal theory. She pioneered the legal claim for sexual harassment and, with Andrea Dworkin, created ordinances recognizing pornography as a civil rights violation and the Swedish/Nordic Model (Equality Model) for abolishing prostitution. Her work with survivors established the first legal recognition of rape as an act of genocide. Professor MacKinnon practices and consults nationally and internationally. She was the first Special Gender Adviser to the Prosecutor of the International Criminal Court (ICC) from 2008 to 2012. Professor MacKinnon's books include Sex Equality (3d ed. 2016), Women's Lives, Men's Laws (2005), Only Words (1993), Feminism Unmodified (1987), Sexual Harassment of Working Women (1979), and Butterfly Politics (2017, 2018). Studies document that Professor MacKinnon is among the most widely cited legal scholars in the English language.

Virginia Marturet, Professor of Law, University of Buenos Aires, is a feminist lawyer, an activist on sexual and reproductive health, women and girls' rights, and a restless fighter for the betterment of human rights in Argentina. She is a graduate of the University of Buenos Aires, Law School, where she specialized in business, non-discrimination law and class actions, communication and social media. Marturet volunteers with NGOs fighting for inclusion, diversity and human rights in different scenarios. She has prepared educational programs about human rights, targeting the information to specific audiences such as national and regional parliamentarians, national judges and judicial officials. She has participated in building territorial networks which assist women and children facing domestic violence. She has participated in the Argentinean #NiUnaMenos movement. Marturet has written and lectured about gender, education and law. She is also a Strategic Marketing Consultant.

Aileen McColgan is a barrister at 11KBW, London and is Professor of Law and Social Justice at the University of Leeds, previously Professor of Human Rights Law and Vice Dean, Academic Staff Affairs at King's College London. She specializes in discrimination/equality, human rights and employment law. She was until 2016 the UK's National Expert on the European Networks of Legal Experts in the Field of Gender Equality and of Experts in the Non-discrimination field and is Honorary Legal Counsel to the International Planned Parenthood Federation. She has published very widely on human rights, discrimination and employment law.

Ruth M. Mestre i Mestre (PhD) teaches legal theory and philosophy of law at the University of Valencia and is part of the European Network of Experts in the field of Gender Equality. With S. Jonhsdotter, Mestre coordinated the report *FGM in Europe: An Analysis of Court Cases* (European Commission 2016), and published *FGM in Europe: Public Discourse Versus Empirical Evidence*, INT'L J. OF LAW, CRIME AND JUSTICE 2017, and *Court Cases, Cultural Expertise and "FGM" in Europe, Studies in Law, Politics and Society* (2019). Other publications include: *GJ vs. Spain and Access to Justice for Victims of Human Trafficking*, Strasbourg Observers BLOG, 2016; *Exploring Intersectionality: FGM/C at the Istanbul Convention* in Niemi, Stoyanova, and Peroni (eds.): INTERNATIONAL LAW AND VAW: EUROPE AND THE ISTANBUL CONVENTION, Routledge (in press).

Amelia Miazad is the founding director of the Business in Society Institute and a member of the business law faculty at the University of California Berkeley School of Law. The Institute studies the changing role that companies are playing in society and how this evolution of corporate purpose impacts corporate governance. Professor Miazad leads the Institute's research, curriculum development, and programming. She publishes research and teaches courses at Berkeley Law. Professor Miazad also teaches in executive education programs and speaks at conferences around the world, which informs Berkeley Law's research and provides opportunities for practitioners to engage in this emerging and impactful area.

Shivangi Misra is an India-trained lawyer currently residing in Ottawa, Canada. She works with the Canadian Feminist Alliance for International Action, managing projects and policy on the implementation of international women's rights law within Canada. Prior to relocating to Canada, she worked with Senior Advocate Indira Jaising in India at Lawyers Collective of New Delhi, a leading public interest organization working to protect and promote the rights of the most marginalized. Misra's areas of research and advocacy are anti-discrimination law and intersectional feminist legal issues. She currently serves as an advisory board member with the Berkeley Center for Comparative Equality and Anti-discrimination Law.

Marianna Muravyeva is a Professor of Russian Law and Administration at the University of Helsinki. Her research is interdisciplinary, bringing together history, social sciences and law to examine long-term trends and patterns in social development with a special focus on normativity, gender and violence. Some of her most recent projects focus on human rights of women and austerity, conservative jurisprudence, violence against women, and family violence (violence against parents and domestic violence). Professor Muravyeva co-chairs Women and Gender Network of the European Social Sciences History Conference and a founding member of the Russian Association of Women's Historians (RAIZhI). She has published extensively, including edited volumes PARRICIDE AND VIOLENCE AGAINST PARENTS THROUGHOUT HISTORY: (DE)CONSTRUCTING FAMILY AND AUTHORITY? (London: Palgrave Macmillan, 2017), DOMESTIC DISTURBANCES, PATRIARCHAL VALUES: VIOLENCE, FAMILY AND SEXUALITY IN EARLY MODERN EUROPE (New York: Routledge, 2015); WOMEN'S HISTORY IN RUSSIA: (RE)ESTABLISHING THE FIELD (Cambridge: Cambridge Scholars Publishing, 2014); GENDER IN LATE MEDIEVAL AND EARLY MODERN EUROPE (London and New York: Routledge, 2013) and numerous articles and books chapters.

Ann M. Noel, Co-editor, is the Co-Director of the Berkeley Center's Sexual Harassment Working Group. She is the founder of Noel Workplace Consulting, specializing in legal advice and training on California and federal employment law compliance, especially sexual harassment prevention, disability and leave laws. Through the end of 2012, Noel was the California Fair Employment and Housing Commission's General Counsel, crafting California's regulations on mandatory sexual harassment training, disability and pregnancy discrimination, and its chief administrative law judge, adjudicating employment and housing cases, including sexual harassment cases. Noel has written extensively about employment and housing discrimination law, writing and editing practice guides on the Violence Against Women Act, fair employment, fair housing, public accommodations, and hate crimes. She frequently lectures and trains about effective anti-harassment training and investigations, and disability and leave laws.

Caroline Joelle Nwabueze is a Doctor of Law from Douala University in Cameroon, where she obtained her Ph.D. in law with first class honors. She is a graduate from the University of Torino in Italy, and Handong International Law School in Korea where she obtained her Master in intellectual property and LLM in international law. Dr. Nwabueze specializes in the field of law and development, advocating for the use of international legal frameworks as tools to enhance the capacity development of unnoticed communities. She has served as intern at the World Intellectual Property Organization, and as legal consultant at UNESCO-ICHCAP Korea. She has been a postdoctoral research fellow at the College of Law, University of South Africa under the South African Research Chair in Law, Society, and Technology. She is currently Senior Lecturer at Enugu State University of Science and Technology in Nigeria, where she has held the positions of head of the Public Law Department and a member of the University Ethics Committee. Dr. Nwabueze is the Chairperson of Advocates International African Task Force on Rule of Law and Integrity. In addition, she leads the African Research and Study Group on equality and non-discrimination laws.

Karen O'Connell is an Associate Professor in law at the University of Technology Sydney (UTS) with expertise in sex and disability discrimination, sexual harassment and equality laws. Her current research focuses on inequality and the biosciences, including the biological impact of discrimination and sexual harassment, in order to develop proposals for law reform. With Professor Isabel Karpin (UTS Law) she recently completed a large Australia Research Council Discovery project on "The Legal Regulation of Behaviour as a Disability" (2015-2019). Dr O'Connell was formerly employed in senior roles at the Australian

Human Rights Commission (AHRC), where she worked on national human rights inquiries and wrote federal guidelines, including on sexual harassment. As well as her experience on large professional and academic research projects, Dr O'Connell has consulted on social justice projects for gender, disability and human rights organizations.

Amy Oppenheimer is an attorney with over 35 years of experience in employment law, as an attorney, workplace investigator, expert witness, arbitrator, mediator, trainer and administrative law judge. She is the founder and past President of the Board of the Association of Workplace Investigators, Inc. (AWI), is on the California Department of Fair Employment and Housing Task Force on Sexual Harassment, and is Past Chair of the Executive Committee of the Labor and Employment Section of the State Bar of California. Amy is co-author of INVESTIGATING WORKPLACE HARASSMENT, HOW TO BE FAIR, THOROUGH AND LEGAL (Society of Human Resource Management, 2003). She leads a law firm that is dedicated to conducting impartial investigations, training and mediation.

David B. Oppenheimer, Co-editor, is a Clinical Professor of Law, the Director of the Berkeley Center on Comparative Equality and Anti-Discrimination Law, and the Faculty Co-Director of the Pro Bono Program at Berkeley Law. He was the founding director of the Boalt Hall Employment Discrimination Law Clinic. He is the author of numerous books, book chapters and articles on anti-discrimination law and civil rights history, focusing on U.S. and comparative law, and has lectured on anti-discrimination law at scores of universities around the world. Professor Oppenheimer has litigated sexual harassment, pay equity and other forms of sex discrimination cases, as well as cases of race discrimination, ethnicity discrimination, disability discrimination, religious discrimination, and age discrimination, and has filed amicus curie briefs in the California and United States Supreme Courts. He earned a juris doctor degree from Harvard University. He is a member of the California and United States Supreme Court bars.

Isabelle Rorive is Professor of Law and President of the Centre Perelman for Legal Philosophy of the ULB (Université Libre de Bruxelles, Belgium). Her research focuses on theoretical and practical developments of the right to equality and non-discrimination in a comparative perspective, the imprint of legal cultures on the development of law, as well as on the contemporary challenges that human rights are facing in a global and numerical world (see her website, http://www.philodroit.be/_Rorive-Isabelle_?lang=en). As the advisor of the Vice-Chancellor and the President of the ULB for the equality and diversity policy, a senior expert member of the European Equality Law Network and of the Berkeley Center on Comparative and Anti-Discrimination Law, Isabelle Rorive pursues many of her research projects in a European or international setting with a multidisciplinary approach. With Professor Emmanuelle Bribosia, she launched the Equality Law Clinic (ELC) in 2014.

Purna Sen is Executive Coordinator against sexual harassment at UN Women, where she was formerly Policy Director. Sen's experience is in policy, advocacy, teaching, research and publishing in education, inter-governmental work, local government and NGOs. Her work has covered violence against women, human rights, trafficking, sexuality and sexual control, development and race equality in the United Kingdom. She has been on management/advisory groups of NGOs including the Refugee Women's Resource Project, Southall Black Sisters, the Kaleidoscope Trust (LGBT rights), RISE (domestic abuse) and the Commonwealth Human Rights Initiative. Purna was previously Deputy Director of the LSE Institute of Public Affairs, Head of Human Rights for the Commonwealth and Programme Director at Amnesty International. Her PhD (Bristol) researched domestic violence. Sen received the Sir Brian Urquhart Award for Distinguished Service to the UN in 2018 and was included in 100 most influential people in global gender policy in 2018, 2019.

Giorgia Serughetti is a Research Fellow at the Department of Sociology of the University of Milano-Bicocca, Italy. She is a lecturer in "Politics and policies", and co-coordinator of postgraduate course "Violence against women and children: knowing and combating the phenomenon" and of undergraduate course "Training operators/social workers to combat gender violence" (Social Work degree program). She is the author of several essays in academic journals and in collective volumes, and of the books: "Uomini che pagano le donne. Dalla strada al web, i clienti nel mercato del sesso contemporaneo" [Men who pay for sex. From the street to the web, clients in the contemporary sex market] (Ediesse, 2013; 2nd ed., 2019), "Libere tutte. Dall'aborto al velo, donne nel nuovo millennio" [All women free. From abortion to the veil, women in the new millennium], with Cecilia D'Elia (Minimum fax, 2017).

Colleen Sheppard is a Professor at McGill University, Faculty of Law, and former Director of the McGill Centre for Human Rights and Legal Pluralism. She has an honors B.A. and LL.B. from the University of Toronto, and an LL.M. from Harvard University. Following her legal studies, she clerked for Chief Justice Dickson at the Supreme Court of Canada. Her teaching and research focus on human rights law, equality, discrimination law, comparative constitutional law and feminist legal theory. Selective publications include, INCLUSIVE EQUALITY: THE RELATIONAL DIMENSIONS OF SYSTEMIC DISCRIMINATION IN CANADA (McGill-Queen's University Press, 2010) and *Mapping Anti-discrimination law onto Inequality at Work: Expanding the Meaning of Equality in International Labour Law*, 151 Int'l Lab. Rev. 1 (2012). Colleen Sheppard served as a Commissioner on the Quebec Human Rights and Youth Rights Commission from 1991 to 1996. She was elected a fellow of the Royal Society of Canada's Academy of Social Sciences in September 2016.

Isabel C. Jaramillo Sierra is Full Professor of Law at Universidad de los Andes, Bogotá. Her work focuses on the effects of feminist legal reform and the distributional effects of family law. Her recent publications in English include: *Finding and Losing Feminism in Transition* in GOVERNANCE FEMINISM: NOTES FROM THE FIELD (2019) (Halley et al., eds.); *Latin American Feminist Legal Theory: Taking Multiple Subordinations Seriously* in ROUTLEDGE HANDBOOK ON LAW AND SOCIETY IN LATIN AMERICA (2019) (Ansolabehere et al., eds.); and (with Ana Cristina González Vélez) *Legal Knowledge as a Tool for Social Change: La Mesa por la Vida y la Salud de las Mujeres as an Expert on Colombian Abortion Law* in 19 HARV. HEALTH & HUM. RTS. J. (2017) pp. 109-118.

Ramya Kannabiran Tella received her PhD in Geography from King's College London in 2019. Her research interests lie at the intersections of gender studies, environmental anthropology and science and technology studies.

Maryamossadat Torabi is an associate at Ashrafi & Partners Law Firm residing in the Islamic Republic of Iran. She attained her LL.B. and LL.M. from the Faculty of Law at Shahid Beheshti University which is the leading law faculty in the country. Maryam is an independent researcher focusing on the relationship between Islamic law/Sharia and the international human rights law system in addition to environmental law. Her research interests and activities include children rights, legal clinics, Islam and the environmental crisis, religion and politics in Central Asia. She is a member of Global Alliance committed to achieving Justice through Education (GAJE).

Lining Zhang is a freelance researcher, activist and lecturer in China. Her research and projects focus on women's and girls' rights to education, freedom of choices and freedom from violence. She has researched and worked on issues of sex equality with grassroots NGO and activist groups. She teaches Chinese high school students and college students on issues of sex equality through various online courses and schools. Before going freelance, she ran the clinical office in Peking University's School of Transnational Law, working on public interest cases in both the U.S. and mainland China. Zhang studied law at Peking University, Harvard University and UTS in Sydney. Before returning to China, she worked briefly in Sanctuary for Families in New York and the ACLU headquarter Women's Rights team.

The Global
#MeToo Movement

CHAPTER 1

Global #MeToo[1]

Catharine A. MacKinnon[2]

We are in the middle of the first mass movement against sexual abuse in the history of the world. Global #MeToo sprung from the law of sexual harassment, quickly overtook it, and is shifting law, cultures, and politics everywhere. It also electrifyingly demonstrates in action what I'm calling "butterfly politics."

In 1972, the scientist Edward Lorenz, trying to grasp how small seemingly insignificant things become cataclysmically big, asked, "Does the flap of a butterfly's wings in Brazil set off a tornado in Texas?"[3] Considering this, he

---

1. Some of the themes and locutions included in this talk have previously appeared in op-eds published in the *Guardian* and the *New York Times*. Catharine A. MacKinnon, *How Litigation Laid the Ground for Accountability After #MeToo*, GUARDIAN, Dec. 23, 2017, https://www.theguardian.com/commentisfree/2017/dec/23/how-litigation-laid-the-ground-for-accountability-after-metoo; Catharine A. MacKinnon, *#MeToo Has Done What the Law Could Not*, N.Y. TIMES, Feb. 4, 2018, https://www.nytimes.com/2018/02/04/opinion/metoo-law-legal-system.html. Aspects of this material are also discussed in CATHARINE A. MACKINNON, *Butterfly Politics, Introduction to* BUTTERFLY POLITICS 1 (2017) [hereinafter MACKINNON, *Introduction*]; CATHARINE A. MACKINNON, *Preface to the Paperback Edition* of BUTTERFLY POLITICS: CHANGING THE WORLD FOR WOMEN ix (2019) [hereinafter MACKINNON, *Preface*]; and Catharine A. MacKinnon et al., *'This Moment Turned Out to Be Fleeting': Nine Reflections on #MeToo, One Year On*, N.Y. TIMES, Oct. 6, 2018, https://www.nytimes.com/2018/10/06/opinion/me-too-weinstein-one-year.html; and in an interview conducted by Brock Colyar, *The Ms. Q&A: Catharine MacKinnon Weighs in on the #MeToo Movement*, MS. MAG. BLOG, July 30, 2018, http://msmagazine.com/blog/2018/07/30/ms-qa-catharine-mackinnon-weighs-metoo-movement/.

2. Elizabeth A. Long Professor of Law, University of Michigan Law School and The James Barr Ames Visiting Professor of Law, Harvard University since 2009.

3. EDWARD N. LORENZ, THE ESSENCE OF CHAOS 14 (1994), *quoted in* Robert C. Hilborn, *Sea Gulls, Butterflies, and Grasshoppers: A Brief History of the Butterfly Effect in Nonlinear Dynamics*, 72 AM. J. PHYSICS 425, 425 (2004).

conceived the "butterfly effect,"[4] which charmingly models how some tiny simple actions, properly targeted within structural dynamics under the right conditions, can come to have complex large effects.[5] Butterfly politics, applied to
change in the gender system, including through law, means that the right small
intervention in the structure of an unstable political system can ultimately produce systemic change. It proposes a theory of social change in power relations
through activist law.[6]

The early openings of the butterflies' wings on sexual harassment were the
legal, political, and conceptual innovations of the 1970s,[7] setting the stage for
the collective social intervention of the #MeToo movement that is shifting gender hierarchy's tectonic plates.

To start with the why now question—to ask what made #MeToo possible—is to ask what, for the first time, made it harder to keep the sexual abuse
inside than to put it out? The reverse has always been the case. It is also to look
into #MeToo's elements, what will extend it, what will keep it going.

One beginning point was the legal breakthrough that defined sexual
harassment as sex discrimination, calling the experience and violation what it
is: a vector and dynamic of structural inequality, specifically gender, with major
white supremacist and class-based (poverty, economic vulnerability) dimensions. Sex inequality is both complex and unstable. Complex due to its multiple
interacting unequal variables: race, ethnicity, religion, class, disability, sexuality,
and age. These do a lot of their work through gender, and gender does a lot of
its work through them. Unstable because it is based on a lie: that women are
men's natural inferiors, men women's natural superiors, commonly termed "difference." Life refutes the lie of inferiority every day, which means it takes a lot
of force to hold it together. This hierarchical system—superiority being above
inferiority in value, worth, status, resources, power, despite some acknowledgment of its injustice, the human and civil right to equality supposedly makes it
illegal—has proven extraordinarily tenacious.

Framed as inequality, sexual harassment stopped being something women
(or anyone) just had to live through, breaking the age-old rule of impunity that
the more power a man has, the more sex he can exact from those with less power.

---

4. See "Does the Flap of a Butterfly's Wings in Brazil Set off a Tornado in Texas?"
LORENZ, *supra* n. 3, at 14. The original talk appears as Appendix 1 *in* LORENZ, *The Butterfly Effect, id.* at 181.

5. Robert E. Scott, *Chaos Theory and the Justice Paradox*, 35 WM. & MARY L. REV. 329, 348 (1993).

6. This analysis is further developed in MACKINNON, *Introduction, supra* note 1.

7. *See* CATHARINE A. MACKINNON, SEXUAL HARASSMENT OF WORKING WOMEN: A CASE OF SEX DISCRIMINATION (1979) (laying the foundation for and chronicling the early stages of these developments).

In this system, because sexual abuse is about power, it is about sex. If all the sexual abuse reported in the #MeToo movement starting in late 2017 had remained effectively legal for the past forty-some years—as without sexual harassment law, most of it would have—this explosive movement against it would have been unthinkable, nor could it have been so volcanically effective. Without law delegitimizing sexual harassment, calling it out for what it is in law—this is how law actually works in life—powerful men (and men have power) would not be losing their jobs, political and academic positions, deals, and reputations today.[8]

The #MeToo moment also, obviously, built on decades of collective work against sexual abuse by groups and individuals, the leading ones being African American women: all the early legal cases; Professor Anita Hill's testimony in 1991 against Clarence Thomas;[9] Tarana Burke's 2006 use of the phrase "me too" to call out the abuse of African American women and girls in particular;[10] and the #SayHerName campaign.[11] The "campus sexual assault" movement of the last decade or two is also a forerunner of #MeToo, combining legal initiatives with social media intervention, inspiring the investigation by President Barack Obama's administration of several hundred schools for inadequate response to sexual abuse on campuses.[12]

---

8. According to the New York Times, "at least 200 prominent men have lost their jobs after public allegations of sexual harassment" since the #MeToo movement began in 2017. Audrey Carlsen et al., *#MeToo Brought Down 201 Powerful Men. Nearly Half of Their Replacements Are Women*, N.Y. TIMES, Oct. 29, 2018, https://www.nytimes.com/interactive/2018/10/23/us/metoo-replacements.html.

9. For discussion, see CATHARINE A. MacKINNON, *Speaking Truth to Power, in* WOMEN'S LIVES, MEN'S LAWS 277 (2005).

10. *See #MeToo: A Timeline of Events*, CHI. TRIB. (June 13, 2019), http://www.chicagotribune.com/lifestyles/ct-me-too-timeline-20171208-htmlstory.html; Tarana Burke, *The Inception*, JUSTBEINC., https://justbeinc.wixsite.com/justbeinc/the-me-too-movement-cmml. Burke describes creating a MySpace page for the nascent "Me Too" movement, but recent attempts to locate it have been unsuccessful. *See* Abby Ohlheiser, *The Woman Behind 'Me Too' Knew the Power of the Phrase When She Created It—10 Years Ago*, WASH. POST, Oct. 19, 2017, https://www.washingtonpost.com/news/the-intersect/wp/2017/10/19/the-woman-behind-me-too-knew-the-power-of-the-phrase-when-she-created-it-10-years-ago/?utm_term=.21a2452bb83c.

11. #SayHerName is a movement organized since 2014 by the African American Policy Forum (AAPF) to lift up Black women and girl victims of police brutality and other anti-Black misogynist aggression, historical and contemporary. Among other actions, it organizes vigils, demonstrations, meetings, and marches, issues reports, and features a Mothers Network for survivors of murdered Black women and girls. See Homa Khaleeli, *#SayHerName: why Kimberlé Crenshaw is fighting for forgotten women*, THE GUARDIAN, May 30, 2016, https://www.theguardian.com/lifeandstyle/2016/may/30/sayhername-why-kimberle-crenshaw-is-fighting-for-forgotten-women.

12. Although the campus sexual assault numbers are a moving target, as investigations are closed upon their completion, as of September 22, 2017, there were 360 open investigations. Sarah Brown, *What Does the End of Obama's Title IX Guidance Mean for Colleges?* CHRON.

Another crucial moving part in the U.S. awakening was the 2016 presidential election. Claims of sexual harassment by President Bill Clinton had, for many, previously identified the issue of sexual harassment with the Right's use of it for political gain: a morality crusade rather than a matter of coercion and exploitation. The election of Donald Trump reversed the relation of sexual harassment to conventional political alignments, redefining the democratic and liberatory potential of publicly claiming sexual victimization. Instead of interfering with a respected president's desired policies and leadership,[13] exposing these violations in one's own life became a means of resisting the forces of darkness—misogyny, racism, authoritarianism, lies, stupidity, you name it. Even as the movement revealed that perpetrators of sexual abuse were not just those ugly men over there, but our nice men right here, this reversal of the conventional politics of the issue released a tsunami of enraged women.

This history placed Hillary Clinton in an awkward position as a presidential candidate. Who even knows what confronting sexual abuse on behalf of violated women, what Michele Dauber in this context calls "electoral kryptonite," could have mobilized for her campaign? But what contributed to creating Trump as president—indifference to reports of sexual abuse—fueled #MeToo in no small part because of its role in creating Trump as president. The point here is, for myriad reasons, if Hillary Clinton had been elected President, #MeToo would not have occurred. In other words, we are the backlash.

The allegations against Harvey Weinstein threw a match into this tinderbox. Ashley Judd's willingness to be named, as reported by the *New York Times*,[14] then the further reports in the *New Yorker*,[15] set off the butterfly effect that is #MeToo, transnational in scope and showing no signs of slowing. High quality journalism touched off this movement, followed by survivors in the millions

---

HIGHER EDUC., Sept. 22, 2017, https://www.chronicle.com/article/What-Does-the-End-of
-Obama-s/241281. *See also* Nick Anderson, *At First, 55 Schools Faced Sexual Violence Investigations. Now the List Has Quadrupled*, WASH. POST, Jan. 18, 2017, https://www.washingtonpost
.com/news/grade-point/wp/2017/01/18/at-first-55-schools-faced-sexual-violence-investiga
tions-now-the-list-has-quadrupled/?utm_term=.15977fc8d3a1.

13. The presidency of Bill Clinton was derailed by sexual harassment charges that culminated in impeachment. The cases of Monica Lewinsky and Paula Jones are considered in CATHARINE A. MACKINNON, *Afterword* to DIRECTIONS IN SEXUAL HARASSMENT LAW 687 (Catharine A. MacKinnon and Reva B. Siegel eds., 2004).

14. Jodi Kantor & Megan Twohey, *Harvey Weinstein Paid Off Sexual Harassment Accusers for Decades*, N.Y. TIMES, Oct. 5, 2017, https://www.nytimes.com/2017/10/05/us
/harvey-weinstein-harassment-allegations.html.

15. Ronan Farrow, *From Aggressive Overtures to Sexual Assault: Harvey Weinstein's Accusers Tell Their Stories*, NEW YORKER, Oct. 10, 2017, https://www.newyorker.com/news
/news-desk/from-aggressive-overtures-to-sexual-assault-harvey-weinsteins-accusers-tell-their
-stories.

taking to social media airwaves. Sexual abuse was finally being reported in the established media, and still is, as pervasive and endemic rather than sensational and exceptional.[16] This makes it real. Women have been talking with each other about this outrage for millennia. Social media could have become just a digital echo chamber in which a million whispers of sexual abuse went to die. A major part of the response, including the cultural and legal changes that are occurring, is because the legacy media—the reality and consciousness machine, whose reports have not been confined to privileged women or to prominent men—is continuing its ethical, sometimes inspired, reporting.[17]

Notice: #MeToo is cultural, driven principally by forces other than litigation, and is surpassing the law in changing norms and providing relief for human rights violations that the law did not—in some ways in current form could not, although law is embedded in culture and can and will change with it.

Over the past couple of years, survivors in numbers and gorgeous diversity, perfectly displaying the kaleidoscope that a collectivity of butterflies is called, have begun to erode the two biggest cultural barriers to ending sexual harassment (and all forms of sexual abuse) in law and in life: the disbelief and trivialization of its victims. Before, even when she was believed, nothing he did to her mattered so much as what would be done to him if his actions were taken seriously. In some ways, it is even worse to be believed and to have what he did not matter. It means you don't matter.

---

16. I tried to get journalists to do this over twenty years ago in a Keynote Address at the Journalism and Women Symposium (JAWS) (Sept. 12, 1998). For the published version, see MacKinnon, *Mediating Reality, in* Women's Lives, Men's Laws, *supra* note 9, at 289, 293 ("What women in the media can do, and sometimes win the fight to do, is place their stories of men's sexual mistreatment of women in real context. Sexual abuse is an everyday event—common, systematic, nonexceptional. Talk about it as if you know what you are talking about. Women in the press have been abused just as vast numbers of women in every profession have. Report and analyze events as if you live in the world we know we live in, in which sexual use, manipulation, and abuse can be believed to happen because they do happen. Talk about it as if it hurts and as if it matters because it does hurt and it does matter.").

17. Large-scale surveys of working women estimate that approximately one in every two women will be harassed during their academic or working lives. *See* Louise F. Fitzgerald, *Sexual Harassment: Violence Against Women in the Workplace*, 48 Am. Psychol. 1070, 1070, 1073 (1993). When asked whether they have been "sexually harassed," fewer respondents answer affirmatively than when asked about specific sexual behaviors and experiences. Louise F. Fitzgerald et al., *Measuring Sexual Harassment: Theoretical and Psychometric Advances*, 17 Basic & Applied Soc. Psychol. 425 (1995). Women who are harassed, but do not label their experiences as such, evidence "similar negative psychological, work, and health consequences" as those who do label them correctly. Vickie J. Magley et al., *Outcomes of Self-Labeling Sexual Harassment*, 84 J. Applied Psychol. 390, 399 (1999). For further information on sexual harassment, see generally Catharine A. MacKinnon, Sex Equality 1002-1207 (3d ed. 2016).

This precise choreography was retraced in the final Senate hearing for Judge Brett Kavanaugh's Supreme Court nomination. Dr. Christine Blasey Ford provided remembered facts of a sexual attack by him: He did this. When questioned on those facts, Judge Kavanaugh repeatedly provided . . . his résumé: I matter.[18] These exact dynamics of inequality drive the system of sexual politics in which the more power a man has, the more sexual access he can get away with compelling.

It used to be that women accusing men of sexual abuse were the ones thrown overboard. Women's voices recounting sexual abuse being heard, believed, and acted on—and some men being thrown overboard, despite setbacks like the Kavanaugh confirmation[19]—is real change. Don't ask me what's next. This is it, this right here. It has arrived. The alchemy of #MeToo is beginning to transform what has been a privilege of power into a disgrace so despicable that not even many white upper-class men feel they can afford it around them.

While it's a miracle when anyone claiming sexual violation is believed, the odds have long been irrelevantly improved by any form of privilege—dominant race, ethnicity, religion, class, celebrity, nationality, caste, sexuality, age, gender, or combinations, although they did not keep it from happening. Harasser prominence and celebrity accuser stoked some of the media fire initially but have not confined the movement. An attack on these hierarchies, including by white women celebrities, is also an attack on the fact that women's work, like the rest of women's lives, is often denigratingly sexualized. Working for tips in a restaurant to make anything close to a living wage, for example, largely requires women in effect to sell themselves sexually. The entertainment industry outright commodifies the sexuality of the women in it. It's no coincidence that so many of the exposed harassers in entertainment reportedly subjected their victims to a pornographic spectator sexuality, masturbating over them in real life like consumers do over women in pornography. This also partly explains why Time's Up women—actors frequently used and abused to create the sexualized culture in which we are buried, and who as working women, almost no matter how well-known or successful, must please powerful men to continue to get that work—are so perfectly positioned to attack it.

---

18. *Nomination of the Honorable Brett M. Kavanaugh to be an Associate Justice of the Supreme Court of the United States (Day 5): Hearing Before the S. Comm. on the Judiciary*, 115th Cong. (2018), https://www.judiciary.senate.gov/meetings/nomination-of-the-honorable-brett-m-kavanaugh-to-be-an-associate-justice-of-the-supreme-court-of-the-united-states-day-5.

19. Sheryl Gay Stolberg, *Kavanaugh Is Sworn In After Close Confirmation Vote in Senate*, N.Y. TIMES, Oct. 6, 2018, https://www.nytimes.com/2018/10/06/us/politics/brett-kavanaugh-supreme-court.html.

If the same cultural inequalities are permitted to operate in law as operate in the behavior the law prohibits—as exemplified by the rape myth that women who have had sex are inherently not credible, for instance, having apparently lost our credibility along with our virginity—equalizing attempts such as sexual harassment law encounter systemic drag. This logjam is finally being broken, or starting to be, by the #MeToo movement, by survivors being believed and valued as the law seldom has. Again, women have been saying these things forever. It is the response to them that is changing.

As #MeToo moves the culture beneath the law of sexual abuse to make it potentially a far more effective tool than it has ever been, some conventional systemic legal processes are shifting. Examples are Bill Cosby's conviction in his second trial, Judge Aaron Persky's recall by the voters, Larry Nassar's conviction and sentencing.[20] The surfacing of allegations against Catholic priests and bishops by adult survivors of childhood sexual abuse, many of them men,[21] which began before #MeToo, increasingly including complaints of official cover-ups as well as direct acts of sexual aggression,[22] has arguably taken inspiration and

---

20. On the conviction of Bill Cosby, see Tray Connor, *Cosby Trial: Juror Says it was a 'True Deadlock,'* NBC NEWS (June 22, 2017, 12:24 P.M.), https://www.nbcnews.com /storyline/bill-cosby-scandal/cosby-trial-juror-says-it-was-true-deadlock-n775666, and Jen Kirby, *Cosby Defense Attorneys Used Personal Attacks to Try to Discredit Witnesses,* VOX (Apr. 13, 2018, 8:12 P.M.), https://www.vox.com/2018/4/13/17234172/bill-cosby-trial-accusers -janice-dickinson-testimony. For discussion of the Persky recall, see Maggie Astor, *California Voters Remove Judge Aaron Persky, Who Gave a 6-Month Sentence for Sexual Assault,* N.Y. TIMES (June 6, 2018), https://www.nytimes.com/2018/06/06/us/politics/judge-persky-brock -turner-recall.html, and Katie J.M. Baker, *Here's the Powerful Letter the Stanford Victim Read to Her Attacker,* BUZZFEED NEWS (June 3, 2016, 4:18 P.M.), https://www.buzzfeednews.com /article/katiejmbaker/heres-the-powerful-letter-the-stanford-victim-read-to-her-ra. Information on the conviction of Larry Nassar may be found in Christine Hauser, *Larry Nassar is Sentenced to Another 40 to 125 Years in Prison,* N.Y. TIMES (Feb. 5, 2018), https://www.nytimes.com /2018/02/05/sports/larry-nassar-sentencing-hearing.html.

21. *See, e.g., Catholic Church Child Sexual Abuse Scandal,* BBC, Feb. 26, 2019, https:// www.bbc.com/news/world-44209971 (referencing a Church-commissioned report concluding that "more than 4,000 US Roman Catholic priests had faced sexual abuse allegations in the last 50 years, in cases involving more than 10,000 children—mostly boys"). Needless to say, the numbers have only increased in the intervening years, the total victimized worldwide almost certainly unknowable.

22. For a survey of the problem as of early 2019, see Nicole Winfield, *A Global Look at the Catholic Church's Sex Abuse Problem,* ASSOCIATED PRESS, Feb. 21, 2019, https://www .apnews.com/8cb4daf509464bad8c13ef35d44a0fc5. Of the many contributions to the global conversation regarding child sexual abuse in the Roman Catholic Church, see, e.g., Paul Elie, *What Do the Church's Victims Deserve?,* NEW YORKER, Apr. 8, 2019, https://www.newyorker .com/magazine/2019/04/15/what-do-the-churchs-victims-deserve, and Emma Green, *Why Does the Catholic Church Keep Failing,* ATLANTIC MAGAZINE, Feb. 14, 2019, https://www .theatlantic.com/politics/archive/2019/02/sean-omalley-pope-francis-catholic-church-sex -abuse/582658/. *See also* Collected Articles, Roman Catholic Church Sex Abuse Cases, N.Y.

heart, and derived potency and momentum, from adding its voices to a rising MeToo.[23]

And so much legal change is needed. #MeToo is exposing the lack of freedom, including sexual freedom, that prevails under conditions of inequality. In the United States and elsewhere, rape law continues to be infused with rape myths. Critical light has been shed on criminal law's burden of proof and standards for due process rights of the accused, for instance, confrontation and cross-examination, which are inappropriately often imported, tacitly or explicitly, into civil and administrative processes without putting them into inequality context or exhibiting any awareness that sex equality standards have never been applied to these areas. Processes for investigating and interrogating sexual violation in most settings remain within the chain of command of the institution that is, in essence, or sees itself as, being investigated, rather than being independent. In any other setting, this would be called corruption. Transparency is not the usual rule here. Secrecy is, protecting organizational brand. In any other context this would be understood as being a cover-up.

Liability standards for employers and educational institutions remain unrealistically stacked against sexual harassment survivors. Standards for retaliation—one of the biggest fears behind nonreporting—are not realistic in this context. Even before a case can get started in the United States, the federal law of discrimination has a statute of limitations of mere months, the shortest in law, which expires before almost any victim of sexual violation is past trauma, far less post-traumatic stress. What does this mean, if not that legislators know discrimination is rampant and want to disappear it? The damage caps for harassment only minimize the extent of its harm by suppressing its measure and can

TIMES, https://www.nytimes.com/topic/organization/roman-catholic-church-sex-abuse-cases. *See, e.g.,* Pascale Bonnefoy & Austin Ramzy, *Pope's Defense of Chilean Bishop in Sex Abuse Scandal Causes Outrage,* N.Y. TIMES, Jan. 19, 2018, https://www.nytimes.com/2018/01/19/world/americas/pope-sex-abuse-chile.html.

23. This is especially evident in the case of Catholic nuns and other women who have adopted the hashtag #NunsToo. *See, e.g., The Catholic Church is Headed for Another Sex Abuse Scandal as #NunsToo Speak Up,* THE CONVERSATION (Feb. 14, 2019, 9:08 P.M.) (reporting that women theologians "influenced by the success of the #MeToo movement" ... convened a meeting—called Voices of Faith—in Rome to share their stories of sexual harassment and abuse at the hands of male clerics, and decry the patriarchy of the Catholic hierarchy"), http://theconversation.com/the-catholic-church-is-headed-for-another-sex-abuse-scandal-as-nunstoo-speak-up-111539; Sylvia Poggioli, *After Years of Abuse by Priests, #NunsToo Are Speaking Out,* NPR (Mar. 18, 2019, 7:22 A.M.) (quoting a Belgian expert on the sexual abuse of minors and vulnerable adults who opined that "the movement of #MeToo has absolutely [had] an influence" on the willingness of Catholic nuns to speak out), https://www.npr.org/2019/03/18/703067602/after-years-of-abuse-by-priests-nunstoo-are-speaking-out.

discourage contingent representation.[24] No motion to change any of this exists in the US Congress or anywhere else to my knowledge, although some of it is better under California law.[25]

Practical steps to capture the movement's insights could include limits on various forms of secrecy and nontransparency that hide the extent of sexual abuse and enforce survivor isolation, such as forced arbitration, silencing non-disclosure agreements, especially in cases of physical attacks and multiple perpetration, and settlements forcibly made confidential. Being able to sue individual perpetrators and their enablers, jointly with institutions, as California allows,[26] could shift perceived incentives when it comes to the actual abuse. Legal standards for reasonableness and unwelcomeness, which themselves refer to social standards, need to shift and are shifting. But the only legal change in US law that matches the movement's scale would be the passage of an Equal Rights Amendment and application of substantive equality standards to its interpretation. It would expand the congressional power to legislate against sexual abuse. It could and should renovate constitutional interpretation in a more substantive, including intersectional, direction, reconfiguring legal equality itself.

Supported by law, sincere revulsion against sexually harassing behavior, as opposed to revulsion at reports of it, could change workplaces and schools, even streets. It could restrain repeat predators as well as the occasional and casual exploiters, as the law so far has not. Shunning perpetrators as sex bigots who take advantage of the vulnerabilities of inequality could transform societies. Many social sectors could recognize their obligation to foster environments free from sexual objectification, pressure, or aggression, in which reporting of sexual abuse is welcomed rather than punished, accountability not impunity prevails for individuals and institutions that engage in or enable such abuse, and excellence and inclusion rather than hierarchy and fear—imagine that—operate as real rather than rhetorical standards.

---

24. Ctr. for Justice & Democracy, Fact Sheet, *The Unintended Consequences of State Tort Limits: Caps on Damages and Statutes of Limitations in Sexual Assault Cases*, Fact Sheet, Feb. 14, 2019, CTR. FOR JUSTICE & DEMOCRACY, https://www.centerjd.org, http://centerjd.org/system/files/CAPSSOLSEXASSAULTF4.pdf.

25. Ramit Mizrahi, *Sexual Harassment Law After #MeToo: Looking to California as a Model*, YALE L.J. FOR., June 18, 2018, https://www.yalelawjournal.org/pdf/Mizrahi_fdk1ngup.pdf.

26. Harassment claims can be brought against individual defendants in California under the Fair Employment and Housing Act, *Reno v. Baird*, 18 Cal. 4th at 644, 76 Cal. Rptr. 2d 499, 957 P.2d 1333 (Cal. 1998), although discrimination claims cannot. California separately legislated against discrimination and harassment, making harassment actionable "by an employer … or any other person." § 12940, subd. (j)(1), which liability can extend to nonsupervisory coworkers. Cal. Gov. Code § 12940(j)(3).

Sexual harassment's links to other issues are becoming increasingly visible during this explosive time. For one, sexual harassment is an especially appropriate vehicle for a worldwide movement not only because it affects women of all cultures, groups, and classes, but also because it encompasses, builds in, parallels, or evokes so many other abuses of women and children, from simple discrimination to other abuses of authority or trust or power. It often includes rape and raises all the issues of undesired sexual interactions that are acquiesced to under conditions of unequal power.

#MeToo has opened a wider discussion of the place of power in coercing sexual interactions that links with developing international legal understandings. The international definition of rape in the International Criminal Tribunal for Rwanda's (ICTR) *Akayesu* case is based on coercion, consent being so irrelevant as not to require mention.[27] Domestic laws of rape in many jurisdictions, and sexual harassment trainings in schools, typically turn on "consent," the legal meaning of which ranges from actual desire affirmatively expressed to lost fights to despair to passive acquiescence to frozen fright to coma to death. Making "consent" central to rape law is what puts the victim on trial. It is why the British conviction rate (with its all-consent law) is an appalling 5.7 percent of cases reported, itself a small fraction of the total perpetrated.[28] Consent as a concept is rooted in the active/passive model of sex as something someone with more power does to someone with less, who lets it happen or tries not to. If sex happened, non-consent has to be proven, meaning the assumption was that it was consensual unless proven otherwise. "Yes" can be coerced. Consent is thoroughly sex stereotyped. As a concept, it is given its fullest expression in the British political theory that justifies rulers in ruling the ruled. It means acquiescence whether or not a choice is real, it is what is attributed to you when you are rolled by power. It is an intrinsically unequal concept, including when it works the way it is supposed to work, riding under the cover of desire but virtually never invoked when desire is real. In the international law of sex trafficking, which prohibits sexual exploitation in among others, circumstances of vulnerability or abuse of power, consent is, by statute, no defense.[29]

Sexual harassment law in the United States, for all its inadequacies, has grasped from the outset that inequality is not consented to. Accepting unequal pay, for instance, doesn't make it equal. Sexual harassment law does not use

---

27. Prosecutor v. Akayesu, Case No. ICTR 96-4-T, Judgment, ¶¶ 688 (Sept. 2, 1998).

28. Liz Kelly et al., A Gap or a Chasm? Attrition in Reported Rape Cases 25 (Home Office Research Study No. 293, 2005) (UK).

29. U.N. General Assembly, Protocol to Prevent, Suppress and Punish Trafficking in Persons, Especially Women and Children, Supplementing the United Nations Convention against Transnational Organized Crime, art. 3 (a)-(b), Nov. 15, 2000, TIAS 13127, 2237 U.N.T.S. 319, ("Palermo Protocol"), [https://perma.cc/K5KK-RQ8B].

consent and never has; it uses unwelcomeness.[30] Sexual assault is a crime of inequality. One potential insight of #MeToo is that consent needs to come out of rape law as well. Domestic laws of rape should be based on coercion, reconfiguring definitions of force to extend beyond physical force to encompass all the forms of inequality, meaning vulnerability, that make rape possible, including race, class and poverty, sexual orientation, gender identity, disability in a major way, immigration status, state power, military occupation, colonialism, and the consequences of climate change, with age as well as gender stereotypes, when actively deployed to force sexual interactions. Deterrence, not incarceration, is the goal, which is why this concept is focused on those with the most power, as opposed to existing law, which targets those perpetrators who have the least.

A second link rising in visibility is the fact that sexual harassment makes women's real work into a form of prostitution: forced trading of sexual access for economic survival, which is what prostitution is. In its fundamental dynamics, sexual harassment turns real work into an arm of the sex trade, termed "serial rape" by its survivors. The imperative to exchange sex for survival, or its possibility held out whether the survival is real or not, governs women's inequality, hence women's lives, worldwide. In prostitution, virtually all of women's and girls' options are precluded by individuals or social forces—for instance, white supremacy, poverty, misogyny—except for this one, making her so-called consent to it, or so-called choice of it, almost always fraudulent and illusory, as is "sleeping her way to the top."

Women who supposedly have rights, including equality rights in employment and education, are reduced to this floor of women's status when tolerance of sexual harassment, or sexual delivery in any form from objectification to rape, is made a requirement of the paid labor force, including in paid housework, where sexual predation is widespread. The same applies to educational or career advancement. As a formerly prostituted woman colleague once cogently observed to me, "… and you have to do all that other work, too." Precisely this—sexual harassment in its pure form, meaning prostitution—is what is being widely rejected by women and some men in the international #MeToo movements today.

The way butterfly politics seemingly comes out of nowhere to suddenly be everywhere is illustrated by the Nordic model on prostitution, which penalizes the buyers (johns) and sellers (pimps and traffickers) of sex, eliminating any penalties for the bought and sold, the prostituted people.[31] In Sweden, where it was passed first in 1999, it has virtually eliminated sex trafficking and reduced

---

30. Meritor Sav. Bank v. Vinson, 477 U.S. 57 (1986).

31. For discussion, see Catharine A. MacKinnon, *Trafficking, Prostitution, and Inequality*, 46 HARV. C.R.-C.L. L. REV. 271 (2011).

prostitution by massive percentages by supporting prostituted people who want to leave prostitution, which by international measures is 89 percent of them.[32] This equality model on prostitution is now embraced in many countries (Norway, Iceland, Northern Ireland, Canada, France, the Republic of Ireland, and Israel), despite well-funded sex industry opposition. Like all good human rights work, and everything I have ever done, it is directly based on the experiences, needs, and insistent demands of survivors. Prostituted people are not the criminals. Those who buy and sell them are.

If requiring sexual use as the price of survival is a human rights violation when combined with a real job or as with education, another entitlement, it certainly violates human rights when imposed all by itself, when it is the only thing a woman is permitted to be valued or paid for, even if her value approximates pond slime and the lion's share of the payment of the approximately 84 percent who are, on average, under the control of third parties goes to others.[33] Yet it is not effectively illegal to buy a person for sexual use in most places. When buyers call forth revulsion and rejection when sexual harassment's dynamic in its pure form—prostitution—is exposed; when those who report it—women and girls, men and boys, transgender persons, disproportionately women of color and indigenous women—are no longer stigmatized, shamed, and blamed as their violators are vaunted and defended and kept invisible; when this form of unequal predation is seen as the opposite of freedom, and those who outright buy others for sexual use are unmasked as the predators they are—let's call #MeToo prostitution and trafficking maybe #NotSexNotWork—this will be the transformation the present one has prepared.

A third link reveals lessons in #MeToo for gender as an inequality per se in its conceptual and practical links to sexual abuse of children. Sexual harassment is like sexual abuse in childhood in manipulating trust and dependency and institutionally betraying those who report. Sexual abuse of children is arguably the foundational practice of the whole gender system, ground zero of sex inequality. Andrea Dworkin called incest "boot camp."[34] Sexual abuse in childhood is the practical foundation of prostitution and sex trafficking, in that most people used in prostitution, the destination of sex trafficking, were sexually abused as children and entered prostitution as children. Pimps, who know what they are doing, select formerly sexually abused children on purpose.

---

32. Melissa Farley et al., *Prostitution and Trafficking in Nine Countries: An Update on Violence and Posttraumatic Stress Disorder*, 2 J. TRAUMA PRACTICE 33, 34, 51, 56, 65 (2003).

33. Melissa Farley et al., *Online Prostitution and Trafficking*, 77 ALB. L. REV. 1039, 1042, 1042 n.14 (2014).

34. Andrea Dworkin, *Prostitution and Male Supremacy*, 1 MICH. J. GENDER & L. 1, 4 (1993).

Both children and prostituted people are barely surviving through serial rape and molestation under circumstances in which they have no realistic options and from which they have few possibilities of escape.

Sexual abuse in childhood is about what rape and sexual harassment and prostitution are about: *sex forced on those with less power by those with more*, made definitive of masculinity and femininity. This is also the dynamic pornography sexualizes. And many if not most rapists were sexually abused as children. To escape this being done to them, a choice they are given, many men become masculine, sexualizing power over others. To survive under it, girls are taught to acquiesce in femininity, sexualizing power over us, sometimes calling it "empowerment."

Sexual abuse in childhood explains more about the gender system, that is, more about male violence, meaning violence, and more about sexual politics, meaning politics, than any other single thing does. If you put the best studies together, it affects about half of girls in the United States in contact forms before we reach the age of majority,[35] and likely at least a quarter of boys.[36] Data varies by country so we don't even know its real incidence and pervasiveness around the world—based on data we do have, rates in South Africa are by far the highest for both men (60.9 percent) and women (43.7 percent), next are Jordan and Tanzania, with prevalence rates of 27 percent and 25 percent respectively, for men, they are followed by Israel, Spain, Australia, and Costa Rica, and for women, Australia (37.8 percent), Costa Rica (32.2 percent), Tanzania (31

---

35. This is a conservative extrapolation derived from combining Diana E.H. Russell, THE SECRET TRAUMA: INCEST IN THE LIVES OF GIRLS AND WOMEN 62 (1986) (finding that 38 percent of subjects in a study conducted in San Francisco in 1977 had been sexually abused by physical contact before the age of majority), with Linda Meyer Williams, *Recall of Childhood Trauma: A Prospective Study of Women's Memories of Child Sexual Abuse*, 62 J. CONSULTING & CLINICAL PSYCHOL. 1167, 1170 (1994) (reporting that 38 percent of women studied did not recall "sexual abuse that they experienced in childhood and that had been documented in hospital records").

36. *See* David Finkelhor, *Boys as Victims: Review of the Evidence*, CHILD SEXUAL ABUSE: NEW THEORY AND RESEARCH 150 (David Finkelhor ed., 1984) (presenting evidence showing that 2.5 to 8.7 percent of adult male subjects had been sexually victimized as children); Stefanie Doyle Peters et al., *Prevalence*, in A SOURCEBOOK ON CHILD SEXUAL ABUSE 15 (David Finkelhor ed., 1986) (reviewing studies finding prevalence rates of child sexual abuse among boys ranging from 3 to 31 percent). For illuminating comparative data on the lifetime prevalence of sexual abuse in children of both sexes, see Amy Young et al., *Alcohol-Related Sexual Assault Itemization Among Adolescents: Prevalence, Characteristics, and Correlates*, 69 J. STUD. ALCOHOL & DRUGS 39 (2008) (finding that 11.5 percent of women and 6.1 percent of men reported intercourse and other sexual violence as children; 46.2 percent of women and 26.2 percent of men reported other contact abuse such as fondling, touching and kissing; 48.4 percent of women and 26.6 percent of men reported mixed abuse or an unspecified type of sexual abuse; and 67.3 percent of women and 40.9 percent of men reported sexual abuse that did not involve contact, such as indecent exposure and inappropriate sexual solicitation).

percent), Israel (30 percent), Sweden (28.1 percent), the United States (25.3 percent), and Switzerland (24.2 percent)[37]—only that there doesn't seem to be any place it certainly doesn't happen. And although some valiant steps have been made against some institutions (churches, residential schools, schools, period), virtually nothing is being done about it, despite laws against it. Blackstone said better ten perpetrators go free than one innocent accused suffers,[38] as if these were alternatives. With sexual assault, we have both. And this starts before one even grows up enough to have one's sexual abuse recognized as harassment or exposed through #MeToo. Until we figure out how to address sexual abuse of children for real, we will not have done what we need to do.

With all this to be concerned about, women frequently shift our attention to "backlash": their response to our response to their abuse of us. Often neglected is that there is no backlash without a frontlash. Whenever we stand up, whenever we are found in other than supine or prone positions, any bit of power we gain will be called "too much," "going too far." Anytime abusers don't get away with violating us without consequences, it will be called "bias" or "lack of due process." Anytime we say what he did, making perpetrators look like who and what they are, it will be called "defamatory." Any sanction we win will be likened to the death penalty. Anytime we insist on being treated as equals, including going to lunch with the boss, we will find they are incapable of seeing women as other than sexual objects. Yes, they intend to keep their sexual access to us. Yes, their access is established by power and entrenched in institutions and doctrines to support them. All this means is, yes, we haven't won yet. But we are winning.

To continue the frontlash, for agents of social change for human rights, acting consciously, knowing that extremely small initial conditions can be amplified exponentially over time through systemic repetition to ultimately radically shift the way a system behaves—this presents the risk, the caution, and the hope of the butterfly effect. It supports the activist mantra: what you do matters. You are all butterflies.

The #MeToo mobilization, this uprising of the formerly disregarded, has made increasingly untenable the assumption that the one who reports sexual abuse is a lying slut. That already is changing everything. With #MeToo, we have our tornado, and not only in Texas. And a lot of the sexual harassment that has been a constant condition of women's lives is probably not being inflicted at this very moment.

---

37. Noemí Pereda et al., *The Prevalence of Child Sexual Abuse in Community and Student Samples: A Meta-Analysis*, 29 Clinical Psychol. Rev. 328, 333, 334 tbl. 4 (2009).

38. 4 William Blackstone, Commentaries *358.

As butterflies take flight from beneath the shadow of the law, we are living through the first systemic uplift in women's status since the vote. Imagine a revolution without violence against domination and aggression. Envision a moment of truth and a movement of transformation for the sexually violated toward a more equal, therefore more peaceful and just world. It is happening all around the world, all around us, right now.

The Americas

CHAPTER 2

The #MeToo Movement in the United States: Reckoning with the Law's Failure

Jessica A. Clarke[1]

The #MeToo movement has brought the problems of sexual harassment and assault in the United States into sharp focus, exposing the systemic failure of the law for survivors. In October 2017, the *New York Times* and *The New Yorker* magazine reported that media mogul Harvey Weinstein had been sexually harassing women in the entertainment industry since the 1990s.[2] On social media, an overwhelming number of people responded with the hashtag #MeToo, telling their own stories of sexual assault and harassment.[3] In the year after the Weinstein story, more than 200 prominent American men lost their positions as a result of accusations of sexual misconduct.[4] The movement

---

1. Professor of Law, Co-Director, George Barrett Social Justice Program, Vanderbilt University, Nashville, TN.

2. Jodi Kantor & Megan Twohey, *Harvey Weinstein Paid Off Sexual Accusers for Decades*, N.Y. TIMES (Oct. 5, 2017), https://www.nytimes.com/2017/10/05/us/harvey-weinstein -harassment-allegations.html; Ronan Farrow, *From Aggressive Overtures to Sexual Assault: Harvey Weinstein's Accusers Tell Their Stories*, NEW YORKER (Oct. 23, 2017), https://www.new yorker.com/news/news-desk/from-aggressive-overtures-to-sexual-assault-harvey-weinsteins -accusers-tell-their-stories.

3. #MeToo, TWITTER, https://twitter.com/hashtag/metoo. The hashtag made reference to a campaign started twenty years earlier by activist Tarana Burke to provide survivors of sexual abuse with solidarity and resources. Sandra E. Garcia, *The Woman Who Created #MeToo Long Before Hashtags*, N.Y. TIMES (Oct. 20, 2017), https://www.nytimes.com/2017/10/20/us/me -too-movement-tarana-burke.html.

4. Audrey Carlsen et al., *#MeToo Brought Down 201 Powerful Men. Nearly Half of Their Replacements Are Women*, N.Y. TIMES (Oct. 29, 2018), https://www.nytimes.com/interac tive/2018/10/23/us/metoo-replacements.html. A few accused women have also been in the headlines. *See* Hannah Giorgis, *Asia Argento, #MeToo, and the Complicated Question of Power*,

brought new attention to the then-pending criminal prosecutions of actor Bill Cosby[5] and USA Gymnastics doctor Larry Nassar,[6] both accused of a series of sexual assaults spanning decades. During the September 2018 hearings to confirm Justice Kavanaugh to the U.S. Supreme Court, Dr. Christine Blasey Ford testified about being sexually assaulted by Kavanaugh when the two were teenagers in the 1980s.[7] After politicians expressed doubts about Dr. Ford's credibility because she had failed to come forward earlier, survivors began using the social media hashtag #WhyIDidntReport to explain their reasons for not availing themselves of the legal system.[8]

This chapter offers a brief summary of some of the key features of U.S. law on sexual assault and harassment in an attempt to explain why the law has been such a profound failure for survivors. It also discusses legal reform efforts that have been undertaken as a result of the #MeToo movement.

Criminal Law

In the United States, rape and sexual assault are, for the most part, defined by the governments of individual states.[9] Historically, U.S. law treated rape claims with extraordinary skepticism, both because women were thought to fabricate accusations and because the crime was penalized by the harshest of sanctions, including the death penalty.[10] The law therefore imposed a number of special requirements on victims, including physical resistance, prompt reporting, and corroboration.[11] Moreover, because the offense was seen "as an injury to the husband or father of the raped woman" it could not be committed "against

---

ATLANTIC (Aug. 21, 2018), https://www.theatlantic.com/entertainment/archive/2018/08/asia-argento-allegations/568018/.

5. Jen Kirby, *Bill Cosby Found Guilty of Sexual Assault*, VOX (Apr. 26, 2018), https://www.vox.com/2018/4/26/17272470/bill-cosby-trial-verdict-guilty-sexual-assault-andrea-constand.

6. Kerry Howley, *Everyone Believed Larry Nassar*, THE CUT (Nov. 19, 2018), https://www.thecut.com/2018/11/how-did-larry-nassar-deceive-so-many-for-so-long.html.

7. *Read Christine Blasey Ford's Prepared Statement*, N.Y. TIMES (Sept. 26, 2018), https://www.nytimes.com/2018/09/26/us/politics/christine-blasey-ford-prepared-statement.html.

8. #WhyIDidntReport, Twitter, https://twitter.com/hashtag/metoo.

9. In the U.S. federal system, violent crime is generally a state matter. *See* United States v. Morrison, 529 U.S. 598, 618 (2000).

10. Model Penal Code: Sexual Assault and Related Offenses 10 (Am. Law Inst., Tentative Draft No. 1, 2014). The laws were not applied in a racially neutral manner, and black men accused by white women were more likely to be convicted. Id.

11. *Id.* at 9.

a female victim of previously unchaste character."[12] As a result of feminist advocacy beginning in the 1970s, these requirements now find themselves on shaky legal footing.[13] But outdated ideas continue to have an influence over what cases are reported to law enforcement, what cases are pursued by the prosecutors who have the discretion to decide whether to bring charges, and what cases are convincing to the juries who must determine that a defendant is guilty beyond a reasonable doubt.[14]

Early American courts borrowed their definition of rape from English common law: "carnal knowledge of a woman forcibly and against her will."[15] In recognition of the harms of same-sex assaults and assaults by women against men, most U.S. jurisdictions now define offenses in gender-neutral terms, by reference to particular acts and body parts.[16] While historically a victim was required to resist "to the utmost," that requirement has now given way.[17] But the roles of force and consent remain debated. A majority of states now penalize sex without consent, even in the absence of force.[18] But many still define rape to require that the perpetrator used force in addition to requiring sexual penetration, even in the absence of consent.[19] Definitions of force vary, with some states defining force broadly to include "circumstantial coercion or intimidation."[20]

In 2012, the American Law Institute (ALI), a nongovernmental organization of U.S. legal professionals, began revising the sexual assault provisions of the Model Penal Code, an influential set of model criminal laws. The ALI's 2017 draft includes "sexual penetration or oral sex without consent" as a separate offense, apart from "forcible rape."[21] This offense would require that the perpetrator acted "knowingly" or "recklessly."[22] The ALI has approved a defi-

---

12. *Id.*

13. Michelle J. Anderson, *Campus Sexual Assault Adjudication and Resistance to Reform*, 125 YALE L.J. 1940, 1946-49 (2016).

14. *Id.* at 1950–53.

15. 4 WILLIAM BLACKSTONE, COMMENTARIES ON THE LAWS OF ENGLAND *210 (1765).

16. MODEL PENAL CODE: SEXUAL ASSAULT AND RELATED OFFENSES 7–9 (Am. Law Inst., Tentative Draft No. 3, 2017).

17. *Id.* at 26. Eight states still have "a formal resistance requirement, meaning that resistance is required unless it would be futile or likely result in injury." *Id.* In these states, resistance may be verbal. *Id.* at 27.

18. *Id.* at 40–41 (surveying U.S. state statutes and case law as of October 2016).

19. *Id.* at 23.

20. *Id.* at 23–24.

21. *Id.* §§ 213.1-.4, at 49, app. A. The proposed definition of "forcible rape" includes "using physical force or restraint, or making an express or implied threat of bodily injury of physical force or restraint." *Id.* § 213.1, at 13.

22. *Id.* § 213.4, at 50, app. A.

nition of consent to mean "a person's willingness to engage in a specific act of sexual penetration, oral sex, or sexual contact. Consent may be express or it may be inferred from behavior—both action and inaction—in the context of all the circumstances."[23] "A clear verbal refusal—such as 'No,' 'Stop,' or 'Don't,'—establishes the lack of consent";[24] but consent may be absent even without such a statement.[25] This concept is known as "contextual consent."[26] There remain disagreements over what circumstances might "nullify apparent consent" such as "force, fraud, and coercion," among other issues.[27] The ALI's project has been controversial due to specific policy arguments as well as generalized opposition to rape reform "attributable to misogyny."[28]

U.S. law once required a victim's "prompt complaint" as a prerequisite to a sexual assault prosecution, on the theory that victims who did not immediately report could not be trusted.[29] While this rule has been abandoned, many U.S. states still have statutes of limitations that bar claims if they are not brought within a certain time period, sometimes ten years or less.[30] These time limitations were reportedly the reason that, out of the sixty women who had accused Bill Cosby of rape and other crimes, prosecutors could only bring one case, that of Andrea Constand.[31] Although they could not bring charges, several accusers were permitted to testify at Cosby's re-trial about how he had drugged and sexually assaulted them, lending support to Constand's accusations.[32]

---

23. *Id.* § 213.0(a)-(b), at 51, app. B.

24. *Id.* § 213.0(e).

25. *Id.* § 213.0(c) ("Neither verbal nor physical resistance is required to establish that consent is lacking, but their absence may be considered, in the context of all the circumstances, in determining there was consent.").

26. *Id.* at 44.

27. Stephen J. Schulhofer, *Reforming the Law of Rape*, 35 LAW & INEQ. 335, 344–46 (2017). For critique of the proposed rules, *see* Catharine A. MacKinnon, *Rape Redefined*, 10 HARV. L. & POL'Y REV. 431, 474 (2016).

28. Schulhofer, *supra* note 27, at 336.

29. MPC Tentative Draft No. 1, *supra* note 10, at 86.

30. RAINN, State by State Guide on Statutes of Limitations, https://www.rainn.org /state-state-guide-statutes-limitations.

31. Jen Kirby, *Bill Cosby Found Guilty of Sexual Assault*, VOX (Apr. 26, 2018), https:// www.vox.com/2018/4/26/17272470/bill-cosby-trial-verdict-guilty-sexual-assault-andrea -constand.

32. Jeannie Suk Gerson, *Bill Cosby's Crimes and the Impact of #MeToo on the American Legal System*, NEW YORKER (Apr. 27, 2018), https://www.newyorker.com/news/news-desk /bill-cosbys-crimes-and-the-impact-of-metoo-on-the-american-legal-system. Cosby was retried because his first trial, which occurred before the #MeToo movement, ended with a hung jury. *Id.* At the first trial, only one additional accuser testified, while at the re-trial, five did. *Id.*

Historically, U.S. law required "corroborative evidence" such as physical injuries for claims of rape,[33] and even with that evidence, jurors were instructed to regard a victim's testimony with particular caution.[34] While these rules have been eliminated or curtailed,[35] the criminal justice system continues to impose an informal "credibility discount" on victims in rape cases.[36] Some researchers estimate that only 7 to 27 percent of rapes that are reported to law enforcement are prosecuted, and only 3 to 26 percent result in conviction.[37] Surveys reveal that law enforcement officers believe reports of rape are much more likely to be false than reports of other crimes, despite the lack of evidence to support this assumption.[38] The criminal justice system imposes a particular credibility discount on "women of color, immigrants, LGBTQ individuals, women in poverty, and sex workers."[39] Even prosecutors who do not personally discount the credibility of survivors may decide not to bring cases because they predict that jurors will not believe survivors.[40] One of Harvey Weinstein's accusers caught Weinstein admitting to sexually assaulting her on tape, yet prosecutors still thought there was not enough evidence to bring a case.[41]

While U.S. rape law once turned on the victim's chastity, inquiries into the victim's sexual history are now barred by evidentiary rules called "rape shield laws."[42] And yet defense lawyers can still "re-victimize the complainant through subtle, but still dehumanizing, cross-examinations" about the victim's dress and behaviors leading up to the rape, implying that the victim was to blame.[43]

---

33. MPC Tentative Draft No. 1, *supra* note 10, at 87–88.

34. *Id.* at 89.

35. *Id.* at 88–89.

36. Deborah Tuerkheimer, *Incredible Women: Sexual Violence and the Credibility Discount*, 166 U. PA. L. REV. 1, 2 (2017).

37. Kimberly A. Lonsway & Joanne Archambault, *The "Justice Gap" for Sexual Assault Cases: Future Directions for Research and Reform*, 18 VIOLENCE AGAINST WOMEN 145, 156 (2012).

38. In one survey of 891 police officers, 53 percent believed that between 11 and 50 percent of women falsely report rape, and 10 percent believed that between 50 and 100 percent of women make false reports. Amy Dellinger Page, *Gateway to Reform? Policy Implications of Police Officers' Attitudes Toward Rape*, 33 AM. J. CRIM. JUST. 44, 55 (2008).

39. Tuerkheimer, *supra* note 36, at 31.

40. Lonsway & Archambault, *supra* note 37, at 159.

41. Farrow, *supra* note 2.

42. MPC Tentative Draft No. 1, *supra* note 10, at 91–94.

43. Corey Rayburn, *To Catch a Sex Thief: The Burden of Performance in Rape and Sexual Assault Trials*, 15 COLUM. J. GENDER & L. 437, 446 (2006).

Studies demonstrate that sexual assaults are the most underreported of all serious crimes.[44] As the #WhyIDidntReport discussion revealed, survivors have many reasons for not coming forward, including concerns that they will be not be believed by police and fear of reprisals from their perpetrators and communities.[45] Consider Maryville, Missouri, where, in 2012, after a 14-year-old girl reported that she had been raped by a 17-year-old football player, the girl's family was subjected to vitriolic harassment, her mother was fired from her job, and the family's home was burned down under suspicious circumstances.[46]

While rape is no longer a crime punishable by death, a punitive movement in criminal justice reform has succeeded in implementing draconian penalties for those convicted of sex offenses, such as onerous public registration requirements.[47] Some opposition to rape reform today is driven by legitimate concerns about these draconian penalties, as well as the general dysfunction of the U.S. criminal justice system in terms of dramatic racial disparities, stark class biases, and mass incarceration.[48] The image of the assailant that underlies punitive reforms is that of a predatory stranger, rather than the more common experience of rape by intimates and acquaintances.[49] This view may paradoxically make efforts to recognize abuse more difficult. For example, for decades, Bill Cosby's accusers "were met, mostly, with skepticism, threats, and attacks on their character," perhaps because of Cosby's sitcom image as America's dad.[50] And one curious aspect of the Larry Nassar case is that gymnasts had long been reporting his sexual abuse, but because it was difficult to square their stories with Nassar's generous personality and effective medical care, the gymnastics

---

44. Studies show varying reporting rates between 16 and 42 percent. MPC Tentative Draft No. 1, *supra* note 10, at 14.

45. For survey evidence on reasons survivors do not report, see DEPARTMENT OF JUSTICE, OFFICE OF JUSTICE PROGRAMS, BUREAU OF JUSTICE STATISTICS, FEMALE VICTIMS OF SEXUAL VIOLENCE, 1994-2010, at 7 tbl. 9 (2013), https://www.bjs.gov/content/pub/pdf/fvsv9410.

46. Dugan Arnett, *Nightmare in Maryville: Teens' Sexual Encounter Ignites a Firestorm Against Family*, KANSAS CITY STAR (Oct. 12, 2013), https://www.kansascity.com/news/special-reports/maryville/article329412.html.

47. Anderson, *supra* note 13, at 1953.

48. Schulhofer, *supra* note 27, at 350–51.

49. According to one survey, only 14.1 percent of women and 15.1 percent of men who reported they were raped said that their assailant was a stranger. MICHELE C. BLACK ET AL., THE NATIONAL INTIMATE PARTNER AND SEXUAL VIOLENCE SURVEY: 2010 SUMMARY REPORT 22 (2011), http://www.cdc.gov/violenceprevention/pdf/nisvs_report2010-a.pdf.

50. Noreen Malone & Amanda Demme, *"I'm No Longer Afraid": 35 Women Tell Their Stories About Being Assaulted by Bill Cosby, and the Culture That Wouldn't Listen*, THE CUT (July 26, 2015), https://www.thecut.com/2015/07/bill-cosbys-accusers-speak-out.html#barbara-bowman.

community did not turn against him until a police officer found his cache of child pornography.[51]

The #MeToo movement has drawn attention to the lack of resources devoted to rape and sexual assault by law enforcement.[52] A 1994 federal law, the Violence Against Women Act (VAWA) provides funding to law enforcement agencies, courts, and private organizations to address domestic and sexual violence.[53] These funds have supported the creation of special law enforcement units devoted to sexual violence, services for victims, and community education, among other things.[54] VAWA requires that state and local governments pay for sexual assault survivors to undergo forensic medical examinations to collect DNA, photographic, and other evidence.[55] This evidence is stored in containers known as "rape kits."[56] Because sexual assault investigations were not prioritized for many decades, a backlog developed in which thousands of kits were left unanalyzed.[57] State and local governments have recently devoted funds to reduce these backlogs and used rape-kit evidence to open new investigations.[58] In the wake of #MeToo, a number of U.S. states have passed laws to ensure that rape-kit evidence is analyzed in a more timely manner.[59]

---

51. Howley, *supra* note 6.

52. *See, e.g.*, Rebecca Beitsch, *#MeToo Has Changed Our Culture. Now It's Changing Our Laws*, Pew Stateline (July 31, 2018), https://www.pewtrusts.org/en/research-and-analysis/blogs/stateline/2018/07/31/metoo-has-changed-our-culture-now-its-changing-our-laws.

53. 34 U.S.C. § 12291 (2012).

54. U.S. Dep't of Justice, Office on Violence Against Women, The 2016 Biennial Rep. to Congress on the Effectiveness of Grant Programs Under the Violence Against Women Act xi-xvii (2016), https://www.justice.gov/ovw/page/file/933886/download.

55. 34 U.S.C. § 10449.

56. Office of Manhattan Dist. Attorney, Test Every Kit: Results from the Manhattan District Attorney's Office's Sexual Assault Kit Backlog Elimination Grant Program 4 ("Manhattan Dist. Attorney") (2019), https://www.manhattanda.org/wp-content/uploads/2019/03/Test-Every-Kit-Results-from-the-Manhattan-District-Attorneys-Offices-Sexual-Assault-Kit-Backlog-Eliminaton-Grant-Program.pdf.

57. *Id.* at 6; Steve Reilly, *Tens of Thousands of Rape Kits Go Untested Across USA*, USA Today (July 16, 2015), https://www.usatoday.com/story/news/2015/07/16/untested-rape-kits-evidence-across-usa/29902199/.

58. *See, e.g.*, Manhattan Dist. Attorney, *supra* note 56, at 2–3, 17–18.

59. *See, e.g.*, 2019 Tex. Sess. Law Serv. Ch. 408 (H.B. 8) (Vernon's); 2019 Md. Laws Ch. 33 (S.B. 767) (West); 2019 Wash. Legis. Serv. Ch. 93 (S.S.H.B. 1166) (West).

Antidiscrimination Law

In addition to criminal justice, U.S. law also addresses sexual abuse as a civil rights issue. This is as a result of the work of feminist lawyers and activists in the 1970s, such as Catharine MacKinnon and Lin Farley.[60] Sexual harassment law in the United States first developed as an interpretation of Title VII of the Civil Rights Act of 1964, a federal statute that prohibits employment discrimination "because of … sex."[61] Under Title VII, victims of sexual harassment may bring civil suits against their employers. A federal administrative agency, the Equal Employment Opportunity Commission (EEOC), is also authorized to bring suit on behalf of victims. But the statute's reach is limited by a number of substantive, procedural, contractual, and practical barriers. While some individual states have passed laws to fill the gaps left by Title VII, many have not, leaving a patchwork of protection throughout the United States.

One limitation of sexual harassment law is that Title VII applies only to certain employer/employee relationships, leaving many workers out in the cold.[62] Although independent contractors, such as most sharing-economy workers, freelancers, vendors, and consultants, make up 10 percent of the American workforce, they are beyond the law's reach.[63] For this reason, most of the actors who spoke out against Harvey Weinstein would not have claims under Title VII. In addition to exempting many workers, Title VII also exempts certain employers such as the federal judiciary,[64] the military,[65] and those businesses that employ fewer than fifteen people.[66] Low-wage and immigrant workers, although ostensibly permitted to bring claims, are unlikely to have the information, time, access to counsel, or resources to do so.[67] While the EEOC may bring claims on behalf of these workers, its resources are limited.

---

60. Reva B. Siegel, *Introduction: A Short History of Sexual Harassment, in* DIRECTIONS IN SEXUAL HARASSMENT LAW 1–39 (Catherine A. MacKinnon & Reva Siegel eds., 2004).

61. 42 U.S.C. § 2000e-2(a)(1) (2012).

62. *See, e.g.*, Murray v. Principal Fin. Group, Inc., 613 F.3d 943, 944 (9th Cir. 2010).

63. Bureau of Labor Statistics, Economic News Release, Contingent and Alternative Employment Arrangements Summary (June 7, 2018), https://www.bls.gov/news.release/conemp.nr0.htm.

64. Nancy Gertner, *Sexual Harassment and the Bench*, 71 STAN. L. REV. ONLINE 88, 89 (2018).

65. Michael I. Spak & Alice M. McCart, *Effect of Military Culture on Responding to Sexual Harassment: The Warrior Mystique*, 83 NEB. L. REV. 79, 99 (2004).

66. 42 U.S.C. § 2000e(b) (2012).

67. Elizabeth Kristen et al., *Workplace Violence and Harassment of Low-Wage Workers*, 36 BERKELEY J. EMP. & LAB. L. 169, 180 (2015).

Even plaintiffs with the wherewithal to bring suit may conclude it is a losing proposition. Litigating a sexual harassment claim can be time consuming and emotionally devastating; U.S. discovery rules require that plaintiffs repeatedly recount the details of their abuse to hostile adversaries in a process that can take years.[68] Under Title VII, victims may be entitled to reinstatement, lost wages, and other such restitution, but sexual harassment does not always result in these types of damages.[69] The law also allows compensatory damages for harms such as emotional distress, and punitive damages to penalize and deter employers, but those types of damages are capped, up to a combined maximum of $300,000.[70] Moreover, to win punitive damages, a plaintiff must make the extraordinary showing that her employer "discriminate[d] in the face of a perceived risk that its actions will violate federal law."[71] These limits not only reduce a plaintiff's incentive to bring suit, they also undermine the deterrent value of sexual harassment law.[72]

If a victim does decide to bring a case, her claim will have to meet a stringent set of substantive requirements. To prove a claim of sexual harassment, a plaintiff must generally establish that: (1) the harassment was because of sex; (2) the harassment was severe or pervasive; (3) the harassment was unwelcome; and (4) there is a basis for employer liability. Federal courts analyze these elements mechanically and often dismiss a plaintiff's case before trial if she lacks sufficient evidence of any one of them.

Because sexual harassment is a species of sex discrimination under federal law, a plaintiff must demonstrate that she was targeted "because of sex."[73] Both men and women can be targeted because of sex, and there is no requirement that the harasser be of a different sex than the victim.[74] Courts generally presume that harassment motivated by sexual desire was because of sex.[75] But there is no requirement that the harassing words or conduct be of a sexual nature.[76] Courts have also found harassment was because of sex where the harasser expressed hostility toward men or women in the workplace, where men or women were

---

68. For one account of the toll sexual harassment litigation can take on plaintiffs, see CLARA BINGHAM & LAURA LEEDY GANSLER, CLASS ACTION: THE STORY OF LOIS JENSON AND THE LANDMARK CASE THAT CHANGED SEXUAL HARASSMENT LAW (2002).

69. 42 U.S.C. § 1981a (2012).

70. *Id.*

71. Kolstad v. Am. Dental Ass'n, 527 U.S. 526, 536 (1999).

72. *See* Joni Hersch, *Efficient Deterrence of Workplace Sexual Harassment*, 2019 U. CHI. L.F. 147.

73. Oncale v. Sundowner Offshore Servs., Inc., 523 U.S. 75, 80 (1998).

74. *Id.*

75. *See* Jessica Clarke, *Inferring Desire*, 63 DUKE L.J. 525, 536 (2013).

76. *Oncale*, 523 U.S. at 80.

singled out for worse treatment, and where the harasser targeted the victim because of the victim's failure to conform to gender stereotypes.[77]

Despite the many ways that harassment can be because of sex, courts myopically focus on sexual desire and sexualized harms. This myopia obscures how sexual harassment is also a manifestation of "workplace sexism": "a way for dominant men to label women (and perceived 'lesser men') as inferior and shore up an idealized masculine work status and identity."[78] For example, harassers might target a woman with misogynist insults that are not sexual but are certainly sexist. Some male supervisors who feel uncertain about how to interact with women as a result of the #MeToo movement might exclude women from networking opportunities, refuse to mentor women, or not invite women to dine or travel with them.[79] This is also harassment because of sex.

Moreover, the judicial preoccupation with sexualized harassment makes it more difficult to see how race-based and sex-based harassment might overlap and coincide, or how LGBTQ plaintiffs can be victims of sexual harassment by straight coworkers.[80] Some courts construe a claim of sexual harassment to require a plaintiff to be a member of a "protected class," even though there is no such requirement in Title VII, which covers all "individual[s]."[81] These courts reason that LGBTQ plaintiffs are bringing claims based on sexual orientation or transgender status, rather than as members of the protected classes of men or women.[82] At the time of this writing, the U.S. Supreme Court is considering whether discrimination on the basis of sexual orientation or gender identity is "because of ... sex" under Title VII.[83]

A second element is that the harassment was "severe or pervasive," both as an objective matter, meaning in the estimation of a reasonable person, and as a

---

77. *See* Clarke, *supra* note 75, at 535–39. On similar theories, nonbinary people can also be targeted for harassment because of sex. *See* Jessica Clarke, *They, Them, and Theirs*, 132 Harv. L. Rev. 894, 924–25 (2019).

78. Vicki Schultz, *Reconceptualizing Sexual Harassment, Again*, 128 Yale L.J.F. 22, 24 (2018).

79. *See, e.g.*, Gillian Tan & Katia Porzecanski, *Wall Street Rule for the #MeToo Era: Avoid Women at All Cost*, Bloomberg (Dec. 3, 2018, 4:00 AM), https://www.bloomberg.com/news /articles/2018-12-03/a-wall-street-rule-for-the-metoo-era-avoid-women-at-all-cost.

80. *See, e.g.*, Brian Soucek, *Queering Sexual Harassment Law*, 128 Yale L.J.F. 67, 67–69 (2018).

81. Jessica Clarke, *Protected Class Gatekeeping*, 92 N.Y.U. L. Rev. 101, 123–26 (2017).

82. *Id.*

83. Bostock v. Clayton Cty. Bd. of Comm'ners, 723 F. App'x 964 (11th Cir. 2018), *cert. granted*, 139 S. Ct. 1599 (2019); Equal Employment Opportunity Comm'n v. R.G. &. G.R. Harris Funeral Homes, Inc., 884 F.3d 560 (6th Cir. 2018), *cert. granted*, 139 S. Ct. 1599 (2019); Zarda v. Altitude Express, Inc., 883 F.3d 100 (2d Cir. 2018), *cert. granted*, 139 S. Ct. 1599 (2019).

subjective matter, meaning in the victim's own estimation.[84] Harassment need not cause psychological or tangible economic harm to meet this standard.[85] Courts consider factors including "the frequency of the discriminatory conduct; its severity; whether it is physically threatening or humiliating, or a mere offensive utterance; and whether it unreasonably interferes with an employee's work performance."[86] A single incident—such as sexual assault or a quid-pro-quo demand for sexual favors—may be sufficient.[87]

Notoriously, lower federal courts have raised the bar for what counts as "severe or pervasive."[88] Many of the incidents exposed by the #MeToo movement would not qualify as harassment under this harsh standard. For example, in one case, a female law enforcement officer alleged that her male supervisor had tried to kiss her and called her a "frigid bitch" when she refused him, showed up at her home to tell her he loved her, commented on her appearance, chased her around the office, picked her up and lifted her over his head, rubbed against her, and attempted to look down her shirt, among other incidents over the course of her four years working in his department.[89] The court dismissed the case because the conduct "was not that frequent."[90] Another problem is that courts often disaggregate allegations of harassment into separate categories for analysis—for example, separating racial and sexual harassment,[91] or sexual and non-sexual forms of harassment[92]—in order to find that no one category meets the "severe or pervasive" standard.

A third element of a harassment claim is that the harassment be unwelcome. Early on, U.S. courts recognized that it is not a defense to sexual harassment that the victim voluntarily submitted to sexual interaction; it is sufficient that the harassment was unwelcome.[93] This was an improvement over a doctrine that would have allowed a victim's consent to be a defense. While the unwelcomeness element is not an issue in many reported cases, it may still focus undue attention on the victim's personal history and response to the harassment,

---

84. Harris v. Forklift Sys., Inc., 510 U.S. 17, 22 (1993).

85. *Id.*

86. *Id.* at 23.

87. Sandra Sperino & Suja Thomas, Unequal: How America's Courts Undermine Discrimination Law 33 (2017).

88. *Id.* at 33–38.

89. Mitchell v. Pope, 189 F. App'x 911, 913 n.3 (11th Cir. 2006).

90. *Id.* at 913.

91. Clarke, *supra* note 81, at 127–29.

92. Vicki Schultz, *Reconceptualizing Sexual Harassment*, 107 Yale L.J. 1683, 1713–29 (1998).

93. Meritor Sav. Bank v. Vinson, 477 U.S. 57, 68 (1986).

limiting the cases plaintiff's lawyers are willing to bring and inviting defense attorneys to engage in intrusive and humiliating discovery into a plaintiff's personal life.[94]

A final element is employer liability. One quirk of U.S. harassment law is that under Title VII, only employers are liable; individual harassers may not be sued.[95] There are three tiers of employer liability. The highest level is automatic liability. An employer is automatically liable if (a) the harasser took a "tangible employment action" against the victim, meaning some sort of official act of the enterprise, such as a demotion, or (b) the harasser is one of the company's highest officials.[96] Thus, if the victim lost her job, or if her harasser were Harvey Weinstein and she was an employee of the Weinstein Company, liability would be automatic. But much harassment is informal, and most harassers do not have their names on the building.

A second tier of employer liability is known as the *Faragher/Ellerth* standard.[97] It applies if there is no basis for automatic liability, but the harasser was the victim's supervisor. Under this standard, the employer has the burden of proving that it "exercised reasonable care to prevent and correct promptly any sexually harassing behavior, and that the plaintiff employee unreasonably failed to take advantage of any preventive or corrective opportunities provided by the employer or to avoid harm otherwise."[98] The lowest tier of liability applies when the harasser was a coworker, customer, or other person who was not the plaintiff's supervisor, in which case it is the plaintiff who has the burden of proving the employer was negligent.[99]

This complicated employer liability scheme renders sexual harassment law ineffective in a wide swath of cases. When liability is not automatic, claims will be barred unless victims took advantage of their employer's "preventative or corrective opportunities" by promptly reporting the harassment. Yet studies have

---

94. Grace S. Ho, *Not Quite Rights: How the Unwelcomeness Element in Sexual Harassment Law Undermines Title VII's Transformative Potential*, 20 YALE J.L. & FEMINISM 131, 151–52, 155 (2008).

95. Victims of sexual harassment may bring common-law tort claims against individual perpetrators under state law, but they seldom do for a variety of reasons, notably the lack of liability insurance funds that might provide compensation should they prevail. Martha Chamallas, *Will Tort Law Have Its #Me Too Moment?*, 11 J. TORT L. 39, 47–48, 52–53 (2018).

96. Burlington Industries, Inc. v. Ellerth, 524 U.S. 742, 758, 761–63 (1998).

97. *Id.* at 753; Faragher v. City of Boca Raton, 524 U.S. 775, 807 (1998).

98. *Burlington Industries, Inc.*, 524 U.S. at 765.

99. *See, e.g.*, Carr v. Allison Gas Turbine Div., Gen. Motors Corp., 32 F.3d 1007, 1009 (7th Cir. 1994). This same negligence standard often applies in common-law tort claims against institutions that employed perpetrators of sexual abuse, making it difficult for survivors to win their cases. *See* Martha Chamallas, *Vicarious Liability in Torts: The Sex Exception*, 48 VAL. U. L. REV. 133, 136 (2013).

found that 70 percent of sexual harassment victims never complain internally.[100] Victims do not complain because "they fear disbelief of their claim, inaction on their claim, blame, or social or professional retaliation."[101] Moreover, "employers often create policies and grievance procedures that are ineffective or inaccessible or involve fear of retaliation. And courts, for their part, often fail to distinguish between effective and ineffective organizational policies."[102]

According to one study, 75 percent of employees who complained faced some sort of retaliation.[103] While Title VII forbids retaliation, the U.S. Supreme Court has made it more difficult to prove than other violations of the statute.[104] As a general matter, plaintiffs are only protected if they have filed an official complaint with a federal agency or if they had a reasonable belief that the harassment was illegal.[105] This can put victims in a double bind: if a victim complains about her supervisor's harassment too early, and then that supervisor fires her in retaliation, a court may conclude she did not have a reasonable belief her harassment was severe or pervasive, and so her firing was permissible.[106] But if that plaintiff waits until the supervisor's harassment becomes severe or pervasive, a court may conclude that she failed to promptly take advantage of corrective opportunities provided by the employer, and therefore the *Faragher/Ellerth* defense immunizes the employer from liability.

In addition to these substantive requirements, there are unusual procedural hurdles for sexual harassment claims. Before bringing suit, a plaintiff must first file a "charge" with the EEOC or state agency, so that agency can attempt to resolve the case or decide whether it should bring suit on the plaintiff's behalf. Plaintiffs have a short time frame, generally 300 days, but sometimes as few as 180 days, in which to bring that charge.[107] By contrast, a typical statute of

---

100. Lilia M. Cortina & Jennifer L. Berdahl, *Sexual Harassment in Organizations: A Decade of Research in Review*, *in* 1 THE SAGE HANDBOOK OF ORGANIZATIONAL BEHAVIOR 469, 469–96 (J. Barling & C. L. Cooper eds., 2008).

101. CHAI R. FELDBLUM & VICTORIA A. LIPNIC, U.S. EQUAL EMP'T OPPORTUNITY COMM'N, REPORT OF THE CO-CHAIRS OF THE SELECT TASK FORCE ON THE STUDY OF HARASSMENT IN THE WORKPLACE (2016), https://www.eeoc.gov/eeoc/task_force/harass ment/report.cfm.

102. LAUREN B. EDELMAN, WORKING LAW: COURTS, CORPORATIONS, AND SYMBOLIC CIVIL RIGHTS 62 (2016).

103. Lilia M. Cortina & Vicki J. Magley, *Raising Voice, Risking Retaliation: Events Following Interpersonal Mistreatment in the Workplace*, 8:4 J. OCCUPATIONAL HEALTH PSYCHOL. 247, 255 (2003).

104. *See* Univ. Tex. Sw. Med. Ctr. v. Nassar, 570 U.S. 338, 352 (2013).

105. Clark County Sch. Dist. v. Breeden, 532 U.S. 268, 271 (2001).

106. Deborah L. Brake, *Retaliation in an EEO World*, 89 IND. L.J. 115, 139 (2014).

107. 42 U.S.C. § 2000e-5(e)(1) (2012).

limitations for breach of contract is six years, with no requirement that a charge be filed with any agency first.[108]

On top of the substantive and procedural barriers, there may also be contractual barriers to suit. As a condition of hire, many U.S. employers require that their employees sign agreements limiting their rights to pursue sexual harassment claims. These agreements may require that charges of sexual harassment be settled in arbitration rather than litigation,[109] or they may bar class-wide claims,[110] and they may require confidentiality.[111] Whether or not there is an agreement to arbitrate, employers often require nondisclosure agreements as a condition of any settlement of a sexual harassment claim, shielding harassers and the company from public scrutiny.[112] Many commentators blamed confidentiality agreements for the persistence of Harvey Weinstein's harassment.[113]

As a result of the #MeToo movement, some U.S. states have passed laws limiting the use of nondisclosure agreements.[114] Others have attempted to limit mandatory arbitration agreements,[115] even though federal courts have struck down similar laws as preempted by a federal statute, the Federal Arbitration

---

108. *See, e.g.*, MASS. GEN. LAWS ch. 260 § 2 (2019).

109. ALEXANDER J.S. COLVIN, ECON. POLICY INST., THE GROWING USE OF MANDATORY ARBITRATION 1 (Sept. 27, 2017), https://www.epi.org/files/pdf/135056.pdf.

110. *See* Epic Systems Corp. v. Lewis, 138 S. Ct. 1612, 1619 (2018).

111. Steven Davidoff Solomon, *Arbitration Clauses Let American Apparel Hide Misconduct*, DEALBOOK (July 15, 2014), https://dealbook.nytimes.com/2014/07/15/arbitration-clauses-let-american-apparel-hide-misconduct/. While arbitration and other such agreements do not bind the EEOC, the EEOC can bring only a fraction of meritorious cases. EEOC v. Waffle House, Inc., 534 U.S. 279, 295–96 (2002).

112. Alexia Fernández Campbell, *A New House Bill Would Bar Companies from Using Nondisclosure Agreements to Hide Harassment*, VOX (July 18, 2018), https://www.vox.com/2018/7/18/17586532/sexual-harassment-bill-ban-nondisclosure-agreements-ndas-congress-metoo.

113. *See, e.g.*, Daniel Hemel, *How Nondisclosure Agreements Protect Sexual Predators*, VOX (Oct. 13, 2017), https://www.vox.com/the-big-idea/2017/10/9/16447118/confidentiality-agreement-weinstein-sexual-harassment-nda.

114. CAL. CIV. PRO. § 1001 (West 2019) (forbidding nondisclosure agreements if a victim has filed a civil or administrative complaint); N.Y. GEN. OBLIG. § 5-336 (McKinney 2018) (forbidding nondisclosure agreements unless it "is the complainant's preference"); N.J. STAT. ANN. § 10:5-12.8 (West 2019) (providing that nondisclosure agreements are unenforceable against current or former employees). Some states have forbidden certain nondisclosure agreements as conditions of employment. CAL. GOV'T CODE § 12964.5 (West 2019); TENN. CODE ANN. § 50-1-108 (2018); MD. CODE ANN., LAB. & EMPL. § 3-715 (West 2018); VT. STAT. ANN. tit. 21, § 495h(g)-(h) (2018); WASH. REV. CODE 49.44.210 (2018). A California law nullifies any agreement that would prevent a person from testifying about alleged criminal conduct or sexual harassment at the request of an administrative agency, legislature, or court. CAL. CIV. CODE § 1670.11 (West 2019).

115. *See, e.g.*, N.Y. C.P.L.R. § 7515 (McKinney 2019).

Act.[116] A new provision of the U.S. tax code forbids employers from deducting settlement payments if the settlement included a nondisclosure agreement, which may reduce the incentives to include these provisions.[117]

Some individual U.S. states and localities have passed laws providing remedies for sexual harassment where Title VII would not.[118] For example, California and New York have extended their laws to cover independent contractors.[119] California has gone further to forbid sexual harassment by any person with a "business, service, or professional relationship" with the victim or who "holds himself or herself out as being able to help the plaintiff establish a business, service, or professional relationship with the defendant or a third party."[120] This includes doctors, lawyers, teachers, elected officials, directors, and producers.[121] California's legislature has also clarified that workplace harassment does not have to meet the "severe or pervasive" standard to be illegal; an employee need only prove that "a reasonable person subjected to the discriminatory conduct would find … that the harassment so altered working conditions as to make it more difficult to do the job."[122] Some state courts, including New York's, have declined to adopt the *Faragher/Ellerth* defense, imposing automatic liability for harassment by supervisors.[123] Some states have also extended the statute of limitations, for example, New York's is three years.[124] Political polarization at the federal level in the United States makes state-level change a more likely reform strategy for feminists. But state-level change will be piecemeal.

Although legal reforms have been limited, the #MeToo movement has had a major impact in prompting voters, corporate leaders, and other institutional actors to remedy the lack of gender diversity in leadership. In the first mid-term election after the movement went viral, an unprecedented number of

---

116. *See, e.g.*, AT&T Mobility LLC v. Concepcion, 563 U.S. 333 (2011).

117. Tax Cuts and Jobs Act of 2017, Pub. L. No. 115-97, § 13307, 131 Stat. 2054.

118. Another popular reform is to increase required trainings by employers. *See, e.g.*, CAL. GOV'T CODE § 12950.1 (West 2019). But research on the efficacy of training programs is mixed. *See, e.g.*, Frank Dobbin & Alexandra Kalev, *Training Programs and Reporting Systems Won't End Sexual Harassment. Promoting More Women Will*, HARV. BUS. REV. (Nov. 15, 2017), https://hbr.org/2017/11/training-programs-and-reporting-systems-wont-end-sexual-harass ment-promoting-more-women-will.

119. CAL. GOV'T CODE § 12940(j)(1) (West 2018); N.Y. EXEC. L. § 296-d (McKinney 2018).

120. CAL. CIV. CODE § 51.9(a)(1).

121. *Id.*

122. CAL. GOV'T CODE § 12923(a) (quoting Harris v. Forklift Sys., 510 U.S. 17, 26 (1993) (Ginsburg, J., concurring)). The legislature has also clarified that "[h]arassment cases are rarely appropriate for disposition on summary judgment." *Id.* § 12923(d).

123. *See, e.g.*, Zakrzewska v. New Sch., 928 N.E.2d 1035, 1038–39 (N.Y. 2010).

124. N.Y. C.P.L.R. 214(2) (McKinney 2018).

women won seats in the U.S. House of Representatives.[125] The *New York Times* estimates that almost one-half of the 201 prominent men who lost positions as a result of #MeToo-related allegations were replaced by women.[126] In 2018, California passed a law mandating gender diversity on corporate boards—the first such law in the United States.[127] These changes reflect the recognition that one structural cause of sexual harassment is the gendered power imbalance in American institutions.[128]

The #MeToo movement has also prompted new efforts by the nonprofit sector to make harassment law more effective, such as the launch of the Time's Up Legal Defense Fund, an organization that connects victims of workplace sexual harassment with legal representation and public relations assistance, particularly low-income women and people of color.[129] In its first six months, the Fund "allocated more than $5 million to 75 cases."[130]

In addition to Title VII's bar on sexual harassment in employment, federal statutes also forbid sex discrimination in education,[131] housing,[132] and health care.[133] Interpretations of Title VII often influence the interpretations of these other statutes, for better or worse.[134] Courts have interpreted Title IX, a 1972 law that forbids sex discrimination in educational programs receiving federal funding, to require schools to stop students from sexually harassing other

---

125. Mary Jordan, *Record Number of Women Heading to Congress*, Wash. Post (Nov. 8, 2018), https://www.washingtonpost.com/politics/record-number-of-women-appear -headed-for-congress/2018/11/06/76a9e60a-e1eb-11e8-8f5f-a55347f48762_story.html?utm _term=.817eac07048e.

126. Carlsen et al., *supra* note 4.

127. Cal. Corp. Code § 301.3 (West 2019). The law applies only to certain public corporations with principal executive offices in California. *Id.* The rule defines who is a woman based on self-identification, not sex assigned at birth. *Id.* § 301.3(f)(3).

128. *See* Dobbin & Kalev, *supra* note 118; Vicki Schultz, *Open Statement on Sexual Harassment from Employment Discrimination Law Scholars*, 71 Stan. L. Rev. Online 17, 22–24 (2018) (collecting studies on the links between sex segregated workplaces and harassment).

129. About Time's Up Legal Defense Fund, Nat'l Women's Law Ctr., https:// nwlc.org/times-up-legal-defense-fund/about-times-up-legal-defense-fund/ (last visited Apr. 28, 2019).

130. Time's Up Legal Defense Fund, Time's Up Annual Report 6 (2018), https://nwlc-ciw49tixgw5lbab.stackpathdns.com/wp-content/uploads/2018/12/TIMES-UP -2018-Version-2.pdf.

131. 20 U.S.C. § 1681 (2012).

132. 42 U.S.C. § 3604 (2012).

133. 42 U.S.C. § 18116(a) (2012).

134. *See, e.g.*, Rigel C. Oliveri, *Sexual Harassment of Low-Income Women in Housing: Pilot Study Results*, 83 Mo. L. Rev. 597, 604 (2018).

students.[135] In 2011, the Obama Administration began aggressively enforcing this law, advising schools that they were required to establish procedures for the fair and prompt resolution of complaints of sexual violence, defined broadly; to designate an employee to coordinate compliance efforts; and to evaluate charges based on the "preponderance of the evidence standard," which asks whether an event was "more likely than not" and is the general rule in civil cases in the United States.[136] In November 2018, the Trump Administration announced that it planned to pull back on the Obama-era rules in the interests of protecting the due process rights of the accused.[137] Despite changes in U.S. presidential administrations, many of the reforms that were prompted by the 2011 guidance have proven popular with school administrations and student activists, and are therefore likely to have staying power.[138]

Conclusion

As a result of feminist reform movements, U.S. law has made tremendous strides in redefining sexual assault and creating remedies for sexual harassment. But these laws remain riddled with loopholes, limitations, and traps for the unwary victim. The #MeToo movement has demonstrated that sexual harassment and assault remain at crisis levels in the United States. But it now seems more likely that incidents will be exposed through investigative journalism, blog posts, or social media, than through formal legal complaints. The new threat of public exposure may better deter and even incapacitate perpetrators. But media attention does not suffice to compensate survivors, to help the many victims whose harassment does not make headlines, or to change underlying structures and attitudes that result in abuse. Sexual entitlement, misogyny, and sexism have proven resilient, often infused with racism, classism, and homophobia. Meaningful change in the United States will require the rethinking of criminal justice and antidiscrimination rules, as well as creative new legal strategies.

---

135. *See* Davis v. Monroe County Bd. of Educ., 526 U.S. 629, 649–51 (1999).

136. Office for Civil Rights, *Dear Colleague Letter from Assistant Secretary for Civil Rights Russlynn Ali*, U.S. Dep't Educ. (Apr. 4, 2011).

137. U.S. Dep't of Educ., Press Release, *Secretary DeVos: Proposed Title IX Rule Provides Clarity for Schools, Support for Survivors, and Due Process Rights for All* (Nov. 16, 2018), https://www.ed.gov/news/press-releases/secretary-devos-proposed-title-ix-rule-provides-clarity-schools-support-survivors-and-due-process-rights-all. At the time of this writing, the proposed rules have not been finalized.

138. Suzanne B. Goldberg, *Is There Really A Sex Bureaucracy?*, 7 Cal. L. Rev. Online 107, 114–17 (2016).

CHAPTER 3

#MeToo Canada: Toward a Culture of Equality

Colleen Sheppard[1]

Introduction: The Emergence of #MeToo in Canada

Even before the rise of the #MeToo movement in Canada, sexual harassment, sexual assault, and the gendered abuse of power had attracted significant media, institutional, and political attention, particularly when high profile and powerful men in society were implicated. Two important examples riveted Canadians: the 2016 widely publicized firing and subsequent sexual assault trial of Jian Ghomeshi—a radio broadcasting "superstar" at the Canadian Broadcasting Corporation (CBC);[2] and the 2015 resignation of Marcel Aubut, head of the Canadian Olympic Committee (COC), following numerous allegations of sexual harassment.[3]

Beyond highlighting the egregious nature of individual misconduct, these cases revealed the need to examine institutional and societal contexts that too often allow sexual abuse to occur and to continue. In the wake of both the Ghomeshi scandal at CBC and the Aubut resignation at the COC, independent investigations were conducted into the workplace practices at both

---

1. Professor, Faculty of Law & Centre for Human Rights & Legal Pluralism, McGill University. I wish to thank Esther Dionne Desbiens and Rebecca Jones for their invaluable research assistance in preparing this chapter and the Social Sciences and Humanities Research Council for providing financial support.

2. Chris Young, *Ghomeshi acquitted: Read the verdict and catch up on what you missed*, THE GLOBE AND MAIL, Mar. 28, 2016, http://www.theglobeandmail.com/news/national/jian-ghomeshi/article28476713/ (last visited May 9, 2019).

3. *COC president Marcel Aubut resigns after harassment complaint withdrawn*, CBC NEWS, Oct. 3, 2015, http://www.cbc.ca/news/canada/montreal/marcel-aubut-coc-sex-harass ment-complaint-1.3255535 (last visited May 9, 2019).

organizations. These investigations confirmed that sexual harassment and abuse were not simply aberrant individual problems, but rather linked to broader systemic and institutional failures. As noted in one of the reports, the "CBC failed to live up to its obligations to provide its employees a workplace that is free from disrespectful and abusive behaviour."[4] The host culture, structures of governance, and supervision all contributed to this hostile work environment.[5] While Ghomeshi was terminated once the allegations of criminal wrongdoing surfaced, his subsequent acquittal prompted concerns about the limits of the criminal justice system's ability to address the complexities of sexual misconduct.[6] In the case of the COC, the independent law firm report concluded that:

> [T]here exists a perception amongst the COC staff that the SLT (Senior Leadership Team) were aware of information that suggested that harassment was occurring in their workplace and they were unable or unwilling to take steps to address it. As such, many COC staff feel that the Board and the SLT failed in their obligation to provide a safe environment for COC employees.[7]

Although Aubut had resigned, the survivors of his harassment in the workplace were fearful about coming forward to speak out about their experiences.

Given these controversies, when the Harvey Weinstein scandal broke in the United States, and the #MeToo movement gained momentum,[8] the ripple effects in Canada were significant. Many women felt more empowered to speak out about their experiences of sexual harassment and abuse. For example, the former Executive Director of the COC, Leanne Nicolle, was inspired to tell her

---

4. JANICE RUBIN AND PARISA NIKFARJAM, RUBIN THOMLINSON LLP, PRIVILEGED AND STRICTLY CONFIDENTIAL REPORT: CBC WORKPLACE INVESTIGATION REGARDING JIAN GHOMESHI 26 (Apr. 13, 2015), https://assets.documentcloud.org/documents/1894581/report-april-2015-en-1.pdf (last visited May 9, 2019).

5. *Id.*

6. Following highly publicized criminal trials, Ghomeshi was acquitted of the criminal charges. For some, his acquittals reinforced a perception that the criminal justice system is a difficult and often hostile venue for bringing claims of sexual violence. *See* Anne Kingston, *Jian Ghomeshi: How he got away with it*, MACLEAN'S, Nov. 6, 2014, https://www.macleans.ca/news/canada/jian-ghomeshi-how-he-got-away-with-it/.

7. CHRISTINE THOMLINSON, RUBIN THOMLINSON LLP, PRIVATE AND STRICTLY CONFIDENTIAL SUMMARY REPORT PREPARED FOR THE CANADIAN OLYMPIC COMMITTEE ON THE RESULTS OF THE INDEPENDENT REVIEW CONSTITUTED UNDER TERMS OF REFERENCE DATED OCTOBER 6, 2015, 3 (Jan. 4, 2016), https://cdn.prezly.com/9a/502fc0ba2911e59bde230b615d1538/Summary-Report-English.pdf (last visited May 9, 2019).

8. *See* Sandra E. Garcia, *The Woman Who Created #MeToo Long Before Hashtags*, N.Y. TIMES, Oct. 20, 2017, https://www.nytimes.com/2017/10/20/us/me-too-movement-tarana-burke.html.

story of sexual harassment publicly.[9] And women in the entertainment industry began going public about sexual abuse and harassment that were eerily similar to the experiences of women in the US #MeToo movement. In October 2017, ten women accused the founder of a major Quebec summer comedy festival (Just for Laughs) of sexual misconduct, prompting his resignation as president and the sale of his shares in the company.[10] In January 2018, the director of the well-known Soulpepper Theatre in Toronto resigned after four women actors "said … that they had been sexually harassed, groped, touched and repeatedly propositioned by him over 13 years."[11] Allegations of sexual harassment and abuse against Canadian politicians were also emerging, prompting calls for resignation and more effective protections against sexual misconduct.[12]

Similar to many other countries, Canadian social media was functioning as a powerful tool for raising awareness about the risks and realities of sexual abuse and harassment. Between 2016 and 2018, there was a substantial increase in the number of police-reported sexual assaults coinciding with the rise of the #MeToo movement.[13] The movement was helping to expose pervasive sexual abuse and harassment in women's lives. It was also making a difference in terms of concrete results—forcing men accused of abuse to resign or be discharged from their positions of power and influence. Social media campaigns were

---

9. Josh Dehaas, *Exclusive: Leanne Nicolle goes public with Marcel Aubut harassment allegations*, CTV NEWS, Oct. 16, 2017, https://www.ctvnews.ca/canada/exclusive-leanne -nicolle-goes-public-with-marcel-aubut-harassment-allegations-1.3635204 (last visited May 9, 2019).

10. The Canadian Press, *Sex assault complaint filed against Just for Laughs founder Gilbert Rozon*, CTV NEWS, Oct. 23, 2017, https://www.ctvnews.ca/entertainment /sex-assault-complaint-filed-against-just-for-laughs-founder-gilbert-rozon-1.3645128.

11. Catherine Porter, *Toronto Theater Director Resigns Amid Sexual Misconduct Accusations*, N.Y. TIMES, Jan. 4, 2018)\, https://www.nytimes.com/2018/01/04/world/canada/soul pepper-theater-toronto-albert-schultz.html.

12. Rachel Aiello & Glen McGregor, *Patrick Brown denies sexual misconduct allegations from two women, resigns as Ontario PC leader*, CTV NEWS, Jan. 24, 2018, https://www .ctvnews.ca/politics/patrick-brown-denies-sexual-misconduct-allegations-from-two-women -resigns-as-ontario-pc-leader-1.3774686; Lama El Asrak, *Latest sexual assault allegation towards a Canadian politician a reminder of work to be done: N.S. advocate*, STARMETRO HALIFAX, Apr. 23, 2018, https://www.thestar.com/halifax/2018/04/23/latest-sexual-assault-allegation -towards-a-canadian-politician-a-reminder-of-work-to-be-done-ns-advocate.html; Meagan Campbell and Catherine McIntyre, *Sexual harassment has long festered on the Hill. Now, female MPs from all parties are saying "enough"*, MACLEAN'S, Mar. 7, 2018, https://www.macleans.ca /politics/ottawa/sexual-harassment-on-parliament-hill/ (last visited May 9, 2019).

13. CRISTINE ROTENBERG AND ADAM COTTER, STATISTICS CANADA, POLICE-REPORTED SEXUAL ASSAULTS IN CANADA BEFORE AND AFTER #MeTOO, 2016 AND 2017 (Nov. 8, 2018), https://www150.statcan.gc.ca/n1/pub/85-002-x/2018001/article/54979-eng .htm (reports to police peaked in October 2017, a 46 percent increase from the previous year with the province of Quebec seeing the largest increase, 61 percent).

proving more efficient and effective in some ways than formal legal processes set up to redress sexual violence. While questions of fairness and due process were raised with respect to social media allegations, traditional legal protection, processes, and remedies also came under scrutiny.

During this time, Canadian women also created their own versions of #MeToo, supporting the general #MeToo movement, but looking to the future through #AfterMeToo in English and #EtMaintenant? (AndNow?) in French. Both hashtags communicated a concern with taking action to respond to emerging stories of widespread sexual misconduct. A symposium on sexual misconduct in the entertainment industry was held in December 2017, leading to a series of recommendations published in the #AfterMeToo Report released on International Women's Day, 2018.[14] One important aspect of this report was its recognition of the systemic vulnerability of actors in the entertainment industry, as a result of precarious job security, long and irregular hours, and working conditions in remote locations. It highlighted the particular vulnerability of actors of color and trans actors, who already experience significant barriers in accessing work and visibility in the entertainment industry. In Quebec, women mobilizing around #EtMaintenant? emphasized the need to be inclusive of the concerns of *all* working women and to connect with political movements like Black Lives Matter and Stella, a grassroots organization mobilizing on behalf of sex workers.[15]

Indigenous women have also voiced the importance of the #MeToo movement in their communities.[16] In so doing, they have highlighted a tension between keeping silent about sexual abuse because of concerns about solidarity with Indigenous men in the face of colonialism, and the need to confront abuse to heal and develop healthy communities. Indigenous women have also mobilized to contest the egregious sexual violence perpetrated by non-Indigenous men. The disproportionate number of missing and murdered Indigenous women and girls attests not only to private violence, but also to systemic inequalities embedded in policing and in the criminal justice system.[17] #MeToo

---

14. David Butt and Chi Nguyen, AfterMeToo (Mar. 6, 2018), https://docs .wixstatic.com/ugd/1766c7_398ee90fdbb047af951203f20a5f3db3.pdf.

15. *See* the Common Declaration of Et Maintenant (and Now) at http://web.archive .org/web/20180223155956/https://www.etmaintenant.net/ (archived website); *see also*, *About Stella*, Stella, http://chezstella.org/en/about-stella/.

16. *See, e.g.*, Lindsay Nixon, *#MeToo and the Secrets Indigenous Women Keep*, The Walrus, Mar. 8, 2019, https://thewalrus.ca/metoo-and-the-secrets-indigenous-women -keep/; Angela Sterritt, *Indigenous #MeToo catching fire in B.C. First Nations communities*, CBC News (Oct. 26, 2018), https://www.cbc.ca/news/canada/british-columbia/indigenous -metoo-movement-slowly-catching-fire-in-bc-1.4878759.

17. *See* Amnesty International, Stolen Sisters: A Human Rights Response to Discrimination and Violence against Indigenous Women in Canada (2004),

mobilization across Canada thus reflects important differences in women's experiences of sexual violence and underscores the need to take into account intersecting structures of subordination, racism and legacies of colonialism.

Legal Protections: From Retroactive Complaints to Proactive Prevention

In Canada, there are both criminal and civil protections against sexual assault and misconduct. The federal *Criminal Code* prohibits sexual assault and in many of the #MeToo cases, criminal charges have been brought in the wake of allegations.[18] However, given the high standard of proof in the criminal context (beyond a reasonable doubt), evidentiary challenges, and the lack of any tangible remedies for the survivors of the misconduct, many victims choose civil avenues for redress.[19]

Legislation in all jurisdictions across Canada prohibits sexual harassment in the workplace, and provides complaint mechanisms and remedies.[20] Increasingly, legislative provisions provide express protection from harassment based on sex, gender identity or expression, sexual orientation, racial or ethnic origin, disability, or a combination of these grounds.[21] Back in the 1980s, the Supreme

---

https://www.amnesty.ca/sites/amnesty/files/amr200032004enstolensisters.pdf; AMNESTY INTERNATIONAL, NO MORE STOLEN SISTERS: THE NEED FOR A COMPREHENSIVE RESPONSE TO DISCRIMINATION AND VIOLENCE AGAINST INDIGENOUS WOMEN IN CANADA (2009), https://www.amnesty.ca/sites/amnesty/files/amr200122009en.pdf; *see also, Our Mandate, Our Vision, Our Mission*, NATIONAL INQUIRY INTO MISSING AND MURDERED INDIGENOUS WOMEN AND GIRLS, http://www.mmiwg-ffada.ca/mandate/.

18. Criminal Code, R.S.C. 1985, c C-46, §§ 271-273.2, http://canlii.ca/t/7vf2.

19. *See Due Justice for All Project*, METRAC ACTION ON VIOLENCE, http://www .metrac.org/what-we-do/project-highlight/ (a collaborative, evidence-based research project exploring alternative justice methods for survivors of sexual violence).

20. For an overview of Canadian anti-discrimination and harassment laws, see Colleen Sheppard, *Canada, in* COMPARATIVE PERSPECTIVES ON THE ENFORCEMENT AND EFFECTIVENESS OF ANTIDISCRIMINATION LAW 83-109 (Marie Mercat-Bruns, David B. Oppenheimer & Cady Sartorius eds., 2018).

21. *See, e.g.*, Canadian Human Rights Act, R.S.C. 1985, c H-6, http://canlii.ca/t/52zkk, which states that it is a discriminatory practice to harass someone based on any of the protected grounds of discrimination, including: race, national or ethnic origin, color, religion, age, sex, sexual orientation, gender identity or expression, marital status, family status, genetic characteristics, disability, and conviction for an offence for which a pardon has been granted or in respect of which a record suspension has been ordered (see sections 3(1), 3.1 and 14 of the Act). *See also*, Charter of Human Rights and Freedoms, C.Q.L.R. c C-12 (Can. Que.), http://canlii .ca/t/52t34, which includes protection against discrimination or harassment on the basis of race, color, sex, gender identity or expression, pregnancy, sexual orientation, civil status, age except as provided by law, religion, political convictions, language, ethnic or national origin,

Court of Canada held that sexual harassment constitutes a form of sex discrimination. In describing sexual harassment, Chief Justice Dickson explained:

> [S]exual harassment in the workplace may be broadly defined as unwelcome conduct of a sexual nature that detrimentally affects the work environment or leads to adverse job-related consequences for the victims of the harassment. It is ... an abuse of power. When sexual harassment occurs in the workplace, it is an abuse of both economic and sexual power. Sexual harassment is a demeaning practice, one that constitutes a profound affront to the dignity of the employees forced to endure it. By requiring an employee to contend with unwelcome sexual actions or explicit sexual demands, sexual harassment in the workplace attacks the dignity and self-respect of the victim both as an employee and as a human being.[22]

Hundreds of human rights cases involving sexual harassment have been channeled through federal and provincial human rights commissions and tribunals.[23] While critically important, recurrent concerns have been voiced about time delays, low damage awards, and the retroactive nature of the legal process.[24] Of significance in the context of the #MeToo movement, is the increase in complaints about sexual harassment being channeled through the human rights system in jurisdictions all across Canada, and the need for resources to support survivors through the legal processes. Civil litigation strategies, such as class action tort claims for systemic negligence in failing to protect employees from workplace harassment, are also emerging in the Canadian context.[25] These claims involve significant damage awards that should provide important financial incentives for systemic change.

---

social condition, or disability. The Ontario Human Rights Code, R.S.O. 1990, c H.19, http://canlii.ca/t/2fd (last visited May 10, 2019), also provides comprehensive protection against harassment on the basis of race, ancestry, place of origin, color, ethnic origin, citizenship, creed, sex, sexual orientation, gender identity, gender expression, age, marital status, family status, or disability (see sections 5 and 7 of the Code).

22. Janzen v. Platy Enterprises Ltd., [1989] 1 SCR 1252 at 1284.

23. For a general review of sexual harassment law in Canada, see Arjun Prakash Aggarwal & Madhu M Gupta, Sexual Harassment in the workplace (3rd ed. 2000).

24. *See* Colleen Sheppard, Inclusive Equality: The Relational Dimensions of Systemic Discrimination in Canada 141-6 (2010); *see also*, Pearl Eliadis, Speaking Out on Human Rights: Debating Canada's Human Rights System 51-52 & 75-78 (2014).

25. *See* Davidson v. Canada (Attorney General), 2015 ONSC 8008 (Can. Ont. Sup. Ct. J.) http://canlii.ca/t/gmnv5; Merlo v. Canada, 2017 FC 533 (Can. Fed. Ct.) http://canlii .ca/t/h52tm (last visited May 10, 2019); Lisa Johnson, *WestJet faces potential class-action lawsuit over alleged workplace harassment*, CBC News, Apr. 4, 2016, http://www.cbc.ca/news/canada /british-columbia/westjet-class-action-mandy-lewis-1.3520515.

Beyond the availability of legal recourse in the wake of sexual misconduct, there have been growing concerns about strengthening proactive regulatory approaches aimed at preventing harassment or sexual violence from occurring in the first place. Rather than putting the burden on the victim of harassment to pursue legal remedies retroactively, legislative initiatives imposing proactive obligations to establish sexual harassment and violence policies in workplaces and educational institutions, and to prevent sexual violence, have been introduced over the past few years.[26] These initiatives pre-date the most recent #MeToo developments. The province of Ontario, for example, launched "It's Never Okay: An Action Plan to Stop Sexual Violence and Harassment," in March 2015, "to help change attitudes, provide more support for survivors and make workplaces and campuses safer and more responsive to complaints of sexual violence and harassment."[27] As part of this initiative, in 2016, Ontario passed the *Sexual Violence and Harassment Action Plan Act (Supporting Survivors and Challenging Sexual Violence and Harassment)*, which requires organizations to take concrete steps to address, redress, and prevent sexual violence.[28] The law defines sexual violence as, "any sexual act or act targeting a person's sexuality, gender identity or gender expression, whether the act is physical or psychological in nature, that is committed, threatened or attempted against a person without the person's consent, and includes sexual assault, sexual harassment, stalking, indecent exposure, voyeurism and sexual exploitation."[29] In Quebec, more proactive protections were introduced to address sexual violence in colleges and universities in December 2017.[30] In the workplace context, in addition to protections against sexual harassment and provisions in occupational

---

26. *See, e.g.*, Bill 176, *An Act to amend the Act respecting labour standards and other legislative provisions mainly to facilitate family-work balance*, 1st Sess., 41st Leg., Quebec, 2018 (assented to Jun. 12, 2018), SQ 2018, c 21, http://www.assnat.qc.ca/en/travaux-parlementaires /projets-loi/projet-loi-176-41-1.html (last visited May 10, 2019); *see also*, Bill 132, *An Act to amend various statutes with respect to sexual violence, sexual harassment, domestic violence and related matters*, 1st Sess., 41st Leg., Ontario, 2016 (assented to Mar. 8, 2016), SO 2016, c 2, https://www.ola.org/en/legislative-business/bills/parliament-41/session-1/bill-132.

27. *It's Never Okay: An Action Plan to Stop Sexual Violence and Harassment Progress Update 2016-2017*, GOVERNMENT OF ONTARIO, https://www.ontario.ca/page/its-never -okay-action-plan-stop-sexual-violence-and-harassment-progress-update-2016-2017.

28. Bill 132, *An Act to amend various statutes with respect to sexual violence, sexual harassment, domestic violence and related matters*, 1st Sess., 41st Leg., Ontario, 2016 (assented to Mar. 8, 2016), SO 2016, c 2, https://www.ola.org/en/legislative-business/bills/parliament -41/session-1/bill-132 .

29. *Id.* at § 17(1).

30. Bill 151, *An Act to prevent and fight sexual violence in higher education institutions*, 1st Sess., 41st Leg., Quebec, 2017 (assented to Dec. 8, 2017), SQ 2017, c 32, http://www .assnat.qc.ca/en/travaux-parlementaires/projets-loi/projet-loi-151-41-1.html.

health and safety laws, Quebec was at the forefront in providing protection against "psychological harassment" and bullying.[31]

At the federal level, legislation was introduced to provide comprehensive protection against sexual misconduct and to ensure that employers take steps to prevent sexual misconduct by utilizing a model that draws on occupational health and safety protections.[32] Workplace harassment and violence are defined broadly as "any action, conduct or comment, including of a sexual nature, that can reasonably be expected to cause offence, humiliation or other physical or psychological injury or illness to an employee, including any prescribed action, conduct or comment."[33] The Canadian Parliament's initiatives appear to have been a response to recent recognition of gaps in protection from sexual harassment in the workplace, particularly sexual misconduct by politicians. Similarly, in direct response to widespread problems in the entertainment industry, federal policy initiatives now require that arts organizations commit to providing a workplace free of sexual misconduct to access federal funding.[34]

This regulatory shift toward imposing proactive obligations on employers and educational organizations to prevent sexual misconduct is to be applauded; however, it is still too early to tell if it has been effective. In other contexts, proactive regulatory initiatives have failed to be adequately monitored—resulting

---

31. Act respecting labour standards, C.Q.L.R., c N-1.1 §§ 81.18-81.19 (Can. Que.) http://www.legisquebec.gouv.qc.ca/en/showdoc/cs/N-1.1; *see also, Seven-Year Recap: Psychological Harassment in Quebec*, McMILLAN LLP, https://mcmillan.ca/Seven-Year-Recap-psychological-harassment-in-Quebec; *see also*, Occupational Health and Safety Act, R.S.O. 1990, c O.1 §§ 32.0.1-32.0.8 (Can. Ont.); Bill 219, *The Workplace Safety and Health Amendment Act (Harassment and Violence in the Workplace)*, 4th Sess., 39th Leg., Manitoba, 2009, https://web2.gov.mb.ca/bills/39-4/pdf/b219.pdf; The Saskatchewan Employment Act, S.S. 2013, c S-15.1, http://canlii.ca/t/8sws; The Occupational Health and Safety Regulations, 1996, R.R.S. c O-1.1 Reg 1 (Can. Sask.), https://www.canlii.org/en/sk/laws/regu/rrs-c-o-1.1-reg-1/131521/rrs-c-o-1.1-reg-1.html.

32. Bill C-65, *An Act to amend the Canada Labour Code (harassment and violence), the Parliamentary Employment and Staff Relations Act and the Budget Implementation Act*, 1st Sess., 42nd Parl., 2017, No. 1 (as passed by the House of Commons May 7, 2018) (Can.), https://www.parl.ca/DocumentViewer/en/42-1/bill/C-65/third-reading#enH517.

33. As noted in the New York Times, "Unlike the government in Washington, the federal government in Canada under Prime Minister Justin Trudeau, a self-described feminist, has been leading the push to address sexual harassment." Ian Austen and Catherine Porter, *In Canada, a 'Perfect Storm' for a #MeToo Reckoning*, N.Y. TIMES, Jan. 29, 2018, https://www.nytimes.com/2018/01/29/world/canada/metoo-sexual-harassment.html.

34. Teresa Wright, *Arts organizations must commit to harassment-free environment or forego funding: Joly*, THE TORONTO STAR, Apr. 25 2018, https://www.thestar.com/news/canada/2018/04/25/arts-organizations-must-commit-to-harassment-free-environment-or-forego-funding-joly.html.

in slow or non-existent progress toward greater equity.[35] While regulatory innovation is critical, it alone is insufficient to transform workplace, societal and organizational culture.[36]

Conclusion: Toward a Culture of Equality

While it is important to reform our laws to ensure maximum and effective protection for survivors of sexual violence, there is growing recognition that we need to examine institutional practices and interactions outside of the formal purview of law. The #MeToo movement alerted us to the power of non-traditional approaches to seeking vindication for the violation of rights. By amplifying the courageous voices of those who had historically been ignored or not believed, it awoke a collective spirit of solidarity capable of reinforcing the dawning power of survivors' voices. When formal law failed and even re-victimized survivors, social media provided a platform for survivors to curate their own narratives, spread awareness and receive support.

The political and legal responses to #MeToo have begun to usher in a new era—one that may not be characterized by an either/or approach. It may no longer be a question of utilizing *either* formal law *or* social media to prevent and respond to sexual violence. Rather, we need to work to make our legal protections and processes more effective, innovative, fair, and accessible, while ensuring that we listen to the stories and voices of survivors expressed through all our modern and creative means and channels of communication.

---

35. *See, e.g.*, Nan Weiner, *Employment Equity in Canada: What Do the Data Show About Its Effectiveness?*, *in* EMPLOYMENT EQUITY IN CANADA: THE LEGACY OF THE ABELLA REPORT 29 (Carol Agócs, ed., 2014); *see also*, Linda Hamilton Kreiger, *Afterword: Socio-Legal Backlash* 21 BJELL 475 (2000).

36. *See* Colleen Sheppard, *Systemic Inequality and Workplace Culture: Challenging the Institutionalization of Sexual Harassment* 3 CLELJ 249 (1995).

CHAPTER 4

What's Past Is Prologue: #MeToo in Mexico

Estefanía Vela Barba[1]

How has "#MeToo" helped shape sexual harassment law for the workplace in different countries? In order to answer this question as it pertains to Mexico, this article is separated into four sections. In the first, I will review the "public conversations" that were happening in the country before the arrival of "MeToo." Then, I will briefly outline sexual harassment law in Mexico as it applies to the workplace. In the third section, I will examine the conversation "MeToo," specifically, sparked in the country. And finally, I will present my conclusions.

The Discussions Before "MeToo"

Mexico is, like many other countries, a place in which feminist activism has been present for decades.[2] And, like in many other countries, this activism has been partially focused on battling gender-based violence and discrimination against women through policy reform.[3] Sexual harassment law was born out of these efforts and its first iteration dates all the way back to 1991.

---

1. Estefanía Vela Barba is Executive Director of Intersecta, a feminist research and advocacy organization committed to ending gender discrimination in Mexico.

2. The modern feminist movement in Mexico is considered to have begun in the 1970s, more than a decade after women's suffrage was recognized. *See*, for instance, Eli Bartra, *Mujeres y política en México. Aborto, violación y mujeres golpeadas*, 1 POLÍTICA Y CULTURA (1992); Lourdes Arizpe, *El feminismo: del grito de los setenta a las estrategias del siglo XXI*, in FEMINISMO EN MÉXICO. REVISIÓN HISTÓRICO-CRÍTICA DEL SIGLO QUE TERMINA (Griselda Gutiérrez Castañeda ed., 2002).

3. Regina Larrea Maccise, *Transforming Rape Law: Legal Chronicles of the Mexican Feminist Movement* (Apr. 29, 2013) (unpublished LL.M. Long Paper, Harvard Law School) (on file with author).

Although sexual harassment law has been changing since 1991, these reforms were rarely accompanied by broad public discussions or demonstrations.[4] These are instead relatively new, and most of them include, in one way or another, the use of online media, particularly by young feminists.

The first notable use of online media in this sense is the case of the hashtag "#RopaSucia" (which translates as "dirty laundry"), which was launched in July 2015 by three poets—Maricela Guerrero, Paula Abramo, and Xitlálitl Rodríguez—to denounce "sexism in the cultural world." "We must air the #Dirty Laundry," Guerrero wrote on Twitter on July 13, 2015: "Do you remember a misogynistic phrase uttered by a public servant, artist, editor, or writer?" "Put it here," she instructed. By April 2016, over 15,000 messages had been written using the hashtag, including messages regarding harassment women experienced in the cultural world. This hashtag started a conversation, which was, in my view, their purpose.[5]

The second notable use of online media to specifically address sexual harassment occurred in April 23, 2016, with the launching of the hashtag #MiPrimerAcoso ("my first harassment," in English). This hashtag came to be after more than a month of public discussion regarding sexual harassment that started, precisely, on March 8, 2016, on International Women's Day, of all days. What happened then?

A young reporter, Andrea Noel, was walking the streets of Mexico City, going about her day, when a random guy ran up to her from behind, lifted her skirt, pulled down her underwear, and ran away. Per her narration,[6] she noticed that there was a security camera right where it happened. She was able to recover the tape and decided to post it online. "If someone recognizes this idiot," she tweeted, "please identify him. Women should be able to walk safely. #HappyWomen'sDay." The video went viral and unleashed a discussion never seen before.

There were those that thought she deserved to be raped, of course (and told her so); there were those that thought it wasn't really harassment; or that

---

4. Many policy reforms have been made since 1991 regarding sexual harassment and many other issues. However, these reforms were not always accompanied by broad public discussions, nor public manifestations. This does not mean, however, that there were none. There were many, though most were focused on the specific issues of "femicides" (the murders of women "because they are women") and abortion.

5. For an interview with the poets, see Ainhoa Suárez Gómez & Jorge Cano, "#Ropa Sucia: misoginia y machismo en el medio cultural," *Horizontal*, Apr. 8, 2016.

6. I suggest reading her directly, in the recount she published a year after "The Incident," as she calls it. It is a three-part saga, that can be found online: Andrea Noel, *A Viral Sex Crime That Shocked a Nation: The Victim's Story*, DAILY BEAST, Mar. 12, 2017; *How I Hunted My Sex-Assault Suspect Online and on Mexico Streets*, DAILY BEAST, Mar. 13, 2017; and *The Web Nailed the Wrong Man for My Sex Assault in Mexico*, DAILY BEAST, Mar. 14, 2017.

she was, ultimately, exaggerating. But there were also voices showing support as well. And, as the days went by, more and more women started talking about their own similar experiences. The stories included everything from catcalling to being masturbated on in the subway, having men take pictures of them without their consent, or having professors or bosses harass them with impunity.[7]

After many stories were told and reported on by the media, another common thread began to emerge: the authorities' appalling response to this violence, especially criminal law authorities (which were the focus in most of the stories). Either women were outright dismissed by them, if they dared denounce the violence, or authorities were incapable of properly investigating and dealing with the cases.

The data available confirms this reality. People rarely report harassment to criminal authorities, according to the National Survey on Victimization and Perceptions of Public Security (ENVIPE).[8] According the ENVIPE, there are several reasons why people don't report the harassment, the most common of which are a distrust in authorities, a lack of evidence to back up their claim, and the fact that they consider it to be a waste of time. The second problem is that, even if people try to file a complaint, authorities do not always open an investigation. The most cited reason for this is that authorities, according to those surveyed, decided that no crime was committed or that there was no proof of the crime.

And finally, even if an investigation is opened, that does not guarantee that it will reach the courts, nor that it will result in a conviction. Although it is impossible to individually track every case that enters the criminal justice system in Mexico,[9] aggregates show that there is a huge gap between the number

---

7. For some of the stories, *see* Estefanía Vela Barba, *No nos van a romper*, EL UNIVERSAL, Mar. 31, 2016.

8. The ENVIPE measures five different types of sexual violence: rape, attempted rape, "exhibitionism," "offensive touching," and "harassment" ("hostigamiento"). ENVIPE shows three crucial things: women are disproportionately the victims of these types of violence (depending on the conduct, they represent between 82.5 percent to 92.8 percent of the victims); men are disproportionately those who commit these acts of violence (both against men and women); and these forms of violence are rarely denounced (in 2018, for instance, with the exception of rape, the other forms of violence were the *least* denounced crimes of which women were the victims).

9. There are two big problems in Mexico regarding access to public information. First, as the NGO EQUIS Justicia para las Mujeres has been denouncing over the years, most courts in the country do not publish their rulings. Thus, it is impossible to access the cases individually. (*See Transparencia en la publicación de sentencias*, EQUIS JUSTICIA PARA LAS MUJERES, Dec. 2017, http://equis.org.mx/wp-content/uploads/2018/02/Informe_Transparencia_Sentencias .pdf). The other problem is that statistics regarding the criminal system are compiled in problematic ways. For instance, it is impossible to track a case from start to finish. What we have are aggregates published separately by prosecutors' offices and courts.

of investigations opened and those that result in formal accusations. Those that conclude with people being actually sentenced are even fewer. Between 2013 and 2016, for instance, according to the National Census on Criminal Justice, only 91 people were sentenced for harassment in the entire country. Considering that ENVIPE registers between 220,000-548,000 crimes of sexual harassment every year, that number is appalling.

In this context of impunity, women decided to take to the streets on April 24, 2016. Marches were organized in over ten cities in the country, from Hermosillo, Sonora, in the north, to Tuxtla Gutiérrez, Chiapas, in the south. Precisely one day before the march, (e)stereotipas, a feminist group to which I belonged, launched the hashtag #MiPrimerAcoso, directly inspired by the Brazilian #MiPrimerAsedio.[10] Two hours after it was launched, it became viral.[11] When women took to the streets the next day, in what became the biggest demonstration in feminist Mexican history to date, it was still a trending topic.[12]

It ended up being, in other words, our own "#MeToo."

This "conversation" led to some policy changes, but these were mostly focused on harassment in the streets.[13]

For instance, after the April 24 march, the Mexico City government decided to respond with the strategy known as "30-100": implementing thirty different actions over the course of 100 days to fight gender violence against women in the streets and in the public transportation system. They decided to focus solely on street harassment despite the fact that women were denouncing harassment in a variety of places, including the workplace.

---

10. The story of #MiPrimerAcoso is recounted in Catalina Ruiz-Navarro, *#MiPrimerAcoso: la historia detrás del Trending Topic*, VICE MÉXICO, Apr. 25, 2016.

11. According to an analysis by DISTINTAS LATITUDES, in two days, over 19,000 tweets used the hashtag. When retweets, bots, and people who used the hashtag without telling their own stories were discounted, however, approximately 1,100 testimonies were left. *See* *#MiPrimerAcoso: la etiqueta que destapó la cloaca de las agresiones sexuales*, DISTINTAS LATITUDES, May 24, 2016.

12. For a historical analysis of this march, *see* Karla Motte, *Una perspectiva histórica de la #PrimaveraVioleta*, ANIMAL POLÍTICO, May 3, 2016.

13. It is not that changes did not occur in the workplace context. For instance, the National Women's Institute published in March 2017 the Protocol for the prevention, attention, and punishment of sexual harassment that would cover *all* of the federal public administration. "Sensitivity trainings" were implemented in a variety of public institutions (the Ministry of Exterior, the General Attorney's Office, etc.). But, as I mentioned previously, these strategies were already in place. And their "new" implementation was not generally accompanied by public protests or media discussions as they were in the case of street harassment and harassment occurring in public universities.

The "strategy" became viral when the then-Mexico City governor, Miguel Ángel Mancera, decided to brag about one of its components: a whistle,[14] a pink one, at that. In a city of over 8 million people, where 4.3 million trips are made daily in the public transportation system, a whistle was seen as a solution to the problem of harassment. To make matters worse (or funnier), a "whistle" in Spanish is called a "pito," which also means penis. So, basically, the government's solution to the problem of sexual harassment was giving women a "pito." That irony—believe me—*was* stressed by many. The whistles since then were known as #LosPitosDeMancera: Mancera's whistles.

There were many more problems with the government's 30-100 strategy.[15] For starters, they had no clear diagnosis of the problem (where it happened most, how it happened, why it happened).[16] In spite of this, they proposed reinforcing their policy of having "separate" subway cars and buses for women and having more police officers patrolling the stations. And they presented a campaign that told women that their "complaint was their best defense."[17] This campaign, though, inviting women to make formal complaints, was not accompanied by

---

14. *See* Kate Linthicum, *Why Mexico is giving out half a million rape whistles to female subway rides*, L.A. TIMES, Oct. 23, 2016.

15. The Sexual and Reproductive Rights Area of the Right to Health Program at the Centro de Investigación y Docencia Económicas, of which I was a part, was one of the organizations that decided to evaluate the 30-100 strategy. The full report can be found online. *See Estrategia 30-100. Informe de seguimiento*, EQUIS JUSTICIA PARA LAS MUJERES, ÁREA DE DERECHOS SEXUALES Y REPRODUCTIVOS, GRUPO DE INFORMACIÓN EN REPRODUCCIÓN ELEGIDA & ALA IZQUIERDA, Nov. 2016, http://equis.org.mx/wp-content/uploads/2018/02/INFORME-FINAL_web.pdf.

16. The government, together with UN Women Mexico, published a report almost a year after these measures were announced. *See Diagnóstico sobre la violencia contra las mujeres y las niñas en el transporte público de la Ciudad de México*, GOBIERNO DE LA CIUDAD DE MÉXICO, EL COLEGIO DE MÉXICO, ONU MUJERES MÉXICO, Feb. 2017, https://mexico.unwomen.org/es/digiteca/publicaciones/2017/03/diagnostico-ciudades-seguras.

17. Given the lack of space, I cannot address another problematic campaign the government issued together with UN Women Mexico a year after #MiPrimerAcoso. This is the campaign known as "#NoEsDeHombres," which roughly translates as: "It is not a man's thing to do." This campaign had three components: two videos and several boards, plastered all over the subway system. In one video, they showed people waiting for the subway. At the same time, screens in the platform would light up, showing men's asses being recorded. Men, of course, reacted by covering themselves. Finally, the screen projects a message: "This is what women suffer every day." On another video, they featured men reacting in a subway to a seat that was shaped in a man's body, penis and all. Above the seat, a sign read: "Exclusive for men." Some would sit down, inadvertently, until they would jerk up after feeling "it." On the floor below, a sign read: "It is uncomfortable to travel here, but it is nothing compared to the sexual violence women suffer in their daily commutes." Finally, the "graphic materials" featured men making "lewd faces." "This is how they look at your daughter/mother/sister/partner/friend every day," the boards read. "Sexual violence is a crime. It can take you to prison. Respect." *See Evaluación de la Campaña #NoEsDeHombres*, ONU MUJERES MÉXICO, June 26, 2018. The campaign was, of

an improvement of the institutions charged with processing those complaints, which was one of the things women were denouncing in the first place.

In some universities, at the same time, students were organizing to denounce sexual violence and demand clear rules of action, that would ensure they were heard and properly protected.[18] In the case of the National Autonomous University of Mexico (UNAM), which is the biggest and one of the most important universities in the country (it has around 250,000 students), after many protests—and media stories—students succeeded. The UNAM published its own "Protocol for the Attention to Cases of Gender Violence" in August 2016. They presented the Protocol together with UN Women Mexico, tying their actions to the #HeForShe campaign.[19] Other universities, such as the Centro de Investigación y Docencia Económicas (CIDE)[20] and the Universidad Iberoamericana, followed suit, publishing their own protocols. The actual rules, however, have been criticized by many for a variety of problems.[21] Protests to these days continue, now under the banner of "#AquíTambiénPasa," this too happens here.[22]

---

course, critiqued for several reasons. *See* Carolina Torreblanca, *El efecto de la campaña #NoEsDeHombres*, ANIMAL POLÍTICO, May 31, 2018.

18. *See*, for instance, *Violencia sexual en las universidades de América Latina: omisiones, obstáculos y opacidad*, DISTINTAS LATITUDES, Nov. 27, 2016.

19. *See La UNAM se adhiere a la plataforma 'He for She' de ONU Mujeres para la Igualdad de Género*, BOLETÍN UNAM-DGCS-580, Aug. 29, 2016.

20. In December 2015, just before #MiPrimerAcoso, the head of the economics department at CIDE was denounced by many students for harassment. Just as he was about to be fired, though, he quit. In November 2016, CIDE published its own Protocol for harassment. In July 10, 2017, *Buzzfeed Mexico* ran the story about the economics professor, calling attention to the fact that he was now working in the federal government. *See* Yuriria Ávila, *Este profesor de Universidad acosó sexualmente a sus estudiantes y sigue trabajando en el gobierno mexicano*, BUZZFEED MEXICO, July 10, 2017, https://www.buzzfeed.com/mx/yuririaavila/este-profesor -de-universidad-acoso-sexualmente-a-sus-estudia. One day later, Buzzfeed ran another story about another professor who also quit right before he was to be fired for harassment. *See* Yuriria Ávila, *Otro profesor del CIDE renunció tras comprobarse que acosó sexualmente a sus alumnas*, BUZZFEED MEXICO, July 11, 2017, https://www.buzzfeed.com/mx/yuririaavila/otro-profesor -del-cide-renuncio-tras-comprobarse-que-acoso. In response, CIDE decided to upgrade its Protocol and general strategy to combat "gender inequality." *See* "Comunicado del CIDE sobre la protesta #AquíTambiénPasa," CIDE, Nov. 26, 2018, https://www.cide.edu/saladeprensa /comunidad-del-cide-sobre-la-protesta-de-aquitambienpasa/.

21. The Protocols adopted in universities are problematic for several reasons and have been criticized by student groups and feminist groups. *See*, for instance, Guayaba Quemadora, *Conoce 33 formas en que el Protocolo de la UNAM viola los derechos humanos de las mujeres*, LA QUE ARDE, Nov. 30, 2016, https://www.laquearde.org/2016/11/30/protocolo-unam/.

22. *See* VV.AA., *#AquíTambiénPasa: contra el acoso en universidades*, NEXOS, Nov. 22, 2018, https://cultura.nexos.com.mx/?p=17071; Almudena Barragán, *#AquíTambiénPasa: la*

Given this context, when the *New York Times* and the *New Yorker* published their reports on Harvey Weinstein's harassment, I was excited at the possibility of witnessing a conversation that specifically addressed harassment in the workplace. Maybe the time had finally come, I thought, to have a conversation around the law's shortcomings in reducing this particular problem.

Why would a conversation addressing harassment in the workplace, specifically, be necessary?

For the case of Mexico, there are several reasons, and to understand them, it is important to know the basic tenets of the law's regulation of sexual harassment.[23]

The Law Before "#MeToo"

The first-time sexual harassment was regulated in Mexico, in 1991, it was introduced as a crime in the Federal Criminal Code. This novel regulation was part of a broader reform to this code that sought to recognize the variety of ways in which women were subjected to "sexual violence," so as to ensure their "access to justice."[24]

In this first iteration, sexual harassment was called "*hostigamiento*" and was defined as the act of "sieging," in a "reiterated" way and with a "lascivious intent," a person with whom there is a hierarchical relationship. This hierarchical relationship could be born out of a domestic, labor, or school relationship, or "any other that implies subordination." Thus defined, sexual harassment was not limited to acts that occurred in a workplace. No matter where it happened, as long as there was "subordination," it was punishable. Although some legislators

llamada de auxilio de las universitarias contra el acoso sexual en México, EL PAÍS: VERNE, Nov. 16, 2018, https://verne.elpais.com/verne/2018/11/16/mexico/1542336241_631947.html.

23. For a full description (in Spanish) of law governing employment discrimination in Mexico, including sexual harassment, *see* Estefanía Vela Barba, *La discriminación en el empleo en México*, INSTITUTO BELISARIO DOMÍNGUEZ & CONSEJO NACIONAL PARA PREVENIR LA DISCRIMINACIÓN, 2017, https://www.conapred.org.mx/documentos_cedoc/completo Discriminacion08122017.pdf. For a shorter version of sexual harassment law (in Spanish), *see* Estefanía Vela Barba, *#MeToo en México*, NEXOS, Feb. 26, 2018, https://www.nexos.com .mx/?p=36297.

24. In "Employment Discrimination or Sexual Violence? Defining Sexual Harassment in American and French Law," Abigail C. Saguy analyzes the differences in framing that exist between the United States and France with regards to sexual harassment. The first regulated harassment using civil law, concretely *anti-discrimination* law as applied to the employment context, while the second one regulated harassment through criminal law, as a form of sexual violence. Applying these terms, Mexico clearly went the French way. *See* Abigail C. Saguy, *Employment Discrimination or Sexual Violence? Defining Sexual Harassment in American and French Law*, 34 LAW & SOC. REV. 4 (2000).

linked it to broader patterns of discrimination suffered by women, what was ultimately punished was only *sexual* conduct by individuals. In concrete terms, this meant that the law covered only sexual conduct committed by individual persons who could be fined or, in case of public servants, be removed from office. Companies or universities, for instance, in this legal scenario, could not be sued, only the individual perpetrators sued.

Throughout the 1990s and the first decade of the 2000s, all states (there are thirty-two in Mexico) criminalized "sexual harassment" in similar ways.[25] The most important differences with the Federal Criminal Code are the fact that states also criminalized harassment that occurs outside of *formally* hierarchical relationships and contemplated *prison* as a punishment for harassment. Other than that, the framing is similar: harassment is a *sexual crime* that occurs in a variety of settings, committed by individual persons who deserved to be punished for their behavior.

It was not until this last decade, 2010 and beyond that other forms of regulation, besides criminal law, began to be adopted and used, and with these new tools, sexual harassment *in the workplace* began to be regulated as something separate from harassment that occurs in other scenarios.

For instance, by the end of the first decade of the 2000s, "protocols" for punishing sexual harassment in the public administration began appearing.[26] These protocols are, basically, norms that establish procedures for public offices

---

25. In some cases, what was criminalized by Mexican states was called "hostigamiento"; in others, "acoso sexual," "asedio sexual" or "aprovechamiento sexual." Definitions vary in important ways. What some states define as "hostigamiento," others call "acoso." In some cases, harassment needs to occur in a "hierarchical relationship" for it to be punished. In others, it doesn't. With the exception of one code, there are no distinctions between the places where harassment happens: it is a crime, regardless of whether it occurs in the workplace, at school, in the street, or some other place. In most cases, it warrants time in prison (unlike the Federal Criminal Code, where the punishment is a fine). And, in all cases, what is punished is, once again, "sexual conduct."

Which conduct in particular? It is not always clear. The easiest way to understand what harassment is, is by responding that it is an "unwanted" sexual conduct that does *not* involve touching (that is the crime of "sexual abuse") or penetration (that is the crime of "rape"). Some state codes specify that asking someone for sexual favors is included in sexual harassment; others don't. Some codes establish that it needs to be "reiterated" for it to be punished; others don't. Most codes explicitly state that it is necessary to prove that the conduct provoked "damage" or "psycho-emotional suffering" in the victim. That is, it is necessary not only to prove that the conduct happened, but that it had a pernicious effect on the victim. In all cases, again, it is a conduct that can only be committed by an individual. Companies or schools, once again, cannot be sued.

26. The oldest one I have been able to find is the *Protocolo de intervención para casos de hostigamiento y acoso sexual*, published by the National Women's Institute in 2009, http://cedoc .inmujeres.gob.mx/documentos_download/101154.pdf.

to deal with *internal* cases of sexual harassment. They apply exclusively to public servants, for acts they commit while on the job.[27]

In addition to these protocols, in 2012, the Federal Labor Law was reformed to explicitly address sexual harassment. This law applies to labor relationships between private companies and their employees, and it is binding in the entire country. With this reform, harassment was explicitly included in the law as a violation that employees *and employers* could commit "in the place

---

27. To date, laws that regulate "administrative responsibilities" and those that regulate labor relationships between the government and its employees, do not *explicitly* include sexual harassment as an offense. These protocols are thus designed to fill that void. They are based on public servants' and employees' general obligation to conduct themselves with "respect" toward others. Sexual harassment is thus understood as a breach of that obligation. *See*, for instance, *Ley General de Responsabilidades Administrativas*, Diario Oficial de la Federación, July 18, 2016, https://www.dof.gob.mx/nota_detalle.php?codigo=5445048&fecha=18/07/2016; *see also Ley Federal de los Trabajadores al Servicio del Estado, reglamentaria del Apartado B) del Artículo 123 Constitucional*, Diario Oficial de la Federación on Dec. 28, 1963 (last reform published on June 22, 2018), http://www.diputados.gob.mx/LeyesBiblio/pdf/111_010519.pdf.

Now, most protocols are focused on one of two things. Either they are focused exclusively on "sexual harassment," which is defined in terms that are similar to those established in criminal codes. Or they focus on harassment and "labor violence" or "labor harassment," which are defined more broadly, to include non-sexual conducts as well. In these cases, however, "labor harassment" is not necessarily linked—as it is in the United States, for instance—with discrimination. That is, it is not necessarily directed at people because of their race, sexual orientation, disability, or some other analogous "category." It is just "violence," period. An example of the first model is the *Protocolo para la prevención, atención y sanción del hostigamiento sexual y acoso sexual*, published on August 31, 2016, https://www.dof.gob.mx/nota_detalle.php?codigo=5450530&fecha=31/08/2016, that is applicable to the entire federal public administration. This protocol was designed by the National Women's Institute, one of the leading authorities on this issue. An example of the second model is the Supreme Court of Justice's Protocol (*see* Acuerdo General de Administración Número III/2012 of the Comité de Gobierno y Administración de la Suprema Corte de Justicia de la Nación, published on July 3, 2012, https://www.sitios.scjn.gob.mx/codhap/sites/default/files/banner/archivos/AGA-III-2012.pdf) as well as the National Electoral Institute (*see* Protocolo para prevenir, atender y sancionar el hostigamiento y acoso sexual o laboral, published in 2014, https://portalanterior.ine.mx/archivos2/DS/recopilacion/JGEor201406-27ac_01P04-04x01.pdf).

As it happens with criminal law, these protocols are designed to punish individual harassers. The punishment can generally range from a public admonition, to a fine, a suspension, or being "fired." Public servants can even be "barred" from public office for some time. The thing is, though, not all the procedures established in these protocols lead to such sanctions. In some cases, the protocols create "Committees" that *do not* have the power to establish these disciplinary measures. These powers remain with the "Controlarías," the "internal organs of control," which are bound to administrative laws. The most these committees can do is issue "recommendations" and try to begin the disciplinary procedure before the *Controlaría*. In this sense, rather than "solve" the problem, these Protocols have created unnecessary procedures.

of work."[28] This was the first law that explicitly recognized the possibility of directly suing employers (as opposed to individual harassers) for "tolerating" harassment.

In addition to labor law, criminal law, and administrative law, civil law can also be used to fight workplace harassment. Practically all civil codes in the country allow private parties to sue others for "moral damage" ("daño moral"). This is generally understood as any damage—physical, emotional, and social—that is suffered by an individual because of another's actions. "Moral damage" is an old civil precept, not originally designed for harassment, but it has nonetheless been used in recent years to fight it.[29] Civil law is important because it also allows workers to sue employers for allowing or tolerating harassment.

---

28. The Federal Labor Law defines "hostigamiento" as an "exercise of power" in a "relationship of real subordination" between the victim and the aggressor, that is expressed in "verbal or physical" conduct, or a mixture of both. It is not necessarily sexual in nature. What does an "exercise of power" entail? The law is not clear. "Acoso sexual" is defined as "a form of violence" in which, although there is "no subordination," "there is an abusive exercise of power" that leads to a state of "helplessness and risk for the victim," "regardless of whether it is realized in one or several events." What, exactly, does that mean? It is not clear.

Now, what are the consequences for harassment, according to the Federal Labor Law? There are several, two of which I want to highlight. If the harasser is an employee, the employer can legally fire that person, "without responsibility." This means that a person who is fired can successfully sue the employer for wrongful termination, unless the employer can prove that there was just cause for the firing (in this case, that the person harassed another). The employer, however, can also be "punished," in two ways. If the employer is the one doing the harassment, a fine can be imposed by labor authorities. If the employer "permits or tolerates" acts of harassment, a fine can also be imposed. In both cases, the fine imposed can range from anything between US$1,000 to US$25,000. This was the first time, in Mexican law, that employers were explicitly held accountable for "tolerating" or "permitting" harassment.

29. In 2014, the Supreme Court decided its first case regarding the use of civil law to fight harassment and confirmed that such a use was valid. The case involved a woman who worked in a labor court (*Junta de Conciliación y Arbitraje*), of all places, and she sued the court for harassment. This case is important because it officially opened the possibility of suing *employers*, be they public or private, for larger amounts of money (at least larger than those established in the Federal Labor Law). *See* Amparo Directo 47/2013, decided by the First Chamber of the Supreme Court of Justice, on February 7, 2014, https://archivos.juridicas .unam.mx/www/bjv/libros/9/4404/5.pdf.

Finally, there is "human rights law"[30] and "anti-discrimination law."[31] Under human rights law, people can file complaints before Human Rights Commissions if their rights have been violated by *public* servants or *public* institutions. Under anti-discrimination law, they can file a complaint before Anti-Discrimination bodies if their rights have been violated by public *or* private parties. Both have been used to fight harassment as well.

This is, in a nutshell, the law governing sexual harassment in the workplace in Mexico that has been built up over the years. And it has many problems that need to be addressed.

To begin, it is incredibly complex, as I hope is obvious by its mere description. Although harassment in the context of employment is prohibited by many different laws and can be challenged through many different means, these means vary according to the person's employment. The resources available for public servants, for instance, are not the same as those available to people that work in private companies; those that work in the informal sector do not, of course, have the same resources as those that work in formal settings. Just figuring out where a person can go to is the first problem.

The second problem is that all these different pathways have different evidentiary standards, procedures, time frames, and sanctions, which, even when considered in tandem, fail to give victims proper redress. For instance, let's suppose a woman decided to quit her job as a result of harassment. If she decided to sue the company using labor law, the company might get fined and she might get her job back, but she cannot get punitive damages. If she goes to civil court, she can get punitive damages, but not necessarily get reinstated. If she goes to criminal court, the *individual* harasser can be imprisoned, but that does not necessarily ensure that she gets her job back or that the company gets punished

---

30. I am using the term "human rights law" in this paper, to refer to a very specific form of law: the law that falls under the purview of human rights commissions. The National Human Rights Commission, the most important of these bodies, was created in 1990; there are also state commissions, created throughout the 1990s. These commissions are meant to be "independent" from the governments, precisely because their point is to review government acts to ensure that they respect human rights. People can directly sue governments before these commissions for human rights violations. Sexual harassment, in this sense, is interpreted as a human rights violation. The problem with these commissions is that their "rulings" are not legally binding. They are not even called "rulings", but "recommendations."

31. Anti-discrimination law in Mexico is relatively new. The law that "inaugurated" this branch of law was the Federal Law to Prevent and Eliminate Discrimination, published in 2001. This law created the National Council to Prevent Discrimination (CONAPRED). People can sue both public and private parties before the CONAPRED for acts of discrimination. Originally, CONAPRED's punishment powers were very limited. At worst, if a person was deemed to have discriminated, they had to issue a formal apology and submit to sensitivity training. After 2014, however, the CONAPRED acquired the power to impose more severe sanctions, such as restitution measures.

or is forced to change in any way. It becomes almost necessary for a victim to sue an employer through every means possible—with all the costs that such a litigation strategy entails, especially if lawyers with different specialties need to be retained—to see if, together, she might be able to get proper redress.

The third problem—perhaps not surprising given the complexity of the law—is that most of these means are ineffective in actually punishing harassment. As I previously stated, people are rarely punished through criminal law. And what little data is available regarding the other pathways (the fact that there is less data available for civil law or labor law when compared to criminal law is itself a problem) shows that these other mechanisms are just as ineffective as criminal law in addressing the problem. For instance, according to the response I got from the Labor Ministry through a petition for access to public information, between 2013 and 2017, not a single company in the entire country was fined for harassment in the workplace.[32]

It is clear that impunity, in Mexico, is not limited to criminal law, but this rarely gets discussed. The focus generally remains on criminal law. In my view, the potential of MeToo, given its focus of harassment in the context of *employment*, was to push the conversation toward these other systems of law, especially labor law.

Beyond the problems that each complaint pathway has, there are other issues to address as well. Although harassment happens in many places and relationships, which suggests it is practically "universal," it is nonetheless highly contextual. It can be reduced or exacerbated by a variety of factors, that change depending on the setting in which it happens and the relationship within which it takes place. For example, the specific *type* of harassment that is most prevalent changes depending on *who* is doing the harassment (a boss or a coworker).[33] The prevalence of harassment can also change depending on how segregated a workspace is.[34] Places in which there is "subjective, unconstrained authority,"

---

32. Dirección General de Asuntos Jurídicos, Dirección de Evaluación, Rendición de Cuentas y Responsabilidad Pública, Unidad de Transparencia, Oficio No. STPS/UT/44/18, Mar. 5, 2018, Respuesta a Solicitante con el Folio 0001400004418, information available in *Shadow Report on Employment Discrimination Against Women in Mexico*, Área de Derechos Sexuales y Reproductivos Programa de Derecho a la Salud División de Estudios Jurídicos Centro de Investigación y Docencia Económicas, 6, June 2018, https://tbinternet.ohchr.org/Treaties/CEDAW/Shared%20Documents/MEX/INT_CEDAW_NGO_MEX_31406_E.pdf.

33. *See* Sonia M. Frías, *Hostigamiento, acoso sexual y discriminación laboral por embarazo en México*, 73 Revista Mexicana de Sociología, no. 2, 343, 2011; Adriana Ortega, *La (invisibilidad de la) violencia laboral en México*, Animal Político, Jan. 28, 2020, https://www.animalpolitico.com/blog-de-intersecta/la-invisibilidad-de-la-violencia-laboral-en-mexico/.

34. *See* Vicki Schultz, *Reconceptualizing Sexual Harassment*, 107 Yale L.J., 1998, and Vicki Schultz, *Reconceptualizing Sexual Harassment . . . Again*, Yale L.J. Forum, June 18, 2018.

as scholar Vicki Schultz argues, are also ripe for harassment. And in Mexico, another important factor to consider is that most people—57 percent, to be precise—work in an informal setting (without benefits, employment stability, etc.) and that only 40 percent of women are economically active.[35]

It is important to take into account all these factors because it forces us to broaden the scope of our solutions. If we believe harassment is the product of a few "bad apples," our solutions will most likely be focused on punishing individuals. If we believe harassment is fostered by "industry dynamics and organizational conditions," as professor Schultz says, or is affected by broader economic policies that foster work precariousness and informality, we will look beyond individual punishment and into broader policies. The point is to begin discussing all of this.

And the Harvey Weinstein story *could have* prompted such a conversation. But, at least in Mexico, it did not.

#MeToo in Mexico

There are three moments that show, in my view, where the conversation around #MeToo turned to in Mexico.

The first is related to the publication by *Le Monde* of a "letter" signed by 100 "prominent" French women, including actress Catherine Deneuve and writer Catherine Millet, on January 9, 2018. The letter, as many others have recounted, critiqued the "#MeToo movement,"[36] arguing that it basically went "too far," confusing sexual violence with gallantry, while demonizing "men" and victimizing "women."

In Mexico, the letter got the media's attention. The high point was when one of the most important morning television programs in the country ("Despierta con Loret") invited Marta Lamas[37] and Catalina Ruiz-Navarro, both renowned feminists, to discuss the French manifesto. The program, of course, was set up to highlight their differences, making them "debate" over the excesses of "#MeToo." The program was watched online by hundreds of

35. For data on employment discrimination and how it affects women in Mexico, *see* Vela Barba, *supra*, note 23, pp. 52-76.

36. Valeriya Safronova, *Catherine Deneuve and Others Denounce the #MeToo Movement*, N.Y. TIMES, Jan. 9, 2018, https://www.nytimes.com/2018/01/09/movies/catherine-deneuve -and-others-denounce-the-metoo-movement.html.

37. At the end of 2018, Marta Lamas published a book devoted to sexual harassment. *See* MARTA LAMAS, ACOSO: ¿DENUNCIA LEGÍTIMA O VICTIMIZACIÓN?, Fondo de Cultura Económica, 2018.

thousands of people and ended up trending on Twitter.[38] It divided people into two groups: those decrying the disqualification of victims and those applauding "moderation."

A month after this program, in February 2018, something else happened. Carmen Aristegui, one of the most respected journalists in the country, devoted one of her television programs to #MeToo. She interviewed three actresses—Karla Souza, Stephanie Sigman, and Paola Núñez—and one comedienne—Sofía Niño de Rivera—about their own experiences.[39]

Although Karla Souza never divulged the name of the man that she claimed raped her, Televisa, one of the country's most important television broadcasters, decided to fire Gustavo Loza, a director, for the incident. Loza snapped back, claiming to have had a "sentimental relationship" with Souza, but denying any claim of rape. He also criticized Aristegui for not reaching out to him. At the same time, an old interview of Souza reappeared in which she affirmed that she sometimes used her "charms" to "get ahead."

In the case of Sofía Niño de Rivera, things got heated as well. She had claimed that a famous journalist, Ricardo Rocha, had harassed her on set before an interview. He also protested, claiming that he had gone over that interview several times and that in no moment did he treat her the way she said he treated her. He also denounced Aristegui for failing to do her due diligence with him. A hundred "prominent" women—including some feminists—published a letter supporting Rocha. "We have only received respect, love, and support" from him, they claimed.

In this context, the debate was focused, again, on a critique of women and "MeToo." If women were harassed, why didn't they speak up? Was it really even harassment? Weren't they demonizing men? Wasn't it a "witch hunt?" What about due process?

Finally, after more than a year had passed, in March 2019, women, once again, used social media to denounce harassment, on this occasion specifically using the banner of "MeToo."[40] There were some differences with prior iterations.

---

38. *See* Francisco J. Trejo Corona, *Se debatió feminismo en cadena nacional y ardió Twitter por las declaraciones de Marta Lamas*, Tercera Vía, Jan. 12, 2018, http://terceravia .mx/2018/01/se-debatio-feminismo-en-cadena-nacional-la-republica-tuitera-esta-contenta -marta-lamas/.

39. *See* Carmen Aristegui, *#MeToo en México: mujeres compartieron en "Aristegui" sus denuncias de acoso sexual*, CNN en Español, Feb. 23, 2018, https://cnnespanol.cnn.com/ video/me-too-mexico-aristegui-karla-souza-paola-nunez-nino-de-rivera-loza-rocha-orig -digital-pkg/.

40. *See* Paulina Villegas, *How a Young Activist Set Off a #MeToo Avalanche in Mexico*, N.Y. Times, Mar. 28, 2019, https://www.nytimes.com/2019/03/28/world/americas /mexico-metoo.html; Nina Lakhani, *#MeToo reaches Mexico: majority of women in media report harassment at work*, The Guardian, Mar. 27 2019, https://www.theguardian.com/world

Earlier, most women referred to the violence to which they had been submitted but refused to identify their aggressors. This time, women named names. A second important difference is that anonymous Twitter accounts were created to group complaints by professional sectors. There were accounts focused on writers, musicians, lawyers, and scholars, for instance.[41] They published the victims' testimonies, including anonymous ones. Testimonies included everything from lewd remarks to intimate partner violence. Not surprisingly, the conversation again shifted to the "excesses."

In reviewing the history of sexual harassment law in Mexico, what is striking is that this is the exact same conversation that occurred when sexual harassment was first criminalized in 1991. The reform did spark a discussion in the Chamber of Deputies. According to the records of this discussion, one representative in particular, Guadalupe Gómez, voiced the concerns of many others.

The first "problem" with the reform, as identified by representative Gómez, was that this "conduct"—harassment—was an "Anglo-Saxon import" that did not correspond at all to "our idiosyncrasies and cultural values." In "North America," she said, a woman cannot be the object of "*piropos*," which are still defined by the Spanish Royal Academy as "compliments." If she wants, the representative (inaccurately) affirmed, this woman can call the police, so the "*piropeador*" can be taken to the commissary. "Why," she asked, "must we kill the *piropo*, that literary expression of the street, that gallant form of courtship that is a part of the emotional substance of the Latino man?" "How many relationships," she asked, "began with an evident harassment on the part of the man, who sought to be admitted and appreciated?"

The second "problem" with the reform she identified was that it actually demeaned women, by "over protecting them." In her view, what women should do when faced with harassment was talk back, so they could "stop" it and "evade" it. Besides, she claimed, "what one woman can define as harassment, another can see it as a manifestation of interest, affection, or love." And, she added, let us not forget that "women can and do harass men" too.

The pushback to this came from two representatives, Hilda Anderson and Amalia García, who both expressed one simple idea: this "conduct" was not "new," nor an "import." It happened in Mexico "too" and had been happening for quite some time. "Thousands" of women suffered it, women who worked in factories and in government institutions, women who studied in the university

/2019/mar/27/mexico-metoo-workplace-abuse-sexual-harassment-media; Alida Piñón, *The Feminist Movement Is Taking Over Mexico*, EL UNIVERSAL, Apr. 7, 2019, https://www.eluniversal.com.mx/english/feminist-movement-taking-over-mexico.

    41. *See* Yuriria Ávila, *¿Cómo surgió el movimiento Me Too y cómo revivió en México?*, ANIMAL POLÍTICO, Mar. 27, 2019, https://www.animalpolitico.com/elsabueso/como-surgio-el-movimiento-me-too-y-como-revivio-en-mexico/.

and in high school. "Sexual harassment happens everywhere" and it can affect "all the women," "regardless of their age, civil status, physical appearance, level of education or professional state." And it is not "flirting based on mutual appreciation," it is not "sending a bouquet of flowers." It is generally a "manifestation of power," used to "intimidate, coerce or humiliate" another person. And yes, they responded, men are harassed too, but women represent "95% of the victims." All we are trying to do, they argued, is include "in law the concerns of many people." In spite of this, they said, our colleagues feel "attacked" and some "even feel like potential harassers." But this is not what we want. We just want to stop "the commission of more crimes."

To date, these represent the two "frameworks" that are still used to discuss sexual harassment. On one side, sexual harassment is seen as a sexual conduct that is part of a broader pattern of sexual violence that is disproportionately suffered by women. Yes, sexual harassment happens in the workplace, but it happens everywhere else as well. Distinctions are erased to highlight the prevalence of the problem. And the pushback to date is the same: women, critics affirm, are calling "violence" behavior that is really just an expression of "seduction" or "affection." Women are victimizing themselves and demonizing men. And in order to stop old injustices, new ones are—critics claim—being committed.

We cannot seem to get past these framings.

And "MeToo" is itself an example of this.

"#MeToo" became a *global* phenomenon after the story regarding Harvey Weinstein's harassment broke. Weinstein's story is the story of a variety of abuses *in the workplace*. Not, perhaps, an ordinary workplace. But a workplace, nonetheless. It had the potential to spark a discussion about the failures of sexual harassment law in reducing *these* particular abuses.

At the same time though, the truth is that "MeToo" transcended the workplace discussion. The millions that responded, "MeToo" did so to a question of whether they had ever been "sexually harassed or assaulted," *regardless of place and time.* Thus framed, "MeToo" allowed commonalities to become visible, so much so, that it became a *global* phenomenon, but in doing so, it has also erased many differences, many of which are particularly relevant to law and public policy. And when one considers the backlash, and the amount of attention it demands, the task of getting into the details seems impossible. All the while, authorities are simply let off the hook. And it's understandable: when women's credibility is supposedly on the line, who has time to get into the nitty gritty of labor law?

What's clear, though, is that if we truly want to reduce sexual harassment in the workplace through legal reform, we need to push the conversation toward this point.

CHAPTER 5

The Healing Power of Telling Stories? Some Unforeseen Effects of #MeToo in Colombia

Isabel C. Jaramillo Sierra[1]

When Alyssa Milano encouraged the use of the tag #MeToo to mobilize against sexual assault after the Harvey Weinstein scandal, she probably never imagined that she would spark a global phenomenon. In Colombia, the global campaign materialized in complex ways with, unfortunately, few tangible results. Feminist NGOs have used the Spanish version to support, in the abstract, the fight against sexual harassment, and express solidarity with victims. Young college students have used the hashtag to denounce the sexual violence they endure at home, in the streets, and on campuses around the country. Finally, some reporters and broadcasters have shared their own stories in the media.

Notwithstanding the number of stories and the solidarity of women from different ages and professions, there is already a sense of frustration as men continue to harass with impunity in the wake of the movement. In fact, the latest news on sexual harassment involved the acquittal of former Ombudsman (officer in charge of the promotion and protection of human rights) Jorge Otálora based on evidence that the woman who had accused him had at some point sent him a gift with a card suggesting that they had a relationship.[2]

This chapter provides an account of the uses of #MeToo and its Spanish version #Yotambién, proposes an interpretation of Colombian law on sexual harassment currently in force, and points to some of the weaknesses in the legal framework that could explain why the campaign has failed. I argue that the

---

1. Profesora Titular, Universidad de Los Andes, Bogota, Colombia.

2. *No es explicable que la víctima termine en brazos del agresor: Corte sobre caso Otálora*, Semana, May 28, 2018, https://www.semana.com/nacion/articulo/corte-absuelve-a-jorge -armando-otalora-por-supuesto-acoso/569154.

campaign has actually been costly to the efforts of feminists mobilizing to transform Colombian law on gender violence, but also has produced an opportunity for feminists to engage a younger generation of women.

Colombian Women Too ...

Colombian women have connected in different ways to the #MeToo movement. Roughly speaking, there have been three dominant interpretations of what to do with the hashtag and what the movement is about.

One interpretation, shared by Colombian women in elite NGOs and center-to-left-wing intellectuals, is that the tag is about exposing gender violence in media, and that the movement is about ending all forms of gender violence. In this way, they connect the accusations against Harvey Weinstein to a larger agenda of reducing gender violence in Colombia. These women then use the tag when referring to their own campaigns—old and new—and to every case of gender violence they wish to make more visible. This use is both innovative and deceptive. It connects local concerns to a global agenda and brings light to very important work. Most of this work is oriented to the legal reform of Colombian gender violence law through litigation and increased awareness. These Colombian feminists have been building a model for the defense of victims that uses international and regional law to demand that judges and prosecutors consider the delicate situations that women confront when they seek protection from authorities. These NGOs have worked hard with government authorities to introduce special legislation on gender violence,[3] to increase sentencing for femicides, and to obtain punishment for cases that otherwise might not have been noticed, particularly the kidnap, rape, and murder of indigenous girls by white professional males.[4] However, their campaigns have little to do with the media, professional, and academic elites that #MeToo mobilized in other parts of the world, and the fact that they are using the tag has not changed this focus or orientation. Actually, these NGOs rely almost completely on funding from international aid that stresses assisting vulnerable populations. These agencies only consider poor women to be in such situations.

A second interpretation of #MeToo, or #Yotambien, has originated among college students who have understood #MeToo as a space for voicing experiences of sexual abuse and violence. The Facebook page "Confesiones

---

3. Law 1257 of 2008.

4. *Aumentan a 58 años la condena contra Rafael Uribe Noguera*, Semana, Nov. 2, 2017, https://www.semana.com/nacion/articulo/condena-a-rafael-uribe-aumento-a-58-anos-de -carcel/545779.

Universitarias" (University Confessions) has become a forum for stories about the abuse and violence perpetrated by family members—boyfriends, friends, or former boyfriends as well as stories about the abuse and violence faced in the streets and public transportation. As opposed to the NGO use of the tag, here women tell detailed stories in the first person and without any punitive goal in mind. Although there is a flavor of reproach and a tone of disillusionment, narrators explain that they are not seeking to put anyone in jail but rather to find comfort in finally being able to admit to themselves and their support networks that it happened. These are two examples of the posts by young women in Confesiones Universitarias:

> "Hello All. Since #metoo has become stronger and I am not capable of telling this story out loud, I decided to tell it here.
>
> A little more than a year ago I was going through a rough patch with the guy who was my boyfriend at the moment, and I felt very guilty about it. One day he went to my house and got into a huge fight with me, I don't even remember why. Out of nowhere he unzipped his pants, grabbed my hair, threw me onto the floor and forced me to give him a blow job. [...]
>
> I stayed on the floor crying and shocked. I had never been so humiliated in my life. I felt dirty, I felt repulsed. [...]
>
> When I read what so many other women wrote, all the feelings I had that day came back to me. I just wanted it out of my system. Thanks for reading." [Translation by the author]

This is the second story:

> Hello, my abuse story is this: I left the University and got on a bus; I sat in a window seat, leaving the aisle seat free. A 70-year-old man got on the bus in one of the stops. When I saw him come up, he gave me a bad impression, but I did not move. He looked at me and sat in the free seat next to me. Five minutes later he began to touch himself. I felt uncomfortable but I didn't do anything; I thought he would eventually stop. A few minutes later, he decided to take out his penis and masturbate. At that point I decided I would change seats, but he grabbed my hand, showed me a knife, and told me that if I moved, he would stab me. [...] The most frustrating part of this experience for me has been that the people I have shared this story with have not taken it as seriously as I felt it was. My parents listened but didn't do anything about it, their attitude was "those things happen" [...] Thanks for Reading." [Translation by the author]

The Facebook page has now received these kinds of stories for over a year. Small groups of young college students mobilizing around sexual violence in elite universities have felt paralyzed by the outpouring of stories. On the one hand, these stories are anonymous, and it is not clear that it would be ethical or safe to try to find the women who wrote them. At some points, the stories do not even seem to be real. On the other hand, their efforts over the last five years have focused on sexual violence in universities, and on moving away from the discourse of violence toward a discourse of equality and mobilizing for consciousness-raising instead of punishment. The group posting the stories, then, has become a large but anonymous group that has embraced the mode of sharing their truths without claiming any particular identity or connecting to any larger plan or scheme.

Finally, #MeToo has encouraged women in media to use their stories to evoke public reactions. Three cases have been especially prominent. Two of these cases involved young women (one news anchor and one model/actress) physically abused by their boyfriends who decided not only to press charges, but also to talk about their cases in newspapers and on talk shows.[5] Their prevailing message was that "even if the police and prosecutors do not believe you, you have to say no, you have to speak up, you have to seek help." They harshly criticized the men involved, other young actors and models, and the authorities and defense lawyers who disregarded the women's cries for help. To date, there have not been any changes in the legal situation of any of the accused.

The third case had the potential of roiling the waters a little more. This case concerned Claudia Morales, the former communications director of President Álvaro Uribe Vélez. Morales disclosed that an unidentified previous boss raped her. She told the story in the preliminaries of the presidential elections, and although Álvaro Uribe Vélez was not running, he was certain to have a big influence in the elections. Morales systematically refused to name the perpetrator, stating that she had to protect her family and that legally, there was nothing that could be done to stop him. She defended her right to silence, saying that what was important was how her testimony could empower women and shame men in general. She wanted her story to demonstrate that beyond judicial redress, we need to create spaces for these stories to be believed. Her story

---

5. *Actriz colombiana denuncia agresión de su pareja: polémica, una campaña de apoyo y una contradenuncia*, CNN Español, Sept. 14, 2018, https://cnnespanol.cnn.com/2018 /09/14/eileen-moreno-alejandro-garcia-actriz-colombiana-agresion-pareja-polemica-campana -apoyo-colombia-mexico/. *Las agresiones de Gustavo Rugeles según los relatos de Marcela González*, WRadio, Dec. 27, 2017, https://www.wradio.com.co/noticias/actualidad/las -agresiones-de-gustavo-rugeles-segun-los-relatos-de-marcela-gonzalez/20180110/nota /3685366.aspx.

was strongly contradicted by the political party of Álvaro Uribe Vélez, which ended up, in effect, winning the elections.

Legal Responses to Sexual Harassment in Colombia

Mobilization and legal reform surrounding sexual harassment in Colombia has been building for more than twenty years. The 1994 General Law on Education[6] first established sexual harassment as a serious offense in the context of primary and secondary education. The particular article on sexual harassment, however, was abolished when the 1995 General Disciplinary Code[7] came into force, according to the Constitutional Court ruling on this matter in 1997.[8] The Court, in its decision, explained that sexual harassment of students by professors was a serious disciplinary offense, and should be understood as such under the new statute even if the statute did not explicitly mention sexual harassment. Nonetheless, it noted that the legislator's intention of unifying all disciplinary codes should be taken seriously and given the weight it deserved. Protection against sexual harassment could be obtained through interpretation of the clauses included in the statute. To better illustrate the effect of this decision, it is worth noting that Law 115 of 1994 defined sexual harassment as disciplinable bad behavior occurring in the education system in article 125:

> Sexual Harassment. The bad behavior causes established in article 46 of decree 2277 of 1979 are hereby added to include sexual harassment and, consequently, whomever incurs in this conduct will be sanctioned in accordance to what is provided in article 53 of such decree and will be definitively excluded from the ranking, according to the teacher's statute.

Law 200 of 1995, which replaced decree 2277 of 1979, does not mention sexual harassment as "bad behavior" in disciplinary terms, and does not refer explicitly to the type of sanctions to be imposed to teachers in particular.

In 2006, the Colombian Congress adopted for the first time a Law on Harassment in the Workplace,[9] applicable to both private employees and public officials. The Law introduced some language relevant to the struggle to end sexual harassment in the workplace. Article 7, which illustrates some conduct

---

6. Law 115 of 1994.
7. Law 200 of 1995.
8. Decision C-210 of 1997.
9. Law 1010 of 2006.

that constitutes workplace harassment, includes gender-based slurs, requiring employees to perform duties not included in the labor contract, discrimination, and revealing intimate information. This article does not explicitly mention that requiring sexual favors is a type of harassment, but it does establish that the list is not exhaustive, and that other conduct may be understood as workplace harassment. The law clarifies that if the harassment is public and repeated, the victim does not need more proof than testimony.[10] Nevertheless, the law also recognizes that just one act could be constitute harassment and that harassment may take place in private.[11] Employees are granted protection against dismissal for six months after the presentation of a harassment claim[12] and have the right to be compensated for wrongful dismissal if the harassment is proven.[13] The individuals found guilty of harassment may be fired without any compensation,[14] while the company may be subjected to fines from roughly $300 to $2,000.[15] Any disciplinary or punitive measure, as well as any compensation, must be adopted by a Labor Judge if the case does not involve a public servant, according to Article 13. The same article provides for the intervention of the Solicitor General's office and application of the General Disciplinary Code if a public servant is involved. Individuals suffering from harassment may also ask for the intervention of the Labor Inspector, who may admonish the employer and the company, and demand that they carry out sensitivity trainings and other pedagogical interventions to increase the employee's welfare.[16] Article 9 also provides for the creation of Coexistence Committees in every company. These committees are in charge of adopting preventive and pedagogical measures pertaining harassment in the workplace.[17]

The 2008 Law on Gender Violence[18] included some provisions applicable to workplace sexual harassment and introduced a reform of the existing

---

10. Article 7.

11. Article 7.

12. Article 11.

13. Article 10.

14. Article 10.

15. Article 10.

16. Article 9.

17. According to the only study on the effectiveness of the law that has been published, the Ministry of Labor has not been able to persuade companies to create the Coexistence Committees and there are no records of the type of pedagogical activities used. See Carmen Marina López Pino and Ernesto Ortiz, "Effectiveness of the law 1010/2006 on harassment in the workplace in Colombia, interpreted from a sociological point of view" in Revista de Derecho, No. 44, 2015, http://dx.doi.org/10.14482/dere.44.7171.

18. Law 1257 of 2008.

Criminal Code establishing the crime of "Sexual Harassment."[19] The 2008 Law defined "sexual harm" in article 3 as: "Consequences that derive from forcing someone to have sexual contact, either physical or verbal, or to participate in other sexual interactions [...]. Sexual harm may also derive from forcing the victim to engage in a sexual act with third persons." According to article 12, to prevent and to eradicate gender violence, government should work with employers to ensure equal pay for equal work and to end sexual harassment. Finally, article 29 established the crime of sexual harassment by adding article 210 A to the Criminal Code. Article 29 provides that:

> Whoever uses, in his own benefit or that of a third party, his manifest superiority or relations of authority or power derived from age, sex, or labor, social, family or economic position, to harass, persecute, stalk or besiege physically or verbally, to obtain non-consensual sexual ends, another person, will be sentenced to 1 to 3 years in prison.

The Colombian Constitutional Court has intervened to moderate the interpretation of legislation concerning sexual violence against women in three ways that are relevant for sexual harassment in particular. First, it has denounced the introduction of information about a victim's sexual history at trial as a violation of the right to privacy and the right to due process.[20]

Second, the Constitutional Court has established that women who are victims of gender violence may not be fired for the inconveniences that this situation may cause the employer. Thus, in the case of *Esperanza v. Fundación Universitaria Tecnológico Comfenalco de Cartagena*,[21] the court ordered the respondent to reinstate the plaintiff to her job as secretary in the law school, demanded that the University's president and law school staff take courses on gender and the law, and ask the plaintiff's forgiveness. The respondent had argued that under Colombian labor law, it could fire any employee at will, as long as it duly compensated her according to the legal guidelines. The court, nonetheless, pointed out that employers could not freely fire an employee suffering from gender violence to avoid related inconveniences (e.g., missing work for having to go to the police or prosecutor's office, going to the doctor, or

---

19. Law 599 of 2000.

20. For example, in Decision T-453 of 2005, Judges Manuel José Cepeda, Jaime Córdoba, and Rodrigo Escobar, unanimously ordered the trial judge to exclude a particularized list of evidence that violated the victim's rights.

21. Decision T-878 of 2014, with Judges Jorge Iván Palacio, Gloria Stella Ortiz, and Jorge Ignacio Pretelt.

securing the protection of their children). It established the duty of all employers to protect women victims of gender violence.

Finally, the Constitutional Court has determined that women who voice the concerns and advocate for victims of sexual violence cannot be fired for this reason, even if duly compensated. In *Mónica Godoy v. Universidad de Ibagué*, the Court unanimously ordered the University of Ibague to reinstate Professor Mónica Godoy to her position, after being fired for being "conflictive."[22] This assessment of her behavior resulted from her defense of women in cleaning services and men in security services from sexual harassment and unjust terminations.

The Supreme Court, for its part, has established that the definition of sexual harassment adopted by the International Labor Organization—any behavior that is "unwanted and offensive"—should be used to complement Colombian labor law on harassment in the workplace. In a decision by the Labor Chamber, Justice Clara Cecilia Dueñas established that an employer could fire an employee occupying a supervisory position based on his sexual demeanor toward his female employees.[23]

#MeToo's Failings

As discussed in the introduction, in the last year there have been no convictions or falls from prominence for Colombian men accused of sexual harassment. Jorge Armando Otálora, the Ombudsperson that resigned after the Solicitor General's office decided to suspend him for accusations of sexual harassment, was exonerated of all charges in September of this year.[24] He submitted some text messages in which his accuser had been nice to him and this was enough to negate his threats. According to the Supreme Court's Criminal Chamber that ordered a halt to all investigations, the accuser's expressions of affection "outweighed" the threats he manifested.

I argue that this result may be attributed to the shortcomings of the legal framework concerning the responsibility of public officials who fail to investigate cases of sexual violence involving adult women, and the protection of victims of sexual harassment in particular. I also argue, nonetheless, that the highest costs of the #MeToo campaign as it has manifested locally may be related to the

---

22. Decision T-239 of 2018, with Judges Fernando Reyes, Cristina Pardo, and Gloria Stella Ortiz.

23. SL648-2018-55122.

24. *Procuraduría suspendió a Jorge Armando Otálora como defensor del Pueblo*, EL ESPECTADOR, Jan. 28, 2016, https://www.elespectador.com/noticias/judicial/procuraduria-suspendio-jorge-armando-otalora-defensor-d-articulo-613241.

undermining of efforts to reform the law and the re-inscription of the inevitability of sexual harm as young women find no respite for their suffering.

The Colombian framework on sexual harassment and violence in civil, labor, and criminal law has two counterproductive characteristics. The first is that it is vague in defining prohibited behavior. Although the Supreme Court recently intervened to explain that all sexual conduct that is "offensive and unwanted" constitutes disciplinary offenses, this interpretation has not trickled down to judges and other officials in charge of investigating sexual harassment.[25] The Criminal Chamber of the Supreme Court has clarified that the crime of sexual harassment needs to involve conduct that is repetitive and produces "suffering" in the victim but does not involve the consummation of a sexual act.[26] This definition not only contradicts the one upheld by the Labor Chamber, this contradiction could be explained away using ideas of local priority, but makes it impossible to find real life situations to which the law could be applied.[27]

The same court actually says that if the act is a verbal invocation, it becomes an insult punishable as a crime against honor, and if the act involves touching, it becomes sexual abuse. It provides no examples of situations where sexual harassment would take place. The vagueness in the definition and the contradictory interpretations make it difficult for potential victims to find support for their allegations in the law. Further, it makes it easy for public officials in charge of investigations to claim that the particular situation of the victim is not included under the law.

The second characteristic of this framework is that it is intended to protect women formally employed. However, less than 50 percent of working women in Colombia meet these criteria, though many more work.[28] Informal employment spreads into sectors as varied as tourism, communications, and transportation.[29]

Feminist NGOs and college students had been working separately to reform this legal framework through litigation and awareness campaigns. As

25. SL648-2018-55122.

26. SP107-2018-49799.

27. Contradictions between civil and labor law, and criminal law, can be explained away by saying that the determinacy requirements of criminal law and civil law are different, as sanctions in civil and criminal law are different.

28. *El 47 % de los ocupados del país son informales*, PORTAFOLIO, Apr. 10, 2017, https://www.portafolio.co/economia/empleo/el-47-de-los-ocupados-del-pais-son-informales-504878.

29. *Ibid.* Informality in employment includes individuals working as entrepreneurs, working without affiliation to social security, working in companies with less than 10 employees or working as domestic employees. *Boletín Especial. Medición del Empleo Informal*, DANE, Dec. 31, 2009, https://www.dane.gov.co/files/investigaciones/boletines/ech/ech_informalidad/bolet_ech_informalidad_sep_nov2009.pdf.

pointed out above, feminist NGOs' efforts have been oriented to specify the harm of sexual violence and to make visible and important gender violence in the media and among public officials. For this, they choose cases that can be won both because of the characteristics of the case and because of the willingness of victims to endure the process. As in other cases of strategic litigation, they focus on cases that may be easily won, and they focus on few cases because their resources are few. #MeToo introduces a lot of noise because it brings to the public consciousness the stories of victims who are not willing or interested in litigation. Bringing these cases to light produces reactions in the public that cannot be predicted or contested effectively. The result is that some reactions about victims' accounts of sexual violence and sexual harassment are reiterated without being challenged: they tell lies; they seek revenge; and they were not harmed.

College students, for their part, had been working on awareness campaigns that sought to mobilize young women toward collective goals and change the violence frame for an equality frame. #MeToo worked on the logic of violence and individualized crime and punishment that they were trying to subvert. Awareness campaigns seemed trivial compared to the amount of suffering endured by the women who were speaking up. Yet the "anonymous mass" did not seem interested at all in joining already existing groups or mobilizing beyond their brave acts of telling their stories.

These negative effects should not be the whole story about #MeToo, though. As the tag is still being used, and we learn from the victories of our friends and allies in the United States, it seems important to reflect on the possibilities this campaign has opened up to engage young women and elite women in feminist mobilization. In the Colombian case, where feminism has been in the margins of politics, not only because of undemocratic institutions, but also because of the power of the Catholic Church, reaching some parts of the population has been historically very difficult. Elite women in general have avoided involvement and stayed away from the mire of professional feminists. Universities have been strongholds for conservatives. #MeToo seems to have cut through apathy and denial. Our challenge is to transform stories into actions. All ideas are welcome.

CHAPTER 6

#MeToo in Argentina: Stop Killing Us, Please, #NiUnaMenos!

Virginia Marturet[1]

"There is a privileged minority and its mere existence should not offset nor excuse discrimination that other people face."

— Simone de Beauvoir

On June 3, 2015, a coalition of women from academia and journalism organized a massive march in Buenos Aires to address violence against women, calling it, NiUnaMenos (NUM), or Not One [Woman] Less. The march

---

1. Professor of Law, University of Buenos Aires Law School, Argentina.

2. Graphic by Romina Lerda created to advance the #NiUnaMenos movement and used with the artist's permission.

gathered thousands of women to protest femicide[3] (gender-based violent crimes against women)[4] in the city. The NUM movement worked as the main driving force to put feminist debates and calls for change in common usage in Argentina, rather than just in academic circles.[5]

Argentina Before #MeToo and #NiUnaMenos: Progress and Challenges

According to Simone de Beauvoir:[6] "Feminism is a way of living individually, by fighting together." In Argentina, NUM and the later #MeToo and Time's Up movements have profoundly changed the dialogue about women's place in society, leading to daily discussions in different contexts, either virtually on social media, or at work, on TV or with family and friends. These conversations have raised women's and girls' consciousness so that behavior that might have been ignored before is no longer tolerated.

From time to time these conversations can be friendly but sometimes they are heated. In Argentina, we are beginning to put a stop to sexist situations by raising awareness and creating a culture where the established norms are constantly questioned to create new rules of social coexistence. The ongoing dialogue has produced, from the public and private sectors, more policies to address the claims at stake.

In Argentina, the feminist movement dates back almost a century. Prior to 2015, the recognition of women's rights has made significant progress, not only with specific legislation, but also by complying with related human rights legislation, while utilizing international standards of full enjoyment of such rights.

- Human Rights Laws: The 1994 Constitutional Reform introduced new approaches to people's rights and the adoption of

---

3. In Spanish the terminology of this word is similar to "homicidio" (murder). However, it only refers to the murder of women, whereas "femicide" as the Mexican politician and activist Marcella Lagarde defines it, includes the lack of governmental protection to women in cases of violence.

4. This is a word first used in 2010 to define these crimes after Wanda Taddei's murder by her boyfriend Eduardo Arturo Vazquez. This awakened the awareness of gender-based violence in Argentina and the issue of femicides. In 2012 the law barring femicides was passed and this has led to a greater gender perspective in entering judgments.

5. To accurately describe the NUM movement in Argentina, the author interviewed women living in Argentina, from different settings (academic, political, housewives, students, and professionals), socioeconomic status, nationalities, and ages.

6. SIMONE DE BEAUVOIR, EL SEGUNDO SEXO (THE SECOND SEX) (Debolsilo, ed., Argentina, 2016).

international Treaties on Human Rights, such as the Universal Declaration on Human Rights. The Reform established Argentina as a country committed to develop policies and to coordinate projects in recognition and fulfillment of minorities' rights, or in the words of Roberto Gargarella,[7] "disadvantaged groups," which includes women, despite their being a majority of the population.

- Gender Equality: Since 1992, under a federal gender equality law, electoral lists for the National Congress must contain a minimum of 30 percent female candidates, but in reality, the figure has been much higher, up to 35 to 39 percent.
- Comprehensive Sexual Education: In 2006, the federal government approved the National Comprehensive Sexual Education Plan (ESI for its acronym in Spanish), with age-appropriate information for children from three to seventeen years old in public, private, and religious schools.[8] Younger children between three and five years old, learned self-care habits, caretaking of other people, and values of coexistence. Moreover, they were taught to respect personal privacy and that under no circumstance should anyone touch their private parts, unless otherwise needed in cases of specific hygiene. Nonetheless, because of resistance from conservative and religious groups and parents, ESI was not uniformly implemented.
- Gender Violence: Violence against women in Argentina has been a long-standing problem, despite many laws addressing the problem. The civil society organization La Casa del Encuentro reported that between January and September 2013, 209 women died as a result of domestic or gender-based violence, and from 2008 to 2015, there were 2,224 reported cases of femicide.[9]

In 2006, the City of Buenos Aires, mobile phone operators and the National Government entered into an agreement whereby mobile operators would provide support for women facing or experiencing violence, calling for free the country's 144 emergency hotline.

---

7. ROBERTO GARGARELLA, DERECHOS Y GRUPOS DESAVENTAJADOS (Rights and Disadvantaged Groups) (Gedisa, ed., 1999).

8. *Programa Nacional de Educación Sexual Integral, Ley 26.150*, INFOLEG, Oct. 23, 2006, http://servicios.infoleg.gob.ar/infolegInternet/anexos/120000-124999/121222/norma .htm.

9. Reported in U.S. State Dept. Human Rights Reports for 2015, Argentina, https:// 2009-2017.state.gov/j/drl/rls/hrrpt/humanrightsreport/index.htm#wrapper.

In 2009, the government enacted "Law 26.485," the **National Plan of Action to Prevent, Assist and Eradicate Violence Against Women** (Plan Nacional de Acción para la Prevención, Asistencia y Erradicación de la Violencia contra las mujeres). Notwithstanding enactment of this law and others to prevent femicides and sexual harassment and to help victims, the rate of gender-based violence has not decreased.[10]

- Bans on Abortions: When the first Criminal Code was enacted in Argentina in 1886, all abortion, with no exceptions, was banned. In 1921, the law was amended to allow abortions where the life of the mother was endangered or if a rape victim was mentally disabled. In 2012, the Argentine Supreme Court held that when any pregnancy resulted from a rape, abortion was also lawful.[11]

The NUM Movement

Even with the progress made toward gender equality, there were still significant challenges in every part of women's lives that the NUM movement sought to address. Thus, in 2015, the NUM organizers started with a very ambitious political agenda including efforts to:

- Increase women's pay. Women earn 27 percent less than men and are considered second-class citizens;
- Guarantee and enforce the **National Comprehensive Sexual Education Plan** (Educación Sexual Integral, ESI) in all areas of education, by training teachers and directors in schools;
- Reduce sexual harassment at work, other places, and street harassment; and
- End violence against women.

The anti-violence agenda aimed to implement the necessary means and control from the Government for the 2009 **National Plan of Action to Prevent, Assist and Eradicate Violence Against Women**, Law 26.485. Activists sought to:

---

10. *Política públicas: Incidencia, sensibilización y legislatura*, LA CASA DEL ENCUENTRO, http://www.lacasadelencuentro.org/politicaspublicas.html.

11. *Historia del aborto en Argentina*, FUNDACIÓN HUÉSPED, https://www.huesped .org.ar/informacion/derechos-sexuales-y-reproductivos/tus-derechos/interrupcion-legal-del -embarazo/historia-del-aborto-en-argentina/.

- Guarantee access to legal counseling for victims;
- Guarantee protection to victims by using electronic controls to prevent aggressors from breaching measures issued by the court ordering them to stay away from the victims; and
- Establish a National Record of violence against women to generate true and up-to-date statistics of femicides, which would help the government to develop efficient public policies.

In the subsequent four years, this political agenda has expanded to address the prohibition on abortion, judicial stereotyping, and promoting LGBTQ equality.[12]

Examples from the NUM Movement

Lucia O., twenty-nine years old, with a Bachelor of Psychology degree, and working in a well-respected Buenos Aires hospital, experienced and witnessed harassment of her colleagues. At the beginning, however, she did not consider these issues to be crimes. "That the interns were touched, groped, or assaulted was common. Today it is considered harassment and the hospital has even received a complaint. Everyone should now be more careful about what they do or say. But this is happening because everyone is talking about it. Among the women interns working in hospital, there are burning talks about feminism, and despite having different points of view, we all agree that we have stopped considering certain behaviors as natural," she commented.

This is not an isolated reaction; the changes introduced as a consequence of the NUM debate are evident and profound. These debates reflect and modify the topics from sexual harassment as agreed upon by professionals from different workplaces, as illustrated below.

Since the beginning of the NUM movement, men are being more careful with what they say, do, and ask women in the workplace and in private settings. Mercedes M., fifty-two years old, a health professional working in a hospital and in private practice, comments that men's behavioral carefulness is "something that didn't happen before and even some men avoid sexist jokes."

"The issue is all over. All hell breaks loose when there is a sexist comment," Florencia S., thirty-nine years old, added. 'There's always a turned-on TV in the kitchen of the company I work for and when femicides are on the news, inner

---

12. *La FALGBT se suma a #NiUnaMenos y convoca a marchar contra la violencia hacia las mujeres*, FEDERACIÓN ARGENTINA LGBT, http://www.falgbt.org/slider/la-falgbt-se-suma-a-niunamenos-y-convoca-a-marchar-contra-la-violencia-hacia-las-mujeres/.

debates kick off and sometimes they become heated. But I always feel I learn something new." It is important to highlight the phrase "heated discussions," because it defines the Argentinean culture in a way, where everyone gets excited about everything.

Advancing Gender Equality

This awakening of society and feminism through social media paved the way to create the public support for the federal government to introduce a variety of measures to address gender equality, including programs in the last few years in the nation, provinces, and municipalities. All of this was achieved thanks to the NUM movement.

For example, in the past, the percentage of women in leadership positions in public and private entities has shown inequality, but it is improving dramatically. The Ministry of National Modernization (Ministerio de Modernización Nacional), an entity created in 2015, reported that 40 percent of those who hold public office or are directors of the Public Administration in Argentina are women.

In 2017, the Argentinean National Congress amended the federal gender equality law[13] for electoral lists, effective for the 2019 elections.

Combating Gender Violence

Heightened awareness about violence against women is perceived, but male and female equality is still a long way off and gender-based violence rates in Argentina are still alarming. After three years of the NUM movement, one woman is murdered every 30 hours, according to data published in June 2018 from the Monitoring Center for Violence against Women (Observatorio de la Violencia contra las Mujeres) in Mumalá.[14] In a September 26, 2017, Monitoring Center survey, 80 percent of women reported feeling insecure on the streets, especially at night.[15]

---

13. The Gender Parity Law in Areas of Political Representation in Argentina, sanctioned on November 23, 2017 by Law No. 27.412, https://es.wikipedia.org/wiki/Ley_de_ Paridad_de_G%C3%A9nero_en_%C3%81mbitos_de_Representaci%C3%B3n_Pol%C3 %ADtica.

14. https://www.facebook.com/MuMaLaNacional/photos/a.233475650860831 /330990267776035/?type=3&theater.

15. https://www.losandes.com.ar/article/espacio-publico-8-de-cada-10-mujeres-se -sienten-inseguras.

In 2017, the City of Buenos Aires enacted the "Ankle Bracelets Secured Women" law (Tobilleras Mujeres Seguras), enforced by the Ministry of Justice and Security of the City of Buenos Aires, to ensure compliance with judicial restraining orders for male partners to remain or not to get near a specific address. The "Victims against Violence Plan" (Las Víctimas contra las Violencias) recorded 5,433 victims of sexual harassment in the last three years.

Moreover, the National Government created in September 2017 the **National Women's Institute** (INAM, for its acronym in Spanish) to issue policies, develop projects, and take steps to empower women, eradicate gender-based violence, and promote gender equality in Argentina.[16]

When the 2009 National Plan of Action to Prevent, Assist and Eradicate Violence Against Women (the Plan) was first introduced, there was a clear understanding in Argentinean society that the Plan be implemented with a very clear, and unequivocal gender perspective in the whole nation.

The Plan has two main central themes: (1) the prevention and comprehensive assistance of women threatened with gender-based violence; and (2) the prevention and comprehensive assistance of women experiencing gender-based violence. The Plan also has three keystones: (1) to educate the public about gender issues; (2) to coordinate such education; and (3) to permanently monitor and assess public policies to be aware of whether they are preventing gender violence.

The Secretariat on Human Rights and Cultural Diversity of Argentina (Secretaría de Derechos Humanos y Pluralismo Cultural de la Nación) under the Ministry of Justice and Human Rights (Ministerio de Justicia y Derechos Humanos de la Nación) develops projects and carries out action plans for women's rights. The latest National Plan[17] for 2017-2020 has five main topics, including inequality and discrimination. The aim is to address Human Rights policies in the long term, and to better control its implementation, monitoring, and assessment.

At the municipal level, in March 2018, the City of Buenos Aires Legislature introduced a bill to grant women facing or experiencing gender-based violence a leave of absence and "to update, on the grounds of gender equality, leaves of absence, sick leaves, adoption, school adaptation under the Labor Relationships of the City of Buenos Aires." Finally, in November 2018, the bill passed. The legislature also changed and increased leaves for pregnancy, adoption, childbirth for women and men, even adding leave for gender-based and

---

16. *Plan Nacional de Acción 2017-2019*, INAM, https://www.argentina.gob.ar/inam /plandeaccion.

17. *Plan Nacional de Acción de Derechos Humanos*, YouTube, Dec. 11, 2017, https:// youtu.be/E_elo6RWjqg.

intrafamily violence. This is a further step to reduce the gender gap and promote equal distribution in tasks related to childcare between women and men.[18]

National Campaign for the Right to Legal, Safe, and Free Abortions

Women's claims for sexual and reproductive health, including legal abortions, began in 1983, when democracy and the establishment of human rights returned in Argentina, after two years of military dictatorship. However, it was the February 19, 2018 massive march of NUM activists carrying green handkerchiefs to symbolize the campaign to legalize abortion (pañuelazo) that finally brought it before Congress.

A 2018 survey showed that 70 percent of Argentineans wanted a comprehensive abortion bill to be passed.[19] In March 2018, the bill to legalize abortion was submitted to Congress for debate with seventy-one signatures of Deputies from all parties. The Argentinean President, Mauricio Macri, who himself opposed abortion, nonetheless called for Congress to debate this bill on the voluntary termination of pregnancy (hereafter, VTP). The debate on VTP had been pending for years and had not occurred during the eight-year term of a female president, Cristina Fernandez de Kirchner. Note that, since July 17, 1980, Argentina had committed to comply with international treaties on Human Rights and Women's Rights in CEDAW, and unrestricted abortion is one of the rights set forth therein.

As Sabrina Cartabia Groba[20] expressed, "We cannot think of the debate to legalize abortion and its significance but for the contribution of NUM. There was a huge social mobilization, choosing whether to be in favor or not carried out by politicians and participants. The NUM movement paved the way to discuss the legalization of abortion, an issue affecting women, girls and

---

18. DECTO 2018- 365- AJG. EE No. 30.202.871/MGEYA-DGALE/2018 - s/Ley No. 6025. https://documentosboletinoficial.buenosaires.gob.ar/publico/20181121.pdf.

19. *Una encuesta asegura que el 70% de los argentinos quiere que se debata la legalización del aborto*, LA GACETA, Mar. 2, 2018, https://www.lagaceta.com.ar/nota/763015/actualidad /encuesta-asegura-70porciento-argentinos-quiere-se-debata-legalizacion-aborto.html.

20. Sabrina Cartabia Groba is a recognized feminist lawyer, activist on sexual and reproductive health, and a relentless fighter for the betterment of women's and girl's rights in Argentina and especially for the legalization of abortion. She is a Cum Laude University of Buenos Aires graduate and the president of the group of companies fighting for diversity and women's rights. She was a member of the NiUnaMenos movement from October 2016 to January 2018. In 2018 she became the first Argentinean woman to be recognized by TIME magazine, which defined her as a leader of generations to come.

teenagers (51 percent of the Argentinean society) given the structural differences in Argentina, which is why there should be social change."[21]

The NUM debate also opened the door to discussions in the society, politicians from different parties, trade unions, state agencies and departments, the legislative, the executive and the judicial powers about unfettered abortion rights and gender equality in general.

Although narrowly passing in the Chamber of Deputies, the more conservative Senate defeated the bill to legalize abortion.

The Argentinean Constitution provides that the Federal Government supports the Roman Catholic religion. For this reason, the debate in Congress about legalizing abortion was blocked by pressure from the Catholic Church. This is a different, necessary debate that the Federal Congress owes to Argentinean society—amend the Constitution to eliminate involvement by the Catholic Church.

NUM members are analyzing their tactical mistakes in failing to pass the bill, so that there will be a different result next time the abortion bill is discussed in Congress.

Position of Women at Work

In Argentina, women's positions and pay at work are gradually improving as policies to promote gender equality are resulting in higher pay and more senior positions for women.

"Companies under societal pressure are promoting women who had experience and could do better," commented María José Sucarrat, the Co-founder and Executive Director of the group of companies fighting for diversity (RED, for its acronym in Spanish) quoted in a Gender-Equality Guide for Companies and published by Di Tella University in 2017.[22] She added that "the average position of directors can reach 50 percent of women but this percentage decreases to 35 percent of women in the average managerial position."

Sabrina C added: "The Deputy Chamber, Federal and Provincial Congresses are treating the gender equality on electoral lists to create gender equality

---

21. Interview by the author with Cartabia, October 18, 2018; for more about Cartabia and the anti-abortion movement in Argentina, see Suyin Hayes, *Warrior for Women's Rights*, TIME, Oct. 10, 2018, https://time.com/collection-post/5414037/sabrina-cartabia-next -generation-leaders/?utm_campaign=time&xid=time_socialflow_twitter&utm_source= twitter.com&utm_medium=social.

22. Universidad Torcuato di Tella, https://www.utdt.edu/, *Guía de género para empresas. Hacia la paridad* (2017), UTDT, ESCUELA DE NEGOCIOS, EDUCACIÓN EJECUTIVA, https:// www.utdt.edu/ver_contenido.php?id_contenido=11972&id_item_menu=21543.

in the Chamber of Deputies and Senators. Moreover, as for trade unions, they created Gender Commissions. As for Political Parties and Social Movements, they are working hard to prevent and assist women in case of violence."

In a 2018 interview, Helena Estrada, Director of the **Women's Economic Development Center,**[23] told local media that according to research carried out by her Center, the women's participation in the economy should increase and to achieve this, Helena promotes the economic empowerment of women. That means, for instance, more women working outside the home, having control over their own finances, making more money at work, etc. She states that "[G]enerally speaking, women invest more money at home, in her family and in the education of their sons and daughters. This shows the positive impact of the economic empowerment of women not only in the society, but also in the economy: it is said that when this gender inequality ends, the Argentinean GDP will grow to 16 percent. This is because there is an idle capacity: today there are two and a half million of inactive women."[24]

The increase in women in company leadership positions is occurring because "gender measures taken in the public sector have a cultural impact on the private sector," according to Georgina Sticco, a co-founder with Carolina Villanueva, of GROW, a consulting firm[25] specializing in workplace gender bias. "It is a fact that there are more and more women holding office and that the enactment of gender equality law in Congress—for example—makes changes in the position for directors in the private sector." Sticco also stated that the decision of former Argentine President Mauricio Macri to allow debate on the bill to legalize abortion showed that feminists today are being heard thanks to the efforts of the NUM movement and the previous feminist movements over the last forty years.

The #NiUnaMenos (not One [Woman] Less) and #MeToo.

Social activism against sexism has been growing since 2015 in Latin America thanks to two separate sociocultural campaigns different from the U.S. 2017 #MeToo movement. These campaigns were the perfect opportunity to publicize and protest against diverse crimes women face, especially in the workplace.

---

23. Centro de Desarrollo Económico de la Mujer, https://www.argentina.gob.ar/produccion/cedem.

24. *Economía machista: las mujeres ganan hasta un 45% menos que los hombres,* INFOBAE, Dec. 13, 2019, https://www.infobae.com/sociedad/2018/01/27/las-mujeres-ganan-hasta-un-45-menos-que-los-hombres/.

25. GROW, https://generoytrabajo.com.

In the words of Sabrina C., "there are similarities between these movements because they intend to break social taboos surrounding gender-based violence: MeToo is against sexual harassment done by a Hollywood director, and this marked the shower of related complains; NiUnaMenos is a movement intended to break silence [about violence against women] in history."

The #ArgentineanMeToo (#MeTooArgentino)

The #MeToo movement initially erupted in Argentina in September 2018. Numerous female employees working for Greenpeace in Argentina and Chile had complained to Greenpeace about sexual harassment and other offenses by their Executive Director, Martín Prieto.[26] The women filed criminal complaints against Prieto. Greenpeace thereafter carried out an internal investigation and dismissed Prieto for the crimes of sexual and labor harassment and "violence to the detriment of women."

In the subsequent criminal case, the court did not initially dismiss the claims but established that some of the claims did not constitute the crime of sexual harassment (as defined by the Criminal Code) while others were barred by the statute of limitations. The case has been dismissed.

On a larger scale, the #ArgentineanMeToo (#MeTooArgentino) arrived in the country in December 2018 as a consequence of a deep revolution like a liberation cry from different generations of women. On December 11, 2018, an organization of Argentine actresses held a press conference to announce a criminal accusation of rape and sexual harassment by Juan Darthés, an actor, of Thelma Fardín, an actress, during a tour with the cast of a soap opera teen TV show in which they had both starred. The show was for two years playing at prime time, reaching high ratings in its teen audience. Fardín posted a video with the accusation that nine years earlier, when she was sixteen years old, the only adult actor on tour, Juan Darthés, then forty-five, had forced her to touch his penis, performed oral sex on her despite her repeated requests for him to stop, and raped her.[27]

Fardín filed her accusation in Nicaragua, where the alleged events occurred, and she commented that thanks to three other actresses who had already spoken out against Darthés, she decided to break her nine-year silence. On December 13, 2018, Mauro Viale, a famous journalist in Argentina, interviewed Darthés.

---

26. Mariano Carbajal, *El efecto Me Too llegó a la Argentina*, Página 12, Sept. 12, 2018, https://www.pagina12.com.ar/141597-el-efecto-me-too-llego-a-la-argentina.

27. *El relato de Thelma Fardin contra Juan Darthés*, INFOBAE, YOUTUBE, Dec. 11, 2018, https://www.youtube.com/watch?v=zstw3PdVcoI.

He accused Fardín, a minor at the time of the events, of having initiated the request for sex, which he had refused. Other members of the cast then began accusing other members of the soup opera's production of sexual abuse. Juan Darthés was isolated in Brazil, his home country, awaiting the outcome of the case of Nicaragua. On October 16, Nicaragua accused him legally and formally. So, the Nicaraguan Justice asked for his international capture.

The mass media reported that after Thelma Fardín's public accusation, the number of calls to the #114 help line set up to report gender-based violence episodes increased by 240 percent. A specialist on this issue explained that an official accusation like this one supported by all actresses made it easier for women to break their silence and report abuse.[28] The Argentinean Organization of Performers (SAGAI for its acronym in Spanish) reported another alarming finding: 66 percent of women and 32 percent of men confessed to have been abused at the workplace, in the set, casting, and/or performance.

Fardín's accusation led many others to reveal they had been victims of abuse and sexual harassment. There have also been governmental accusations. This is a new era of awareness and activism for which we should be prepared. The Fardín story implies the need to work with care to create strong protocols to protect children and teenagers working in show business from abuse. And with renewed activism, we find a massive group of women have joined forces since March 2018 to legalize the voluntary termination of pregnancy (abortion).

On December 14, 2018, the President announced a new **Plan for Equal Opportunity and Rights** (Plan de Igualdad y Derechos) to promote gender equality in Argentina. The Plan aims to promote everyone's right to equal opportunities to live freely in a fair society, regardless of their gender.

Moreover, the National Congress passed the **Micaela Law** (Ley Micaela), named after a femicide victim, which creates the **Permanent National Program of Institutional Training in Gender and Violence against Women** (Programa Nacional Permanente de Capacitación Institucional en Género y Violencia contra las Mujeres). Such training is for all state officials and workers to prevent and handle cases of gender inequality and gender-based violence.

The domino effects of the #MeToo movement are still being seen around the world, including Argentina. The ways in which men and women treat each other are changing for good. As stated by Argentinean actresses, "This is only the beginning!"

---

28. *Aumentaron las llamadas a las líneas de violencia de género tras la denuncia contra Juan Darthés por violación*, Todo Noticias, Dec. 12, 2018, https://tn.com.ar/sociedad/se-dispararon-las-llamadas-las-lineas-de-violencia-de-genero-tras-la-denuncia-contra-juan-darthes_923954.

Future of the Movements

The future is quite promising for the empowerment, recognition, strengthening, and development of women's rights inspired by #MeToo and #NiUnaMenos. These movements are similar and yet different, reflecting the countries where they originated, their aftermath, impact, and agendas. They are similar because they fight for women's rights, create spaces for dialogue/debate, and push for equality of opportunities and rights. Women increasingly expect politicians to listen, to observe their problems, and to make the world a suitable place for women, regardless of their age, race, religion, nationality, ideology, political or trade union opinion, financial situation, or physical features.

In Argentina, it seems there is a new way of thinking and speaking that "challenges the structures of a strong, powerful and violent patriarchy." These fights bring up questions about power relationships in all settings.[29]

As for the challenges, Sabrina C, points out that, "Since feminism has a quite extensive agenda on the grounds of gender, it should be included in all and every setting where important decisions affecting society are made. There is a lot to do in many other places. The movement is part of different places and even though things against women are still happening, they feel protected for being part of NiUnaMenos." We need to take note and think about why the Senate rejected the bill on legalizing abortion, Sabrina kept on saying, and I agree, "not to make the same mistake again." It is also important to support the comprehensive sex education to benefit society; it is the needed weapon to fight against violence.

Among the movements in each country, the issues at stake join women from different parts of the world. I consider it a positive development that there are variations in feminist movements, each with its own distinctive features depending on the difficulties women face every day around the world. This makes the agenda broader and brings more claims for women's rights. We should think positively about the fact that there are more places where women can express that they have suffered from assault, harassment, and violence.

The NUM movement is diverse, and only women are members. There is no doubt that the women's cry is being heard and is demanding a fair place in the world.

Sabrina C. pointed out that "We cannot see what NUM will do in the future, and we get surprised every minute when we see the strength and potency of this movement. New generations are growing in settings, where political debate, free thought, factual changes and experience of harassment;

---

29. Carmen Beramendi, Director, Latin America University of Social Sciences in Uruguay, and Senator substitute of Casa Grande, part of FrenteAmplio, Uruguay.

settings different from previous generations among daughters, mothers and grandmothers in relationship to seeing gender-based violence as natural. Young women no longer consider gender-based violence as something natural and they are more willing to ask for assistance and to gather with other women to make changes in different scenarios, from university, family and political areas."

We should all learn from the success and the mistakes made from these movements. We can join their strengths, thanks to globalization and technology, so that in a not so distant future, we can look back and see that today the world is a place where women are included, where all humans living around the world can fully enjoy their human rights.

As explained herein, most of the laws and amendments to reduce and eradicate sexual harassment and violence against women are very recent in Argentina, in place not more than six years. These very recent changes make more understandable why there is an alarming number of femicides. There is yet a lot to do, as the new laws and plans are not yet giving the expected results. Undoubtedly, the feminist movement has a lot to do with the changing of rules that other people thought and saw as normal when they were not. We need to continuously demand education and equality for women in Argentina.

However, much was achieved in 2018, the year of feminism, with a new door opened for an infinite set of possibilities for Argentinean women in redesigning cultural values, power roles, and laws enforcing gender equality. Current and future generations of Argentinean women can feel proud of the women who preceded them and what they have achieved. These new opportunities are what I, and many other women living in this era of change, are experiencing right now, embracing feminist values, upending traditional gendered power roles, and struggling for equality in social, political and structural opportunities.

Finally, I would like to share some "good news" about the number of femicides in Argentina. This is an update of the Argentinean situation since #MeToo and #NiUnaMenos came into the picture.

In comparison with the statistics previously mentioned, 2019 has been a better year for women in Argentina. In my opinion, this is the consequence of the feminist movement in the country and social mobilizations.

In August 2019, Argentina was recognized by Spotlight Initiative[30] as one of the Latin American countries with records of data and numbers about femicides.[31]

---

30. The Spotlight Initiative is a program to eliminate violence against women and girls, launched by the European Community and the United Nations.

31. *La Iniciativa Spotlight: Para eliminar la violencia contra las mujeres y las niñas,* UNITED NATIONS, https://www.un.org/es/spotlight-initiative/.

In the later part of 2019, the rate of femicide dropped from once every 30 hours to every 32 hours, giving Argentinian women hope that feminist movements were beginning to change society in a good way. Yet in the beginning of 2020, the femicide rate jumped to a record high of a femicide every 23 hours. Thus, despite positive changes to Argentinian society brought by feminist movements, there is still much work to be done. *So, please Stop Killing Us!*

Simone de Beauvoir said—and I agree—*"Change your life today, don't invest in the future. Act now, don't wait."*

CHAPTER 7

Brazilian Sexual Harassment Law, the #MeToo Movement, and the Challenge of Pushing the Future Away from the Past of Race, Class, and Social Exclusion

Denise Neves Abade[1]

———————

Say it say it say it
Tell it like it is

What breaks your heart
What keeps you awake at night
What makes you want to breakdown and cry

But say you'll never turn your back
Say you'll never harden to the world
Say you'll never try to still the rhythms in your breast
Say you'll never look at the evil among us and try to forget
Say you'll tell it like it is

> —"Tell It Like It Is" (a song by Tracy Chapman)[2]

Introduction

The sex scandal surrounding Hollywood producer Harvey Weinstein, which broke in October 2017, has spread the #MeToo campaign to the world,

———————

1. Senior Federal Prosecutor and Professor of Law, Mackenzie University Law School, São Paulo.

2. © Purple Rabbit Music. Reprinted with permission.

with famous actresses and anonymous women alike revealing that they have been abused in the past. The hashtag #MeToo gains momentum every day.

At first, the #MeToo movement resulted in the denunciation of an impressive number of powerful men accused of committing sexual abuse in all professional sectors. Many of them saw their careers take a dramatic downturn, seemingly overnight.

But with the growth of the movement, women took additional action, relying on one another to prosecute their abusers and expand their fight against all kinds of discrimination, including wage inequality.[3]

In Brazil, many artists named the violence against women using the hashtag #EuTambém. Brazilian artists like Monica Martelli, Marina Person, Deborah Secco, Bruna Barros, Luka, and Alice Santana showed their support by telling their own stories and pointing to the growing need to talk about sexual harassment.[4]

In actuality, Brazilian women's empowerment preceded #MeToo and had inspired reforms in national laws.

In 2015, the Brazilian social media campaign *#PrimeiroAssedio* ("first harassment") spread to other countries, with women encouraged to report when they experienced sexual harassment for the first time. The hashtag, meaning in English, "my first harassment," was a sly send-up of a once-popular advertisement for trainer bras. More than 80,000 women responded.

In early 2017, months before the Harvey Weinstein case, a leading actor in Brazilian soap operas, Jose Mayer, was in the spotlight for reasons other than his acting when one of his studio's custom designers, Susllem Tonani, accused him of harassment. Scores of celebrities rallied to her defense in T-shirts emblazoned with "Mexeu com uma, mexeu com todas" ("Mess with one woman, you mess with us all").

---

3. It should be noted that this was not the first time that a campaign against sexual abuse has become global. In 2014, the hashtag *#YesAllWomen* trended on social media worldwide after shooter Elliot Rodger killed six people and wounded 14 others near the campus of the University of California, Santa Barbara. In a video Rodgers uploaded on the internet just before the attack, Rodger said he would commit the hate crime against women because he was involuntarily celibate.

4. The newspaper *O Globo* gave voice to the women in a series of reports. A video produced by the newspaper with actresses' testimony was posted online with some repercussions, available at https://youtu.be/Mbox_tZg52o. After this initiative, other women started to post on social networks testimonies with *#eutambem*. According to Keyhole—a Hashtag Analytics and Social Media Analytics internet site that provides real-time data with hashtag tracking for Twitter, Instagram, and Facebook—*#eutambem* was on the 20 trending hashtags between February and March 2017, just after the actresses' video was released. See https://keyhole.co /hashtag-tracking/posts/msWEH9/eutambem.

The Mayer case had great repercussions in the national media. The newspaper *Folha de São Paulo* released a letter using the hashtag *#agoraéquesãoelas*,[5] in which Tonani accused the actor of sexual abuse. At first, the actor denied any involvement in the incident, but later issued a public apology and said his actions were wrong. Soon, there were numerous comments, moral judgments, opinions, and controversies. Many supported the designer and some the actor.

Despite these advances and the boldness of protests, protecting women is still fraught with systemic barriers and victims push back at considerable risk.

If, on the one hand, denunciations are not new, on the other, the effects of the public denunciations are novel. Through internet campaigns, women have gained power that they have never had at any other time in history.

Words mobilize, foster comfort and empathy, and promote change. But we have to recognize that in Brazil, empowerment against sexual harassment is a privilege of a minority armed with information, aware of their rights, who discovered how to arm themselves, and know that they will have protection if they do not accept this type of violence.

The question is how to create a world where even the most vulnerable and under-resourced, with a less profound understanding of the subordination of women, can protect themselves. Those afraid of judgment, harassment, losing their jobs or reputations: the vast majority of Brazilians.

The current movement is promising, but it gives us the false notion that societal change has come for all. It has not. There is still a gulf between the awareness of the minority and the reconstruction necessary to push the future away from the past.

As will be seen in this chapter, for more than twenty years, Brazilian law has steadily reinforced measures to eliminate discrimination against women and against sexual harassment. But in a country with a predominantly macho culture, there are still many obstacles to overcome.

First, education that promotes gender equality is needed so this transformation can be extended to the next generation. Second, profound change in the culture of business is essential. Currently, companies favor men to the detriment of women in leadership positions, and human resources departments continue to ignore harassment as if it were not a chronic problem.

We will see that at least in theory the legislative evolution of Brazil regarding sexual harassment is undeniable. New laws have empowered the government to protect women, but enforcement is still a big problem.

---

5. *"Agora é que são elas"* could be translated as "now, it's time for the women," but the expression in Portuguese also means "now comes the difficult part."

Despite the deeper understanding of the universality of human rights,[6] through the recognition of the difference as an instrument of inclusion and the consequent deepening of its understanding in theoretical and practical aspects, hegemonic human rights practices continue to marginalize women and blacks in certain situations. This occurs either because they are based on a one-dimensional, white, and androcentric perspective, or because they presuppose the manipulation of homogeneous and mutually exclusive categories, or because of a vertical construction, constituted from above and below. Therefore, there is an urgent need to implement policies that adopt, prevent, and combat these different intensities of rights violations based on the paradigm of intersectional analysis, which recognizes that it is part of the concept of universality of human rights and equality to recognize the right to difference and diversity, with the development of mechanisms to protect the most vulnerable groups.[7]

The Italian legal philosopher and journalist Norberto Bobbio said that there are three main sources of inequality: ethnic, sexual and social: "Any overcoming of this or that discrimination is interpreted as a stage of the progress of civilization. The three main sources of inequality among men: race (or, more generally, participation in an ethnic or national group), sex, and social class."[8] Viewed in these terms, it is going to take some time until Brazil reaches an adequate level of "civilization." As is true in other countries, the struggle against the "macho" culture is a work in progress.

The Beginning: Historical Development of Gender Discrimination Law in Brazil That Leads to Sexual Harassment Law

According to the United Nations General Recommendation 19 to the Convention on the Elimination of all Forms of Discrimination Against Women (CEDAW), sexual harassment includes "such unwelcome sexually determined behavior as physical contact and advances, sexually colored remarks, showing pornography and sexual demands, whether by words or actions. Such conduct can be humiliating and may constitute a health and safety problem; it

---

6. The Brazilian author André de Carvalho Ramos affirms that the foundation of the right to equality is the universality of human rights, which determines that all human beings are equal and must enjoy conditions that enable the enjoyment of these rights. See ANDRÉ DE CARVALHO RAMOS: CURSO DE DIREITOS HUMANOS 615 (6th ed. 2019).

7. Denise Neves Abade, *Perspectiva Transversal de Gênero no Enfrentamento da Corrupção*, in PERSPECTIVAS DE GÊNERO E O SISTEMA DE JUSTIÇA BRASILEIRO, ESMPU, 111, 105-122 (2019).

8. NORBERTO BOBBIO, IGUALDADE E LIBERDADE 43 (4th ed. 2000).

is discriminatory when the woman has reasonable ground to believe that her objection would disadvantage her in connection with her employment, including recruitment or promotion, or when it creates a hostile working environment."[9] The Inter-American Convention on the Prevention, Punishment, and Eradication of Violence against Women states that sexual harassment is a kind of violence against women.[10]

Sexual harassment can also be understood to be a form of sexual discrimination, considering that, under Brazilian law, discrimination is any distinction, exclusion, restriction, or preference based on sex, gender, sexual orientation, disability, religious, political, or philosophical belief, race, color, descent, national, or ethnic origin, the purpose of which is to annul or restrict the recognition, enjoyment, or exercise, under equal conditions, of human rights and fundamental freedoms in the political, economic, social, cultural, or any other field of public or private life.[11]

The first steps taken by Brazil to empower women and protect them against workplace discrimination was Law no. 9,029, in 1995.[12] Law 9,029/1995 forbids discrimination (in an employment setting) because of sex, national origin, race, color, marital status, familial situation, disability or age, among others. In addition to prohibiting the adoption of any discriminatory and restrictive practice for access to (or maintenance of) employment relationships on the basis of sex, origin, race, color, marital status, family status, disability, occupational

---

9. Committee on the Elimination of Discrimination against Women, General Recommendation 19, Violence Against Women (11th sess., 1992), U.N. Doc. A/47/38 at 1 (1993), reprinted in Compilation of General Comments and General Recommendations Adopted by Human Rights Treaty Bodies, U.N. Doc. HRI/GEN/1/Rev.6 at 243 (2003).

10. Inter-American Convention on The Prevention, Punishment and Eradication of Violence Against Women—"Convention of Belem Do Para" states in Article 2:

"Violence against women shall be understood to include physical, sexual and psychological violence:

a. that occurs within the family or domestic unit or within any other interpersonal relationship, whether or not the perpetrator shares or has shared the same residence with the woman, including, among others, rape, battery and sexual abuse;

b. that occurs in the community and is perpetrated by any person, including, among others, rape, sexual abuse, torture, trafficking in persons, forced prostitution, kidnapping and sexual harassment in the workplace, as well as in educational institutions, health facilities or any other place; and

c. that is perpetrated or condoned by the state or its agents regardless of where it occurs."

11. This is the legal definition of discrimination in Brazil, according to Law no. 12.288/2010, article 1º, I (Racial Equality Statute).

12. Act no. 9,029 of April 13, 1995.

rehabilitation or age, the act established that discriminatory practices against pregnant women constitute a crime.[13] This was the first Brazilian legal anti-harassment policy.

Shortly thereafter, to respond to the Global Action Platform of the Beijing Fourth World Conference on Women, the Brazilian Congress included a gender quota mechanism in Act no. 9,100, of September 29, 1995, enacting rules for the implementation of regional legislative elections. The platform recommended affirmative action acceleration to reduce legislative gender imbalances—until then women were almost entirely excluded from the centers of political power. Law no. 9,100 established that at least 20 percent of the list of each party or coalition should be filled by women candidates. Two years later, Act no. 9,504 established quotas for nominations also for federal proportional elections, increasing the stipulated quota to 30 percent. This law will take time to generate results, but it shows the importance of the subject.

An important legal framework for combating gender discrimination in Brazil is the so-called "Maria da Penha Act," enacted in 2006 to combat domestic violence in Brazil. After the Maria da Penha Act became law, Brazil established new facilities, women's police centers, to provide comprehensive support to victims of domestic violence.

"Delegacias Especializadas de Atendimento à Mulher (DEAMs)," literally translated as specialized police services for women, are part of the Civil Police and are focused on crimes such as rape and domestic violence that target women. Although not a legal requirement, the units are primarily staffed with women. Among other responsibilities, similar to those of a regular police

---

13. The statute says: "Art. 2—The following discriminatory practices are a crime:

   I.   the requirement of test, examination, expertise, report, certificate, statement or any other procedure related to sterilization or pregnancy;

   II.   the adoption of any measures, of initiative of the employer, that configure;

     a.   induction or instigation of genetic sterilization;

     b.   promotion of birth control, thus not considering the provision of services and counseling or family planning, carried out through public or private institutions, submitted to the standards of the Unified Health System (SUS).

Penalty: one to two year detention and fine.

Active subjects of the crimes referred to in this article are:

   I.   the employer individual;

   II.   the employer's legal representative, as defined in labor legislation;

   III.   the director, direct or by delegation, of public bodies and entities of direct public administrations, indirect and foundational work of any of the Powers of the Union, the States, the Federal District and the Municipalities."

station, DEAMs are charged with requesting urgent protective measures from the judge in case of domestic violence. [14]

The Maria da Penha law arose in a context in which typically, an abused woman's economic subordination would lead her not to report domestic violence, fearing loss of financial support of her children.[15]

The law's name was chosen to honor Maria da Penha Maia Fernandes, who was subjected to domestic violence for twenty-three years by her ex-husband and became paraplegic after he attempted to murder her. Her ex-husband's trial was delayed due to the lack of clear and unambiguous legislation addressing violence against women. Today, the Maria da Penha Act[16] considers crimes of domestic and family violence against women "any action or omission based on gender that causes death, injury, physical, sexual or psychological suffering and moral or property damage."

The evolution of legislation to combat discrimination and gender violence culminated in the 2015 establishment of the crime of femicide, which gave a proper name to the murder of women in contexts marked by gender inequality. The new law[17] defines femicide as "the murder of a woman committed on the grounds of the female sex" and the predicted penalty ranges between twelve and thirty years of imprisonment.

Every day in Brazil, thirteen women are murdered. Brazil has the fifth highest rate of femicide in the world: 4.8 homicides for every 100,000 women.[18]

---

14. Women's police centers have been gaining popularity over the last decade. So far, such police centers have been adopted by Argentina, Bolivia, Ecuador, Ghana, India, Kosovo, Liberia, Nicaragua, Peru, the Philippines, Sierra Leone, South Africa, Uganda and Uruguay. Within Latin America, Brazil has the largest operation with more than 500 stations. See the data in the World's Bank study about the subject in Elizaveta Perova and Sarah Reynold, *Women's Police Stations and Domestic Violence -Evidence from Brazil*, WORLD BANK GROUP, http://documents.worldbank.org/curated/pt/441331467987820782/pdf/WPS7497.pdf.

15. In 2016, a third of women in Brazil, 29 percent, reported having suffered some type of violence. Of these, only 11 percent sought assistance at a women's police station. See the statistics in the Handbook, *Visível e Invisível: A vitimização das mulheres no Brasil* (Visible and Invisible: The victimization of women in Brazil), an initiative of the NGO Forum Brasileiro de Segurança Publica (March 2017), http://www.forumseguranca.org.br/wp-content/uploads/2017/03/relatorio-pesquisa-vs4.pdf.

16. Act 11,340/2006.

17. Act 13,104/2015.

18. According to two major studies: (1) Kevan Guilherme Nóbrega Barbosa et al., *Epidemiological and spatial characteristics of interpersonal physical violence in a Brazilian city: A comparative study of violent injury hotspots in familial versus non-familial settings, 2012-2014*, PLOS ONE, Jan. 7, 2019, https://doi.org/10.1371/journal.pone.0208304, and (2) Pinheiro Rodrigues et al., *The increase in domestic violence in Brazil from 2009-2014*, 22 REVISTA DE CIÊNCIA E SAÚDE COLETIVA, n. 9, Rio de Janeiro (Sept. 2017), http://dx.doi.org/10.1590/1413-812320 17229.09902016.

The 2015 Brazilian "Map of Violence" that covers the murder of women shows that 106,093 women were murdered between 1980 and 2013, with 4,762 just in 2013. In 2015 the number decreased only slightly: 4,621 women were murdered in Brazil, accounting for 4.5 deaths per 100,000 women.[19]

Brazilian Sexual Harassment Law

The unequal power dynamic between men and women is a worldwide phenomenon. Discrimination against women and gender inequality drive violence and sexual harassment against women. For this reason, there is pressure to increase state protection measures to balance the power. Since the feminist movements of the 1970s, feminists have advocated for government measures to curb sexual harassment.[20]

It is important to note that Brazilian courts make a clear distinction between moral damages, moral harassment, and sexual harassment.

Thus, harassment in the workplace refers to the abusive conduct of the employer when exercising its power, managerial or disciplinary, attacking the dignity or physical or psychological integrity of an employee. Harassment constitutes a kind of moral damage that has some unique characteristics.

Moral harassment is "the exposure of workers to humiliating, degrading and embarrassing, repetitive and prolonged circumstances during their working hours and in the exercise of their functions."[21] Some state laws prohibit moral harassment in the public sector.[22] Unfortunately, there is still no specific law covering private sector employees in Brazil.

Moral damage, on the other hand, happens when an individual "feels affected in his psychic, moral and intellectual mood, either by affliction to his honor, privacy, intimacy, image, name or in his own physical body."[23] In this

---

19. All the data are in the study *Atlas of Violence/2017*, 36-42, published by the Institute of Applied Economic Research, a public foundation linked to the Ministry of Planning, available at http://www.ipea.gov.br/portal/images/170602_atlas_da_violencia_2017.pdf.

20. André Boiani, *Assédio Sexual—aspectos gerais*, CURITIBA: JURUÁ, 2005; and Bruno Salles Pereira Ribiero, *Delineamentos sobre o crime de assédio sexual*, REVISTA LIBERDADES, SÃO PAULO, 131, Sept.-Dec. (2013).

21. As decided by the Superior Labor Court—(Tribunal Superior do Trabalho—TST) Recurso de Revista (appeal): RR no. 1096-91.2010.5.10.0003.

22. Brazil is a federation and as such its citizens are governed by both federal and state laws. As an example of laws that foresee administrative punishments in the sphere of state public service, there are Law 12.250/06 of the State of São Paulo and Law 117/11 of the State of Minas Gerais.

23. Superior Labor Court—(Tribunal Superior do Trabalho—TST)—Recurso de Revista (appeal): RR 656-25.2016.5.12.0005.

case, the injured person must gather evidence and demonstrate the impact of the injury on his personal life and repercussions on work. Contrary to harassment, it is not necessary that there be a repetition of the offenses in order for moral damage to be established.

The Brazilian Civil Code defines damage in the following terms: "Art. 186—The one who, by voluntary action or omission, negligence or imprudence, violates rights and causes harm to others, even if only moral, commits an illicit act."

Finally, for the Brazilian courts, sexual harassment is not confused with moral harassment. In sexual harassment, embarrassment is directed exclusively at those who would obtain sexual advantage or favor. Such conduct is addressed by the Penal Code and, like any criminal conduct, also leads to civil compensation: indirect termination of harasser's employment and compensation of the victim for moral damages.

Sexual harassment can occur in a variety of settings, including in workplaces, on public transportation, and in public spaces. The problem of harassment on public transportation is a constant issue, leading Brazil to criminalize such conduct.[24] In the streets, the debate started by an American NGO called "Stop Street Harassment" began to be discussed in Brazil with the 2013 "Chega de fiu fiu" ("no more whistles") campaign.[25]

Women have the fundamental right to a life free of violence.[26] This right is provided in the Inter-American Convention on the Prevention, Punishment, and Eradication of Violence against Women (Convention of Belém do Pará).[27] The Convention defines violence against women broadly in Articles 1 and 2. The Convention details the context in which such violence may occur and also specifies some forms of violence such as rape, sexual abuse, and others. Thus, for the purposes of the Convention, violence against women is understood to mean any act or conduct based on gender that causes death, injury, or physical, sexual

---

24. In the São Paulo subway, the campaign, "There is no silly hand—only lack of character. Break the silence," has led to reports of sexual harassment growing by 9 percent in the first four months of 2018, compared to the previous year. See in https://catracalivre.com.br /cidadania/casos-de-abuso-sexual-no-transport-publico-aumentam-9-em-2018/.

25. Started on July 24, 2013, "Chega de Fiu Fiu" is a campaign to combat sexual harassment in public spaces launched by Project Think Olga, see the details in https://thinkolga .com/2018/01/31/chega-de-fiu-fiu/.

26. See Monica Melo, *Assédio sexual: um caso de inconstitucionalidade por omissão*, 143 REVISTA DE INFORMAÇÃO LEGISLATIVA, 85/100 (Jul-Sep. 1999).

27. Text in English available at https://www.oas.org/juridico/english/treaties/a-61 .html.

or psychological suffering to women, both in the public and private spheres (art. 1°).[28]

Sexual harassment brings with it the component of abuse of power. This abuse, transforming the art of seduction into blackmail, makes the victim of this type of violence often feel gagged. The phrase "abuse of power" also encompasses a feeling in the much less powerful female that she has no ability to say "no" to the sexual overtures because of fear of losing her job, job status, or reputation—so there is both an inability to say no to the seduction, and once the man is successful, the potential for blackmail and other negative consequences.

As seen above, in Brazil, it is possible to denounce this abuse in the labor, administrative, and civil sphere, with compensation to the victim to repair the damage suffered. Further, sexual harassment began to be considered a crime in Brazil in 2001, when Law no. 10,224 added a new article to the Criminal Code, article 216, that defines harassment as follows: "Constrain someone with the purpose of taking advantage or sexual favor, with the agent prevailing in his hierarchical superior form, or ascendancy inherent in the exercise of employment, position or function: Penalty: detention from one (1) to two (2) years." The criminal statute requires that there is hierarchical superiority, or economic dependence of the harassment victim.

Harassment is characterized by sexually suggestive speech or action, lack of receptivity on the part of the recipient, and a concrete threat. As the author Paulo Viana de Albuquerque Jucá says, "[It] is repetitive when it comes to verbal harassment and not necessarily when harassment is physical—the so-called groping in the butt between people who do not share intimacy and with sexual intent, is enough to establish sexual harassment, without the need for repetition—in order to cause an unpleasant work environment, jeopardizing one's job, as well as undermining the integrity and dignity of the person, making it possible to request compensation for physical and moral damages."[29] If there is violence or serious threat, the conduct may characterize a more serious crime: rape.[30]

On September 24, 2018, Law 13,718 was enacted, adding to the Criminal Code the crimes of sexual harassment and the dissemination on social media of a filmed rape or pornography.

---

28. Article 1: For the purposes of this Convention, violence against women shall be understood as any act or conduct, based on gender, which causes death or physical, sexual or psychological harm or suffering to women, whether in the public or the private sphere.

29. Paulo Viana de Albuquerque Jucá, *O Assédio sexual como justa causa típica* in 61 Revista LTR, n. 2, 175–182 (Feb. 1997).

30. Article 213 of the Criminal Code provides that rape is: "to constrain a person, by violence or serious threat, to have a carnal conjunction or to practice or allow him to practice another libidinous act."

The proposal to amend the Criminal Code concerning crimes against sexual dignity is intended to combat violence against women. The proposal was developed after two cases of great notoriety. In the first, a man ejaculated on the neck of a girl when they were both inside a bus at Avenida Paulista, in São Paulo, in 2017. The second involved the gang rape of a sixteen-year-old girl in Rio de Janeiro in 2016, which was filmed and posted on the Internet.

According to the September 2018 law, sexual harassment constitutes the practice, against someone and without their consent, of a libidinous act to satisfy one's own lust or that of a third party.[31] The crime of sexual harassment is punishable by up to five years in prison.

The new law closed a large legal loophole to hold abusers accountable in cases of sexual harassment in public spaces. However, in the case mentioned earlier of ejaculation on the bus, the person involved was not convicted because the judge understood that the law was in limbo between the old law, where the act would be an offense against modesty, a criminal offense punished only with a fine, and the new law, which repealed the modesty-offense law.

The new law also punishes the conduct of *frotteurism*. *Frotteurism* consists of "touching and rubbing yourself at a person without their consent." The behavior usually occurs in places with a large concentration of people, from which the individual can more easily escape from detection (e.g., busy sidewalks or public transport vehicles). The offender rubs his genitals against the thighs and buttocks or caresses the genitalia or the victim's breasts with his hands.[32]

The law was also clear that if the conduct constitutes a more serious crime, it will not be charged as the lesser crime of sexual harassment and can be classified as a crime of rape, which is more serious and more specific (for example, if you practice libidinous acts using violence or a serious threat).

Finally, it is important to note that the option of the Brazilian legislature was to criminalize the conduct of sexual harassment that implies a hierarchical situation between the victim and the agent. For conduct of constant attacks and insinuations that cause disturbance to the victim, the legal reprimands follow in

---

31. Sexual harassment:

Art. 215-A. To practice against someone and without their consent a libidinous act with the purpose of satisfying one's own lewdness or that of a third party:

Penalty—imprisonment, from 1 (one) to 5 (five) years, if the act does not constitute a more serious crime....

§ 5 The penalties provided for in the head of the article and §§ 1, 3 and 4 of this article apply regardless of the victim's consent or whether he or she has had sexual intercourse prior to the crime.

32. https://psiquiatria.com/glosario/frotteurismo.

the scope of civil law, administrative law and labor law, in generic previsions, as explained above.[33]

Measures to criminalize sexual harassment constitute an important step forward in a reality of "macho criminal law," which often results in impunity for perpetrators for crimes against sexual freedom. The culture of rape—no doubt present in Brazil—warrants state attention. Hopefully, legislative advances, encouraged by global campaigns like the #MeToo movement, will continue to achieve results.

Conclusion: Expanding #MeToo

There is no doubt that the #MeToo Movement has prompted many to reexamine the conditions that have allowed harassment and violence to flourish.

Even with favorable laws, most women in Brazil bear a patriarchal mind-set and misogyny, rooted deeply across Brazilian culture. At the same time, when we talk about sexual harassment, gender is not the only variable in shaping individuals' experiences of harassment. Race, class, age, and ethnicity are also very important factors in determining the different possibilities of access to the means of protection offered to these victims.

Black, young, and ethnic minority women and girls suffer violence in ways similar to other women. This includes child harassment and abuse, sexual violence, trafficking and exploitation, intimate partner violence, and so on. There are, however, differences in forms of sexual harassment and violence that will disproportionately impact women taking into account a combination of multiple forms of discrimination, based on systems of inequalities that feed on each other—especially gender, race, ethnicity, class, and sexual orientation and identity.

Certainly, it is still necessary to fight for the equality of men and women—but it is now time to reflect how far away this equality is for black women, who are still struggling to be considered equal to other women, the white women.[34] #MeToo cannot be alien to this debate, especially in Brazil.

Considering the historical context of the situation of blacks in the world, black women are more likely to suffer various types of violence. Black women are prone to suffer at least two types of oppression: racism and machismo.

---

33. The distinctions between the types of harassment was made by JUAN ANTONIO ALTÉS TÁRREGA, EL ACOSO SEXUAL EN EL TRABAJO 29 (Tirant lo Blanch, ed., 1st ed. 2002).

34. About this inequality, see Zelma Madeira and Daiana de Oliveira, *Persistentes desigualdades raciais e resistências negras no Brasil contemporâneo*, REVISTA SERVIÇO SOCIAL & SOCIEDADE 133, Sept.-Dec. 2018, http://dx.doi.org/10.1590/0101-6628.154.

According to this woman's particularities, she may suffer others (for example, lesbophobia, biphobia, transphobia, fat phobia, class bias, etc.).

According to the "Dossier Black Women: portrait of the living conditions of black women in Brazil,"[35] in 2009 black women accounted for about a quarter of the Brazilian population. There were almost 50 million women in a total population that, in that year, reached 191.7 million Brazilians.

The study "Map of Violence 2015," produced by the Latin American Faculty of Social Sciences with the support of the United Nations,[36] gives an indicator of the very different reality among black and white women. In 2015, there was a drop of 11.9 percent in the homicide rate of white women. In the same year, the homicide rate of black women grew by 19.5 percent. In absolute numbers, the study revealed that between 2003 and 2013, 46,186 women were killed. Of this, 25,637 were black or 55 percent. White women murdered during the same period totaled 17,500, or 37 percent. We note that such disparities are more severe for black women, youth and children.

The picture of racial inequalities is not much better when it comes to average income, where wages for black women are much lower not only in relation to wages for men, but also in relation to wages for white women. The average income of black women in 2009 was equivalent to 40 percent of the income of white men, while that of white women was equivalent to 68 percent of the income of white men.[37]

Facts like these have prevented black women from developing their potential and achieving mobility and social advancement, as they occupy disadvantaged positions in terms of occupation and income, education, and entry into higher education and the labor market, while domestic work is predominant. The data provided by the Brazilian Economic Research Institute in the portrait of gender and race inequalities from 1995 to 2015[38] are illustrative: despite some advances, we are faced with persistent inequality for the black population group, the worst positions being for black women.

---

35. MARIANA MAZZINI MARCONDES, ET AL., DOSSIÊ MULHERES NEGRAS: RETRATO DAS CONDIÇÕES DE VIDA DAS MULHERES NEGRAS NO BRASIL 19 (2013).

36. Júlio Jacobo Waiselfisz, Mapa da violência 2015: *homicídio de mulheres no Brasil*, FLASCO, BRASILIA, 2015, https://www.mapadaviolencia.org.br/pdf2015/MapaViolencia_2015_mulheres.pdf.

37. *Afro 2011: Ano Internacional das e dos Afrodescendentes*, ORGANIZAÇÃO DAS NAÇÕES UNIDAS, ONU, p. 7 (2011), http://unesdoc.unesco.org/images/0021/002140/214060por.pdf.

38. Daniel Cerqueira, et al., Atlas da Violência 2016, *Nota técnica n. 17*, IPEA, Mar. 2016, https://www12.senado.leg.br/institucional/omv/entenda-a-violencia/pdfs/atlas-da-violencia-2016.

With regard to barriers to finding better positions in the labor market, black women accumulate disadvantages: in Brazil, they constitute the majority in domestic employment, historically marked by precariousness, exploitation, and oppression. The category of domestic workers is formed by approximately 7 million professionals, and among women, 61.7 percent are black. Historically, domestic work is the main gateway for black women to enter the labor market, and it is where the violation of rights is most evident: practically 75 percent of domestic workers in Brazil are in irregular employment situation.[39]

Black women also have less access to education: analyzing the rate of illiteracy, which has been falling in an important way in Brazil in recent decades, there is a racial differential: in 2015, among white women fifteen years old or more, only 4.9 percent were illiterate; in the case of black women, this number was double, 10.2 percent. Among men, the gap is similar when white and blacks are compared.[40]

Between 1995 and 2015, the white adult population with twelve years or more of education doubled, from 12.5 percent to 25.9 percent. In the same period, the black population with twelve years or more of education went from an unbelievable 3.3 percent to 12 percent, an increase of almost four times, but that does not hide that the black population has attained only now the educational level that is twenty years behind the white population.[41]

The 2017/2018 annual report of the National Mechanism for Preventing and Combating Torture also makes explicit the necessity of an intersectional vision[42] when we speak of inequality between men and women and between white and black people in the Brazilian prison system.[43]

---

39. *Afro 2011, supra*, note 37.

40. *Retrato das desigualdades de gênero e raça—1995-2015*, IPEA, 2017, p. 2, http://www.ipea.gov.br/portal/images/stories/PDFs/170306_retrato_das_desigualdades_de_genero_raca.pdf.

41. *Ibid.*

42. The concept of intersectionality was introduced by law professor Kimberlé Crenshaw in 1989 in her classic article, *Demarginalizing the Intersection of Race and Sex: A Black Feminist Critique of Antidiscrimination Doctrine, Feminist Theory and Antiracist Politics*, 1 U. Chic. Legal F., art. 8 (1989), http://chicagounbound.uchicago.edu/uclf/vol1989/iss1/8. Intersectionality was formulated as a metaphor to represent the situation of African American women simultaneously subordinate in terms of race and gender to the multidimensionality of their experiences, and their exclusion from U.S. feminist and anti-racist anti-discrimination legislation and policies. She highlighted how they experienced qualitatively different discriminations against women in general and but also against African American men.

43. The report is available for download at https://www.mdh.gov.br/informacao-ao-cidadao/participacao-social/mecanismo-nacional-de-prevencao-e-combate-a-tortura-mnpct/relatorios-1/RelatrioAnual20172018.pdf.

The study points out that about 64 percent of the total number of people deprived of freedom in Brazilian prison establishments is composed of black men and women,[44] reflecting the systemic marks resulting from slavery, perceptible throughout the 131 years after abolition. All women in prison are especially vulnerable to torture and other cruel, inhuman, or degrading treatment or punishment, adding to the violence in general existing in the prison system also those resulting from machismo and misogyny—but conditions of vulnerability.[45]

The general picture of economic and social vulnerabilities, the lack of economic opportunities and exclusion from the formal labor market, early sexual exploitation, and the growing record of murder and rape of such women are worrying. When, even though they are aware of the risks, they enter the world of crime, they still experience the process of patriarchal domination, a fact that is also reproduced within the walls of the Penitentiary, mainly through the treatment at the hands of penitentiary agents who often lack the necessary training for contact with the prisoners under their responsibility.

The concretization of citizenship that is manifested in movements such as #MeToo, points to the need to broaden the scope of this concept considering the paradigm of human rights, understood as universal and indivisible.

Citizenship must be extended beyond access to civil and political rights to incorporate social, economic, cultural, and environmental dimensions. It is therefore a question of reconciling the universalist principle of equality with the recognition of the specific needs of groups historically excluded from social wealth and culturally discriminated against.

In a country like Brazil, the struggle is to bring the social change wrought by movements like #MeToo to women of various intersecting identities, including but not limited to ethnicity, socio-economic status, and sexual orientation.

The Brazilian student and social activist Stephanie Ribeiro expressed her dissatisfaction with the #MeToo on seeing the famous cover of *Time* magazine in December 2017 ("Person of the year—The silence breakers") in which celebrities were appointed as leaders of the movement, and only one black woman (Tarana Burke) was in the main photo: "Many actions are based on

---

44. BRASIL. Ministério da Justiça e Segurança Pública. Relatório sintético do Levantamento Nacional de Informações Penitenciárias—INFOPEN, July 2016.

45. Mechanismo Nacional De Prevenção e Combate À Tortura: Relatório Anual 2017, https://www.mdh.gov.br/informacao-ao-cidadao/participacao-social/mecanismo-nacional -de-prevencao-e-combate-a-tortura-mnpct/relatorios-1/RelatrioAnual20172018.pdf; .Relatório sintético do Levantamento Nacional de Informações Penitenciárias—INFOPEN, July 2016, https://www.justica.gov.br/news/ha-726-712-pessoas-presas-no-brasil/relatorio_2016_junho .pdf; and Mulheres em Prisão (Women in Prison), 2017, http://ittc.org.br/wp-content/uploads /2017/03/relatorio_final_online.pdf.

a non-intersectional idea of feminism and place, as usual, only white women with a role. Some white women, who even—many times because of their liberal behaviors—support more white men than we, black feminists (…). So when I saw the cover right away, I was already bothered by the fact that Taylor Swift was there, a singer who already had racist behaviors at various times. I wonder: how can a person who does not review her racial privileges be pointed out as a symbol of female empowerment? Empowerment for whom? I'm a woman and I'm black, I don't feel good and I don't even feel empowered with people who aren't able to see their white privileges. Besides Taylor, it bothers me, as always, like most covers, advertising campaigns, and even soap operas, which always create the narrative of the one black surrounded by white individuals. There is a gigantic problem in the narrative of the single black man who is there in that cover when only one black woman appears. We are always represented as an exception on an island surrounded by whites."[46]

Gender equality requires facing unpleasant facts: we can no longer pretend that things are better than they are. We need to truly face them to move forward.

---

46. Stephanie Ribeiro, *A capa da Time só representa o racismo do feminismo branco,* MARIE CLAIRE BRASIL, Dec. 8, 2017, https://revistamarieclaire.globo.com/Blogs/BlackGirl Magic/noticia/2017/12/stephanie-ribeiro-capa-da-time-so-representa-o-racismo-do-feminis mo-branco.html.

Europe

CHAPTER 8

The #MeToo Movement in France: A Wave of Ambivalence

Marie Mercat-Bruns[1]

———————

Right before the #MeToo hashtag was posted by Alyssa Milano on October 15, 2017,[2] Sandra Muller, a French journalist, in New York at the time, reacted to the Harvey Weinstein sexual abuse allegations made in the *New York Times* and the *New Yorker* articles. Using the hashtag "#squeal on your pig" ("#BalanceTonPorc," in French), on October 13, she encouraged French women to reveal their story of sexual harassment at work, to express their indignation, and to describe and name their aggressors.[3] In a second post, she herself revealed TV producer Eric Brion's verbal misconduct at a professional event one evening: "You have big breasts. You are my type of woman. I am going to make you come all night."[4] Several months later, he issued apologies. Brion ascribed his behavior to his heavy drinking that night and explained that he was flirting

———————

1. Affiliated Professor, Sciences Po Law School (Copilot, CNAM Gender Program LISE, CNRS).

2. In 2006, Tarana Burke began using the phrase "Me Too" to raise awareness of the pervasiveness of sexual abuse and assault in society, and the phrase developed into a broader movement, following the 2017 use of #MeToo as a hashtag after the Harvey Weinstein sexual abuse allegations, see https://www.businessinsider.com/how-the-metoo-movement-started -where-its-headed-tarana-burke-time-person-of-year-women-2017-12?IR=T.

3. #balancetonporc! Toi aussi raconte en donnant le nom et les détails d'un harcèlent sexuel que tu as connu dans ton boulot. Je vous attends. English translation: #squeal on your pig! You too tell your story with names and details on sexual harassment you have experienced at work. I am expecting your reactions.

4. Rachel Donadio, *Balance Ton Porc is France's #MeToo*, The Atlantic, Oct. 18, 2017, https://www.theatlantic.com/international/archive/2017/10/the-weinstein-scandal-seen-from -france/543315/.

with her inappropriately. He, nevertheless, filed suit against her for defamation and won.[5]

This chapter aims to assess: (1) what occurred in France when the #MeToo movement emerged in worldwide news in 2017; (2) what laws protected persons from harassment and assault, especially in the workplace before this event; (3) in practice, if these laws were enforced and if barriers existed in filing complaints; and (4) if the movements triggered changes both in law and in civil society for better effectiveness of norms, access to justice, and implementation of rights.

The French Paradox After the #MeToo Movement

After Muller's call, a flow of tweets followed in France[6] with narratives of assaults. Tweets often just described verbal or non-verbal acts, either sexual harassment, sexist remarks, or sexual assaults, named the perpetrator, or just situated him in all walks of life: gynecologists, directors of a summer camp, lifeguards, instructors, diplomats, and TV producers. In a recent book, Sandra Muller describes the outpouring of tweets after her hashtag (900,000 as of July 2018).[7] Some are also from men like Aurélien: "Of course the feminist and legal battles are important. But let's face it. They have failed completely. Complaints are rejected by the District Attorney, victims are liable for defamation. Feminist movements are ridiculed."

From the beginning, the #MeToo movement triggered very ambivalent reactions in France. Some observers considered this was due to the different

---

5. Fanny Bobille, Saskya Vandoorne, and Bianca Britton, *French #MeToo founder must pay thousands in damages after losing defamation case*, CNN, Sept. 25, 2019, https://edition.cnn.com/2019/09/25/europe/french-metoo-founder-defamation-intl/index.html.

6. This chapter does not discuss Europe, but members of the European Parliament also reacted. In September 2017, before #MeToo, the European Parliament member from Germany and Green Party politician Terry Reintke described how she had been a victim of a sexual attack in the German city of Duisburg. On October 25, 2017, in the aftermath of the #MeToo debate, the EU Parliament decided to deal with similar occurrences within its walls. The legislature passed resolution P8_TA(2017)0417 "Combating sexual harassment and abuse in the EU European Parliament" resolution of October 26, 2017 to combat sexual harassment and abuse in the European Union as well as the EU Parliament (2017/2897(RSP)): Cases of harassment and assault within the Parliament were to be investigated, cleared up and sanctioned.

7. Sandra Muller, #BALANCETONPORC 32 (2018). Muller gives this example of one social media poster, Nathalie: "There are forms of violence that are ignored in our society, social networks are new tools to take into our voices and free ourselves from the suffering. Facing perverts who act with impunity, the law does not always favor victims, we need all the resources to combat this phenomenon. Victims are not sufficiently protected or taken into account." Fear must change sides." pp. 67-68.

nature of the French hashtag.[8] Unlike the Quebec translation of #MeToo, #moi aussi, the French hashtag was perceived by a part of French public opinion as fostering accusations, instead of a more positive message about bonding of survivors,[9] even though French citizens also tweeted #MeToo.[10] The risk of false accusations was compared to the infamous denunciations of Jews by their neighbors in Vichy France.[11] However, other journalists reacted strongly by saying this view puts the Jewish victims of Nazi Germany and the presumed perpetrators of sexual harassment in the same bag. Furthermore, this associated women who denounced their aggressors with the Nazis or the French who collaborated with them. Even French President Emmanuel Macron, who, from the beginning, took a strong stand against sexual harassment, sexism, and sexual violence, warned citizens against a "culture of informers."[12]

Government Support for #Movement Except When Two Ministers Are Targets of Accusations

From its outset, the # movement was explicitly supported as "liberating" by the President Macron[13] and backed by his wife Brigitte Macron.[14] The Secretary of State for Equality, Marlène Schiappa, reacted quickly: "Under #MeToo, women describe terrible cases of abuse as well as cat calls. However, the type of violation isn't what's at the heart of the sexism debate, it's the fact that men

---

8. Annette Lévy-Willard, Chroniques d'une onde de choc: #MeToo secoue la planète 96 (2018).

9. Laure Murat, Une révolution sexuelle? Réflexions sur l'après-Weinstein 34 (2018).

10. Louis Germain, *1.7 million #MeToo tweets*, Les Ateliers du CFJ, Jan. 31, 2018, https://ateliers.cfjlab.fr/2018/01/31/meeto-une-vague-de-tweets-une-hausse-des-plaintes/.

11. Laure Murat, *supra*, note 9, pp. 34-35, quoting the reaction of a journalist of the far right, E. Zemmour: "This way of proceeding reminds me of the way Jews were denounced during Vichy."

12. Laure Murat, *supra*, note 9, p. 34, and Barbara Krief, *Macron déçoit certaines féministes avec son plan d'égalité femmes-hommes*, L'Obs, Nov. 25, 2017, https://www.nouvelobs.com/politique/20171125.OBS7836/macron-decoit-certaines-feministes-avec-son-plan-d-egalite-femmes-hommes.html. Even on November 25, the international day against sexual violence, the President makes reference to a normalization of accusations (day to day). For some authors, the President confuses denunciation (the act of informing about something (often disagreeable)) and informing as a denunciation dictated by vile and odious motives. See L. Murat, p. 34.

13. "There has been a liberation of women in terms of their freedom of speech on this issue," according to President Macron, Annette Lévy-Willard, *supra*, note 8, p. 109.

14. Sandra Muller, *supra*, note 7, pp. 69 and 70.

take the liberty of all sorts of transgressions."[15] From the beginning, Schiappa considered the need for legal reform and new sanctions like on-the-spot fines against people harassing women in the streets.[16]

Macron, on November 25, 2017, also felt the importance of the turn of events. He organized with the Secretary of State a specific ceremony at the Elysée Palace, inviting all the feminist NGOs to pay tribute, with one minute of silence, to the 123 women who were abused and killed by their husbands or partners in 2016 and gave a long speech launching a new policy for women deciding that equality would be the great national cause of his term: "Our society as a whole is ill with sexism. Shame has to change sides. The Republic has to do what it takes to cleanse herself too. Criminals who, on a daily basis, harass, insult, touch, assault, should not be excused but spotted, vilified, brought to justice, strongly condemned, without complacency. This is a condition of our Republican pact and France should no longer be one of those countries where women are fearful...."[17]

However, when two ministers, the Minister for the Environment, Nicolas Hulot,[18] and the Minister for the Budget, Gérald Darmanin, were accused of rape in the past or through ongoing legal proceedings, which in both cases were

---

15. Marlène Schiappa, *Violences sexuelles et sexistes: Marlène Schiappa face aux auditeurs,* France Inter, Nov. 27, 2017, https://www.franceinter.fr/emissions/le-telephone-sonne /le-telephone-sonne-27-novembre-2017.

16. *Marlène Schiappa: "Nous rendrons réelle l'infraction de harcèlement de rue,"* La Depeche, Sept. 23, 2017, https://www.ladepeche.fr/article/2017/09/23/2651363-marlene -schiappa-rendrons-reelle-infraction-harcelement-rue.html.

17. *Discours du Président de la République à l'occasion de la journée internationale pour l'élimination de la violence à l'égard des femmes et du lancement de la grande cause du quinquennat,* ÉLYSÉE, Nov. 25, 2017, https://www.elysee.fr/emmanuel-macron/2018/01/09/discours -du-president-de-la-republique-a-l-occasion-de-la-journee-internationale-pour-l-elimina tion-de-la-violence-a-l-egard-des-femmes-et-du-lancement-de-la-grande-cause-du-quinquennat, A. Lévy-Willard, *supra,* note 8, p. 109.

18. The District Attorney of the town of Saint Malo confirmed in a press release that there had been a complaint of rape against Nicolas Hulot in 2008 but the case was closed because the statute of limitations had expired. The accusation by the granddaughter of former President François Mitterrand, a photographer from a famous agency who was 20 at the time, dated back to June 1997. The complaint described an act without violence but passive and unde- sired with Nicolas Hulot, a quick affair under no pressure.

unsuccessful for different reasons,[19] the whole government, including the Secretary of State for Equality, stood behind their colleagues.[20]

Mixed Support for the #Movement from Journalists, Writers, and Artists

This hint of ambivalence within the government is reflected also in the writing of journalists, authors, artists, and politicians. For example, women journalists were some of the first to denounce the inappropriate behavior of colleagues.[21] However, on October 17, on a famous "France Culture" radio show, the writer Christine Angot reflected on the underlying rhetoric of power in France like the one present in gender-blind labor relations and Marxist thought: "I do not think the question is correctly framed … by saying that men are pigs and women are only victims. I think men are human. And women are also human. However, these humans all live under a regime of power. And those who profit, men or women regardless, have a serious tendency to abuse it. So, we are amidst abuse of power." "The challenge is not talking about it as one

---

19. Gérald Darmanin, Minister of Public Funds (Budget), was accused of raping Sophie Patterson-Spatz in May 2017 and having requested sex in exchange for an apartment. The case was closed when the plaintiff did not respond to further investigations. She filed a new claim for rape, supported by feminist Caroline De Haas, in January 2018, accusing Darmanin in 2009 of imposing sex with her when she requested that he intervene with the government to erase from her criminal record a suspended sentence of 10 months of prison in 2007. Despite criminal investigations pending and texts showing sex was linked to what the minister had promised, the government stood by Darmanin. On February 16, 2018, the District Attorney closed the case, explaining that absence of consent could not be established. On February 28, a new sexual harassment and breach of trust claim was filed, but the investigative judge granted a motion to dismiss the case. Apparently Darmanin might still be indicted following a subsequent November 14, 2019 decision of the French Supreme Court which considered that Sophie Patterson-Spatz's appeal of the investigative judge's motion to dismiss was still viable. See *Plainte pour viol: la justice va réexaminer le non-lieu de Darmanin*, L'Obs, Nov. 14, 2019, https://www.nouvelobs.com/justice/20191114.OBS21093/plainte-pour-viol-contre-darmanin-la-justice-va-reexaminer-le-non-lieu.html.

20. Xavier Patier, *Tribune de Marlène Schiappa dans le JDD ou le retour de la bonne vieille politique*, LE FIGARO VOX, Feb. 11, 2018, http://www.lefigaro.fr/vox/politique/2018/02/11/31001-20180211ARTFIG00082-tribune-de-marlene-schiappa-dans-le-jdd-ou-le-retour-de-la-bonne-vieille-politique.php.

21. Examples include Anne Saurat-Dubois, BFMTV (statute of limitations results in dismissal of case); Giulia Fois, France 5 (accusation triggers dismissal of a head figure at Radio France); Astrid de Vilaines. LCP, the Parliament Channel(accuses Frédéric Haziza of inappropriate gestures, he is sanctioned but then returns; she resigns and he is only condemned to "a reminder of the law" (rappel à la loi), S. Muller, *supra*, note 7, pp. 74-82.

would think. What is difficult is to free oneself from this power struggle."[22] A journalist concludes on this shock wave: "It has shaken up the power structures" in France.[23]

This critique of the #MeToo approach, as sharing publicly experiences of male assault or harassment, should not negate the massive positive reaction of women in France. For example, on November 7, 2017, petitions were introduced by 100 women to request from Macron an urgent plan for reform. The call was signed by 50,000 people.[24]

Outright Backlash From Other Journalists, Philosophers, Psychiatrists, Politicians, and Celebrities

Outside of journalist Eric Zemmour's comparison of the use of the hashtag "Squeal on your pig" with the practices of Vichy informers,[25] there are those like conservative philosopher Alain Finkielkraut who considered that "this movement is the end of the presumption of innocence required for defendants at trial, the end of an era; a happy mix between the respect of manners and the heart of civilization of mores." He added that "he is proud to be French." For him, "there will always be individuals with perverted behaviors."[26] In other words, for some commentators, *#balance ton porc* serves only to denounce these "twisted minds," the product of individual volition, and not the direct effect of collective sexist norms women and men internalize unconsciously.

This resistance also comes from women, and not only from the far right like Marine Le Pen, who consider the French #squeal on your pig brutal and insulting and street harassment being only perpetrated by immigrants.[27] As expressed by a journalist, Maya Kadra in the newspaper *Libération*, "Limiting

---

22. *Tribune de Marlène Schiappa dans le JDD ou le retour de la bonne vieille politique*, France Culture, Oct. 17, 2017, https://www.franceculture.fr/emissions/le-journal-de-la -philo/le-journal-de-la-philo-mardi-17-octobre-2017.

23. Annette Levy-Willard, *supra*, note 8, p. 84.

24. Annette Levy-Willard, *supra*, note 8, p. 99.

25. Laure Murat, *supra*, note 9, pp. 34-35.

26. "A young woman in a news report said a man masturbated in front of her in a bus. It is uncomfortable, a pain, maybe atrocious but is this harassment? Perverts exist in front of schools with their coats and as long as there are men with twisted minds and these behaviors will never be completely eradicated but they say nothing about the relationships between the sexes in our society." Alain Finkielkraut & Elisabeth Levy, *#Balance Ton Porc: L'esprit d'escalier*, Causeur, RCJ, Oct. 22, 2017, https://www.youtube.com/watch?v=aXBmGdCBCFA.

27. Marine Le Pen, *"Le harcèlement de rue est en immense majorité le fait de ressortissants de l'immigration,"* Jan. 16, 2018, http://www.contre-info.com/marine-le-pen-le-harcelement-de -rue-est-en-immense-majorite-le-fait-de-ressortissants-de-limmigration.

the cry of these assaulted women to #balance ton porc, is extracting women's rights from the legal and societal framework.[28] The struggle for women takes the form of an emotional, almost irrational, subjectification of the problem. Women appear humiliated but the hashtag can be equated to massive indignation. Collective violence is a retaliation of the victim vis-à-vis her aggressor but, in this way, the victim identifies with him. This violence traps verbal expression and destroys the principle of equality.... One cannot start from particular situations to create general slogans. Women's struggle must be rational, tempered, not doxing."[29]

On January 9, 2018, a more formal and organized backlash was organized by women themselves: French film star Catherine Deneuve, writers Catherine Millet and Catherine Robe-Grillet, journalist Elisabeth Levy, and 100 other French female celebrities published an open letter in the newspaper *Le Monde*, harshly criticizing the "denunciation campaign" against men.[30] They spoke out against the *#balance ton porc* hashtag: "We defend the freedom to be bothered, essential to sexual freedom, trying to pick up someone with insistence is not a crime or a misdemeanor, gallantry is not a chauvinistic assault." "Rape is a crime, but insistent or clumsy flirting is not an offense." "We cannot be reduced to our bodies. Our internal/intrinsic freedom cannot be violated."[31]

---

28. Maya Kadra, *Balance ton porc: non merci!*, LIBÉRATION, Oct. 19, 2017, https://www.liberation.fr/debats/2017/10/19/balance-ton-porc-non-merci_1603799.

29. *Ibid.*

30. Since the article, Catherine Deneuve has written that she wanted to write about the collateral effects on art of #name your pig but is sorry if the letter shocked victims of sexual assault that she supports wholeheartedly: https://www.liberation.fr/debats/2018/01/14/catherine-deneuve-rien-dans-le-texte-ne-pretend-que-le-harcelement-a-du-bon-sans-quoi-je-ne-l-aurais_1622399.

31. Here are some excerpts: "The facts after #MeToo have triggered in the press and in social networks a campaign of public denunciations of individuals.... This summary justice already has its victims, the men sanctioned in their jobs, forced to resign, etc., because all they did was touch a knee, steal a kiss (....) This fever to send the pigs to the slaughterhouse serves in reality the interests of the enemies of sexual liberty. Today, men are required to search retrospectively in the depth of their conscience an inappropriate behavior they had 10, 20, 30 years ago and they should repent for. This public confession, this intrusion of self-proclaimed district attorneys in the private sphere, this is what creates a type of climate akin to a totalitarian society.... We are conscious that the human person is not monolithic: a woman can, in the same day, head a professional team and enjoy being the sexual object of a man, without being a "bitch" or a vile accomplice to patriarchy. She can make sure her pay is equal to that of a man, but not feel traumatized by someone who rubs his penis against women in the subway, even if this is a misdemeanor. She can even consider this as the expression of sexual deprivation, a non-event." *"Nous défendons une liberté d'importuner, indispensable à la liberté sexuelle,"* LE MONDE, Jan. 9, 2018, https://www.lemonde.fr/idees/article/2018/01/09/nous-defendons-une-liberte-d-importuner-indispensable-a-la-liberte-sexuelle_5239134_3232.html.

The Emergence of the French Feminist Divide in the Press—Or a Strong Need for an Open Conversation Between French Women on Power, Gender, and Sexuality?

However, the next day, a group of 30 prominent feminists, most of them presidents of NGOs for women led by Caroline de Haas reacted on a national news radio station, France Info. This reaction shows both an intergenerational conflict on the issue of sexual harassment and a strong divide in the feminist movement in France, but it at least started an open conversation on the issue. According to de Haas, "Every time rights of women progress and consciousness rises, resistance appears. In general, it takes the form of 'Yes, it is true, but….' What we have in the *Le Monde* backlash Deneuve group article[32] is what you hear at the coffee break or in family dinners when the colleague or the uncle doesn't understand what is happening."

Caroline de Haas refutes each argument of the article:

- First, reacting to the fear that, with the *#balancetonporc* hashtag, "We might be going too far" de Haas responds, "When equality advances, excessiveness is always held up as a risk." "In France, there are thousands of sexual assaults and hundreds of rapes: this is the caricature" we should be worrying about.
- When the backlash group article complains "We can't say anything anymore," de Haas retorts, "As if the fact society is less tolerant to sexism, racism homophobic acts is a problem. Accepting insults against women is authorizing violence. Controlling our language is a sign our society is progressing."
- To the accusation, "This is puritanism," for de Haas, "Saying feminists are prudes or frustrated sexually is disconcerting. Violence is a burden for women … on our spirit, our bodies, our pleasure and our sexuality. How can we imagine an instance that our society is liberated sexually for women when one out of two women consider they have suffered from sexual violence?"

---

32. Since the Le Monde article on the "right to bothered," Deneuve has distanced herself from some authors and says her position, defending freedom of expression in the arts and a form of political correctness, does not condone in anyway sexual harassment, sexual assault, and rape, and she said she did not want to offend victims of these acts she condemns. Catherine Deneuve, *"Rien dans le texte ne prétend que le harcèlement a du bon, sans quoi je ne l'aurais pas signé,"* Libération, Jan. 14, 2018, https://www.liberation.fr/debats/2018/01/14/catherine-deneuve-rien-dans-le-texte-ne-pretend-que-le-harcelement-a-du-bon-sans-quoi-je-ne-l-aurais_1622399.

- When the backlash article objects, "We cannot flirt anymore," de Haas answers, "This is confusing, deliberately [equating] seduction based on respect and pleasure with violence."
- For the backlash group, "Harassment or aggression is inappropriate, but flirtation, on the other hand, is not serious." De Haas refutes, "This is not true: it is not a question of degree between flirting and harassment but a difference in nature. In one instance, both are considered as equals and in the other, one individual [the female] is considered as an object regardless of one's desire or consent."
- Last, on the changes needed, "It is women's responsibility," says the backlash group. De Haas counters, "When the backlash group says that it reflects a need of education for girls, so they do not feel intimidated, women are held responsible for not being assaulted. When will we ask the question of men's responsibility for rape and assault and boys' education? Women are human beings like others. We have a fundamental right to live our lives safely. In France, in the United States, in Senegal, in Thailand or in Brazil: it is not the case today. Nowhere."[33]

Commentators wonder whether this conversation reflects an intergenerational conflict between feminists. This does not seem to be the case because Françoise Héritier, one of France's most famous feminist anthropologists commented in *Le Monde* favorably about the #movement just before passing away: "Victims, instead of staying underground and distraught, use #MeToo.... This is what [women victims] lacked for centuries; understanding that we were not alone.... We must rethink the question of the relations between the sexes, confront the male domination and annihilate the idea that there is an irrepressible male desire. It is a gigantic project of construction that lies ahead."[34]

So, for some commentators, outside of raising awareness about sexual violence in France, the #MeToo movement exposed an irreconcilable divide in the French feminist movement since the sexual revolution in the 1960s.[35] This might also epitomize the ongoing debate in society at large between those who think that accepting unconditional individual sexual liberty as an inherent

---

33. See *TRIBUNE*. *"Les porcs et leurs allié.e.s ont raison de s'inquiéter": Caroline De Haas et des militantes féministes répondent à la tribune publiée dans "Le Monde,"* France TV Info, Oct. 1, 2018, https://www.francetvinfo.fr/societe/droits-des-femmes/tribune-les-porcs-et-leurs-allie-e-s-ont-raison-de-sinquieter-caroline-de-haas-et-des-militantes-feministes-repondent-a-la-tribune-publiee-dans-le-monde_2553497.html.

34. Annette Levy-Willard, *supra*, note 8, p. 16.

35. Laure Murat, *supra*, note 9, pp. 37-39.

power struggle is a condition of equality between the sexes and those who consider enforcing structural equality is the condition of sexuality without violence.

Before #MeToo, the Laws Protecting Sexual Harassment and Assault in France

Sexual harassment law in France first developed in 1992 focused on quid pro quo harassment. Initially it prohibited only acts of a sexual nature linked to an abuse of authority, similar to the gender-neutral bullying legislation more often enforced. As a result of European law, the legal framework on antidiscrimination had to expand to prohibit sexual harassment as a form of discrimination. The scope of sexual harassment law was extended to cover hostile environment sexual harassment in 2012. Recent legislative reforms in 2015 and 2016, before #MeToo, already improved the sanctions and the tools for preventing sexual harassment as a professional risk at work. Criminal law on rape and sexual assault developed as a separate legal framework.

Definition of Sexual Harassment Before #MeToo: A Slow but Progressive Expansion Under EU Influence

The EU Commission in 1991 invited Member States to "protect the dignity of women and men at work [by] considering unacceptable behavior with sexual connotation or behavior linked to sex which affect women and men at work and … [as] contrary to the principle of equal treatment, regardless of the fact it is perpetrated by supervisors or colleagues."[36]

In France, rape is defined[37] as "an act of sexual penetration[38] without the consent of the victim, regardless of its nature,[39] committed against a person with

---

36. Recommendation of November 27, 1991 (92/131/CEE).

37. The Criminal Code of 1810 punished rape but did not define it (art 332 Penal Code); case law had made efforts to try to define it, Cass Crim June 25, 1857, Dubas Decision.

38. The law of December 23, 1980 offered a definition of rape including any form of penetration (mouth, anal, oral, vagina); D. Mayer, *La réforme de la répression du viol en France par la loi du 23 décembre 1980*, RDPC 1983, p. 277.

39. All forms of penetration (even incomplete penetration, ejaculation or even finger penetration) with or without an object. A lot of cases discuss those objects (candle, handle of shovel, stick, bottle, even vegetables, spoons....).

violence, force, threat or surprise"[40] and sexual assault as "any sexual abuse committed with violence, force, threat or surprise."

A 1992 reform[41] was the first to introduce a narrow definition of sexual harassment, (essentially by supervisors), as "the act of harassing using orders, threats and coercion in an attempt to obtain sexual favors, perpetrated by a person abusing his/her authority."[42] In 2001, the law[43] extended its scope to include as victims persons refusing such acts, witnesses of these acts, job applicants, interns, and trainees in companies of all sizes. Case law recognized harassment of men by women[44] and same-sex harassment.[45]

It was not until 2002 that the condition of abuse of authority was eliminated[46] and sexual harassment was described more vaguely as "the act of harassing another person to obtain sexual favors."[47] That same year, EU law offered a wider definition of sexual harassment: "Where any form of unwanted verbal, non-verbal or physical conduct of a sexual nature occurs, with the purpose or effect of violating the dignity of a person, in particular when creating an intimidating, hostile, degrading, humiliating or offensive environment,"[48] adding that "harassment and sexual harassment was discrimination on the grounds of sex."

This broad EU definition inspired the expansion of the French definition of sexual harassment in 2012:[49] sexual harassment now consists "of repeated words or behavior with a sexual connotation, which undermine his or her dignity by reason of their degrading or humiliating nature or create against him

---

40. Rape included in article 222-23 Criminal Code carried a fifteen-year prison sentence if there were no aggravated circumstances. For a long time, feminists fought hard to obtain, in practice, judicial recognition of rape as a crime and not a misdemeanor as indecent exposure with violence (five-year sentence, article 333 Criminal Code). On March 1, 1994, a new Criminal Code replaced the notion of indecent of exposure with sexual assault.

41. Law no. 92-684 of July 22, 1992. It also modified the law for civil servants: loi no. 83-634 of July 13, 1983.

42. Art. 222-33 Penal Code. Law no. 98-468 June 17, 1998 added: "use of serious pressure to obtain sexual favors."

43. Law no. 2001-397 of May 9, 2001 on equality between women and men at work.

44. The principle of this type of harassment was acknowledged in one case but not proven, Soc. 2 Oct. 1997 no. 95-41322.

45. Court of Appeal of Besançon June 27, 2000 no. 1999/01016.

46. Both in the French criminal and the labor codes.

47. Law no. 2002-73 January 17, 2002 on social modernization; The extension of the scope of the definition did result in increasing the number of sentences from thirty to forty a year between 1994 and 2003 to seventy to eighty-five a year after 2005.

48. Directive 2002/73/CE, article 1(2), now in Recast Directive 2006/54/CE July 5, 2006.

49. Law no. 2012-954 of August 6, 2012: A change both in the Criminal Code and the Labor Code.

or her an intimidating, hostile or offensive situation and "any form of serious pressure, even if not repeated, exerted with the real or apparent goal of obtaining an act of a sexual nature, if it is sought for the benefit of the actor or the benefit of a third party." So, the French definition now covers both quid pro quo harassment *and* sexual harassment creating hostile "*situations*," not "hostile *environments*," which is still contrary to EU law.[50]

The unique 2012 French legal framework still distinguishes[51] sexual harassment from harassment[52] as discrimination based on sex,[53] prohibited in a separate statute.[54] This might be due to the fact that moral harassment, bullying, was already a strong model with extensive case law, constructed as an infringement on the dignity of the person regardless of gender without reference to equality or discrimination.[55] Public and private employees are protected against acts of retaliation if they denounce any violations.[56] In 2015, a ban was added on sexist acts in employment.[57]

---

50. See directive 2006/54 article.

51. This distinction between discrimination and harassment is confirmed in the guidelines of the Ministry of Justice following the adoption of the 2012 law: Taubira Guidelines (*circulaire*) no. 2012-15 August 7, 2012, mentions that the goal is to protect victims, "who are mostly women."

52. French law also prohibits moral harassment (bullying): art.1152-1 of Labor Code, art. 222-33-2 Penal Code.

53. M. Mercat-Bruns, *On harassment as discrimination based on prohibited grounds (sex, race) and prevention, Racisme au travail: nouveaux modes de détection et outils de prévention*, DROIT SOCIAL 361 (2017).

54. Article 1 of Law no. 2008-496 of May 27, 2008 Law no. 2008-496 transposing the directive in European law on harassment as a form of discrimination.

55. Hebert, L. Camille, *Dignity and Discrimination in Sexual Harassment Law: A French Case Study*, Wash. & Lee J. Civ. Rts. & Soc. Just., Vol. 25/1 (Aug. 1, 2018); Forthcoming, Ohio State Public Law Working Paper No. 455, p.1. Available at SSRN: https://ssrn.com /abstract=3239557; C. Hebert, L. Lerouge, *The law of workplace harassment of the United States, France, and the European Union: comparative analysis after the adoption of France's new sexual harassment law*, 35 Comp. Lab. Law & Pol'y J. 93 (2013).

56. Art. L.1153-2, L.1153-3 Lab. Code, art. 6 ter Law July 13, 1983.

57. Any act linked to the sex of a person, with the purpose or effect of violating her/his dignity or creating an intimidating, hostile, degrading, humiliating, and offensive environment; The term in French: *agissement sexiste*, see Law no. 2015-994 of August 17, 2015 (known as Rebsamen Law). M. Becker, Les agissements sexistes et le harcèlement sexuel, 1743 Semaine Sociale Lamy 21 (2016).

Sanctions and Enforcement of Sexual Harassment Law Before the #MeToo Movement

Outside of rape and sexual assault both punishable by law,[58] sexual harassment is a misdemeanor.[59] Since 2016,[60] the employer must include sexist acts in professional risks covered in its implemented prevention policies[61] and include it in the company's binding code of conduct.[62] In any case,[63] since sexual harassment is a form of sex discrimination, any presumed victim can alert the French Defender of Rights who investigates cases of discrimination and can enlighten the courts as amicus curiae.[64]

As for civil remedies, a successful claim of sexual harassment requires payment of back pay,[65] and employers can be liable under the new class action suit against discrimination[66] but other efforts to expand financial sanctions have encountered resistance. The minimal damages awarded had been increased

---

58. Article 222-23 of the Criminal Code sanctions rape: fifteen-year prison sentence; 20 years with aggravated circumstances (art. 222-24).

59. It can lead to two years of incarceration and a €30,000 fine (Art. L 222-33 Criminal Code); Aggravating circumstances can lead to three years of incarceration and a €45,000 fine if the worker took more than eight days of sick leave; the victim is less than 15-years-old; the victim is particularly vulnerable because of his/her age, her health, a mental or physical infirmity, a pregnancy, apparent or known.

60. Law no. 2016-1088 of August 8, 2016 (Law El Khomri).

61. Article L. 4121-2 of the Labor Code as part of the employer's duty in terms of health and security (*obligation de sécurité*): awareness raising campaigns and training; article L. 4612-3 of the Labor Code: health and security employee representatives must be involved in the prevention.

62. Article L. 1321-2 of the Labor Code.

63. Civil or criminal.

64. https://www.defenseurdesdroits.fr/sites/default/files/atoms/files/150715_-_depli ant-harcelement_sexuel_web.pdf. In terms of the burden of proof, it was not until the August 8, 2016, law that the less stringent standard of proof for discrimination was duplicated exactly for sexual harassment: Article 1154-1 of Labor Code reads "the employee **presents facts** that can infer the existence of sexual harassment" instead of the previous more rigorous standard: "the employee **established** facts that can infer...": more than ever, this is a burden of production of evidence now.

65. Since any dismissal or other acts are considered null and void.

66. The law covers harassment as a form of discrimination based on a prohibited ground: Law no. 2016-1547 November 18, 2016, on the modernization of Justice (art. 62).

in 2014[67] from six to twelve months[68] but the provision was later abolished.[69] Again, in 2016,[70] a law reintroduced a right to minimal damages of six-months back pay, but this was eliminated in a 2017 labor law reform.[71]

In terms of enforcement, since 2002, the extension of sexual harassment law beyond abuse of authority to cover harassment between colleagues resulted in an increase in the number of sentences from thirty a year in 1994 to seventy in 2003.[72] This relatively low number shows the challenge of bringing a claim, when, according to a 2014 survey, one out of five women declared they had been harassed at work.[73] Harassment was perpetrated by colleagues (41 percent), by the employer (22 percent), and by the immediate supervisor (18 percent).[74] In only three out of ten cases did the victims complain to their employer, and 30 percent of the victims did not confide in anyone.[75] In 40 percent of the cases brought to the employer's attention, the solution was unfavorable for the plaintiffs, with a direct effect on their employment (labor contract not renewed, negative effect on their career).[76] Conversely, only 40 percent of victims indicated that the presumed perpetrator was sanctioned, and the survey reveals only 5 percent of victims filed a claim in court.[77]

The case law, before the #MeToo movement, confirms that it was very difficult to prove sexual harassment in the workforce,[78] often construed as an

---

67. Law on Real Equality between women and men of August 4, 2014.

68. See Maude Becker, *Le harcèlement sexuel doit être sanctionné plus lourdement*, SEMAINE SOCIALE LAMY, Dec. 3, 2018, p. 11.

69. The Constitutional Council considered this minimal remedy had nothing to do with the law on equality (*cavalier legislatif*) that it was included in, see Maude Becker, *supra*, note 68, p. 11.

70. El Khomri Law of August 8, 2016, already cited in footnote 60.

71. See Macron's Labor Reform through several Executive Orders on September 22, 2017 (Journal Officiel Sept. 23, 2017) followed by their ratification by Parliament (Law of March 28 no. 2018-217) and after Constitutional Review, Constitutional Court Decision, Mar. 21, 2018).

72. Legislative history of the law of 2012: http://www.senat.fr/rap/r11-610/r11-6103. html.

73. According to a March 26, 2015 survey of the Defender of Rights, https://www .defenseurdesdroits.fr/fr/publications/etudes/enquete-sur-le-harcelement-sexuel-au-travail.

74. *Ibid.*, Defender of Rights survey, note 73.

75. *Ibid.*

76. *Ibid.*

77. *Ibid.*

78. See Marie Mercat-Bruns, *Harcèlement sexuel au travail* in S. Hennette-Vauchez, D. Roman, M. Pichard, LA LOI ET LE GENRE, CNRS 2014, p. 2018.

individual act in exchange for sexual favors[79] and more recently, before 2012, as part of a sexist environment.[80] Negating consent to prior sexual relations increased the challenge to prove that acts were unwelcome.[81] Judges also had difficulty distinguishing "feelings of love" from inappropriate sexual conduct.[82] Moreover, some judges resisted for some time before admitting that sexual relations with colleagues or a supervisor during lunch or after work could come under the realm of sexual harassment law instead of providing immunity for the perpetrator under privacy laws.[83]

Changes in the Law and Enforcement Since the #MeToo Movement

The French government reacted quickly to the worldwide #MeToo/#squeal on your pig movements with proposals of concrete legislative reform. Nevertheless, questions remain about the focus of the changes in the law, and a series of activists' protests and articles reflect the persistent challenges to tackling sexual harassment and sexual assault in France.

Macron's Reform Against Sexual Violence: More Criminal Sanctions and Information Circulated but Limited Structural Changes in Equality at Work

On November 25, 2017, the International Day for the Elimination of Violence against Women, President Macron in a televised speech at the Elysée Palace in front of the main feminist groups and major stakeholders on gender issues noted that in 2016, 123 women died in France at the hands of their

---

79. Court of Appeals of Metz, May 27, 1997, no. 1996/03038; Court of Appeals of Bourges, April 11, 1997, no. 1996/01545; Court of Appeals of Paris, October 2, 1996, no. 1995/31878; Court of Appeals of Poitiers, January 15, 1999, Jurisdata no. 004540; Court of Appeals of Grenoble, November 18, 2002, no. 1999/02793); Court of Appeals of Douai, September 29, 2006, no. 2005/03239), Court of Appeals of Paris, January 18, 1996, *Dr. Ouv.* 1997, p. 76; Court of Appeals of Dijon, February 6, 2001, no. 2000/00227.

80. Soc. December 15, 2009, no. 08-44848; Soc. Feb. 9, 2010, no. 08-44632.

81. Soc. November 30, 2005, no. 04-41206; Court of Appeals Nancy March 28, 1990, JData no. 043339; Court of Appeals of Douai, December 16, 1994, no. 1994/10914.

82. Court of Appeals of Metz, September 1, 2003, no. 1999/03537.

83. Soc. November 30, 2005, no. 04-13877; the Supreme Court finally reversed the case law and concluded that harassment outside of work could be generated by the work relationship regardless of the time and place: Soc. March 3, 2009, no. 07-44082; Soc. October 19, 2011, no. 09-72672.

husbands or boyfriends. The public recognition of recurring violence against women set the tone and explains the nature of the current legislation based on sanctions.

In his speech, Macron made the solemn commitment that equality between women and men would be one of the country's major national initiatives with three priorities: cultural education and battle for equality; more support for victims; and a reinforcement of criminal sanctions for sexual violence.[84] Feminists groups hailed the president's good intentions and commitment to zero tolerance for sexual violence, proposing online filing for sexual assaults, police training on sexual assault, and trauma support centers for victims, while criticizing the limited budget awarded to implement the legislative measures proposed.[85]

In accordance with this presidential agenda for reform, the minister of justice and the Minister in charge of equality between women and men introduced a bill on March 21, 2018, to reinforce the struggle against sexual and sexist violence. In August 2018, the French Parliament passed a new law against sexual and gender-based violence.[86] It extends the statute of limitations for sexual offenses against children to thirty years,[87] facilitates the proof of mental coercion or surprise in cases of sexual assault or rape of minors of fifteen or younger,[88] enacts new criminal sanctions against street harassment,[89] against

84. https://www.elysee.fr/emmanuel-macron/2017/11/25/discours-a-loccasion-de-la-journee-de-lutte-contre-les-violences-faites-aux-femmes.

85. Macron déçoit certaines féministes avec son plan d'égalité femmes-hommes, L'Obs, Nov. 25, 2017, https://www.nouvelobs.com/politique/20171125.OBS7836/macron-decoit-certaines-feministes-avec-son-plan-d-egalite-femmes-hommes.html.

86. LOI no. 2018-703 du 3 août 2018 renforçant la lutte contre les violences sexuelles et sexistes, https://www.legifrance.gouv.fr/affichTexte.do?cidTexte=JORFTEXT000037284450&categorieLien=id.

87. Article 7 Code of Penal Procedure.

88. Article 222-22-1 Penal Code, following the acquittal of an adult on rape charges who had had sexual relations with a minor who was eleven years old, https://www.francetvinfo.fr/sante/enfant-ado/acquittement-dans-une-affaire-de-relation-sexuelle-avec-une-mineure-il-faudra-changer-la-loi_2463214.html.

89. Article 621-1 Penal Code targets "outrage sexiste et sexuel," sexist or sexual indignation: the act of imposing a verbal or non-verbal act with sexual or sexist connotation that either affects the dignity of the person because of its degrading and humiliating nature or because it creates an intimidating, hostile, or offensive situation. It can lead to fines from €750 up to €3,000 or impose rehabilitation training.

cyber harassment,[90] and extended the Penal Code's prohibition on sexual harassment to include sexist acts.[91]

Some of these changes are seen as counterproductive because they just pile up more criminal sanctions related to different forms of sexual violence and sexism and might create confusion or limit harsher sentencing. For example, street harassment is now sanctioned with a fine up to 3,000 euros even though the law already prohibits sexual harassment with a harsher punishment.[92] Sexist insults are already prohibited with a fine of 45,000 euros and one year in jail.[93] Furthermore, as some French academics observe, sanctioning street harassment in certain neighborhoods might serve as a pretext for racial profiling and fining young individuals of foreign origin, instead of enforcing sexual harassment law at work or in posh neighborhoods.[94]

In reaction, more recently, specific obligations at work were imposed in companies to fight employment-related sexual harassment and to raise awareness about violations, complaint procedures, and enforcement. Effective January 2019, the 2018 law sets forth new obligations for French companies in the fight against sexual harassment and sexist behaviors. The companies must: display in all company locations a poster on sexual harassment and the means for legal action; designate a "sexual harassment and sexist practices" contact person in companies of at least 250 employees; and designate a "sexual harassment and sexist practices" contact person within all workers' councils (CSE).[95]

---

90. See article 222-33 Penal Code: "sexual harassment also occurs when words or behaviors are imposed on the same person by several persons, in a concerted manner, at the instigation of one person, or successively with the knowledge that the words or behaviors are being repeated. It also "increases to the penalties for violation of the statute when the conduct is committed using a public online communication service or an electronic or digital medium."

91. Sexual harassment is the act of imposing on a person, in a repeated manner, words or behavior with a sexual or gender-based connotation, which undermine his or her dignity by reason of their degrading or humiliating nature or create against him or her an intimidating, hostile, or offensive situation.

92. The Penal Code already prohibits sexual harassment with a similar definition, see note 53.

93. Loi du 29 juillet 1881 sur la liberté de la presse; art. 32, See Interview of Maude Beckers, Le harcèlement sexuel doit être sanctionné plus lourdement, Semaine Sociale Lamy, Dec. 3, 2018, no. 1839, p. 12, https://www.legifrance.gouv.fr/affichTexteArticle.do?idArticle= LEGIARTI000006419738&cidTexte=LEGITEXT000006070722.

94. https://www.liberation.fr/debats/2017/09/26/contre-la-penalisation-du -harcelement-de-rue_1599121.

95. The law no. 2018-771 of September 5, 2018, aims to make companies and employees aware of the fight against sexual harassment and sexist behavior. It requires the display in the company of the text on sexual harassment and access to litigation. As of January 1, 2019, employers will have to inform, by any means, employees, trainees, and interns, as well as candidates for recruitment, training, or work placement, of the text of the Article 222-33 of the

All these initiatives to inform and internalize procedures on sexual harassment at work are useful tools but fall short of tackling the systemic barriers to equality between men and women at work in France. In short, Macron's plan against sexual violence construes sexual harassment as an issue of violence and more often quid pro quo harassment and less as a question of gender discrimination. The new provisions on sexism[96] are symbolic because they only add a criminal sanction to existing provisions on hostile environment sexual harassment and sexism,[97] included before the #MeToo movement. Measures to combat the glass ceiling and sex segregation in certain job sectors require more proactive measures by bystanders of sexual harassment, promoting equal pay or hiring a critical mass of women in certain professions to reduce the risk of harassment.

Enforcement After the #MeToo Movement: More Complaints, Defamation, Protests, and a National Platform to Facilitate Implementation

Since January 2018, the number of claims of sexual violence registered by the police has risen by 23.1 percent according to the French Minister of

---

French Penal Code (text defining sexual harassment) as well as civil and criminal actions and information about the competent authorities and services (defined soon by a decree). This obligation applies in the workplace and at the door of the place of recruitment (Article L. 1153-5 paragraph 2 of Labor Code, article 105 Law, September 5, 2018). In companies with twenty or more employees, the internal regulations must already recall "the provisions relating to moral and sexual harassment and sexist behavior." (Article L. 1321-2 of Labor Code). Designation of Social and Economic Council (CSE) contact person in companies employing at least 250 employees: as of January 1, 2019, the CSE must designate, from among its members, a contact person to combat sexual harassment and sexist acts, in the form of a resolution adopted, for a period ending with that of the mandate of the employee delegate (see Article L. 2314-1, paragraph 4).This contact person will benefit from training in health, safety, and working conditions (L. 2315-18 of French Labor Code).The training is paid by the employer under the conditions defined by a decree (not yet adopted). A "sexual harassment and sexist behavior" contact person in companies employing at least 250 employees: As of January 1, 2019, in every company employing at least 250 employees, a referent is appointed to guide, inform, and help employees fight sexual harassment and sexist behavior. (Article L. 1153-5-1 new). The text does not specify the mode of designation of the "sexual harassment and sexist acts" contact person. Sexual Harassment on the Agenda of the (sector/industry) collective bargaining: unions will now have to negotiate at the industry level on "tools for companies to prevent and act against sexual harassment and sexist behavior" (Article L. 2241-1, 2 ° of the Labor Code). This negotiation must take place at least every four years.

96. In the Penal Code [Article 222-33].
97. In the Labor Code [L. 1142-2-1].

the Interior.[98] The government had earlier published statistics on the growing number of claims of rape and sexual assault since 2017, noting that claims had increased from 10 to 12 percent in a year, especially in the final months of 2017, with an increase of 31.5 percent, due to the #MeToo movement and a desire to report assaults, which had occurred in the past.[99] There has also been an increase in successful sexual harassment cases in employment[100] that includes sexist insults in precarious job settings.[101]

In practice, the informal reporting of #squeal on your pig since October 13, 2017, does not always conform to the exact information needed in the judicial process as the president of the union of judges explained in an interview.[102] "The #movement expresses a need. The District Attorney can prosecute on his own or only after a formal request. So, it is not enough if the presumed victim says: 'I have been assaulted by this person in a tweet.' He/She must say more specifically: 'I have been assaulted by this person who works here.'"[103]

There has definitely been "legal" backlash in reaction to the movement. Some silence-breakers who have used the hashtag have been the target of claims for defamation, including the author of the first #squeal on your pig, Sandra Muller. In a tweet, as previously mentioned, she had revealed TV producer Eric Brion's verbal misconduct at a professional event: "You have big breasts. You are my type of woman. I am going to make you come all night."[104] Several months later, he issued apologies and explained that, due to heavy drinking that night, he was flirting with her inappropriately.

However, on September 25, 2019, the French lower civil court in Paris ordered Muller to pay €15,000 ($16,500) in damages to Brion, as well as €5,000

98. http://www.lefigaro.fr/flash-actu/2018/09/06/97001-20180906FILWWW 00139-forte-hausse-des-violences-sexuelles-en-2018.php.

99. https://www.lepoint.fr/societe/forte-hausse-des-plaintes-pour-viol-et-agression -sexuelle-en-2017--25-01-2018-2189532_23.php.

100. Labor Court 10 November 2017, no. 15-03130 (cleaning women in trains); Court of Appeals of Orléans: Feb. 7, 2017, no. 15-02566 (desk assistant of journalists); Administrative Court of Appeals, Marseilles, Jan. 15, 2019, no. 2602002 (police department); Court of Appeals Grenoble, 22 Mars 2018, no. 16/01339 (employee in movie theater); Court of Appeals of Paris May 2, 2018, no. 16/15715 (bus driver sexually harassed and retaliation).

101. Supreme Court Cass. Soc. 30 Janvier 2019, no. 17-28905: sexist harassment of a cook in a short-term job who was the target of sexist and sexual comments and who had trash thrown at her without any reaction from her supervisor.

102. Ibid. https://www.lepoint.fr/societe/forte-hausse-des-plaintes-pour-viol-et-agres sion-sexuelle-en-2017--25-01-2018-2189532_23.php.

103. Ibid. The DA can prosecute or not; a feminist NGO locally can ask DA to prosecute indicating what was written so it is not just the survivor.

104. See Donadio, *supra*, note 4.

($5,500) in legal fees.[105] She also had to delete the tweets and share the court's statements on her Twitter account. The court recognized that "all violence perpetrated by men against women is without any doubt an issue of public interest." However, the court concluded that, by accusing Brion of sexual harassment, Muller was liable for defamation—because according to the law, the harassment violation consists of "repeated acts or serious pressure," and Muller could not be exonerated from liability based on "good faith," since "she did not have a sufficient factual base" or "proof of the truthfulness of her accusations."[106]

According to the court, Sandra Muller "lacked prudence in her tweet, using strong terms like 'pig' to qualify the plaintiff, assimilating him in this context to Harvey Weinstein," and the term "squeal" (in French, *balance*), "exposed him to societal disapproval." Muller "exceeded the limits admissible in terms of freedom of expression; her comments constituted a personal attack." The judges underlined in their decision "the global and exceptional impact of the tweet" and their effect on Eric Brion: "social isolation" and deep depression. Muller's lawyers argued the fact that her tweet *#squeal on your pig* had liberated women and their voices whereas Brion's lawyers pleaded this was a form of "denunciation." His lawyers attacked "the lie" that the tweet was allegedly based on since Eric Brion "was not a harasser." They contended that "*#squeal on your pig*" was a wonderful phenomenon but outside of that, there are rumors and slander. Muller's lawyers argued that sanctioning their client would in fact "gag" those

---

105. *Sandra Muller, l'initiatrice de #balancetonporc, condamnée pour avoir diffamé l'homme qu'elle accusait de harcèlement*, LE MONDE, Sept. 25, 2019, https://www.lemonde.fr/societe/article/2019/09/25/l-initiatrice-de-balancetonporc-condamnee-pour-avoir-diffame-l-homme-qu-elle-accusait-de-harcelement_6013008_3224.html.

106. Law of July 29, 1881, on freedom of the press, article 32: in French law, defamation is the allegation or accusation of a fact that is prejudicial to the honor or consideration of a person. The fact may be true or false, but it must be detailed enough to be verified without difficulty and the subject of cross-examination. The two defenses to avoid liability are: the "exception of truth" (which must be total, perfect, and complete and linked to the defamatory comments; and the defense of "good faith" which implies four cumulative requirements: prudence and measure in the expression without exaggeration; absence of personal conflict with the victim; the existence of a legitimate goal (informing on a public health scandal for instance); and the seriousness of the investigation which is distinct from the truth of the comments made. The accusations of the author, journalist or not, should be based on solid facts, even if ultimately an error was made. The plaintiff can prove that the accusations are randomly made or based on a deliberate lie.

whose voices have been liberated.[107] Muller and her lawyers since then have appealed, temporarily suspending the fines and other court orders.[108]

Some recent case law is also ambivalent.[109] In September 2019, the Supreme Court only qualified as a wrongful conduct and not sexual harassment, sexual comments made by a manager in text messages to his female employee who then responded and adopted at work a "very seductive attitude." For the court, this "ambiguous attitude" and "voluntary participation in a game of seduction" excludes sexual harassment. This is a narrow interpretation of the law, focusing on investigating the explicit or implicit consent and behavior of the victim, despite the now larger legal framework since 2012 which includes any single act of quid pro quo harassment or repeated acts that create sexually hostile environments.

On a more positive note, the younger generation of French girls have noticed some positive changes in the behavior of boys after the #MeToo movement.[110] Moreover, evidence in France of the impact of the #MeToo movement on the enforcement of sexual harassment and sexual assault came with the International Day on the Elimination of Violence Against Women. A new hashtag #All of us (women) (#noustoutes) gathered 50,000 people on November 24, 2018, in protests across the country against sexual violence.[111] The next day, Prime Minister Edouard Philippe announced the creation of an online alert platform on sexual and sexist violence.[112] It will allow victims or witnesses to

---

107. S. Muller, *supra*, note 7, p. 159; Thibaut Solano, *#Balancetonporc: ces plaignantes désormais accusées*, L'EXPRESS, Apr. 10, 2018, https://www.lexpress.fr/actualite/societe /balancetonporc-ces-plaignantes-desormais-accusees_2038045.html.

108. Aurelian Breeden, *French #MeToo Movement's Founder Loses Defamation Case*, N.Y. TIMES, Sept. 25, 2009, https://www.nytimes.com/2019/09/25/world/europe/france-sandra -muller-verdict.html.

109. Supreme Court of France, Cour de Cass. Soc. Sept. 5 2019, no. 17-31171.

110. Arièle Bonte, *#MeToo: elles racontent ce que ce mouvement a changé dans leur quotidien*, RTL, Apr. 10, 2018, https://www.rtl.fr/girls/identites/metoo-elles-racontent-ce-que -ce-mouvement-a-change-dans-leur-quotidien-7795019237.

111. Anais Moran, *Marche contre les violences faites aux femmes: "Aujourd'hui, c'était notre moment à nous toutes,"* Libération, Nov. 24, 2018, https://www.liberation.fr/france /2018/11/24/marche-contre-les-violences-faites-aux-femmes-aujourd-hui-c-etait-notre -moment-a-nous-toutes_1694079. Catherine Mallaval & Anais Moran, *Une marche dans les pas de #MeToo*, Libération, Nov. 22, 2018, https://www.liberation.fr/france/2018/11/22 /une-marche-dans-les-pas-de-metoo_1693694. *"Ras le viol": les féministes en nombre dans la rue contre les violences sexists*, L'Obs, Nov. 25, 2018, https://www.nouvelobs.com/topnews /20181125.AFP9158/ras-le-viol-les-feministes-en-nombre-dans-la-rue-contre-les-violences -sexistes.html.

112. The platform launched on Tuesday, November 27, 2018, in the presence of the Secretary of State for Women, Marlène Schiappa, the Minister of Interior and the Minister of Justice.

talk, around the clock, with a police officer especially trained to help them file their complaint. As the Prime Minister said: "Now in a couple of clicks this can help each one (woman) start fresh, anew: for herself and for her family. And maybe avoid the worst." This is intended to make sure sanctions are effective, and it was promised over a year ago by the president in his speech on gender equality.

In the meantime, a senator from Macron's new party "En marche" was accused of sexual harassment.[113] And, two French actresses, Valentine Monnier and Adèle Haenel, have recently gone to the press alleging that movie directors Christophe Ruggia and Roman Polanski presumably fondled or raped them when they started in the profession. The actresses argue that these directors' recent movies cannot serve as a defense[114] or a remake with young actors.[115] Haenel, who was under 15 years old at the time, explains in the interview that her statement is a political act, beyond an individual accusation, to raise awareness in society. Her former director Ruggia is now under criminal investigation[116] and the First Lady[117] has publicly given her full support to the actress. Ronan Farrow, interviewed by the French press, sees these new public accusations in

---

113. *"Pot de maquillage": accusé de sexisme, le député LREM Joachim Son-Forget est recadré par son groupe*, FRANCE INFO, Dec. 26, 2018, https://www.francetvinfo.fr/politique /la-republique-en-marche/pot-de-maquillage-accuse-de-sexisme-le-depute-lrem-joachim-son -forget-est-recadre-par-son-groupe_3117535.html.

114. Actress Valentine Monnier accused Roman Polanski of raping her at the age of 18. She strongly objects to Polanski's making an analogy of his situation—accused of raping her and also a fugitive from an American rape conviction of a 13-year-old girl—and that of the subject of his new film, Alfred Dreyfus, in "J'accuse" showing the unfair anti-Semitic prosecution of a Jewish military officer, https://www.vanityfair.com/hollywood/2019/08/roman-polanski-an -officer-and-a-spy-rape-allegations-interview.

115. See Cesar prize winning actress Adèle Haenel interviewed by journalist Edwy Plenel from MediaPart. Haenel explains that she cannot watch Christophe Ruggia in another movie with adolescent actors, and that she was encouraged to come out with her story because of the #MeToo movement and the film "Leaving Neverland" about Michael Jackson, https:// www.youtube.com/watch?v=QFRPci2wK2Y.

116. *Accusations d'Adèle Haenel: ouverture d'une enquête pour "agressions sexuelles,"* LE PARISIEN, June 11, 2019, http://www.leparisien.fr/faits-divers/accusations-d-adele-haenel -ouverture-d-une-enquete-pour-agressions-sexuelles-06-11-2019-8187426.php. Haenel has finally decided to file suit against Ruggia after first considering that "justice ignores victims and we ignore justice," Coline Vazquez, *Accusations d'Adèle Haenel: ouverture d'une enquête pour "agressions sexuelles",* L'EXPRESS, Nov. 27, 2019, https://www.lexpress.fr/actualite/societe /justice/agressions-sexuelles-ce-que-va-changer-la-plainte-d-adele-haenel_2109106.html.

117. *Les infos de 18h—Brigitte Macron apporte son soutien à Adèle Haenel*, RTL, Nov. 7, 2019, https://www.rtl.fr/actu/debats-societe/les-infos-de-18h-brigitte-macron -apporte-son-soutien-a-adele-haenel-7799412997.

the French movie business as "promising."[118] Since then, the selection committee in charge of the Cesar film competition (like the Oscars) has resigned after
all the members nominated Polanski for best director despite the new accusations of rape. Polanski still won the prize for best director.

These two recent stories have led to a new Le Monde investigation on the
effect of #MeToo on enforcement, which recognizes a rising number of criminal
claims. However, interviews of sexual violence plaintiffs confirm the challenges
posed by lengthy and difficult criminal investigations in which cases are often
closed because of issues relating to the possible "consent" of the plaintiff or lack
of DNA evidence.[119] As long as sexual harassment claims, other sexual assault,
and feminicides[120] still surface, this reflects how France, like many other countries, requires in-depth monitoring and action to deal with structural inequality
in the workplace,[121] the political sphere, and society as a whole.

---

118. *Ronan Farrow: "Ce qui se passe autour de Roman Polanski et d'Adèle Haenel est pro-
metteur,"* LE MONDE, Nov. 18, 2019, https://www.lemonde.fr/societe/article/2019/11/18
/ronan-farrow-ce-qui-se-passe-autour-de-roman-polanski-et-d-adele-haenel-est-prometteur
_6019534_3224.html.

119. According to the Ministry of Justice, in 2016 just before #MeToo, of the 32,700
sexual assault claims processed, 73 percent of the cases were closed with no further action, *Le
toujours très difficile traitement des plaintes pour violences sexuelles*, LE MONDE, Nov. 6, 2019,
https://www.lemonde.fr/societe/article/2019/11/06/deux-ans-apres-metoo-le-difficile-traite
ment-des-plaintes-pour-violences-sexuelles_6018168_3224.html.

120. On November 23, 2019, 49,000 people marched in Paris, as well as in 30 other
cities in France, in protest against sexual violence and femicides (there have been 116 murders
in France since January 2019). The march was organized by an informal group on social media
using a new hashtag, #NousToutes [#All of Us], *Violences faites aux femmes: 49,000 personnes
défilent à Paris*, LE PARISIEN, Nov. 23, 2019, http://www.leparisien.fr/societe/violences-faites
-aux-femmes-des-milliers-de-personnes-defilent-dans-le-pays-23-11-2019-8200047.php.

121. M. Mercat-Bruns, *Systemic discrimination: rethinking the tools of gender equality*, 2
European Equality Law Review 1 (2018).

CHAPTER 9

#MeToo in Belgium: Confronting the Failure of Criminal Law

Emmanuelle Bribosia, Chloé Leroy, and Isabelle Rorive[1]

"Femme de la rue" and the First Signs of Awareness

According to a recent survey, 95 percent of women living in Belgium have already faced sexist behavior in public spaces and 94 percent in the work sphere. Furthermore, one out of two women has already been the victim of sexual assault on the street or in public transport.[2] If these numbers prove the magnitude of sexual harassment in Belgium, it is only recently that this phenomenon has been brought to the public's attention.

The launch of the documentary "Femme de la Rue" ("Woman of the Street") by Sofie Peeters in July 2012 became a turning point. In this thirty-minute short-film, Sofie Peeters films herself while walking in the streets of Brussels. Many men catcall her, follow her, insult her, and make comments and propositions that are sexual in nature. Once released, the documentary went viral. It has been criticized for presenting an ancient phenomenon as new, for inciting women to flee "bad" neighborhoods, and for designating men of Northern African origin as the main culprits of street harassment. Nevertheless, this documentary caused such a stir that a legislative response followed. The law aiming to combat sexism in public spaces was adopted on May 22, 2014 (see below).

While sexual harassment in public places had largely been ignored until 2012, Belgium has been part of the worldwide movement to fight gender

---

1. Emmanuelle Bribosia, Professor of Law and Vice-President of the Institute for European Studies; Isabelle Rorive, Professor of Law and President of the Centre Perelman for Legal Philosophy of the ULB; and Chloé Leroy, former PhD student and legal researcher, all at the Université de Bruxelles, Belgium.

2. *Sexisme, Bientôt Fini? Where Do We Stand on Sexism?*, JUMP, 2017, https://jump .eu.com/wp-content/uploads/2016/11/Full_Report-Sexisme-French_Englishweb.pdf.

inequality. Since 2001, a National Action Plan to combat domestic violence, female genital mutilation, forced marriages, honor-related violence, and sexual violence has been in place. Again in 2002, the fight against gender inequality in political representation became a matter of constitutional import. As part of that effort, a series of laws were enacted to ensure strict gender parity on the ballots. Since 2011, public companies and companies listed on the stock market have been required to implement quota systems to ensure that one-third of the board of directors are women. With females constituting 60 percent of graduates, all Belgian universities have adopted gender policies to ensure equal representation in the academic world. Furthermore, these last years, two inter-university Masters in Gender Studies were launched.[3]

Despite all those laws and policies, inequality levels remain high in real life, and have been extensively documented by statistics and gender benchmarks.[4]

A Comprehensive Legal Armory

Anti-discrimination Legislation Derived from European Law

The fight against sexual harassment has been part of Belgian anti-discrimination law for several decades. At the end of the 1990s, Belgium adopted a sophisticated legal framework to combat gender inequality in the workplace. Driven by the European Union, this framework was extended, at the early aughts, to goods and services. The prohibition of discrimination targets not only direct and indirect discrimination, but also harassment and the instruction to discriminate. The law distinguishes between sexual harassment and harassment on the basis of sex.[5] The law also provides for a shared burden of proof in the case of discrimination or harassment on the basis of sex: if the veracity of the claims of such behavior, established by the victim, can be presumed, it is for the respondent to prove that there has been no discrimination.

---

3. In 2014 for Dutch-speaking universities and in 2017 for French-speaking universities.

4. See last numbers published by the Belgian Institute for the Equality of Women and Men: Femmes et hommes en Belgique: Statistiques et indicateurs de genre (Institut pour l'Egalité des Femmes et Hommes, 3rd ed., 2018) https://igvm-iefh.belgium.be /fr/publications/femmes_et_hommes_en_belgique_statistiques_et_indicateurs_de_genre _troisieme_edition.

5. Harassment is defined as "where an unwanted conduct related to the sex of a person occurs with the purpose or effect of violating the dignity of a person and of creating an intimidating, hostile, degrading, humiliating or offensive environment." Sexual harassment has the same definition regarding "unwanted verbal, non-verbal or physical conduct of a sexual nature."

In addition to those classic tools, European Union law also put in place gender mainstreaming policies, as well as the creation of a gender equality body. In Belgium, this duty has been carried out since 2002 by the Institute for the Equality of Women and Men (IEWM), which collects and manages complaints of victims of discriminations on the grounds of sex, and which can initiate legal proceedings in defense of gender equality. In 2017, the IEWM received 295 complaints and brought twenty-six legal proceedings, 12 percent of the complaints concerned sexual harassment.

While Belgian antidiscrimination law provides for a high level of protection, it still suffers from a lack of effectiveness. Discrimination remain commonplace, and victims' access to justice is fraught with difficulties: lack of knowledge of their rights; high costs and the lengthiness of the procedures; fear of retaliation; and difficult burden of proof. The challenge for the authorities is no longer the adoption of new anti-discrimination legislation, but making sure existing laws are being enforced and facilitating access to justice.[6]

Ambitious Yet Ineffective Criminal Law

The criminal legal framework in Belgium is rather classic when it comes to sexual harassment. The Belgian Criminal Code prohibits voyeurism, indecent behavior, and rape.[7] These infractions, as well as procuring and bigamy, are included under the chapter relating to "crimes and offences against family order and public morality"; this title dates back to the adoption of the text in 1867. Insult and harassment are also infractions,[8] and the sentence can be doubled if the offence was motivated by the sex of the victim, which is then deemed an aggravating circumstance.[9]

The documentary of Sofie Peeters demonstrated the limited effectiveness of these provisions. Several measures have been taken to try to contain sexual harassment. As of September 2012, several cities, including Brussels, began allowing public officials to impose administrative fines up to €250 for sexist slurs in public spaces. At the federal level, Belgium was the first country in the

---

6. Françoise Tulkens & Marc Bossuyt, *Commission d'évaluation de la législation fédérale relative à la lutte contre les discriminations, Premier rapport d'évaluation*, Feb. 2017, https://www .unia.be/files/Documenten/Aanbevelingen-advies/Commission_d%C3%A9valuation_de _la_l%C3%A9gislation_f%C3%A9d%C3%A9rale_relative_%C3%A0_la_lutte_contre_les _discriminations.pdf.

7. Art. 371/1 to 378bis Criminal Code.

8. Art. 448 and 442bis Criminal Code.

9. Art. 453bis Criminal Code, inserted by 25 February 2003 pertaining to the combat of discrimination.

world to adopt legislation (the law of May 22, 2014) to combat sexism in public spaces. This law sought to reinvigorate the existing legal framework by proposing an autonomous criminalization of sexism, which is defined as any deed or behavior in a public[10] space that clearly seeks to express disdain toward another person due to their sex, or to consider them, for that same reason, inferior or essentially reduced to their sexual dimension, severely harming their dignity.

While it was very little debated in the Federal Parliament and a large majority voted in favor of it, the law has been heavily criticized since its adoption. The first problem was the restriction of the definition of sexism to acts aimed toward a particular person or group of persons. By doing so, the law disregards the possibility that the victim could be a more global group (hypothetically, all women), and not necessarily one particular woman. The law offers thus no remedy, for instance, against sexist jokes targeting women in general or against sexist advertisements.[11] This choice is not incidental. The antiracism act, for instance, condemns incitement to racial discrimination, violence or hatred, and the diffusion of ideas supporting racial supremacy.[12] It is therefore not necessary to have a particular victim.[13]

The effectiveness of this law has also been called into question from its inception. The creation of a new infraction to combat sexism was especially contested, since the most pressing need was an increase of police and judicial resources to apply the already existing laws. Lacking those, this new law would only lead to confusion of the population, frustration of victims, and a sense of impunity among perpetrators.[14] Finally, some people considered this law a threat to fundamental freedoms. As with the anti-discrimination laws, annulment of this law has been sought before the Constitutional Court, on grounds that it violates freedom of expression, the principle of legality of criminal offenses, the principles of equality and non-discrimination, and freedom of religion.[15]

---

10. The law mentions art. 444 of the Criminal Code, regarding behaviors that take place in meetings or public spaces; in the presence of several persons, in a place which is non-public but opened to a certain number of persons having the right to assemble and attend the place; in any place in the presence of the offended person and with witnesses; by printed or non-printed writings, pictures or symbols displayed, distributed or sold, offered for sale or exposed to public scrutiny; or by non-public writings addressed or communicated to several persons.

11. Franklin Kuty, *L'incrimination du sexisme*, 1 Rev. Dr. Pén. Crim. 41 (2015).

12. Law of July 30, 1981, on the punishment of certain acts inspired by racism or xenophobia.

13. Jimmy Charruau, *Une loi contre le sexisme? Étude de l'initiative belge*, 7 Rev. Dr. H. 1 (2015).

14. Kuty, *supra*, note 11.

15. Cour constitutionnelle, May 25, 2016, no. 72/2016.

Four years after the passage of the law aiming to combat sexism in public spaces, the results are mixed, to say the least. In 2016, only fifty complaints were filed based on this law, and the first conviction took place in November 2017. There are several reasons for this lack of effectiveness: first, the burden of proof is particularly difficult to support in cases of sexual harassment, and the trivialization of sexism discourages women from coming forward. Second, the law is often unknown to citizens: only half of women know they can file complaints of sexual harassment in public places and that this behavior can be punished by the law. Third, the small number of complaints that actually result in a sentence discourages victims from pressing charges, especially since interaction with the police can be a negative experience and lead to secondary victimization.

In conclusion, Belgium still struggles to efficiently combat sexual harassment, despite a developed legal framework, an Equality Body specifically dedicated to gender equality, and the adoption of a law aimed at combating sexism in public spaces. The Belgian State recently was condemned by the European Court of Human Rights due to the passivity of its authorities when handling rape charges.[16] The applicant had pressed charges against a colleague in 1998 for two counts of rape and indecent behavior. After a lengthy, ten-year procedure, the Council Chamber—an examining court—dismissed the case. The European Court of Human Rights considered that the passivity of the authorities compromised the investigation, which hadn't been led seriously or thoroughly. The European Court unanimously found the Belgian State violated Article 3 of the European Convention of Human Rights, which prohibits torture and inhuman and degrading treatment.

#MeToo, the Social Turmoil

From October16, 2017, the hashtag #MeToo was massively shared in Belgium, especially in Brussels and the Dutch-speaking part of the country. In the French-speaking part of Belgium, the hashtag #BalanceTonPorc, prompting women to publicly denounce their aggressors, was more popular starting on October 15. On October 17, 2017, both key words peaked in different search engines.

The debate mounted quickly. On October 23, 2017, an op-ed entitled "#MeToo, One Must Be Willing to Not See It"[17] was published in one of the

---

16. B.V. v. Belgique [May 2, 2017] Eur. Ct. H.R.

17. Florence Hainaut and Myriam Leroy, *#MeToo, pour ne rien voir, il faut le vouloir*, Le Soir, Oct. 23, 2017, https://plus.lesoir.be/120713/article/2017-10-23/carte-blanche-metoo -pour-ne-rien-voir-il-faut-le-vouloir.

main French-speaking news outlets. On November 9, 2017, three Care Centres for Victims of Sexual Violence were opened (which had been in the pipeline for a long time) and accommodated in a couple of months a much higher number of victims than expected, presumably because of #MeToo.

But #MeToo didn't elicit unanimity: on January 9, 2018, an opinion piece was published in the French newspaper *Le Monde*, called "Women Release Another Voice," [18] and was co-signed by several Belgian women, including an eminent university professor. This opinion piece saw in #MeToo a new form of puritanism, reducing women to "poor little things," and its release sparked a massive controversy, especially among Belgian academics.

Despite the criticism of the #MeToo movement, the testimonies of victims of sexual harassment and sexual assault rapidly increased in multiple sectors. Several female politicians, including the President of the Senate, denounced the sexist behavior of their male colleagues. The media are also concerned, and in November 2017, the Dutch-speaking part of the country was in shock when a star television presenter was dismissed on grounds of harassment.

The controversies continued when the Belgian Football Union announced at the end of November that rapper Damso would be writing the official Belgian Red Devils theme song for the 2018 World Cup. A feminist group condemned this choice, on the grounds that his songs were degrading and promoted violence against women. In March 2018, the Football Union announced they would no longer collaborate with Damso and said there would be no official World Cup song (which, in Belgium, is no small detail).

It is however in the artistic and cultural sphere that #MeToo had the greatest impact, when 150 people co-signed an open letter that led to the dismissal of the head of a Brussels theatre. This was followed by an important mobilization and a comprehensive reflection on the place of women in the performing arts, which lead to several initiatives in matters of policy and a profound reform of the Belgian artistic sector.

It is beyond doubt that the #MeToo movement has had a profound impact on Belgium. Testimonies, controversies, initiatives, and profound reflections in the academic, political, media, artistic, cultural, and sports communities: the contributions to civil society are countless.

However, #MeToo had very limited legal consequences in Belgium. The legal impact that followed the #MeToo movement in many countries had already happened in Belgium in 2012, following the "Woman of the Street" documentary. It is important to note, however, that the IEWM recorded a

---

18. *Des femmes libèrent une autre parole*, LE MONDE, Jan. 9, 2018, https://www .lemonde.fr/idees/article/2018/01/09/nous-defendons-une-liberte-d-importuner-indis pensable-a-la-liberte-sexuelle_5239134_3232.html.

post-#MeToo increase in reporting of sexism and sexual harassment as forms of discrimination, which certainly is no mere coincidence.[19]

The #MeToo movement did lay bare the inadequacies of Belgian law in terms of sexual harassment. A motion for resolution was submitted in February 2018, asking the Belgian government to proceed with an evaluation of the 2014 law to combat sexism in the public spaces. However, more than an evaluation of the law, the resolution insists on the need to raise public awareness about the dangers of sexism, to educate young people on gender equality, to support organizations in the field, and to train teachers, police officers, and workers in the legal and psycho-medical field, as well as workers in public transport, on sexual harassment.

And perhaps that is where the true challenge lies in matters of sexual harassment. It is unrealistic to expect that the law will solve a problem that is so ingrained in our culture and society. The solution does not lie in always more developed legal provisions, but in a profound change in our mentalities, which evolves from civil society. The problem cannot be reduced to sexual harassment, as that is grounded in the power relationship between men and women.[20] In Belgium, where 90 percent of chief executive officer positions are occupied by men, and where women are systematically a minority in decision-making circles, the fight against sexual harassment becomes more meaningful when it is part of a global movement of gender equality claims. And maybe this is #MeToo: denouncing the power imbalance between men and women in the public sphere, which mirrors social structures. If that is the case, it is probably more useful to wait for profound changes in the social dynamics initiated in the framework of the #MeToo movement, rather than for any legislative change, no matter how ambitious.

---

19. *Annual Report*, Institute for the Equality of Women and Men, 2017, https://igvm -iefh.belgium.be/sites/default/files/rapport_annuel_egalite_2017_fr_web.pdf.

20. Motion for resolution aiming at reinforcing combat against sexism in public spaces, *Doc.*, Sén., 2017-2918, no. 6-404/1. This motion for resolution has been introduced by members of the Socialist Party and was not voted before the end of the legislature.

CHAPTER 10

A Changing Landscape: Ireland and the #MeToo Movement

Ivana Bacik[1]

The Advent of the #MeToo Movement in Ireland

When news of the #MeToo movement hit Ireland in October 2017, there had already been significant public focus on gender discrimination in Irish society, notably in the arts sector. In November 2015, the grassroots campaign #WakingTheFeminists was formed by a group of women working in theatre to protest the male-dominated lineup in the Abbey (Irish National Theatre) centenary program marking 100 years since the 1916 Easter Rising, a formative moment in the birth of the Irish State. The campaign mobilized women in the arts, the media, and elsewhere to highlight discrimination, marginalization, and harassment issues.

In October 2017, directly inspired by #MeToo, writer/director Grace Dyas published online allegations of sexual harassment against the former director of another leading Dublin theatre, the Gate; more women then came forward publicly with similar allegations against him.[2]

---

1. Irish Labour Party Senator; Reid Professor of Criminal Law, Criminology and Penology, Trinity College, Dublin, Ireland.

2. See Kathy Sheridan, *Grace Dyas: "Do Nothing Until You Know Exactly What to Do,"* THE IRISH TIMES, Jan. 23, 2018, https://www.irishtimes.com/culture/stage/grace-dyas-do -nothing-until-you-know-exactly-what-to-do-1.3364626. The Gate commissioned a report, published in March 2018, that found that a culture existed in the theatre "whereby too much power was vested in one individual and people felt unable to speak out": Deirdre Falvey, *Release of Gate Report into Colgan Behaviour*, THE IRISH TIMES, Feb. 28, 2018, https://www.irishtimes .com/culture/stage/release-of-gate-report-into-colgan-behaviour-not-in-my-remit-expert -1.3408073. Allegations against one high-profile male presenter/comedian caused him to step aside from public performance and broadcasting: *Al Porter Sex Pest Claims*, THE TIMES, Nov. 18, 2017, https://www.thetimes.co.uk/article/al-porter-sex-pest-claims-6ds8q9jfn.

Until relatively recently, a culture of secrecy and repression around sex had persisted for many decades in Ireland, a country in which the Catholic Church has traditionally dominated public life and private ethics.[3] The power of the Church has been waning in recent years, as was powerfully symbolized in the passage of the marriage equality referendum in 2015 and the 2018 referendum to allow for legal abortion in Ireland.[4] This decline in the power of the Church has been particularly evident since the publication of reports documenting widespread sexual abuse of children in religious-run institutions.[5]

The true extent of sexual harassment and abuse is greatly under-reported, in Ireland as elsewhere.[6] The #MeToo Movement may well have influenced many victims and survivors to speak out for the first time about their abuse. Reports late in 2019 showed the number of sexual crimes reported to police reaching a record high, with speculation about the effect of #MeToo in bringing about this marked increase.[7]

The #MeToo movement was unlikely, however, to have been the only catalyst for upswing in reports of sexual abuse. The proceedings of a Belfast rape trial, in which the accused men were all well-known rugby players, dominated the Irish media over nine weeks in early 2018.[8] When the men were all acquitted, thousands came out on Dublin streets to protest at the verdict, using the hashtag #IBelieveHer. Though tried in Northern Ireland, the case was credited with generating Ireland's own #MeToo movement across the whole island.

Following the public outcry surrounding the verdict, the government initiated a review of the investigation and prosecution of sexual offenses, chaired

---

3. See, for example, DIARMUID FERRITER, OCCASIONS OF SIN: SEX AND SOCIETY IN MODERN IRELAND (2009).

4. Referendum on the Thirty-Fourth Amendment of the Constitution passed, May 2015; Referendum to repeal the Eighth Amendment to the Constitution, passed May 2018.

5. See, for example, the "Ryan Report": *Report of the Commission to Inquire into Child Abuse*, GOVERNMENT PUBLICATIONS, May 2009, http://www.childabusecommission.ie/rpt/.

6. See HANNAH MCGEE, REBECCA GARAVAN, MAIREAD DE BARRA, JOANNE BYRNE & RONAN CONROY, THE SAVI REPORT: SEXUAL ABUSE AND VIOLENCE IN IRELAND (2002), which found that while more than 25 percent of women had experienced contact sexual assault or unwanted non-contact sexual experiences as adults, only 8 percent had reported their experiences to the Gardaí (the Irish police).

7. Ian Begley, *Reporting of Sexual Offences Hits Record in Wake of #MeToo*, IRISH INDEPENDENT, Sept. 28, 2019, https://www.independent.ie/irish-news/reporting-of-sexual-offences-hits-record-in-wake-of-metoo-38542007.html; Conor Lally, *Sexual Crimes Reported to Gardaí Reach Record High, CSO Finds*, THE IRISH TIMES, Sept. 27, 2019, https://www.irishtimes.com/news/crime-and-law/sexual-crimes-reported-to-garda%C3%AD-reach-record-high-cso-finds-1.4032456.

8. Conor Gallagher, *Inside Court 12: The Complete Story of the Belfast Rape Trial*, THE IRISH TIMES, Mar. 28, 2018, https://www.irishtimes.com/news/crime-and-law/inside-court-12-the-complete-story-of-the-belfast-rape-trial-1.3443620.

by expert Tom O'Malley, to report on and recommend changes needed in the criminal justice system.[9] Thus, a general awareness now exists among policy-makers of the need to reform and update Irish law on sexual harassment and abuse.

Legal Protections

In October 2017, when the #MeToo movement made news, Ireland already had extensive laws against harassment and assault, although some clearly require updating in light of legal and political developments.

Criminal laws protect both men and women in Ireland against rape,[10] sexual assault,[11] and other forms of sexual abuse.[12] Sexual assault means an assault in circumstances of indecency; this would include acts of sexual groping or threatened groping, as well as any unwanted sexual contact or abuse that falls short of intercourse. Harassment (including sexual harassment) is criminalized under § 10 of the Non-Fatal Offences Against the Person Act 1997, defined as "persistently following, watching, pestering, besetting or communicating with" a person, so as to "seriously interfere" with their "peace and privacy" or to cause "alarm, distress or harm" to them.

Sexual harassment that does not fit the criminal definitions either of sexual assault or of harassment under § 10 of the 1997 Act can, however, be actionable under civil law. Under civil law all employers in Ireland have a legal duty of care under the Employment Equality Acts 1998-2015 and the Safety, Health

---

9. *Minister Flanagan Publishes Terms of Reference for Review of the Investigation and Prosecution of Sexual Offenses*, Dept. of Justice & Inequality, Sept. 7, 2018, http://www.justice .ie/en/JELR/Pages/PR18000279. A major review into trials of serious sexual offenses in Northern Ireland was conducted in 2019 by Sir John Gillen following the Belfast rape trial. See Sir John Gillen, *Report into the law and procedures in serious sexual offences in Northern Ireland: Recommendations*, GILLEN REVIEW, https://www.justice-ni.gov.uk/sites/default/files/publica tions/justice/gillen-report-recommendations.pdf.

10. The gender-specific offense of rape (requiring the perpetrator be male and the victim female) is criminalized under § 2 of the Criminal Law (Rape) Act 1981; a gender-neutral offence of rape (penetrative sexual assault) is criminalized under § 4 of the Criminal Law (Rape) (Amendment) Act 1990. See further TOM O'MALLEY, SEXUAL OFFENCES (2nd ed., 2013).

11. The offenses of sexual assault and aggravated sexual assault are criminalized under § 2 and § 3 of the Criminal Law (Rape) (Amendment) Act 1990.

12. A range of other sexual offenses are provided for in different legislation, for example the Criminal Law (Sexual Offences) Act 2017, which criminalizes certain behaviors under the heading "Sexual Exploitation of Children." Part 4 of the 2017 Act also reforms the law on prostitution, making it a criminal offence to purchase sex (while effectively decriminalizing those engaged in prostitution themselves).

and Welfare at Work Act 2005 to have adequate policies in place to ensure dignity at work is safeguarded.

The employment equality legislation covers nine different grounds of discrimination: gender, civil status (such as being single, married etc.), family status (parenting responsibility), sexual orientation, age, disability, race (including nationality), religious belief, and membership of the Traveller community.[13] Trade union membership, economic status, and political opinion are among the grounds not covered. Harassment based on any of the nine specified grounds is regarded as an unlawful form of discrimination related to conditions of employment.

Under Section 14A of the 1998 Act, harassment is defined as "any form of unwanted conduct related to any of the discriminatory grounds."[14] In the same section, sexual harassment is defined as covering "unwanted verbal, non-verbal of physical conduct of a sexual nature." To constitute either harassment or sexual harassment, the conduct must have "the purpose or effect of violating a person's dignity and creating an intimidating, hostile, degrading, humiliating or offensive environment for the person." The statutes protect employees and independent contractors and also cover third party harassment of an employee.

Other equality legislation (Equal Status Acts 2000-2015) covers consumers and protects them against sexual and other harassment on the same nine grounds in the provision of goods and services.[15]

Under the employment equality legislation, employees can file complaints of discrimination or harassment with the Workplace Relations Commission (WRC), which is a free service. Complaints must be brought within six months of the last act of harassment. This time limit can be increased to twelve months if "reasonable cause" for the delay can be shown. Complaints can be dealt with by mediation if both sides agree, or else will be dealt with by the WRC adjudication service. Remedies available from the WRC are back pay and compensatory damages. In addition, there are strong protections against victimization provided for in the Employment Equality Acts, so an employer cannot treat an employee badly for taking a claim or being a witness in a claim. The WRC also

---

13. See MARGUERITE BOLGER, CLAIRE BRUTON & CLIONA KIMBER, EMPLOYMENT EQUALITY LAW (2012). The Traveller Community is an indigenous Irish ethnic minority group, making up approximately 0.5 percent of the national population, whose culture and way of life, of which nomadism is an important factor, distinguishes them from the settled population; see www.itmtrav.ie (website of the Irish Traveller Movement).

14. § 14A of the 1998 Act (inserted by § 8 of the Equality Act 2004): "Harassment and Sexual Harassment."

15. Equal Status Acts 2000-2015. § 11of the 2000 Act (amended by § 51 of the Equality Act 2004) protects against sexual and other harassment in the provision of goods and services.

deals with complaints relating to harassment or discrimination under the Equal Status Acts.

The Code of Practice on Sexual Harassment and Harassment at Work, produced by the government in 2012, aims to give practical guidance to employees and employers on appropriate procedures for preventing and dealing with sexual harassment at work.[16] The Irish Human Rights and Equality Commission has a general remit to promote equality and can provide advice, and in some cases legal assistance, where a complainant brings a harassment claim before the WRC.

The Reality

Before the beginnings of the #MeToo movement, very few complaints of gender discrimination or sexual harassment were made each year. The Workplace Relations Commission annual report for 2018 discloses that only 13 percent of complaints made before it that year related to discrimination/equality grounds.[17] The report does not specify how many of these related specifically to claims of harassment. A total of 595 complaints were made under the Equal Status Acts, but it is notable that, while membership of the Traveller Community and race remain the two main most commonly cited discrimination grounds, there was a notable rise in gender-related claims between 2016 and 2017, and a small rise again in 2018.[18]

The 2018 report notes an enormous (116 percent) increase in the number of complaints brought under the Employment Equality Acts, from 671 in 2017 to 1,449 in 2018. Notably, while the number of gender-related employment claims rose by 61 percent from 2016 to 2017, they fell by 11 percent in 2018 (while claims based on age, religion, and/or disability rose that year).[19]

The 2018 report also provides a summary of two sexual harassment cases dealt with by the WRC that year. In the first, decided in March 2018, a car parts company was ordered to pay €46,000 compensation to a receptionist for the sexual harassment she had suffered; and in the second, decided in May 2018,

16. SI 208/2012; Employment Equality Act 1998 (Code of Practice) (Harassment) Order 2012.

17. *Workplace Relations Committee Annual Report 2018*, Workplace Relations Committee, https://www.workplacerelations.ie/en/news-media/workplace_relations_notices/annual-report-2018.pdf: 2,138 out of 15,451 complaints made.

18. The gender ground was only indicated in Equal Status Acts claims 20 times in 2016, but in 2017 it was cited on 101 occasions and in 2018 on 116 occasions.

19. The gender ground was indicated in an Employment Equality Acts' claim 219 times in 2016, and on 353 occasions in 2017.

a contact center company was ordered to pay a female technical support agent €35,000 compensation for harassment, and a further €10,000 for victimization. It is too soon to say whether the #MeToo movement is responsible for any rise in gender-related claims, given that at least some of these cases are known to include claims of harassment, but some commentators have speculated on its influence.[20]

Changes in the Law or Enforcement

In November 2017, inspired by #WakingTheFeminists and #MeToo, the Amplify Women group published a "Harassment Toolkit" for women experiencing sexual harassment in the workplace.[21]

The Irish Supreme Court's recent decision in *Hickey v. McGowan*[22] is likely to have a significant effect on sexual harassment law. The effect of the judgment is likely to broaden vicarious liability principles, under which employers are liable for the actions of their employees, including in cases of sexual abuse or sexual harassment. Previously, employees who suffered harassment had to prove that their employers had failed in an established duty of care toward them, for example by placing them in a dangerous situation or failing to introduce written anti-bullying polices. It appears however that the broader test would apply even outside day-to-day employment activities. For example, in the entertainment sector, it has been speculated that strict liability would now apply if harassment took place during auditions for a role.

In addition, recent legislative reforms through the Criminal Justice (Victims of Crime) Act 2017, the Criminal Law (Sexual Offences) Act 2017, and the Domestic Violence Act 2018 have strengthened protections for victims of violence, including gender-based violence, and have introduced new offenses

---

20. Kathy Sheridan, *The MeToo Movement Is Far From Over*, THE IRISH TIMES, Mar. 28, 2018, https://www.irishtimes.com/opinion/kathy-sheridan-metoo-movement-is-far-from-over-1.3442194, reporting on a case in which an Irish car parts company was ordered to pay €46,000 compensation to a receptionist who was sacked after refusing to have sex with her boss.

21. http://www.fishamble.com/uploads/1/1/3/7/113713777/wtf_harassment_tool kit_amplifywomen-1.pdf.

22. Hickey v. McGowan [2017] IESC 6 (Ireland); on February 9, 2017 the Supreme Court by a 4:1 majority found that a religious order was liable for sexual abuse of a child by a teacher in a school under its patronage, adopting the "close connection" test which tends to broaden the range of circumstances in which an employer may be liable for actions on the part of an employee, even in very extreme circumstances such as the sexual abuse in this case. The test is based upon whether there was a "close connection" between the acts in question and the work which the employee was engaged to perform.

concerning the purchase of sex;[23] and the crime of 'coercive control' within intimate relationships.[24]

Further legislative reform is also likely. In addition to the legal changes that may follow the publication of the O'Malley review, ongoing concerns have been expressed about the capacity of existing laws to challenge online harassment. Opposition politicians have put forward legislation to strengthen harassment offenses, and to criminalize cyber-bullying and so-called 'revenge porn' behaviors.[25] It is clear from these and other recent legal and political developments that the #MeToo, #WakingTheFeminists, and #IBelieveHer movements have undoubtedly helped to generate a renewed focus on laws and procedures to address the incidence of sexual harassment and abuse in Ireland.

---

23. Part 4 of the Criminal Law (Sexual Offences) Act 2017; §§ 25-27 "Purchase of Sexual Services."

24. § 39 of the Domestic Violence Act 2018.

25. The Labour Party's Harassment, Harmful Communications and Related Offences Bill 2017, passed Second Stage in the Dáil on January 31, 2018; see *Dáil Éireann Debate*, Oireachtais, Jan. 31, 2018, https://www.oireachtas.ie/en/debates/debate/dail/2018-01-31/28/.

CHAPTER 11

The #MeToo Movement in Italy: Chronicle of a Death Foretold?[1]

Costanza Hermanin[2] and Giorgia Serughetti[3]

Preamble: Why Italy Ought to Be a Centerpiece in #MeToo

Italy has something to do with the beginning of the #MeToo movement but is probably also among the countries where the movement encountered the strongest backlash.

This chapter analyses the relation of Italy to the beginning of #MeToo and then describes the societal and cultural characteristics that determined the emergence of Italy's specific provisions on sexual harassment and sexual violence. This background, together with the identification of the movement with Italian actress Asia Argento, help explain why #MeToo did not bring about positive change for harassment victims in Italy.

Unknown to most, two of the key figures among the women who determined the beginning of #MeToo, exposing sexual misconduct by movie director Henry Weinstein are Italian. The first, actress Asia Argento, is probably the best-known among the women who went on record with the *New Yorker* in the groundbreaking article by Ronan Farrow on October 10, 2017. The second is Ambra Battilana Gutierrez, the model who, back in 2015, reported Weinstein for sexual assault and worked with the New York City Police Department by wearing a wire in an attempt to extract a confession from him.

---

1. Paraphrasing Gabriel Garcia Márquez, winner of the 1982 Nobel Prize in Literature.

2. Costanza Hermanin, Visiting Professor at the Department of Political Science and International Affairs of John Cabot University, Rome.

3. Giorgia Serughetti, Research Fellow, Department of Sociology and Social Research, University of Milano-Bicocca.

But what is even less known is that, on October 13, 2017, before #MeToo became a worldwide phenomenon, another Italian woman, journalist Giulia Blasi, asked women to share on Twitter their experiences of sexual misconduct. The hashtag that Blasi used, *#quellavoltache*, translates the English phrase "that time when" and opened the door to 10,000 tweets in the space of a few hours.

One might think that these three brave Italian women were nurtured in a culture of respect and rejection of abuse of power and sexual violence.

Unfortunately, quite the opposite is true. Italy is a country where, until 1981, charges of rape could be dropped by legal authorities if a rape victim agreed to marry her rapist. Until 1996, furthermore, sexual violence was defined by law as an offense to public morals, not against sexual freedom and physical integrity.

Thus, social movements have mainly targeted violence against women, rather than harassment at the workplace, which only featured—and keeps being featured—as a secondary concern for many NGOs.

Data on female murders and domestic violence in Italy are amongst the most worrying in Western countries. According to the latest survey by the Italian National Institute of Statistics (ISTAT),[4] violence affects about one in three women between sixteen and seventy years old: 6.8 million women have suffered some form of physical or sexual violence during their lives. In 41 percent of the cases (2.8 million) violence was committed by partners or former partners. The latter group, along with relatives and friends, is responsible for most of the more serious violence, such as rape and physical violence.

Violence against women is still a largely hidden phenomenon. A high percentage of women do not speak to anyone about the violence they have suffered, do not report it (reporting rates cover 12.2 percent of partner violence and 6 percent of non-partner violence), and do not seek help. According to ISTAT, women do not report such abuse because they believe they can handle the situation by themselves or they think that the fact is not serious.[5] But also, they do not report for fear of retaliation, shame and embarrassment, or distrust in law enforcement agencies.

Although the first anti-violence centers run by women date back to the 1980s, and women have mobilized against violence since then, the cultural obstacles to the emergence of an anti-violence movement remain very high. This also has implications for the possibility of bringing cases of sexual harassment within #MeToo and beyond.

---

4. *Violenza dentro e fuori la famiglia*, ISTAT, https://www4.istat.it/it/violenza-sulle -donne/il-fenomeno/violenza-dentro-e-fuori-la-famig.

5. *Ibid.*

Moreover, this cultural reluctance also explains why the most significant feminist movements in Italy have focused on the issue of violence against women from the start. This is the case of *Non Una di Meno* (NUDM—"Not one woman fewer"), which since 2017 has organized major public events on the International Day for the Elimination of Violence against Women (November 25) and International Women's Day (March 8).[6] Since the beginning of the #MeToo campaign, NUDM has sought to forge a link with it and supporting an effort to turn it into a collective battle through the slogan "WeTo(o)gether." However, this was not enough to prevent the extreme specificity of #MeToo, which was reduced to the personal stories of its best-known characters.

Legislative Loopholes and the Limits of Criminalization

Criminal Law

The pervasive nature of violence against women has had an effect on Italian legislation as well. Over the past decades, criminal law and jurisprudence on different forms of violence, including sexual violence and stalking, has evolved to a much greater extent than civil norms on harassment at work.

The real turning point was 1996 when, as mentioned earlier, the present criminal law framework was enacted. The three basic features of this legislation[7] have been very relevant also in the context of #MeToo. The legislation implies, first, that rape and other forms of sexual violence can only be prosecuted following a complaint, and not *ex officio*. Second, the complaint needs to be filed within six months from the assault. Third, a victim cannot withdraw a complaint of sexual violence—even to avoid consequences of victimization or intimidation by the perpetrator. Although some, especially in the context of #MeToo, have criticized the six-month deadline as too restrictive, some feminist lawyers accept it as a reasonable safeguard against false complaints and blackmail. Penalties for sexual violence range from five to ten years in prison.

The boundaries between sexual violence and sexual harassment are blurred under the present penal law framework. Sexual harassment does not feature as such in the Criminal Code; thus, case law takes as a reference Article 660 on "Simple Threats." In addition, the Supreme Court of Cassation has provided a

---

6. Rachel Martin, *Non Una di Meno: Exploring the Women's Strikes in Italy*, Ms. Magazine, Mar. 29, 2017, https://msmagazine.com/2017/03/29/non-una-di-meno-exploring-womens-strikes-italy/.

7. Law 66/1996.

broad interpretation of the notion of "sexual violence,"[8] for example, defining as attempted sexual violence to include acts that do not imply physical contact.[9]

In judgment no. 2742/2010, the Supreme Court established that "vulgar expressions with a sexual background, or invasive and insistent courtship acts, other than sexual abuse, are to be considered sexual harassment." In a prior case, it had specified that harassment can be equated "with all those behaviors, sexually connoted, different from sexual abuse, which go beyond complimenting a woman or proposing a personal relationship."[10]

A 2009 Law Decree established stalking as a distinct offense. Article 612 bis of the Criminal Code defines stalking as "repeated conduct that threatens or harasses anyone in a way that causes a persistent and severe state of anxiety or fear, or a well-founded alarm for the safety of one's own, or of a close relative, or of a person connected to him by an emotional relationship, or that forces one to alter his own habits of life." Different from harassment and sexual violence, stalking can be prosecuted *ex officio* in specific cases. When compared to harassment and sexual violence, the distinctive element of stalking as an offense is its psychological impact on the victim. Criminal statistics of the past years have shown a strong correlation between stalking and sexual harassment. According to a 2014 research by the Ministry of Justice on first instance rulings based on Article 612 bis, in 91 percent of the cases the convicted stalker is a man, in 74 percent of the cases a former partner, and in half of the cases the stalker's goal was to get back in a sentimental relationship with the victim.[11]

Last, in 2013, the Italian government adopted through an emergency procedure a Law Decree (later voted by Parliament into Law 119/2013), dubbed the "Law on Femicide." The government acted after statistics showed that, at least after 2000, Italy registered one murder perpetrated by a man on a woman every third day, bringing Italy closer to Mexico than to its European counterparts. The Law on Femicide addresses violence against women in general, not just murder, and increases penalties for crimes. It establishes preventive measures as well as programs specific to female victims of violence. To date, unfortunately, it has not changed the death rate significantly.[12]

---

8. Art. 609-bis of the Criminal Code.

9. Cassazione Penale No. 38719/2012.

10. Cassazione Penale No. 27762/2008.

11. *Indagine statistica attraverso la lettura dei fascicoli dei procedimenti definiti con sentenze di primo grado*, MINISTRY OF JUSTICE, 2014, https://webstat.giustizia.it/Analisi%20 e%20ricerche/2014%20-%20Rilevazione%20procedimenti%20di%20Stalking.pdf.

12. According to law enforcement data acquired by the Parliamentary Committee of Inquiry on Femicide (Final Report, 6 February 2018), the number of murders with female victims decreased slightly between 2011 and 2016, albeit with an inconstant trend: 170 in 2011, 161 in 2012, 180 in 2013, 153 in 2014, 143 in 2015, 149 in 2016. However, the rate of decrease

Civil Law

Up until 2005, sexual harassment did not have a space in civil law. Thus, a victim of sexual harassment could only resort to criminal charges for sexual violence or general harassment in order to seek redress. It is thanks to European Union anti-discrimination law that the Italian Code of Equal Opportunities includes harassment as a legal category. A first EU Directive[13] established penalties for sexual harassment at the workplace and in employment more generally. A few years thereafter, EU Directive 2006/54 and a new Legislative Decree (5/2010), expanded the scope of this legislation to include harassment experienced during access to public services. This includes, for instance, sexual harassment at school or in public transportation. Alongside harassment, the latest definition of gender-based direct and indirect discrimination have been included in the National Code for Equal Opportunities and in a new article of the Civil Code, Article 2087.

In the National Code, sexual harassment is defined as "any form of unwanted verbal, non-verbal or physical conduct of a sexual nature that has the purpose or effect of violating the dignity of a person, in particular when creating an intimidating, hostile, degrading, humiliating or offensive environment." The Italian definition uses the adjective *unwanted*, not *unwelcome*.

Women can thus sue perpetrators, who can be held individually liable, as well as companies for failing to protect them, in civil courts and benefit from strong protection from retaliation. With Ruling 7097 of 2018, the Labor Section of the Supreme Court of Cassation decided that the employer is jointly responsible with the perpetrator if it does not take action to prevent sexual harassment to the detriment of a worker. In keeping with European Union law, claimants can benefit from a shift in the burden of proof, and trade unions and local gender counselors (a network of about 100 public officials) can stand in support or on behalf of them in court or through alternative dispute resolution. The 2018 Budget Law (No. 2015/2017) also established that no one can be dismissed, transferred, or demoted before or after filing a complaint for sexual harassment. It also established incentives for companies who hire victims of gender violence.

But as civil legislation on sexual harassment is very recent the hurdles are many.

(–14%) is much lower than the total number of homicides (–39%). Moreover, extrapolating only the data of homicides committed within the family (which are the vast majority for those with female victims), an even smaller downward trend can be observed: 124 (2011), 112 (2012), 125 (2013), 117 (2014), 111 (2015), 111 (2016).

13. Directive 2002/73, transposed with Legislative Decree 145/2005.

The main hurdle is awareness of the civil laws' existence: women still resort to criminal charges of sexual violence, and very few cases based on recent civil provisions have yet reached the higher courts.

There is also a frequent misuse of the legal terminology used to refer to sexual harassment in official documents as well as in statistics and in the media. For instance, journalists tend to prefer the term mobbing, as well as the notion of "stalking at the workplace," which they use interchangeably with harassment. Such a confusion in terminology hampers a victim, rather than helping her.

Prevention

With respect to prevention, only very few companies, mainly multinationals, have designed procedures or identified people to whom a worker can report sexual harassment. In 2007, the main business and trade union confederations of Europe (ETUC, BUSINESSEUROPE, UEAPME, and CEEP)[14] signed a framework agreement on harassment and violence at work. It concerned the implementation, Europe-wide, of specific procedures and practices in the workplace.[15] The framework agreement is an official document issued by the European Social Dialogue and formally transmitted to the main institutions of the European Union.[16]

Although all of the signatories have Italian members, the Italian Confederation of Industry and the three main trade unions took almost ten years to transpose the European framework into a national agreement.[17] Some have explained this delay saying that "the Italian industrial structure is characterized

---

14. European Trade Union Confederation, Business Europe, Union européenne de l'artisanat et des petites et moyennes entreprises, European Centre of Employers and Enterprises Providing Public Services.

15. The agreement requires enterprises to have a clear statement against harassment and specific procedures to target emerging cases. It also determines that the responsibility to prevent and target harassment rests with the employer.

16. *Communication from the Commission to the Council and the European Parliament transmitting the European framework agreement on harassment and violence at work*, Commission of the European Communities, August 11, 2007, 686, http://www.europarl.europa.eu /hearings/20071121/femm/framework_agreement_en.pdf.

17. *Accordo su molestie e violenza sui luoghi di lavoro*, Tra Confindustria e CGIL, CISL e UIL, Jan. 25, 2016. http://www.cgil.it/admin_nv47t8g34/wp-content/uploads/2016/01 /Accordo_su_molestie_e_violenza_luoghi_lavoro_25.01.2016.pdf.

by small and micro businesses, for whom it is not straightforward to implement internal procedures, as compared to large and well-structured companies."[18]

In addition to the ten-year delay, the signatories did not add any specificity to its original provisions. As of today, it has been simply translated word-by-word, a fact that further stresses the limited relevance of the document.

#MeToo Gets to Italy

When #MeToo got to Italy, papers mainly attacked Argento and other women speaking out, by frontloading pictures of them kissing or hugging Weinstein under titles such as "the slow memory of divas."[19] The baseline was: they knew what they were doing and they were looking for it.

What is most striking, is that this #MeToo backlash did not come from men only. Many, perhaps most, Italian women openly engaged in some form of stigmatization of victims of sexual violence in the context of #MeToo.

In Italy, the letter by French actress Catherine Deneuve (who later retracted her statement)[20] has galvanized not only those who denounced the risks of summary justice when men are accused of harassment, but also the vast array of those who characterized #MeToo as a moralist and puritanical movement, carried on by privileged women whose problems are of no interest to the vast majority of the female population.

This was not, however, the political significance of the chorus of complaints that arose within the campaign, according to the feminist movements that have looked positively at #MeToo. Indeed, they have often pointed out that, rather than a question of sexual morality, a major political and social issue was at stake: the power relations between men and women in a country where the employment gap is of almost 20 percentage points—one of the highest in the European Union, and mean monthly earnings of men are 18 percent higher than those of women.[21] In an economic system and a job market afflicted by

---

18. European Commission, *Study on the implementation of the autonomous framework agreement on harassment and violence at work*, 2016, https://ec.europa.eu/social/BlobServlet?docId=16191&langId=en.

19. *Le violenze di Harvey Weinstein: l'ambizione rallenta la memoria delle dive*, Affaritaliani.it, Oct. 11, 2017, http://www.affaritaliani.it/cronache/le-violenze-di-harvey-weinstein-l-ambizione-rallenta-la-memoria-delle-dive-503809.html also one of the main Italian newspapers, La Repubblica, published similar titles and the same picture.

20. *Nous défendons une liberté d'importuner, indispensable à la liberté sexuelle*, Le Monde, Jan. 9, 2018 https://www.lemonde.fr/idees/article/2018/01/09/nous-defendons-une-liberte-d-importuner-indispensable-a-la-liberte-sexuelle_5239134_3232.html.

21. EIGE, *Gender Equality Index 2019: Italy*.

such visible inequalities, the problem of harassment ceases to be an individual fact but takes on structural features.

This structural reality is what was claimed by more than one hundred actresses and show-business workers who signed in February 2018 the *Dissenso comune* (Common Dissent) manifesto.[22] Even though the manifesto came out embarrassingly late, months after the outbreak of the Weinstein case, it had the merit of clarifying the systematic nature of the problem:

> Sexual harassment is a transversal phenomenon. It is a system. It is part of an arrangement under the eyes of all, one that contemplates the absolute male majority in places of power, the difference in compensation for equal work, the constant and permanent sexualization of workspaces. Gender inequality in workspaces makes women, all women, at risk of harassment because they are always subjected to implicit blackmail. It happens to the secretary, the worker, the immigrant, the student, the intern, the domestic helper. It happens to everyone.

In fact, far from being a problem that afflicts show business alone, harassment in Italy is widespread in all working environments: a survey by ISTAT (2018) estimates that there are 1.404 million women (8.9 per cent of the 14-65 age group) who have suffered physical harassment or sexual blackmail in the workplace during their lifetime; 425,000 (2.7 percent) in the last three years. The survey also reports that 1.173 million women (7.5 percent) have been victims of sexual blackmail throughout their lives in order to be employed, to maintain their jobs, or to obtain career progressions; 167,000 women have suffered these forms of blackmail in the last three years (1.1 percent).[23]

In the course of their lives, female employees with college degrees appear to be the most susceptible to harassment or sexual blackmail at work. Over the last three years, it has been more common for a woman to be blackmailed, either in order to be hired or to keep her job, if she is an employee (37.6 percent and 39.4 percent, respectively) or a skilled worker in the trade and services sector (30.4 percent and 34.9 percent) than in other cases. In nearly all the cases, the perpetrator of sexual blackmail of women is a man.[24]

---

22. *Lettera al Presidente della Republica Sergio Mattarella*, Bridge, Feb. 2018, http://dissensocomune.it.

23. *Le molestie e i ricatti sessuali sul lavoro*, Istat, 2018, https://www.istat.it/it/files/2018/02/statistica-report-MOLESTIE-SESSUALI-13-02-2018.pdf.

24. *Ibid.*

The Forms of the Backlash

"In Italy, #MeToo Is More Like 'Meh'" was the title of a *New York Times* article dated December 16, 2017.[25] In the United States, the mobilization has triggered a historic change, and for this reason has been recognized as a revolution of similar scope to the great movements of the late sixties. In contrast, in Italy, it appears buried under a blanket of disinterest, almost a loud yawn.

Not only that, but in the pages of Italian newspapers and on television, to defuse the destabilizing charge of women's speech, #MeToo has been made the object of derision, biting attitudes of "mansplaining," or discredit.

The particular discrediting commitment on this front of the right-wing press, traditionally in favor of Silvio Berlusconi, has given rise to suspicions that the former prime minister's return to the limelight has had an influence on the backlash.[26] Between 2009 and 2011, Berlusconi himself was accused of several abuses of power aimed at obtaining sexual favors from young women.[27]

But many skeptical or openly denialist voices have been raised, even in liberal newspapers and magazines. The main rhetoric has been one about the end of courtship, seduction, desire.

So, for example, the comedian Enrico Brignano declared to *Corriere della Sera*: "We are men, we like women, if a woman does not say no, it means she agrees to it."[28] Singer Francesco De Gregori went on record with *Vanity Fair* affirming that: "The discussion has taken an absurd turn, muddling things. Stalking, harassment and violence are areas other than courtship. I will never be convinced that a hand that touches the leg of a friend of yours at the cinema is to be sanctioned with jail."[29]

---

25. Jason Horowitz, *In Italy, #MeToo is More Like 'Meh'*, N.Y. TIMES, Dec. 16, 2017, https://www.nytimes.com/2017/12/16/world/europe/italy-sexual-harassment.html.

26. Simona Siri, *Having a misogynist leader has consequences. And no, I don't mean Trump*, THE WASH. POST, Dec. 14, 2017, https://www.washingtonpost.com/news/global -opinions/wp/2017/12/14/the-MeToo-movements-disturbing-failure-in-italy/?noredirect =on&utm_term=.ff4fee0ecd5c.

27. Tara John, *Italy's Silvio Berlusconi Is Back in the Spotlight and So Are His Sexist Comments. Here Are Some of His Worst*, TIME, Mar, 1, 2018, https://time.com/5179379 /italy-silvio-berlusconi-sexist-remarks-women/.

28. Chiara Maffioletti, *La versione di Brignano: "Condanno le molestie ma le fake news esistono,"* CORRIERE DELLA SERA, Dec. 17, 2017, https://www.corriere.it/spettacoli/17 _dicembre_11/versione-enrico-brignano-comico-cinepanettone-film-poveri-ricchissimi -fausto-brizzi-accuse-molestie-ma-fake-news-esistono-2738873a-dde0-11e7-8c94-7eddeb 8854ff.shtml.

29. Malcom Pagani, *Francesco De Gregori: Non è più tempo di raccontarsi storie*, VANITY FAIR, Dec. 9, 2017, https://www.vanityfair.it/music/storie-music/2017/12/09/francesco-de -gregori-intervista-canzoni.

Other recurring topics in the newspapers cast #MeToo as a witch hunt and condemned "media trials" of men accused of harassment. However, the only damage during #MeToo was suffered by those women who raised their voices and made accusations.

The most prominent high-profile men accused of sexual misconduct in Italy were Giuseppe Tornatore and Fausto Brizzi, both movie directors. About ten women told very similar stories on television about being harassed by the latter during film auditions, and his name was removed from the posters for his movie *Poveri ma ricchissimi*. A week later, however, the controversy seemed to have died down in the mainstream press. Some months later, Brizzi was cleared by the court of all charges. As for Tornatore, accused by the actress Miriana Trevisan, the world of cinema was solidly behind him, while Trevisan was accused of being out only for the publicity.[30]

This state of affairs led Simona Siri to state in the *Washington Post*, that: "Instead of having their voices amplified, Italian women supporting the #MeToo movement are constantly mocked online by men and even other women who see them as uptight feminists."[31]

The Barriers

According to the above mentioned ISTAT survey (2018), in 80.9 percent of cases women who suffer from sexual blackmail in the workplace do not talk about it with anyone. Only 15.8 percent of those who have been blackmailed in their lifetime reported their experience and spoke about it mainly with colleagues (8.2 percent), rather than the employer (4.1 percent), managers or workplace administrators (3.3 percent), or with trade unions (1.0 percent). Almost none have reported to the police.[32]

Why do women not report what happened? According to the ISTAT report, in many cases (27.4 percent) the women did not report what happened because: the incident was not considered a serious one; they lacked confidence in the police (23.4 percent); they chose not to accept blackmail and instead quit their jobs (19.8 percent); they decided to deal with the situation by themselves or with the help of family members (18.6 percent); or they feared being judged and treated badly at the time of reporting (12.7 percent). Looking at the data

---

30. Gloria Satta, *Tornatore difeso dalle sue attrici: "É un signore, accuse improbabili,"* Il Messaggero, Nov. 5, 2017, https://www.ilmessaggero.it/pay/edicola/giuseppe_tornatore _difeso_dalle_sue_attrici_e_un_signore_accuse_improbabili-3346062.html.

31. Siri, *supra*, note 26.

32. *Le molestie e i ricatti sessuali sul lavoro, supra*, note 23.

for the last three years prior to the survey, the percentage of those who did not report because they consider the episode to be minor (18 percent) decreased: an indication of raising awareness of the fact that such practices are unfair, abusive, and intimidating.[33]

The barriers that prevent the reporting of cases of harassment and sexual blackmail in the workplace are thus many. They include the lack of adequate support and procedures, but also the costs—both economic and emotional—of civil and criminal cases. Prejudices toward accusers and a low propensity to give victims credibility often make police investigations and court proceedings a secondary victimization experience for women.

In 1979, the documentary "Processo per stupro" (*Rape trial*), which was broadcast on national public television, revealed for the first time how the victim, in proceedings for sexual violence, could be transformed into a defendant. Today, although awareness of the problem of violence against women has grown considerably, it is not uncommon for women to be exposed to new traumas in the course of trials. A recent example of this is the recent case of two American students who, in Florence, accused two *carabinieri* (military police) of rape, and for this reason found themselves subjected to a twelve-hour interrogation by the defendants' lawyers, and obliged to answer a number of degrading and offensive questions.[34]

The risks of secondary victimization are certainly a disincentive for victims to bring their cases to justice. This is particularly true when there is a clear imbalance of power between the claimant and the offender, as the latter can deploy much greater means of defense than those available to the victim to present her case.

Counterclaims for defamation or slander can also constitute significant barriers. For example, the actress Miriana Trevisan, mentioned earlier, was indicted for defamation in 2018 after she spoke of harassment in show business, accusing the film producer Massimiliano Caroletti.[35]

But an even more important risk, for cases of harassment and sexual blackmail in the workplace, is the fragility of the position held by women in precarious jobs. In particular, for younger workers (fifteen to thirty-four years old), one in three women holds a temporary job or freelances and is therefore not covered

---

33. *Ibid.*

34. Barbie Latza Nadeau, *They Accused Cops of Rape. Then the Smear Campaign Began*, THE DAILY BEAST, Sep. 12, 2017, https://www.thedailybeast.com/they-accused-cops-of-rape-then-the-smear-campaign-began.

35. Adnkronos, *Miriana Trevisan a processo*, Oct. 11, 2018, https://www.adnkronos.com/fatti/cronaca/2018/10/11/miriana-trevisan-processo_J7tdIECgKRt92Z0nAjFL3H.html.

even by the measures that are intended to protect claimants from retaliatory dismissals.[36]

Social Movements

Faced with the state of affairs described so far, many associations and groups in Italy are working for change. However, they clash with strong resistance in the corporate world, the media, show business, and the growing hostility of politics.

As seen above, the #MeToo campaign has found relevant support in a feminist movement that for some years now has experienced a new vitality. Feminism in Italy has often been described as a discontinuity,[37] a movement that appears and reappears in alternate phases, mobilizing its many and diverse currents against threats to women's freedom or advancing new visions and political practices. Violence against women has been one of the most significant targets in recent years.

The anti-violence centers and women's shelters, originated from the experience of feminism, play a prominent role in the fight against gender-based violence, acting as essential nodes in the network to support victims as well as to prevent and fight abuse. Centers and shelters, which are currently number over 550,[38] help women to recognize violence in relationships and offer legal, psychological and social support. They also aim at fostering cultural change and advocate for more effective policies at both the national and the local level.

Although workplace harassment is not the main focus of anti-violence centers and women's shelters, they present themselves as a reference point also for women affected by this type of abuse. The president of the D.i.Re. network, which brings together 80 anti-violence centers in Italy, declared in October 2017: "We are with Asia [Argento], with the Swedish ministresses who denounced harassment at the European Summits, with the athletes abused to gain access to the Olympics, with all the women who overcome silence even

---

36. ISTAT, *Young people into the labour market*, 2017, https://www.istat.it/en/archivio/205090.

37. Consuelo Corradi and Daniela Bandelli, *Women's Movements and Policies to Fight Gender Violence. Analyzing Political and Social Factors in Italy*, 1 SOCIOLOGIA E POLITICHE SOCIALI, 27-43 (2018).

38. See *Centri antiviolenza e case rifugio*, ISTAT, https://www4.istat.it/it/violenza-sulle-donne/la-fuoriuscita/centri-antiviolenza.

within their home, freeing themselves from the fear and shame of the violence they suffered."[39]

Other important actors are trade unions, which in recent years have increased their activism on this matter and have stimulated policies to combat sexual harassment in various business sectors.

However, bottom-up activism and organizations have to confront an ever more visible and widespread hostility toward gender equality, civil rights, and progressive social transformation.[40] The government in office in Italy in 2018-2019, composed of two parties frequently defined as "populist" (the League and the Five Star Movement), promoted a political agenda that opposed the rights and freedoms that women gained over the past 50 years.

The most striking example of this retrenchment is the bill on the reform of child custody in the event of separation promoted by League Senator Simone Pillon, a prominent character in an integralist or identity-based Catholicism that leads battles against "gender ideology" and against legal and assisted abortion.[41] The draft law enshrines the end of consensual separation; requires family mediation; abolishes the maintenance allowance for the poorer parent (generally the woman); and ignores the problem of intra-family violence, forcing children to stay with their fathers even when they are accused of violence by the mother (without any consideration for the problem of minors witnessing domestic violence). The ultimate aim of the bill does not seem to be to ensure fairer separations, but rather to harm women who intend to divorce, to make divorce an increasingly inconvenient option, and therefore to restore a *de facto* indissoluble marriage.

The then Minister for the Family, Lorenzo Fontana, is also a promoter of the "traditional family" model—the heterosexual, married, white family—against what he describes as a feminist, homosexual, and multiculturalist "drift." He is another active opponent of the law that legalized abortion in Italy.

In this political climate, the transformative demands of feminism, in its many expressions, find it increasingly hard to bring about change at the political and legislative level.

---

39. *Ricatti sessuali nello sport, nella politica, nello spettacolo. I Centri Antiviolenza al fianco delle donne*, Di.Re., Oct. 26, 2017, https://www.direcontrolaviolenza.it/ricatti-sessuali -nello-sport-nella-politica-nello-spettacolo-centri-antiviolenza-al-fianco-delle-donne/.

40. See Jane Fae, *As Italy indulges a nationalist agenda, women's rights are being steadily eroded*, THE INDEPENDENT, Dec. 22, 2018, https://www.independent.co.uk/news/long_reads /italy-womens-rights-abortion-gender-equality-feminism-lega-politics-a8690541.html.

41. Anna Lavizzari and Massimo Prearo, Massimo, *The anti-gender movement in Italy: Catholic participation between electoral and protest politics*, EUROPEAN SOCIETIES, 1-21 (2018).

Conclusion

In a sense, the large debate around the #MeToo movement in Italy ended up almost backfiring. It unveiled the persistence of a sexist culture despite the evolution of the law.

What should then activist do, in this context? The first thing is acknowledging this (provisional) failure and research its deep causes. Second, they should also work through the international movement and mount pressure to expose the peculiarity of their country. Last, but first, is fighting for education. To date, everything that discusses sex and gender at school has been almost totally barred in the name of an alleged Catholic morality.

In conclusion, what some brave Italian women did at the very beginning of the #MeToo campaign was probably driven more by total resentment of their native culture, rather than empowerment. Unfortunately, #MeToo was then met mainly with skepticism and defiance in Italy. Nonetheless, in a context where equality, abortion, and divorce are cast into doubt on the global stage, our hope is that women's movements will again join forces. Not only to preserve and enforce the existing law, but also to walk that further step that Italy did not make thanks to #MeToo.

CHAPTER 12

Silent Women? Non-Disclosure Agreements and the #MeToo Movement in the United Kingdom

Aileen McColgan[1]

In October 2017, the Harvey Weinstein scandal generated domestic #MeToo headlines when Weinstein's former UK assistant, Zelda Perkins, first revealed harassment she suffered by Weinstein in 1998, as well as Weinstein's sexual assault of a fellow Miramax worker. Perkins detailed how the two women had been subjected to extraordinary pressure by Miramax's UK law firm to sign a non-disclosure agreement (NDA) in 1998 when they resigned from their jobs, silencing their exposure of Weinstein's conduct for decades.[2] Perkins later told Parliament's Women and Equality Committee that Weinstein had been physically present at the 1998 post-employment discussions between the two women and Miramax. Negotiations had taken place over several occasions, including a twelve-hour session that ended at 5:00 A.M., and neither woman was permitted to retain a copy of the NDA, whose terms included a requirement that the women use their best efforts not to disclose anything in any criminal proceedings that might be taken against Weinstein.[3]

The Perkins case has not been the only example of #MeToo outrage focused on the operation of NDAs. In January 2018, the *Financial Times* sent several female journalists to work as undercover waitresses at a men-only

---

1. Aileen McColgan, 11 KBW and Leeds School of Law.

2. Matthew Garrahan, *Harvey Weinstein: How Lawyers Kept a Lid on Sexual Harassment Claims*, FINANCIAL TIMES, Oct 23, 2017, https://www.ft.com/content/1dc8a8ae-b7e0-11e7-8c12-5661783e5589.

3. WOMEN AND EQUALITIES COMMITTEE, SEXUAL HARASSMENT IN THE WORKPLACE, 2017-19, HC 725, 39-40 available at https://publications.parliament.uk/pa/cm201719/cmselect/cmwomeq/725/725.pdf.

fundraising "President's Club" dinner, held annually in London. Dinner organizers instructed the all-female waiting staff to dress in skimpy black outfits with
matching underwear and high heels and required the women to sign NDAs
in advance of the evening. The *Financial Times* reported that guests sexually
harassed and assaulted many of the staff members. Attendees included leading
names in the UK's business, media, legal, and political spheres.[4]

Parliament's Women and Equalities Committee concluded in July 2018
that NDAs had been used unethically by some employers and lawyers to silence
victims of sexual harassment, and that there was insufficient oversight and regulation of their use.[5] The Committee accepted that NDAs could be appropriate in settlements of sexual harassment claims if a "victim makes the judgment
that signing an NDA is genuinely in their own best interests, perhaps because it
provides a route to resolution that they feel would entail less trauma than going
to court, or because they value the guarantee of privacy." But, the Committee
expressed grave concerns about the widespread and unethical use of NDAs
"to silence victims of sexual harassment in the workplace" from reporting serious wrongdoing to the police, assisting with criminal investigations or prosecutions, and discussing matters of public interest. The Committee referenced
fears of criminal prosecution expressed by women who had signed NDAs and
demanded that the legal professions' regulators "demonstrate that [lawyers]
will face serious sanctions if they sexually harass clients or colleagues or if they
misuse NDAs to silence victims of sexual harassment." The Committee recommended a variety of legal changes to require that NDAs be clear, that they set
out the disclosures that signatories are legally entitled to make, that the scope
of permissible disclosures be extended, and to make it an offense for employers
and their professional advisers "to propose a confidentiality clause designed or
intended to prevent or limit the making of a protected disclosure or disclosure
of a criminal offence."

In October 2018, the Women and Equalities Committee published a
report on the sexual harassment of women and girls in public places.[6] It found
that sexual harassment "affects the lives of nearly every woman in the UK,"
with many experiencing it routinely, serving to "affect[] women's behaviour and
choices and restrict[] their freedom to be in public spaces." The Committee
called for the introduction of a "comprehensive plan or programme of work"

4. See, e.g., Madison Marriage, *Men Only: Inside the Charity Fundraiser Where Hostesses Are Put on Show*, FINANCIAL TIMES, Jan. 23, 2018, https://www.ft.com/content/075d679e-0033-11e8-9650-9c0ad2d7c5b5; *Presidents Club: Scandal-Hit Charity Dinner Organiser Quits Post*, BBC ONLINE, Jan. 24, 2018, https://www.bbc.co.uk/news/business-42801178.

5. SEXUAL HARASSMENT IN THE WORKPLACE, *supra* note 3, 37 §106.

6. WOMEN AND EQUALITIES COMMITTEE, SEXUAL HARASSMENT OF WOMEN AND GIRLS IN PUBLIC PLACES INQUIRY, Sixth Report of Session 2017–19, HC 701.

to achieve the commitment made by the government to eliminate sexual harassment of women and girls by 2030, stating that the governmental "foot appears to be almost entirely off the pedal" and that the government "has not caught up with the huge social changes reflected in the #MeToo movement. Instead it risks giving the impression that it thinks sexual harassment is either too trivial to address, or that the problem is immune to policy intervention."

Among the recommendations made by the Committee were: the collection of data by the government on sexual harassment in public places; the development of educational strategies based on "a robust understanding of why [sexual harassment] happens, who perpetrates it, and how men and women differ in their understandings and experiences of the problem [which] must understand the cultural attitudes and social norms that lead to or enable sexual harassment, and how to go about challenging and changing them"; consideration of whether sexual harassment should be categorized as a hate crime; and the regulation of sexual harassment in online spaces and on public transport.

Also, in October 2018, the British media reported that billionaire retail businessman Sir Philip Green had entered into non-disclosure agreements with five former employees who accused him of sexual harassment. The NDAs were upheld by the Court of Appeal, but Lord Peter Hain used Parliamentary Privilege to name Green in the House of Lords, as a result of which the businessman's identity was widely published. In January 2019 Green abandoned legal action against the *Telegraph* newspaper in connection with the disclosures, and in February 2019 the media reported that Green had paid several former employees at least £1 million not to disclose allegations of sexual assault or racial denigration. Green denied that his conduct amounted "to any type of crime, or anything that would amount to gross misconduct, or a serious risk to health and safety."[7]

The #MeToo movement in the United Kingdom has generated increased awareness of the extent and nature of sexual assault. It has spurred action by (largely) female journalists[8] and barristers.[9] The Royal Court theater issued a behavior code for the theater industry in November 2017 and the following month scrapped plans for the production of a play whose co-director was accused of sexual harassment.[10] The doctors' union has called for a #MeToo movement

---

7. *Sir Philip Green 'Paid Employee £1m over Harassment Claims',* BBC ONLINE, Feb. 9, 2019, https://www.bbc.com/news/uk-47179344.

8. Holly Watt, *Journalists Set up Second Source Group to Tackle Harassment*, THE GUARDIAN, Nov. 2, 2017, https://www.theguardian.com/world/2017/nov/02/journalists-second-source-sexual-harassment-women.

9. Frances Gibb, *Taking a Stand for Women at the Bar*, THE TIMES, May 24, 2018, https://www.thetimes.co.uk/article/taking-a-stand-for-women-at-the-bar-cx3t3mpnv.

10. See *Royal Court Theater Scraps Play after Harassment Complaint against Director*, BBC ONLINE, Dec. 13, 2017, https://www.bbc.co.uk/news/entertainment-arts-42337504.

to stamp out sexual harassment of female doctors, many of whom experience bullying and harassment.[11] The Law Society and Bar Standards Board, which regulate solicitors and barristers respectively, have warned lawyers that they may be subject to disciplinary action if they are involved in the misuse of NDAs, and the Law Society has initiated such proceedings against the solicitor who acted for Weinstein in relation to the NDA imposed on Zelda Perkins.[12]

Evidence of a backlash against #MeToo is emerging in the form of defamation claims designed to silence allegations of harassment. One recent example concerns a number of women sued for defamation by an (unnamed) prominent musician after accusing him of unacceptable behavior toward women.[13] Another was the decision in *Stocker v. Stocker* in which an award of £5,000, with £200,000 costs, was made against a woman who accused her ex-husband in a Facebook post of having tried to "strangle" her after an incident in which he left handprints on her neck that were visible to the police two hours later.[14] The judge who ruled against Ms. Stocker is quoted as having accepted that her husband had been guilty at least of assaulting her, that there were "gun issues," and that he had made threats "though not of immediate violence against her," but ruled that she had defamed him by suggesting that he was a dangerous man. It is worth noting that Mr. Stocker had been arrested on three occasions, one of which related to the breach of a non-molestation order, while another concerned a firearm.[15] The judge further ruled that, although the definition of strangulation did not necessarily involve death, the fact that Ms. Stocker had accused her husband of *attempting* to strangle her when he had in fact left marks on her neck meant that she was accusing him of attempting to kill her.[16] The

---

11. And see the October 2019 report of the independent investigation commissioned by the doctors' union (the British Medical Association or BMA) into sexual harassment within the BMA: *Action Under Way to Bring about Cultural Change within the BMA*, British Medical Association, Nov. 27, 2019, https://www.bma.org.uk/about-us/equality-diversity-and-inclusion /independent-investigation-into-sexism-and-sexual-harassment-at-the-bma.

12. See Jemma Slingo, *Allen & Overy's NDA Prosecution Delayed*, THE LAW SOCIETY GAZETTE, June 3, 2019, https://www.lawgazette.co.uk/news/allen-and-overys-nda-prosecu tion-delayed/5070471.article.

13. Catherine Baksi, *Courts "Are Silencing Abused Women,"* THE TIMES, Feb. 14, 2019, https://www.thetimes.co.uk/article/courts-are-silencing-abused-women-95hrdjqnq.

14. Hayley Dixon, *Woman Found to Have Defamed Ex-Husband Takes Fight to Supreme Court*, THE TELEGRAPH, Jan. 23, 2019, https://www.telegraph.co.uk/news/2019/01/23 /woman-found-have-defamed-ex-husband-facebook-takes-fight-supreme/.

15. Helena Spector, *Stocker v. Stocker: A Greenlight for Men Who Abuse Women*, THE JUSTICE GAP, Jan. 28, 2019, https://www.thejusticegap.com/stocker-v-stocker-a-greenlight-for -men-who-abuse-women/.

16. *Stocker v. Stocker* [2016] EWHC 147 (QB) (United Kingdom), [2016] All ER (D) 235 (Jan) (HC) (United Kingdom); [2017] EWCA Civ. 381 (CA) (United Kingdom); Dixon, *supra* note 14.

Supreme Court eventually overturned the judge's decision in this case, unanimously ruling that he had erred in adopting an overly formalistic approach to the meaning of Ms. Stocker's words and failing to take account of the fact that Facebook is a medium for casual conversation.[17] The decision, while welcome in that particular case, will not prevent defamation claims from being used in the future to counter complaints of violence against women.

In February 2019, the *Press Gazette* reported that a former senior employee at Linklaters, a major London law firm, had been enjoined from disclosing information about "the current culture at Linklaters" and the "ongoing struggle Linklaters has with women in the workplace."[18] The former senior employee had intended to disclose "specific examples" of the alleged problems which were listed as "the 'Munich incident,' the 'NY settlement' and the 'London Settlement.'" The judge was satisfied that such disclosures would have amounted to breaches of the employee's contractual obligations of confidence because "the information referred to was of an inherently sensitive and confidential nature." The Linklaters' case may be an example of one in which the interests of staff who had complained of harassment or similar conduct was in preserving confidentiality. The same could have been said of the Phillip Green case, in which at least some of the former staff who had signed NDAs do not appear to have favored disclosure by the press, but the public interest may nevertheless be in favor of disclosure.

Legal Protections Against Harassment

Harassment is prohibited across the United Kingdom by the Equality Act 2010 and the equivalent Northern Ireland provisions that apply to work,[19] education, access to goods, facilities, and services, including premises, the delivery of public functions, and the conduct of associations. Harassment is defined to include unwanted conduct that is related to sex or gender reassignment[20] or which is of a sexual nature, and which has the intentional or unintentional effect

---

17. *Stocker v. Stocker* [2019] UKSC 17 (United Kingdom).

18. PA Mediapoint, *Law Firm Wins Gagging Order Against Former Director Seeking to Expose Its Alleged "Struggle ... with Women in the Workplace,"* PRESS GAZETTE, June 2, 2019, https://pressgazette.co.uk/judge-grants-gagging-order-against-former-linklaters-director-seeking-to-expose-law-firms-culture/.

19. Including many independent contractors but not volunteers.

20. S26 of the Equalities Act 2010 (United Kingdom). Similar (though not identical) provisions apply in Northern Ireland. Harassment related to age, disability, race, religion or belief, or sexual orientation is also regulated, though harassment connected to religion or belief or sexual orientation is not expressly prohibited in some contexts.

of, violating the harassed person's dignity or creating an intimidating, hostile, degrading, humiliating, or offensive environment for him or her. Where the effect is unintended, a court or tribunal must take into account, in determining whether the conduct had the effect of violating the harassed person's dignity or creating an intimidating, hostile, degrading, humiliating, or offensive environment for him or her, the perception of the person complaining of harassment, the other circumstances of the case, and whether it is reasonable for the conduct to have that effect.

The type of harassment outlined above is generally referred to as "hostile environment" harassment. The Equality Act also prohibits "quid pro quo" harassment, defined as unwanted conduct of a sexual nature or which is related to gender reassignment or sex, which has the intentional or unintentional effect of violating the harassed person's dignity, or creating an intimidating, hostile, degrading, humiliating, or offensive environment for him or her, and as a result of his or her submission to or rejection of which, the harassed person is treated less favorably. Employers are responsible for harassment by staff and agents, but in the former case can use an "all reasonable steps" defense. Individual harassers are jointly liable.

The harassment provisions have existed in more or less their current form since 2005. Third-party harassment was briefly covered between the implementation of the Equality Act 2010 and the repeal of the relevant provision in October 2013. (This repeal followed a consultation exercise in which only 20 percent of respondents favored this step, but the government insisted upon it in the interest of deregulation and on grounds that "nothing in the consultation responses has persuaded us that there is a case for retaining" the provision.) Work-related harassment claims must be brought in the employment tribunal, others in the county court. The advantage of the former is that costs awards are relatively rare, and thus the deterrent they would otherwise pose to litigation is absent. Having said this, the fact that costs are not recoverable adds an additional hurdle to claimants given the relatively modest damages typically awarded and the practical necessity of instructing lawyers in harassment cases.

The Reality

In July 2018, Parliament's Women and Equalities Committee reported that, while there are no official statistics on sexual harassment in the workplace:

"Surveys commissioned by media and other organisations ... [give the] impression ... of a widespread problem across many sectors ... borne out by evidence we have received about, for example, the entertainment industry, teaching, journalism, hospitality, retail, healthcare, the music industry and the international charity sector. Throughout the world of work, in spite of the law, sexual harassment is an everyday, common occurrence … [and] women are significantly more likely to experience sexual harassment than men. Perpetrators are disproportionately men.… Specific groups are disproportionately affected or susceptible to sexual harassment at work, such as young women between the ages of 18 and 24, employees with a disability or long-term illness, and members of sexual minority groups. Workers with irregular, flexible or precarious employment contracts, common in the services sector, and freelancers are more likely to experience sexual harassment._Specific factors may affect different racial groups, and experience of sexual harassment can be bound up with racial harassment. TUC research found that no BME women who had reported an incident to their employer felt it had been dealt with satisfactorily, compared to seven per cent of white women."[21]

The UK's *Guardian* newspaper reported in August 2016 that 52 percent of women in Britain had been sexually harassed at work, citing a survey carried out by the TUC and the Everyday Sexism Project.[22] The figure for women aged sixteen to twenty-four was 63 percent. One in eight of those surveyed reported that they had experienced unwanted sexual touching of their breasts, buttocks, or genitals, or attempts to kiss them at work, which would amount to criminal sexual assault. One percent reported having been raped or seriously sexually assaulted at work. Eighty percent of women did not report the harassment to their employers, generally because they were concerned about damaging workplace relationships or not being taken seriously. Very few of those who reported sexual harassment brought claims to a tribunal regardless of how unsatisfactory the outcome of the complaint to their employers. At the time of the survey, tribunal fees were in place and a woman seeking to bring a sexual harassment claim would have had to expend £1200 in tribunal fees to do so, not including the costs of legal representation. Although tribunal fees have since been removed, the fraction of sexual harassment that results in legal action is very small indeed.

Nor are those familiar with the legal process more likely than others to complain about sexual harassment. In July 2016, the Bar Standards Board (BSB), which regulates barristers, found that 40 percent of women barristers who responded to an online survey reported having experienced sexual harassment

21. See SEXUAL HARASSMENT IN THE WORKPLACE, *supra* note 3. The TUC (Trade Union Congress) is the national association of trade unions. "BME" indicates black and minority ethnic.

22. Alice Ross, *Half of Women in UK Have Been Sexually Harassed at Work, Study Finds*, THE GUARDIAN, Aug. 10, 2016, https://www.theguardian.com/lifeandstyle/2016/aug/10/half-of-women-uk-have-been-sexually-harassed-at-work-tuc-study-everyday-sexism.

at work.[23] Only 20 percent of the barristers who experienced sexual harassment had reported it, citing fears that the report would damage their careers. Half of those who did report were unsatisfied with the response.[24] More recently, and despite the obligation of barristers to report serious professional misconduct, including sexual harassment, by other barristers to the BSB, that body reported that it had received only two complaints of sexual harassment.[25]

In March 2017 the *Guardian* alleged that sexual harassment was endemic in British universities with approximately 300 formal complaints having been made by students and staff, but the paper reported that many other victims of harassment had been deterred from bringing formal complaints by concerns about their education or careers.[26] A number of universities had entered into NDAs to settle complaints:

> A senior lecturer at a university in the north of England told the Guardian she had raised an allegation of sexual harassment against a co-worker as an informal complaint but was told it would have to be treated as a formal grievance. The university went ahead with its own investigation and said it had found evidence of a relationship between the complainant and the accused, so it could not be sexual harassment. She denies there was any relationship. She was asked to withdraw her complaint in order to keep her position.

Legal Changes

The #MeToo movement has not resulted in any legal changes in the United Kingdom yet, though it has triggered two investigations by Parliament's Women and Equalities Committee that may result in legal reform. Having conducted its inquiry into sexual harassment at work, in 2018 the Committee called for the imposition of a new employer duty to protect workers from harassment and victimization. This duty would be supported by a statutory code of practice; a greater role for regulators; improved enforcement processes

---

23. 25 percent of all women barristers responded to the survey.

24. Owen Bowcott, *Female Barristers Report High Level of Sexual Harassment at Work*, THE GUARDIAN, Jul. 12, 2016, https://www.theguardian.com/money/2016/jul/12/female-barristers-report-high-level-of-sexual-harassment-at-work.

25. Owen Bowcott, *Fear Stops Reporting of Sexual Harassment at the Bar, Says Top QC*, THE GUARDIAN, Dec. 2, 2018, https://www.theguardian.com/world/2018/dec/02/sexual-harassment-at-the-bar-not-being-reported-over-career-fears-says-barrister.

26. David Batty, Sally Weale & Caroline Bannock, *Sexual Harassment 'at Epidemic Levels' in UK Universities*, THE GUARDIAN, Mar. 5, 2017, https://www.theguardian.com/education/2017/mar/05/students-staff-uk-universities-sexual-harassment-epidemic.

for employees; reform of the use of NDAs; and improvements to the collection of government data.

The government agreed in December 2018 to seek to act on most, but not all, of the Committee's recommendations. The government agreed: to introduce a new statutory code of practice;[27] that NDAs required better regulation, including a clearer explanation of the rights that a worker cannot abrogate by signing one; that regulators should clarify that workplace sexual harassment is unacceptable; that sexual harassment should be considered when assessing the fitness of the individuals and employers they regulate; and that employers "have a responsibility to take reasonable steps to protect their staff from third party harassment where they know that their staff are at risk." The government also agreed to gather data on the prevalence and nature of workplace sexual harassment at least every three years, with a view to launching survey questions in 2019, though it declined to impose an employer duty to protect workers from harassment and victimization or to increase sanctions for poor employer practices. The survey was completed in October 2019 and the government is analyzing the responses at the time of this writing. The promised Code of Practice on harassment is still awaited, as is legislative action on NDAs.

In June 2019 the Women and Equalities Committee published its report *The use of non-disclosure agreements in discrimination cases*.[28] Among its findings were that NDAs were used "routinely" to cover up allegations of workplace discrimination and harassment and that employees often felt that they had no choice but to agree to a settlement, including an NDA, because of the difficulties of pursuing litigation and the imbalances of power between employers and employees. The Committee reported "shocking evidence [of] ... the detrimental effect an NDA can have on the lives of ordinary people," including "emotional and psychological damage ... which can affect their ability to work again or to move on," as well as financial losses resulting from job losses and litigation. It called upon the government to ensure that NDAs could not continue to be abused to prevent legitimate discussion of allegations of unlawful discrimination or harassment; to require the use of plain language in NDAs; to strengthen corporate governance requirements to require that employers protect staff from discrimination and harassment; and to require named senior managers at the board level or similar to oversee antidiscrimination and harassment policies and procedures and the use of NDAs in discrimination and harassment cases. The Committee also reiterated its previous calls for government to place a mandatory duty on employers to protect workers from harassment and victimization

---

27. See SEXUAL HARASSMENT IN THE WORKPLACE, *supra* note 3.

28. WOMEN AND EQUALITIES COMMITTEE, THE USE OF NON-DISCLOSURE AGREEMENTS IN DISCRIMINATION CASES, 2017-19, HC 1720.

in the workplace and to improve the remedies which employment tribunals can award as well as the costs regime applicable in tribunals.

The following month the government published its response to a consultation paper it issued in March 2019 on the use of NDAs,[29] reporting that it would legislate to ensure that NDAs may not prevent disclosure to the police, regulated health and care professionals, or legal professionals; that the limitations on the duties of confidentiality imposed by NDAs would have to be clear to those signing them; that improved independent legal advice must be available to an individual signing an NDA; and that it would issue guidance on drafting requirements for NDAs.[30] Three months later, the government responded to the Women and Equalities Committee's June 2019 report, declaring that it would consult on whether employers should be required to provide references for former employees as part of the wider package to control the use of NDAs that it had announced in July.[31]

29. *Confidentiality Clauses: Measures to Prevent Misuse in Situations of Workplace Harassment or Discrimination*, Dept. for Business, Energy, and Industrial Strategy, Apr. 29, 2019, https://assets.publishing.service.gov.uk/government/uploads/system/uploads/attach ment_data/file/783011/confidentiality-clauses-consultation.pdf.

30. *Confidentiality Clauses: Response to the Government Consultation on Proposals to Prevent Misuse in Situations of Workplace Harassment or Discrimination*, July 2019, Dept. for Business, Energy, and Industrial Strategy, https://assets.publishing.service.gov.uk/government /uploads/system/uploads/attachment_data/file/818324/confidentiality-clause-consultation -govt-response.pdf.

31. The Use of Non-Disclosure Agreements in Discrimination Cases: Government Response to the Committee's Ninth Report of Session, 2017–19, HC 215.

CHAPTER 13

Over 75,000 Voices Raised in Sweden

Laura Carlson[1]

The disintegration of the Swedish Academy and the subsequent decision not to award the 2018 Nobel Prize in Literature[2] are perhaps the most palpable fallouts of the Swedish #MeToo movement. Manifestations in Sweden against sexual harassment had begun already in October 2017, triggered by the renewal of the American #MeToo movement due to the Harvey Weinstein allegations[3] A cascade of over thirty different Swedish hashtags from different sectors followed, signed in total by over 75,000 individuals sharing their own experiences of, or witness to, rape, sexual assault, and harassment. The first Swedish hashtag included over 800 women working in film and theatre (#tystnadtagning—lights, camera, action). The three largest hashtags to date cover more than 15,000 female teachers (#ickegodkänt—failed), 12,000 women in law (#medvilkenrätt—by what right), and 10,000 physicians and medical students (#utantystnadsplikt—without a duty of confidentiality).

Other entertainment industry sectors came out with hashtags: over 600 female opera singers (#visjungerut—we're singing out), 2,000 female singers (#närmusikentystnar—when the music stops), 600 dancers (#tystdansa—dancing in silence), and 1,600 backstage employees (#metoobackstage) gave accounts. Other cultural sectors joined as well, with over 1,600 women, trans- and non-gendered persons in the art world (#konstnärligfrihet—artistic freedom), 2,000 women and non-gendered persons in the restaurant industry

---

1. Laura Carlson is a professor in private law, specializing in labor and discrimination law at the Department of Law, Stockholm University.

2. The decision was later made to award both the 2018 and 2019 Nobel Prizes in literature in 2019.

3. "MeToo" was first coined in 2006 by Tarana Burke, a Black woman activist, to empower survivors of sexual harassment.

(#vikokarover—we're boiling over), and 400 women and non-gendered persons within the night club industry (#listanärstängd—the queue is closed).

Women in other branches also came forth with examples and calls for change. Two concerned political power, with over 1,300 female politicians (#imaktenskorridorer—in the corridors of power) and 1,400 women in the Swedish Church (#vardeljus—let there be light). Other sectors included more than 2,400 female academics (#akademiuppropet—academic appeal), 7,000 female journalists (#deadline), 2,000 women in the PR sector (#sistabriefen—the last briefing), and almost 400 women within archeology (#utgrävning-pågår—excavation underway). Women in male-dominated sectors also participated, with more than 4,000 women in the construction industry (#sistaspikenikistan—the last nail in the coffin), 1,600 women in the tech industry (#teknisktfel—technical error), 1,500 women in the labor union movement (#inteförhandlingsbart—non-negotiable), and 1,800 women within the military (#givaktochbitihop—salute and be quiet).

Voices outside of the employment sectors were raised under hashtags encompassing more vulnerable groups, including seventy women and girls living with drug addiction, criminality and prostitution (#utanskyddsnät—without a safety net), 400 women in prostitution (#intedinhora—not your whore), and 133 women living under honor oppression (#underytan—under the surface). Five hundred persons within the temperance movement (#nykterfrizon—sober free zone), 630 hearing impaired persons (#slådövörattill—turn a deaf ear), and between 50 and 100 individuals reporting health care patient violations (#vårdensomsvek—the healthcare that failed) also responded. Two hundred schoolgirls (#tystiklassen—quiet in the classroom), 2,300 women in sports (#timeout), and 1,089 women in the horse world (#visparkarbakut—we are bucking) also signed. The accounts given included not only reports of individual acts but also revealed widespread institutional acceptance and even facilitation of rape, sexual assault, and harassment in many different sectors. By way of example, one woman in military officer training gave an account of returning to her quarters after leave to find her bathroom mirror covered in the dried sperm of several men.[4]

The Fallout in the Swedish Academy

The Swedish #MeToo movement had its most notorious effect on the Swedish Academy, the institution that among other things awards the Nobel

---

4. *Vittnesmål från värnplikten: Grova trakasserier krossade officersdrömmarna*, SvT Nyheter, Nov. 30, 2017.

Prize in literature. Criminal charges of unlawful sexual conduct were brought against a few high-profile Swedish actors and persons in the "culture" business, but the most public case involved rape charges against Jean-Claude Arnault, a well-known Swedish photographer referred to as *kulturfiguren*, the "culture figure." These charges raised questions concerning both the passivity of, and the facilitation by, the Swedish Academy, common themes in the #MeToo movement worldwide. In November 2017, eighteen women published their experiences of sexual harassment and repeated sexual assaults by Arnault beginning in 1996 and up to 2017 in the daily newspaper DN.[5] One of these women had informed the Academy in 1996 of Arnault's sexual harassment of several women. A series of articles focusing on Arnault's conduct was written by Niklas Svensson in 1997, published under the heading, "Sexual Terror in the Cultural Elite" in one of Sweden's national daily newspapers, Expressen. The Academy decided not to investigate the claims.

Many of Arnault's alleged assaults occurred at his club, which was supported by funds from the Swedish Academy, or at the Academy apartments used by Arnault. Even after the 1996 reporting of Arnault's conduct to the Academy, it continued for two decades to provide generous funding and support to Arnault. This Academy support can further be questioned as Arnault during this period was (and still is) married to one of the Academy's directors, Katarina Frostenson, raising issues of corruption. Arnault's use of the Academy's apartments (to such an extent that he even put his own name on the door) directly violated the Academy's rule that only Academy directors were permitted to use the apartments.

The Academy Secretary, Sara Danius, hired a law firm in 2017 to investigate the relationships of the Academy Directors to Arnault and related matters such as leaks regarding the Nobel laureates in literature. The law firm's recommendation was that the Academy file police charges against Arnault's club, which the Academy declined to do. Several directors stopped being active Academy members in protest either to Danius's investigation, viewing it as disloyal, to the Academy's failure to act on these recommendations, or to the conflicts of interest that existed in the situation.

Danius was voted out of office as secretary by the Academy due to her initiation of the investigation and the fact that the situation was made public. The Academy decided to not award the 2018 Nobel Prize for literature that year, citing as its reason the fact that the general public confidence for the Academy was too low. The Academy published a 2018 commentary to its 1786 bylaws stating that directors are to "avoid criticizing the Academy and colleagues publicly" as

---

5. Johanna Palm, *Arton kvinnor anklagar en central person i svenskt kulturlivet för sexuella trakasserier och övergrepp*, DAGENS NYHETER KULTUR, Nov. 21, 2017.

part of their duty of loyalty to the Academy (which Danius's actions were seen to be in violation of). The rules regarding conflicts of interest have also now been clarified in response to the awarding of funds and benefits to Arnault while he was married to an Academy Director. Directors themselves are still required to assess and report whether they believe they have any conflicts of interest without any external mechanism in place to check their findings.

A Swedish district court found Arnault guilty of rape in October 2018. Both Arnault and the prosecutor appealed the judgment, which the Court of Appeals upheld that same year, while increasing the prison sentence to two and a half years. The Swedish Supreme Court denied Arnault's petition to appeal in 2019.[6] Frostenson has now stepped down as an academy director. Even though Arnault was successfully prosecuted for sexual assault, the backlash against Danius as the secretary calling for an investigation and disclosing the situation was extreme.

Swedish Legislation Concerning Criminal Sexual Conduct

The complacency of the Academy for over two decades can in part be seen as a reflection of the legal treatment, both criminal and civil, of rape, sexual assault, and sexual harassment under Swedish law. If we use the Arnault case as a timeline, the law concerning rape when the first complaints were made in 1996 required a very high evidentiary showing of violence or the threat of violence to prove rape.[7] The Swedish word for rape, *våldtäkt*, literally means to take (*täkt*) with violence (*våld*). The law was amended in 2005 to remove the requirements of "violence" or "threats of violence" to prove rape, and a 2010 amendment broadened the definition of rape to include situations in which the victim was in a helpless condition.[8] Statistics from 2014[9] show that one in ten women, and one in a hundred men, over the age of eighteen, have been subjected to serious sexual assault or attempted assault defined as involving threat, violence, or the victim being in a helpless state. Approximately 20 percent of women and

---

6. *Dom i Högsta domstolen i dag—fängelsestraffet för kulturprofilen står sig*, AFTONBLA-DET, Apr. 25, 2019.

7. Section 6.1 of the Criminal Code (Brottsbalken, BrB 1962:700). An English translation of Chapter Six of the Swedish Penal Code can be found at the website of the Swedish Government Offices at government.se.

8. *Lag* (2005:90) *om ändring i brottsbalken* and *Lag* (2010:371) *om ändring i brottsbalken*.

9. Nationellt centrum för kvinnofrid, *Våld och hälsa: En befolkningsundersökning om kvinnors och mäns våldsutsatthet samt kopplingen till hälsa*, UPPSALA UNIVERSITET, 2014.

5 percent of men over the age of eighteen have been subject to lesser sexual assault. Twenty-two thousand cases of sexual assault were reported in 2017, of which 7,370 were classified as rape, an annual increase of 8 percent for reports and 10 percent for cases involving rape. Of those 22,000 reports, approximately 1,100 were successfully prosecuted, resulting in conviction rate for 2017 of 5 percent.[10]

Sweden again amended its rape legislation effective July 1, 2018, to encompass in the definition of rape a certain type of sexual act in which the other person is not participating voluntarily, with the sanction of a prison sentence of two to ten years depending upon the severity of the crime.[11] Two additional crimes, negligent rape and negligent sexual assault, were added. These two crimes occur when the perpetrator has been grossly negligent as to whether the person with whom the perpetrator is having sexual intercourse is participating voluntarily, with a maximum prison sentence of four years. Requiring a showing of consent as proven by the perpetrator, as opposed to the victim proving that the perpetrator knew there was a lack of consent by the victim, has been intensely debated in Sweden in the past decades.

However, given the low number of reports and even lower number of successful prosecutions, the Swedish Government finally determined that shifting the burden of proof was necessary. It can also be briefly mentioned that Sweden does not have a robust tort system. Bringing a civil action based on sexual assault, while technically legally possible, is seldom done, aside from in connection with the criminal case. When the tort claim is combined with the criminal prosecution, the burden of proof applied to the tort claim typically is beyond a reasonable doubt. Given the fairly low damages awarded in tort cases and the application in Sweden of the English rule, where the losing party has to pay the prevailing party's legal costs and fees, the economic risks are simply too great for most plaintiffs to bring civil tort cases based on unlawful sexual conduct.

Swedish Civil Legislation Concerning Sexual Harassment

Using the Arnault case again as a timeline, by 1996, specific civil sexual harassment legislative prohibitions had been in place in Sweden for only five years. Harassment has been a "stepchild" in questions of sex equality in general. The original 1979 Equal Treatment Act contained no specific provisions dealing

---

10. Brå, *Våldtäkt och sexualbrott*, BRÅ, 2018 available at the website of Swedish National Council for Crime Prevention, Brottsförebyggande rådet (Brå) at bra.se.

11. *Lag* (2018:618) *om ändring i brottsbalken*.

with harassment, with such claims falling instead within the general provisions concerning sex discrimination. Section 6 of the 1991 Equal Treatment Act was enacted to address this deficiency in part, at least with respect to reprisals for reporting sexual harassment. Section 6 was amended in 1998 as part of a government investigation concerning violence against women, mandating now that employers take measures to prevent employees from being subjected to sexual harassment or harassment resulting from a complaint about sex discrimination. A duty for the employer to investigate claims of sexual harassment was prescribed in a new § 22a, arising when the employer received knowledge that an employee had been subjected to sexual harassment by another employee, as well as a duty to take steps that reasonably could be required to prevent continued sexual harassment. The failure to perform these obligations could result in an award of damages to the employee under § 27a. The categories of harassment were further refined in 2005 with § 6 amended to state that the employer is to take the measures necessary to prevent any employee from being subjected to: harassment based on sex; sexual harassment; or retaliatory harassment. The 2005 law also prohibited an employer from giving instructions to harass.

The current 2008 Discrimination Act (2008:567)[12] has kept this structure with respect to employers. The 2008 Act has, however, expanded the law to include sectors other than employment: education; labor market policy activities and employment services; professional recognition; membership in certain quasi-public organizations such as labor unions; the provision of goods, services and housing; health and medical care and social services; the social insurance system; unemployment insurance and student financial aid; national military and civilian services; and public employment. Generally, these sectors are to work to prevent harassment on any of the now-protected grounds: sex, transgender identity or expression, ethnic origins, religion, disability, sexual orientation, or age. Sexual harassment is defined in § 1:4(5) as conduct of a sexual nature that violates someone's dignity. Instructions as to third party harassment are included in the definition of discrimination. There is a duty for certain of these actors to take active measures to prevent discrimination, as well as to investigate claims of harassment under § 2:3 of the Discrimination Act.

---

12. Diskrimineringslag (2008:567). An English translation of the Discrimination Act can be found at the website of the Swedish Government Offices at https://www.government.se /information-material/2015/09/discrimination-act-2008567/.

The Case Law Concerning
Sexual Harassment

Few sexual harassment cases are litigated in Sweden. The most recent case successfully brought to the Labor Court was in 2016.[13] There the Labor Court found that a fellow employee had sexually harassed the plaintiff, and that the plaintiff had clearly stated to the harasser that such attention was unwanted. This is a twist in Swedish harassment cases. There is no actual requirement in the legislation that a plaintiff prove that she or he has informed the harasser that such attention was unwanted. But, there also is no objective standard applied by the courts to such behavior. In other words, under the law, there is no reasonable person that would have known such conduct was unwanted, in this case staring at plaintiff's breasts and commenting on her body. The courts have thus generally required that plaintiffs themselves inform harassers that the behavior is unwanted. Otherwise, the plaintiff has to prove that the harasser actually knew that such behavior was unwanted by the plaintiff under a subjective standard (a reasoning parallel to the Swedish rape legislation and the former requirement that victims prove that the defendant knew there was a lack of consent). The Labor Court awarded damages in the 2016 case of SEK 10,000 (approximately €960 or $1,100.00).

In an earlier 2016 case, the Labor Court found that the employer had acted in a sexually harassing manner by requesting that the employee sit in his lap and kissing her on the cheek and neck while giving her an employee evaluation. The Labor Court awarded SEK 50,000 in damages.[14] The same court has also found harassment on the basis of sex, where the employer forced female employees to wear a name tag stating their bra size at work, awarding SEK 50,000 in damages.[15] The most recent Labor Court case concerning retaliation was in 2013, where an employer terminated a fixed term contract due to the employee's reporting of sexual harassment, awarding damages in the amount of SEK 75,000.[16]

---

13. *DO v. Nya Möler Bageri & Konditori AB*, Arbetsdomstolens domar 2016 no. 56.

14. *DO v. Carlos-Mina AB*, Arbetsdomstolens domar 2016 no. 38.

15. *Handelsanställdas förbund v. Svensk Handel and Change of Scandinavia Sweden AB i Farum*, Arbetsdomstolens domar 2013 no. 29.

16. *DO v. ABC Trafikskola AB*, Arbetsdomstolens domar 2013 no. 71.

The Employer's Duty to Investigate and Constructive Termination

Another aspect of the sexual harassment jurisprudence concerns the employer's duty to investigate and constructive termination, that is, whether the employer, through a failure to act, has caused the constructive termination of an employee subjected to sexual harassment. The first such case was brought in 1987 under the 1979 Equal Treatment Act.[17] A female employee had reported to her employer sexual harassment by a fellow employee in November 1984. At a general personnel meeting held the next day, the alleged perpetrator stated that he would not want to have sex with her even if he could. After meetings to discuss the issue, the supervisor told the plaintiff to seek employment elsewhere as she was disrupting the workplace, and all the male employees had threatened to quit. The Labor Court found that the actions of the supervisor were not based on plaintiff's sex (as required by the law at that time) but rather the disruptions she caused in the workplace.

In the most recent constructive termination case, the Labor Court found that the employer did not fail in its duty to investigate nor did the employer have a duty to encourage plaintiff to resume her employment.[18] The twenty-two-year-old female plaintiff was serving in the Swedish military and sent to Kosovo, the sole woman in a group of six. Of the 600 troops there, fifty were women. The plaintiff alleged that she was subjected to both oral and physical sexual harassment and also excluded from decision-making processes. She informed her platoon officer of the harassment and eventually requested a transfer. The plaintiff alleged that she was told either to accept the situation or leave. She chose the latter. On her return home to Sweden, she informed the personnel department of the situation as she experienced it, but no investigation was initiated. The Labor Court found that the employer had a basis for finding that the plaintiff's termination was not based on the reasons she gave, but rather that she simply did not like Kosovo and wanted to go home. The court also found that her supervisor's statement, that she needed to decide whether she wanted to stay or leave, could not be seen as an ultimatum. Because of this, according to the court, the employer could not be seen as having acted in a way that conflicted with good practices in the labor market, and thus did not cause the plaintiff's termination. The Labor Court found that the plaintiff most likely was subjected to sexual harassment, but that she never explicitly informed her employer of this. As such, the defendant had no knowledge and thus no duty, the court said,

---

17. *JämO v. City of Stockholm*, ARBETSDOMSTOLENS DOMAR 1987 no. 98.

18. *JämO v. The State of Sweden through the Swedish Armed Forces*, ARBETSDOMSTO-LENS DOMAR 2005 no. 63.

a reasoning consistent with the subjective assessments conducted by the courts with respect to criminal sexual conduct.

The Lawfulness of the Harasser's Employment Termination

Historically, the majority of cases in which the issue of sexual harassment has been raised have concerned the lawfulness of employment terminations of the harasser. Two very strong and different interests collide in such cases, the rights of an employee not to be harassed and the rights of the harassing employee to employment protection under the Employment Protection Act (EPA).[19] This issue was first squarely raised in 1996 under the new provision in the 1991 Equal Treatment Act.[20] A fifty-nine-year old male teacher argued that he was unlawfully terminated for sexually harassing students. The Labor Court found that no one had informed the plaintiff of the inappropriateness of his behavior and that the employer had failed in its duty to correct the problem and rehabilitate the teacher. Thus, the Labor Court said, lawful grounds for the termination did not exist under EPA §7.

The Labor Court changed this assessment a decade later, reaching more of a balance between the interests of the victim and the employment protection of the harasser.[21] A thirty-six-year-old male plaintiff alleged that his termination was not lawful as based on his sexual harassment of a nineteen-year-old female. The Labor Court noted that according to the preparatory works to the 1974 EPA,[22] the standard for lawful termination was where an employee had grossly neglected his duties or committed an act so intentional or grossly negligent that it could not reasonably be tolerated in a legal relationship. Stating that violence or the threat of violence does not belong in the workplace,[23] the Labor Court found that the male employee's actions were of such a serious nature in violation of the 1991 Equal Treatment Act that he could be seen as having grossly neglected his duties. As seen from the summaries above with respect to both criminal and civil legislation, individuals claiming sexual harassment and assault

---

19. Anställningsskyddslag (1982:80). An English translation of the Employment Protection Act can be found at the website of the Swedish Government Offices at government.se.

20. *The Union of Swedish Civil Servants v. The University College of Film, Radio, Television and Theatre in Stockholm*, ARBETSDOMSTOLENS DOMAR 1996 no. 10.

21. *A. S. v. Skånemejerier Economic Association*, ARBETSDOMSTOLENS DOMAR 2006 no. 54.

22. Prop. 1973:129 *Kungl. Maj:ts proposition med förslag till lag om anställningsskydd, m.m.* at 254.

23. Citing Prop. 1981/82:71 *om ny anställningsskyddslag m.m.* at 72.

have faced high legal thresholds in order to successfully litigate any such claims. And even where successful, the sanctions and remedies available, particularly with respect to damages, have been minimal.

The Legal Aftermath of the Swedish #MeToo

The legal impact of the Swedish #MeToo movement, aside from a few criminal convictions, has been minimal. The government dedicated SEK 120 million in the 2019 budget to educate judges, lawyers, police, teachers, and students as to issues of sexual harassment and criminal offenses. However, the same pattern can be traced in most sectors, first denial, then shock that such problems actually exist, and then calls for greater educational efforts. Aside from the labor unions, few strong civil society organizations have taken up this issue. And, as seen earlier, one of the Swedish #MeToo hashtags concerned sexual harassment within the labor union movement itself.

A survey was conducted a year after the initial Swedish #MeToo responses to gauge the effect of the phenomenon. The results showed that seven out of ten Swedish employees perceived there to be significant equality problems at workplaces.[24] Problem areas identified in the survey included gender wage gaps, pay equity, glass ceilings, and targeted recruitment. The Swedish laws concerning criminal sexual conduct and civil sexual harassment and reprisals have been lagging. This has been exacerbated by the courts requiring subjective proof of intent because they are reluctant in general to find such behavior proven—a result easily seen in the statistic that only approximately 5 percent of all reported rapes are successfully prosecuted. One theory about the extent of the Swedish #MeToo, with over 75,000 voices raised, is that this significant response was due to the inability of Swedish law to address this behavior. A greater legal awareness of procedural hurdles such as the burden of proof can be detected, but progress is still at best slow.

---

24. Johan Carlo Olsson, *Studie: arbetsplatser upplevs ojämställda*, Svenska Dagbladet, Oct. 13, 2018 *citing* Sofia Rasmussen and Madeleine Sultan Sjöqvist, Equality Swedish 2018.

CHAPTER 14

Spain: #Justiciamachista, #Cuéntalo, and Stop Eating Strawberries!

Ruth M. Mestre i Mestre[1]

There's no Weinstein case in Spain. Indeed, if #MeToo is only about sexual harassment, then one could argue there is no such thing as a Spanish #MeToo. A case of sexual harassment against Moroccan women working in Spain hit the media in 2018, but it did not receive as much attention as other cases of gender-based violence.

This was not the first time that harassment went unnoticed. In 2016, two major cases received media attention, one concerned the human resources director of a public TV station (Canal 9) who was accused by three female co-workers; another concerned a university professor who was sexually harassing female colleagues. Important as these cases were, they did not provoke a response from the general public or the feminist movement. However, one would have expected a different reaction two years later, because if #MeToo is about making sexual violence visible, then its impact in Spain was extraordinary.

The case that put violence against women back on the Spanish political agenda, generating indignation, reaction, street demonstrations, social mobilizations, and legal changes began in 2016. During the San Fermines "running of the bulls" event in Pamplona, five young men gang-raped an eighteen-year-old girl, filmed the rape, and shared the video through a WhatsApp group called "La Manada" (the Wolfpack). She reported the rape to the police that night and the five men were arrested the following morning (July 2016). By November 2017, the trial was receiving immense media attention. On November 17, the defense lawyer submitted as evidence to the court a report by a private detective showing the victim's behavior *after* the alleged rape, presumably revealing that

1. Universitat de València, Project Transformaciones de la justicia DER2016-78356-P, Ministerio de Ciencia, Innovación y Universidades.

she was not particularly traumatized, thus "proving" that the accusations of rape were false. The court decided to accept the report for evaluation, and women from all over the country spontaneously demonstrated, chanting: "We are your pack" and "I believe you." Those November 17 demonstrations were the first of a series of feminist protests that continued into 2018.

The global #MeToo movement put those protests in a broader context of protesting against sexual violence. The Spanish feminist movement successfully claimed that sexual violence is a painfully common experience; that the legal system and legal process revictimizes us; that social agreements subordinate women in many different ways and settings; and that we have had enough. There is, however, an urgent need yet to be addressed regarding the sexual violence and harassment that seasonal migrant women face in Spain.

Legal Framework for Sexual Violence and Sexual Harassment

The fight against violence against women in Spain had two important moments before 2018. In December 1997, Ana Orantes was burnt alive by her ex-husband after she denounced forty years of abuse on a television program. For many, this was the awakening from a delusion of equality, that started with the death of the dictator Francisco Franco in 1976, and the recognition of equality between men and women in the new Spanish Constitution (1978). Her murder put violence against women (VAW) on the political agenda and set the road to a major achievement: the passing of the Comprehensive Protection Measures Against Gender-Based Violence Act (2004).[2]

With this act, the law moved away from previous conceptualizations by clearly stating that gender-based violence is a manifestation of inequality. The act includes provisions on labor law, healthcare, social work, education, and criminal law, and builds a comprehensive framework protecting women who suffer violence. The act states that its purpose is to: "combat violence against women by their present or former spouses or by men with whom they maintain or have maintained analogous affective relations ... as an expression of discrimination, the situation of inequality, and the power relations prevailing between the sexes." Thus, although it appropriately points to the cause of violence being the structural power relations of men over women, the law only protects women

---

2. In 1989, the Criminal Code introduced the crime of "physical violence in the family" that only addressed constant violence against family members (spouse, children, and others). The 1995 "Criminal Code of the Democracy" did not substantially modify those provisions. Although further modifications were introduced in 2003, a comprehensive reform was undertaken with the Comprehensive Protection Measures Act in 2004.

from intimate or domestic violence,[3] leaving all other forms of gender-based violence against women outside this equality framework.

The second moment for framing certain forms of VAW as a matter of equality was in 2007 when the Effective Equality of Women and Men Act (the Effective Equality Act) passed as a result of the European directives on equality.[4] Both, the Spanish Criminal Code and the Labor Code had contained provisions against sexual harassment since 1995. However, the Effective Equality Act introduced the idea that sexual harassment was a form of discrimination.[5] The act established several preventive measures regarding harassment, such as the requirement that companies, state administrations, and every public service create protocols to prevent and punish sexual harassment in the workplace. Unfortunately, the effectiveness of such protocols is questionable.[6] Further,

---

3. This narrowing of the category *gender* to a "woman in a relationship" (Elena Larrauri, Criminología crítica y violencia de género (1st ed., 2007)) has been extensively criticized. It has led to a confusion among politicians, lawyers, and scholars that use the term gender as synonymous with woman and "gender violence" as synonymous with violence against woman. The act included children and other *vulnerable* victims, and so the act contains many contradictions as it covers gender-based violence against women, as well as domestic violence (see Ruth M. Mestre i Mestre, María José Añón Roig, Violencia sobre las mujeres: discriminación, subordinación y derecho, La nueva ley contra la violencia de género (J. Boix & E. Martinez (eds.) LO 1/2004 de 28 de diciembre 2005); Larrauri, supra; Derecho, Género e Igualdad. Cambios en las estructuras jurídicas androcénctricas, Vol. I (Daniela Heim, Encarna Bodelón González, eds., 2009.); and María Luisa Maqueda Abreu, Razones y sinrazones para una criminología feminista (1st ed., 2014)).

4. Directive 2006/54/EC of the European Parliament and of the Council of 5 July 2006 on the implementation of the principle of equal opportunities and equal treatment of men and women in matters of employment and occupation (recast).

5. The Spanish Act reproduces the definitions of the directive, classifying as indirect discrimination any apparently neutral provision, criterion, or practice that puts persons of one gender at a disadvantage compared with persons of the other gender, unless that provision, criterion, or practice is objectively justified by a legitimate aim, and the means of achieving that aim are appropriate and necessary. Sexual harassment is defined as occurring when any form of unwanted verbal, non-verbal, or physical conduct of a sexual nature occurs, with the purpose or effect of violating the dignity of a person, in particular when creating an intimidating, hostile, degrading, humiliating, or offensive environment.

6. In 2012 a study on the implementation of such measures in public universities revealed that thirty-six universities out of forty-five had an equality unit, and four were creating such a unit. Only eleven universities with equality units had programs to fight VAW: thus, only thirty-four of forty-five universities complied with the law. (Esperanza Bosch Fiol, *El acoso sexual en el ámbito Universitario: elementos para mejorar la implementación de medidas de prevención, detección e intervención*, Instituto de la Mujer (2012), http://www.inmujer.gob.es/areas Tematicas/estudios/estudioslinea2014/docs/El_acoso_sexual_ambito_universitario.pdf.) Valls concluded that "Spanish Universities tend not to intervene in situations of violence against women and they simply delegate the responsibility to take actions to other institutions, such as the police." (Rosa Valls et al., *Breaking the silence at Spanish Universities: Findings from the first*

many companies and organizations do not take measures until cases reach the threshold of a criminal offense and other actors intervene.

Thus, by 2017-2018, the legal framework was being criticized from different perspectives, as protection against gender-based VAW was limited to "women in relationships"; the legal system re-victimized women, accepted victim-blaming arguments in rape cases; while sexual harassment measures and preventive actions were ineffective. For some, referring to all this as "indirect discrimination" (the only legal concept available), or even "structural discrimination," seemed inappropriate. The Spanish professor M. Barrère proposes reformulating and re-labeling anti-discrimination legislation under the term "subordiscrimination," because it highlights better than other terms (such as structural, systemic, or institutional discrimination) the "power over" element of the treatment, and the fact that discrimination is not a *situation* but an action (or an omission) that acquires a certain meaning through one or various systems of power that minimize the status of some social groups, reproducing their subordination in a particular context.[7]

8 March 2018—#Nosotrasparamos (8 March—We Strike!)

Public protests about the "Wolfpack" case had spontaneously occurred across the country for months, and the call for a general strike by the feminist movement in March 2018 prospered in this ambience. As in other countries, Spanish women were called to a general strike from productive work, reproductive work, consumption of resources, and student studies, articulating the different ways in which neoliberalism and capitalism oppress women.

Over five million women did not attend their workplace and over six million demonstrated in massive protests across the country. Seven thousand journalists signed a "We strike" manifesto, provoking blank screens on television channels, thin newspapers, and empty media studios. Those who could not participate in the strike were invited to participate in other ways, and men were invited to organize care work instead of demonstrating.

The groundwork for this successful event started in 2009, when the national feminist congress redirected the focus of concern towards complex and intersecting power relations, including class, race, or migratory status. In

---

study of violence against women on campuses in Spain, 22 (13) Violence Against Women 2016, 1533, 1519-1539).

7. María Angeles Barrere Unzueta, *Filosofías del derecho antidiscriminatorio: ¿Qué derecho y qué discriminación?: Una visión contra-hegemónica del Derecho Antidiscriminatorio*, Anuario de filosofía del derecho, Tomo XXXIV, p. 11-242 (2018).

2011, the *15M movement* against austerity,[8] and the 2014 fight for reproductive freedom,[9] contributed to a shift in the feminist movement, adding a new generation of feminists with a far more complex agenda than that promoted by *official* feminism.[10]

The Wolfpack Decision: #Justiciamachista (Patriarchal Justice)

After the huge success of the protests on March 8, the court's decision in the Wolfpack case was a tremendous disappointment. On March 20, the members of the Wolfpack were found guilty of sexual abuse and sentenced to nine years in prison. The court did not find "intimidation" to be established,[11] even though the perpetrators took advantage of their numbers and strength. The court declared the sexual acts to be unconsented sex, but not rape. The decision generated social anger, feminist concern, and protests against patriarchal justice: "It's not abuse but rape," "rape is rape," "patriarchal justice," and "I believe you" were heard again on the streets.

A few days later, a journalist published her own rape story, twittered under #cuéntalo (talk about it), and her story was quickly shared by many women telling their own rape stories.

---

8. On May 15, 2011, Spain was, in the words of Ramón A. Feenstra, et al., "convulsed by one of the most spectacular popular uprisings in its history" (RAMÓN A. FEENSTRA ET AL., REFIGURING DEMOCRACY: THE SPANISH POLITICAL LABORATORY (1st ed. 2017)). About eight million citizens took part in occupations of public squares in at least sixty municipalities across the country, in the middle of a great social, economic, and political crisis. The protests and occupation of public squares for discussing and organizing social alternatives lasted several months, and some of the *asambleas populares* (popular assemblies) are still working in many neighborhoods.

9. In 2010 an act was passed to guarantee sexual and reproductive health that decriminalized abortion in the first 14 weeks of pregnancy and established the conditions for abortion before and after week 22. The previous 1985 legislation considered legal abortion only in cases of risk for the mother, rape, or malformation of the fetus. In 2014, the government announced its intention to re-establish the case-based legislation, and this caused protests and the resignation of the Minister of Justice.

10. Justa Montero, *La huelga feminista del 8M: haciendo historia*, in NURIA ALABAO ET AL., UN FEMINISMO DEL 99%, (2018) pp. 33- 43, http://feministas.org/IMG/pdf/articulo_huelga_feminista_justa-1.pdf.

11. The Spanish Criminal Code distinguishes rape (penalties up to twelve years prison) from sexual abuse (nine years), requiring violence or intimidation for rape, and "mere" unconsented sex for sexual abuse. Two judges found the Wolfpack members guilty of sexual abuse. The third judge believed that the victim's whole story was untrue and that the parties were just having fun.

The gap between women's understanding of rape, and the response of the criminal justice system produced a social outcry. The point was not whether the rapists had been sentenced to an appropriate number of years in prison. Rather, the elements of concern were how the legal system had dealt with the case; how the testimony of the victim was translated into a legalese that was incomprehensible for most people; and whether the court was or was not obliged to interpret intimidation or violence with a gender perspective. Could the court not see that intimidation for a woman in the context of a sexual threat needs to be construed differently from intimidation in any other violent or crime-related context?

The outcry was so great, and the protests so large, that the conservative government led by the *Partido Popular* announced an immediate revision of the criminal provisions by the Criminal Codification Commission.[12] In November 2018, the commission met for the first time, and although it agreed that the term "rape" needed to be reintroduced in the Criminal Code, it has not yet reached an agreement on whether there should be one or two crimes, or how to adapt the criminal provisions to the Istanbul Convention.[13] The discussion on the need to modify the Criminal Code was reflected in the election campaign in April 2019.

Although the party that won the elections (the Socialist Party) included a modification of the provisions regarding rape in its manifesto, it is unclear if and when this discussion and modification will be implemented in the law. New general elections were held in November 2019 with a quite different political scenario, in which for the first time after Franco's dictatorship, an extreme right-wing party that opposes sexual equality and LGBTQ rights has parliamentary representation.[14]

On appeal in 2019, the high court found the five members of the Wolf-pack guilty of rape and sentenced them to nine years in prison.

---

12. This was again subjected to great criticism because, among other things, the commission at the time was formed of nineteen men and one woman. Many members refused to participate in the commission if more women were not appointed, and finally, the commission was changed to consist of twelve women, thirteen men, and three female experts especially appointed for this revision.

13. Council of Europe Convention on Preventing and Combating Violence Against Women and Domestic Violence (Istanbul Convention), 2014.

14. At present, the ideological lines of extreme right parties in Europe reject equal rights for migrants and racialized groups of citizens and reject policies of equality. A number of European countries (Poland, Bulgaria, Hungary, and Turkey) are seriously considering withdrawing from the Istanbul Convention because it reflects this "gender ideology" that they want to eradicate.

Strawberry Fields Forever

Every now and then there is an article in the Spanish press about sexual harassment against seasonal workers in the strawberry fields in Huelva, Spain. Spanish migration legislation in 2000 added the "temporary foreign worker" system within the established annual quotas as the legal admission procedure for seasonal migrant workers.

Seasonal workers are recruited abroad, sign a three-, six-, or nine-month contract and return to their homes when it expires. They live on the farm where they work. According to Palumbo and Sciurba, all Moroccan agricultural seasonal workers in Huelva in 2012 were middle-aged women; only 5.4 percent had a secondary level education; only 3.8 percent were without dependent children, and more than 75 percent were illiterate.[15] Seasonal workers have very poor working conditions and are controlled by *manijeros* (taskmasters) who may be local workers or settled migrants recruited to control other migrant workers.

These conditions ensure that the women return home only after the season is done, and that they remain isolated and under close supervision while working.[16] In this context of dependency, migratory women suffer abusive working conditions that range from arbitrary wage deductions to sexual harassment and abuse. Romanian women recruited by foreign agencies endure very similar conditions, and arguably, these two groups of women are victims of human trafficking for labor exploitation.[17]

In June 2018, a group of Moroccan women working strawberry fields in Moguer (Huelva) reported sexual harassment and sexual abuse by their *manijero*. Even though temporary foreign worker contracts are monitored by state agencies, measures to prevent or punish sexual harassment have not been implemented and are not mandatory for employing seasonal workers. Although their case received much more attention than on previous occasions, their situation did not give rise to massive demonstrations: no #MeToo; no feminist revolt; and no extensive media coverage.

This shows that the Spanish feminist movement, and Spanish society in general, has failed to address VAW from a wider perspective and within a

---

15. Palumbo, L. and Sciurba, A. (2018): *The vulnerability to exploitation of women migrant workers in agriculture in the EU: the need for a human rights and a gender-based perspective*, 29, Policy Department for Citizens' Rights and Constitutional Affairs- Directorate General for Internal Policies of the Union, European Parliament (2018).

16. Margarita Miñarro Yanini, *Excelencia económica e inmigración femenina: la "explotación" de temporeras del "oro rojo,"* 427 CEF—Trabajo y Seguridad Social, Oct. 2018, p. 5-15.

17. Palumbo and Sciurba, *supra*, note 15.

framework of equality and anti-discrimination. After #MeToo, #cuéntalo, and "#justiciamachista," Violeta Assiego remarked that white feminists must stop eating Spanish strawberries and join with Moroccan feminists in denouncing the sexist-racist-classist treatment Moroccan women receive in Spanish fields from employers and *manijeros*,[18] as well as by state agencies and migratory legislation.

In March 2019, the organization Women's Link Worldwide began giving legal representation to four Moroccan women who had denounced sexual harassment in Moguer (Huelva, Spain), and the case is under investigation.[19]

If 2017-2018 was a turning point in Spain for sexual violence in general, and for showing the many ways the system fails women, then 2019 has been a worrying year. The extreme right entered the political scenario expressing belligerent resistance and rejection of equality policies, including those that combat sexual violence. In addition, the general political paralysis in Spain is delaying the legal modifications needed to adapt legislation on sexual violence to international standards. It seems as if the window of opportunity is closing without having achieved effective changes in law or society, and without a discourse or policy regarding the different power relations that shape inequality and VAW, including the power relations expressed in feminist dynamics.

---

18. Violeta Assiego, *Zona Crítica: Las feministas blancas comemos fresas*, ELDIARIO .ES, Nov. 6, 2018, https://www.eldiario.es/zonacritica/feministas-blancas-comemos-fresas _6_781181891.html.

19. See *Women's Link is representing four female migrant workers who suffered labour exploitation and sexual harassment while harvesting strawberries in Spain*, WOMEN'S LINK WORLDWIDE, Oct. 3, 2019, https://www.womenslinkworldwide.org/informate/sala-de -prensa/women-s-link-representa-a-cuatro-trabajadoras-de-la-fresa-que-sufrieron-explota cion-laboral-y-acoso-sexual-en-espana.

CHAPTER 15

Much Backlash Against Nothing: #MeToo in Czechia

Barbara Havelková[1] and Zuzana Andreska[2]

Introduction

A definition and a prohibition of harassment, initially only in labor law, entered Czech law in 2000.[3] The law was introduced in Czechia solely to fulfill EU membership obligations.[4] This has meant that the reasons for adoption and aims of harassment provisions, and anti-discrimination law more generally, have not been adequately understood by the Czech public. And this ignorance has negatively impacted the effectiveness of its judicial application.[5] Because of this external driver for legislation, the process of adoption of the new provisions was not accompanied by testimonies of Czech women who had experienced it.

---

1. Associate Professor of Law, Faculty of Law and Tutorial Fellow in Law, St Hilda's College, University of Oxford.

2. Law Student and Gender Studies Graduate, Charles University, Czech Republic.

3. The provision on sexual harassment was part of EU implementation obligations, specifically Equal Treatment Directive as amended by the Amending Directive art 2(2); now Recast Directive, art 2(1)c, d and 2(2)a. The original transposing Czech provision in Act No 65/1965 Coll, Labour Code, s 7(2), enacted in 2000, covered only quid pro quo sexual harassment and was not compliant with the EU harassment definition. A new definition was introduced in 2004, to comply with the Amending Directive. With the adoption of a new Labour Code, Act No 262/2006 Coll, Labour Code, which counted on the contemporaneous adoption of the first proposed Antidiscrimination Act, which would cover the issue of harassment, the protection disappeared. This situation was only remedied in 2009 when the second proposed version of an Antidiscrimination Act was passed and entered into force (Act No 198/2009 Coll, Anti-Discrimination Act, s 2(2), 4(1,2)).

4. BARBARA HAVELKOVÁ, GENDER EQUALITY IN LAW: UNCOVERING THE LEGACIES OF CZECH STATE SOCIALISM (Hart/Bloomsbury. 2017), hereinafter "BH," 225-238.

5. BH, 243-273.

Indeed, both in Parliament and more widely in public debates, the discussion has always been driven by those who doubt and minimize the phenomenon. Those who have experienced it have mostly remained silent.

The situation was not changed by the worldwide #MeToo phenomenon. Indeed, rather than a bottom-up movement based around individual testimonials, #MeToo has galvanized those in Czechia who misinterpret its content and aims and who generate fear about it and its repercussions. For these reasons, the #MeToo movement not only did not lead to any legal change, but none was even raised or debated despite the fact that the legal framework, as well as its insufficient enforcement, are ripe for improvement.[6]

In the following, we briefly present the legal protections and highlight some of their deficits. We claim, however, that, despite the issues with the legal framework as well as its enforcement, the problem mostly remains a general lack of understanding of the phenomenon of gendered abuse of power and violence, in the legal community and beyond. For that reason, we dedicate a separate, and substantial, part of our chapter to public debates. For this analysis, we draw on print media[7] as well as material generated by the legal community (lawmakers and lawyers), such as parliamentary debates and court decisions.[8] Particular attention is given to the conference "Legal Aspects of the MeToo Campaign" that took place in Prague in March 2018 (hereafter "MeToo Conference") in the context of a prominent wider legal gathering, the "Permanent Conference of Czech Law."[9]

The MeToo Conference was probably the most high-profile public event in Czechia on the topic of #MeToo and the law. It took place in the central building of Charles University and had the patronage of the President of the

---

6. See, e.g., Barbara Havelková, Zuzana Andreska, Násilí na ženách. In Petra Kubálková (ed.), Ženy a česká společnost: Hodnocení implementace pekingské akční platformy na národní a mezinárodní úrovni (Peking +20) (2016) (Cz.); Klára Kalibová, Stereotypní představy o "Pravém znásilnění" a důvěryhodnosti poškozené trestný čin znásilnění v interpretační praxi českých soudů. In Petra Kutálková, Lubica Kobová (eds.), Sexuální násilí, proč se nikdo neptá? (2014) at 53ff (Cz.).

7. Here, Jana Valdrová's media analysis has been particularly useful, and we draw on it below. Jana Valdrová, *Jak se v Česku píše a mluví o #metoo*, Jana Valdrová's Blog (Dec. 6, 2017), http://www.valdrova.cz/2017/12/jako-koza-petrzeli-aneb-kdyz-nekdo-nevi-o-cem-je -metoo/ (Cz.), hereafter "Valdrová."

8. These have previously been analyzed in BH.

9. The Permanent Conference of Czech Law has the goal of formulating important doctrinal opinions in the field of law and legal theory and has the patronage of, among others, the President of the Constitutional Court, Pavel Rychetský, the President of the Chamber of Deputies, Radek Vondráček, the Mayor of the City of Prague, Adriana Krnáčová, and the Rector of Charles University, Tomáš Zima.

Committee on Constitutional Law of the Chamber of Deputies, Marek Benda, and the Vice President of the Supreme Court, Roman Fiala. The conference was organized by a former Minister of Justice, Daniela Kovářová,[10] and among its speakers were—aside from Kovářová and Fiala—a Constitutional Court judge (David Uhlíř), a former Cabinet Minister (Cyril Svoboda), several ordinary court judges and prominent attorneys, and well-known sexologists. Although the MeToo Conference presented itself as an expert event, the invited speakers had no relevant expertise in gender or gender-based harassment or violence; the only female speakers—apart from the organizer Kovářová—were an actor, and an Olympic skier who previously criticized #MeToo. The overwhelming majority of the contributions were hostile and/or dismissive. While the MeToo Conference was of course not representative of the opinions of the entire legal community, it is worth noting that while there was some criticism of it from a few journalists and students of Charles University, the event and its output was never disavowed by the Permanent Conference organizers or its patrons, or condemned by any other part of the legal community. From the MeToo Conference's contributions, as well as other public debates, nine themes[11] emerge, which underlie the difficulties that any fight against harassment and gender-based violence encounters in Czechia.[12]

Legal Protection

At the moment, gender-based violence is addressed in the Criminal Code, while harassment, in labor relations and in access to goods and services, is prohibited under the Anti-Discrimination Act ("A-DA"). In terms of criminal law, the coverage of gender-based violence has been steadily improving: a specific crime of domestic violence was inserted in 2004,[13] the new Criminal Code adopted in 2009 newly criminalized stalking[14] and introduced a more comprehensive

---

10. Kovářová is a long-term critic of gender analysis of the law. She established and currently serves as the President of the Union of Family Lawyers, which promotes the idea of state non-interference with the institution of the family.

11. Similar themes have been identified by other authors: Jana Valdrová and Hana Maříková in her analysis of interviews with trade union officials. Hana Maříková, *Analýza přístupu odborových svazů ČMKOS k obtěžování a sexuálnímu obtěžování, in* Obtěžování žen a mužů a sexuální obtěžování v českém systému pracovních vztahů. Rozsah, formy, aktéři, řešení (Alena Křížková et al., eds., 2006), pp. 67-75, hereafter "Maříková."

12. The discourse regarding #MeToo is familiar from previous debates about gender-related issues.

13. Act No 40/1961 Coll, Criminal Code, as amended by Act No 91/2004 Coll, s. 215a; now Act No 40/2009 Coll, Criminal Code, s 199. For detail, see BH, p. 181.

14. Act No 40/2009 Coll, Criminal Code, s 354, entitled "dangerous pursuit."

definition of trafficking.[15] The definition of rape has also been subject to several, overwhelmingly positive, developments. Since 2001, rape against any person (not only women) is covered, and any sexual intercourse comparable to genital intercourse (also anal, oral, or digital) is included.[16] The 2009 Criminal Code widened the definition further, to include any other sexual intercourse-action by which the perpetrator achieves sexual gratification using the body of another person (groping of genitals, breasts, etc.).[17] Moreover, a new offence of "sexual coercion" was also added, which covers also coercion to "self-gratification, denudation or similar behavior" or persuasion of various sex acts by a person in a position of power or authority.[18] Problems remain, however: the definition of rape turns to the concept of violence (or defenselessness) rather than lack of consent. This means that an act of resistance is required; a mere refusal of intercourse is insufficient. Rape is considered a violent crime affecting the dignity of its "victims;"[19] an understanding of the harm to sexual autonomy seems to be absent. The debates surrounding #MeToo echo these limitations.

The Anti-Discrimination Act, which was adopted in 2009, defines harassment and sexual harassment as a form of discrimination.[20] Harassment is defined as "unwanted conduct related to discrimination grounds (incl. sex[21]) which has the purpose or effect of violating the dignity of a person, and of creating an intimidating, hostile, degrading, humiliating or offensive environment, or (conduct) which can be interpreted as a condition for a decision impacting the exercise of rights and duties arising from employment."[22] Sexual harassment is then understood as harassment of a "sexual nature."[23] Both definitions, as well as their scope of application, basically follow those of EU directives. While transposition obligations appear fulfilled by Czechia, full implementation is another matter. Despite the fact that some definition of harassment has been in the legal order for close to two decades and almost a decade has passed since the adoption of the A-DA, the number of cases on sexual harassment remains low.

---

15. Ibid, s 168. The definition of trafficking evolved gradually: in 2002, it was gender-neutralized, and in 2004, its scope was expanded beyond sexual exploitation to other forms of acts such as forced labor. BH p. 181 fn. 301.

16. Act No 144/2001 Coll. amending the Criminal Code.

17. Ibid, s 185.

18. Ibid, s 186.

19. This point is based on the letter of the law, in terms of the place of the crime within the structure of the Criminal Code. It is also true of understandings within the legal community.

20. Act No 198/2009 Anti-discrimination Act, hereafter "A-DA", s 2(2).

21. The exhaustive list is in A-DA, s 2(3).

22. Ibid, s 4(1).

23. Ibid, s 4(2).

The two judgments[24] available to us focus disproportionately on the claimant and blame her. In both cases, the courts went out of their way to assess the personality of the claimant and show that she might have been difficult, one court assessing her as "arrogant,"[25] with "communication problems."[26] No such examination of the harasser was undertaken. Despite the fact that in both cases the female employees were harassed by their superiors, the power disparity, as well as complete lack of investigative and remedial procedures by the employer, were ignored by the courts. Harassment that does not reach the gravity of crimes or happens outside of legally relevant relationships (employment or access to goods and services), such as all street harassment, is not specifically addressed by the law.

Socio-Cultural Obstacles to Fighting Harassment and Gender-Based Violence

The #MeToo campaign entered Czechia in the fall of 2017 through Twitter. However, the number of posts remained low and no prominent women joined the movement. Despite this, a vigorous backlash soon followed. It evinced several characteristics, essential to the understanding of the lack of success of #MeToo, as well as of the fight against gender-based harassment and violence, and even gender inequality, in Czechia more generally.[27]

Three aspects of patriarchy, essential for understanding the problem of harassment, which were relatively widely debated and illustrated in English-speaking media, are not widely known and understood in Czechia: (1) that harassment is not driven by "natural" human sexual instincts, but is deeply cultural; (2) the fact that harassment is about power, not sex; and (3) that it is not an individual problem of "deviants." but a structural problem, enabled by a particular cultural environment.

First, in Czechia, sexual harassment is often interpreted as a type of natural sexual behavior and a way of communication between women and men. Evolutionary biologists are therefore invited to comment on it, and they predictably defend it as survival mechanism of the species ("We are all descendants of men and women, who behaved 'biologically effectively,' because sexuality

---

24. Judgment of the District Court for Prague 1, AB v. Ministry of Foreign Affairs, Sept. 6, 2007, Ref No 27C 90/2004-123. Judgment of the District Court in Pardubice, PS v. Fire Department, Mar. 12, 2008, Ref No 8C 373/2006-107.

25. Judgment of the District Court in Pardubice, P.S. proti Hasičskému záchrannému sboru, Mar. 12, 2008, Ref No BC 373/2006-107.

26. Ibid.

27. The following quotations are all from the MeToo Conference.

leads to growth. Women offer something (sex) and men have to make an effort. Who does not make effort (harass), their genes will disappear."[28] A senator[29] stated that "had it not been for sexual harassment, [he] would have never met [his] wife, with whom [he] is still happily married." This take on harassment blithely accepts coercion; in the words of a prominent Czech sexologist, Radim Uzel: "a certain level of sexual coercion has always been an adequate part of human interaction."

There is, second, a clear inability or unwillingness to distinguish between unwanted behavior (which is harassment) and wanted behavior (which is not). Most commentators collapse the difference between mutual flirting and abuse of power.[30] This was exemplified by a statement by a former Constitutional Court judge,[31] who claimed to also be a survivor of sexual harassment because a wife of his colleague danced too close to him at a Bar Association formal dinner and whispered that he was the best dancer in the world. The power dimension—be it in the concrete situation that often involves a male employer, superior, teacher, gatekeeper, etc., let alone the general power inequality inherent in patriarchy— is not understood. The strong neo-liberalism of Czech public discourse[32] means that most instances of harassment are interpreted as unproblematic *quid pro quo* arrangements. In this "market exchange," women's sexuality is seen as their power or they are seen to exchange their sexuality for men's power ("A market is always based on a (free) choice and everyone has to take responsibility for their actions."[33]; "I consider it inappropriate to mix the victims of very serious criminal offences (such as rape) with those, who used sex to get a career."[34]).

Third, the last statement shows another common theme: the only situation in which sexual harassment and violence is unambiguously condemned is in the context of criminal law. This is arguably connected with the perception that these acts are exceptional, individual aberrations only committed by deviants. The structural aspect of "normal" men enabled by patriarchy to abuse power simply because they can, on the other hand, is ignored.[35] The consequence of this is that harassment is widely perceived as not something that ought to be legally regulated. This thesis was the underlying argument and conclusion of the MeToo Conference. The argument that law should stay out of "private"

---

28. Petr Hampl.
29. Jaroslav Kubera.
30. See also analysis in Valdrová.
31. Stanislav Balík.
32. BH, 199-200.
33. Laura Janáčková, psychologist.
34. Miroslav Krutina, attorney.
35. BH, 180ff.

relations is familiar from parliamentary debates about the criminalization of domestic violence, as well as anti-discrimination law.[36] One of the organizers of the MeToo Conference, Karel Havlíček, claimed in his introductory speech that the law has become so intrusive that "it is difficult now to claim whether there actually is any private sphere anymore."

Barbara Havelková has argued elsewhere[37] that this lack of understanding has partly to do with the missing "second wave feminism" in Czechia and in East Central Europe more generally. Radical feminism, with its ability to identify the gendered nature of social structures, would be especially helpful. But its rise in the "West," from 1970s onward, coincided with particularly harsh intellectual isolation of Czechoslovakia and a suppression of any bottom-up social movements. A gender analysis of power has yet to truly come into being.

These three issues are accompanied and supported by the several other "arguments" and moves, many not specific to Czechia. A fourth, and familiar, argument deployed against most gender progressive legislation and feminism, is that of cultural specificity of Czechia.[38] #MeToo also was identified as something un-Czech, a foreign import.[39] In the fifth strategy, the acts of harassment are misrepresented and ridiculed.[40] The former mostly by using examples that no #MeToo testimonials identify as a problem, such as opening doors for women and helping them into coats.[41] The latter notably by a specific use of the Czech term "harašení," which—although phonetically similar to English[42]—actually denotes (harmless) rustling and thus makes a joke of harassment. Sixth, the motives of those who speak up are questioned ("those who share their stories on social media are driven by revenge, but while using criminal law is a civilized way of exacting revenge, using campaigns on social media is not").[43] Seventh, the survivors of harassment are blamed for its occurrence. Two women speakers pointed out that women's use of make-up is a signaling of sexual availability and thus an invitation,[44] and it was pointed out that it is women's responsibility to "create and protect their personal space."[45] Eighth, those few women who

---

36. BH, 202-4 fn 90.

37. BH, 128, 292-5.

38. BH, 289.

39. Statements by the President of the Supreme Court, Roman Fiala, and a former Constitutional Court judge, Stanislav Balík. Similar observations have been made by Maříková and Valdrová.

40. Daniela Kovářová, Lukáš Bohuslav.

41. These examples were gathered from newspaper articles by Valdrová.

42. Valdrová.

43. Tomáš Sokol, attorney.

44. Laura Janáčková, psychologist.

45. Kateřina Neumannová, Olympic skier.

have decided to share their stories, as well as their tone, are being "policed" (the #MeToo campaign has been described as "aggressive" in its "moral mentoring tendency, which spoils the lives of the rest of the society"[46]). Ninth, fear of abuse of any legal regulation by survivors is prominent.[47]

For all these reasons, #MeToo might have had the opposite effect in Czechia than it has had elsewhere: rather than encouraging those who have experienced gender-based violence and harassment to speak up, it has shown them that society, including many in legal professions, are not ready to listen. Any supportive legal response is thus also far from being on the books.

---

46. Libor Vávra, the President of the Municipal Court in Prague.

47. This point was implied by many speakers at the MeToo Conference and is a staple of the media discourse (Valdrová). See also Maříková, 73.

CHAPTER 16

Early Start, Slow Progress, Racist Takeover, but Destined Not to Yield: The #MeToo Movement in Germany

Ulrike Lembke[1]

The Advent of the #MeToo Movement

Germany's #MeToo moment occurred some years before the #MeToo movement crossed the Atlantic. On the night of January 24, 2013, three feminists—Nicole von Horst, Anne Wizorek, and Jasna Strick—met on Twitter to discuss an article about daily sexism and street harassment. Motivating their meeting was the newspaper publication of sexist remarks by the liberal party's top candidate for the federal parliamentary elections directed at a young female journalist interviewing him as well as an article about misogyny within the newly founded Pirates' Party.[2] There were also nationwide preparations for the "one billion rising" day, a global campaign to end violence against women and girls.[3]

---

1. Professor for Public Law and Gender Studies, Humboldt University, Berlin.

2. Uta Steinwehr, *Sexismus: Der Aufschrei bleibt*, Deutsche Welle, Jan. 23, 2018, https://www.dw.com/de/sexismus-der-aufschrei-bleibt/a-42278374. When interviewed, the liberal party's top candidate for the federal parliamentary elections, Rainer Brüderle, said to the young female journalist Laura Himmelreich that she "could well fill out a dirndl" (Laura Himmelreich, *Der Herrenwitz*, Stern, Feb. 1, 2013, https://www.stern.de/politik/deutschland /stern-portraet-ueber-rainer-bruederle-der-herrenwitz-3116542.html). Another young female journalist, Annett Meiritz, described misogyny within the newly founded Pirates' Party, especially sexist remarks and rumors calling her a prostitute who received her inside information by offering sexual services (Annett Meiritz, *"Man liest ja so einiges über Sie,"* SpiegelOnline, 2013, https://www.spiegel.de/spiegel/annett-meiritz-ueber-die-frauenfeindlichkeit-in-der -piratenpartei-a-877558.html).

3. "One billion rising" is a global campaign to end violence against women and girls, organizing public events on February 14 every year with many German women's groups participating (https://www.onebillionrising.org/).

Following the example of the hashtag #ShoutingBack,[4] Anne Wizorek suggested they establish the Twitter handle #aufschrei ("outcry") to share experiences about sexual harassment. Within days, about 57,000 Twitter messages were published that reported mostly female experiences of sexism, harassment, and sexual violence.[5] The "sexism-debate" entered the media, newspapers, and newsrooms in Germany and was even reported in the *New York Times*.[6]

On June 21, 2013 #aufschrei was awarded the German Grimme Online Award,[7] the first hashtag receiving such a (or rather, any) prestigious award.[8] The jury emphasized that no discussion initiated in social media had met with such a broad response in the traditional media and in politics before. The response had demonstrated the importance of social media for societal debate and public opinion. All users who had constructively discussed the problems of existing everyday sexism had, at the same time, paved the way for a new, dovetailed online and offline debate culture. In 2014, Anne Wizorek published a book on everyday sexism and how to tackle gender discriminatory structures.[9]

The #aufschrei movement not only produced broad public and policy debate about everyday sexism and sexual harassment but also strengthened other movements for a fundamental reform of sexual assault law. Many women's rights organizations in Germany, especially the Federal Association of Rape Crisis Centers and Women's Counselling Centers,[10] campaigned for the implementation of a "No means No" concept in German criminal law, meaning that sexual assault and rape should be punishable without further requirements, such as establishing coercion by the perpetrator or helplessness or defense by the victim. Despite broad public debate on the topic and the fact that the Council of Europe Convention on Preventing and Combating Violence Against Women

---

4. British author Laura Bates initiated the Everyday Sexism Project in 2012 (http://everydaysexism.com/) to offer the opportunity to share experiences of sexism and sexual harassment, including the 2013 hashtag #ShoutingBack, focusing on street harassment of women.

5. Available under http://aufschrei.konvergenzfehler.de/timeline/.

6. Melissa Eddy & Chris Cottrell, *German Politician's Remark Stirs Outcry Over Sexism*, N.Y. TIMES (Jan. 28, 2013), https://www.nytimes.com/2013/01/29/world/europe/29iht-germany29.html.

7. Since 2001, the Grimme Institute, a non-profit research and public services facility, has awarded the Grimme Online Award to high-quality online content (https://www.grimme-online-award.de/).

8. See https://www.grimme-online-award.de/archiv/2013/preistraeger/p/d/aufschrei/.

9. ANNE WIZOREK, WEIL EIN #AUFSCHREI NICHT REICHT. FÜR EINEN FEMINISMUS VON HEUTE (Fischer 2014).

10. See https://www.frauen-gegen-gewalt.de/en/.

and Domestic Violence[11] explicitly required such law reform, the governing parties did not take action. That is, they did not take action before New Year's Eve 2015-16, when a large number of women became victims of sexual harassment and assault at the Cologne main station.

The perpetrators in Cologne were described by the police—which had been obviously unable to handle the situation adequately and guarantee safety in this public space—as young male North Africans. Despite discussing the safety problems, politicians of both the governing party as well as other German parties, among them right-wing populist parties, started a racist debate about foreign sexual offenders, refugees and migrants threatening the German female population.[12] Now, even the conservative parties advocated for amendments to the Penal Code, but only if coupled with a tightening of German asylum law. Members of left-wing parties and the Greens[13] as well as many civil society organizations had to consider stopping campaigning for the "No means No" concept due to its racist takeover. As it became obvious that conservative and right-wing political stakeholders would continue no matter what, German feminists took various political actions to fight for sexual autonomy and against racism at the same time. But neither the #ausnahmslos ("without exception"/"no excuses")[14] movement nor a multitude of civil society actions could prevent a majority of the federal parliament from enacting amendments to German asylum law that significantly lowered the requirements for expulsion and deportation immediately, after all factions of parliament had passed unanimously the amendments to the Penal Code.

---

11. See https://www.coe.int/fr/web/conventions/full-list/-/conventions/rms/090000 168008482e for the articles of the convention and https://www.coe.int/en/web/istanbul-con vention/home for the Council of Europe homepage for the convention.

12. For further analysis of the racist takeover of feminist politics "after Cologne" denying the extent of domestic violence in Germany, barring women from public spaces, letting *white* German perpetrators off the hook, and discounting women of color affected by (sexual) violence, see the excellent contributions under https://streit-wert.boellblog.org/. For more analysis including aspects of space and legal discourse, see Ulrike Lembke, *Weibliche Verletz-barkeit, orientalisierter Sexismus und die Egalität des Konsums: Gender-race-class als verschränkte Herrschaftsstrukturen im öffentlichen Raum*, ZtG (ED.) GRENZZIEHUNG VON "ÖFFENTLICH" UND "PRIVAT" IM NEUEN BLICK AUF DIE GESCHLECHTERVERHÄLTNISSE, 30-57 (2017), https://www.gender.hu-berlin.de/de/publikationen/gender-bulletins/bulletin-texte/texte-43 /bulletin-texte-grenzziehungen-von-oeffentlich-und-privat-im-neuen-blick-der-geschlechter verhaeltnisse.

13. The "Greens" (in German, *Bündnis 90/Die Grünen*) is a 1993 merger of the German Green Party (founded in 1980) and the Alliance 90 (based upon GDR civil rights movements). The party focuses on ecological, economic, and social sustainability.

14. The group describes itself, in English, as "Against sexualised violence and racism. Always. Anywhere. #ausnahmslos ("noexcuses")." See https://ausnahmslos.org/english.

Until today, conservative politicians, right-wing populists, and women from the far-right Identitarian movement ("Daughters of Europe") alike have based their political and electoral campaigning on images and legends of the dangerous strangers from African or Arab "cultures" threatening the (of course, white) German female. Racist takeovers of feminist politics and the toxic entanglement of racism and feigned fighting for women's human rights are among the major obstacles for feminist politics concerning sexual autonomy of women in Germany.

Another form of backlash to the #aufschrei and later #MeToo movement was and still is the narrative of sexual harassment being a question of morals. In March 2013, just before International Women's Day, the federal president of Germany joined the "sexism debate" by stating that when "such a fury of virtue [*Tugendfuror*[15]] prevails," he was "less moral than one would perhaps expect from him as a former clergyman."[16] Feminist movements strongly contested this approach,[17] but the buzzwords of "morality politics" and "moral panics" continued to influence or even shape public debate, and, partly, the German legal debate about sexism, sexual harassment, and criminal law reform concerning sexual assault and rape.[18]

The actual #MeToo Movement hit Germany late. There was the initial coverage of the Harvey Weinstein revelations in the German press, as there had been worldwide, but it was not before January 2018 that the first German perpetrator was named in public. The newspaper *Die Zeit* published sexual assault and rape allegations against the famous German film director Dieter Wedel.[19] Three actresses, two of them identified by their names, claimed that Dieter Wedel had raped or tried to rape them in the 1990s, and many others reported

---

15. The term "*Tugendfuror*" did not exist before in the German language. It is a portmanteau of an old-fashioned term for (female) virtue (*Tugend*) and an unusual term for (female) rage and hysterics (Furor). The very similar term "*Tugendterror*" was coined by civil law professors, lawyers, and politicians when campaigning against the implementation of European anti-discrimination law in 2005 and 2006. It fulfills the same function as "political correctness terror" and comparable terms.

16. *Gauck beklagt "Tugendfuror" im Fall Brüderle*, SPIEGELONLINE, Mar. 3, 2013, https://www.spiegel.de/politik/deutschland/sexismus-debatte-gauck-beklagt-tugendfuror-im-fall-bruederle-a-886578.html.

17. E.g., *Open Letter to the Federal President*, March 3, 2013, published by #aufschrei activists. See Fabian Reinbold, *#Aufschrei gegen Gauck*, SPIEGELONLINE, Mar. 6, 2013, https://www.spiegel.de/politik/deutschland/sexismus-debatte-aufschrei-gegen-gauck-a-887170.html.

18. For an excellent analysis of legal discourse, see Anja Schmidt, *Zum Zusammenhang von Recht, Moral, Moralpolitik und Moralpanik am Beispiel der Reform des Sexualstrafrechts*, 38 ZEITSCHRIFT FÜR RECHTSSOZIOLOGIE 2, 244-271 (2019).

19. Jana Simon & Annabell Wahba, *Im Zwielicht*, ZEITONLINE, Jan. 3, 2018, https://www.zeit.de/zeit-magazin/2018/02/dieter-wedel-regisseur-sexuelle-uebergriffe-vorwuerfe.

that he humiliated and harassed actresses on set. *Die Zeit*'s coverage attempted to distance itself from the "hysterical features that the #MeToo debate has occasionally exhibited" as deputy editor-in-chief Sabine Rückert wrote.[20] Alas, this was in vain as *Die Zeit* faced immediate criticism by other newspapers as well as legal discourse that focused on the statute of limitations and the presumption of innocence and lodged accusations of "trial/execution by media" and, of course, of "morality politics."[21]

Dieter Wedel resigned as artistic director of the Bad Hersfelder Festival[22] but denied all accusations. Due to the statute of limitations that applied to the accusations dating from the 1990s, criminal prosecution could not clarify the allegations. But more and more actresses came forward and accused him of sexual assault in the 1970s and 1980s. Documents from a public television broadcaster showed that some incidents were known but declared to be private matters. In early 2018, there was broader media coverage, but the analysis of power structures remained tedious and tenuous, and the television and film industry stayed mostly silent.[23] In contrast, the #MeToo Movement was featured at the international film festival Berlinale with a complaint and support system as well as a panel discussion about #MeToo where important members of the film and television industry were greeted by the federal minister responsible for gender equality.[24]

In May 2018, six women, including author and presenter Charlotte Roche, accused Gebhard Henke, program director of the public broadcaster WDR, of several instances of sexual harassment between 1990 and 2015.[25]

---

20. Sabine Rückert, *Verdacht und Berichterstattung*, Zeit Online, Jan. 11, 2018, https://www.zeit.de/kultur/film/2018-01/dieter-wedel-vorwuerfe-zeit-magazin-verjaehrung. Sabine Rückert later became (in)famous for her campaigning against sexual law reform. She not only made sure that a Federal Court of Justice (criminal law) judge could campaign weekly against sexual law reform, including naming and shaming feminist activists (for an astounding fee!), but she herself produced headlines such as, "Whether It Was Rape or Not Is Now in *Her* Discretion the Morning After."

21. E.g. Gisela Friedrichsen, *Mediale Hinrichtung per #MeToo—Schluss damit!*, Welt, Jan. 4, 2018, https://www.welt.de/vermischtes/plus172184533/Nun-auch-Dieter-Wedel-Mediale-Hinrichtung-per-MeToo-Schluss-damit.html.

22. A famous annual summer theater and opera festival, held under the auspices of the Federal President and for an audience of up to 1,600 persons.

23. See Friederike Zoe Grasshoff, Violetta Simon & Claudia Tieschky, *Alle, alle, alle sollen es gewusst haben*, Süddeutsche Zeitung, Jan. 25, 2018, https://www.sueddeutsche.de/panorama/vorwuerfe-gegen-dieter-wedel-alle-alle-alle-sollen-es-gewusst-haben-1.3840777.

24. See Berlinale press releases for 2018: https://www.berlinale.de/de/archiv/jahresarchive/2018/08_pressemitteilungen_2018/08_pressemitteilungen_2018detail_42068.html.

25. *Charlotte Roche wirft WDR-Filmchef Belästigung vor*, Süddeutsche Zeitung, May 4, 2018, https://www.sueddeutsche.de/medien/sexuelle-uebergriffe-beim-wdr-charlotte-roche-wirft-wdr-filmchef-belaestigung-vor-1.3967611.

Henke denied the accusations. After examination by the WDR, Henke was dismissed based on credible allegations of at least ten women. He sued WDR; the legal dispute was later settled amicably, but Henke was not reemployed. Henke also brought an injunctive action against the newspaper *Der Spiegel* and Charlotte Roche. He was supported in an open letter from more than twenty women from the film and television industry, who described working with him as controversial, but never abusive.[26] Yet two days before the oral hearing in February 2019, Henke withdrew his complaint when given the information that there were seven (prominent) women from the film industry ready to report more cases of sexual harassment.[27]

Legal Protections

In October 2017, when the #MeToo Movement made news, sexual harassment and harassment on the grounds of sex were prohibited in the workplace by anti-discrimination law, and the recently amended Penal Code prohibited rape, sexual assault, sexual harassment through touching, and any sexual interaction against the noticeable will of another person. In a landmark decision in June 2017, the Federal Labor Court had stated that "sexual harassment in the workplace" is often "an expression of hierarchies and the exercise of power and not of sexual pleasure."[28]

While earlier German law covering sexual assault and sexual harassment in the workplace had solely focused on the violation of dignity,[29] modern German

---

26. See the letter at *Offener Brief pro Henke*, MEDIABIZ, May 4, 2018, http://www .mediabiz.de/film/news/offener-brief-pro-henke/429476.

27. *Gebhard Henke zieht Klage gegen Charlotte Roche und "Spiegel" zurück*, SÜDDEUT- SCHE ZEITUNG, Feb. 21, 2019, https://www.sueddeutsche.de/medien/metoo-henke-wdr -roche-1.4340872.

28. Federal Labor Court, judgment of June 29, 2017, 2 AZR 302/16, http://juris .bundesarbeitsgericht.de/cgi-bin/rechtsprechung/document.py?Gericht=bag&Art=en&nr =19424.

29. Germany's first statutory regulation against sexual harassment in the workplace, the Employees' Protection Act (*Beschäftigtenschutzgesetz*, see https://de.wikipedia.org/wiki/Bes- chäftigtenschutzgesetz), entered into force in 1994 and had nearly no effect. The law required proving intent on the part of the harasser and "recognizable rejection" by those affected, and it focused solely on a violation of dignity. In 1995, German legal scholar Susanne Baer, now a Federal Constitutional Court judge, criticized the law, noting that the difficulties of German legal jurisprudence in dealing with sexual harassment were a homemade problem, mainly based on the erroneous construction of sexual harassment as a violation of dignity. The protection of dignity led to individualization, muddled the context, favored a paternalistic or perpetrator per- spective, suggested ideal victim behavior, and just missed the point. In contrast, Baer suggested that sexual harassment should be understood as a form of gender discrimination that maintains

law has been shaped by conforming with international human rights law (German's criminal law covering sexual assault[30]) and European Union directives (covering anti-discrimination law). The European Union Gender Equality Directives explicitly named sexual harassment as discrimination based on sex,[31] which had important legal consequences such as a shift of the burden of proof in favor of those affected, no requirement of intent on the part of the harasser, and a ban on upper limits for compensation claims. EU Directives covered both sexual harassment in the workplace[32] and sexual harassment in access to and supply of goods and services.[33] After lengthy discussions about the dangers of anti-discrimination law, the federal parliament passed the General Equal Treatment Act (*Allgemeines Gleichbehandlungsgesetz*[34]) to implement the European Equality Directives in 2006.

Thanks to the directives, Germany has detailed definitions of harassment and sexual harassment: under Section 3(3) of the General Equal Treatment Act (GETA), harassment shall be deemed to be discrimination when unwanted conduct in connection with race or ethnic origin, gender, religion or belief, disability, age, or sexual orientation takes place with the purpose or effect of violating the dignity of the person concerned and of creating an intimidating, hostile, degrading, humiliating, or offensive environment. Under Section 3(4) of the GETA, sexual harassment shall be deemed to be discrimination in relation to access to employment, recruitment conditions, and working conditions when unwanted conduct of a sexual nature—including unwanted sexual acts

---

or creates hierarchical gender relations in working life. See SUSANNE BAER, WÜRDE ODER GLEICHHEIT? ZUR ANGEMESSENEN GRUNDRECHTLICHEN KONZEPTION VON RECHT GEGEN DISKRIMINIERUNG AM BEISPIEL SEXUELLER BELÄSTIGUNG AM ARBEITSPLATZ IN DER BRD UND DEN USA (Nomos, 1995).

30. TATJANA HÖRNLE, MENSCHENRECHTLICHE VERPFLICHTUNGEN AUS DER ISTANBUL-KONVENTION. EIN GUTACHTEN ZUR REFORM DES § 177 STGB (Deutsches Institut für Menschenrechte, 2015), https://www.institut-fuer-menschenrechte.de/publikationen /frauenrechte/.

31. Directive 2002/73/EC of the European Parliament and of the Council of September 23, 2002, on the implementation of the principle of equal treatment for men and women as regards access to employment, vocational training and promotion, and working conditions; Council Directive 2004/113/EC of 13 December 2004 implementing the principle of equal treatment between men and women in the access to and supply of goods and services; Directive 2006/54/EC of the European Parliament and of the Council of 5 July 2006 on the implementation of the principle of equal opportunities and equal treatment of men and women in matters of employment and occupation (recast).

32. European Equality Directives 2002/73/EC and 2006/54/EC.

33. European Equality Directive 2004/113/EC (not implemented concerning sexual harassment).

34. General Act on Equal Treatment, Aug. 14, 2006 (FEDERAL LAW GAZETTE I p. 1897), https://www.gesetze-im-internet.de/englisch_agg/englisch_agg.html.

or requests to carry out sexual acts, physical contact of a sexual nature, comments of a sexual nature, and the unwanted showing or public exhibition of pornographic images—takes place with the purpose or effect of violating the dignity of the person concerned, in particular where it creates an intimidating, hostile, degrading, humiliating, or offensive environment.

The GETA is directly applicable to all employment relationships between private parties. The Act covers all persons in dependent employment, including part-time, fixed-term, probationary or temporary employment, and persons of similar status on account of their economic status ('quasi-subordinate'). It further covers vocational apprentices, job applicants, or recently terminated employees. Non-civil servant employees in the civil service are equally protected. Volunteers might be covered by interpreting the act in the light of European Union law. The Act promises protection against third-party harassment of employees, but this does not work out in practice.[35]

Under the GETA, the employer has the duty to take the measures necessary to ensure protection against discrimination, including (sexual) harassment. Where employees violate the prohibition of discrimination, including (sexual) harassment, the employer shall take suitable, necessary, and appropriate measures to stop the discrimination; this may include cautioning, moving, relocating, or dismissing the perpetrator employee in question. When discriminated or harassed against, employees have the right to lodge a complaint with the appropriate department in the firm, company, or authority. When the employer takes obviously unsuitable measures or no measures at all to stop the (sexual) harassment in the workplace, the affected employees have the right to stop working without loss of pay if necessary for their protection. The rejection or toleration of sexual harassment must not be the basis for disciplinary measures against the person concerned.

Employees can file a complaint before the competent labor court (or, when working for the state, administrative court) to oblige the employer to take necessary measures, and they can claim damages or compensation. Employers must pay compensation if they themselves harass, but also if they do not

---

35. The comprehensive assessment of the General Equal Treatment Act by SABINE BERGHAHN, MICHA KLAPP & ALEXANDER TISCHBIREK, EVALUATION DES ALLGEMEINEN GLEICHBEHANDLUNGSGESETZES (Antidiskriminierungsstelle, 2016), pp. 107ff, with many references, finds that the act offers no effective protection against discrimination, especially in the form of (sexual) harassment, by supervisors or superiors who are not employers, by colleagues, and by third parties such as business partners, customers, or clients, since the only person liable is the employer, and only in case of fault. Although third parties are indeed mentioned in Section 12(4) of the General Equal Treatment Act, the scope of this regulation is highly debated. The focus of debates lies upon the tolerability for the employer if he had to take measures against important clients or business partners, and there is no case law yet.

effectively prevent (sexual) harassment by other employees. (In violation of European Union law, the Act requires establishing fault against the employer.)

In practice, (alleged) harassers bring the vast number of complaints when they are facing legal consequences such as reprimand or dismissal. Therefore, German case law on sexual harassment in the workplace has mainly developed in unfair dismissal suits. Nevertheless, courts have ruled that a single assault suffices to constitute sexual harassment,[36] and that the employer is obliged by law to prevent any repetition by whatever means necessary, including warning, moving, or transferring the harasser to another workplace. Exploiting a superior position or a special dependency affects the sanction's gravity.[37] While the question of whether harassment through touching shall result in termination without notice is still judged inconsistently depending on the circumstances,[38] courts have clearly stated that verbal harassment can justify an extraordinary dismissal without notice.[39]

However, to date, German case law deals solely with (sexual) harassment in the workplace and in no other area. The GETA shows some pitfalls and shortcomings concerning its scope of application. Under Section 2, the prohibition of discrimination, including harassment, seems to cover all areas of employment, as well as social security, social benefits, education, and access to and supply of goods and services.[40] But further clarifications and especially concrete statutory entitlements are lacking in the areas of social protection and education. And the protection in access to and supply of goods and services is considerably weakened by statutory requirements not in compliance with the European law.

---

36. Federal Labor Court, judgment of June 9, 2011, 2 AZR 323/10.

37. E.g., Administrative Court of Meiningen, judgment of Dec. 8, 2011, 6 D 60012/11 Me.

38. Pro: State Labor Court of Mecklenburg-Pomerania, judgment of Aug. 14, 2012, 5 Sa 324/11 (the harassment was particularly threatening, and repetition was to be expected); State Labor Court of Hesse, judgment of Feb. 27, 2012, 16 Sa 1357/11 (the victim was a trainee, and the transferal of the harasser to another workplace was impossible); State Labor Court of Hesse, judgment of Nov. 17, 2010, 6 Sa 640/10 (particularly threatening). Contra: State Administrative Court of Bavaria, judgment of July 13, 2011, 16a D 10.565 (life crisis and true regret of the harasser); State Labor Court of Düsseldorf, judgment of June 12, 2013, 7 Sa 1878/12 (one-time misconduct of the harasser and offender-victim mediation successful).

39. Federal Labor Court, judgment of June 9, 2011, 2 AZR 323/10; State Labor Court of Schleswig-Holstein, judgment of Mar. 4, 2009, 3 Sa 410/08; Administrative Court of Augsburg, judgment of Nov. 11, 2011, AU 2 K 09.1369.

40. For an overview of legal protection in different times and fields, see Ulrike Lembke, *Sexuelle Belästigung: Recht und Rechtsprechung*, 8 AUS POLITIK UND ZEITGESCHICHTE, 35-40 (2014).

Moreover, in clear violation of EU law, the prohibition of sexual harassment under Section 3(4) of the GETA is explicitly restricted to employment. According to the prevailing opinion of German legal commentaries, this restriction is not applicable to the civil service (partly regulated by special administrative law) and must be eliminated for the field of education and for the provision of goods and services by a directive-consistent interpretation. There is no case law to support this opinion. However, legislation concerning education falls under the jurisdiction of the German states, and rules concerning the conduct on campus are subject to academic self-administration. Although female students are disproportionately affected by sexual harassment, their legal protection is fragmentary, inconsistent, and often based upon the goodwill of the individual university's president or administration.[41]

In 2016, sexual harassment through touching became a criminal offense under the new Section 184i of the Penal Code. Prior to this enactment, legal protection against sexual harassment had generally been restricted to the workplace. Under the Penal Code before the reform, sexual assault and rape required violence, coercion, or grave threats, or a specially defined helpless situation, but no other forms of sexual assault were considered, e.g., unexpected touching or grabbing. Moreover, courts disagreed about which types of touching or grabbing would constitute sexual assault, depending on the body parts concerned as well as the kind of clothing worn by the victim. Grabbing between the legs would always constitute sexual assault but touching the breast of a woman might not if she was wearing a winter coat or a thick sweater.[42]

Therefore, many of the Cologne 2015-2016 New Year's Eve sexual assaults (see earlier discussion) were just not punishable under German criminal law. The 2016 Penal Code amendments not only introduced the offence of sexual harassment in Section 184i but extended the definition of sexual assault to include assault by means of surprise and unexpected touching or grabbing. If courts previously wanted to reach a verdict of guilty for sexual harassment, they had to resort to an offense outside of criminal law on sexual offenses and convict

---

41. EVA KOCHER & STEFANIE PORSCHE, SEXUELLE BELÄSTIGUNG IM HOCH-SCHULKONTEXT—SCHUTZLÜCKEN UND EMPFEHLUNGEN (Antidiskriminierungsstelle des Bundes, 2015), https://www.antidiskriminierungsstelle.de/SharedDocs/Downloads/DE/publikationen/Expertisen/Expertise_Sexuelle_Belaestigung_im_Hochschulkontext.html.

42. The Federal Court of Justice, judgment of Mar. 20, 2012, 1 StR 447/11, regarded the touching of clothed genitals as a punishable sexual offence, but only because the person concerned was physically abused before. In its judgments of July 8, 2014, 2 StR 175/14, and of July 23, 2013, 1 StR 204/13, the Federal Court of Justice stated that touching parts of the body other than the primary sex organs (here, the breast of a girl and a boy clothed in a shirt) would not necessarily constitute a criminal offence. The Higher Regional Court of Brandenburg, judgment of Oct. 28, 2009, 1 Ss 70/09, suggested that a forced French kiss would not amount to sexual assault.

on the basis of physical insult.[43] This workaround, however, had the undesirable side effect that the judgment had to contain reflections upon the "sexual honor" of the victim.[44]

The 2016 criminal law reform implemented the "No means No" concept by fundamentally amending the Penal Code.[45] With this reform, any sexual act against the noticeable will of another person became a criminal offense without further requirements. Violence, coercion, joint action, severe or general threatening, surprise, or the exploitation or taking advantage of a person in a vulnerable, defenseless, or helpless position constitute offenses with aggravated penalties. While the 1997/98 criminal law reform was supported by International Human Rights debate,[46] the 2016 criminal law reform was strongly influenced by the Council of Europe Convention on Preventing and Combating Violence against Women and Domestic Violence.[47] However, there is a considerable gap between public discourse and feminist movements campaigning for effective legal protection against sexual assault and harassment on the one hand, and legal discourse, including case law dwelling on "morality politics" and "moral panics," on the other. As it was mainly the courts and influential legal literature that made the 1997/98 criminal law reform fail in practice, it remains to be seen what impact their hostile stance and stereotyping will employ this time.

---

43. E.g., Higher Regional Court of Nürnberg, judgment of Nov. 3, 2010, 1 St OLG Ss 219/10; Higher Regional Court of Bamberg, judgment of Sep. 28, 2006, 3 Ss 48/06.

44. Ambivalent: Federal Court of Justice, judgment of Sep. 18, 1986, 4 StR 432/86; in the affirmative: Higher Regional Court of Karlsruhe, judgment of June 6, 2002, 1 Ss 13/02.

45. Former criminal law reforms had not been successful in effectively protecting sexual autonomy and integrity. It was not until the 1997/98 criminal law reform that marital rape became a criminal offence, that male adults were recognized as possible victims of rape or sexual assault, and that the law covered other forms of committing these crimes than forced sexual intercourse alone. Since 1997, rape or sexual assault could be committed by coercion, severe threatening, or by "exploiting a vulnerable/defenceless position," which should have significantly extended the protection. But the Federal Court of Justice ruled out all cases of practical importance, especially sexual assault committed in apartments (the most common crime scene) and cases where the victim did not exhibit "fight or flight," and introduced extra-legal reduced penalties for spouses and intimate partners.

46. SARAH ELSUNI, GESCHLECHTSBEZOGENE GEWALT UND MENSCHENRECHTE (Nomos, 2011).

47. See *supra*, note 10.

The Reality

In the beginning, the legal protection against sexual harassment in the workplace did not work.[48] First small changes only occurred after the General Equal Treatment Act had entered into force. Although only through the (biased) framing of dismissal suits, the labor courts nonetheless started to develop stronger and stronger case law protection against sexual harassment at the workplace, culminating in the 2017 Federal Labor Court's recognition that "sexual harassment in the workplace" is often "an expression of hierarchies and the exercise of power and not of sexual pleasure."[49]

But despite the advancing insights of the courts, workplace sexual harassment victims obviously refrain from taking legal action, although sexual harassment remains a widespread problem. A 2015 study shows that while employees and HR managers are generally aware of the prohibition on sexual harassment, they are unaware of the employer's specific obligations and workers' rights under the GETA, and less than half can name concrete protection measures in their own company.[50] Works councils, too, have too little knowledge of the specific legal protections and still make too little use of works agreements as a means to prevent sexual harassment in the workplace.[51] Thus, while legal protections have improved significantly, progress in practice is still very slow.

The 1997/98 criminal law reform was one of Germany's most important law-making efforts, not only due to its gestational duration of over thirty years, but to its mobilization ability and paradigmatic changes. But the hopes and expectations of these legal reforms were not fulfilled: the reporting of rape and

---

48. Almut Pflüger, Susanne Baer et al., Beschäftigtenschutzgesetz in der Praxis (BMFSFJ, 2002), https://www.bmfsfj.de/bmfsfj/beschaeftigtenschutzge-setz-in-der-praxis/80792, showed that the 1994 Employees' Protection Act remained almost completely ineffective: only a fraction of the incidents were reported at all, the law was hardly known to those responsible in companies, administrations, and courts, and even in relevant court proceedings it was almost never applied. Instead, stereotypes about the allegedly private nature of sexual harassment shaped the judiciary's decision-making.

49. Federal Labor Court, *supra*, note 28.

50. Federal Anti-Discrimination Agency, "Sexual harassment in the workplace": Results of a representative survey among employees in Germany (ADS 2015), and "Sexual harassment in the workplace": Survey of 667 HR managers and works councils (ADS 2015), both available under https://www.antidiskriminierungsstelle.de/DE/ThemenUndForschung/Geschlecht/sexuelle_Belaestigung/sexBelaestigung_node.html.

51. Federal Anti-Discrimination Agency, "Sexual harassment in the workplace": Survey of 667 HR managers and works councils (ADS 2015).

sexual assault decreased while the attrition rates continued to rise.[52] The main obstacles hampering the prosecution of sexual harassment cases were (and still are) rape myths, gender stereotypes, and victim blaming, as well as misconceptions about the substantial difference between morals and intimacy on the one hand and gender-based discrimination and violence on the other.[53] As a Federal Court of Justice judge and influential author of a legal commentary as well as several criminal law professors were among the strongest opponents of the 2016 reform, it remains to be seen how the reform will be put into practice.

Criminal proceedings for rape and sexual assault are rare and very often an ordeal for the victims, who report the proceedings to be characterized by gender stereotypes, blaming the victim, rape myths, secondary victimization, and obstructions of the work of the legal counsel whose support they are entitled to. The association of defense lawyers is campaigning against victim's statutory rights in criminal proceedings and stressing the myth of the "lying woman." In 2017, the Regional Court of Münster decided on an unusually high amount of compensation for a rape victim to be paid by the perpetrators because, inter alia, the victim had been forced to watch the perpetrators' recording of her own rape during the court proceedings in the presence of the rapists and suffered severe trauma from this experience.[54] The judge who ordered the viewing, at the request of the defense lawyers, and who forced the victim to watch the recording until the very end, did not face any consequences for this inhuman and degrading treatment of a rape victim in court.[55]

---

52. Jo Lovett & Liz Kelly, Different systems, similar outcomes? Tracking attrition in reported rape cases across Europe (Metropolitan University, 2009), http://fellowship.birn.eu.com/en/file/show/jelena_blog4_lizkellyreport.pdf. "Attrition" refers to the failure of a rape case to proceed through the criminal justice system.

53. Ulrike Lembke, *Vergebliche Gesetzgebung. Die Reform des Sexualstrafrechts 1997/98 als Jahrhundertprojekt und ihr Scheitern in und an der sog. Rechtswirklichkeit*, 34 Zeitschrift für Rechtssoziologie 1+2, 253-283 (2014).

54. Regional Court of Münster, judgment of Dec. 7, 2017, 02 O 229/17, http://www.justiz.nrw.de/nrwe/lgs/muenster/lg_muenster/j2017/02_O_229_17_Teil_Versaeumnis_und_Schlussurteil_20171207.html.

55. See German Women Lawyers' Association, Submission to the UN Committee against Torture (CAT)—parallel report to the Sixth State Report of Germany, 27 March 2019, https://www.djb.de/verein/Kom-u-AS/K6/st19-09/. Concerning the (legal) situation of victims of gender-based violence in criminal proceedings in general, see German Women Lawyers' Association, Policy Paper "Opferrechte in Strafverfahren wegen geschlechtsbezogener Gewalt," 22 November 2018, https://www.djb.de/verein/Kom-u-AS/K3/st18-18/.

Changes in the Law and Its Enforcement?

As German legislation and case law had fundamentally been amended immediately prior to the #MeToo Movement making news in Germany, further fundamental legal changes could not be expected soon. But not every change needed is of a legal nature. New laws and statutory amendments need societal change to become legal practice. Everyday sexism and sexual assault cannot be eradicated by laws alone, and the same is true for gender stereotypes, rape myths, and victim blaming. The #aufschrei and the #MeToo movements made sexism and sexual harassment an issue in the public and the media, in social and family debates, and in legal and political discourse, and it was about time. Right-wing populism is rising in Germany, as it is nearly everywhere in Europe, and its nationalist and racist agenda is inextricably linked with hierarchical gender orders, gender stereotypes, sexism, violence, and anti-feminism.[56]

Since many debates had just taken place, the influence of #MeToo—when viewed in isolation—was limited to certain areas, in particular to cultural arts and media and the people working in these fields. Harassers, who had ruled like kings in their cultural profession, were questioned and criticized, but more importantly, the gender hierarchies and structures supporting power abuse for decades were tackled. Culture and media leaders had viewed themselves as outside of normal working life for a long time, producing tremendous creative output on the one hand and unbelievable structures of power abuse on the other.

As a first result of the #MeToo Movement, a "trust center against sexual harassment and violence" was set up where persons working at theaters or in the film and television industry could seek counseling and support.[57] The "pro-quota film movement"[58] is destined to further gender equality in film and television with the expectation that more women telling their stories means less gender stereotypes on and off screen.

The #MeToo Movement encouraged a broader critique of sexism and gender stereotyping as the basis for gender hierarchies, oppression, and violence in many branches of the cultural professions. One example is the fundamental critique of the body-shaming casting show Germany's Next Top Model under the hashtags #NotHeidisGirl and #keinbildfuerheidi, and by a great music video scripted, starred and produced by girls and young women from

---

56. Henning von Bargen & Barbara Unmüßig, *Antifeminismus—Scharnier zwischen rechtem Rand und Mitte*, GWI Blog, Sep. 28, 2016, https://www.gwi-boell.de/de/2016/09/28/antifeminismus-scharnier-zwischen-rechtem-rand-und-mitte.

57. See Themis Vertrauensstelle, https://themis-vertrauensstelle.de/.

58. See Pro Quote Film, https://proquote-film.de/#object=page:216.

the target group.[59] Another example is the broad public debate about sexist advertisement.[60]

When the creative industry is targeted, the demand for change is not restricted to some power- abusing alphas or to "creative" products overflowing with gender stereotypes. Attention has recently turned to the fact that all these great artists, musicians, and actors, and editors and directors have to be trained somewhere. Universities offering musical, artistic, or acting education and training in Germany sometimes have considerable problems with sexual harassment. The lecturers are often famous artists, musicians, and actors who are hired because of their creativity and genius rather than because of their self-reflection or didactic skills. The teaching takes place in very small groups or with the teacher and student alone. There is a masculine cult of genius and a certain kind of rape culture asserting that "sexual liberality" and "crossing your boundaries" would naturally unleash creativity. The training is often very intimate, and the students are extremely dependent on their lecturers and professors for grades, evaluations, and job referrals. It is impossible to tackle these power structures, and their inherent possibilities of abuse, assault, harassment, and violation, without a fundamental change of institutional culture and a new understanding of how to train for creative professions.

In 2016 and 2017, the former president of the Munich conservatory, famous concert pianist Siegfried Mauser, was sentenced for the sexual coercion of a female colleague.[61] A further sentencing for additional cases of sexual assault was rendered in October 2019.[62] The hearing with dozens of witnesses drew the picture of a male leader continuously abusing his powers. However, a larger

---

59. For the video and more information, see *Not Heidi's Girl*, PINK STINKS, https://pinkstinks.de/notheidisgirl/.

60. E.g., BERIT VÖLZMANN, GESCHLECHTSDISKRIMINIERENDE WIRTSCHAFTSWERBUNG (Nomos, 2015). And in a rant by feminist comedian Carolin Kebekus about the most stupid examples of sexist advertisement, she mentions that two years of MeToo should not have been for naught. See https://www.facebook.com/Carolinkebekus.pttv/videos/281798415990200/UzpfSTI5NzU1MTUyMzY2MjAyMToyMzE2MTUxMjg1MTM1MzU4/.

61. See Andreas Salch, *Ex-Rektor der Musikhochschule bestreitet sexuelle Nötigung*, SÜDDEUTSCHE ZEITUNG, Mar. 16, 2017, https://www.sueddeutsche.de/muenchen/prozess-ex-musikhochschulrektor-bestreitet-sexuelle-noetigung-1.3421642.

62. See *Neue Anklage gegen Ex-Rektor der Münchner Musikhochschule*, SÜDDEUTSCHE ZEITUNG, Apr. 19, 2017, https://www.sueddeutsche.de/muenchen/muenchen-neue-anklage-gegen-ex-rektor-der-musikhochschule-1.3469576, and *Ehemaliger Musikhochschul-Präsident muss ins Gefängnis*, FRANKFURTER ALLGEMEINE ZEITUNG, Oct. 9, 2019, https://www.faz.net/aktuell/gesellschaft/kriminalitaet/muenchen-ehemaliger-musikhochschul-praesident-muss-ins-gefaengnis-16424327.html.

number of famous authors, musicians and artists still either support this abuse as normal behavior of an intellectual and creative elite and/or lament the "hypocritical new puritanism of American provenance," "witch hunts," "malicious intrigue," a "poisoned and hysterical climate," and how "women whose advances are rejected are treacherous like mines" because of their "vindictiveness."[63]

In 2016 and 2017, the Munich conservatory enacted guidelines against sexual discrimination and harassment, established anonymized monitoring as well as a procedure for requesting a teacher change in urgent cases, and provided for free psychological and initial legal counseling outside the conservatory in cases of sexual harassment.[64] In June 2019, the Berlin University of Arts adopted guidelines on the protection against (sexualized) discrimination, harassment, and violence.[65] The Berlin conservatory is still discussing the adoption of similar guidelines.

In July 2018, the Academy of Media Arts Cologne (where Gebhard Henke—the second sexist harasser publicly named in the context of the #MeToo Movement—continued to be a professor) adopted principles to prevent humiliation, discrimination, sexual harassment, violence, and abuse of power.[66] In February 2019, students demanded the resignation of Henke, who became less and less visible at the academy. The latest news is that, in July 2019, the Academy Senate met with Henke and discussed his continued employment in view of the considerable loss of trust—behind closed doors.[67] The students announced that they would continue their protests. To start, they organized an action day on the topic of sexualized violence and abuse of power. To their

63. See Heidi Ruhbaum, "*Böswillige Intrige*," BR KLASSIK, Nov. 30, 2018, https://www.br-klassik.de/aktuell/news-kritik/nike-wagner-meeto-siegfried-mauser-intrige-100.html and Hans Magnus Enzensberger, *Münchens Kulturwelt ist entsetzt: Tückische Tellerminen*, SÜD-DEUTSCHE ZEITUNG, May 27, 2016, https://www.sueddeutsche.de/muenchen/nach-dem-urteil-gegen-ex-rektor-der-musikhochschule-muenchens-kulturwelt-ist-entsetzt-1.3009189.

64. See the conservatory's guidelines at *Maßnahmen gegen sexuelle Belästigung und Machtmissbrauch*, HOCHSCHULE FÜR MUSIK UND THEATER MÜNCHEN, https://website .musikhochschule-muenchen.de/de/index.php?option=com_content&task=view&id=2017 &Itemid=1.

65. See the university's guidelines at *Richtlinie zum Schutz gegen (sexualisierte) Diskriminierung, Belästigung und Gewalt*, UNIVERSITÄT DER KÜNSTE BERLIN, https://www.udk-berlin.de/universitaet/gleichstellungspolitik/grenzueberschreitungen/richtlinie -zum-schutz-gegen-sexualisierte-diskriminierung-belaestigung-und-gewalt/.

66. See the Academy's policy on equal treatment and discrimination at *Gleichbehandlung/Diskriminierung*, ACADEMY OF MEDIA ARTS COLOGNE, https://www.khm.de/gl _gleichbehandlung/.

67. Armin Himmelrath, *Proteste gegen den unsichtbaren Professor*, SPIEGELONLINE, Jul. 8, 2019, https://www.spiegel.de/lebenundlernen/uni/koeln-kunsthochschule-streit -um-vorwuerfe-gegen-professor-gebhard-henke-a-1275898.html.

surprise, members of the academy presidency and teaching staff also appeared and participated in the discussion. As Jasna Strick, one of the initiators of #aufschrei, said: to effectively combat sexism and sexual harassment, every generation needs its own sexism debate, their own #MeToo moment and their own experiences and activism.[68]

---

68. See Steinwehr, *supra*, note 2.

CHAPTER 17

I Am Not Afraid to Tell: The #MeToo Movement in the Russian Federation

Marianna Muravyeva[1]

When the #MeToo Movement hit Twitter and the internet, Russia was ready to participate. A year before, in summer 2016, Anastasia Melnichenko, a Ukrainian activist, started her own virtual flash mob. In response to a Facebook post that blamed women for rape, Melnichenko shared her own story of sexual assault with the hashtag #янебоюсьсказати/ть (in Ukrainian/Russian, "I am not afraid to tell"). The post went viral across Ukrainian- and Russian-language social media: hundreds of women shared their own stories of sexual assault and sexual harassment at work. In the first two months alone, there were 12,282 original posts and over 16 million views.[2] The post also saw wide coverage in mainstream media and attracted a number of comments from public figures, experts, local and international civil society organizations, and human rights defenders. At the same time, the posts provoked a tremendous backlash that led to Facebook blocking Melnichenko's account due to fake complaints that the account and posts were generated by an internet bot to infest Russian Facebook. It was unblocked a week later, after verifying the account's authenticity.[3] The campaign successfully increased the visibility of the problem of sexual violence in Russia, which finally became public and provoked a public debate due to the active participation of women. The many posts by women also raised awareness

---

1. Professor of Russian Law and Administration, Aleksanteri Institute, Faculty of Law, University of Helsinki.

2. Feruza Aripova & Janet Elise Johnson, *The Ukrainian-Russian Virtual Flashmob against Sexual Assault*, 16 J. OF SOC. POL'Y STUD. 487, 487-500 (2018).

3. *Facebook заблокировал аккаунт организатора флешмоба #яНебоюсьСказать [Facebook Blocked Flash Mob Organizer Account #I'mNotAfraidToSay]*, MEDUZA, July 14, 2016, https://meduza.io/news/2016/07/14/facebook-zablokiroval-stranitsu-organizatora-fleshmoba-yaneboyusskazat.

of the very low reporting of sexual violence incidents as well as poor legal protection and enforcement of existing legislation.

The Harvey Weinstein revelations in October 2017 and the subsequent #MeToo movement received wide coverage by Russian press and social media. However, some Russian responses to both the accusations of harassment against Weinstein and the #MeToo movement included ambivalence, seeing it as a "Hollywood celebrity" problem. Russian activists noted that for Russians, the 2016 virtual flash mob was much more important and relevant than #MeToo, due to the latter's being perceived as far from local reality.[4] As a result of the 2016 virtual flash mob, Russian activists and the public were particularly engaged with the February 2017 campaign against "decriminalization" of domestic violence, when the Russian Parliament relegated assault that did not require hospital treatment (broken bones or a concussion), including assault committed by "close persons," to administrative law, impacting the prosecution of domestic violence.[5]

Despite ambivalence about #MeToo, according to a poll conducted by the Public Opinion Fund (FOM) in December 2017, the majority of people thought that sexual harassment in Russian show business was systemic, as bad as in America. People also insisted that sexual harassment should be a criminal offence and harshly prosecuted.[6]

Russian's #MeToo movement finally took off in February 2018, when Daria Zhuk, a producer and a reporter at the opposition-leaning television network Dozhd TV; Farida Rustamova, the BBC Russian Service correspondent; and Yekaterina Kotrikadze, the deputy chief editor of RTVI television, based in New York, came forward with their stories of being harassed and assaulted by a prominent member of the State Duma (lower house of the parliament, or Federal Assembly), Leonid Slutsky, the chairman of the Committee on Foreign Affairs. Farida Rustamova published the transcript of an audio recording in which she tried to resist Slutsky's advances.[7] Duma deputies, including women,

4. *Dvizhenie #MeToo god spustia: zhenskaia solidarnost' ili kholivar? [The #MeToo Movement a Year Later: Women's Solidarity or Holy War?]*, THE BBC: RUSSIAN DESK, Aug. 23, 2018, https://www.bbc.com/russian/features-45247219.

5. Madeline Roache, *Russia's Version of #MeToo Has Struggled to Take Off—Until Now*, TIME, Aug. 2, 2019, https://time.com/5636107/metoo-russia-womens-rights/.

6. *Сексуальные домогательства: Следует ли судить виновных в сексуальных домогательствах? Часты ли случаи домогательства в России? [Sexual Harassment: Should Sexual Harassment be Judged? Are Sexual Harassment Cases Frequent in Russia?]*, PUBLIC OPINION FUND, Dec. 3, 2017, https://fom.ru/Bezopasnost-i-pravo/13882.

7. Masha Gessen, *Russia Finally Gets Its #MeToo Moment*, THE NEW YORKER, Mar. 23, 2018, https://www.newyorker.com/news/our-columnists/russia-finally-gets-its-metoo -moment.

supported Slutsky against these accusations, and the Duma's Ethics Committee cleared him of all accusations in any misconduct. However, journalists called for a boycott of the Duma and received support among the journalist community. Alena Popova, a Russian activist who herself had worked as an accredited Duma journalist, called for a campaign to deprive Slutsky of his deputy status.[8] Despite pickets and public protests, he continues to serve in the Duma. The website *Net Domogatel'stvam* (Stop Harassment) that Alena created was shut down by the government. Alena was arrested six times for picketing the Duma with a cardboard life-size dummy of Slutsky.[9]

In 2018, other sexual harassment accusations appeared in the media: Daria Komarova, another journalist, accused Stanislav Govorukhin, a Duma deputy and a famous producer, of sexual harassment, and Renat Davletgildeev, yet another journalist, shared his story of harassment by Vladimir Zhiriniovskii, the leader of one of Russia's parliamentary parties. Nothing came of either accusation.

At the time of the "I am not afraid to tell" hashtag and #MeToo movements, Russian legislation contained some measures to prosecute sexual violence, including sexual harassment. Russia has had a long tradition of prosecuting harassment, with the first laws going back to the seventeenth century. The Russian Legal Code of 1649 punished sexual coercion of slaves by their masters (owners) (XX:80).[10] The second Soviet Criminal Code of 1926 introduced the specific article on sexual harassment, defining it as coercing a woman into sexual relations by a person on whom she is dependent economically or at work, with a punishment of five-years' incarceration (art. 154).[11] In the 1960 Criminal Code, the punishment was reduced to three years (art. 118).[12]

Chapter 18 of the current Criminal Code prosecutes rape (art. 131); other forced acts of sexual nature, including homosexual and lesbian acts (art. 132); coercing someone into sexual relations (art. 133); coercing someone into

---

8. *Активистка Алёна Попова запустила сайт о домогательствах Слуцкого [Activist Alena Popova Launches Slutsky Harassment Site]*, WONDERZINE, Apr. 6, 2018, https://www.wonderzine.com/wonderzine/life/news/234395-net-domogatelstvam.

9. Ена Барышева, *"Слуцкие ворота": год после сексуальных домогательств в Госдуме ["Slutsky-Gate": A Year After Sexual Harassment Scandal in the State Duma]*, DEUTSCHE WELLE, Feb. 2, 2019, https://p.dw.com/p/3DoU5.

10. Соборное Уложение (The Conciliar Legal Code) 1649 Chapter XX art. 80, see English translation here: http://individual.utoronto.ca/aksmith/resources/ulozh/Chapter_20.htm.

11. Уголовный кодекс РСФСР (Criminal Code of the RSFSR) 1926 art. 154, available here: http://law.edu.ru/norm/norm.asp?normID=1241189.

12. Уголовный кодекс РСФСР (Criminal Code of the RSFSR) 1960 art. 118, http://www.consultant.ru/document/cons_doc_LAW_2950/6d8a39804bfe82e851812361be108dd1296a042c/.

sex work (art. 240); and sex trafficking (art. 127.1).[13] Article 133, *Coercing into Actions of Sexual Nature*, provides prosecution for sexual harassment, which is understood as sexual intercourse (*polovoe snoshenie*) or other acts of a sexual nature (*inye deistviia seksual'nogo kharaktera*) that are forced by blackmail; threat to destroy, damage or remove property; or by using economic or other dependence of the victim on the perpetrator. The punishment for such acts is either a fine (equal to the perpetrator's annual salary or other annual income up to 120,000 rubles), or a variety of labor or incarceration alternatives: compulsive labor (up to 480 hours), corrective labor (up to two years), penal labor (one year), or incarceration for one year. It is significant that the current 1996 Code significantly reduced the punishment for sexual harassment compared to the earlier Soviet-era legislation.

Adjudication for sexual harassment is rather complicated. Article 133, which covers coercing someone into sexual relations, belongs to the class of "public prosecution" cases, which means that state enforcement and prosecuting agencies are obligated to pursue prosecution based on communication of the crime committed, i.e., not necessarily on the official complaint of a victim. The prosecution cannot be stopped with reconciliation or withdrawal of the complaint. The burden of proof also lies with the state, and the state prosecutor acts as a plaintiff in court. However, articles 131 (rape) and 132 (other forced acts of sexual nature) are private-public prosecution, meaning that the investigation can only be initiated upon an official complaint by the victim, but cannot be stopped by the victim upon the withdrawal of the complaint.[14] In addition, civil litigation can be used to compensate for moral harm or unlawful dismissal, but it does not contain any specific definition of sexual harassment or grounds for its prosecution.

Both Russian labor law and criminal law contain antidiscrimination provisions (art. 3 of the Labor Code and art. 136 of the Criminal Code) as well as for the prosecution of the abuse of power by officials and managers. In the private sector, Russian companies and state agencies provide protection against sexual harassment in their company's rules and guidelines, called "*Pravila vnutrennego trudovogo rasporiadka*" ("Internal Labor Guidelines") or "*Pravila povedeniia v kampanii*" ("Rules of Conduct"). These guidelines often contain a section on a company's working environment principles and its behavior code. Almost all

---

13. Уголовный кодекс Российской Федерации (Criminal Code) (UK RF), http://pravo.gov.ru/proxy/ips/?docbody&nd=102041891. Unauthorized English translation here: https://www.wipo.int/edocs/lexdocs/laws/en/ru/ru080en.pdf.

14. Уголовно=процессуальный кодекс Российской Федерации (Criminal Procedural Code) (UPK RF) art. 20 and 146, http://www.consultant.ru/document/cons_doc_LAW_34481/f58a4b0cb77f034412407f9f39928eaffbbac5d1/.

these documents include the explicit prohibition of sexual harassment under threat of dismissal.[15]

Activists, scholars, and legal practitioners agree that in its current state, Russian legislation is insufficient, poorly enforced and biased against women who come forward.[16] It is very difficult to register a complaint and even more difficult to see it through the investigation to trial. Attorneys attest that without a clear definition of sexual harassment in Russian legislation, it is very difficult to prosecute.[17] Activists point out that harassment culture is very much in place in Russia and that there is an acute need to fight gender stereotypes and call out those responsible for it.[18]

Accusations of sexual harassment can easily backfire. According to available case law, male officials and managers accused of sexual harassment can easily manipulate the judicial system to their advantage by filing a defamation suit against the female accuser. In a 2016 Moscow case, women who had filed a complaint against Sergey Durygin, the head of the military orchestra, withdrew their charges under the threat of criminal prosecution. Durygin initiated a defamation civil suit against the women, insisting that they had spread lies and undermined his reputation. The judge ruled in his favor. Case files show that the main complainant, an orchestra accountant, found herself resented by others in the orchestra for asking authorities to audit the orchestra. She acknowledged that there was no independent evidence of harassment, as all of it happened when she and Durygin were one-on-one.[19]

According to the State Automated Database "Justice," which contains all Russian court decisions and judgments since 2010 in a digital format, administrative and civil law is the main tool for prosecuting sexual harassment: almost 8,000 cases have been decided under the civil law and 12,500 under administrative law.[20] The Judicial Department of the Supreme Court's statistics for

---

15. See, for example, *Employee Code of Conduct*, HEMPEL, https://www.hempel.ru/~/media/Global/files/code-of-conduct/Hempel-CodeofConduct-RU.pdf.

16. Иван Клейменов, Сексуальное домогательство: криминологический и уголовно-правовой аспекты *[Sexual Harassment: Criminological and Legal Analysis]*, 32 ВЕСТНИК ТОМСКОГО ГОСУДАРСТВЕННОГО УНИВЕРСИТЕТА. ПРАВО, 42, 42-54 (2019), https://cyberleninka.ru/article/n/seksualnoe-domogatelstvo-kriminologicheskiy-i-ugolovno-pravovoy-aspekty.

17. Елизавета Маетная и Любовь Чижова, *"Где-то на грани нормы". Почему в России допустимы сексуальные домогательства ["Somewhere Borderline": Why Sexual Harassment is Acceptable in Russia]*, RADIO SVOBODA, Mar. 29, 2018, https://www.svoboda.org/a/29117588.html.

18. Barysheva, *supra*, note 9.

19. Durygin v. Gorshkova [2016] case N 2-2299/2016 - M-14984/2015, Odintsovo City Court, Moscow Region, GAS Pravosudie (Russia), https://sudrf.ru/.

20. ГАС "Правосудие," https://sudrf.ru/.

2018 provides the following number of convictions: art. 131 (rape)—2,049; art. 132 (other forced acts of sexual nature)—2,044; and art. 133 (coercing into sexual relations)—30.[21] A 2014 SuperJob's Research Center poll shows that 11 percent of women experienced sexual harassment at work, which is rather low.[22] In 2017, the poll conducted by Levada Center found that 20 percent of women and 16 percent of men acknowledged that sexual harassment occurs in their place of work, but 71 percent and 62 percent, respectively, insisted that it never happens.[23] Both polls asked a direct question ("Have you ever experienced sexual harassment at work?") without any clarification as to what kind of actions could be treated as sexual harassment. Therefore, the low percentages are not surprising. This data highlights that people are unaware of the problem and do not recognize the elements of sexual harassment because they do not have sufficient information about it. When researchers conduct more nuanced polls, the numbers of women who experienced sexual harassment are much higher.[24]

In 2012, a group of activists organized a movement called *RosNakhal* ("Russian Jerk" or "RusJerk"; #roshakhal). Started as a Vkontakte group (the Russian equivalent of Facebook), RosNakhal targeted men who sexually harassed women on the streets and at the workplace. The members of the group recorded harassment and posted those videos online. From the beginning, activists led by Yulia Kolyadina, a journalist and hostess at the World Fashion Channel, had a very clear legal reform agenda: to amend both the Code of Administrative Offences and art. 213 (hooliganism) of the Criminal Code to include a punishment for sexual harassment.[25] They picketed the State Duma and found some response from the deputies. Oleg Nilov, the deputy from the party Just Russia, initiated a bill to introduce a separate article to the Code of Administrative Offences titled "harassment," in which the definition followed the International Labour Organization standards.[26] It was rejected on the first reading by the Duma.

---

21. *Statistics*, Russian Federation Supreme Court (Verkh. Sud RF), the Judicial Department, 2018, http://www.cdep.ru/index.php?id=79&item=4894.

22. *6% мужчин и 11% женщин в России жалуются на харассмент [6% of Men and 11% of Women in Russia Complain of Harassment]*, SuperJob, Jan. 28, 2015, https://www.superjob.ru/research/articles/111691/6/.

23. *Sexual Harassment*, Levada Center, Dec 20, 2017, https://www.levada.ru/en/2017/12/20/sexual-harassment/.

24. Deborah Erdos Knapp, Cathy LZ DuBois, Mary Hogue, Marina N. Astakhova, and Robert H. Faley, *Russian workers' experiences with and perceptions of sexual harassment severity*, 30 The Int'l J. of Hum. Resource Mgmt 2049, 2049-2076 (2019).

25. *РосНахал: Кто и зачем? [RosNakhal: Who and Why?]*, Ридус, Sep. 19, 2012, https://www.ridus.ru/news/46017.

26. See the bill here: О внесении изменений в Кодекс Российской Федерации об административных правонарушениях в части установления защиты прав женщин от

In 2016, a group of feminist lawyers led by Marina Davtyan campaigned for the explicit criminalization of domestic violence after the State Duma decided to relegate some types of assault not resulting in injuries or health damage to administrative law, thus making the prosecution of physical assault easier to establish. The feminists and their Duma allies succeeded in amending art. 116 "Assault" of the Criminal Code to include an assault on behalf of "close persons," thus explicitly making it possible to prosecute domestic violence in Russia for the first time since 1918. Seven months later, however, this amendment was reversed. The new February 2017 version of the code excluded "close persons" from the article and assault against any family members not resulting in serious injury was relegated to the status of "petty offense," punishable under the Administrative Code of the Russian Federation.[27] In 2018, the gender equality law, which had been pending in the Duma since 2002, was finally rejected.

However, due to the 2016 virtual flash mob and the #MeToo movement that made discussions about violence against women visible and widespread, female leaders, including Russian Parliament representative Oksana Pushkina and Federation Council head Valentina Matvienko, have vowed to promote a women's agenda. Pushkina assured the mass media in September 2019 that two bills will be introduced to the Duma that fall: "On Equality Between Women and Men in Labor Relations" and "On Sexual Harassment."[28] Together with a bill on prevention of domestic violence, these three legislative initiatives will create the new legislative framework for combating violence against women.

Activists are determined to see this legislation through the Duma now, when they have powerful allies. Russia, however, has a long way to go to make public and private spaces safe for women.

сексуальных домогательств [On amendments to the Code of the Russian Federation on administrative offenses in terms of establishing the protection of women's rights from sexual harassment], https://sozd.duma.gov.ru/bill/467782-6.

27. Marianna Muravyeva, *"Should Women Have More Rights?" Traditional Values and Austerity in Russia*, Rosa Luxemburg Stiftung, 2018, https://www.rosalux.eu/en/article/1272.should-women-have-more-rights-traditional-values-and-austerity-in-russia.html.

28. *Домогательства преодолимой силы [Overcoming Harassment]*, Коммерсантъ, Sep. 30, 2019, https://www.kommersant.ru/doc/4110374.

CHAPTER 18

Public Campaigns, the Reception of #MeToo, and the Law Concerning Sexual Harassment in Turkey

Kadriye Bakirci[1]

Introduction

For decades, Turkish feminists have played an important role in raising awareness about gender-based violence utilizing a variety of publications,[2] activities, protests, and campaigns.

In 1980, the Turkish women's movement launched the "Campaign Against Battering" to stop domestic violence and wife battering, followed by movements to stop honor killings and to stop subjecting young women to virginity checks, and to halt forced and child marriages.

Since 1989, various women's advocates and groups in Turkey also have initiated activities and campaigns such as "Our Bodies are Ours, Say No to Sexual

---

1. Professor of Employment and Social Security Law, Hacettepe University, Faculty of Law.

2. See Kadriye Bakirci, "How Sexual Harassment of Employees Is Treated Under Turkish Law," (1999) Istanbul Technical University and Technical University of Berlin, Joint Conference, Istanbul; Kadriye Bakirci (2000a), Is Hukuku Acisindan Isyerinde Cinsel Taciz, Yasa Yayinlari, Istanbul; Kadriye Bakirci (2000b), "Isyerinde Cinsel Taciz ve Turk Is Hukukuna Iliskin Cozum Onerileri," Turhan Esener'e Armagan, Ankara; Kadriye Bakirci (2000c), "Iscilerin Ucuncu Kisilerin Saldirisina Ugramalari Halinde Isverenin Sorumlulugu," Cimento Isveren, C.14, S.3; Kadriye Bakirci, "Sexual Harassment of Working Women in the United Kingdom," Nuri Celik'e Armagan, Beta Yayinlari, Istanbul (2001).

Harassment,"[3] "Purple Needle Campaign Against Street Sexual Harassment,"[4] "Campaign Against the Categorization of Women as 'Respectable Women' and 'Easy Women' by The Previous Criminal Act of 1926,"[5] "Campaign and Struggle to Intervene as a Third Party in the Court's Proceedings,"[6] "Woman's Statement is Sufficient" Campaign,[7] and the "Campaign Over 13 Year Old Girl Rape Case."[8] All of these campaigns played an important role in raising public awareness about the issue of sexual violence and street sexual harassment.

------

3. This was the first campaign against street sexual harassment, started in 1989 in Istanbul. With this campaign, women attempted to question and uncover the sexist norms and morality that prevailed in society. It used the slogan "we demand back the streets and the nights," indicating women's wish to claim public spaces free of harassment.

4. The "Purple Needle Campaign" against street sexual harassment is a very important feminist activity, also originally started in 1989. After sexual harassment perpetrators in a 2008 New Year's crowd at Taksim Square were let off with a paltry fine, feminists decided to speak out every Friday evening and revive the earlier campaign. They gathered next to Taksim Square, every Friday and handed out 7-centimeter (2 ¾ inch) needles with purple ribbons to women on the street to stick into harassers who made unwelcome sexual advances. See https://bianet.org /english/gender/104137-purple-needle-action-against-sexual-harassment.

5. This public campaign was also held in 1989 when the Antalya 2nd Court of Serious Crimes granted four rapists reduced sentences using the previous Criminal Act (CA) of 1926 (No.765) Article 438, because the victim known as "N.T." was claimed to be a prostitute. Feminists protested using Article 438, and the court's decision, since the aim was to protect only "respectable women" and the ruling violated the principle of equality guaranteed by the current Turkish Constitution of 1982 (Article 10). The mounting reaction led to the Constitutional Court's annulment of Article 438, which had allowed a reduced sentence for those who raped prostitutes. The Criminal Act of 1926 (No.765) was replaced by the current Criminal Act (No.5327) in 2004.

6. There is no regulation allowing women's associations and/or non-governmental organizations to intervene in civil and/or criminal proceedings involving female victims. Therefore, women's NGO's have long been campaigning to intervene as a third party in cases involving violence against women and girls. See Canan Arin, *"Gender Based Violence: A Present to Women of Turkey,"* REFLECTIONS TURKEY, Apr. 9, 2012, http://www.reflectionsturkey.com/2012/04 /gender-based-violence-a-present-to-women-of-turkey/.

7. See subsection "Burden of Proof" below.

8. This was another big campaign in 2011 when Turkey was faced with a major legal and children's rights scandal. The 14th Criminal Division of the Court of Cassation upheld a lower court's ruling that a thirteen-year-old girl—known only as "N.C."—who was raped by twenty-six men in 2002, had given her "consent" to the sexual violence that she was subjected to over the course of seven months. Men paid two adult women for access to the girl. In November 2011 two women accused of having sold the girl for sex were sentenced to nine years in prison, but the twenty-six men, including teachers, civil servants, and a village elder, were given sentences ranging from one to six years. Judges from the Court of Cassation agreed that the sentences of the twenty-six men convicted of having sex with the thirteen-year-old girl should be reduced because the girl consented. The court sentenced the twenty-six accused rapists based on the previous CA of 1926, which was in force until 2004. Although the ruling was condemned by feminist activists, lawyers, NGOs, the previous president, and some ministers and politicians, it was not overturned, and the case has been taken to the European Court of Human Rights

Two years before the #MeToo Movement caught on in the West, women in Turkey had started a social media campaign on Twitter to share their accounts of sexual harassment and violence, in the very powerful #SenDeAnlat ("YouTellToo" or "TellYourStoryToo") Twitter campaign after twenty-year-old female psychology student Ozgecan Aslan was brutally murdered in 2015.

On February 11, 2015, Ozgecan Aslan was traveling on a minibus in the south-east seaside province of Mersin, when the minibus driver tried to rape her. Aslan pepper-sprayed the driver before he stabbed her and beat her to death with an iron bar. He then enlisted the help of his father and a friend to dispose of her body in a river in Tarsus. The body was found showing evidence of burns as well as the fatal injuries. The driver was arrested on February 16, 2015, confessed to the crime, and his father and friend were also arrested. All three were convicted and ordered to serve life imprisonment. The driver was killed in prison the next year.[9]

Ozgecan Aslan's murder sparked mass protests in Turkey and prompted women to share their stories of sexual harassment, violence, and fear in a growing Twitter campaign.[10] Using the hashtag #SenDeAnlat, women have told of their experiences of violence, intimidation and harassment, as well as tactics that they have resorted to, such as wearing a wedding ring or getting off a bus early to avoid being the last passenger.[11]

Since February 16, 2015, more than 440,000 tweets have been shared under the hashtag #SenDeAnlat, and it was the third highest trending topic worldwide on February 17, 2015. Another hashtag, #OzceganAslan, was even more popular, trending as the highest topic worldwide on February 16 and 17, 2015, with more than 2.5 million tweets.[12]

(ECtHR) by the female lawyer of "N.C." (See Constanze Letsch, *"Turkish court reduces sentences for men accused of raping 13-year-old,"* THE GUARDIAN, Nov. 4, 2011, https://www.theguard ian.com/world/2011/nov/04/turkish-court-reduces-rape-sentences).

9. See *"Man convicted of-murdering Turkish girl shot dead in prison,"* HURRIYET DAILY NEWS, Apr. 11, 2016, http://www.hurriyetdailynews.com/man-convicted-of-murdering -turkish-girl-shot-dead-in-prison-97640.

10. See Helen Davidson, *"Rape and murder of young woman sparks mass Twitter protest in Turkey,"* THE GUARDIAN, Feb. 17, 2015, https://www.theguardian.com/world/2015/feb /17/turkish-woman-ozgecan-aslans-sparks-anti-violence-campaign-sendeanlat.

11. See Charlotte Alfred, *"Women In Turkey Share Devastating Stories Of Sexual Harassment In #Sendeanlat Twitter Campaign,"* HUFFINGTON POST, Feb. 25, 2015, https://www .huffingtonpost.com/2015/02/17/turkey-sendeanlat-twitter-campaign_n_6699702.html ?ncid=tweetlnkushpmg00000067&utm_content=buffer7d1d2&utm_medium=social&utm _source=twitter.com&utm_campaign=buffer.

12. See Davidson, *supra*, note 10.

These devastating first-hand accounts of victims showed that no female was immune to sexual harassment; it affects minors, hijabis,[13] the elderly and disabled, those living in urban and rural areas, those with little education and those with graduate degrees, the rich and poor, and tourists and locals. All these women had been taught since early childhood to hide in shame and to remain quiet in the face of rape and sexual harassment. Now it was out in the open.

Beren Saat, a Turkish actress and celebrity, wrote via Twitter about her own experiences and how hard it was to be a woman in Turkey. Saat wrote about the sexual abuse she has faced, starting from her school years up until very recently, even as a well-known actress. "All the cat-calls at me while I was returning home from school with a school uniform skirt … my accelerated steps in the dark while returning home from preparatory school … the face of the child who showed his erect penis to me inside our apartment building and me running home with trembling hands and not telling this story to anyone … my fight with a drunk broadcasting manager who grabbed my butt during the TV channel's celebration night …" were examples of some of the abuse Saat related.[14] She did not name her harassers.

Didem Soydan, a well-known Turkish model, tweeted that she had received anonymous abusive text messages, which started with "so you're a model," after she had testified and given her cell phone number to police in the case of a woman who was forced into a car after being beaten.[15]

Among the stories shared under the #SenDeAnlat, many women related either their own harassment stories or shared tactics that women had to take to avoid sexual harassment. "Not being able to turn the light on immediately when you enter your house to avoid being spotted at which flat you live," or "Is there any man (in Turkey) who tells his mother to keep talking on the phone because a group of women are standing in his way?" and "We cannot wear lipstick, mini-skirts, grow our hair long, go out at night, laugh because we are women, right?" were a few examples of the many shared experiences which women in Turkey face.[16]

Meanwhile, during a rally condemning Aslan's murder in the Central Anatolian province of Kayseri, a woman cried for justice as she related by megaphone the story of her rape. "Enough already! What is the end to the murders, rapes and all these things? The judge said there is 'consent' because (the rape

---

13. Hijabis are Muslim women who wear a head covering in public.

14. See "*Turkish women relate sexual harassment stories via social media*," Hurriyet Daily News, Feb. 16, 2015, http://www.hurriyetdailynews.com/turkish-women-relate-sexual -harassment-stories-via-social-media--78413.

15. *Id.*

16. *Id.*

victim) was over 16, said M.N., the rape victim, referring to her own rape case, during which the rapist walked free from court because the judge ruled that consent to sex had been given because she was over sixteen years old.[17]

In June 2017, three women decided to set up a HarassMap in Turkey inspired by the Egyptian HarassMap initiative, and they asked Egyptian volunteers to help them to start their own version of the HarassMap Platform. The Egyptian HarassMap is an award-winning volunteer-based initiative founded in late 2010.[18] HarassMap is based on the idea that if more people start taking action when sexual harassment happens in their presence, this epidemic can be ended. By taking a collective stand against sexual harassment, re-establishing social consequences for harassers—and making role models of people who stand up to them—it is believed that harassers can be deterred from harassing again.[19]

The Egyptian HarassMap initiative is trying to create a global movement of HarassMap-inspired initiatives against sexual harassment.[20]

"Sendeanlat.harassmap.org" platform was launched in Turkey in October 2017. It is an open data platform that aims to contribute to advocacy by keeping data on sexual harassment and sexual assault incidents reported to the site through a crowdsourcing method. The platform gets its name from the #sendeanlat tag that appeared on social media after the murder of Ozgecan Aslan.[21]

Although women in Turkey had begun to share their accounts of sexual harassment and violence long before the #MeToo Movement, the #MeToo Movement itself—calling out harassers by name and holding them accountable—was stillborn in Turkey.

To commemorate November 25, the International Day for the Elimination of Violence Against Women, in 2017 the *Hurriyet* daily newspaper interviewed famous women who shared their memories of domestic violence. The interviews were published on November 27, 2017, under the headline "Ben De Siddet Gordum (I Have Experienced Violence Too) and started trending on social media. Most of these prominent women confessed their memories of beatings and humiliation from men close to them: boyfriends, husbands, fathers, or colleagues, as well as violence from random strangers. They advised

---

17. *Id.*

18. See "HarassMap: Stop Sexual harassment together," https://harassmap.org/en.

19. *Id.*

20. *Id.*

21. See *"Sen de Anlat!,"* https://sendeanlat.harassmap.org/tr; Secil Epik, *"Güvenli alanlar yaratmak için: Sen de Anlat* (To Create Safe Spaces, Tell Me Too)," K24, Aug. 2, 2018, http://t24.com.tr/k24/yazi/sen-de-anlat,1896.

others not to stay quiet, to join feminist organizations, and to set an example that humiliation should be brought to the perpetrators, not their victims[22]. Although *Hurriyet's* interviews got public attention, none of those interviewed named their attackers. Without names, there were no consequences. No one was prosecuted; no one resigned from their jobs; no one provided a public apology. #MeToo movement has not encouraged more victims to speak up.

The Struggle to Enact Laws That Protect Women Against Harassment in Turkey

Turkey did not have any specific laws or statutory provisions on sexual harassment until 2003. However, general provisions of the Turkish Constitution, and civil and criminal statutes were applicable to sexual harassment.[23]

After the Helsinki European summit in 1999 granted Turkey official European Union candidate country status, the ensuing reform process in Turkey brought many legislative changes for women's rights. As a candidate country, Turkey was required to harmonize its existing legislation and practices concerning the equal treatment of men and women in the labor market with those of the European Union. The accession criteria require Turkey to fully adopt the legal framework of the European Union (called "Acquis Communautaire").[24]

In 2004, Turkey passed certain constitutional amendments to bring the country more closely in line with the European Union, including ratification of international treaties. According to the amended Turkish Constitution,[25] where a conflict between ratified international treaties covering fundamental rights and freedoms and domestic law exists, the international treaties shall prevail. These treaties are binding upon Turkey's legislative, executive, and judicial branches, the administrative authorities, and other institutions and individuals.[26]

---

22. See "*#Ben de şiddet gördüm (I have experienced violence too)*," HURRIYET, Nov. 27, 2017, http://www.hurriyet.com.tr/gundem/-ben-de-siddet-gordum-40659092.

23. The Civil Code (CC) of 2001 (No. 4721), the previous CC of 1926 (No. 743), the previous Employment Act (EA) (No. 1475) of 1971, the previous Obligations Act (OA) (No. 818) of 1926, and the previous Criminal Act (CA) (No.765) of 1926 applied to sexual harassment. See Kadriye Bakirci, "Remedies against sexual harassment of employees under Turkish law," EUROPEAN PUBLIC LAW, 3: 473–484 (2001).

24. See Kadriye Bakirci, "Gender Equality in Employment in Turkish Legislation with Comparisons to EU and International Law," Journal of Workplace Rights, Vol. 15(1) 3-25 (2011). "Acquis Communautaire" is the accumulated legislation, legal acts, and court decisions that constitute the body of European Union law.

25. Article 90.

26. Article 11.

Turkey therefore underwent a period of rapid legislative change and development between 2002-2010 to comply with the EU's acquis communautaire and with Council of Europe (COE), International Labour Organisation (ILO), and United Nations (UN) conventions, all now ratified by Turkey.[27]

Among the international and regional instruments in this field binding for Turkey are UN, ILO, and COE Conventions and Declarations, which include protections against violence against women and promote gender equality.[28]

Under the COE Revised Social Charter, Turkey must promote awareness of, information on, and prevention of sexual harassment in the workplace, or in relation to work, and to take all appropriate measures to protect workers from such conduct and also to promote awareness of, information on, and prevention of recurrent reprehensible or distinctly negative and offensive actions directed against individual workers in the workplace or in relation to work.[29]

---

27. See Bakirci (2011), *supra*, note 24; Bakirci, K./Uygur G./Yalcin Sancar T., "*Aile Ici Siddete ve Yetkili Kurum ve Kuruluslara Iliskin Mevzuat ve Degerlendirme Raporu (Uluslararasi, Avrupa ve Turk Hukuk Mevzuati), Kadına Yonelik Aile Ici Siddetle Mucadele Projesi, BM ve Basbakanlik Kadinin Statusu Genel Mudurlugu Projesi, (Yayimlanmamis Rapor)*" (The International, European & Turkish Legislation on Violence Against Women in the Domestic Sphere, The Research Project for the Turkish Prime Ministry, Department of Women's Status, 2007.

28. These include: the UN Convention on the Elimination of All Forms of Discrimination against Women (CEDAW); the Optional Protocol of CEDAW, the UN Convention on the Protection of the Rights of All Migrant Workers and Members of Their Families; the UN Convention on the Rights of Persons with Disabilities; the COE Revised Social Charter; the European Convention on Human Rights; the COE Convention on Preventing and Combating Violence against Women and Domestic Violence (Istanbul Convention); the ILO Convention No. 111 concerning Discrimination in Respect of Employment and Occupation and Recommendation, 1958; ILO Convention No. 158 concerning Termination of Employment at the Initiative of the Employer, 1982; and ILO Declaration on Fundamental Rights and Principles at Work, 1998.

The European Court of Human Rights has also developed a body of jurisprudence concerning the positive obligations of states to prevent, prosecute, punish, and provide remedies for acts of violence committed by private individuals or entities. (See Andrew Clapham, Human Rights Obligations of Non-State Actors, OUP, ch. 9 (2006).)

For more information about the Istanbul Convention, see Kadriye Bakirci, "Istanbul Sozlesmesi," Ankara Barosu Dergisi, 2015/4, pp.133-204 (2015), http://www.ankarabarosu .org.tr/siteler/ankarabarosu/tekmakale/2015-4/7.pdf.

For more information about the ILO conventions and declarations which specifically prohibits sexual harassment in the workplace, see Kadriye Bakirci, "*Indigenous Women's Issues (The ILO's Indigenous and Tribal People's Convention, 1989)*" in Encyclopedia of Women in Today's World, Vol. 2 (No. 169) (Z. Stange, C.K. Oyster, J.E. Sloan, eds., Sage Publication, USA, 2011), and see Kadriye Bakirci, "*Domestic Workers* (the Domestic Workers' Convention, 2011)" in Encyclopedia of Women in Today's World, Vol. 1 (No. 189) (Z. Stange, C.K. Oyster, J.E. Sloan, eds., Sage Publication, USA, 2011).

The amendments to the Maritime Labour Convention, 2006 (No. 186), include issues of bullying and harassment. None of them have been ratified by Turkey.

29. Article 26.

Turkey has also modernized its civil, criminal, and family laws, taking major steps forward toward gender equality.[30] Turkey introduced the offence of sexual harassment for the first time in its Employment Act of 2003,[31] followed by similar additions in other statutes.[32] [33]Stalking by anyone (by a family member, a colleague, or an employer, etc.) was regulated for the first time in the Protection of the Family and Prevention of Violence Against Women Act in 2012.[34] Furthermore, the Turkish Higher Education Board adopted sexual harassment as a disciplinary offence in the Regulation on Students' Disciplinary Offences in Higher Education Institutions in 2012.[35]

On the other hand, a reporting person might be victimized by retaliation for filing a complaint or for participating in compliance proceedings. Retaliation might take different forms such as mobbing (moral or psychological harassment), bullying, stalking, dismissal, etc.[36] Although protection against retaliation has been implicitly provided by the general provisions of Turkish

---

30. See the new CC (OJ 8.12.2001, No.24607), the EA (No. 4857—OJ 10.6.2003, No. 25134), the CA (No. 5237—OJ 12.10.2004, No. 25611), the OA (No. 6098—OJ 4.2.2011, No. 27836), and the Human Rights and Equality Institution Act (HREIA) (No. 6701—OJ 20.4.2016, No. 29690).

31. See Kadriye Bakirci, "*Isci Kadinlarin Insan Haklari (Human Rights of Women Employees)*," ANKARA BAROSU HUKUK KURULTAYI, C.III, Ankara Barosu Yayini, Ankara (2006).

32. The CA in 2004, the OA in 2011, and HREIA in 2016. For more information about these additions, see Kadriye Bakirci, "*Isyerinde Cinsel Taciz ve Turk Ceza Kanunu On Tasarisi (Sexual Harassment in the Workplace and the Draft Criminal Code)*," ISTANBUL BAROSU DERGISI, S.1, Mart (Criminal Act additions) (2001) and Kadriye Bakirci, "*Kadınlara Yonelik Hukuksal Ayrimciligin Bir Baska Urunu: Borclar Kanunu Tasarisi'nda Cinsel Taciz ve Ayrimcilik (A Legislative Type of Discrimination: Harassment and Discrimination in the Draft Obligations Law)*," Is Mufettisleri Dernegi II. Calisma Yasami Kongresi (Apr. 26-27, 2008) Tartisma ve Panel Notlari, Is Mufettisleri Dernegi, Ankara, 2008 (Obligations Act additions).

33. Article 105 of the CA states that: (1) Any person who harasses another person with sexual intent shall be sentenced to a penalty of imprisonment of three months to two years or a judicial fine, upon a complaint being made by the victim. (2) Where these acts are committed by misusing the influence derived from a hierarchical, service, education/training, or familial relationship, or where such acts are committed by taking advantage of working at the same workplace, the penalty to be imposed under the above section shall be increased by one half. Where the victim has had to leave his/her employment or school or separate from his/her family, the penalty to be imposed shall not be less than one year. If the perpetrator did not have sexual intent, or it cannot be proven, then the offence will consist of an insult, regulated by Article 125 of the CA.

34. The Protection of the Family and Prevention of Violence Against Women Act (PVAWA) (No.6284 - OJ 20.3.2012, No. 28239).

35. OJ 18.8.2012, No. 28388.

36. See Kadriye Bakirci, "*Work-Related Whistleblowing in Democratic Societies Context: A Comparative Study of International, EU and Turkish Law*," 26 J. of Financial Crime, No. 4, pp. 1165-1202 (2019), https://doi.org/10.1108/JFC-09-2018-0090.

civil and criminal statutes,[37] the EA and HREIA explicitly provided protection against retaliation in relation to sex discrimination (including sexual harassment) complaints in its scope in 2016.

These developments demonstrate that the EU accession process in Turkey has brought positive changes. However, during this rapid process, many issues have not been addressed, and some problems have been encountered, such as contradictory arrangements arising from a sexist attitude evident in the legislation because of the underrepresentation of women. There are mistakes and contradictions due to errors made in the translation of EU regulations by unqualified people. Piecemeal amendment of related regulations has resulted in an ill-fitting patchwork of legislation caused by commissions that are unaware of each other's work.[38]

Law Concerning Sexual Harassment and Retaliation (Victimization) in Turkey Today

Definition of Sexual Harassment and Retaliation (Victimization)

The only definition of sexual harassment in Turkish law exists in the HREIA. Article 2/j defines sexual harassment as a form of harassment and states that harassment including sexual, psychological, and gender-based forms is any painful, degrading, humiliating, and disgraceful behavior that intends to undermine the dignity of a person or distress the person or lead to such consequence. Under the HREIA sexual harassment is a form of discrimination. On the other hand, the Istanbul Convention Article 40 defines sexual harassment as "any form of unwanted verbal, non-verbal or physical conduct of a sexual nature with the purpose or effect of violating the dignity of a person, in particular when creating an intimidating, hostile, degrading, humiliating or offensive environment."[39] This definition is binding on Turkish law.

---

37. The Civil Code (Article 2), the Employment Act (Articles 17, 18) and the Criminal Act. See Kadriye Bakirci, *Uluslararasi Hukuk, AB ve ABD Hukuku Ile Karsilastirmali Calisma Yasaminda Kadin Erkek Esitligi Arayisi, Cinsiyet Ayrimciligi Yasagi ve Turkiye (Searching for Gender Equality and the Non-Discrimination Principle Based on Gender Equality in Employment in International, European Union, United States and Turkish Law)*, 2. Bası, Seckin Yayincilik, Ankara (2012).

38. See Bakirci (2011), *supra*, note 24.

39. A definition of sexual harassment is given by the Recast Directive 2006/54/EC (Article 2). See Kadriye Bakirci, "*Sexual harassment in the workplace in relation to EC legislation*," INTERNATIONAL JOURNAL OF DISCRIMINATION AND THE LAW, 1: 3–28 (1998).

The Istanbul Convention obliges parties to prevent secondary victimization.[40]

Under the HREIA, retaliation is the adverse reaction to a complaint or to proceedings aimed at enforcing compliance with the equality principle and constitutes a form of discrimination.[41] HREIA also defines mobbing (moral/psychological harassment) at the workplace:[42] "actions which intend to alienate a person from a job, exclude or distress the person on the basis of gender, race, color, language, religion, faith, sect, philosophical or political opinion, ethnic origin, wealth, birth, civil status, medical condition, disability or age." Under the HREIA discrimination also includes mobbing.

Individual or Vicarious Liability for Sexual Harassment and Retaliation in Employment

Sexual harassment and/or retaliation can involve employers, employers' representatives (managers/ supervisors), workers, contractors, volunteers, clients, customers, and others connected with or attending a workplace. It can happen at work, at work-related events, or between employer and employee or colleagues outside the work environment.

While the person who sexually harasses someone else and/or retaliates is individually liable for their own behavior under civil,[43] employment,[44] criminal,[45] or administrative law;[46] individual employers or public or private entities can also be held vicariously liable in civil,[47] occupational health and safety,[48] employment,[49] HREIA,[50] or administrative law,[51] for acts of sexual harassment

---

40. Articles 15, 18.

41. HREIA Article 4.

42. See Kadriye Bakirci, "*Universite Calisanlari ve Universitede Psikolojik Siddet ve Yildirma (Mobbing) (University Workers: Psychological Violence and Mobbing at the Universities)*," Donusturulen Universiteler ve Egitim Sistemimiz, Egitim Sen Yayinlari, Ankara (2008).

43. CC Articles 24-25; OA Articles 49, 56, and 58.

44. EA Article 25/II.

45. CA Articles 105, 102, 103, 225, 226, and 122.

46. Civil Servants Act (CSA) (No.657), Articles 124-145—OJ 23.7.1965, No. 12056.

47. OA Article 417/1, CC Article 25. See Bakirci (2001).

48. Occupational Health and Safety Act (No.6331)—OJ 30.6.2012, No. 28339.

49. EA Articles 24/II, 5, 18.

50. Article 4/d.

51. CSA Articles 6-31, 10, Regulation on the Principles of Ethical Behavior of Public Officials and the Application Procedures and Essentials, the Establishment of the Council of

and retaliation by their representatives (managers/ supervisors), workers or clients, customers, and others connected with or attending a workplace.

If sexual harassment takes the form of stalking, the claimant may ask the family court to make a restraining order prohibiting the perpetrator from doing anything described in the order under the PVAWA.[52]

Burden of Proof

Under the EA and HREIA, the employee/claimant has the burden of proving discrimination by the employer. However, if there is a strong likelihood of such a violation, the burden of proof that the alleged violation has not happened shall rest on the employer.[53]

In civil,[54] administrative, and criminal law, the burden of proof is on the claimant.

A few landmark decisions by the Court of Cassation Criminal Divisions reveal that the court will require a different standard of proof to establish workplace sexual harassment. For instance, the Court of Cassation 5th Criminal Division in a 2004 decision held that a professional woman's evidence (in this case the testimony of an intern woman lawyer) should be treated as having satisfied the necessary burden and standard of proof for the court to find that sexual harassment had occurred. The court reasoned that for a professional woman to lie about being the victim of sexual harassment was against the "ordinary flow of life," because the female claimant would endanger her career and her reputation in a traditional society like Turkey, and that no professional woman would risk this damage if no harassment had occurred.[55] The same court has required a higher standard of proof for a finding of the occurrence of sexual harassment in lawsuits filed by nonprofessional employees[56] and treats women differently based on their social status or class.

Ethics for Public Officials Act (No. 5176)—OJ 8.6.2004, No.25486; HREIA Article 4/d; OHSA.

52. Article 5.

53. EA Article 5; HREIA Article 21.

54. OA Article 50/1.

55. Court of Cassation 5th Criminal Division, 2003/4048, 2004/2528. See also Court of Cassation 14th Criminal Division, 22.10.2018, 2018/6176.

56. See Bakirci (2011), *supra*, note 24; Court of Cassation Assembly of Criminal Divisions, 9.11.2010, 2010/8-134, 2010/217; Court of Cassation Assembly of Criminal Divisions, 19.4.1993, 1993/6-79, 1993/108; Court of Cassation 14th Criminal Division, 30.06 2014, 2012/11463, 2104/8940; "*Yargıtay'dan tartışma yaratacak karar: Sanığın beyanı esas*" (*The Decision to Create a Debate From the Supreme Court*), VATAN, June 6, 2015, http://www.gazete vatan.com/yargitay-dan-tartisma-yaratacak-karar-sanigin-beyani-esas-798992-yasam/.

After this decision, women's groups started a campaign titled "A Woman's Statement is Sufficient," advocating that a woman's statement should be accepted as sufficient without any differential treatment based on a woman's professional class, especially with allegations of sexual crimes and even during the trial process.[57] Although the campaign was criticized for violating the principle of presumption of innocence in criminal cases,[58] it had a positive impact on raising awareness of the need for women's allegations to be taken seriously by the police, prosecutors, and by the courts.[59]

On the other hand, in a recent rape case, the court did not find liability despite the testimony of an intern woman lawyer against a male lawyer.[60]

Yet in some decisions when there is no "direct" proof of sexual harassment, the court has established liability by exploring and assessing all the facts and surrounding circumstances. For instance, in a 2005 decision, the Court of Cassation 9th Criminal Division decided that the chronological story of sexual harassment without any contradiction was enough to establish that sexual harassment had occurred.[61]

---

57. See "*Delil Aramayin Kadinin Beyani Esatir*" (*Do Not Look for Evidence, the Statement of the Woman Is Essential*), EVRENSEL, May 3, 2012, http://www.evrensel.net/haber /28271/delil-aramayin-kadinin-beyani-esastir; "*Kadının beyanı esastır, tersini ispat yükümlülüğü erkeğe aittir . . .* (The declaration of the woman is essential and the obligation to prove the opposite belongs to the man)," Sosyalist Feminist Kolektif, Dec. 18, 2012, https://www.sosyalist feministkolektif.org/eylem-etkinlik/sfk-imzal-metinler/kadinin-beyani-esastir-tersini-ispat -yukumlulugu-erkege-aittir/.

58. Court of Cassation Assembly of Criminal Divisions, 25.11.2014, 2013/9-610, 2014/512.

59. Also this campaign led to the introduction of a provision in the PVAWA that no evidence or report proving the violence occurred is required to take preventive cautionary decisions by the public authorities or the courts (Article 8/3).

60. See "*Cinsel saldiridan yargilanan avukat Yurtdasa delil yetersizliginden beraat*" (Lawyer Yurtdasa, who was tried for sexual assault, was acquitted based on 'insufficient evidence'), Gazette Karinca, Jul.10, 2017, http://gazetekarinca.com/2017/07/cinsel-saldiridan-yargila-nan-avukat-yurtdasa-delil-yetersizliginden-beraat/; for opposite decisions see Atakan Uslu, "*Mahkeme 'Kadının Beyanı Esastır' Dedi: Tecavüzcü Kocaya 18 Yıl Hapis*" (*Court Says "Woman's Declaration Essential': 18 Years in Prison for Rapist's Husband*), Onedio, Nov. 23, 2016, https:// onedio.com/haber/mahkeme-kadinin-beyani-esastir-dedi-tecavuzcu-kocaya-18-yil-hapis -740583 (The court accepted a wife's rape claim against her husband); "*Yargıtay tecavüz davasında beraati bozdu: Kadının beyanı esastır*" (Supreme Court Overturned Acquittal in Rape Case: Woman's Declaration is Essential), SPUTNIK TURKEY, Apr. 12, 2018, https:// tr.sputniknews.com/turkiye/201812041036456482-yargitay-tecavuz-davasi-beraat-karari -bozma/ (The court accepted the testimony of a woman who was raped at the historical city walls of Alanya by a man she met the same day.).

61. Court of Cassation 9th Criminal Division, 2004/13286, 2005/7706; See also Court of Cassation Assembly of Criminal Divisions, 26.05.2009, 2008/5-187, 2009/128; Court of Cassation 5th Criminal Division, 27.10.2009, 2007/7587, 2009/12054.

Voluntary and Mandatory Alternative Dispute Resolution in Sexual Harassment Cases

The claimant of sexual harassment or victimization in Turkey can resort to the appropriate legal jurisdiction if they think their rights are being abused, and they can also apply to various authorities to have these abuses assessed or corrected.

Employees also have the right to make complaints to the Labour Inspectorate of the Ministry of Family, Employment and Social Services for violation of the sexual harassment provisions of the EA and OA (Articles 91-97).

Turkish law also provides for alternative dispute resolution (ADR) processes in criminal, employment, and civil law.

Sexual harassment victims can make a complaint to the Committee on Equality of Opportunity Between Men and Women for the Grand National Assembly of Turkey,[62] the Public Auditing Institution (Ombudsperson),[63] the Human Rights and Equality Institution of Turkey or the Human Rights Boards of cities or towns,[64] or the Presidency Communication Centre (CIMER).[65] These are voluntary channels.

The Istanbul Convention prohibits mandatory alternative dispute resolution processes including mediation and conciliation, for all forms of violence allegations covered by the scope of the Convention.[66] The Istanbul Convention prohibition recognizes that although voluntary ADR might present advantages in some criminal and civil law cases, ADR has negative effects in cases of violence against women, in particular if participation in such ADR methods is mandatory and replaces adversarial court proceedings. Victims of gender-based violence can never enter the ADR processes on a footing equal to that of the perpetrator. With these offenses, victims are invariably left with a feeling of shame, helplessness, and vulnerability, while the perpetrator exudes a sense of power and dominance. To avoid the re-privatization of violence against women and to enable the victim to seek justice, it is the responsibility of the state to provide access to adversarial court proceedings presided over by a neutral judge and carried out on the basis of the national laws in force.

---

62. Act No.5840, OJ 24.3.2009, No.27179.
63. Act No.6328 OJ 29.6.2012, No.28338.
64. Regulation on Human Rights Boards of the Cities or Towns, OJ 23.11.2003, No.25298.
65. http://cimer.gov.tr.
66. Article 48/2.

However, in Turkish law, mandatory conciliation is used in criminal law[67] and mandatory mediation is used in employment law.[68] These provisions are in violation of the Istanbul Convention.[69]

ADR also prevents the monitoring of the international conventions on gender equality that are ratified by Turkey.[70]

Defamation Cases

There are no figures on how many individuals have been prosecuted for allegedly making false sexual violence allegations, but under Turkish law it is possible to pursue criminal and civil cases against a sexual—harassment accuser for false allegations if it is targeted at a person.[71]

Defamation is a felony under the Criminal Act, and an accuser can be jailed if found guilty.[72] Under the Criminal Act, "no punishment is imposed if the written or verbal declarations before the courts or administrative authorities contain concrete accusations or negative evaluations about the persons within the scope of plea/defenses. In order to achieve such consequence, the accusations and evaluations should be based on real and concrete facts and also be related with the dispute between the parties."[73] However criminal defamation provisions are contrary to the guarantee of freedom of expression, the right to disclose wrongdoings, the right to mount a defense, and they restrict the free flow of information and ideas. Unduly harsh penalties represent a breach of these rights even if circumstances justify some sanction for abuse of these rights. Therefore, criminal defamation provisions should be abolished.

Monetary and moral compensation can be claimed from the accuser for the false allegations under the civil laws.[74]

The big challenge here is to find the delicate balance between guaranteeing the fundamental right to freedom of expression, the right to disclose

---

67. Criminal Procedure Act (No.5271)—OJ 17.12.2004, No.25673, Articles 253, 254, 255.

68. Labour Courts Act, Article 3.

69. See Bakirci (2015), *supra*, note 28; Kadriye Bakirci, "*Towards an Alternative Employment Law Through the Use of Alternative Dispute Resolution by Mediation*," TURKIYE BAROLAR BIRLIGI DERGISI, 140, pp. 355-392 (2019).

70. See Bakirci (Whistleblowing), *supra*, note 36; Bakirci (2019), *supra*, note 69.

71. Court of Cassation 9th Criminal Division, 12.12.2012, 2012/2994, 2012/14875; 30.4.2013, 2013/2885, 2013/6734.

72. CA Articles 125 and 267.

73. CA Article 128.

74. CC Articles 24, 25; OA Articles 49, 56.

wrongdoings, right to a defense, and the right to protect the honor and reputation of persons[75].

Conclusion

Sexual harassment is a form of gender-based violence and gender-based discrimination premised on the unequal status of women. This type of violence is deeply rooted in the social and cultural structures, norms, and values that govern society, and is often perpetuated by a culture of denial and silence.

In contrast to many countries in the region, Turkish women in general are legally protected against sexual harassment, but most of the women are silent and the #MeToo movement has failed to launch.

It seems that disclosure does not deliver justice. For example, the #SenDeAnlat movement never manifested into meaningful reform or accountability. In the wake of Ozgecan Aslan's murder, women were speaking out, but no one was held accountable, and no justice was achieved.

There have been no high-profile men like Harvey Weinstein, who have faced repercussions or public scrutiny for their actions in Turkey.

Sexual harassment charges against an actor in June 2018 was not pursued by the public prosecutor because of the "lack of evidence."[76]

In August 2018, an executive assistant (known as "T.O.") has claimed that she was "exiled" after she filed a sexual harassment complaint against her director at a state university. Another colleague of "T.O." came forward and filed a criminal complaint, claiming that she also became a target of sexual harassment by the same director. The director was removed from his office after the complaints but was later appointed by the university as the Director of an Institution. While the man was not even suspended by the university, "T.O." claims that she was "exiled" by the administration that appointed her, first as a cleaner, and then as the only female worker at a public canteen. "I am the one who was

---

75. In recent case law of the Turkish Constitutional Court related to freedom of speech in employment or mobbing, free expression has outweighed all other considerations. The Court has repeatedly underlined that "freedom of expression constitutes one of the essential foundations of a democratic society" (Turkish Constitutional Court, Ilter Nur Judgment, Application No: 2013/6829, 14.6.2016; Metin Yalcin Judgment, Application No. 2014/5959, 6.2.2019; Tuncer Yigci Judgment, Application No. 2015/5402, 6.2.2019; Hulusi Ozkan Judgment, Application No. 2015/18638, 15.11.2018), See Kadriye Bakirci, "*Work-related whistle-blowing in democratic societies context: A comparative study of international, EU and Turkish law*," JOURNAL OF FINANCIAL CRIME, Vol. 26, No. 4 (2019).

76. See "*Prosecutor drops sexual abuse charges against Turkish TV series actor Talat Bulut*," HURRIYET DAILY NEWS, Aug. 7, 2018, http://www.hurriyetdailynews.com/prosecutor-drops-sexual-abuse-charges-against-turkish-tv-series-actor-talat-bulut-135540.

sexually harassed and then punished because of it. My psychology has been ruined. They put pressure on me to make me quit," she claims.[77]

Therefore, until the abusers are brought to justice, and most importantly until men initiate campaigns against gender-based violence[78] and perpetrators accept their guilt, it would not be easy for ordinary women to come forward with their own stories.

---

77. See Fevzi Kızılkoyun, "*Turkish woman 'exiled' after sexual abuse complaint at university*," HURRIYET DAILY NEWS, Aug. 4, 2019, http://www.hurriyetdailynews.com/turkish -woman-exiled-after-sexual-abuse-complaint-at-university-135418.

78. There are some examples of men initiating campaigns and protests against sexual violence and sexual harassment such as a campaign called "This is not being a man," and men marching against and protesting sexual harassment by wearing skirts in Istanbul.

Middle East/Asia/Oceania

CHAPTER 19

Sexual Harassment Law in Israel and the #MeToo Challenge

Daphne Barak-Erez[1]

Introduction

In the two decades since the enactment of the Israeli Prevention of Sexual Harassment Law in 1998,[2] the president of the state was indicted for rape and sent to prison for several years, the minister of justice was indicted for indecent assault and pushed to resign, and several high-level military commanders were indicted and forced to quit successful careers. This analysis focuses on that law, its implementation, and the controversies surrounding it,[3] trying to assess its impact as well as the limitations of the change it brought about. To paint a fuller picture of the legal landscape, I will also review former approaches to resisting and combating sexual harassment and the interpretation of previous legislation in light of the #MeToo movement.

---

1. Justice, Supreme Court of Israel. Formerly Professor of Law and Dean, Tel Aviv University. I would like to thank Shira Anderson, Anat Ovadia-Rosner, Sarah Scharf, and Shachar Tal for their comments and assistance.

2. Prevention of Sexual Harassment Law, 5758–1998 [hereinafter Prevention of Sexual Harassment Law]. Symbolically, the bill's final vote took place on March 10, just after International Women's Day.

3. This analysis borrows partially from a previous article. See generally Daphne Barak-Erez & Jayna Kothari, *When Sexual Harassment Law Goes East: Feminism, Legal Transplantation, and Social Change*, 47 STAN. J. INT'L L. 175 (2011).

Pre-1998 Law

Prior to 1998, sexual harassment was only partially regulated by employment law, criminal law (which largely proscribed physical aspects of unwanted sexual behavior),[4] and the law regulating disciplinary provisions for state employees.[5]

In the area of employment legislation, the only relevant provision was section 7 of the Equal Opportunities in Employment Law.[6] This provision prohibited "sexual harassment" (using this terminology) but was quite narrow. It originally applied solely to employer-employee relations. In 1995, the legislature amended the provision to include sexual harassment of prospective employees.[7] Still, the protection provided remained rather flimsy because the text did not contain any details regarding the nature of the prohibited behavior.

As for criminal law, the provisions in place before 1998 only covered relatively severe cases of unwanted sexual behavior. Section 348 of the Penal Law, which prohibits "indecent assaults," applies to unwanted sexual advances of a physical nature, such as a coerced kiss. In addition, section 346(b) of the Penal Law, which prohibits "forbidden intercourse by consent," applies to sexual conduct in the context of employment-based power imbalances, such as when a boss exploits his or her "authority in employment or service" to have sexual intercourse with an employee. It applies regardless of whether the exchange was technically consensual. Though these provisions cover many forms of sexual harassment, they hardly reach the full gamut because they are limited to physical acts.

The law applicable to state service—which establishes the state's power to initiate disciplinary proceedings against state employees—served as a third layer of protection. More specifically, one disciplinary offense was defined as behavior in which an employee "conduct[ed] himself in a manner unbecoming of his office as a State employee."[8] Unfortunately, for many years the exact meaning of "unbecoming" in the context of sexual behavior remained undefined.

Ironically, the state disciplinary proceedings' potential as a tool to curb sexual harassment only really began to manifest in 1998—just before the enactment of the new law. Specifically, that year the Supreme Court, in its appellate

---

4. Penal Law, 5737–1977 [hereinafter Penal Law].

5. State Service (Discipline) Law, 5723–1963 [hereinafter State Service Law].

6. Equal Opportunities in Employment Law, 5748–1988 [hereinafter Equal Opportunities in Employment Law]. At the time, this was a general prohibition that did not specify its scope and exact meaning.

7. Equal Opportunities in Employment Law (Amend. No. 3), 5755–1995.

8. State Service Law § 17(3).

capacity, convicted a state college professor of engaging in unwanted advances toward a female student, overturning part of the state disciplinary tribunal's decision.[9] Since, this judgment, together with the 1998 law that reinforced its main holdings, has served as precedent for many other decisions in which both the disciplinary tribunals and the Supreme Court have found state employees guilty of sexual harassment.[10]

The pre-1998 laws were insufficient because they were largely focused on criminal law and administrative disciplinary law, under which the state has sole enforcement power. In contrast, in civil litigation, the power to sue rests in the hands of the injured individual. In addition, the pre-1998 criminal and disciplinary procedures were focused on punishing the wrongdoer, not compensating the victim.[11]

The New Sexual Harassment Law—20 Years of Revolution

The Prevention of Sexual Harassment Law of 1998 aims "to prohibit sexual harassment in order to protect human dignity, liberty, and privacy, and to promote equality between the sexes."[12] In a move of symbolic significance, the bill was initiated by all eight women who served, at the time, as members of the Knesset, the Israeli parliament (MKs).[13] In contrast to the way in which sexual harassment law has evolved in the United States as an application of anti-discrimination law, the Israeli law was heavily inspired by the European

---

9. StSA [State Service Appeal] 6713/96 State of Israel v. Ben Asher [1998] 52(1) PD 650, 661 (Israel). The accused hugged and touched the complainant and asked her to "go out" with him.

10. See, e.g., StSA 309/01 Zarzar v. State Service Comm'r [2001] 55(2) PD 830 (Israel); StSA 1928/00 State of Israel v. Bruchin [2000] 54(3) PD 649 (Israel). The Supreme Court used to hear appeals on decisions of the tribunal for disciplinary matters for state employees. Currently, these appeals are heard by the district courts.

11. However, it is worth noting that in Israel, it is possible for the court in a criminal trial to award the victim limited compensation, according to a special provision in the Penal Law.

12. Prevention of Sexual Harassment Law, § 1.

13. The ninth female MK, Limor Livnat, was then a Government Minister and under Israeli constitutional law could not therefore initiate a non-governmental bill. The Knesset consists of 120 members. The representation of women has since significantly increased. It has reached more than 30 women in the 20th Knesset, which was elected in 2015, but this achievement has not since been equaled. This is far from equal or adequate representation, but it is still more significant compared to the past.

concept of human dignity.[14] Despite the influence of other systems, the law did not confine itself to existing models of anti-sexual harassment legislation. In fact, at the time of its enactment, it was probably the most comprehensive and far-reaching law of its kind in the world.[15]

In contrast to previous provisions, the 1998 law provides a broad and detailed definition of sexual harassment. It also prohibits many specific acts, such as repeatedly making sexual references or propositions to a person who shows that he or she is not interested in them, making such comments to a subordinate, even if the subordinate does not show that he or she is not interested,[16] and making disparaging remarks to a person because of his or her sex or sexual orientation. In addition, in its definition of sexual harassment the law also includes the traditional criminal offenses of sexual assault, and the use of blackmail to demand the performance of a sexual act, as defined by the Penal Law.[17]

The law provides three enforcement channels—in criminal, civil, or labor courts—through which individuals can proceed. It defines sexual harassment as both a criminal offense[18] and a cause for a civil suit.[19] Notably, not only does the law permit civil litigation, but it also eases plaintiffs' paths to success because it does not require a showing of concrete damages. In addition, violation of the

---

14. See generally Orit Kamir, *Dignity, Respect, and Equality in Israel's Sexual Harassment Law*, DIRECTIONS IN SEXUAL HARASSMENT LAW 561 (Catharine A. MacKinnon & Reva Siegel eds., 2004) (discussing the role of the concept of human dignity in Israeli sexual harassment law); Orit Kamir, *Rethinking Sexual Harassment in Terms of Human Dignity-Respect*, 29 MISHPATIM 317 (1998) (comparing U.S. sexual harassment law and Israeli sexual harassment law). For criticism of this choice, see generally Noya Rimalt, *Stereotyping Women, Individualizing Harassment: The Dignitary Paradigm of Sexual Harassment Law Between the Limits of Law and the Limits of Feminism*, 19 YALE J.L. & FEMINISM 391 (2007) (arguing that the Israeli conceptualization of sexual harassment as a dignitary harm has had the unintended effect of reinforcing existing patriarchal social norms).

15. *See* Tsili Mor, *Law as a Tool for a Sexual Revolution: Israel's Prevention of Sexual Harassment Law—1998*, 7 MICH. J. GENDER & L. 291, 292 (2001) ("Today, Israel boasts an extraordinary law, billed as one of, if not the most, progressive laws of its kind in the world").

16. The question of who qualifies as a subordinate was addressed by the Supreme Court in subsequent cases. See, e.g., StSA 1599/03 Tapiro v. State Service Comm'r [2003] 58(2) PD 125 (Israel).

17. At the same time, the Prevention of Sexual Harassment Law refrained from including the serious criminal offenses that refer specifically to sexual intercourse, such as the offense of "forbidden intercourse by consent," prohibited under Penal Law, § 346(b). However, in fact, victims of such offenses were indirectly empowered by the enactment of the new law.

18. Prevention of Sexual Harassment Law, § 5.

19. Prevention of Sexual Harassment Law, § 6.

law serves as a basis for disciplinary proceedings under the law applicable to state employees.[20]

The law also imposes specific obligations on employers to prevent sexual harassment, and failure to comply renders employers liable to suit.[21] Among other things, the law requires employers to take reasonable care to prevent sexual harassment in the workplace; to appoint an employee responsible for receiving and investigating complaints, as well as preparing reports concerning them; and, in any workplace with more than twenty-five employees, to publicize "sample rules" that explain the prohibition on sexual harassment and procedures for filing complaints.

Importantly, this is just one aspect of the law. It actually applies far beyond the workplace context, and in this regard is broader than U.S. law. In fact, the Israeli law does not mention employer-employee relationships specifically, and instead uses broad language to define and proscribe sexual harassment generally.[22] Later amendments have broadened its application still further, as legislators try to update the law to changing background circumstances. For example, one of these recent amendments included in the definition of sexual harassment the publication of pictures, movies, or recordings that focus on an individual's sexuality, where this publication may humiliate or degrade the portrayed person and was made without his or her consent.[23] This provision was drafted to combat a new type of harassment made possible by technologies that did not exist when the law was originally enacted.

Implementation and Enforcement

Israel's sexual harassment law is certainly not limited to words on paper. It has frequently been applied to real cases. Simultaneously, the state continues to prosecute cases of sexual violence under more traditional sexual offenses, such as rape and sodomy. The number of sexual harassment cases that have found their

---

20. See generally StSA 43/01 Darwish v. State Service Comm'n [2001] 55(3) PD 817 (Israel); StSA 1934/03 Falach v. State Service Comm'n [Nov. 18, 2003] (Israel); StSA 4193/06 Chai-Cohen v. State Service Comm'n [Oct. 5, 2006] (Israel); StSA 2192/06 Rahmani v. State Service Comm'n [Apr. 5, 2007] (Israel); StSA 11976/05 Halil v. State Service Comm'n [Apr. 11, 2007] (Israel) (Throughout, cases cited only with dates are not published in hard copy but are available online).

21. Prevention of Sexual Harassment Law, §§ 7–8.

22. Prevention of Sexual Harassment Law, § 4 ("A person shall not harass another sexually nor persecute such person").

23. Prevention of Sexual Harassment Law (Amend. No. 9), 5773–2013 (adding § 3(a)(5a) to the Prevention of Sexual Harassment Law).

way to the courts—through criminal indictments, employment law litigation, and disciplinary proceedings—demonstrate a generally robust, working legal framework.[24] In addition, the state has promulgated regulations regarding the implementation of employers' duties under the Prevention of Sexual Harassment Law.[25]

Of course, this does not necessarily mean that victims feel empowered enough to report harassment, or that complaints are always handled effectively.[26] From a formal perspective, however, the law has established procedures that largely enable them to do so. Specifically, victims are protected from shaming and retaliation in the public sphere through prohibitions on publishing their names.[27] The fact that women can file lawsuits while remaining, in most cases, anonymous outside of the legal proceedings is an important safeguard that points to the law's pragmatism and efficacy.

Another important aspect of Israel's sexual harassment legal framework has been the willingness of state prosecutors to indict high-level officials.

One of the first landmark cases in this context was the trial of Yitzhak Mordechai, who, at the time, was the minister of transportation. He had previously served as a Major General and was considered a renowned war hero. One of his female subordinates filed a complaint against him for sexual harassment and indecent assault. Eventually, two other women came forward and filed additional complaints. He was charged with three counts of sexual assault and found guilty on two of them. Ultimately, he received a relatively lenient punishment, which did not include prison time (but rather only a suspended sentence). His appeal against his conviction, as well as the prosecution's appeal requesting a harsher punishment, were both dismissed, as was his request to appeal to the Supreme Court.[28] At any rate, he resigned, and his successful public career was effectively terminated.

---

24. For an early case in which a court reviewed, and partially invalidated, a decision not to prosecute, see HCJ [High Court of Justice] 4869/01 Anonymous v. Military Judge Advocate Gen. [2002] 56(3) PD 944 (Israel).

25. See generally Prevention of Sexual Harassment (Employers Duties) Regulations, 5758–1998.

26. It is worthwhile to mention that the #WhyIDidntReport movement also manifested in Israel, with publications addressing specific concerns shared by potential complainants.

27. See Penal Law, § 352 (prohibiting the publication of information that identifies individuals as persons who were injured by or complained they were injured by a sex offense). See also Prevention of Sexual Harassment Law, § 5(e) (prohibiting publication of information that identifies persons harmed by an offense under this law). In addition, lawsuits against employers are regulated by Equal Opportunities in Employment Law, § 10A, which grants labor courts discretion to order a closed trial (adopted by Prevention of Sexual Harassment Law, § 10(c)).

28. RCrimA [Request for Criminal Appeal] 332/02 Mordechai v. State of Israel [Nov. 18, 2004] (Israel).

Another public affair that proved decisive in this context was the trial of former Minister of Justice Haim Ramon.[29] Ramon was indicted for "indecent assault" when he kissed on the mouth a young female officer who served in the Prime Minister's Office. During the trial, the court focused on the question of consent. The court, relying on the officer's version of events, found Ramon guilty and sentenced him to community service.[30] Although Ramon was technically convicted under the "traditional" offence of engaging in "indecent assault," that offense has been incorporated into Israel's modern sexual harassment law—and this case provided a meaningful contribution to the sexual harassment landscape.

A particularly significant case was the so-called *Katzav* affair. It concerned Moshe Katzav, a long-time Israeli public figure, who at the time was serving as the President of the State of Israel (an important, even if largely symbolic, title).[31] During his term in office, several female employees filed complaints against Katzav for sexual offenses that allegedly occurred both during his time as president and while he had previously held other public service positions. The Attorney General initiated an investigation and eventually filed several serious criminal charges against Katzav for sexual harassment and rape. After rejecting a plea bargain, Katzav was found guilty of two counts of rape and was sentenced to prison for seven years.[32] His appeal to the Supreme Court was dismissed.[33]

Though the *Katzav* affair was by no means a standard sexual harassment case, it served as a meaningful turning point in the Israeli public sphere and signaled an increased willingness by women to file complaints regarding sexual harassment and other forms of sexual violence. Indeed, several other high-level police and military officers were indicted for sexual offenses following the case.[34]

In addition to state-based enforcement, victims have challenged public appointments of their alleged harassers under administrative law doctrines that enable judicial review of such appointments.

---

29. CrimC [Criminal Case] (TA) 5461/06 State of Israel v. Ramon [Jan. 31, 2007, the conviction] and [Mar. 29, 2007, the sentence] (Israel).

30. In addition, the court ordered Ramon to pay his victims damages, according to special rules that apply to awarding compensation in criminal trials, as explained above.

31. See Basic Law: The President of the States, § 1 ("A President shall stand at the head of the State"). This is in contrast to the role of Prime Minister, who serves as head of the executive branch.

32. In addition, he received a deferred judgment ordering additional penalties if he commits similar offenses in the future. He was also ordered to pay his victims damages.

33. CrimA [Criminal Appeal] 3372/11 Katzav v. State of Israel [Nov. 10, 2011] (Israel).

34. See, e.g., RCrimA 10002/17 State of Israel v. Mor [July 18, 2018] (Israel) (convicting the former Deputy Chief of Police of breach of trust and sexual harassment for his sexual relations with three policewomen).

The first high profile case of this sort was the *Galili* affair.[35] That case concerned the intended promotion of Brigadier General Nir Galili, who had a sexual relationship with a young female soldier serving under his command as his personal secretary. Galili was charged in military disciplinary proceedings for participating in that relationship. He was reprimanded and subjected to an administrative sanction that "froze" any possibility of promotion for two years. Following the completion of this period, the Minister of Defense and the Commander-in-Chief of the IDF decided to make Galili the commander of a division and to promote him from the rank of one-star general to two. Galili's former secretary filed a petition to the Supreme Court, in its capacity as the High Court of Justice, arguing that Galili's conduct as a commander made him ethically and morally unfit for promotion. The Supreme Court accepted the petition and held that it would be unreasonable to give Galili a higher rank, considering his past abuse of power (although it refrained from intervening in the decision to make him a commander of the division). In some ways, Galili was still relatively lucky, in the sense that he only had to face disciplinary proceedings and was not forced to retire immediately after his misconduct was exposed. This is to a large degree a result of the case being one of the early ones of its kind. In later cases, the perpetrators were forced to retire and faced charges in military courts.[36]

The *Ramon* affair returned to the Supreme Court, sitting as the High Court of Justice, when the then-prime minister offered Ramon a new ministerial position—a decision that was approved by the Knesset. NGOs committed to the protection of women's rights filed a petition against Ramon's new appointment. However, the majority of a Supreme Court panel declined to accept the petition, basing its decision on the court's very limited power to intervene in a decision regarding ministerial appointments.[37]

Last but not least, the *Ritman* case proves relevant.[38] Here, the case dealt with a complaint concerning the behavior of one of the Israel Police's most high-ranking commanders, the chief of the main investigative unit, who was accused of sexually harassing a female officer serving under him. The petition attacked the Israel Police's decision not to remove him from his position following the complaint. The Supreme Court accepted the petition, declaring the

---

35. See HCJ 1284/99 Anonymous v. Chief of General Staff [1999] 53(2) PD 62 (Israel).

36. A much later case involved Brigadier General Ofek Buchris who committed sexual acts with a subordinate female soldier. In this matter, dealt with during 2016, Buchris had to retire and face charges. His punishment included demotion to the rank of Colonel.

37. HCJ 5853/07 Emunah the Movement of the Nat'l Religious Women v. Prime Minister [2007] 62(3) PD 445 (Israel).

38. HCJ 3884/16 Anonymous v. Minister of Internal Defense [Nov. 20, 2017] (Israel).

decision invalid because the chief of police made it without reviewing all of the Policemen Investigation Unit's reports and relevant testimony. Thus, the court did not directly intervene with the Israel Police's decision—it did not order Ritman's removal—but it made clear that findings of sexual harassment are highly relevant to promotional decisions. A few months later, Ritman announced his retirement.

Legal Implementation vis-à-vis Public Attitude

Law does not exist in a vacuum, and public opinion also plays an important role in the struggle against sexual harassment. Here, there is some tension between the law's formal narrative and public opinion. Indeed, the public's attitude toward the law is quite complex,[39] despite the fact that the law followed the trajectory of earlier legislation and was introduced through the democratic legislative process, making it more likely to enjoy public legitimacy than rules made through judicial lawmaking.

One major reason for this is the way that the new law challenges entrenched public norms. The law rejects the notion that there can ever be consent in the context of a superior-subordinate relationship. In the eyes of its critics, this normative choice has cast a cloud of doubt on the law's legitimacy since its enactment. More specifically, when the legislature first introduced the law, critics focused on three main concerns: that the law signaled "the end of romance and flirting"; that women would use the law to blackmail and take revenge on men, especially male employers; and that there was a wide gap between common, accepted societal standards—arguably standards also accepted by Israeli women—and those that the law endorsed. As the law has been enforced, these initial concerns have intensified.

This debate first manifested in the legislative process, though the law eventually passed by a majority of eighteen to one (that is, with a clear plurality of votes—the majority of the Knesset's 120 MKs were not in attendance). At the time, MK Rechav'am Ze'evi, former Israel Defense Forces (IDF) General, remained the lone dissenter. In the Knesset debate prior to the vote, he declared the law "demonic"[40] and said that while he certainly opposed sexual harassment, he was afraid that the law would serve as a tool for women to take revenge on

---

39. See generally Sergio Herzog, *Public Perceptions of Sexual Harassment: An Empirical Analysis in Israel from Consensus and Feminist Theoretical Perspectives*, 57 SEX ROLES 579 (2007) (explaining that this ambivalence exists despite the fact that the public generally perceives sexual harassment as a serious matter).

40. DK (1998) 5901.

men, especially in the workplace against the employer.[41] Quoting from the Biblical Song of Songs and Proverbs, Ze'evi also warned that the law would destroy
romance and that "wooing would be forbidden."[42]

In the following years, the law has continued to generate controversy—
perhaps paradoxically—because it has been effectively applied. This may be the
curse of success. The relatively high level of awareness, public debate, implementation, and enforcement that the law has generated have created a partial
backlash.

One important aspect of the controversy concerns the sexual harassment
law's criminal enforcement. Some of the most heated arguments against it
have arisen in this context. In fact, several commentators who claim to support
the law's underlying purpose have fiercely criticized its criminal components,
arguing that it should only be enforced through civil actions and disciplinary
proceedings.[43]

In practice, the most controversial criminal cases have proven to be those
that dealt with ambiguous issues of consent and those that involved relatively
minor physical overtures. Many critics of the law do not consider its definition
of sexual harassment vis-à-vis sexual advances legitimate. The *Ramon* case was
controversial in the Israeli public arena exactly for this reason. Many people
were outraged that Ramon could be convicted for an allegedly unwanted kiss,
regardless of the imbalance of power implicit to the relationship. The court
did not hesitate to find that the complainant had not consented to the kiss—
and, accordingly, to convict. However, critics still had mixed reactions to the
judgment. Some vocal commentators, including human rights activists who
usually identify with feminist causes, thought that the court had gone too far
by criminalizing a kiss in such circumstances.[44] The *Ramon* case also served as
a battlefield for the debate regarding the appropriateness of the law's criminal

---

41. *Id.* at 5902.

42. *Id.* at 5903. Ironically, reports regarding sexual misconduct were made against Ze'evi
himself after his death. *See infra* note 46 and accompanying text.

43. See generally Mordecai Kremnitzer & Liat Levanon, *The Criminal Prohibition
on Sexual Harassment—Justifying a Means to an End and Its Price*, 2 SHA'AREI MISHPAT 285
(2001). For the counter argument, see Orit Kamir, *Response: When You Say No—What Do You
Mean?* 2 SHAAREI MISHPAT 307 (2001).

44. Such critics included former MKs Yael Dayan and Shulamit Aloni. See, e.g., Hana
Beit Halachmi, *Ramon's Women Friends [Hachaverot Shel Ramon]*, YNET, Sept. 21, 2006. Yael
Dayan was the Chairperson of the Parliamentary Commission for Women's Rights and was in
fact the speaker who presented the Prevention of Sexual Harassment Bill to the Knesset. Shulamit Aloni was the founder of the left-wing party Ratz, the Movement for Civil Rights.

application[45]—although, again, from a formal perspective, Ramon was charged with a criminal offense that existed before the law's enactment.

The Public Arena and the Legal Aspects of #MeToo

Like other countries, Israel has borne witness to several high-profile cases where allegations of inappropriate behavior were not coupled with litigation or criminal charges—or, if they were, where the case's public fallout far outweighed its legal significance. Many of these allegations refer to acts that occurred in the far past, for which bringing criminal charges or civil suits is no longer feasible, and name men who are or used to be in the public arena. In other words, #MeToo has come to Israel, too.

One example that seemingly preceded the formal start of the #MeToo movement in Israel was a television report by the highly esteemed investigative journalist Ilana Dayan. This report exposed allegations of sexual misconduct against the late Rechavam Ze'evi, previously mentioned as the only MK who voted against the Prevention of Sexual Harassment Law.[46] Ze'evi was assassinated in 2001 by Palestinians while serving as a government minister. He is currently annually honored by a state-supported commemoration ceremony, and many streets and public places bear his name. The report, which predictably raised much public interest, relayed that Ze'evi allegedly committed many acts that would today be regarded as sexual harassment and even as acts of sexual violence. Ze'evi's family responded angrily, arguing that these allegations, made after his death, were impossible to fairly rebut. Both sides had very strong views on the matter and the issue was never resolved.

In October 2017, as the #MeToo movement began to gain public attention in Israel, the popular daily paper "Yedioth Ahronoth" published a cover story that included columns written by female actresses, singers, and writers, sharing their experiences with sexual harassment and sexual violence. This development opened the door for a flow of subsequent publications, covering stories about women from different social backgrounds and their experiences

---

45. See *supra* note 44.

46. This report was broadcast in Ilana Dayan's famous program "Uvda" (in Hebrew, "fact") in April 2016.

with sexual harassment.[47] It is worthwhile to mention that some notable accusations were also made by men who experienced sexual harassment in their past.[48]

From a legal perspective, one major challenge regarding these public allegations relates to the potential for retaliatory defamation lawsuits. In this regard, the difference between the broad American doctrine of freedom of speech, specifically the protections granted by *New York Times Co. v. Sullivan*,[49] and the laws of many other countries is crucial. In Israel, the defendant in a defamation suit bears the burden of proving that his or her statement was truthful and convincing the court that a public interest rationale supported its publication. When an allegation concerns a public figure, the public interest rationale is obvious. However, proving the truthfulness of a complaint is never easy—and especially not many years after the alleged incident occurred.

One illustrative example of this problem is the *Uri Daniel* case.[50] In that case, four women brought lawsuits against a male social acquaintance. All four women claimed that he raped them on different occasions. The man was not a public figure in the narrow sense, but he was a lawyer with a successful career. The man's accusers chose to express their allegations publicly and by filing a complaint to the Israeli Bar Association. They also filed complaints with the police, though the police could not investigate because the statute of limitations had run. Eventually, the women brought suit directly. In turn, the man sued them for defamation.

The resulting litigation was quite complex. To summarize, the women's civil suits were dismissed due to the statute of limitations. However, the Supreme Court, in its appellate capacity, allowed the defamation suit to proceed because the suit against the women's public allegations was timely. The case was further complicated by the question of whether the complaints to the police should be regarded as defamatory. Although the law recognizes a special defense to defamation for bona fide complaints, the Supreme Court upheld the district court's finding that the women were not sufficiently credible. In my dissent, I criticized the district court's reasoning for not finding the women's testimonies credible (for instance, the district court included in its analysis the late filing of

---

47. Allegations made by relatively well-known female reporters against former colleagues who were senior to them at the time the events allegedly occurred also attracted significant public attention. Examples include allegations made by Dana Weiss (against Gabi Gazit) and Oshart Cotler and Neri Livne (against Alex Giladi).

48. One allegation of this sort that gained considerable attention was made in 2018 by Assaf Harel, who, at the time, hosted a popular late-night TV show. Harel shared with his audience his story about being harassed by a teacher when he studied at the prestigious Thelma Yellin High School for the arts.

49. New York Times Co. v. Sullivan, 376 U.S. 254 (1964) (United States).

50. CA [Civil Appeal] 7426/14 Anonymous v. Daniel [Mar. 14, 2016] (Israel).

the complaints—but it is well established that late complaints regarding sexual harassment are extremely common, and that their timing does not necessarily bear on their truthfulness).[51]

Another hotly debated question concerns how the public at large, as well as employers (including private ones), should react toward people accused of sexual harassment or assault. This concern is relevant not only when the individual in question is convicted, but also when no formal proceedings take place and therefore the presumption of innocence still applies. What are the criteria to be applied in these cases? What is the significance of the (generally long) lapse of time between the alleged incident and its publication? What is the significance of the individual's current attitude to these past events?[52] And what weight should be given to the publication's potential harm to the accused's well-being, particularly in extreme cases?[53] These are issues most often relevant in the public arena. Usually they do not involve the legal system, but they may sometimes have legal implications. To a large extent, they illustrate the unique difficulties associated with transformative legal change. Viewed this way, the introduction of sexual harassment law and the #MeToo movement also serve as case-study of transitional justice.

At this stage, it is still too early to assess the full impact of the changes described. It can be said, however, that accusations of sexual harassment have pushed influential people to, at the very least, take a break from their public careers.[54]

Conclusion

What are the lessons to be learned from this story? One lesson is that legal reform does not always go hand-in-hand with social change. It may eventually influence social change, but not instantaneously. The Israeli legal system's progressive approach to sexual harassment affected complementary social

---

51. The nuanced way defamation law applies to these issues is still waiting to be clarified. Regarding one of the incidences mentioned, Alex Giladi indeed brought a defamation suit against the journalist Neri Livne, but eventually, following mediation, he dropped it.

52. One example which forms a later chapter in the Haim Ramon affair was a decision of Tel-Aviv University to hire him to teach as an adjunct lecturer, in 2018. This decision was resisted by a group of feminist students. One of them referred to him in her protest as a "sex offender." Ramon sued her for defamation, and eventually the case was settled, in 2019.

53. In Israel, a notable example from 2018 is the decision of the artist Boaz Arad to commit suicide following the public accusations made against him concerning past sexual relations with female students.

54. Examples include the cases of leading columnists Ari Shavit and Dan Margalit, who stopped writing for the daily *Haaretz* newspaper.

norms, but only partially. Ultimately, public support for repairing social wrongs is stronger when the resulting reform does not challenge society's basic power structures, but rather offers benevolent assistance to so-called deserving complainants. In addition, existing power structures can only be reformed partially through litigation. Other important steps are taken in the public arena, and their legal implications are less important, although not negligible, due to ripple effects such as defamation suits.

CHAPTER 20

Sexual Harassment and Iranian Laws' Coverage

Maryamossadat Torabi[1]

The #MeToo Movement in Iran

The #MeToo Movement began to spread virally internationally in October 2017 as a hashtag on social media in an attempt to demonstrate the widespread prevalence of sexual assault and harassment, especially in the workplace,[2] encouraging victims of sexual harassment to tweet about it and "give people a sense of the magnitude of the problem."[3] Societies with easy access to the internet and social networks have mostly become aware of this movement. On the other hand, countries with limited access to the internet or where social media such as Twitter, Facebook, YouTube, and Telegram are filtered and censored, have not had the same opportunity to engage with and follow such movements like the rest of the world. Unfortunately, the Islamic Republic of Iran, having censored many websites and media, is one of those countries with limited access to the internet, restricting its population of 82 million people from the free flow of information online.

---

1. Associate, Ashrafi & Partners Law Firm, Tehran, Iran.
2. Nicole Smartt, *Sexual harassment in the workplace in a #MeToo world*, FORBES, Jan. 16, 2018.
3. Nadia Khomami, *#MeToo: how a hashtag became a rallying cry against sexual harassment*, THE GUARDIAN, Nov. 21, 2017. With due credit to "Tarana Burke," the founder of the Me Too movement who used the phrase "Me Too" in 2006, on the Myspace social network as part of a campaign to promote "empowerment through empathy" among women of color who have experienced sexual abuse, particularly within underprivileged communities. See Cristela Guerra, *Where'd the "Me Too" initiative really come from? Activist Tarana Burke, long before hashtags*, BOSTON GLOBE, Oct. 17, 2017.

In addition to these restrictions, only a limited percentage of the population can speak English, mostly students who pursue their higher education in universities. Women who have less education, who are stay-at-home mothers, or who work in lower class jobs never learned English during their education in schools and thus have no access to English-based coverage of the international #MeToo movement.

These two reasons are the main causes of diminished enlightenment for Iranian women and men regarding subjects such as sexual harassments, equal rights for women and men, avoiding childhood marriage, and the absence of movements such as #MeToo. Nevertheless, as the society evolves and becomes more educated, its approach toward these matters evolves as well. Many traditional and religious customs change and allow better sexual education and ameliorate women's concerns about demanding their rights. In this context, and bearing in mind the restrictions mentioned earlier, the legal protection in the Islamic Republic of Iran for women experiencing sexual harassments and assaults will be illustrated.

The Legal Protection for Women Facing Sexual Harassment

Since the Iranian Islamic Revolution in 1979, the Iranian legal system is based on Islamic laws. This does not mean that all previous laws are outdated; however, still it does not provide for equal rights for women and men. The Penal Code addresses sexual harassment and any kind of assault toward women and children as will be explained below.

Harassment and Assaults Against Women and Children in Public Places

Under Article 619 of the Iranian Penal Code, anyone who causes any infringement or assault against a child or a woman in a public place verbally or by any kind of action that is contradictory to their dignity and integrity faces imprisonment from two to six months and up to seventy-four lashes. Due to the general nature of this Article, the perpetrator of any assault, including but not limited to sexual harassment, will face charges; however, this Article only addresses a crime if it takes occurs in a public place and does not cover workplaces. Nonetheless, under the circumstances described, the Act enables women and children to seek justice and to make their offender face punishment.

One of the most important aspects of any law is how it can be implemented. With Article 619, it is not very likely that someone would sexually harass a woman in public and if so, it is very unlikely that the abused would be able to drag that person to a police office or be able to inform the officials at the time; one would expect that normally the assaulters would leave the place as fast as possible. Therefore, such general articles do not genuinely help women and prevent them from being sexually harassed. Moreover, to prove the crime in court under the Iranian Code of Criminal Procedure, two witnesses (men), or four witnesses (women), or one man and two women must attest that such crime has taken place. Otherwise, it is very difficult to prove and attain a just order unless the accused confesses.[4]

In addition, the punishment by being lashed is inhuman and brutal itself; also, the punishment for such crimes must include some sort of mental and psychological compensation for the abused. Nonetheless, this law, which passed in April 2013, clearly conveys the message to Iranian society that harassing women is not acceptable or a trivial subject in our society, but a serious crime in the eyes of the law.

All crimes in the Iranian Penal Code are either a "public crime" or a "private crime." If they are a private crime, the culpable can be freed from all charges if the plaintiff consents. But, if it is a public crime, plaintiff's consent could diminish the penalty, but the accused will still be prosecuted, and the culpable will be punished. Article 619 is addressing a public crime; hence, even if the plaintiff gives her consent, which could be due to being threatened by the accused, it will not eliminate the punishment, and the court will give its order due to the gravity of the deed and execute the penalty. This also conveys the unacceptability under the Iranian legal system for sexual harassments against children and women that take place in public.

Molestation by Telephone or Any Telecommunication Device

Article 641 of the Penal Code indicates that anyone who, via a telephone or by any other telecommunication device, molests or harasses another person, shall face incarceration from one to six months, in addition to the punishment indicated by the special regulations of the telecommunication company.

---

4. Section five of the first book of the Penal Code indicates the ways a crime can be proven. Article 160 in this section states that a crime can be proved by witness or by confession alongside other methods, then in Articles 174 and 164, it explains in detail how the procedure works.

This article is also general and protects every woman and man who could be verbally abused via a telecommunication device. This situation could cover some cases in which a person from the workplace is harassing another coworker or subordinate. This Article is more likely to help women to safeguard themselves against communications made by their managers at work and by their colleagues. This is especially true in this era, when most communications are made by phones, and the new devices allow recording messages and phone calls plus texts sent using different online applications.

Thanks to the new technology and devices, much sexual harassment has been possible to prove in court. One example, which made Iranian society more aware of workplace sexual harassment, was a 2016 case in which a woman named Sheena Shirani made allegations against two of her directors for whom she had worked while at the English language for PressTV[5] in Iran. After Shirani left Iran for Scotland, she published a recorded voice message between herself and her superior manager in which she is clearly being sexually harassed.[6] This file, which circulated via social media, put Iranian society at unease and led to suspension of the two men (Hamid Reza Emadi and an anonymous other manager) from PressTV until further investigations. It should be noted that Shirani never officially filed a complaint in Iranian courts, in subsequent interviews on this subject; she claimed that during the years that she worked at PressTV she had constantly been harassed by her superior managers. From this case, we could understand that in situations where there is some strong evidence, the society and the system do not tolerate any abuse against women even if it has not yet been investigated in the judicial system.

Threat to Honor

Article 669 of the Iranian Penal Code protects against honor and could be used to protect women against sexual harassment, even though it is again a general law and does not specifically cover workplace or domicile harassment. This article states that any person who threatens another in any way to hurt their honor and dignity, whether by demanding money or by demanding that a deed

---

5. PressTV is a 24-hour English- and French-language news and documentary network affiliated with the Islamic Republic of Iran Broadcasting (IRIB). PressTV is headquartered in Tehran and was launched on July 8, 2007.

6. Heather Saul, *What it's really like to be a female TV anchor in Iran*, INDEPENDENT, Apr. 30, 2016, https://www.independent.co.uk/news/people/iran-female-tv-anchor-sheena-shirani-press-tv-a6990011.html.

be done or not done, will face the punishment of up to seventy-four lashes or incarceration from two months to two years.

To Commit a *Haram* Act

As explained above, Islamic laws play an important role in the Iranian legal system. In this context, using a general term such as *Haram*, which is an Arabic word meaning "forbidden" by Islam or "sinful," has been used in Article 638 of the Penal Code as a sentence enhancer for other criminal acts. In this Article, if anyone explicitly displays any *Haram* act in public, in addition to facing charges based on the act itself, they face imprisonment of ten days up to two months or up to 74 lashes. Under Article 638, even if the *Haram* act itself is not distinguished by a penalty, but the act harms and injures the public morality and dignity, it shall be penalized by being imprisoned from ten days to two months or up to seventy-four lashes.

Even though Article 638 is trying to protect society from any unlawful and harming deeds, using general terms that are not defined in the Penal Code, such as the word *Haram*, allows the court to condemn and sentence many by its own interpretation of the act and to impact innocent citizens. Also, the law only refers to acts in public places and it does not include workplaces and households where sexual violence usually occurs by someone the woman knows from her family or her work.

The Reality of Iranian Society

In Iranian society, it is not clear whether society distinguishes between sexual harassment—mostly defined by unwanted sexual advances such as touching or verbally requesting sexual favors, implicit or explicit—and sexual assault, which could be defined as is intentional sexual contact, characterized by use of force, threats, intimidation, abuse of authority, or when the victim does not or cannot consent. In Iranian legal texts, rape has been defined as the only sexual assault, and it is punished by death. Any claims regarding sexual harassment depend on the judge in the court and the judge's approach toward women and their vulnerability.

What is more, the laws summarized above are not what women and children would learn through school or by television programs. These laws are only kept in books, and citizens will become aware of them only if they seek advice from a lawyer or a legal adviser.

Recently a few cases have gone public where children who have been sexually assaulted have spoken out and revealed that their teachers and directors have sexually harassed them, such as at a private Tehran school, the case now in court. This shows that the younger generation has received better sexual education and are becoming aware of their rights to protect their bodies and their personal space.

Regarding the traditional system of Iranian families and how women still are not treated equally by law or society, gradually more women are speaking up; however, it is evident that they will need more support from their legislators and policy makers to come out and speak. If the lawmakers ratify such laws, the public will also become more aware of the drastic situation and the awful effects such acts have on the abused person. This will lead Iranian society toward changing its norms, being supportive of the abused, and not blaming women for being harassed due to their appearance or their choice of clothing.

Conclusion

Sexual harassment has not been independently defined in the laws and regulations of the Islamic Republic of Iran; however, using general articles in the Penal Code, it does cover children and women from some public abuses and could be prosecuted. As Iran is a developing country and in recent years women are slowly receiving better education and are achieving better jobs and managerial positions, Iranian policy makers must do better to keep laws updated to be responsive toward the needs of the society. Especially since Iranian society is a traditional and patriarchal community transiting toward a modern society where everyone is treated equally, it is essential that Iranian law makers become equipped with the same approach to help the whole community toward justice and equality, where women have the same peace of mind as men and do not face humiliation and abuse for their will to rise up in the society and to fulfill their full potential in the workplace.

Furthermore, it is important for the legal system of Iran to empower women to safeguard their dignity in their workplace as well as their houses. All kind of sexual harassment, by word or by deed, should be punished the same whether is inflicted by a coworker or a manager in the workplace or it is imposed in the household and domestically by a father, brother, or a husband.

CHAPTER 21

Afghan Woman and #MeToo: A Story of Struggle and Strength

Zulaikha Aziz[1] and Nasrina Bargzie[2]

Afghan Path

In 2017, a group of teenage Afghan girls took the robotics world by storm. An all-girls team from Herat, Afghanistan, in the shadow of war, travel difficulties, and family heartbreaks, went toe-to-toe with teams across the world and took first place in a top robotics competition in Europe.[3] Their challenge was to create a robot that could solve a real-world problem.[4] The girls created a robot that uses solar power to assist with fieldwork on farms.[5] Thousands of spectators who attended the event chose the girls' team as the winner.[6] Despite all the challenges, these Afghan girls rose and won. This is the story of Afghanistan and of Afghan women.

Afghanistan has endured nearly forty years of armed conflict, and yet in a 2018 Survey of the Afghan People by the Asia Foundation, 80.8 percent of

---

1. Zulaikha Aziz is a human rights attorney and an international development specialist, most recently with the Asia Foundation, Kabul, Afghanistan.

2. Nasrina Bargzie is a human rights and business law attorney, and an expert in national security and civil rights.

3. Christine Hauser, *Afghan Girls' Robotics Team Overcomes Setbacks to Win Contest in Europe*, N.Y. TIMES, Nov. 29, 2017, https://www.nytimes.com/2017/11/29/world/afghanistan -girls-robotics.html.

4. *Id.*

5. *Id.*

6. *Id.*

Afghan female and male respondents reported that they were happy.[7] As Afghan women and the Afghan people face challenge after challenge, both the prevalence of harassment of women exposed by the global phenomenon of movements like #MeToo, and the day-to-day challenges of living in a war zone, the resilience and strength of Afghan women amid these realities cannot be understated.

The challenges and harsh realities are many. Violence against women is one of the biggest issues facing not only Afghan women but Afghanistan in general. The severe gender inequality in Afghanistan is directly related to lower health outcomes, lower educational outcome, and lower income inequality overall.[8] We offer a sober assessment of these realities in the pages that follow, but every difficulty is counter-balanced by the sheer will of Afghan women and Afghan people to survive and flourish as independent, free people.

Real Life: Afghanistan

Women across the world are speaking up about their most painful experiences through the #MeToo movement in an effort to further social progress in women's daily lives. Afghan women, too, are part of this movement. Like their sisters across the world, Afghan women have suffered under historic and current-day gender-specific hostilities. Some issues are cross-cutting—abuse of female athletes, street and internet harassment, laws that provide insufficient protection or are not implemented properly. Others are specific to the history and context of Afghanistan—security in war, and patriarchy systems still evolving in the modern context.

Since the removal of the Taliban regime in 2001, women have made substantial legal gains—women's rights were enshrined in the national Constitution

---

7. The Asia Foundation, A Survey of the Afghan People: Afghanistan in 2018, 37 (2018); *Id.* at 37 ("This year, for the first time, women report being generally happy slightly more frequently than men (81.6% vs. 79.9%).").

8. Afghanistan's Human Development Index value for 2017 is 0.498—which put the country in the low human development category—positioning it at 168 out of 189 countries and territories and a Gender Inequality Index (GII) value of 0.653, ranking it 153 out of 160 countries in the 2017 index. The GII reflects gender-based inequalities in three dimensions—reproductive health, empowerment, and economic activity and can be interpreted as the loss in human development due to inequality between female and male achievements in the three GII dimensions. Please see the 2018 Human Development Report for more information on Afghanistan's statistics with regards to Afghanistan's Human Development statistics and Gender Development Statistics. U.N. Dev. Programme, Human Development Indices and Indicators: 2018 Statistical Update, (2018), http://www.hdr.undp.org/sites/default/files/2018_human_devel opment_statistical_update.pdf. *See also* U.N. Development Programme, Human Developments Reports: Afghanistan, (2018), http://www.hdr.undp.org/en/countries/profiles/AFG.

of 2004, and successive national governments have vowed to protect women's rights, eliminate violence against women, and support women's economic empowerment and political participation. In fact, one of the cornerstones of the international community's intervention in Afghanistan was the so-called liberation of Afghan women.[9] The military occupation was coupled with billions of dollars in humanitarian and development aid, of which a substantial portion was explicitly conditioned on implementing projects containing a "gender equality" or "women's empowerment" component.[10] Even with all of the rhetoric, reports by the United Nations, local civil society groups, and international human rights organizations have shown that violence against women remains largely unaddressed by the Afghan criminal justice system.[11] After nearly two decades of democratic governance after the fall of the Taliban, which kept Afghan women effectively out of Afghan society,[12] the Taliban legacy continues to loom over legal and social progress made by Afghans.[13] In 2018, according to the Special Inspector General for Afghanistan Reconstruction, 56 percent of the country is under Afghan government (referred to as the National Unity Government (NUG)) control, 30 percent is contested, and 14 percent is under the control of insurgent groups.[14] The latest reports of peace talks between the United States and the Taliban to potentially bring the Taliban into a power-sharing agreement with the current Afghan government have Afghan women in fear of the further erosion of their existing rights.[15]

---

9. Editorial, *Liberating the Women of Afghanistan*, N.Y. TIMES, Nov. 24, 2001, https://www.nytimes.com/2001/11/24/opinion/liberating-the-women-of-afghanistan.html.

10. *See, e.g.*, Afghanistan: Gender, USAID (2019), https://www.usaid.gov/afghanistan/gender-participant-training.

11. *See, e.g.*, U.N. Assistance Mission in Afg., U.N. Office of the High Comm'r for Human Rights, Injustice and Impunity: Mediation of Criminal Offenses of Violence Against Women, (2018), https://www.ohchr.org/Documents/Countries/AF/UNAMA_OHCHR_EVAW_Report2018_InjusticeImpunity29May2018.pdf; Heather Barr, *Afghan Government Ignoring Violence Against Women*, HUMAN RIGHTS WATCH, May 30, 2018, https://www.hrw.org/news/2018/05/30/afghan-government-ignoring-violence-against-women; AFGHANISTAN INDEPENDENT HUMAN RIGHTS COMMISSION, SUMMARY OF THE REPORT ON VIOLENCE AGAINST WOMEN (2018), https://www.aihrc.org.af/media/files/Research%20Reports/Summerry%20report-VAW-2017.pdf.

12. *See* SURVEY, *supra* note 7, at 165 ("Women's participation in the political process has been, on its face, a great success story since the fall of the Taliban, when women had no rights of participation or representation.").

13. *Id.* at 77.

14. *Id.* at 128.

15. Rod Nordland, Fatima Faizi & Fahim Abed, *Afghan Women Fear Peace With Taliban May Mean War on Them*, N.Y. TIMES, Jan. 27, 2019, https://www.nytimes.com/2019/01/27/world/asia/taliban-peace-deal-women-afghanistan.html.

As Afghan women and girls take up the mantle of inclusion in the global community through academics, sports, working outside the home, and leading their families, the same ills that plague other countries also plague Afghanistan. Without a doubt, sexual harassment of women is widespread in Afghanistan. From public places to educational environments to the workplace, studies show that upward of 90 percent of Afghan women report harassment.[16] Underlying themes that contribute to extreme levels of harassment include the willingness of men to harass, the lack of public intervention when harassment occurs, victim-blaming, and distrust of police and institutions.[17]

Street harassment is a daily experience for Afghan women,[18] including sexual comments and physical attacks, such as groping, pinching, and slapping. Anti-harassment advocates often end up being the subject of harassment themselves.[19] For example, in 2015, an activist walked outside for eight minutes wearing steel armor to protest the groping and leering she endured daily. The activist received so many threats she was forced to leave Afghanistan.[20]

Harassment of women in public institutions is also a problem area. Like the abuse of female gymnasts in the United States,[21] explosive allegations of sexual and physical abuse of players on the Afghan women's national soccer team rocked Afghanistan in late 2018.[22] A former player has alleged that the president of the Afghanistan Football Federation and some trainers "are raping and sexually harassing female players."[23] The response of the NUG was strong and

---

16. Patricia Gossman, *#MeToo in Afghanistan: Is Anyone Listening?*, HUMAN RIGHTS WATCH, Dec. 20, 2017, https://www.hrw.org/news/2017/12/20/metoo-afghanistan-anyone -listening ("A 2016 study found 90 percent of the 346 women and girls interviewed said they had experienced sexual harassment in public places, 91 percent in educational environments, and 87 percent at work.").

17. Danielle Moylan, *When It Comes to Sexual Assault, Afghanistan Is All Talk and No Action*, FOREIGN POLICY, Dec. 21, 2015, https://foreignpolicy.com/2015/12/21/when-it -comes-to-sexual-assault-afghanistan-is-all-talk-and-no-action/.

18. Sune Engal Rasmussen, *Outrage at Video of Afghan Colonel Sexually Exploiting Woman*, THE GUARDIAN, Nov. 2, 2017, https://www.theguardian.com/world/2017/nov/02 /outrage-at-video-of-afghan-colonel-sexually-exploiting-woman.

19. Moylan, *supra* note 17.

20. Rasmussen, *supra* note 18.

21. Christine Hauser & Karen Zraick, *Larry Nassar Sexual Abuse Scandal: Dozens of Officials Have Been Ousted or Charged*, N.Y. TIMES, Oct. 22, 2018, https://www.nytimes.com /2018/10/22/sports/larry-nassar-case-scandal.html.

22. Fahim Abed & Rod Nordland, *Afghan Women's Soccer Team Accuses Officials of Sexual Abuse*, N.Y. TIMES, Dec. 4, 2018, https://www.nytimes.com/2018/12/04/world/asia /afghanistan-women-soccer-abuse.html; *"There was blood everywhere': the abuse case against the Afghan FA president,"* AFGHAN HERALD, Dec. 27, 2018, https://afghanherald.com/?p=3260.

23. Abed & Nordland, *supra* note 22.

unequivocal. President Ashraf Ghani ordered an investigation and noted that the allegations were "shocking to all Afghans."[24]

The internet has also proven to be a source and space of harassment of Afghan women.[25] Facebook is widely used in Afghanistan and has become a source of harassment where women have received rape threats and extortion threats.[26]

Harassment in the workplace is also rampant, with studies suggesting that up to 90 percent of Afghan women have experienced such harassment.[27] In 2017, a video of an Afghan colonel having sexual intercourse with a woman he pressured after she had asked for a promotion went viral.[28] While the colonel was detained and placed under investigation, no formal charges appear to have been brought yet.[29] Other Afghan women have reported that to get grants from United Nations agencies and various Western embassies, they have been told by Afghan staff that their proposals would be approved in exchange for sexual favors.[30]

Violence against women—including "murders, beatings, mutilation, and acid attacks"—remain prevalent, with the Ministry of Women's Affairs reporting an increase in violence against women in areas under effectively-Taliban control.[31] Afghan women continue to lag behind men in literacy, with literacy of young women being only 57 percent of young men.[32] Further, child marriage continues as a widespread issue limiting the opportunities of women.[33]

The #MeToo movement itself has taken a shape formed by the realities of Afghanistan. While a few Afghan women have spoken out, most Afghan women remain silent in the face of this speak-out movement.[34] One activist who has spoken out noted that "[i]n Afghanistan, women can't say they faced sexual harassment. If a woman shares someone's identity, he will kill her or her family. We can never accuse men, especially high-ranking men, without great risk."[35]

---

24. *Id.*

25. Gossman, *supra* note 16.

26. *Id.*

27. Rasmussen, *supra* note 18.

28. *Id.*

29. Rod Nordland & Fatima Faizi, *Harassment All Around, Afghan Women Weigh Risks of Speaking Out*, N.Y. TIMES, Dec. 10, 2017, https://www.nytimes.com/2017/12/10/world/asia/afghan-metoo-women-harassment.html.

30. *Id.*

31. SURVEY, *supra* note 7, at 32.

32. *Id.*

33. *Id.* at 175.

34. Nordland & Faizi, *supra* note 29.

35. *Id.*

Threats come not only from the accused, but also from the victim's families, and society at large.[36]

Afghan activists blame impunity for perpetrators as a key reason that Afghan women do not report harassment or get relief.[37] Activists push back on the argument that misogyny derived from culture and sexual repression is what drives harassment of Afghan women and point out that harassment of women is prevalent in countries with differing cultural backgrounds and that harassment of women is a global problem.[38] That said, because Afghan laws and policies are not appropriately implemented and are rife with politicking, the reality is that Afghan women often remain unprotected in public and private spaces.[39]

The current government is publicly committed to supporting women's empowerment and addressing violence against Afghan women.[40] NUG's adopted National Action Plan includes adoption of UN Security Council Resolution 1325, addressing the effects of war on women.[41] The international donor and development community, which often drives the inclusion of women's rights issues, is highly involved in attempting to bring NUG's goals into effect and with "two-thirds of the population under the age of 24, Afghanistan's youth culture is thriving in major urban areas, and women are increasingly seen in the arts and media, including bold female street artists, painters and musicians."[42] Strident advocacy of Afghan women's rights leaders has led to the passage of a number of laws directly addressing harassment and violence against women. All these efforts are part of a work very much in progress, and an important part of moving the rights of Afghan women forward.

Women's Rights and the Legal System of Afghanistan

Access to justice remains an enormous problem for Afghan women generally, and more particularly in the context of demanding their right to be free from violence, including harassment.[43] Illustrating the on-the-ground reality for Afghan women and the shortcomings of the Afghan legal system to adequately

---

36. *Id.*

37. *Id.*

38. *Id.*

39. *Id.*

40. Survey, *supra* note 7, at 16.

41. *Id.* at 165.

42. *Id.* at 165.

43. United Nations Assistance Mission in Afghanistan (UNAMA), *Access to Justice for Afghan Women Victims of Violence "Severely Inadequate,"* May 29, 2018, https://unama.unmis sions.org/access-justice-afghan-women-victims-violence-'severely-inadequate'---un-envoy.

address violence against women is the excruciatingly tragic story of Farkhunda Malikzada, a twenty-seven-year-old woman beaten to death by a mob in the center of Kabul on March 19, 2015.[44]

The murder happened in the center of a city near a religious site, among police checkpoints, embassies, ministries, even in the shadow of the presidential palace.[45] A religious leader falsely accused Farkhunda of burning a Quran.[46] In fact, Farkhunda, a teacher of the Quran herself, had told the man that his business of selling *tawiz*—small scraps of paper with religious verses that are supposed to be powerful spells—was against Islam.[47] After the religious leader began to yell that Farkhunda had desecrated the Quran, a crowd formed and beat her with sticks, stones, and even their feet.[48] They tied her to a car and dragged her through the streets, then threw her body on the riverbank and set it on fire.[49] The brutal murder of Farkhunda shocked Afghans and prompted massive demonstrations urging the authorities to protect women from violence.[50] After initial statements by the police in Kabul and prominent Afghan clerics that her killing was justified, there were mass demonstrations in the streets of Kabul which led to nearly fifty men being tried in connection with the attack, including police officers accused of failing to stop the assailants.[51] Four men were sentenced to death, but those sentences were later commuted, and most of the lengthy prison terms given to eight others were reduced.[52] Though the men were prosecuted, the proceedings were criticized for being conducted too hastily with the appeals process happening completely behind closed doors.[53]

---

44. Frozan Marofi, *Farkhunda Belongs to All the Women of Kabul, of Afghanistan*, THE GUARDIAN, Mar. 28, 2015, https://www.theguardian.com/global-development/2015/mar/28/farkhunda-women-kabul-afghanistan-mob-killing.

45. *Id.*

46. *Id.*

47. *Id.*

48. *Id.*

49. *Id.*

50. Haroon Siddique, *Farkhunda Murder, Afghan Court Quashes Death Sentences*, THE GUARDIAN, July 2, 2015, https://www.theguardian.com/world/2015/jul/02/farkhunda-murder-afghan-court-cancels-death-sentences.

51. Hamid Shalizi & Jessica Donati, *Afghan cleric and others defend lynching of woman in Kabul*, REUTERS, Mar. 20, 2015, https://uk.reuters.com/article/uk-afghanistan-woman/afghan-cleric-and-others-defend-lynching-of-woman-in-kabul-idUKKBN0MG1ZA2015 0320; Pamela Constable, *It was a Brutal Killing that Shocked Afghanistan*, WASH. POST, Mar. 28, 2017, https://www.washingtonpost.com/world/asia_pacific/it-was-a-brutal-killing-that-shocked-afghanistan-now-the-outrage-has-faded/2017/03/27/e3301f5a-109c-11e7-aa57-2ca1b05c41b8_story.html?utm_term=.08ace350b946.

52. *Id.*

53. Siddique, *supra* note 50.

The Laws

Afghan women's legal rights are addressed expressly by the Afghan Constitution. Article 22 of the Afghan Constitution (2004) declares: "Any kind of discrimination and distinction between citizens of Afghanistan shall be forbidden. The citizens of Afghanistan, man and woman, have equal rights and duties before the law."[54] Similarly, Articles 83 and 84 of the Constitution emphasize women's participation in the upper and lower houses, including placing a mandate on the President who should ensure that 50 percent of the one-third of appointees of the Mishrano Jirga, the Upper House of Parliament, are women.[55]

The Constitution also requires all laws to be compatible with Sharia. Beyond the Constitution, the Afghan government has made various commitments to women's rights and gender equality in the Afghanistan Compact (AC 2006), the Afghanistan National Development Strategy in support of human development goals (ANDS 2008-2013), and most recently the Afghanistan's National Action Plan for the implementation of the United Nations Security Council Resolution 1325 (NAP 1325), which came into effect in June 2015. ANDS provided an analysis of the priority problems that affect Afghan men and women and set out policies, programs, and benchmarks to measure progress. As a result of such developments, the Afghan government drafted the National Action Plan for the Women of Afghanistan (NAPWA, 2008-2018) with the aim of improving women's lives in Afghanistan through a multi-sectorial plan in the areas of education, health, economic security, and political participation.

In addition to the Constitution and guiding policy documents, there are three sets of official laws that exist in Afghanistan regulating acts of violence against women, namely: the Law on the Elimination of Violence Against Women (EVAW), the Anti-Harassment of Women and Children Law (AHWC), and the revised Afghan Penal Code (PC).

In addition to the Constitution and the three sets of official laws that touch on women's rights, there is also an extensive informal justice system that many Afghans turn to for a variety of reasons including access, familiarity, tradition, convenience, and societal pressure. These informal mechanisms are based on cultural and traditional practices as well as interpretations of Sharia but are often in a tense relationship with both official laws and Sharia.

Overall, however, the official laws are hampered by poor enforcement, and as between EVAW, AHWC, and the PC, there is still unresolved confusion as to which law applies and controls in various contexts.

---

54. CONSTITUTION OF AFGHANISTAN, Jan. 26, 2004, art. 22, available at http://www.afghanembassy.com.pl/afg/images/pliki/TheConstitution.pdf.

55. *Id.* at arts. 38, 84.

Elimination of Violence Against Women Law

In an attempt to address the high incidence of violence against women through the law, women's rights advocates, civil society organizations, and their allies backed the drafting of EVAW. The first law in Afghanistan specifically addressing violence against women, EVAW was adopted in August 2009 in a Presidential Decree.[56] Formulated in 44 Articles, Article 2 states its overall purpose is to: provide legal and Sharia-based protection to women; promote family integrity and fight against misogynist traditions and customs that are un-Islamic; provide support to women who have been harmed; prevent violence against women; raise awareness about violence against women and women's legal protection; and prosecute perpetrators of violence against women. In the face of great opposition, EVAW was passed by presidential decree while Parliament was in recess but has not been approved by Parliament since.[57] EVAW identifies five serious offenses set out in Articles 17 to 21 that the state must act on, irrespective of whether a complaint is filed or subsequently withdrawn.[58] These offenses include sexual assault, forced prostitution, publicizing rape victims' identity, setting fire to or attacking with a chemical substance, and forced self-immolation or forced suicide.[59]

In addition to the five enumerated "serious crimes," EVAW covers a wide range of issues affecting women, from physical and verbal violence against

---

56. Under Article 79 of the Constitution, a bill can be approved by Presidential decree if circumstances require the processing of a legislative document during the recess of the Wolesi Jirga, the lower house of Parliament, with the exception of legislation dealing with matters related to budget and financial affairs. A Presidential decree acquires the full force of law but must be presented to the National Assembly within thirty days of the convening of its first session after the decree has been endorsed. It is up to the National Assembly whether to act on the decree. If the decree is rejected by the National Assembly, it becomes void. If the decree is not rejected by the National Assembly or the National Assembly chooses not to act on the decree, it continues to be enforceable law and must be amended or voided by the same process as a law that has been approved by Parliament. *See* USAID, ISLAMIC REPUBLIC OF AFGHANISTAN LEGISLATIVE PROCESS MANUAL, http://www.cid.suny.edu/publications1/arab/Legislative _Process_Manual.pdf.

57. See Fawzia Koofi, *It's Time to Act for Afghan Women: Pass EVAW*, FOREIGN POLICY, Jan. 13, 2015, https://foreignpolicy.com/2015/01/13/its-time-to-act-for-afghan-women -pass-the-evaw/ for a more completed discussion of the attempted process to get EVAW passed in Parliament.

58. Article 39 states that for all crimes listed in Articles 22-39, "the victim may withdraw her case at any stage of prosecution (detection, investigation, trial or conviction) which results in the stoppage of proceeding and imposition of punishment," but a similar allowance is not stated for crimes listed in Articles 17-21, the "5 serious offenses." See Elimination of Violence Against Women (EVAW) Law, art. 39 (Afg.), https://www.refworld.org/pdfid/5486d1a34.pdf.

59. *Id.* at arts. 17-21.

women to legal, medical, and social protection, to provision of reparations to the harmed party, and protective and supportive measures. EVAW criminalizes twenty-two acts of violence against women such as forced and child marriage, beating, harassment, verbal abuse, and withholding of inheritance, among other offenses.[60] The law also specifies punishments for perpetrators and criminalizes the customs, traditions, and practices that lead to violence against women and that are against Sharia including *baad*,[61] the customary practice of giving a woman or girl from the family of a man accused of a crime in compensation to the family of a victim of a crime.[62]

The institutional responsibility for EVAW is with the Afghan Ministry of Women's Affairs (MoWA) and Afghanistan's judicial system including the Ministry of Justice (MoJ), which is responsible for prosecuting crimes, and Afghan courts. They are tasked with providing support to women who bring claims under EVAW, prioritizing cases of violence against women, and taking active preventive measures.[63]

Looking specifically at the issue of harassment, harassment of women is defined in Article 3(7) of EVAW as "using words or committing acts by any means, which cause damage to the personality, body, and psyche of a woman." But these "acts" and "words" remain undefined.[64] According to Article 30, a person convicted of this offense can be sentenced from three to twelve months in prison. In cases where the person who committed the harassment misused his authority, the sentence cannot be less than six months.[65] According to Article 7 of EVAW, the victims or their relatives can register complaints with the police, the Huquq (civil departments within the MoJ), at courts, or in other relevant offices. These institutions must pursue the complaints and inform MoWA.[66] Based on the same Article and Article 16, the High Commission on the Elimination of Violence (HCEV), chaired by MoWA and with participants from all relevant government institutions, is in charge of coordination between the different institutional actors and for developing policies and regulations for the implementation of EVAW.

---

60. *Id.* at ch. 3, arts. 17-38.

61. *Baad* is a pre-Islamic practice of settlement and compensation whereby a woman or girl from the family of one who has committed an offence is given to the victim's family as a servant or a bride. *Afghanistan: Stop Women Being Given as Compensation*, HUMAN RIGHTS WATCH, Mar. 8, 2011, https://www.hrw.org/news/2011/03/08/afghanistan-stop-women -being-given-compensation.

62. EVAW, *supra* note 58, at art. 25.

63. *Id.* at art. 8.

64. *Id.* at art. 3.

65. *Id.* at art. 30.

66. *Id.* at art. 7.

Besides criminalizing acts of violence against women, EVAW includes provisions designed to ensure that government institutions work to address social and cultural patterns of harassment. For example, according to Article 11, the Ministry of Information and Culture is required to broadcast programs on television channels and radio stations and publish articles to raise public awareness about women's rights, the root causes of violence against women, and to create awareness about crimes committed against women.

EVAW is the most robust law in Afghanistan combating violence against women. The infrastructure built in order to implement EVAW—including the EVAW prosecuting offices—continues to be active and certain cases are still brought under EVAW. EVAW, however, is hampered by a number of realities. First, it was an extremely controversial law in its development and implementation and buy-in from the judicial system still appears to be an issue. Second, as explained further below, parts of EVAW are incorporated in the other two official laws addressing women's rights, namely the AHWC and the revised PC. This has resulted in confusion as to which laws to use in addressing claims of assault and harassment, as well as the proper procedural mechanisms by which to bring those claims.

Anti-Harassment of Women and Children Law

Despite the availability of EVAW, in 2016, Parliament passed a second law, the Anti-Harassment of Women and Children Law (AHWC) to specifically address harassment. This overlap has created conflict and confusion as to what law should govern and what law would be best for women. Though AHWC contains provisions negating and superseding the articles of the EVAW law that address harassment, it continues to be unclear for legal practitioners under which law to bring claims.

AHWC defines harassment as "body contact, illegitimate demand, verbal or non-verbal abuse and or any action resulting in psychological or physical harm and humiliating the human dignity of woman and child."[67] The Ministry of Interior (MoI) was tasked with providing a special contact number so that women can report violations, and the Ministry of Labor, Social Affairs, Martyrs and Disabled was made responsible for combating violations of the law by setting up a High Commission for the Prohibition of Harassment Against Women and Children.[68] All government institutions are "obliged to establish a Committee on Combating Harassment Against Women and Children in

---

67. Anti-Harassment of Women and Children Law, art 3(1).
68. *Id.* at arts. 5, 10.

their respective [institutions] within three months after the enforcement of this law."[69] All complaints of harassment in government institutions are to be reported to the Anti-Harassment Committee of the relevant institution.[70] The Anti-Harassment Committees are then responsible for investigating the complaints, determining which ones are credible, and forwarding those to "relevant attorney[s]" for prosecution.[71] It is not clear whether these "relevant attorney[s]" are government prosecutors from the MoJ or whether they are legal aid attorneys or private attorneys. The MoI is responsible for ensuring that police officers prevent harassment of women and children in public spaces.[72] But as one Afghan woman subject to harassment stated to the Institute of War and Peace Reporting, "what would really be a big help is if the policemen themselves didn't harass me."[73]

In addition to the overlap with EVAW and the resulting confusion as to which law applies, another major problem with AHWC is the relatively lenient penalty for violations. Penalties for those convicted of harassment in public places or vehicles include fines in Afghanis equivalent to between US$80 to US$150, while similar behavior in the workplace or educational or healthcare centers can be punished with fines equivalent of between US$150 to US$300. Aggravated circumstances can lead to imprisonment for up to six months.[74] And even with these lax penalties, implementation under AHWC continues to be ad hoc.

Still other concerns relating to AHWC include that the law classifies women with children,[75] and harassment is narrowly defined as an offense that can be committed against women and children. It does not allow for the

---

69. *Id.* at art. 7.

70. *Id.*

71. *Id.* at art. 8.

72. *Id.* at art. 10.

73. Mina Habib, *New Afghan Law Targets Sexual Harassment*, INSTITUTE OF WAR AND PEACE REPORTING, Mar. 8, 2017, https://iwpr.net/global-voices/new-afghan-law-targets -sexual-harassment.

74. AHWC Law, *supra* note 67, at arts. 25-27; Medica Afghanistan, Petition Not to Ratify the Anti-Sexual Harassment Law Dated 19 Akrab 1395 / 9 November 2016 Pursuant to The Afghanistan Constitution, (2016), http://www.medicaafghanistan.org/medica/index.php /en/petition-not-to-ratify-the-anti-sexual-harassment-law-dated-19-akrab-1395-9-november -2016-pursuant-to-the-afghanistan-constitution/.

75. When speaking about this law with a number of Afghan women's rights leaders and students, a point that was consistently made was that harassment is not just a problem impacting women. Many men face harassment both from other men as well as from some women; institutionalizing it as just a problem impacting women and children not only infantilizes women but fails to offer adequate protection for men. American University of Afghanistan (AUAF) discussions with Zulaikha Aziz, Nov. 28, 2018.

prosecution of cases in which men are sexually harassed verbally or physically. Not only does grouping women and children together and excluding men ignore victims of harassment that may be men, it further reinforces the idea that harassment is only a women's issue, as well as stereotypical notions of women being weak and vulnerable and needing to be protected, like children, as opposed to recognizing that the act of harassment is wrong regardless of who is the target.

Penal Code

The PC also addresses violence against women. Led by the MoJ in 2012, the Afghan government began revising the 1976 PC. Apart from incorporating new laws and provisions such as crimes against humanity and war crimes, the revised PC also incorporated all criminal laws and decrees of Afghanistan into one PC. The revision process was deemed necessary for meeting three key objectives: (1) codify all crimes and punishments in one document, (2) modernize the "Code-modern" definitions and concepts, and (3) ensure Afghanistan's compliance with international commitments.[76] The PC was revised and presented in the Official Gazette in an extraordinary issue on May 15, 2017 by Presidential Decree No. 256, coming into force on February 14, 2018.

Though the original draft of the revised PC included a specific chapter on the elimination of violence against women, incorporating provisions to criminalize the majority of the twenty-two acts set out in EVAW, there was great opposition to the incorporation of EVAW into the PC. That draft of the PC also included new provisions prohibiting both the detention of women on charges of running away and the practice of *baad*. However, the final adopted version did not include any reference to criminal offenses of violence against women, with the exception of rape. Ultimately, the opponents of incorporation were successful though a later amendment on March 3, 2018 incorporated the five "serious crimes" specified under EVAW Articles 17 to 21.[77]

Proponents of incorporation argued that including a chapter on crimes related to violence against women in the PC would codify these crimes in Afghanistan's official criminal code and strengthen compliance and implementation, since the PC is the definitive authority on Afghan criminal law. Opponents of incorporation argued that the PC would not incorporate all of the provisions of EVAW and that a stand-alone law is needed to highlight the particularly egregious nature of crimes of violence against women, and to ensure

---

76. MINISTRY OF JUSTICE, OFFICIAL GAZETTE 1260 (2007), https://www.ilo.org/dyn/natlex/natlex4.detail?p_lang=en&p_isn=105003&p_count=12&p_classification=01.

77. AFGHANISTAN PUBLIC POLICY RESEARCH ORGANIZATION, NEW PENAL CODE AND EVAW LAW: TO INCORPORATE OR NOT TO INCORPORATE? 12 (2018).

the current implementing structures of EVAW prosecutors and the MoWA Committee tasked with implementing EVAW would remain in effect. A further argument was that the EVAW provisions, if incorporated in the PC, would not have passed Parliament and would have been removed in order to ensure passage of the PC. In fact, the PC was never reviewed by Parliament, and it is impossible to say whether it would have been had it included the EVAW provisions.

Ultimately the opponents of incorporation were successful in their lobbying efforts, which resulted in EVAW remaining a stand-alone law and the majority of criminal acts of violence against women remaining out of the PC. Discussions with advisors in MoJ responsible for drafting the PC reveal that the original draft did in fact include all of the criminal offenses enumerated under EVAW.[78] Had the EVAW provisions been designated as violations of Afghanistan's criminal code, they would have carried the same weight as all other criminal offenses in the PC rather than being bogged down by the politically complex history of bringing EVAW into effect.[79] Additionally, current efforts to draft a comprehensive commentary on the implementation of the PC would have included commentary on the crimes related to violence against women, serving as an important opportunity for all legal practitioners, including judges, to understand the implementation of the law with respect to such crimes.[80]

Use of Informal Justice System

Most cases involving violence against women, including the five "serious" offenses in EVAW—rape, forced prostitution, publicizing the identity of a victim, burning or using chemical substances against a woman, and forced self-immolation or suicide—are not even prosecuted by or adjudicated in courts but are instead referred to traditional councils called shuras and jirgas, which have a long history of resolving disputes through the many provinces of Afghanistan.[81] The Afghan Constitution, EVAW, AHWC, and the PC are the official legal mechanisms that should be used to address abuses of Afghan women. However,

---

78. Unnamed MoJ Advisor in discussion with authors, Jan. 21, 2019.

79. The unnamed MoJ Advisor also confirmed that there were no threats to oppose passage of the Penal Code with the EVAW crimes incorporated and all indications pointed to passage.

80. The Asia Foundation facilitated the drafting of a comprehensive legal commentary on the revised Penal Code, completed in 2019. The Commentary includes substantial discussion on the provisions related to crimes involving violence against women which will be helpful in informing the application of those provisions in the Penal Code.

81. UNAMA, *supra* note 11, at 19.

it is estimated that over 80 percent of all disputes in Afghanistan are resolved through these informal mechanisms.[82]

Shuras and jirgas, the terminology differs depending on the region and structure of the councils, are based on local custom, tradition, and religious practices and have existed in Afghanistan for centuries. These informal institutions do not enforce the civil or criminal laws of Afghanistan, but rather the councils' interpretation of Sharia, customary law, or the collective wisdom of elders. These mechanisms are not state-actors and are not legally mandated to resolve criminal cases. They largely operate in an unofficial and unregulated capacity, their decisions in criminal cases are unlawful, and as such, are not subjected to any government oversight or scrutiny. The reasons these informal systems are used to such a high degree are complex and varied. However, one reason may be the confusion around which official law prevails.

Afghan authorities can often exacerbate the situation for victims by turning to informal justice mechanisms to mediate serious offenses instead of carrying out their duty to investigate or prosecute offenses through the formal justice system.[83] Often, even EVAW institutions and legal aid organizations refer cases to shuras and jirgas instead of to prosecutors for investigation and initiation of criminal proceedings.[84] Referring such serious criminal cases, let alone lesser offenses of harassment, undermines efforts to promote women's rights, erodes the rule of law, contributes to an expectation of impunity, discourages the reporting of these cases, and increases citizens' perception of a corrupt and unreliable justice system. Further, the referral to informal dispute resolution mechanisms exposes the government's abrogation of its primary responsibility as duty bearer under international law to ensure the effective prevention and protection of women from such crimes and to provide an effective response where they occur.[85]

---

82. The Center for Policy and Human Development (CPHD) at Kabul University estimated in 2017 that 80 percent of all disputes were being resolved in the informal sector. See CENTER FOR POLICY AND HUMAN DEVELOPMENT, AFGHANISTAN HUMAN DEVELOPMENT REPORT 2007: BRIDGING MODERNITY AND TRADITION—THE RULE OF LAW AND THE SEARCH FOR JUSTICE 9 (2017).

83. UNAMA, *supra*, note 11, at 6.

84. *Id.* "In many cases, EVAW Law institutions either coordinated or participated in the traditional mediation process."

85. Afghanistan is a state party to the International Covenant on Civil and Political Rights; the International Covenant on Economic, Social and Cultural Rights; the Convention on the Elimination of All Forms of Racial Discrimination; the Convention on the Elimination of All Forms of Discrimination against Women (signed in 1980 and ratified in 2003); the Convention against Torture and Other Cruel, Inhuman or Degrading Treatment or Punishment; and the Convention on the Rights of the Child. The Committee on the Elimination of Discrimination against Women, General recommendation No. 35 states that the prohibition

The two different types of mediation carried out by traditional dispute resolution mechanisms related to violence against women—the mediation of criminal offenses of violence against women and the mediation of wider disputes leading to decisions that result in violence against women—are both unlawful and constitute human rights abuses.[86] Traditional mediation mechanisms are prohibited legal tools in cases of violence against women in an increasing number of countries as they do not have an official mandate or agreement to abide by laws protecting women from violence and are therefore insufficient to prosecute serious offenses of violence against women. Mainly composed of men, their rulings are often extremely unjust and largely punitive toward women.[87] Still, in the absence of a legal system that is easily accessible to all Afghans, many women and men have no choice but to submit their complaints to shuras and jirgas if they seek resolution of a dispute. In fact, in many matters the shuras and jirgas are often more capable and more efficient in mediation and dispute resolution but in issues related to violence against women, there is a high risk of more damage to victims.

A Path Forward

Although the stories and statistics may seem bleak, much development has occurred in the past two decades and the resilience of Afghan women cannot be understated. They will carry their society forward to a new day of equal rights and protections for women and men, not just on paper but also in practice. To that end, there are a number of key areas where the Afghan government, civil society organizations, academia, and international allies can focus on to work with Afghan women on advancing their rights. Some recommendations are as follows:

---

of gender-based violence against women has evolved into a norm of customary law and General Recommendation No. 33 on Access to Justice, CEDAW/C/GC/33, 23 July 2015 para. 58 (c), designed to: "Ensure that cases of violence against women, including domestic violence, are under no circumstances referred to any alternative dispute resolution procedures." Accessed respectively at https://tbinternet.ohchr.org/Treaties/CEDAW/Shared%20Documents/1 _Global/CEDAW_C_GC_35_8267_E.pdf; https://tbinternet.ohchr.org/Treaties/CEDAW /Shared%20Documents/1_Global/CEDAW_C_GC_33_7767_E.pdf.

86. UNAMA, *supra*, note 11, at 10.

87. There are very few cases of shuras and/or jirgas containing women. There have been incidents of all women shuras and/or jirgas in certain areas of the country but those are not regular and are not generally responsible for resolving disputes involving men and women including cases of violence against women.

Continued Commitment to Democratic Governance

Democratic governance is a key component of advancing Afghan women's rights and must be upheld in Afghanistan. In the face of war and conflict, uncertainty and threats to their lives, the Afghan people have consistently taken the risk and showed up at the polling stations. They have bet on democracy and recognize it as the way forward. Talks of imposing an interim government comprised of the Taliban and acquiescing politicians runs in direct opposition to the notions of democracy for which Afghans have risked their lives. In addition to negotiations with the current official government of Afghanistan and a potential referendum of the people, the Taliban must explicitly recognize the rights of Afghan women and assert that they will uphold the rights of women to be free from violence as enshrined in the official laws of Afghanistan.

Overlapping Laws Should Be Clarified

The overlap between various laws addressing violence against Afghan women should be clarified and corrected through the Afghan legal process. Ideally, EVAW should be elevated entirely into the PC, and any overlapping pieces with the AHWC should be corrected in favor of EVAW. The AHWC and sections of PC should be updated to reflect harassment of men as well.

Public Awareness and Education

An Afghan-led and culturally appropriate awareness and education campaign[88] around women's rights should be formulated and implemented. The basis to do so can be found in the EVAW law that instructs the Ministry of Information and Culture to broadcast programs on television channels and radio stations and publish articles to raise public awareness about women's rights, the root causes of violence against women, and to create awareness about crimes committed against women. Afghans working with Afghans to define and debate harassment is a key component of the legal system's ability to then implement those norms.[89]

---

88. Danielle Moylan, *When It Comes to Sexual Assault, Afghanistan Is All Talk and No Action*, Foreign Policy, Dec. 21, 2015, https://foreignpolicy.com/2015/12/21/when-it -comes-to-sexual-assault-afghanistan-is-all-talk-and-no-action/.

89. *Id.*

Afghan Women Leadership

Afghan women must be given space to further their own agenda without the pressure of outside forces. Confusion and conflict occur due to competing donor aims and funding opportunities with different donors backing different strategies. Afghan women's rights advocates are left in the middle, attempting to access resources needed to further their work and siding with donors based on funding opportunities rather than shared vision. Any funding that is advanced should be in line with goals set by Afghan women, not by donors. Afghan women cannot be represented by only a handful of prominent leaders who have secured access to donors and high-level leaders. The work must be more transparent and in line with the needs of diverse Afghan women. To that end, there should be a focus on including women from rural and remote areas in the development of a comprehensive Afghan women's rights agenda. The voices of women from remote and rural areas, where the majority of informal dispute mechanisms operate, are often drowned out by those of women in cities and in the capital of Kabul.

Untangle the Confusion Between Religious and Cultural Issues

Often cultural perceptions of women's rights are thought to be derived from Islam when the religion says the opposite.[90] There needs to be a greater focus on addressing religious and cultural perceptions that exist with laws related to ending violence against women. For instance, a woman or man who thinks EVAW conflicts with Islam may not attempt to access that law or may not attempt to use that law to advocate for his or her client or may not decide a case in accordance with that law. Actual implementation of the law requires belief in its purpose and legitimacy. This will require a multi-step approach from reforming legal education curriculum, particularly that of the law and Sharia faculties to include more information on women's rights in Islam and the importance of promoting human rights in general. Specific interventions can include:

1. Legal education campaigns at every level, working with Imams in masjids and local shuras and jirgas—training shura and jirga mem-

---

90. One legal aid attorney relayed the case of a man who was being sued for not giving land that his cousin inherited to her, because she was a woman. His case was being heard by a panel of three female judges. When asked why he was not giving his cousin her land, he responded that "it wasn't in his religion" for women to own land. The judges informed him that in fact, both under Sharia and Afghan law, his cousin was entitled to the land. Ahmad Zia in discussion with Zulaikha Aziz, Dec. 10, 2018.

bers in women's rights from an Islamic context but reflective of the official laws of Afghanistan. This must be done with local religious leaders who are seen as legitimate and authoritative, not external/international experts. Great care must be paid to how the information is conveyed and who conveys the information.

2. More comparative work should be done on how other Muslim countries, which have lower incidence of violence against women, have addressed the issue. Best practices should be developed based on Muslim countries' experiences rather than overreliance on Western models.

3. Teaching women's legal rights in law and Sharia faculties as part of the curriculum so all legal practitioners have a basic understanding when it comes to implementation and advocacy around relevant rights. Focusing on legal education not only imparts important knowledge on women's legal rights to all legal practitioners, but it does so in the early stages of their legal development so that they inherently understand the importance of promoting women's right to be free from violence as a foundational legal concept and implement that knowledge in their work as judges, prosecutors, and defense attorneys.

CHAPTER 22

Traumascapes and an Arc of Resistance: #MeToo in India

Ramya Kannabiran Tella[1] and Kalpana Kannabiran[2]

"As Dalit women, we have for long resisted our perpetrators, which include dominant caste men, mixed caste men, men from our own castes and dominant caste women. The approaches to our battles have been varied but our language has always been one that seeks collective transformation. As anti-caste feminists, we aim to dismantle caste and envision a world that strives for gender equity alongside.

To those that may reprimand us for speaking of gender justice before the battle against caste is won, we say that structural violence cannot be separated; neither for analysis nor for action. The intersectional impact of caste and gender is manifold and the appropriate response multi-pronged. Always."[3]

The #MeToo movement in India has sparked an important national debate that emphasizes some key dimensions with implications for international politics. These are: (1) the right to protection from sexual harassment/ violence, (2) the right to privacy, and (3) the materiality of virtual space. As a social movement, #MeToo has breached spatial, temporal, and social divisions to illustrate the extent to which digital spaces can offer normative and emotional recourse to survivors of sexual harassment, even while offline resolutions remain open. In this essay, we trace the intermeshed trajectories of these themes

---

1. Independent Post Doctoral Scholar in Human Geography.

2. Professor of Sociology and Director, Council for Social Development, Hyderabad, India.

3. Dalit Women Fight, *Anti-Caste Feminist Statement on #MeTooIndia from #Dalit WomenFight*, FACEBOOK, Oct. 9, 2018, https://tinyurl.com/y24lmwma.

through conversations on social media platforms and argue that the emergent narratives of #MeToo are enriched by an intersectional approach to the study of social justice. The composition of the #MeToo movement in India is heterogeneous in terms of individuals, social location, gender identities, and experiences and is fluid—in the making, in a sense, not settled; it is a coarse and unstructured space, the undulations of which draw attention to a politics of affect that plays out on a physical-virtual continuum.

The conversations around #MeToo in India have deliberately eschewed the pathways of legal redress, even while keeping ideas of justice at the center. While a detailed analysis of the legal framework is outside the scope of this article, a brief recapitulation is provided to contextualize the movement.[4] Until 1997, when Bhanwari Devi's case triggered the petition by feminist collectives in Rajasthan to the Supreme Court for guidelines to protect women from sexual harassment at the workplace,[5] the only protections in place were under archaic sections of the Indian Penal Code which defined the offence of "outraging the modesty of a woman" (Sections 354 and 509). It was under these sections that the first major feminist battle against sexual harassment at the workplace was won, with the conviction and sentencing in 1996 of a much-decorated police officer KPS Gill to imprisonment for sexual harassment of a senior officer of the Indian Administrative Service, Rupan Deol Bajaj.[6] The *Vishakha* case followed immediately after in 1997, and the Supreme Court issued detailed guidelines that defined sexual harassment and hostile environments, bringing in international standards to set out women's rights at the workplace.

The *Vishakha* judgment led to a series of directives in institutes of education and government offices to set up Committees against Sexual Harassment (CASH), and prescribed complaints mechanisms and penalties. In 2013, the guidelines formed the basis for the *Sexual Harassment of Women at Workplace (Prevention, Prohibition and Redressal) Act*, 2013.[7] The same year saw far-reaching amendments in the law on rape (shifting the definition of rape away from penile-vaginal penetration alone), drawing on the report of the Justice JS Verma Committee set up by the Union Government after the gang rape and murder of Jyoti Singh on the streets of Delhi in December 2012. It was Justice Verma's court that set out the Vishakha guidelines in the Supreme Court in 1997 as well. There were also far reaching amendments to the *Scheduled Castes and*

---

4. Kalpana Kannabiran, Tools of Justice: Non-Discrimination and the Indian Constitution (2012).

5. Vishakha and others v. State of Rajasthan [1997] 6 SCC 241 (India).

6. Rupan Deol Bajaj v. KPS Gill [1996] 1996 AIR 309 (India).

7. Sexual Harassment of Women at Workplace (Prevention, Prohibition and Redressal) Act, No. 14, Acts of Parliament, 2013 (India).

Scheduled Tribes (Prevention of Atrocities) Act that included several forms of sexual violence against Dalit and Adivasi women in the definition of atrocity.[8] This is the legal architecture that offers protection against sexual violence to Indian women today.

The release of the *List of Sexual Harassers in Academia* by Raya Sarkar, a young Dalit scholar, in 2017, marks the formal commencement of the #MeToo movement in India. The List, as it came to be known, consisted of a number of prominent names from within Indian academia, collated through anonymized sources. The debate on due process and the perils of profiling and unsubstantiated allegations through lists has created polarizations at several levels. The experience of feminist and human rights movements in India, with the creation of lists of dissenters by the state, has rendered "listing" deeply problematic. In the current debate however, the polarization in the academy is most evident in the deep shudder at the academic standing of those who had been "listed," and the refusal by primarily young university scholars to defer to "sage" rebukes. These tensions signal the changing composition of the university system in India, as well as significant shifts and the emergence of multiplicities in Indian feminist standpoints.

The second wave of the #MeToo movement in India followed the disclosures about film producer Harvey Weinstein in the United States, and has drawn a substantially greater degree of national coverage, spreading across various institutional and disciplinary confines.[9] In the continuing context of these events, it has become important to engage in a nuanced reading of the unequal cartographies of sexual violence and affect: by speaking truth to power; by drawing attention to moments of discursive insurgency; and by re-assembling notions of civility to reflect the legitimacy of the othered voice.

Binaries as Devices of Socio-Political Articulation

The movement's entrance into the sphere of public discourse symbolized an important moment in the context of some key dualisms that reflect

---

8. The Scheduled Castes and Scheduled Tribes (Prevention of Atrocities) Amendment Act, 2015, No, 1, Acts of Parliament, 2016 (India).

9. In its second coming, the movement was sparked by charges of sexual harassment brought against male actor Nana Patekar by his peer Tanusree Dutta in late September 2018. This ran conterminously with a tweet in early October 2018 by Mahima Kukreja, a young comedian from Bombay, who alleged that a male comedian, Utsav Chakrabarty, had sexually harassed her. The Wire Staff, *All you need to know: Three weeks of #MeToo and its big impacts*, THE WIRE, Oct. 28, 2018, https://thewire.in/women/all-you-need-to-know-three-weeks-of-metoo-and-its -big-impacts.

larger contentions and interrogations in contemporary social movements in India: (1) young/old feminists, (2) Savarna/Dalit-Bahujan-Adivasi feminists, (3) name-and-shame/due process feminists, and (4) Kashmiri women's ideas of freedom ("azaadi")/feminist liberation (the contestation of "nationalism" as a trope for feminist articulation)). First, the "hierarchies of age"[10] point to critical divergences in the construction of feminist norms of participation, trust, and validation, further emphasizing the need to view both the method and message as legitimate, rather than to dismiss these on account of their form and location within virtual spaces;[11] the movement thus invigorated debates on the digital-material divide through the prism of age. The idea that legitimate feminist discourses are determined by their fixity in the offline world is misleading, antiquated, and counterproductive; not only is the digital self an extension of the "real self,"[12] but also carries an equal claim to the shaping of realities.

Second, it draws attention to the modalities of power that manifest equally in offline and online spaces, as representations of discriminatory sociality;[13] is the #MeToo movement complicit in being a carrier of these repressive silences? Contrary to ideas of seeing and knowing the Internet as a vast performative expanse of "disembodiment,"[14] an important characteristic of #MeToo has been its conscious connection to "embodied subjectivities" through both anonymous and identifiable accounts, on social media platforms like Twitter[15] and Reddit. The Indian case points to the need to locate understandings of pain, anger, suffering, and victimization within a broader canvas that treats caste, class, gender, religion, sexual orientation and other forms of identity along with militarization and military occupation, as sites of instructive rupture.

Third, the method of naming and shaming, which has been a hallmark of the movement, necessitates a deeper reflection on the specific circumstances—of sexual harassment, violence and impunity—that have led to the multiplicity of public accounts in the present. It is thus imperative that we be aware of the

---

10. Kalpana Kannabiran, *#WeToo: In the Footprints of Bhanwari Devi*, OUTLOOK INDIA, Oct. 31, 2018, https://www.outlookindia.com/magazine/story/know-gnawing-absences-in-metoo-let-travesty-of-bhanwari-devis-trial-be-a-reminder/300835.

11. Kaitlynn Mendes, Jessica Ringrose, and Jessalynn Keller, *#MeToo and the promise and pitfalls of challenging rape culture through digital feminist activism*, 25 EUROPEAN JOURNAL OF WOMEN'S STUDIES 236, 241 (2018).

12. Joelle Nagle, *Twitter, cyber-violence, and the need for a critical social media literacy in teacher education: A review of the literature*, 76 TEACHING AND TEACHER EDUCATION 86, 89 (2018).

13. See Mendes et al., *supra* note 11.

14. Jessica E. Brophy, *Developing a Corporeal Cyberfeminism: Beyond Cyberutopia* (Sage Journals, 2010), cited in Nagle, *supra* note 12, at 89.

15. Nagle, *supra* note 12; Mendes et al., *supra* note 11.

persistent elisions that are normalized; the voices of Dalits, Adivasis, Muslims, gender, and sexual minorities, Kashmiri women,[16] and persons with disabilities, are conspicuous in their absence, which begs the question, *who does the "Me" in #MeToo actually represent?* The movement raises important questions about understanding difference and vulnerabilities, viewed in the context of a growing mistrust of formal mechanisms of redress; it lays an open challenge to conceptions of due process that are insulated from, and fail to address, experiences of marginality.

Most pointedly, #MeToo forces a reading of experiences through the frame of intersectionality,[17] situating the movement along a historical arc of injustice, from the rape of Bhanwari Devi in 1992 to the unjust morphologies of due process in the present. For Bhanwari Devi, the project of reclaiming her bodily integrity was etched into a concomitant process of challenging the impunity of casteist and majoritarian vocabularies of violence rooted in selective interpretations of the Constitution. Her position, emblematic of both the "me" and the "we," charts a course for discourses of feminist agency that acknowledge marginalities, through a focus on both erased and interstitial bodies.

Within this formulation, there is also a need to understand Bhanwari's struggle as not hers alone, but as that of a collective of nested experiences ousted to the margins. Mondal asks, with reference to the two recent waves of #MeToo in India:

> "Why are Savarna Indians so reluctant to be represented by a Dalit woman, even someone who is a stranger, someone whose work is not specifically for or about Dalits? … Raya Sarkar's list wasn't only for Dalit women, yet Savarna India needed a new, unrelated #MeToo movement to feel comfortable talking about large-scale sexual harassment. What message does that send to us Dalit women?"[18]

A growing assemblage of actors who are internally differentiated are engaged in negotiating the tensions and contestations of making common cause, showing that the rules and norms that regulate participation online are reproductions of offline social asymmetries. Criteria of inclusion and exclusion—caste, religious and gender identity are some of the many factors that

---

16. Decolonial Feminist Statement on #MeToo in Kashmir, 2018, https://docs.google.com/document/d/1wjEW401Vo4LZJ4dK1SPmQbJEAoJDEVbZYDdPCWyTELg/edit?ts=5bba1ed1 (2018).

17. Patricia H. Collins & Sirma Bilge, Intersectionality (2016).

18. Mimi Mondal, *A Dalit woman's thoughts on #MeTooIndia*, The Indian Express, Oct. 15, 2018, https://indianexpress.com/article/opinion/a-dalit-womans-thoughts-on-metooindia-5402538/.

mediate patterns of participation—and by extension, of visibility, are defined in accordance with dominant social structures. Consequently, a number of individuals engaging with MeToo through an intersectional perspective have repeatedly asserted the need to "amplify" rather than speak for and over marginalized persons (*Tweet*):

> "[3] Pass on the mic and amplify the voices of marginalised using your social capital. [4] Instead of coming to us to 'reform/civilize us'—reform your own casteist, racist, transphobic, ableist households."[19]

For queer and disabled persons who have endured harm and abuse, the challenges are numerous; the doors to due process are difficult to access, with the path to justice being further occluded by the persistent and violent stigmatization of non-cis, non-heterosexual individuals. Social location and hierarchies further underwrite public perceptions of legitimacy in ways that invalidate the claims of particular groups to formal procedures of redress. The option of naming and shaming perpetrators is equally harrowing for queer persons who risk being outed against their will, particularly in cases involving the workplace or intimate partner violence. Thus, the Indian #MeToo movement also makes a strong case for the problematization of "collective identity,"[20] by speaking to a broader argument on the non-neutrality of technologies and discourses of collective action.[21]

Traumascapes of #MeToo: Harassment, Privacy, and the Materiality of the Digital World

As Guinier and Torres[22] have shown through the concept of *demosprudence* in the wider context of the impact of social movements on jurisprudence, there is legal insight to be gained from the traumascapes of the #MeToo movement: the social movement is complementary to the judicial apparatus in its ability to contribute to the making of law, by bearing equally, the insignia of the cultural changes and disjunctures that lead up to moments of national

---

19. Divya Kandukuri (@Smashboard_), TWITTER (Oct. 25, 2018, 12:44 AM), https://twitter.com/Smashboard_/status/1055364560008421376.
20. Ulrich Dolata and Jan-Felix Schrape, *Collective Action in the Digital Age: An Actor-Based Typology* in COLLECTIVITY AND POWER ON THE INTERNET 7, 22-23 (2018).
21. Ulrich Dolata, *Social Movements: The Sociotechnical Constitution of Collective Action,* in COLLECTIVITY AND POWER ON THE INTERNET 31, 41-42 (2018).
22. Lani Guinier & Gerald Torres, *Changing the wind: Notes toward a demosprudence of law and social movements,* 123 YALE L. J. 2740, 2740-2804 (2014).

reflection. The traumascapes of #MeToo point thus to a set of anticipatory actions that combine past and present experiences in their attempt to shape future understandings of justice. And while a number of survivors have sought to pursue either restorative or punitive justice, their cases are also indicative of the precariousness and internally exclusionary character of contemporary discourses of justice: do our languages of justice speak to, for, with or after, the survivors of sexual harassment and assault? #MeToo experiences on Twitter have also drawn attention to the labor of performing feminist collective action, by showing, through the experiences of survivors and their interlocutors, the "affective, precarious, and exploitative" environments of activism that prevail;[23] a number of individuals spoke about their encounters with "abuse, [and] burnout,"[24] resulting in their temporary withdrawal from the digital world.

The violation of bodily sovereignty maps onto dynamics of power, authority, and social capital in ways that render certain voices invisible, even as others assume hypervisibility. In this context and building on Nancy Fraser's concept of a "subaltern counterpublic,"[25] Lamont Hill introduces the concept of a "digital counterpublic" as a means of identifying and constituting narratives of resistance that seek to emancipate marginalized bodies.[26] For Hill, social media platforms such as Twitter offer citizens the opportunity of constituting "new surveillances"[27] that speak to contemporary technologies of accountability that enable persons to publicly question injustices. This resonates with experiences from the Indian #MeToo, where the case of the allegations against senior journalist MJ Akbar (who resigned from his position as the Junior Minister of Foreign Affairs), for example, prompt a careful reflection on the vocabularies of sexual violence, unruliness, and respectability; the survivors, having initiated a subversion of the dynamics of power against "a widely respected male journalist," have also been subjected to a crisis of civility that plays out in the language of "criminal defamation."[28] Relatedly, there is also a question to be asked about the specific design of privacy in these cases, given that while the digital world

---

23. Mendes et al., *supra* note 11, at 239.

24. *Id.*

25. Nancy Fraser, *Rethinking the Public Sphere: A Contribution of Actually Existing Democracy*, Duke University Press, 1990, cited in Marc Lamont Hill, *"Thank You, Black Twitter:" State Violence, Digital Counterpublics, and Pedagogies of Resistance*, 53 URBAN EDUCATION 286, 288 (2018).

26. Hill, *supra* note 25, at 288.

27. *Id.* at 290.

28. PTI, *Court to hear M J Akbar's criminal defamation case on Thursday*, THE ECONOMIC TIMES, Oct. 17, 2018, https://economictimes.indiatimes.com/news/politics-and -nation/court-to-hear-m-j-akbars-criminal-defamation-case-on-thursday/articleshow/66262 450.cms.

offers a space of support and solitude to survivors, their safety offline remains a matter of significant concern.

Experiences of invisibility are further amplified for individuals who occupy positions of disadvantage within already disadvantaged social formations—the testimony of a young woman who was raped by a prominent figure in protests against the rape of a child in Kathua in the embattled state of Jammu and Kashmir (2018) is an important example. The question it raises is pertinent—is there a choice to be made between the forced acceptance of bodily incursions in favor of a larger cause or does the architecture of democracy point to the possibility of a nuanced imagination of justice that is able to acknowledge the gradations and deeply gendered contradictions that inhere?

Conclusion

In October 2018, the *Samaj*, a newspaper in the Indian state of Odisha carried an article that branded the #MeToo movement as "an epidemic that would destroy Indian culture and civilization."[29] But, is a culture that seeks to civilize and discipline its citizens by sacrificing justice for women and sexual minorities, a culture worth preserving? As we have tried to show in this essay, #MeToo experiences arrange themselves into an assemblage that is constantly attempting to reconfigure itself both in terms of its relationship to the exterior, but also, in the relationships that prevail within. Far from implying a call for the vilification of respectable men, #MeToo instead marks the beginning of a political act of dismantling the architecture of an unequal order to make way for one that is able to grant freedom, safety, and dignity to the marginalized to determine, on their own, what a just world might look like. This arc of resistance has a long history on the Indian subcontinent: one that begins with anti-caste feminist icons Savitribai Phule and Tarabai Shinde.

---

29. Sandeep Sahu, *#MeToo: Why There Is No Outrage Against This Misogynistic Editorial*, OUTLOOK, Oct. 25, 2018, https://www.outlookindia.com/website/story/metoo-why-there -is-no-outrage-against-this-misogynistic-editorial/319028.

CHAPTER 23

One of the #MeToo Movements in India: The List

Shivangi Misra[1]

The List

In October 2017, Raya Sarkar, a law student at the time, self-identified feminist, and anti-caste activist, published a crowdsourced list (the List) of professors in Indian academia, accusing them of sexually harassing their students. She started by naming two names and then asked women via a Facebook post to come forward or send her the names of professors who have sexually harassed them. She stated that this list was based on first-person accounts shared with her via WhatsApp, text messages, emails, and other mediums. The List in its final form had seventy-nine professors and faculty members from twenty-nine educational institutions. The List, however, did not make public either the context of the accusations or any supporting evidence. Raya explained that she did not have the consent of the women to release the details yet.[2]

The List is no longer available online and presumably has been deleted from its original location. Its memory and impact, nevertheless, have been preserved in the wide spectrum of responses to the accusations on the List. Homogeneity in any form within India is rare, and the responses from men, women,

---

1. Indian lawyer committed to human rights law and advocacy. Policy Counsel at the Canadian Feminist Alliance for International Action, and previously practicing law with the Lawyers Collective, New Delhi, the leading Indian public interest litigation organization, which works to protect and promote the rights of the most marginalized.

2. Shreya Roy Chowdhury and Aroon Deep, Universities respond to Raya Sarkar's list of alleged sexual predators: Mostly silence, some denials, SCROLL.IN, Nov. 04, 2017, https://scroll.in/article/856589/universities-respond-to-raya-sarkars-list-of-alleged-sexual-predators-mostly-silence-some-denials.

feminists, academics, lawyers reflected the diversity.[3] The author of the List, by publishing the names given to her by other women, faced threats of death, rape, and physical assault.[4] Violence or the looming threat of violence against women is the truth as we know it, but the striking element after the List came out was the strong disagreement among feminists, which tried to shut the doors on the method that popularly came to be known as the "name and shame" method. It was under these circumstances that, two years ago, the #MeToo movement in India began—with unease.

The Response

In a written public statement by fourteen well-known feminist lawyers, activists, and influential public figures, the List was strongly condemned, and they urged that the names on the List be withdrawn from the public domain. The short letter, published on an online platform *Kafila*, is reproduced below:

> As feminists, we have been part of a long struggle to make visible sexual harassment at the workplace, and have worked with the movement to put in place systems of transparent and just procedures of accountability. We are dismayed by the initiative on Facebook, in which men are being listed and named as sexual harassers with no context or explanation. One or two names of men who have been already found guilty of sexual harassment by due process, are placed on par with unsubstantiated accusations. It worries us that anybody can be named anonymously, with lack of answerability. Where there are genuine complaints, there are institutions and procedures, which we should utilize. We too know the process is harsh and often tilted against the complainant. We remain committed to strengthening these processes. At the same time, abiding by the principles of natural justice, we remain committed to due process, which is fair and just.
>
> This manner of naming can delegitimize the long struggle against sexual harassment, and make our task as feminists more difficult.
>
> We appeal to those who are behind this initiative to withdraw it, and if they wish to pursue complaints, to follow due process, and to be assured that they will be supported by the larger feminist community in their fight for justice.

3. Nehmat Kaur, How to Make Sense of the Radical Challenge to Sexual Harassment in Academia, THE WIRE, Oct. 25, 2017, https://thewire.in/gender/facebook-sexual-harassment-south-asian-academics.

4. FP Staff, Raya Sarkar faces death, rape threats after sexual predators' list takes academia by storm, FIRSTPOST, Oct. 28, 2017, https://www.firstpost.com/india/raya-sarkar-faces-death-rape-threats-after-sexual-predators-list-takes-academia-by-storm-4181659.html.

It is an undisputable fact that the women who have signed this "Kafila letter" have played an extremely important role in strengthening the legal framework on the subject of sexual harassment. However, to claim that the feminist struggle seemed to have suffered a setback due to women speaking out in their own respective manner puts the blame where it does not belong, with the survivors. The letter begins with, "As feminists …," according to itself this self-recognition, which is well-suited for feminists, except when it mistakenly assumes it includes all women and all personal experiences. Such criticism coming from inside the movement itself, which assumes that naming an accused without any context delegitimizes the process, is not only troublesome but also fails to appreciate the larger goal that the #MeToo movement is aiming to achieve. It needs to be acknowledged that the lack of context with the names of the academics was only one of the main criticisms about the List. Other criticisms included the absence of "due process" and official complaints, as well as the lack of accountability for the women involved. Nivedita Menon, a feminist academic and one of the signatories of the letter, later said in a personal post on the same portal as the letter,[5]

"Had the List been a series of anonymous testimonies providing context and explanation (as Christine Fair did, for example, in the article that Huff Post shamefully, took down), I personally would have celebrated it, make no mistake. Even if the List had simply described the acts of sexual harassment against each name, I would have thought it possible to help the survivor bring the perpetrators to justice…."

Raya Sarkar in another post explained[6] the reason why she did not refer to the context or the details of the allegations:

"But the complainants were really not for that plan, and they were like 'please don't take my name, please let it be anonymous, because I'm scared, because I will be harassed and the person may figure out it's me.'"

The Divide

It would be naïve to expect unity within the feminist movement in India at any point in history, considering the needs of 500 million Indian women and

5. Nivedita Menon, *From Feminazi to Savarna Rape Apologist in 24 hours*, KAFILA— 12 YEARS OF A COMMON JOURNEY, Oct. 28, 2017, https://kafila.online/2017/10/28/from -feminazi-to-savarna-rape-apologist-in-24-hours/.

6. Elizabeth Cassin and Ritu Prasad, *Student's "sexual predator" list names professors*, BBC NEWS, Nov. 6, 2017, https://www.bbc.com/news/blogs-trending-41862615.

the intersectional realities of caste, class, disability, sexuality, and gender. One of the questions, removed from the epicenter of sexual harassment, is the nature of the #MeToo movement in India: it gained traction despite divide, suspicion, or sometimes simply a rebuke from the dominant groups. The critical approach to #MeToo carries a legacy too heavy to ignore—it is by the women who created the environment and the platforms we stand and speak on. However, we are here now, at the point in Indian history of feminist discourse, and we have two seemingly strong ends of the spectrum. Perhaps unity within movements is a fantasy, and "waves" were just euphemism for the dominant feminist group's ideology in the past. The role to develop feminist discourse to be inclusive of agential experiences is often left to the people who experience the harm. It is a divide; it is a divide of methodology; it is a divide of prioritizing values; and it is a divide of law and culture. It is not a generational divide of the age groups; it is not a conversation in spiral; rather, it is just their moment in history (the women who decided to name their harassers publicly).

The "larger feminist group," as allegedly represented in the letter, urged the "people behind the initiative" to withdraw the names from the List as it did not follow "due process." These women claimed that systems of transparency and accountability had been established after arduous and long struggle by the women. These criticisms are all in good faith and represent the view of some feminists, but they dangerously cut the arm of a movement started by students against the men in Indian academia. In order to make "due process" pragmatically possible and not just in the normative theory of substantive equality, students and other list supporters will need more than the promise of an evolving system. In the absence of effective due process mechanisms, is it viable to dismiss social efforts in the name of #MeToo movement because due process was not followed?

"Due Process" Supporters

The undivided focus on due process of law is misplaced in the context of sexual harassment because the burden on women to act according to legal constructs requires that any action in response to oppression must be in accordance to law. That notion has been debunked by successful social movements such as non-cooperation movements, Occupy, and Black Lives Matter, or evolving conceptual frameworks of legal knowledge. The resistance through the "naming and shaming" method, a form of civil disobedience, is conditional to the standard that the oppression exists and is established—which, we believe, is exactly the case in sexual harassment allegations against men. Only if we accept the power dynamics in sexual harassment cases, can we satisfactorily also dismiss any often-used analogies between the List and a sex offenders' list with its reformative shortcomings.

The intrinsic value of due process and its normative function in law does not exist in a vacuum. Due process exists not only in the black letter of the law but also in its practice. The #MeToo movement is a visible indicator and an acknowledgment that the mere existence of due process should not be equated with its effective implementation in substance. Therefore, at this stage of the movement, women should not be burdened by high faith in such due process of law.

"Believing women"—a concept championed by women in cases such as Brett Kavanaugh's confirmation hearing as a United States Supreme Court Justice, or against the Chief Justice of India, who was accused of sexual harassment by an employee of the Supreme Court of India—was significant in that it opened up the discourse to the treatment of women in the strictly due process systems. It brought to light that, if, in reality, there is a one-dimensional way to look at due process, "believing women" will not find a place in the scheme. If we accept this one-dimensional approach that either one believes in due process or one does not, "believing women" can potentially become a moral absolute that does not fit in the due process narrative. One cannot think that you can believe women without due process being ensured until the end. The process itself is not sacrosanct, as we experience that there will be occasions when women warn each other about predatory behaviors of certain men before they go to a formal system with the potential of escalating the complaint of harm. If a woman standing outside an interview room warns the next woman candidate going in that the man sexually harassed her during the interview, it would seem odd to rebuke her for warning the others standing outside, instead of filing a complaint first. If it is the anonymity of the women coming forward that weakens due process, why will a name I am not familiar with transform my treatment of the warning? We all do not have to adhere to the warning; we just do not have to be gatekeepers for the movement or the feminist process from people who want to be warned. The notion that the credibility of the movement is too brittle for possible false allegations, or allegations post-punishment, begs us to think about the sections of the feminist movement that, prior to the List, were not vulnerable to possible misuse.

Due process, unlike some legal rules, is not a technical concept with a fixed content unrelated to time, place, and circumstances.[7] It is an extremely important pillar of the legal infrastructure. However, to become fixated on that when we are called upon to support women who are finally speaking out and have not decided to take on the extremely burdensome legal recourse, can take up all

---

7. Durga Das Basu, Constitution of India, 3084 (8th Ed. Vol. 3, 2009).

the oxygen in the room. Irrespective, due process is the next step. Nevertheless, it is not an "either/or" situation, but it is the option that has, so far, failed to provide effective redress. Naming and shaming might be pushing moral limits, borne out of the anger of Dalit students, disabled students, dependent students; it might not be productive *qua* the List, but drawing up arbitrary borders for aptness of the anger would be slamming the door closed on these women.

What #MeToo has done for women in India, especially for younger women, has been nothing less than revolutionary, in which the discovery in itself was a jolt to the realization that the due process that comes in the form of Internal Complaints Committees does not hold the faith of the women. The navigation of the struggle against sexual harassment became more decentralized from the identities of feminists who have, and continue to, take the issues up to the court, to now also include the more individualized forms of expression such as the List. Feminists who do not associate themselves with the process can safely choose the latter option. The movement manifested itself in so many forms that can hold different meanings for us. The sex panic of the movement, the cultural diversity, the theories around consensual and non-consensual politics, or the office-space romance advocates hold their own people captive, and we do not have the leader of the movement. It is, after all, an outcry, not the norm. Due process existed then and will do so beyond that point. With all its nuanced identity intact, what it can do is take into account the experiences of the women for whom it also exists. If one narrative is fixated on due process and the other on a social movement exclusively, we will be talking past each other.

That *Kafila* letter became a center point of understanding this divide in the feminist movement in India because it did not arise from a point of bad faith but from meaningful concern over defending the legal system, the establishment thereof was itself a feminist struggle. We would be wrong to believe that it resolved all feminist needs of the present and the future. Women, in this case, students, decide how they want to explore this system. It comes from their own place in the oppression and not from a privileged place of "naming and shaming"—as if the shame is theirs to give suddenly. If we do not address the power imbalance, the reason behind public naming of harassment allegations, then what are we addressing?

Courage and bravery to take up due process of law by the students cannot be a factor where the law can deny rights and freedom against oppression and power-driven social norms. Hence, once we move on from this due process fixation *at this point* for the discourse, we can perhaps move on to discuss how to improve due process as it exists for students in the workplace, including educational institutions. Key to the discourse of ending the culture of sexual harassment are acknowledging that the first #MeToo movement revealed a broken system and that women's intersectional identities (Dalit, lower income,

Queer, disabled) do not permit them to secure a future in a social system that has historically worked against them. Fixating on the significance of inaccessible theories, and not on the survival techniques would be a class issue. The *Kafila* letter and the public backlash could have been an attempt at dissociation, either to separate oneself from the method, or, if one happens to have the tools to impact actual change, then an opportune moment to listen and analyze rather than criticize the process arising out of reasons yet unknown. Feminist methods of inclusion and interactive development, such as asking questions of the List supporters and asking for alternatives in the discourse, could be the next stop toward evolving the Indian process and the #MeToo movement.

There is a divide, where the dominant feminist culture and its treatment of this generation of feminists who are taking the fight online and warning other women of harassers who walk among us are at loggerheads. The movement was not designed to be status- quo friendly, and it ran counter to the culture of dependency on law and legality in order to expose the experiences of a student on a private timeline on social media, open, like a conversation at a bus stop. The feminist ideology that extended support in the justice system is quite simply unaffordable or unavailable in the exhaustion of the rampant nature of daily harassment at educational institutions. This is an opportune moment for the feminists who earlier gave the platform to young feminist to speak to now listen to them as well.

#MeToo movement, after all, is not a single point in time (as it spread globally at various times). It is a discourse about culture, power, as much as it is about the legal recourse. In India, with the myriad issues, every power hub has seen sexual harassment, educational institutions being only one of them. While the discourse has only just begun, students need mechanisms in both the legal and the cultural context. There is ample ambiguity in sexual harassment laws in India, a lack of import of the objects and purpose of the law in practice, and a lack of support in the society with respect to the victims. The systemic oppression in society against women hurts students who are in a space that is ideally supposed to empower them against oppressive systems. Economic independence for women in India is a distant dream and the means to that end is corrupt along the way. The first step could be recognizing what we lack in terms of the law, if we seek to judge the students who resort to alternative methods of justice, beyond what the literature has concluded and seem to be asserting monopoly on what is the "just method."

CHAPTER 24

#MeToo (米兔) in China: A Good, Quick Battle Against Sexual Harassment

Lining Zhang[1]

In spring 2018, #MeToo catalyzed a social media battle over sexual harassment in China on "We Media,"[2] a first in the Peoples' Republic of China. Before 2018, feminist grassroots activists had begun to bring the issue into public discourse. They conducted surveys and polls, and gathered reports documenting the prevalence of sexual harassment in public spaces, as well as workplaces and

---

1. Founder of JOE (Women's Rights Organization), Public Interest Experiential Learning Mentor in Ivylabs, MoonShoot Academy, Yes Go Academy.

2. We Media refers to WeChat, Weibo, and Douban. WeChat is a Chinese multi-purpose messaging, and mobile payment app with over 1 billion monthly active users (902 million daily active users). Described as one of the world's most powerful apps by Forbes, it is also known as China's "app for everything" and a "super app" because of its wide range of functions and platforms. The most important feature is Moments. "Moments" is WeChat's brand name for its social feed of friends' updates. Moments allows users to post images, post text, post comments, share music (associated with QQ Music or other web-based music services), share articles, and post "likes." Privacy in WeChat works by groups of friends—only the friends from the user's contacts are able to view their Moments' contents and comments. The friends of the user will only be able to see the likes and comments from other users if they are in a mutual friends' group. For example, friends from high school are not able to see the comments and likes from friends from university. When users post their moments, they can separate their friends into a few groups, and they can decide whether this Moment can be seen by particular groups of people. Contents posted can be set to "Private," and then only the user can view it.

Weibo is a Chinese microblogging (weibo) website. Launched by Sina Corporation on August 14, 2009, it is one of the most popular social media platforms in China. As of the second quarter of 2018, Sina Weibo has over 431 million monthly active users, with surging stocks, advertising sales, revenue, and total earnings in the quarter.

Douban is a Chinese social networking service website allowing registered users to record information and create content related to film, books, music, recent events, and activities in Chinese cities. It can be seen as one of the most influential Web 2.0 websites in China. See https://baike.baidu.com/item/%E5%BE%AE%E4%BF%A1/3905974?fr=aladdin.

schools. ³ Beyond mere data collection, they also gathered personal stories of women's experiences. Activists raised awareness of the issue by hitchhiking all over China wearing a poster with messages decrying sexual harassment.⁴ Amid this uprising, two prominent male professors at renowned Chinese universities were accused of sexually harassing their students, leading to their controversial dismissals.⁵

The number of similar cases increased drastically in 2018. Within half a year, more than thirty perpetrators were named on We Media by victims or bystanders; many were eventually removed from their posts at high-ranking universities in China. These included nationally recognized professors from Peking, WuHan, Nanjing, Beijing, and Xiamen Universities, many of whom were associated with Ministry of Education-sponsored national projects.

---

3. These include:

- "Silent Iron Lion," a 2016 Beijing Normal University Campus Data and Report on Sexual Harassment, authored by a university student, see https://wenku.baidu.com /view/3ed4a80811a6f524ccbff121dd36a32d7375c71e.html;
- 2014 press reports about the "Wu Chunming" case—sexual harassment by a renowned professor at the top 20 Xiamen University toward his female students, see http://culture.ifeng.com/a/20160108/46992733_0.shtml; https://edu.qq .com/a/20151225/043697.htm;
- the "Sunflower Poll" conducted by Guangzhou Women Workers' NGO on sexual harassment toward female factory workers, the author wished to be anonymous and the article not published; and a collection of 13 cases of male professors sexually harassing female students in schools by the then most active feminist We Media "Voice of Women", (the report on "Voice of Women's We Media account was no longer available to the public as the account was shut down in late 2018. See http://wemedia .ifeng.com/10294902/wemedia.shtml).

Note also that this data gathering referred to the most recent efforts from activists since 2014. Before 2014, there were several rounds of efforts toward raising the issue of sexual harassment, including one in the 1990s, and one in the first decade since 2000.

4. In 2017, several activists and a women's rights NGO in Guangzhou attempted to put up a poster against sexual harassment on metro station walls in Guangzhou. After the crowd-sourcing was successful and versions of posters were presented to the local metro offices, the activists had to stop the project because none of the versions were regarded as "presentable to the public" by the local authority. In response, one of the activists started a trip from Guangzhou to Beijing wearing the poster on her as a jacket. The police stopped the trip halfway. https:// gongyi.ifeng.com/a/20171118/44767104_0.shtml.

5. While thirteen cases were investigated, and reported, only three of them led to a brief discussion online, and two of them ended in the perpetrator being dismissed under pressure from activists' constant letters of petition and public discussion on WeChat. https://baijiahao .baidu.com/s?id=1589383542029003828&wfr=spider&for=pc (BeiHang University professor dismissed); https://www.douban.com/group/topic/116935575/ (Nanjing University professor Zhang Kangzhi dismissed); https://www.sohu.com/a/227560241_391471 (Peking University professor Shen Yang under investigation).

The proliferation of anonymous stories of sexual harassment on We Media has cemented its role in the #MeToo movement in China, with university campuses as the primary battlefield. The Chinese media's portrayal of university campuses as a youthful, academic utopia contributes to the shock value and interest in these stories.

There are several forces leading this movement in China, all of which use their We Media accounts, that is, WeChat and Weibo. Activists[6] created hashtags of "MeToo in China" on Weibo, and WeChat group accounts and email accounts, as well as one hotline, all of which are used as channels to receive any reports, stories, and information about sexual harassment incidents from anybody, and spread messages including data, information, and stories as well as ways to join the movement. When We Media censors deactivated these accounts, new ones were created to spread the same messages. Activists found ways to avoid the censorship by posting and sending *images* with words embedded in them, rather than posting words and phrases that can be easily searched and detected.

The global #MeToo movement inspired Chinese activists to explore the power of We Media to investigate and to publicize sexual harassment allegations in innovative ways. When stories of sexual harassment were received, activists, together with the informants, investigated and interviewed the survivors, witnesses, and their friends and family. When survivors were unwilling or unavailable, activists became the first story tellers. The power lay in the activists' control of the narrative; other media outlets might twist or manipulate the story. To control the integrity of the story, the activists released the first version of the story. This allowed them to shape the vocabulary, tone, and perspectives to be repeated by viewers when they discuss the stories. Capitalizing on the public's feelings of outrage and injustice, the activists' strategy was to engage the public, inspire their empathy, and tell them the specific measures to take. Direct bystanders were encouraged to tell stories and incidents of sexual harassment on We Media, with the choice to either name perpetrators or make anonymous accusations. The public, particularly the educated, were invited on We Media to sign their names on letters of petition or letters of request for information written to university leadership, legislators, and People's Representatives. Letters generally garnered at least 500-800 signatures. The Ministry of Education has responded in social media to such letters, promising that they will take measures requested by the writers, including investigations of all cases reported, issuing strict rules for all education institutions on prohibition, prevention, and

---

6. There is a consensus among activists on the strategy of decentralization amongst themselves. Not only do activists use pseudonyms in creating most accounts, they also work in small groups, rather than one centralized group to avoid censorship and attention.

handling cases of sexual harassment. In addition, several People's Representatives have responded to the letters saying that in the National People's Congress annual meeting in the spring of 2020, the issue of sexual harassment will be on the agenda. While not sufficient, these responses were significant progress on the social media battle, as it said loud and clear to the general public, to the perpetrators, and more importantly to the survivors, that "it ain't private or personal anymore," and it IS a national, public issue of law and morality.

Another important strategy that came from the #MeToo movement is the focus on individual stories. The power of individual stories is that people relate to the details of the stories, particularly the emotional and psychological reactions and trauma of victims. This extends to both the victims who were harassed and bystanders who were silenced. The stories also tell the truth of sexual harassment as an imbalance of power and dispel many common myths about sexual harassment.

One example is the story of several female students who were sexually harassed and raped by the same poetry professor at Henan University. Their boyfriends at the time of the assault collectively told their stories in July 2018. The boyfriends shared how they accidentally found out about the sexual harassment, and immediately suspected their then-girlfriends of infidelity. They could not believe that a celebrity, a highly respected poet, an idol for many students, and their own mentors could do such things. As they finally realized that it was true, they felt a strong sense of shock, anger, and betrayal. These feelings silenced and traumatized them. They experienced anxiety, depression, insomnia to varying degrees. One man explained: "I will never forgive myself because I could not protect my girlfriend."[7] Another went on, "His behavior harmed us as a group and destroyed our respect and trust in many things, especially in our dreams and inspirations."

Female classmates of the victims perceived the relationship as consensual, further silencing the victims from coming forward with their stories of suffering. In a similar situation, a victim eventually committed suicide. When feminists can tell these stories, they lead the public to foster engagement and empathy, rather than further gossip and apathy. In a country with a huge population of We Media users, the #MeToo movement was perfectly positioned to dominate the platform. Wide dissemination of #MeToo stories on We Media served to dispel the apathy that Chinese people previously held toward the issue of sexual

---

7. For interviews with the partners of the Henan victims by WeMedia Official Accounts Guangzhou Gender Center, see https://mp.weixin.qq.com/s?__biz=MzI0ODU2Mjc1OQ ==&mid=2247484243&idx=1&sn=b8975601e83c8cc01bee1e23f6e39056&chksm=e99f967 bdee81f6d8ab8cb5dff511509c9fcc90a7f58756d258a4c6aa6d8cccaaae85b498eb2&mpshare =1&scene=24&srcid=0626UXq6b71LZJiVMXkpGjq0&pass_ticket=4TAwaJov9C3mrYxIo vGun1w8ePRTFviCB%2FuHQuGCCYXWm8CwJfD8EvkVgJmpmGqT#rd.

harassment. The power of individual stories demonstrated the necessity of confronting authority and powerful names with good reputations. With a supportive public, fear of retaliation became less of an impediment to pursuing justice.

Before #MeToo, sexual harassment was not a household phrase, nor was sexual harassment explicitly protected by Chinese law. In China, there is no specific legal regulation of sexual harassment, and in the legal provisions referring to the term "sexual harassment," there is no accurate definition of sexual harassment. Chinese law does not recognize that sexual harassment is a separate basis for filing a lawsuit or starting any type of legal proceeding.

Nonetheless, since 2006, there have been many local laws and regulations related to what many countries characterize as "sexual harassment." These are concentrated in three categories under civil law: (1) the Women's Rights Protection Law, (2) the Labor Law, and (3) the Education Law. In addition, the regulations on public security and punishment have also been used as punishments for "rogues" or "disturbing public order," including sexual harassment in public. In both the civil and criminal spheres, China's judicial precedents do not treat sexual harassment as gender discrimination, but as a violation of either personal rights, physical rights, honorary rights, or labor rights. Though a decent starting point, this structure leaves much room for improvement.

The Fourth World Conference on Women, held in Beijing in 1995, promulgated specific legal provisions on sexual harassment in China. After joining as a member to the Convention on the Elimination of All Forms of Discrimination against Women (CEDAW), the first wave of Chinese sexual harassment investigations occurred in domestic academia. The investigation of Tang Can of the Chinese Academy of Social Sciences was the first time that sexual harassment was exposed as a pervasive problem for many women and girls in China.[8]

Ten years later in 2006, the first batch of provincial women's rights protection laws was amended to include the term sexual harassment. In the following ten years, thirty-two provinces joined, and many cities created municipal regulations. Most of these regulations consist of a simple sentence forbidding sexual harassment of women and indicate that the relevant departments should deal with violations. These regulations are intentionally ambiguous and provide no specific protection or cause of action. However, several provinces have defined sexual harassment, and include obscenity, language, words, pictures, electronic information and "other forms" of harassment. Further, they specify the responsibility of the employer in these situations. These regulations are not widely used by the judiciary. In fact, most of the thirty judicial cases that could

---

8. Can Tang, The Existence of Sexual Harassment in China, 1995. In this study, 169 randomly selected women in Shanghai and Beijing were surveyed and 84 percent of them reported being sexually harassed once, and 63 percent, twice or more.

be retrieved are filed under "personality rights" in civil law and "inappropriate dismissal" in labor laws and regulations. Sexual harassment has been exposed, and most of the victims are not litigating, but the alleged sexual harassment perpetrators have filed lawsuits for labor rights when they are punished by their companies' codes of conduct.

In 2018, as a result of #MeToo in China, the American Asia Fund group issued a comprehensive report, which for the first time gathered all thirty-four judicial cases that mentioned sexual harassment in the last ten years, analyzed them, and proposed specific measures for legal reform based on the analyses.

The report recommends that the Chinese Ministry of Human Resources and Social Security issue departmental regulations or normative documents to prevent and stop sexual harassment in the workplace. These regulations should give a definition of sexual harassment in the workplace; establish preventive mechanisms, including training, education, and publicity mechanisms; and establish standardized disposal mechanisms and procedures, including complaint and investigation procedures. The report recommends that the measures pay attention to the confidentiality of the parties, prevent retaliation, and avoid secondary injuries. Most importantly, it recommends that employers be liable for the harm to victims from workplace sexual harassment. In order to achieve this, the report also suggests adding anti-sexual harassment clauses in the Labor Contract Law. Employers' liability would include joint liability for both the employer and the employee harasser, punitive damages, and remedial measures in case of reprisals toward victims such as salary reduction, downgrade, or dismissal.

The report additionally recommends that the Supreme People's Court issue special guidance. The guidance should include special rules to be followed in the trial of harassment cases. For example, specific measures should be taken to prevent victims from being harmed again. In the process of investigation and evidence collection, the People's Courts should pay attention to protecting the privacy of both parties. Evidence of the victim's past sexual behavior should be excluded in order to avoid problematic inferences or victim-blaming. The second recommendation is for special rules in the distribution of the burden of proof, and for the court's criteria for the acceptance of evidence presented by or in favor of a survivor's case.

The report also proposes that the legislators enact a national Anti-Discrimination Act, and implement local anti-discrimination laws to regulate the sexual harassment in the workplace and the public space, as well on campuses, so it would be an umbrella that collected and clarified all the existing provisions that are scattered, insufficiently defined, and largely vague.

These recommendations show that activists are confident that reform of the current law can properly address the issue of sexual harassment in China and legitimize the battle against sexual harassment for victims. This confidence springs, at least in part, from public responses to the #MeToo movement in China. The scope of the movement has now expanded from campuses to the workplace. Several celebrities in the national broadcast industry including CCTV hosts, and NGO leaders were exposed as perpetrators.[9] It has even become common to see a mainstream news report, or a We Media article describing a case of sexual harassment. The progress and growth of this movement is promising, especially considering how the overall political censorship has been more intense in the last decade since the change of leadership.

---

9. Zhu Jun 朱军, one of the most famous CCTV hosts, was revealed to have sexually harassed girls using his authority as a celebrity in the broadcast industry. The case is ongoing. *See* Javier C. Hernandez, *She's on a #MeToo Mission in China, Battling Censors and Lawsuits*, N.Y. Times, Jan. 5, 2019, https://www.nytimes.com/2019/01/04/world/asia/china-zhou-xiaoxuan -metoo.html. Lei Chuang, a celebrity for his organization for discrimination against people with Hepatitis B, was revealed to have sexually harassed several women volunteers, acknowledged such behavior and was removed from all the positions in the NGO world. Feng Yongfeng 冯永 峰, another celebrity in the NGO world as a leader in environmental protection, was revealed to have sexually harassed and raped several colleagues and has acknowledged it. See https://baijia hao.baidu.com/s?id=1606861419469829006&wfr=spider&for=pc.

CHAPTER 25

#MeToo as Catharsis for Hong Kong's Victims of Childhood Sexual Abuse: Confronting Cultures of Silence and Shame and Creating Conditions for Substantive Change

Puja Kapai[1]

In November 2017, Hong Kong's first Asian Indoor Games Gold Medalist, "Queen of Hurdles" Vera Lui Lai Yiu, posted a selfie on her Facebook page with the caption "#MeToo," signing it with her initials "LLY." In the days that followed, Lui shared with the press that her coach sexually abused her when she was thirteen years old on the pretext of massaging her muscles. Lui said she disclosed the abuse now as a "birthday present to herself" as she turned twenty-three.[2] Lui credited U.S. Olympic gold gymnast McKayla Maroney with inspiring her to share her story. A month before Lui's revelations, Maroney had revealed that her team doctor had repeatedly sexually assaulted her from the age of thirteen.[3]

1. Associate Professor of Law and Convener of the Women's Studies Research Centre, Faculty of Law, University of Hong Kong.

2. Su Xinqi, *"Speaking up is my birthday present to myself," Hong Kong hurdler says of sex abuse revelation*, SO. CHINA MORNING POST, Nov. 30, 2017, https://www.scmp.com/news /hong-kong/community/article/2122281/speaking-my-birthday-present-myself-hong-kong -hurdler-says.

3. Su Xinqi and Christy Leung, *Hong Kong hurdler Vera Lui's claim that a coach sexually assaulted her when she was 13 sparks outcry, police probe*, SO. CHINA MORNING POST, Nov. 30, 2017, https://www.scmp.com/news/hong-kong/law-crime/article/2122203/coach-sexually -assaulted-her-when-she-was-13-hong-kong.

Lui's revelations defied widespread expectations that Hong Kong would remain a "silent onlooker in the MeToo movement."[4] Despite Hong Kong's veneer of cosmopolitan modernity, the Chinese Special Administration Region remains deeply patriarchal and misogynistic. The Weinstein scandal was extensively covered in the Hong Kong media, but initial responses from women and women's organizations occurred largely offline, in whispers, behind closed doors, with women sharing guarded disclosures of victimization. Hong Kong women did not seem to think that their disclosures would lead to the downfall of their "Weinsteins." Rather, they feared that perpetrators would not be held to account, and that they, the victim-survivors of sexual harassment and violence, would be blamed as troublemakers and sued for defamation.[5] Thus the initial public reaction to #MeToo and Lui's story was a call to action for parents to protect their children from sexual abuse, rather than naming perpetrators or detailing their acts of sexual harassment and assault.[6]

Nevertheless, Hong Kong women mobilized silently as the #MeToo movement went global. Several editorials in major newspapers discussed the hope that the #MeToo wave would reach Hong Kong and the rest of Asia, where the scourge of such cases is fueled by entrenched patriarchy and relegation of women to the "second" sex.[7] Hong Kong's annual "SlutWalk" march took place in mid-November 2017 and chose as its theme the need to bust rape myths and to highlight the lessons of #MeToo for Hong Kong: that the reality of sexual harassment and abuse is never far from any of us, and we must stop blaming victims.[8]

---

4. Alfred C. M Chan, Editorial, *Why Hong Kong Needs to Join the #MeToo Movement Against Sexual Predators*, So. CHINA MORNING POST, Nov. 28, 2017, https://www.scmp.com/comment/insight-opinion/article/2121880/why-hong-kong-needs-join-metoo-movement-against-sexual

5. Yonden Lhatoo, Editorial, *So many predators and perverts—are there any good men left at all?*, So. CHINA MORNING POST, Nov. 25, 2017, https://www.scmp.com/comment/insight-opinion/article/2121533/so-many-predators-and-perverts-are-there-any-good-men-left. Lhatoo lamented that: "The #MeToo movement is dead in the water here because of the shame and stigma that victims of sexual assault or harassment have to contend with in a traditionally conservative society. What a pity."

6. Angela Baura, *#MeToo victims' campaign highlights need to educate parents and protect children from abuse*, So. CHINA MORNING POST, Nov. 7, 2017, https://www.scmp.com/lifestyle/families/article/2118322/me-too-victims-campaign-highlights-need-educate-parents-and.

7. Editorial, *Turn the tables on those who harass*, So. CHINA MORNING POST, Nov. 26, 2017, https://www.scmp.com/comment/insight-opinion/article/2121577/turn-tables-those-who-harass; Lhatoo, *supra* note 5.

8. Catherine Lai, *SlutWalk protestors to march against sexual violence and victim blaming*, HONG KONG FREE PRESS, Nov. 17, 2017, https://www.hongkongfp.com/2017/11/13/slutwalk-protesters-march-sexual-violence-victim-blaming/.

The first official statement on the issue came from a November 28, 2017, editorial by Dr. Alfred C.M. Chan, Chairman of Hong Kong's Equal Opportunities Commission, a quasi-governmental body[9] which enforces gender-based anti-discrimination law in Hong Kong, including sexual harassment under the Sex Discrimination Ordinance (SDO).[10] In his English media editorial, Chan noted that sexual harassment is a product of a power imbalance. According to Chan, it instills fear in its victims, who feel powerless to speak up and seek help, especially since the subject of sex is taboo in Hong Kong. He gave the example of a district counselor in Hong Kong who was criticized for sharing her account of harassment with online news media as a stunt for gaining greater publicity. Chan called for better social dialogue, government policies, workplace training, and punishment for perpetrators.[11]

In her first interview since her post, Lui shared how her experiences elicited confusing and conflicting emotions. She trusted and respected her coach as an adult mentor and friend whom she never suspected had ulterior motives. The incident left her shocked and in a state of "fight, flight or freeze." During the abuse, she froze and could not respond. Despite the sexual abuse she had endured at the hands of this coach, however, she continued to celebrate her birthday with him annually.

She acknowledged that her continued contact with her coach would appear contradictory to many and raise questions about her "consent" to his actions, her "acceptance" of his behavior, and even, whether the abuse really happened as described. She shared her emotional struggles in attempting to reconcile her respect and trust for her coach with her rational mind while noting that her body would tense up and send distress signals and she would find ways to maintain a physical distance from her perpetrator when they met.

In thanking Maroney for her courage and inspiration, Lui stated that she shared her objectives for coming forward: to raise public awareness of childhood sexual assault, to encourage victims to speak up, and to break the public taboo of talking about sex, which she noted was nothing to be embarrassed or ashamed about. Lui emphasized that she was not ashamed and did not want people's pity but rather hoped that her actions would inspire others to be courageous, just as she had been inspired to be by Maroney. She strongly believed that breaking her silence had freed her, aiding her in a transformative journey from victim to survivor. In the 800 cases handled in the preceding three years by Rainlily, Hong Kong's first rape crisis center, only half of the victims filed a

---

9. Puja Kapai, *Hong Kong's Equal Opportunities Commission: Calling for a New Avatar,* 39(2) HKLJ 339-359 (2009).

10. Cap. 480, Laws of Hong Kong, https://www.elegislation.gov.hk/hk/cap480.

11. Chan, *supra* note 4.

police complaint.[12] This reality reiterates the fundamental drive behind Lui's decision to speak up.

Lui also stressed that any shame should lie with the perpetrator, whom she identified by his initials rather than name. She urged her parents and teachers not to feel responsible, because a person who decides to abuse his power will find a way to take liberties with the trust given to him. Given that over 85 percent of sexually abused children in Hong Kong know their perpetrator,[13] Lui's call to shift societal focus from victim-blaming to their empowerment and to tackle the barriers that prevent children from speaking to trusted adults about sexual abuse resonated strongly with organizations working with victims of sexual abuse, especially children, to turn the tables on the cultural barriers to Hong Kong's receptiveness to #MeToo. Lui's Facebook post garnered thousands of comments and shares.[14] There was an outpouring of support from members of the sports community in Hong Kong and on social media, lauding her bravery.[15] The coach's employers, including the school where the coach trained Lui, suspended the coach pending investigations. The deputy head of the school expressed full support for Lui, lauded her "great courage," "severely condemned" the molester, and expressed sadness that she had to endure this abuse.[16] The revelations also prompted a school crisis response team to meet all track and field members to brief them and to provide counseling support, vowing to protect all pupils from sexual misconduct and promising full cooperation if Lui took legal action.[17]

---

12. Su Xinqi, *Sports associations urged to take action against sexual abuse after Vera Lui's "Me Too" claims*, So. CHINA MORNING POST, Dec. 17, 2017, https://www.scmp.com/news /hong-kong/article/2124622/sports-associations-urged-take-action-against-sexual-abuse-fol lowing. In late December 2017, Hong Kong's cricket associations implemented an anti-sexual harassment code of conduct. *See* Nazvi Careem, *Anti-sexual harassment code for Hong Kong cricket in the wake of hurdler Vera Lui's assault claims*, So. CHINA MORNING POST, Dec. 27, 2017, https://www.scmp.com/sport/hong-kong/article/2125844/anti-sexual-harassment-code -hong-kong-cricket-wake-hurdler-vera-luis.

13. Baura, *supra* note 6.

14. https://www.facebook.com/laiyiului/posts/1613101928711682:0.

15. In the months to come, editorial sections of the SAR's newspapers continued to applaud and encourage survivors of sexual assault to come forward with their stories, despite recognizing the difficult conditions in which victims are doing so. Their calls hailed from the dire need to improve society's awareness around these issues and the opportunity to finally break the culture of silence and stigma attached to such discussions. *See* Letters to the Editor: Katrina Lo, "Sexual abuse victims raise awareness" and Andy Yeung, *Speak out even if allegation is tough to prove*, So. CHINA MORNING POST, Dec. 17, 2018, https://www.scmp.com/comment /letters/article/2124510/letters-editor-december-17-2017.

16. Xinqi & Leung, *supra* note 3.

17. *Id.*

Lui's delayed reporting of her abuse mirrored the usual trajectory of other childhood sex abuse victims. For example, only one out of seven victims of childhood sexual abuse seek help[18] and the ones that do are typically in their twenties and thirties but the abuse was suffered between the ages of eight and twelve.[19] As with many young victims, Lui attested to the challenges she had processing and characterizing the abuse given the conflict between her view of the coach as a trusted person and her body's physiological reaction that proximity to him elicited after the abuse. These emotions seemed impossible for her to reconcile. Despite this behavior being common among victims of abuse, however, Lui's "natural responses" proved detrimental to her case in court.

There is a dire need to create conditions for victim empowerment[20] and to provide them with support rather than focusing on the outing of sexual predators or pursuit of justice for the victim "at all costs." This echoes calls made by several women's rights groups for therapeutic justice in gender-based violence and discrimination to empower victims to make their own choices and to support these choices, without belittling or second-guessing them.

Public Outcry Against Abuse

Lui's revelations sparked a public outcry in Hong Kong, galvanizing many into action, including Hong Kong's first female Chief Executive, Carrie Lam Cheng Yuet-ngor, who expressed her sympathy for Lui's suffering and asked the police commissioner to immediately follow up with the abuse allegations.

This was an unusual step for the Hong Kong police in the absence of a victim filing a police complaint. For Lui, the attention garnered by her case at the highest echelons of Hong Kong's power hierarchy resulted in a police case being filed against the perpetrator without her making a formal complaint. However, she had not set out to turn this into a legal battle. Lam's call to action on behalf of Lui had effectively undermined her autonomy to decide how to seek closure. The prosecution against the coach appeared to proceed without Lui's initiating a complaint. Lam also encouraged other victims of "sexual misconduct" to come forward and seek help, stating that her "government deals seriously with sexual

---

18. Hong Kong Women's Coalition on Equal Opportunities (2013).

19. Raymond Yeung, *Sex abuse reports are 'tip of the iceberg' as few victims go to police, Hong Kong concern groups say amid Vera Lui case*, So. CHINA MORNING POST, Dec. 1, 2017, https://www.scmp.com/news/hong-kong/law-crime/article/2122430/sex-abuse-reports-tip-iceberg-few-victims-go-police-hong.

20. Natalie Chan, *Letter to the Editor: More power to the #MeToo movement*, So. CHINA MORNING POST, Feb. 4, 2017, https://scmp.com/comment/letters/article/2131772/letters-editor-february-4-2018?amp=1.

assaults against children."[21] Secretary for Security John Lee Ka-chiu reiterated this call to victims to speak up and guaranteed support.[22]

Importantly, Lui's revelations also prompted a strong response within the sports industry, with the Sports Federation and Olympic Committee of Hong Kong ("Federation") condemning the molester and vowing to punish him while the Amateur Athletic Association expressed its concern for the coach's violation of integrity and ethics.[23] The Federation revealed that three weeks prior to Lui's revelations, it had collaborated with the International Olympic Committee to develop a tool kit to guide sporting associations on how to form policies to prevent sexual harassment and assault against athletes.[24] Over seventy of Lui's fellow athletes jointly called on the government and sports associations to create stronger protections against sexual abuse, particularly for young athletes.[25] They demanded a transparent system that held perpetrators accountable for their actions and sent a clear message about the consequences of breaching anti-sexual harassment policies. These calls prompted the Federation and EOC to announce a collaboration to explore innovative approaches to train Hong Kong's seventy-five sports organizations and to encourage engagement in EOC surveys to track the extent of sexual harassment in the sector.[26]

---

21. Xinqi & Leung, *supra* note 3.

22. Alice Wu, Editorial, *Brave Vera Lui brings Hong Kong into the #MeToo campaign against sexual assault*, So. CHINA MORNING POST, https://www.scmp.com/comment /insight-opinion/article/2122483/brave-vera-lui-brings-hong-kong-metoo-campaign-against.

23. *Id.*

24. The toolkit was officially launched on November 3, 2017, three weeks prior to Lui's post. Although the toolkit was said to be launched under the auspices of the sports federation, its press release refers instead to the International Olympic Committee, which officially launched the toolkit to assist International Sports Federations and National Olympic Committees to better safeguard athletes against abuse. The toolkit was launched by HRH Prince Feisal, IOC Member and Chair of the IOC prevention of harassment and abuse in sport (PHAS) working group, at the Association of National Olympic Committees (ANOC) General Assembly in Prague, Czech Republic, by HRH Prince Feisal. The toolkit is available at, https://hub .olympic.org/safeguarding/#_ga=2.209685906.1220913992.1572419894-609798683 .1572419894.

25. Peace Chiu, *More than 70 Hong Kong athletes call for better protection against sexual abuse, especially for young sportspeople*, So. CHINA MORNING POST, Dec. 4, 2017, https://www .scmp.com/news/hong-kong/law-crime/article/2122823/over-70-hong-kong-athletes-call -more-protection-against.

26. Xinqi, *supra*, note 12. In late December, Hong Kong's cricket associations joined hands to implement an anti-sexual harassment code of conduct. *See* Nazvi Careem, *Anti-sexual harassment code for Hong Kong cricket in the wake of hurdler Vera Lui's assault claims*, So. CHINA MORNING POST, Dec. 27, 2017, https://www.scmp.com/sport/hong-kong/article/2125844 /anti-sexual-harassment-code-hong-kong-cricket-wake-hurdler-vera-luis.

That same day as Lui's revelations, Ma Fung-kwok, a member of Hong Kong's Legislative Council who represents the sports sector, shared that he received an anonymous letter detailing sexual assault allegations against another coach, prompting him to make inquiries with the Hong Kong Jockey Club ("HKJC"). According to the HKJC, an internal investigation found that an instructor on its Junior Equestrian Team used "sexually explicit language in the course of his duties" and had been fired.[27]

The Backlash and Its Resistance

Lui was widely lauded on social media as a hero and a role model,[28] and credited in the mainstream media with bringing Hong Kong into the #MeToo era. Nonetheless, there were voices of suspicion, who questioned her failure to come forward earlier or make a police report, her inaction in resisting the coach's inappropriate touching, and her decision to continue to meet him afterward. This was the very second-guessing of her choices Lui had alluded to in describing the need to change the public discourse from one of blame—attributed to her, her parents, or her school—to one where the responsibility is placed with the abuser.

As an expression of solidarity with all victims, a few days after Lui's account was published, twelve women's rights NGOs,[29] officially launched #MeTooHK in an online petition.[30] Entitled, *Stop Rubbing Salt in the Wound, Support Survivors, Break the Silence and Respect Choices*, the petition highlighted Hong Kong's toxic culture of victim-blaming. The petition described the cultural context that stigmatizes women for such experiences, implicating their "chastity," which has significant consequences for their prospects for romantic or marital relationships but also leaves them carrying a burden of shame imposed on them by society despite their being the ones who were wronged.

Launched on November 25, 2017, on United Nations International Day for the Elimination of Violence Against Women, the petition called for respect for victims' choices and for recognition of the power dynamics, social stigma,

---

27. Xinqi & Leung, *supra* note 3.

28. Lui garnered 47,000 responses on her Facebook page. Editorial, *From #MeToo to #Respect*, Chinese University of Hong Kong Updates, http://www.iso.cuhk.edu.hk/english/publications/CUHKUPDates/article.aspx?articleid=2151.

29. The petition was led by the Association Concerning Sexual Violence Against Women, the only NGO in Hong Kong providing a one-stop service to survivors of rape and sexual abuse.

30. Available at https://docs.google.com/forms/d/e/1FAIpQLSetp8xsxqb6w3S8wWgw-OjzBvQksnAbYetlxIjxdwAvvn_Sug/formResponse.

and pressures that might explain why victims choose to remain silent and not pursue formal legal actions against perpetrators. The petition sought to prompt Hong Kong's own conversation around sexual harassment rather than to replicate the trajectory of the #MeToo movement globally, which was perceived as focused on a "call-out" culture to bring sexual predators down publicly.[31]

Hong Kong's own #MeToo backlash[32] was crystallized with a prominent political commentator, Chip Tsao, posting a selfie with a #MeToo sign proclaiming himself a victim of sexual assault, alleging that he was sexually harassed by his kindergarten teacher who once touched his cheek without his consent. Though opining that his alleged perpetrator was likely now a grandma, nonetheless, stating that as a worshiper of "Western" culture,[33] he felt empowered to demonize her as his Weinstein simply by declaring "his truth" on Facebook with the #MeToo caption.[34]

Encouraged by Tsao's attack on #MeToo, naysayers commented on the dangers of trial by social media. In particular, they attacked the strategy used to bring perpetrators to justice, arguing that simply holding up a sign with the words "#MeToo" carries the potential to tarnish reputations and impact men's careers and ruin their lives.

Drawing on gendered stereotypes about victims of assault, commentators urged victims with "real" complaints to file their reports with police, questioned victims' decisions not to report assaults for fear of experiencing secondary

---

31. This is likely an erroneous perception and the result of the movement's revival in Hollywood despite its initiation by Tarana Burke over a decade ago. In Burke's view, the movement is not about calling out high-profile perpetrators but rather, about cultivating conditions for empathy and emotional support for victims of abuse.

32. Desmond Chan, *Why #MeToo must be used with care*, SO. CHINA MORNING POST, Feb. 11, 2018, https://www.scmp.com/comment/letters/article/2132737/letters-editor -february-11-2018.

33. Many have rejected the notion that sexual harassment is a Western phenomenon with little relevance in Asia. *See* Lotus Ruan, *To call sexual harassment a western phenomenon is presumptuous and simply untrue*, HONG KONG FREE PRESS, Oct. 19, 2017, https://www.hong kongfp.com/2017/10/19/call-sexual-harassment-western-phenomenon-presumptuous-sim ply-untrue/. The piece was a response to the Chinese state's media assertion that the Weinstein affair demonstrated that Chinese cultural and traditional values protected women against inappropriate sexual behavior, unlike in the West. Ruan notes that the statistical incidence of sexual harassment experienced by women in different sectors is evidence enough of the widespread prevalence of sexual harassment, which is experienced by 53-70 percent of survey respondents across diverse settings: 53.5 percent of females on the Beijing subway; 70 percent of Guangzhou female factory workers; and 60 percent of female college students; further, 22.7 percent of Chinese males admit they have raped a woman.

34. Alex Lo, *Backlash in Hong Kong against the "Me Too" campaign*, SO. CHINA MORNING POST, Dec. 5, 2017, https://www.scmp.com/comment/insight-opinion/article/2122858 /backlash-hong-kong-against-me-too-campaign.

trauma, and stated that #MeToo was the "[d]umbest movement so far of the century." These comments reinforced the idea that the victims' failure to file a timely complaint was reflective of their ulterior motives in leveling the accusations through a "spurious" movement that "cost" them nothing. Other comments placed the onus for self-protection against assaults on victims.

Responding to these criticisms, supporters of the #MeToo movement noted that women fear the impact on loved ones when they report to the police,[35] that they will not be believed in court, and must open intimate aspects of their life to public scrutiny. Thus, sharing stories online provides an opportunity for catharsis without the same negative consequences. #MeToo signals women's turn to be heard, in their own voice, presenting authentic accounts undistorted by legal processes that constrain their narratives and calls to action. Supporters called for sympathy and trust in those who took courage to speak their truths and warned that thoughtless criticism might cause victims to further retreat, further isolating and driving them deeper into their anguish as they watch their worst fears about breaking their silence materialize.[36]

Netizens were also critical of the ignorance that Tsao and his ilk portrayed in ignoring the abuse of power inherent in harassment cases, which has become entrenched and gone unchecked for too long. The fact that the #MeToo movement has global engagement, across gender, race, class, religion, and countries is demonstrative of the pervasiveness of structural forces which empower perpetrators of abuse. Critics of the movement were quick to deploy arguments about fairness, due process, and justice before the law, which they deemed sacrificed to trial-by-social-media as a result of #MeToo.[37] These comments reveal male anxieties that, if this trend were to proliferate, they could easily suffer consequences regardless of their actual guilt.[38]

Commentators fearing a potential #MeToo "lynch mob" ignore the reality of what happens in China when women do come forward with allegations of harassment. In China, for example, as well as in India, those accused of assault and rape have successfully turned the tables on their accusers, suing them for

---

35. Given that a large number of victims know their perpetrator and often times, they are part of the family or extended family network. *See* Baura, *supra* note 6.

36. Lee Wing Yan, Letter to the Editor: *Show respect for hurdling champion*, So. CHINA MORNING POST, Dec. 9, 2017, https://www.scmp.com/comment/letters/article/2123523/letters-editor-december-9-2017; Maggie Tung, Letter to the Editor: *Mistrust will Silence Victims of Sexual Abuse*, So. CHINA MORNING POST, Dec. 8, 2017, https://www.scmp.com/comment/letters/article/2123487/letters-editor-december-8-2017.

37. Chan, *supra* note 32.

38. Lo, *supra* note 34.

defamation.[39] Thus, arguments about fairness and the burden of proof need to be framed against the broader context of a culture where patriarchy and gender inequality threaten fair process due to the personal and professional costs victims bear in coming forward.

In December 2017, the former "2015 Miss Hong Kong" beauty queen, Louisa Mak, came forward sharing multiple incidents where her breasts were groped without consent. [40] She was attacked on Hong Kong social media for seeking attention, based on the "triviality" of her experience of sexual assault, which some remarked she should be used to, given her line of work. Some insinuated that by entering the beauty pageant, she had "asked for" such attention—which are part of the "perks" of being a beauty queen.

Thus, by December 2017, while some women had shared the #MeToo hashtag along with their experiences, #MeToo in Hong Kong had also led people to question the "victim-worthiness" of certain accounts given the wide discrepancy between the "salacious" accusations coming out of Hollywood and what were seen as fairly 'trivial' incidents. The backlash and these attitudes have impacted people's participation in and receptivity to the movement.

---

39. In one such case, M.J. Akbar, former Indian junior foreign minister of the Modi government and now a leading editor at an Indian newspaper, has hired a team of ninety-seven lawyers for a case against his accuser, Priya Ramani, alleging criminal defamation for her accusations against Akbar. In China, similar tactics have been deployed to silence victims, who have been slapped with defamation suits. In the case of Zhu Jun, the Chinese television anchor, Xianzi, his accuser has countersued him for infringement of "personality rights" in an effort not to back down against the double-edged threats faced by her at the hands of patriarchy but also, state authorities who actively sought to dissuade her due to the positive image enjoyed by Zhu. Xianzi has faced numerous hurdles including a social media blackout and other challenges in pursuing justice for herself. This is against the broader context of the dearth of legal claims of this nature in China. Only two cases on the public record have ever been pursued against perpetrators of sexual harassment in the workplace as compared with hundreds of countersuits that have been brought by men accused of sexual harassment against their accusers. This demonstrates clearly the power of the law but also, how male perpetrators feel empowered to use the full force of the law to threaten and muzzle their accusers, rare as it is to have them speak out. *See* Ananth Krishnan, *In India and China, #MeToo has much further to go*, So. China Morning Post, Oct. 19, 2018, https://www.scmp.com/news/china/society/article/2169218/india-and-china-metoo -has-much-further-go. *See also, China's #MeToo movement takes a legal turn as woman applies to counter sue television star Zhu Jun*, So. China Morning Post, Sep. 27, 2018, https://www .scmp.com/news/china/politics/article/2165974/chinas-metoo-movement-takes-legal-turn -woman-applies-counter-sue.

40. Chiu, *supra* note 25.

Alternative Approaches: "Now What?"

In mid-December 2017, four women from diverse backgrounds organized a forum for women to share harassment stories. They encouraged women to respond immediately when they are harassed to signal to perpetrators that their conduct is unacceptable.[41] The organizers also encouraged the broader community to ask, "Now what?" after #MeToo—how do we respond? However, expecting victims to initiate such steps in the immediate aftermath of sexual abuse or harassment has elicited different reactions, particularly given the victim's right to control her narrative. This approach may lack sensitivity toward victims, blaming them for their post-attack inaction to hold the perpetrator responsible. As Lui and numerous other commentators point out, the only person to blame in such circumstances is the perpetrator of the abuse, never the victim.

In the months since #MeToo kicked off in Hong Kong, there has been much discussion about the Hong Kong-specific scourge of sexual harassment. People expressed uncertainties about whether their experiences amounted to sexual assault or harassment, protections they were entitled to, and anxieties about a potential "witch-hunt" of men or a backlash of shunning women to avoid being caught up in the #MeToo "mania." NGOs providing support to sexual assault survivors, however, saw a doubling of reports of sexual harassment and assault. Clearly, #MeToo was instrumental in prompting victims to speak out and to seek help, reigniting a desire for healing and understanding.

A second "Now What" forum focused on a theme that is gaining momentum in line with UN Women's HeforShe Male Champions of Change initiative: enlisting men as part of strategies for change.[42] Further, data from University of Hong Kong (HKU) students using a new app to educate about harassment

---

41. Rachel Leung, *After #MeToo comes Now What? as women host forum to push for change in Hong Kong community*, So. China Morning Post, Dec. 16, 2017, https://www.scmp.com/news/hong-kong/community/article/2124484/after-metoo-comes-now-what-women-host-forum-push-change.

42. Keshia Hannam, *#MeToo movement needs men, say women, plus three ways to respond to sexual harassment*, So. China Morning Post, Jan. 10, 2018, https://www.scmp.com/lifestyle/article/2127590/hong-kongs-metoo-movement-needs-men-say-women-plus-three-ways-respond, discussing the need for male buy-in into the conversation around preventing and addressing sexual harassment. The forum also discussed three response strategies: identify sexual harassment, respond to it, and end it; and Lauren James, *After #MeToo comes Now What? as women host forum to push for change in Hong Kong community*, So. China Morning Post, Mar. 8, 2018, https://www.scmp.com/lifestyle/article/2135943/gender-equality-hong-kong-metoo-milestones-and-why-theres-still-long-way, discussing their formalized male allies program given the opportune moment presented by the #MeToo movement to harness men's attention, particularly those who are committed to gender diversity, equality and changing mindsets.

found that one in six women and one in ten men experienced sexual harass-ment.[43] Therefore, the need to engage both genders equally in prevention and strategies for redress was vital. The data also showed that 55 percent of women who experienced sexual harassment chose not to report it while 75 percent believed that pre-formulated response strategies to harassment would greatly bolster their confidence and prevent harassers from repeating such behavior. The surveyed group believed strongly in the rehabilitative and preventive effect of responding immediately to the perpetrator.

The Women's Foundation, a Hong Kong charity focused on advanc-ing women's rights and leadership, has hosted panel discussions on how the #MeToo momentum in Hong Kong could be translated into tangible progress for Hong Kong women. Although Hong Kong sexual harassment victims' expe-riences and challenges are distinct, harassment remains entrenched in structural and attitudinal manifestations worldwide. Gender stereotypes, unequal power dynamics, unconscious bias, and fears about reporting due to structural and sys-temic barriers prevent victims from speaking out.[44] These discussions focused on examining #MeToo's impact in Hong Kong and specifically, strategies to pro-mote gender equality, with more women in leadership, as role models and to take part in decision-making processes.[45]

Finally, another event focused on experiences of #MeToo among Hong Kong's ethnic minorities,[46] noting cultural challenges that compel silence among many survivors due to the stigma and shame attached to sex for women of ethnic minority backgrounds.

Despite few public accusations in Hong Kong, the #MeToo movement remains alive. For example, Lui's revelations rocked the sports sector and led to "#Churchtoo" taking hold in Hong Kong, with one woman accusing a pastor of inappropriate sexual conduct with churchgoers, male and female, on social

---

43. P-SHOC App, part of the Prevention of Sexual Harassment Online Course (P-SHOC), University of Hong Kong, http://teli.hku.hk/apps/.

44. Lauren James, note 42, quoting Fiona Knott, CEO of The Women's Foundation.

45. This assumes that in general, women are less likely to hold gendered or harmful ste-reotypes and exhibit leadership qualities which do not see them take advantage of less powerful individuals around them. However, research does not bear this out.

46. *#MeToo, Now What? Desi*, Eaton House, March 2018. The panel featured a diverse group of women, including three ethnic minority Hong Kong women, two qualified counselors and the author, who has researched and written on issues impacting Hong Kong's ethnic minori-ties. *See generally*, Puja Kapai, *The Status of Ethnic Minorities in Hong Kong 1997-2014* (2015), http://www.law.hku.hk/ccpl/pub/EMreport.html; Puja Kapai *Minority Women: A Struggle for Equal Protection Against Domestic Violence, in* FEMINIST CONSTITUTIONALISM: GLOBAL PERSPECTIVES (Beverley Baines et al., eds., 2012); and Puja Kapai, *Bringing Intersectionality Home: Delivering Contextualised Justice in Gender Based-Violence in Hong Kong, in* GENDER, VIOLENCE AND THE STATE IN ASIA 148 (Amy Barrow & Joy L. Chia eds., 2016).

media. The accused pastor admitted his transgressions and other pastors are now being investigated. Further, in the recent past, some church leaders have been held accountable for abuses through the legal process.[47] A Hong Kong Christian Council survey of its parishioners found at least another fifty-five cases of this nature, with one in five involving rape or attempted rape and half the perpetrators were church leaders or workers.[48]

These revelations have prompted calls to hold religious leaders accountable for their abuses and to end a history of secrecy, which suppressed such accounts to protect churches' reputations, drawing on biblical texts to persuade victims to show compassion and forgive perpetrators.[49] The reluctance to believe victims and to dissuade them from tarnishing the church's reputation or hurting their community of church-goers, represents an urgent call to action for church leaders to create safer environments for all congregants and workers.

Some schools, corporate entities, and NGOs in the private and public sectors have begun to implement or reexamine policies for handling sexual harassment. Leveraging internal and external resources, these communities are streamlining processes for handling sexual harassment reports and instituting training for relevant personnel so that they are equipped with the skills required to take necessary action in such circumstances. There are, of course, many others who do not see recent events as having anything to do with them.

Although #MeToo has certainly had an impact in raising awareness and social consciousness around sexual harassment and prompted reflection in Hong Kong about culture and workplace dynamics, and cases filed are being investigated, it has not mirrored the avalanche of allegations we have witnessed globally. This is not to say that the problem of sexual harassment and abuse is not as rife here as elsewhere. Numerous studies have confirmed that one in five women experience sexual harassment in the workplace whereas among schools and university settings, half of the female students have encountered sexual

---

47. SCMP Reporter, *Ex-priest found guilty of molesting altar boy*, So. China Morning Post, January 28, 2003, https://www.scmp.com/article/404909/ex-priest-found-guilty-molest ing-altar-boy. *See also*, Bishop Joseph Zen, *Statement regarding the case of former priest Michael Lau*, https://www.catholic.org.hk/document/notice-elau.html.

48. Editorial: *Churches need to act on claims of abuse*, So. China Morning Post, June 30, 2018, https://www.scmp.com/comment/insight-opinion/article/2153195/churches -need-act-claims-abuse#comments. *See also*, Christy Leung, *With sexual harassment, Hong Kong churches face twofold problem, pastors and concern groups say*, So. China Morning Post, June 25, 2018, https://www.scmp.com/news/hong-kong/hong-kong-law-and-crime/article /2152284/sexual-harassment-hong-kong-churches-face.

49. Alfred C. M. Chan, Editorial: *Silenced in God's name: sexual harassment at Hong Kong churches must be stopped*, Hong Kong Free Press, https://www.hongkongfp.com /2018/07/03/silenced-gods-name-sexual-harassment-hong-kong-churches-must-stopped/.

misconduct.[50] In nearly every industry examined thus far by the EOC, more than 50 percent of female respondents reported experiencing sexual harassment, with respondents in the food and beverage industry hit hardest at a rate of nearly 80 percent.[51]

Underlying these findings is the prevalence of gender inequities in Hong Kong society, including the absence of women in senior leadership positions in both the public and private sector, the gender pay gap, lack of family-friendly workplace policies, and unconscious gender bias impacting the advancement and leadership trajectories of women. The root cause of pervasive gender inequality remains the central target in terms of the push for dismantling patriarchy.[52] However, there is also a distinct cultural dimension to the challenge of dealing with sexual abuse and violence in Hong Kong given the narrative reserved for victims of this type of abuse.

Victim-blaming and revictimization by way of secondary trauma are by far the greatest challenges to any gainful impact of the #MeToo movement in Hong Kong. To seek help, a victim must face the prospect of being blamed for her attack, by being in a place she should not have been at, at a time she should not have been out, doing something she should not have been doing, and wearing something she should not have been wearing. Not only during but also post-attack—in essence, reinforcing rape myths and victim stereotypes. The culprits contributing to this toxic culture unfortunately include the police, prosecutors, and judges within the legal system who act as the primary deterrent for most victims but the culprits also can include friends, colleagues and family members, who often second-guess victims' accounts and choices.

The harsh reality of this was apparent when news broke about attempts to dissuade Hong Kong film director, Sharon Lam Suk-ching, from filing a police report when she was attacked by a Hainan Airlines trainee pilot, who climbed through her eighteenth-floor hotel balcony and attempted to rape her. Lam fought him off and escaped but found that on reporting the attack to the police, she was advised to settle with the attacker because of her unfamiliarity with Mainland Chinese law. When she persisted, she was met with a representative of

---

50. *Break the Silence: Territory-wide Study on Sexual Harassment of University Students in Hong Kong*, https://www.eoc.org.hk/EOC/GraphicsFolder/InforCenter/Research/content .aspx?ItemID=16213.

51. Recent research studies commissioned by the Equal Opportunities Commission into various service sectors affirm this trend. *See* https://www.eoc.org.hk/eoc/graphicsfolder /inforcenter/research/default.aspx.

52. Syed Munir Khasru, *After #MeToo Comes Now What? As Women Host Forum to Push for Change in Hong Kong Community*, So. CHINA MORNING POST, Jan. 25, 2018, https:// www.scmp.com/comment/insight-opinion/article/2130347/metoo-momentum-shows-theres -much-more-do-gender-equality.

Hainan Airlines at the police station and advised against pressing charges given the high costs of training a pilot. If the suggestion that her experience was trivial, not recognized as attempted rape, or very difficult to prove under Mainland laws was not enough to dissuade her, she was told that she could potentially face assault charges herself for fighting off the attacker. In essence, the suggestion was that a more effective approach might have been to let herself be raped to maintain a "strong case."[53] Although this example concerns experiences in China, Hong Kong has certainly demonstrated its own culture of victim-blaming.

In 2013, then Secretary for Security Lai Ting-lok came under fire for suggesting that women should consider drinking less and consider having a known male companion drop them home if they are out late in order to avoid being raped.[54] In a city where bystanders are reluctant to intervene[55] and circumstances where witnesses are unlikely to come forward, the case against the accused boils down to the word of the victim against that of the accused.

Hong Kong has legal protections, both civil and criminal, against sexual harassment, abuse, and violence. The Sex Discrimination Ordinance (SDO) prohibits discrimination on the basis of sex and includes sexual harassment or a hostile work environment as a form of sex discrimination. The Hong Kong Equal Opportunities Commission (EOC) carries the mandate as the city's equality body to receive complaints under this law and parties are required to attempt a conciliatory process before the complaint is pursued in court. However, the model has been criticized for entrenching the power imbalance between perpetrators and victims and for forcing victims to directly confront their abusers. On the other hand, the criminal law contains protections against sexual assault, rape, battery, and vaginal penetration with the penis. However, cases seldom end up in court on criminal charges due to the lack of gender sensitivity among police and the actions of lawyers and judges. The legal protections impose a high burden on complainants, making it all the more challenging for victims to achieve justice after battling not only with the sexual assault or harassment but also attacks on their character and choices.

53. Alice Wu, *Attempt to Cover up Sharon Lam's attempted rape should silence #MeToo's critics forever*, So. CHINA MORNING POST, July 30, 2018, https://www.scmp.com/comment/insight-opinion/hong-kong/article/2157119/attemp-cover-sharon-lams-attempted-rape-should?aid=190131336&sc_llid=9182&sc_src=email_2307754&sc-uid=zOohmZYMew.

54. Phila Siu and Lai Ying-Kit, *Security chief Lai Tung-kwok denies blaming rape victims*, So. CHINA MORNING POST, May 15, 2013, https://www.scmp.com/news/hong-kong/article/1238303/security-chief-lai-tung-kwok-denies-blaming-rape-victims.

55. Peter Kammerer, *Proof that Hongkongers are still struggling with the #MeToo movement: I groped a woman by mistake, but no one said anything*, So. CHINA MORNING POST, Oct. 8, 2018, https://www.scmp.com/comment/insight-opinion/united-states/article/2167432/proof-hongkongers-are-still-struggling-metoo.

Case managers and judges have been found largely unsympathetic to the point of dissuading victims from taking their complaints forward, traumatizing victims due to their lack of gender-sensitive perspectives and processes. Never has this been more apparent than when the magistrate in Lui's case second-guessed the choices Lui made as a victim. He suggested that Lui's recent characterization of the incident as sexual abuse did not match her account where she described her positioning on the bed while being massaged, her responses and reactions at different stages of the massage, and her subsequent conduct toward the coach. The magistrate deployed rape myths describing the "perfect" victim to benchmark Lui's behavior to test the veracity of her account. The judge concluded that Lui's account of the incident as sexual abuse simply could not stand factually beyond all reasonable doubt. The judge reasoned that by Lui continuing to lay there while the coach allegedly transgressed her bodily integrity and by maintaining an amicable relationship with him thereafter on subsequent occasions, she had not objected to the massage. His remarks suggested that Lui was aware that this was a massage for the purposes stated, and that there was nothing untoward in the circumstances.

The trajectory of the few public #MeToo stories in Hong Kong does not bode well for the future of the movement, although it has certainly enlightened the community to the brutality of a Hong Kong culture that undermines and suppresses the cries of children who are sexually abused. The outcome and the discourse deployed in Lui's case serves as a wake-up call for Hong Kong's legal system, actors engaged on the front lines of complaints, and the broader community to create conditions that are necessary to better support victims who come forward, to take an intersectional lens to reflect on the impact of different lived experiences and factors triggering unique vulnerabilities, and to develop a substantive model for equal protection against sexual assault for different groups of victims.

Hong Kong's #MeToo owes its youth for shouldering the heavy burdens that the global movement has placed on them, to come out, contend with cultural shame inflicted on victims of sexual abuse, and to challenge entrenched patriarchy and misogyny in a Confucian context which expects obedience, loyalty, and respect for persons in authority. Whether Hong Kong will honor their bravery and resilience in the face of the brutality shown by the court of public opinion and the court of law by addressing these challenges head on, remains to be seen.

CHAPTER 26

"Uncomfortable Courage (불편한 용기)": Trials and Triumphs of South Korea's #MeToo Movement

Yukyong Choe[1] and Jenny Jian Jang[2]

Introduction

South Korea's rising feminism and organizing against sexual harassment and violence were nurtured and inspired by a number of events, different but familiar to those that had fostered the Harvey Weinstein scandal an ocean away. The Korean movement began, first because of highly publicized acts of violence against women in 2016,[3] and then through collective participation in large scale "candlelight rallies" in 2016 and 2017, where women demanded the impeachment and ouster of Korea's President, Park Geun-hye. These protests allowed women to express themselves and to understand the power of their collective voices to change the status quo. And, when Korea experienced its most publicized "#MeToo" case in 2018, the accuser was a highly respected Korean prosecutor. Korean society was shocked, recognizing that if this powerful woman was harassed and unable to speak out about her abuse, this could happen to anyone.

With women's issues at the forefront of public discourse, Korean women have become emboldened in their response to sexual harassment and violence. Now, more than ever, through social media and broadcast news platforms, women have developed a collective, feminist consciousness. Yet still, Korean law regulating sexual misconduct has stymied the success of this movement. While

---

1. Senior Research Fellow, Korea Legislation Research Institute, Seoul, Korea.

2. Berkeley Center on Comparative Equality and Anti-discrimination Law Intern.

3. Steven Borowiec, *A Woman's Slaying in Seoul's tony Gangnam district stirs emotions in South Korea*, L.A. TIMES, May 21, 2016, https://www.latimes.com/world/asia/la-fg-south-korea-woman-killed-20160521-snap-story.html.

the Korean legislature has attempted to address the problems by amending Korean law, these reforms have had mixed success. As a result, the social movement in Korea against sexual harassment and violence remains an uphill battle.

The Origins of the Korean #MeToo Movement

On May 17, 2016, a young woman using a public restroom in Gangnam, an upscale Seoul neighborhood, was stabbed to death by a male suspect who admitted to police after his arrest that he had chosen a woman as his victim because he had felt "ignored and belittled" by women his whole life. The glass subway entrance closest to the murder was soon covered with notes from women expressing solidarity with the victim and numerous rallies were held protesting violence against women.[4] "Through the summer and fall of 2016, a consciousness born of outrage spread among South Korean women and girls, dovetailing with the mass Candlelight Movement that would bring down President Park Geun-hye."[5]

Starting in October 2016, women joined men, in months of well-organized, peaceful candlelight rallies calling for the impeachment of President Park Geun-hye. In May 2017, the Korean Constitutional Court finally impeached the president on corruption charges. This political triumph from large scale mobilization of Korea's citizens to promote civil democracy emboldened and inspired the Korean feminism movement.

Also in October 2016, Tak Soo-jung, an employee at a publishing house, publicly accused her former poetry teacher of sexual abuse and encouraged other women to speak out on social media. Women's basic demands—for physical safety, equal opportunity, and freedom from oppressive standards of femininity—were shared and discussed widely.[6]

These events: outrage over women's murders, social media sharing of sexual harassment, and successful protests against political corruption, catalyzed the #MeToo movement in Korea and fundamentally changed the conversation of sexual harassment and violence—now an extremely visible topic in national media.

In January 2018, prosecutor Seo Ji-Hyun accused her superior Ahn Tae-Geun of groping her during a funeral for a colleague's father in 2010. When Seo immediately reported the abuse to senior prosecutors, the Ministry of

---

4. E. Tammy Kim, *#Korea Too*, N.Y. Review of Books, Mar. 7, 2019, https://www.nybooks.com/issues/2019/03/07/.

5. *Ibid.*

6. *Ibid.*

Justice failed to take action against her perpetrator and instead punished her with career setbacks. Ahn denied the allegations of sexual assault and any role in pulling strings to demote Seo.

Unlike in years past, however, the public support of Seo's account was overwhelming. On January 29, 2018, Seo spoke out in a live interview aired by JTBC, a prominent broadcast news network. On national television, she revealed the sinister underbelly of the Ministry and how power asymmetries rooted in patriarchy perpetuated a harmful workplace culture. She explained that even for a decorated and esteemed prosecutor like herself, mustering the courage to expose her perpetrator took nearly eight years. She feared retaliation and grew cynical of the ministry's inaction. Magnified media coverage bolstered the public backlash against the perpetrator. Following Seo's interview, JTBC produced hundreds of reports and broadcast segments that further investigated the incident—placing great pressure on Ahn and the Ministry. Seo's powerful account inspired the nation at large to denounce Ahn and demand his resignation. Seo's public announcement is largely considered the spark that set flame to the #MeToo movement in Korea.

In February 2018, Choi Young-Mi published a poem titled "Monster," in the *Hwanghae Review* literary journal, and it went viral. "Virtually every Korean news outlet described the poem as an accusation of molestation, coerced sex, and harassment ("He touches every young girl he sees") against the poet Ko Un, now eighty-five and long considered Korea's best hope for a Nobel Prize in Literature."[7] Ko Un filed a defamation suit against Choi Young-Mi, claiming nearly $1 million in damages caused by the poem's publication and Choi's subsequent media appearances.

The momentum of the Korean #MeToo movement reached its peak in March 2018. JTBC broke a story that exposed presidential hopeful Ahn Hee-Jung as a sexual predator. Kim Ji-Eun, Ahn's secretary, recounted multiple accounts of rape by her employer—four times from June 2017 to February 2018.[8] At the time, Ahn served as District Governor in Chung-nam and was the Korean Democratic Party's frontrunning presidential candidate. Kim explained that as his direct employee, she felt she was not in a position to deny or stop his abuse. Not only was Ahn her employer, he was the face of the majority party. Ahn had political clout he could use to intimidate Kim, end her career, and place her in social exile. Like Seo and numerous victims of power-driven sexual assault, Kim feared potential retaliation and did not resist the assault. Kim's

---

7. *Ibid.*

8. *Prominent South Korean politician resigns after rape allegations, asks for forgiveness*, THE STRAITS TIMES, Mar. 6, 2018, https://www.straitstimes.com/asia/east-asia/prominent-south-korean-politician-to-step-down-after-rape-allegations.

public allegations on television moved the nation to condemn the once-revered politician. The Democratic Party immediately expelled Ahn, and the party's chairwoman issued an official apology to Kim and the public. The very next day, Ahn resigned as governor and announced his retirement from public life after admitting to the sexual misconduct.

Following these brave reports, Korean news platforms continued to provide an outlet for victims of sexual harassment and violence. Notably, journalist Sohn Suk-hee produced a segment on JTBC that shared live-streamed #MeToo stories of five different women. Between January and April 2018, JTBC reported around 280 pieces on #MeToo incidents.

In May 2018, on the two-year anniversary of the Gangnam murder of a young woman, 15,000 people rallied in central Seoul to demand government accountability on sex crimes. "It was among the largest women-centered protests in Korean history and was soon repeated and eclipsed—some 60,000 people showed up for a follow-up rally in early July, and the protests have continued, nicknamed 불편한 용기, or 'Uncomfortable Courage.'"[9]

By the end of 2018, a year after the Harvey Weinstein revelations, Korean media and political culture, which had responded to those candlelight vigils against corruption, also began listening to women's experiences of sexual violence and demanding retribution for sexual abuse.[10] Even more encouraging, by fall 2019, the Korean Supreme Court, as discussed later, had also clearly heard the message of #MeToo.

Difficulties of the Korean Legal Framework on Sexual Violence

So, as Korean culture began to give women a voice to describe sexual abuse, was Korean law ready to address their calls for justice?

Korean criminal law codifies many acts of sexual harassment and violence but that does not mean that acts of sexual violence are often prosecuted or won.

South Korean Criminal Code Article 297 [Rape] establishes that "a person who, by means of violence or intimidation, has sexual intercourse with another shall be punished by imprisonment for a limited term of at least three years."

---

9. Kim, *supra*, note 4.

10. Anna Fifield, *Highflying South Korean politician quits after being accused of raping secretary*, WASH. POST, Mar. 5, 2018, https://www.washingtonpost.com/world/high-flying -south-korean-politician-quits-after-being-accused-of-raping-secretary/2018/03/06/04c23130 -20ff-11e8-a589-763893265565_story.html.

Article 298 [**Imitative Rape**] states "a person who, through violence or intimidation, commits an indecent act on another shall be punished by imprisonment for not more than ten years or by a fine not exceeding 15 million won."

Article 303 [**Sexual Intercourse by Abuse of Occupational Authority, etc.**] establishes that "a person who, by means of fraud or by the threat of authority, has sexual intercourse with another who is under his/her protection or supervision for his/her business, employment or other relationship, shall be punished by imprisonment for not more than five years, or by a fine not exceeding 15 million won."

Act on Special Cases Concerning the Punishment, etc. of Sexual Crimes Article 10 [**Indecent Acts through Abuse of Occupational Authority**] states "a person who, through fraudulent means or by a threat of force, commits an indecent act on another person who is under his/her guardianship or supervision by reason of his/her business, employment, or other relationship shall be punished by imprisonment for not more than two years or by a fine not exceeding five million."

While punishment of abuse of authority is repeatedly codified, the Korean legal framework still fails survivors by establishing a high burden necessary to prove rape. The court applies an extremely narrow interpretation of rape and harassment, as offenses of "violence or intimidation." The perpetrator's actions must "make the victim's resistance impossible or remarkably difficult" in order to constitute sexual assault. Further, the burden rests on the victims to show they "actively" resisted their assailant. Therefore, courts deem accounts of victims who deny consent or mildly resist sexual contact insufficient to meet the definition of sexual assault. Under current law, victims who are unable to resist due to intoxication, humiliation, fear for their lives, or retaliation, are left unprotected. Additionally, the law does not consider sexual harassment in the form of sexual humiliation and degradation a criminal offense. Current legislation fails to provide adequate redress for victims of the harmful behavior.

Furthermore, **Criminal Code Article 307** [**Defamation**] (**1**) and **Article 156** [**False Accusation**] allows assailants to countersue victims—with alarming ease—on the grounds of defamation and false accusation, respectively. Korean law recognizes defamation and false accusation as "Crimes Against Reputation." The law punishes individuals who unlawfully harm another person's social reputation. This conception of defamation is problematic for survivors of sexual violence because defamation law does not allow truth as an absolute defense. So long as the perpetrator can prove that the victim: (1) harmed their reputation; (2) published either a true or a false statement of fact; and (3) published the statement with the knowledge that the statements may defame—the perpetrator has a case. The threat of counter lawsuits often prevents victims from speaking

326 The Global #MeToo Movement

their truth in the first place. Defamation suits can tarnish a victim's reputation and credibility, which may expose them to denigrating social shaming.

Courts' rulings on sexual harassment and violence reflect a patriarchal bias. One recent survey shows that less than half of all reported and received cases of sexual violence are prosecuted. Moreover, in only about 40 percent of the prosecuted cases is the defendant actually found guilty.[11] Upon conviction, approximately 38 percent receive a non-deferred probation and a suspended sentence.[12] With the odds stacked against them, victims of sexual violence are discouraged from taking legal action against their perpetrators.

Court Decisions

Several #MeToo cases brought forth by survivors of sexual violence at the beginning of the Korean movement saw great success. The court sentenced former prosecutor Ahn Tae-Gun, accused by Seo Ji-Hyun, to two years in prison during his January 2019 trial.[13] The court assigned prominent film writer and producer Lee Yoon-Taek a six-year sentence in September 2018.[14] Multiple actresses came forth to expose Taek for groping and other predatory behavior. In September 2018, national short track coach Jo Jae-Bum was sentenced to ten months in prison, following multiple allegations of rape brought forth by gold medalist Shim Seok-Hee.[15] And, on February 15, 2019, poet Ko Un lost his defamation suit against Choi Young-Mi, who had suggested in her poem "Monster" that the poet had molested her and others. In its verdict, Seoul Central District Court cited Choi's "detailed and consistent testimonies." "There was no reason to suspect her claims were false."[16]

Nonetheless, not all cases were immediate #MeToo victories. On August 14, 2018, the court acquitted former governor Ahn Hee-Jung of sexual

11. *2018 Judicial Yearbook*, Supreme Court (South Korea), pp. 683-684, 696-697 and pp. 946.-947. https://www.scourt.go.kr/portal/justicesta/JusticestaListAction.work?gubun=10.

12. *2018 Prosecution Yearbook*, Prosecutor Office (South Korea), p.732. https://www.spo.go.kr/site/spo/ex/board/View.do.

13. Suyin Haynes, *How #MeToo Is Taking on a Life of Its Own in Asia*, TIME, Oct. 9, 2018, https://time.com/longform/me-too-asia-china-south-korea/.

14. *South Korean director sentenced for sex assault*, CGTN, Sept. 20, 2018, https://news.cgtn.com/news/3d3d514f34497a4d7a457a6333566d54/share_p.html.

15. Yonhap, *Ex-short track coach sentenced to 10 months in jail for assaulting athletes*, THE KOREA HERALD, Sept. 19, 2018, http://www.koreaherald.com/view.php?ud=2018091900 0527.

16. *Disgraced South Korean poet Ko Un loses defamation suit*, The National, Feb. 15, 2019, https://www.thenational.ae/arts-culture/books/disgraced-south-korean-poet-ko-un-loses-defamation-suit-1.826217.

misconduct. The court cited a lack of evidence on the part of the woman who brought the case to trial, Ahn's secretary, Kim Ji-Eun. The trial court found Governor Ahn not guilty because Korean legislation at the time did not provide criminal punishments for indecent assault or sexual violence-related crimes.[17] Under Korean law, sexual crimes were largely categorized into three parts: (1) non-consensual sexual exchanges by means of violence or intimidation; (2) sexual violence against a minor, who definitionally cannot give consent; and (3) sexual violence in the workplace.

The court noted a gap in this framework, when an employer's non-consensual sexual advances do not necessitate overt violence, intimidation, or coercion. Ahn's case fit into that gap. Therefore, the court ruled that Ahn's actions did not fit the definition of a criminal offense under the current law. The court stated that because Kim did not display an obvious lack of consent in her response to her employer's advances, Ahn should be acquitted. The court further explained that the question of whether non-consensual sex without violence, intimidation, or coercion in the workplace should be criminalized as rape was one for the National Assembly to decide. In other words, redefining crimes of sexual violence required changes to legislation, which lay outside the court's purview.

However, in February 2019, the appellate court reversed this decision and found Ahn guilty of multiple counts of "non-consensual sexual intercourse by abuse of authority," stating "Former Governor Ahn's status and power itself could function as an intangible force enough to restrain the victim's free will."[18] This landmark case established precedent for punishing perpetrators who abused power asymmetries in the workplace. The court acknowledged the difficulties of giving clear and active consent in an employer-employee relationship. The court noted that Ahn, at the time of his sexual advances, was a prominent governor who had the authority to lay-off, dismiss, and take disciplinary action against Kim. Furthermore, Ahn was a distinguished public figure who was recognized as the majority party's presidential candidate. The court ruled that Kim was likely unable to clearly reject Ahn's advances, in fear of occupational or social retaliation. The court noted that while Ahn did not become violent with Kim, his status and authority alone were enough to intimidate her. Thus, the court ruled that Kim was coerced into sexual intercourse and sentenced Ahn to three-and-a-half years in prison.[19] On September 9, 2019, the Korean Supreme Court affirmed the ruling in the second trial and finalized Ahn's sentence.[20] The Supreme Court highlighted the concept of "gender sensitivity" in interpreting

---

17. Seoul Western District Court 2017 Go-hap 75, Aug. 14, 2018 (South Korea).
18. Seoul High Court 2018 No 2354, Feb. 1, 2019 (South Korea).
19. *Ibid.*
20. The Supreme Court 2019 Do 2562, Sept. 9, 2019 (South Korea).

sexual discrimination issues looking at the context of the incident from the woman's point of view and emphasized the importance of upholding gender equality in this case.

Legislative Reforms Post-#MeToo

The National Assembly, in response to the burgeoning #MeToo movement, has amended and enacted legislation. The National Assembly focused on the following issues:

- Eliminating the narrow interpretation of the meaning of "violence and intimidation" and implementing a "No means No" provision to protect victims;
- Increasing criminal sentences and extending the statute of limitations for sexual crimes in the workplace, sexual misconduct by means of leveraging authority, and workplace sexual harassment;
- Establishing a special act that excludes evidence of the victims' sexual history as a defense for sexual harassment; and
- Revising criminal defamation law to better protect victims who bring sexual violence cases to trial.

Lasting Impact of #MeToo

In the wake of the Korean #MeToo movement, we've seen an encouraging shift of the nation's consciousness toward supporting victims of sexual harassment and violence. According to a 2018 Korean Sexual Violence Counseling Center survey, 60.8 percent of victims cited a desire for "legal support" in building their case against their perpetrator. This is a significant increase from 2017, where only 40.2 percent requested legal support.[21] This increase displays a promising shift of victims empowering themselves and increasingly seeking action against their perpetrators.

---

21. Korea Sexual Violence Relief Center, *2018 Counseling Statistics* (Feb. 26, 2019), p. 6, http://www.sisters.or.kr/load.asp?sub_p=board/board&b_code=7&page=1&f_cate=&idx =4848&board_md=view; *2017 Counseling Statistics* (Feb. 28, 2018), p. 8, http://www.sisters .or.kr/load.asp?sub_p=board/board&b_code=7&page=1&f_cate=&idx=3985&board_md =view.

Victims' requests for "mental and emotional support" also jumped between 2017 to 2018, from 53.8 percent to 59.7 percent.[22] In 2018, more than ever before, victims sought out counseling to discuss the trauma they encountered at the hands of their perpetrators and regain their emotional health. Following the #MeToo movement, the topic of sexual violence became less taboo. No longer shrouded in shame, survivors of sexual violence brought their stories to light, and the topic of better serving victims became a part of the national dialogue.

The Korean #MeToo has sparked a feminist resistance across the country unlike ever before. The movement gained momentum with every high-profile perpetrator exposed in the media and punished in the courts. The Ahn Hee-Jung decision set the precedent for redefining sexual harassment and violence in the workplace, recognizing that it is often impossible for victims to clearly and actively reject an employer's advances when they fear occupational retaliation. This bottom-up movement brought together cultural, social, and legal changes that emboldened survivors of sexual harassment and violence to take action against their perpetrators. Yet the fight to protect victims continues.

---

22. Korea Sexual Violence Relief Center, *2018 Counseling Statistics* (Feb. 26, 2019), p. 6, http://www.sisters.or.kr/load.asp?sub_p=board/board&b_code=7&page=1&f_cate=&idx =4848&board_md=view; *2017 Counseling Statistics* (Feb. 28, 2018), p. 8, http://www.sisters .or.kr/load.asp?sub_p=board/board&b_code=7&page=1&f_cate=&idx=3985&board_md =view.

CHAPTER 27

What Happened After the "Black Box" Opened in Japan? We Will Never Be Silent

Kazuko Ito[1]

"Rape is murder of the soul. However, one's soul can gradually be healed. Day by day you'll be able to return to yourself—if you stay alive. Human beings have the power to do so, and each have their own way of healing. For me, that was telling the truth."

—Shiori Ito, *Black Box*[2]

The Advent of #MeToo in Japan

On October 17, 2017, shortly after the #MeToo movement started with the tweet of American actress Alyssa Milano, one Japanese woman published a book, *Black Box*. The author, Shiori Ito, a female journalist, detailed her journey seeking truth and justice after being sexually assaulted by Noriyuki Yamaguchi, a famous senior journalist, former Washington Bureau chief of the Tokyo Broadcasting System (TBS) and Prime Minister Shinzo Abe's biographer. Ito relayed that the incident happened in April 2015, at a meeting she believed was related to her future career. In the book, she described how the Japanese judicial and social system had treated her: humiliation during the police interview reporting the rape, suspicious cancellation of the arrest warrant against the politically well-connected Yamaguchi, as well as the prosecutor's decision not to prosecute the case.

---

1. Attorney at Law, Secretary General, Human Rights Now.
2. Shiori Ito, Black Box (BunGei Shunju, 2018).

In September 2017, the prosecution review committee in Tokyo had decided in favor of the prosecutor's decision not to prosecute the case, but Ito did not give up. Instead, she filed a civil case against Yamaguchi, published her *Black Box* book and held a press conference at the Foreign Correspondence Club of Japan (FCCJ). Exposing both her full name and face in the media, she told her story and broke the silence of sexual violence in Japan.

Ito's behavior was unusually brave as typical Japanese survivors of sexual assault do not report the crime. As a result of her decision to break the silence on sexual violence in Japan, Ito was subjected to severe hate speech and death threats in Japan. This eventually resulted in Ito's relocation to the United Kingdom.

Although international media covered her story, mainstream Japanese media kept silent about the case. However, her fight was shared by social media; her book was widely read and encouraged many Japanese women.

In February 2018, Human Rights Now, a Tokyo-based rights group organized a #MeToo event inviting Shiori Ito, and she publicly shared her story in front of her supporters. In March 2018, young female supporters of Ito, together with Ito launched the #WeToo Movement in Japan. Since Japanese society is prejudiced against victims, there was a need to create widespread support to encourage more victims of sex crimes in Japan to speak up about their experiences, even though societal expectations may continue to hold them back.

With the movement gaining momentum, more high-profile cases began coming to light. KaoRi, the former model and "muse" of celebrated internationally renowned photographer Nobuyoshi Araki accused him of sexual exploitation over a period of sixteen years.[3] A high school girl accused popular J-pop idol Tatsuya Yamaguchi of sexual harassment, which he later admitted. But in patriarchal Japan, women who accuse men of sexual assault have often been met with personal attacks and harassment rather than sympathy.

It was therefore significant when, in April 2018, a Japanese magazine, Shukan Shincho, picked up the breaking scandal centered around Junichi Fukuda, then Vice Finance Minister of Japan.[4] An anonymous TV Asahi female journalist accused Fukuda of sexually harassing her (sharing an audio recording of him propositioning her). Fukuda resigned without acknowledgment, and his resignation was accepted by his boss, Finance Minister Taro Aso, who nonetheless defended Fukuda saying, "There is no sexual harassment crime in Japan."

---

3. Motoko Rich, *When an Erotic Photographer's Muse Becomes His Critic*, N.Y. TIMES, May 5, 2018, https://www.nytimes.com/2018/05/05/world/asia/nobuyoshi-araki-photographer-model.html.

4. Motoko Rich, *Top Finance Official in Japan Resigns Over Harassment Accusations*, N.Y. TIMES, Apr. 18, 2018, https://www.nytimes.com/2018/04/18/world/asia/japan-sexual-harassment-junichi-fukuda.html.

This government response created the momentum among Japanese female to support #MeToo.

In the immediate aftermath of the scandal, women's groups held an assembly and protested the inadequate reaction of the Finance Ministry, holding up posters bearing the #MeToo slogan in the Diet, Japan's Parliament. Less than a week later, a talk rally organized by women on various social media platforms was held in Shinjuku Tokyo, with around 2,000 people protesting sexual violence under the slogan #IWillNotRemainSilent.

Fukuda's scandal revealed a persistent culture of sexual harassment in Japanese media over decades. In April 2018, the Japanese media "Business Insider" conducted an urgent survey about the sexual harassment experience of female workers in media, exposing serious sexual harassment and a culture of impunity that was deeply embedded throughout the media industry.[5] In May 2018, eighty-six female reporters in thirty-one media companies established an association named "Women in Media Network," and called for elimination of sexual harassment in their workplace.[6]

Contemporary Law in Japan: Sexual Harassment and Violence

In 2017, according to a survey conducted by Japan's Gender Equality Bureau Cabinet Office, 7.8 percent of women and 1.5 percent of men answered that they were victims of sexual assault.[7] In contrast, National Police Agency data shows that only 989 claims of rape cases were accepted by police in 2016.[8]

In Japan, people rarely come forward with sexual assault allegations. Feelings of shame and pressures to conform to societal norms mean that those who find themselves victims of sex-based crimes often suffer in silence. Even when they do seek the help of the authorities, the results are far from encouraging.

---

5. Reiko Takeshita,「男性記者は私を差し出した」メディアの女性たちが声を上げられない理由 ["A male journalist has offered me" The reason why women in media cannot raise their voices], BUSINESS INSIDER, Apr. 19, 2018, https://www.businessinsider.jp/post-165969.

6. David McNeill and Chie Matsumoto, *#WithYou: How women journalists in Japan are fighting harassment*, COLUM. JOURNALISM REV., Aug. 7, 2018, https://www.cjr.org/analysis/japan.php.

7. *Research Report on the violence between men and women*, GENDER EQUALITY BUREAU CABINET OFFICE, Mar. 2018, http://www.gender.go.jp/policy/no_violence/e-vaw/chousa/h29_boryoku_cyousa.html.

8. *January–December 2017 Crime Statistics*, E-STAT, https://www.e-stat.go.jp/stat-search/files?page=1&layout=datalist&toukei=00130001&tstat=000001112156&cycle=0&year=20180&month=0.

The prosecution rate of rape cases in 2016 was a low of 36 percent, reflecting a trend of significant declines in prosecution rates for decades.[9] The Japanese criminal justice system fails to bring perpetrators of sexual violence to justice or to hold them to account for their sex crimes.

In 2009, the Committee on the Elimination of Discrimination against Women (CEDAW), in its concluding observation in its sixth national report on Japan, expressed concern over the then existing Japanese rape law and made concrete recommendations urging Japan "to eliminate in its Penal Code the requirement of the victim's complaint in order to prosecute crimes of sexual violence and to define sexual crimes as crimes involving violations of women's rights to bodily security and integrity, to increase the penalty for rape and to include incest as a specific crime."[10]

Eight years later, in June 2017, the Criminal Provision of the Japanese Penal Code was revised for the first time in 110 years.[11] Several major amendments were made: a) the re-definition of rape to include forced anal and oral sex regardless of the gender of the victim; b) the elimination of the clause requiring a victim to file a complaint in order to prosecute an offender; c) the increase in the minimum penalty for rape from three years' imprisonment to five; and, d) the establishment of a new crime involving sexual intercourse by a parent or guardian.

These reforms were far from satisfactory to end impunity of sexual violence. Survivors' groups have been demanding the removal of "violence or threat" required as an element of crimes in the Article 176 (sexual assault) and 177 (Rape) in the Penal Code. The "violence or threat" element must be proved by the prosecutor beyond a reasonable doubt for judges to convict. Often, prosecutors give up indicting rape or sexual assault cases due to insufficiency of evidence no matter how the evidence demonstrates that survivors did not give consent.

The element of "quasi-rape" under Article 178, sexual intercourse with a woman by "taking advantage of loss of consciousness or inability to resist," is also extremely narrowly defined and an escape route for criminals. However, the Legislative Counsel in the Ministry of Justice excluded a discussion of a

---

9. *Ibid.*

10. United Nations Committee on the Elimination of Discrimination against Women, *Concluding observations of the Committee on the Elimination of Discrimination against Women on Japan*, Aug. 7, 2009, https://www2.ohchr.org/english/bodies/cedaw/docs/co/CEDAW.C .JPN.CO.6.pdf.

11. Tomoko Otake, *Japan's expanded sex crime laws go into effect*, JAPAN TIMES, July 13, 2017, https://www.japantimes.co.jp/news/2017/07/13/national/crime-legal/japans-expanded -sex-crime-laws-go-effect/#.Xs8DqDpKhhF.

proposal to remove "violence or threat" and introduce "No Means No" legislation and this change was not incorporated in the 2017 amendment.

Unfortunately, sexual harassment is still not recognized as an offence in Japan. On May 18, 2018, the Cabinet issued a decision declaring that "under the current legal system, 'criminal sexual harassment' does not exist."

Some of the gaps are however filled by current employment regulations. The Act on Equal Opportunity and Treatment Between Men and Women in Employment, Article 11, states that employers must take measures to redress sexual harassment.[12] Though this is a step toward offering employees some form of protection, it only extends to internal company-led procedures. There is no effective administrative and criminal sanction against employees who sexually harass other employees.[13] For those who begin employment and then go on to experience harassment, often they will never make a complaint due to fear of being shamed or expelled from their workplace.

What Happened When #MeToo Arrived?

Surprised by the Fukuda scandal and the subsequent backlash, the Government of Japan has made some moves to address the situation. Deputy Prime Minister and Finance Minister Taro Aso made a grudging apology for his earlier comment that sexual harassment is not a crime, although he remains in his job. Bureaucrats from the Finance Ministry were ordered to take a training course on sexual harassment and inappropriate conduct toward women; the attendees were mostly male bureaucrats, and the minister himself did not attend.

#MeToo has sparked a new kind of outspokenness in Japan. As more and more women have started sharing their stories, almost every month, new #MeToo stories are covered by the media.

---

12. Act on Securing, Etc. of Equal Opportunity and Treatment between Men and Women in Employment, (Act No. 113 of July 1, 1972), http://www.ilo.org/dyn/travail/docs/2010/Act%20on%20Securing%20etc%20of%20Equal%20Opportunity%20and%20Treatment%20between%20Men%20and%20Women%20in%20Employment%201972.pdf.

Article 11 (1) provides:

> Employers shall establish necessary measures in terms of employment management to give advice to workers and cope with problems of workers, and take other necessary measures so that workers they employ do not suffer any disadvantage in their working conditions by reason of said workers' responses to sexual harassment in the workplace, or in their working environments do not suffer any harm due to said sexual harassment.

13. Article 30 of the Act provides that for employers who do not protect their employees against harassment, "the Minister of Health, Labor and Welfare may make a public announcement of such violation." *Id.*, Article 30.

As in many other countries, traditional news outlets have been slow to pick up on the growing #MeToo Movement. But this comes with a parallel push by online media to disseminate stories of sexual harassment. *Buzzfeed Japan*, one of the only outlets to publish Ito's story at the time (aside from weekly magazines), frequently covered #MeToo related articles about the situation and the movement in Japan.

There is still, however, a tendency in the mainstream Japanese media to treat cases that fall within the ambit of #MeToo as "celebrity gossip." Although famous men or women are often covered by #MeToo reports in the media, ordinary females are left behind.

It is hard to say whether #MeToo is affecting women of all races, religions, and classes, partly due to the largely ethnically Japanese and secular nature of Japanese society. What is most evident, however, is that the younger generation of Japanese women appears to have been significantly encouraged and galvanized by the global #MeToo movement, as well the challenges faced by Shiori Ito. There is now more of an open conversation about gender roles, discrimination, and harassment.

Perceptions of Sexual Harassment

Sexual harassment has been deeply embedded in business culture in Japan and associated with discrimination against women. Although discrimination against women in the workplace has been prohibited since 1985 when The Act on Equal Opportunity and Treatment Between Men and Women in Employment was enacted, de facto discrimination against women nonetheless prevails. Due to a hard work environment and lack of public support for working mothers, many women leave work after giving birth, and relatively young and unexperienced women, as well as part-time female workers are often the majority of female workers. As leadership in business, politics, and media is occupied overwhelmingly by males, male culture is predominant in the workplace and female workers are the minority and marginalized. Under male domination, various types of sexual harassment against women, including both verbal and physical conduct, have become part of the culture in the workplace.

This culture is reinforced by the media, which often depict women as sex objects. Pornography magazines are easily accessible for all ages of men including boys while other male magazines, as well as commercial media outlets, also feature women in a sexualized way without respect.

There is a worrying lack of understanding about consent underlying Japanese society, as exemplified by a 2017 study conducted by Japan's national broadcaster, NHK. The study surveyed men on what constitutes "sexual consent." Eating dinner alone as a couple was considered equivalent to consent by 11 percent of responders; wearing clothes that show a lot of skin, 23 percent; getting into a car together, 25 percent; drinking alone as a couple, 27 percent; and an alarming 35 percent of men considered getting drunk to be the equivalent to sexual consent. Decisions made on sexual violence in the judicial system reflect this sort of mind-set among men across Japanese society.

However, such cultural and male perception is rarely questioned by Japanese society, and women must bear a heavy burden to address such cultural and sexual harassment individually. It is hard for women to publicly denounce and criticize male behavior even if it constitutes sexual harassment, as it is seen as a challenge to the status quo. Often, a woman who raises her voice is seen as a "Troublemaker" who breaks solidarity of the workplace and is isolated. It is thus extremely difficult for women to protest day-to-day sexual harassment.

There is a predominant discourse even among working women that it is necessary skill for professional working women to deal with sexual harassment in a "sophisticated manner," rather than fighting or denouncing it. As for a superior's request for a sexual relationship, it is often seen as a personal matter. If women can hardly resist and are subjected to sexual conduct without genuine consent, women are the ones who are often blamed.

Backlash

Victim-blaming is all too common, with many Japanese asserting that it is the survivor's fault for having put herself in a risky situation in the first place.

If a silence-breaker speaks out about her experience, she will be the one who is blamed by the society, such as, "You are the guilty one who dresses in a sexually attractive way;" "You are the guilty one who went for a drink with the man at night;" and "It is shameful for a woman to talk about a sexual experience in public; better to be silent." Thus, Japanese society rarely blames the perpetrator and rarely questions the social norm that condones the sexual violence and harassment.

Mio Sugita, the ruling party LDP legislator, commented on Shiori Ito during her BBC interview: "In her case, there were clear errors on her part as a woman—drinking that much in front of a man and losing her memory." Sugita adds, "If you're working as a woman in society, you'll be approached by people you don't like. Being able to properly turn them down is one of your skills."[14]

---

14. *LDP lawmaker draws fire over comment on alleged rape victim in BBC documentary*, THE MAINICHI, July 7, 2018, https://mainichi.jp/english/articles/20180707/p2a/00m/0na/013000c.

Shiori Ito fled to London to escape public attacks including rape and death threats and online hate speech over her activity. "I was vilified on social media and received hate messages and emails and calls from unknown numbers. I was called a 'slut' and 'prostitute' and told I should 'be dead.' There were arguments over my nationality, because a true Japanese woman wouldn't speak about such 'shameful' things," Shiori wrote on Politico.eu in January 2018.

Regarding the scandal of Junichi Fukuda, though the accuser was anonymous, she was subjected to severe and persistent online harassment. On Twitter, there were attempts to reveal her identity; she was criticized, without proof, for tricking Fukuda; and her personality was blamed based on inaccurate information. Further, Finance Minister Aso referred to these online groundless allegations, and suggested "Fukuda might have been tricked" and insulted victims. Further Aso said that "the reporter followed Fukuda for information" and "if [the Fukuda reporter was] not comfortable, it is better to replace all reporters with men."

Further, there are moves that demonize the #MeToo movement in general. Critics often argue that, "#MeToo in Japan has become extreme, survivors kept being anonymous and blame men without proving based on material evidence. There is the possibility of false accusation and defamation. How can a MeToo supporter be accountable for such groundless allegations?"

Looking to the Future

Other than these psychological barriers, a significant structural barrier exists in that sexual harassment is not recognized as a crime in Japan. The police are incapable of handling rape and sexual assault cases effectively and sympathetically. Apart from the rape law being insufficient for today's global standards, the police too are not efficient in the investigation and collection of evidence in such cases. In the workplace, no effective mechanism to handle or investigate complaints exists to inquire into any alleged sexual harassment by the employer. There is a pressing lack of support centers and anti-rape centers for survivors. "Consent" remains undefined in the Japanese Penal Code.

The good news is that many new #MeToo movement support groups have been established. #WeToo Japan was established by supporters of Shiori Ito, and Spring, a sexual violence survivors' group demanding law reform, was established in Fall 2017. Further, young women started an organization named "I am" in April 2018, and in response to the Fukuda scandal, "Women in Media network" was established in May 2018. Recently, female university student groups achieved a successful petition campaign protesting SPA! Magazine's article "ranking women's universities on how easy it is to convince students to have sex at drinking parties" and created a new group "Voice Up Japan."[15]

In March 2019, four Japanese district courts delivered four verdicts that acquitted defendants accused of rape and quasi-rape. In three of four cases, the judge found the sexual activity was against the will of victims but decided "not guilty" because the cases did not meet the requirement of rape and quasi-rape.

One case involved a nineteen-year-old victim, whose father had sexually abused her since she was fourteen, against her will. In the case, the judge interpreted the definition of the "inability to resist" element of quasi-rape in an extremely narrow way, and decided the situation surrounding the victim did not meet the criminal element.[16] Many people wondered, "If such a case is decided not guilty, what kind of case can be convicted?"

These decisions triggered the anger of women and girls in Japan. To protest, since April 2019, the so-called "flower demonstration" has spread across Japan.[17] The eleventh day in each month, women and girls spontaneously gather around main streets of different cities in Japan. They hold flower expressing solidarity for victims, share their own stories, and demand legal reform to bring justice and accountability of sexual violence in Japan.

In late April 2019, Voice Up Japan, Spring and Human Rights Now started a #Change.org online petition.[18] The petition has now reached over 99,000 signatures. These organizations again submitted the petition to the Ministry of Justice in March 2020. In response, on March 31, 2020, the Justice Minister declared the establishment of a new study committee on reforms of criminal laws on sex crimes.[19]

Despite serious backlash, Shiori Ito brought her case before the civil court, and the trial concluded in October 2019. Significant numbers of citizens in Japan expressed support for her case and challenges.

---

15. Martin Bureau, *Spa! magazine apologizes for women's university 'sex listing,'* JAPAN TIMES, Jan. 9, 2019, https://japantoday.com/category/national/japan-magazine-apologises-for-women%27s-university-sex-listing?comment-order=popular.

16. Editorial, *Not-guilty rulings on sex crimes*, JAPAN TIMES, May 18, 2019, https://www.japantimes.co.jp/opinion/2019/05/18/editorials/not-guilty-rulings-sex-crimes/#.Xs8D7DpKhhF.

17. *Monthly rally against sexual violence spreads to 9 cities*, THE ASAHI SHIMBUM, June 12, 2019, http://www.asahi.com/ajw/articles/AJ201906120046.html.

18. 法務大臣へ、性犯罪における刑法改正を求めます。"We Call on the Minister of Justice to Amend the Criminal Law in Sexual Offenses"), #Change.org, http://chng.it/Jhtb2hJp.

19. 性犯罪の刑法要件を議論 法務省が検討会設置 (Discuss Criminal Law Requirements for Sexual Offenses), NHK, Mar. 31, 2020, https://www3.nhk.or.jp/news/html/20200331/k10012359371000.html.

On December 18, 2019, the Tokyo District Court delivered judgment for Ito. The court found that the defendant, Noriyuki Yamaguchi "had sexual intercourse without the consent of Ito, who was in a state of intoxication and unconscious" and ordered Yamaguchi to pay ¥3.3 million ($30,000; £22,917) for her damages.[20]

The court rejected a counter-lawsuit filed by Yamaguchi seeking ¥130 million in compensation for damage to his social reputation by Ito's publication and public activities. The court said Ito's action "was aimed at serving the public interest, as it was an act pursuing improvement in the situation surrounding sex crime victims," and concluded that "the content (Ito had made public) is true and cannot be considered as defamation."

Though Yamaguchi made clear that he will appeal the case to the high court, Shiori and her supporters see this decision as a victory and an important milestone to change the status of survivors and Japanese social norms. The decision hugely encouraged the younger generation to stand up for justice.

There are signs of progress in criminal cases as well. In February 2020, the Fukuoka high court overturned a lower court decision and convicted a man for quasi-rape.[21] And, in March 2020, the Nagoya high court overturned the lower court's decision which had acquitted a father of raping his 19-year-old daughter and sentenced him to 10 years imprisonment.[22]

Human Rights Now, a Tokyo-based rights group, has also been supporting the #MeToo movement. Together with these new groups, Human Rights Now supports silence breakers and tries to raise awareness and demand policy reform. Japan is not an easy country for the #MeToo movement, as it is still difficult for women to say NO and for survivors to raise their voices due to cultural and structural problems. However, it is important to support women who bravely raise their voices as much as possible and try to achieve a society where a woman can easily raise her voice.

---

20. *Japanese #MeToo figure calls her court victory a 'landmark' case for sex crimes in the country*, JAPAN TIMES, Dec. 19, 2019, https://www.japantimes.co.jp/news/2019/12/19/national/crime-legal/japan-metoo-symbol-surprised-landmark-rape-suit-ruling/#.Xs8EID pKhhF.

21. *"Innocent" rapist convicted by Fukuoka High Court on appeal*, The Asahi Shimbun, Feb. 6, 2020, http://www.asahi.com/ajw/articles/13105765.

22. *Father found guilty of raping daughter, gets 10 years in prison*, The Asahi Shimbun, Mar. 12, 2020, http://www.asahi.com/ajw/articles/13209314.

CHAPTER 28

The #MeToo Movement in Australia: Silenced by Defamation and Disbelief

Karen O'Connell[1]

Introduction: "Women Are Burning with a Kind of Cold Fury"

In October 2018, a state politician, minister David Elliott, made an allegation against his political opponent, Opposition Leader Luke Foley, under parliamentary privilege. He claimed that Foley had harassed a journalist at a function at Parliament House. The incident had never been reported. The journalist, Ashleigh Raper, made a statement following the public airing of the incident, saying that Foley had put his hand down the back of her dress and into her underpants in front of a colleague at the function. She had chosen not to report the harassment because "[i]t is clear to me that a woman who is the subject of such behaviour is often the person who suffers once a complaint is made," and that she feared she would lose her job, which she "cherished."[2] Around the same time, businesswoman Catherine Marriott was publicly revealed to have made a confidential report against another very senior politician, Barnaby Joyce, about an incident at an official function a year earlier. Marriott said that she was motivated in part by #MeToo, but that the leaking of the case to the media and the ensuing publicity was "horrific."[3]

---

1. Associate Professor, University of Technology, Sydney.

2. Ashleigh Raper, *ABC Journalist Ashleigh Raper's Statement in Full*, ABC NEWS, Nov. 9, 2018, https://www.abc.net.au/news/2018-11-08/ashleigh-raper-full-statement/10478012.

3. Leigh Sales, Peter McCutcheon, and Callum Denness, *Catherine Marriott Speaks Out about Alleged Sexual Harassment by Barnaby Joyce*, ABC NEWS, Sep. 19, 2018, https://www.abc.net.au/news/2018-09-18/catherine-marriott-on-alleged-sexual-harassment-by-barnaby-joyce/10255518.

These stories have all the hallmarks of sexual harassment cases in Australia: even egregious cases mostly go unreported; women are scared to speak up for fear of losing their jobs or reputations; and when they try to maintain privacy—or even cover up the harassment—to protect themselves from the fallout, their wishes may be overridden. Both of the women in these cases, despite never making a complaint, were threatened with defamation suits by their alleged harassers. It is hardly surprising, then, that the same day that the Raper statement was released, journalist Julia Baird wrote that "women are burning with a kind of cold fury."[4]

The State of the Law in Australia: Strong on Paper, Weak in Practice

The way that law has been brought to bear on #MeToo allegations in Australia has been markedly different from the experience of countries such as the United States. While some legal cases are still before the courts, it is clear that Australia's strict defamation laws have had a chilling effect on public discussions of specific allegations of sexual harassment or assault and have arguably acted as a further deterrent to individuals reporting harassment.

The negative role that law has played in the #MeToo cases to date is especially disappointing because Australia has, on paper, strong and comprehensive sexual harassment laws. There are legislative prohibitions against sexual harassment in every state and territory jurisdiction, as well as federally. These laws are embedded in a broader antidiscrimination framework, and with no bill of rights or Constitutional guarantee of equality, Australian antidiscrimination laws are our primary means of protecting equality rights.

Sexual harassment is made unlawful at the federal level in the Sex Discrimination Act of 1984, one of four federal anti-discrimination acts.[5] Sexual harassment has a stand-alone provision (s28A), but it is also a form of sex discrimination, and so is additionally covered by the general prohibition on sex discrimination in the same legislation. *Sex-based* harassment, that is, harassment that is because of a person's sex, such as demeaning nicknames or detrimental behavior that is gendered but not sexual, is also covered by sex discrimination prohibitions, but is rarely argued.

---

4. Julia Baird, *Women are Burning with a Kind of Cold Fury*, THE SYDNEY MORNING HERALD, Nov. 9, 2018, https://www.smh.com.au/politics/nsw/women-are-burning-with-a-kind-of-cold-fury-20181109-p50ezj.html.

5. Alongside the *Racial Discrimination Act* 1975, *Disability Discrimination Act* 1992, and the *Age Discrimination Act* 2004.

The key element of sexual harassment is that there is unwelcome conduct of a sexual nature in circumstances in which a reasonable person "would have anticipated the possibility that the person harassed would be offended, humiliated or intimidated." This term was amended in 2011 to make it easier to prove—there only has to be a foreseeable *possibility* that the person targeted would be impacted by the conduct.

The federal sexual harassment law also attempts to address intersectional sexual harassment by stating that the relevant "circumstances" to be considered include factors such as the age, sexual orientation, gender identity, relationship status, religious belief, race or disability of the person harassed, as well as the relationship between the person harassed and the person who engaged in the conduct, along with "any other relevant circumstance" (s28A(1A)). This provision, however, is very rarely used.

The "sexual" element of the conduct has been defined broadly to include, for example, declarations of love, telling jokes, and flicking an elastic band at a colleague's legs (in the context of other behavior).[6] The case law on whether an applicant has shown that the behavior is "unwelcome" is less clear. For example, the fact that a woman participated in a sexually charged workplace culture did not prevent a successful complaint in one case, while a woman responding to sexual comments in a "friendly" way undermined another.[7] A single incident can constitute sexual harassment, and there is no test of seriousness.

Sexual harassment at the federal level is protected in specified areas of public life, such as employment, education, and the provision of goods and services. However, in a state jurisdiction—Queensland—sexual harassment is simply unlawful without any area limitations.

Much effort has been put into crafting sexual harassment laws that are broad and inclusive. However, Australian anti-discrimination laws are overwhelmingly directed at individual redress and as such are reactive: that is, they are set up to respond to individual harms that have already occurred, rather than preventing systemic and institutional sexual harassment. This necessarily means that they are limited in impact.

One area in which institutional change is required is in relation to vicarious liability, where employers would be liable for their employees' sexually harassing behavior unless they took "all reasonable steps" to prevent it occurring. "All reasonable steps" is understood to mean active, preventive measures; a lack of awareness that the harassment was occurring is not in itself a defense

---

6. *Aleksovski v. Australia Asia Aerospace Pty Ltd* [2002] FMCA 81 (Australia); *Djokic v. Sinclair* (1994) EOC 92-643 (Australia); *Shiels v. James* [2000] FMCA 2 (Australia).

7. *Horman v. Distribution Group Ltd* [2001] FMCA 52 (Australia); *Daley v. Barrington* [2003] FMCA 93 (Australia).

for employers.[8] This means that all employers should have a sexual harassment policy, provide anti-harassment training to all workplace participants, and have procedures for dealing with internal sexual harassment complaints, in order to demonstrate "all reasonable steps" and discharge liability.

In terms of process, there is mandatory conciliation for anti-discrimination complaints, including sexual harassment. An individual cannot take a sexual harassment complaint at the federal level directly to court. Complaints under the Sex Discrimination Act are brought to the Australian Human Rights Commission. If the complaint cannot be conciliated, the commission can terminate it, and, once terminated, a case can be brought to the federal court.

In practice, despite these laws, sexual harassment remains a pervasive problem in public life, with 85 percent of women and 57 percent of men surveyed saying they had been sexually harassed since the age of 15. Over a five-year period, 39 percent of women and 26 percent of men said they had experienced sexual harassment at work.[9] Particular groups are disproportionately impacted. People who identified outside of the gender binary and people other than heterosexual were more likely to be harassed. Age is also a significant factor, as rates of sexual harassment are highest among people aged eighteen to twenty-nine. There is also a significant difference between disabled and non-disabled people, and Aboriginal and Torres Strait Islander people are more likely to have experienced workplace sexual harassment than people who are not. Earlier surveys indicated much lower, albeit still significant, rates of sexual harassment. The same survey conducted four years earlier found that one-third of women (33 percent) had been sexually harassed since the age of fifteen, and fewer than one in ten men (9 percent). It is likely that the added publicity and raised consciousness of the #MeToo movement has made both men and women much more likely to both recognize sexually harassing behavior and to acknowledge themselves as having experienced it.

The extremely high incidence of sexual harassment decreases dramatically as it moves through grievance, complaint, and legal processes. Very few incidents of sexual harassment are reported at all: only 17 percent.[10] Of those, even fewer are brought as formal complaints to the equality bodies at the state or federal level, and only a tiny handful of cases go to court or tribunal each year. This could be considered a success if, for example, it was an indication that

8. Australian Human Rights Commission, *Everyone's Business: Fourth National Survey on Sexual Harassment in Australian Workplaces*, Sep. 12, 2018, https://www.humanrights.gov.au/our-work/sex-discrimination/publications/everyone-s-business-fourth-national-survey-sexual.

9. *Ibid.*

10. *Ibid.*

the incidents that are reported are dealt with effectively at a workplace level, conciliated when they reach an equality body, or settled to the satisfaction of the complainant before they reach the courts. However, Allen's research shows that settlements are driven more by complainants' concerns about the time and energy of litigation, problems with proving discrimination, and low levels of compensation. As noted above, the individual enforcement mechanism of conciliated complaints, with recourse to law if unsuccessful, is "passive, retrospective and reactive."[11]

When the #MeToo Movement Arrived in Australia

With this background of silence—strong legislation on paper, but few cases—the impact of the #MeToo movement in Australia was immediate and intense, with widespread participation in the social media hashtag and further public discussion and activism inspired by it. Australian women had a recent history of using social media to fuel gender equality campaigns, most notably with the #destroythejoint campaign. This national movement was inspired by comments made on radio in 2012 by conservative radio presenter Alan Jones, who, attacking female leaders, said that "women are destroying the joint."[12] A witty campaign started in which women tweeted what they were doing to "destroy the joint," which included: "picking their kids up from soccer; making Father's Day lunches; operating on broken hands; delivering babies; working on legislation for improved school funding."[13] Destroy the Joint continues to expand, and now also hosts the campaign "Counting Dead Women," which tracks and tallies women killed by domestic violence.

It was in this fertile digital and activist culture that #MeToo took root in Australia. The Weinstein story in October 2017 was widely reported across Australian media, and many women, beyond contributing to the MeToo hashtag, shared stories, grew angry, and looked for change. Veteran journalist Tracey Spicer sent out a tweet calling on Australians to contact her with their own

---

11. Dominique Allen, *Behind the Conciliation Doors: Settling Discrimination Complaints in Victoria*, 18 GRIFFITH LAW REVIEW, 778 (2009).

12. JESSICA MCLEAN & SOPHIA MAALSEN, DISRUPTING SEXISM AND SEXUALITIES ONLINE? GENDER, ACTIVISM AND DIGITAL SPACES (Catherine Nash & Andrew Gorman-Murray, 2019).

13. Jenna Price, *Destroying the Joint on the Way to the Post-Patriarchy*, THE SYDNEY MORNING HERALD, Sep. 4, 2012, https://www.smh.com.au/politics/federal/destroying-the-joint-on-the-way-to-the-post-patriarchy-20120903-25a7h.html.

#MeToo stories.[14] Her initial target was her own industry of media and entertainment, but the hundreds (now thousands) of responses she received covered all industries and backgrounds. Spicer's reporting on claims of particularly egregious behavior by Don Burke, one of Australia's best known, most loved, and successful television presenters, kept the #MeToo movement in the public eye. In November 2017 a piece of investigative journalism on Burke was published, reporting claims from dozens of women, as well as male bystanders, that he had sexually harassed, sexually assaulted, and bullied women throughout his long career.[15] In 2018, Spicer established "NOW Australia," an organization equivalent to the United States' "Time's Up," which aims to end sexual harassment and abuse in workplaces.[16]

Several other high-profile sexual harassment cases emerged alongside #MeToo, involving nationally recognized public figures. As well as the political cases described above, two significant cases involved reports of sexual harassment against high profile actors, the former television soap star Craig McLachlan and distinguished theater actor Geoffrey Rush. Yet neither actor has had a sexual harassment case brought against them. Instead, the cases were defamation actions brought against media outlets, and, in the McLachlan case, the woman who alleged the harassment.[17] In the Rush case, media comments were made on the basis of a "confidential" informal report of inappropriate behavior made by an actor, Eryn Jean Norvill, that was later leaked to the media.[18] Norvill was a reluctant witness in Rush's case against Nationwide News, and the judge not only failed to give her evidence of harassment any weight, but described her as prone to "exaggeration and embellishment."[19] Justice Michael Wigney found Norvill lacked credibility, in part, for actions that were all too

---

14. Rob Moran, *Tracey Spicer to Name and Shame "Serial Predators" in Local Media Industry*, THE SYDNEY MORNING HERALD, Oct. 19, 2017, https://www.smh.com.au/entertainment/tv-and-radio/tracey-spicer-to-name-and-shame-serial-predators-in-local-media-industry-20171019-gz3w7n.html.

15. Kate McClymont, *"A High-Grade, Twisted Abuser": Don Burke a Sexual Harasser and Bully, Claims Series of Women*, THE SYDNEY MORNING HERALD, Nov. 26, 2017, https://www.smh.com.au/entertainment/tv-and-radio/a-highgrade-twisted-abuser-don-burke-a-sexual-harasser-and-bully-claims-series-of-women-20171126-gzt6d2.html.

16. www.now.org.au.

17. Mazoe Ford, *Craig McLachlan Seeking $6.5 Million in Damages from ABC, Fairfax and Actress*, ABC NEWS, Nov. 26, 2018, https://www.abc.net.au/news/2018-11-26/craig-mclachlan-seeks-6.5-million-in-damages/10555890.

18. Jamelle Wells, *Actress Wanted Complaint About Geoffrey Rush Kept Confidential, Defence Says*, ABC NEWS, Nov. 7, 2018, https://www.abc.net.au/news/2018-11-07/eryn-norvill-wanted-geoffrey-rush-complaint-confidential-court/10473138.

19. Karen O'Connell, *Geoffrey Rush's Victory in His Defamation Case Could Have a Chilling Effect on the #MeToo Movement*, THE CONVERSATION, Apr. 11, 2019, https://

credible to women attempting to negotiate a professional relationship with a harasser, such as sharing a car trip with Rush and inviting him to an event at her home. Potentially corroborating evidence from actor Yael Stone was ruled out by the judge. Norvill, then, arguably had her own reputation tarnished through making what was intended to be a confidential report, while Rush received the highest defamation payout ever awarded by an Australian court. Many women were devastated by the hearing.[20]

In the Australian #MeToo cases, then, women alleging sexual harassment against men in public positions have had defamation cases brought or threatened against them or, as in the Rush case, been a reluctant witness, but none has brought a case of sexual harassment. The damages involved in defamation and discrimination law also reflect a disturbing discrepancy. While McLachlan has claimed AUS$6.5 million dollars and Rush was ultimately awarded a total of AUS$2.9 million (US$2 million) for harm to their reputations, discrimination law damages are notoriously low, with all but a handful of successful federal sexual harassment cases involving payouts of less than AU$30,000 to women complainants.[21]

#MeToo: Stifled Before There Was Time for a Backlash

While there has been talk in other countries of a "backlash" against the #MeToo movement, in Australia opposition to #MeToo and silencing of allegations happened at the same time. This was in part due to Australia's strict defamation laws, and in part because of the kind of ingrained disbelief—evidenced in the Rush case—that is exacerbated by the layers of confidentiality in the grievance, complaints, and legal processes. Endemic as it is, Australians rarely hear stories of sexual harassment.

Australia's strict defamation laws explain why alleged harassers have brought actions rather than those harassed, and these cases fundamentally

---

theconversation.com/geoffrey-rushs-victory-in-his-defamation-case-could-have-a-chilling -effect-on-the-metoo-movement-115127.

20. Jenna Price, *What Women Feel when They Read about EJ Norvill and Geoffrey Rush*, THE SYDNEY MORNING HERALD, Nov. 2, 2018, https://www.smh.com.au/national/what -women-feel-when-they-read-about-ej-norvill-and-geoffrey-rush-20181101-p50dcp.html.

21. Karen O'Connell, *Rush Gets $850,000, but What of the Victims of Sexual Harassment?* THE AUSTRALIAN, May 10, 2019, https://www.theaustralian.com.au/business/legal -affairs/actual-harassment-or-damage-of-allegations-rush-verdict-question/news-story/c8db d46ab8dfe39782f65032ba715fb5.

shaped the way that #MeToo played out in both law and in public conversation.[22] There is no universal right to freedom of speech in Australian law, only pockets of limited protection of certain kinds of speech, and there is a high chance of success when alleged harassers bring defamation actions in response to public statements about their inappropriate behavior. In Australian defamation law the publisher's primary defense is that the publication is true, and—crucially—the burden of proving truth lies with the publisher. Where there is unwelcome sexual behavior, it often takes place in private, with no witnesses, in circumstances where truth can be hard to evidence.

With the negative treatment of women whose experiences were made public, the #MeToo discussion quickly died down. Whether the movement will translate into any significant legal or political change is yet to be seen.

Stepping Forward: We Need More #MeToo

While #MeToo in Australia has faced formidable hurdles, it has still opened up the promise of future law and policy reforms. The movement created an impetus for broader social and institutional change, which resulted in a National Inquiry into workplace sexual harassment currently underway. This Inquiry is being conducted by the Australian Human Rights Commission, Australia's national human rights institution, which is responsible for conciliating complaints of sexual harassment at the federal level but also has a policy and educative role. The Inquiry will consider the economic impact of sexual harassment, what drives it, and how to prevent it, as well as the adequacy of the existing legal framework.[23]

Submissions to the Inquiry have powerfully argued for a regulatory response to sexual harassment that will be positive and proactive, and, alongside the existing system of individual redress, that has the potential to create genuine change. A system that requires workplaces and educational institutions to actively transform gender-hostile cultures without the need for a complaint is the goal.

Australia's strong sexual harassment laws powerfully illustrate the fact that laws on their own may do little to effect actual change. It is the broader structures, institutions, and cultures that law is embedded in that determine

---

22. Jacqueline Maley, *When #MeToo Meets Defamation Law, and a Brutal Political Culture*, The Sydney Morning Herald, Nov. 9, 2018, https://www.smh.com.au/politics/fed eral/when-metoo-meets-defamation-law-and-a-brutal-political-culture-20181109-p50f3j.html.

23. Australian Human Rights Commission, *National Inquiry into Sexual Harassment into Australian Workplaces*, Dec. 20, 2018, https://www.humanrights.gov.au/our-work/sex -discrimination/projects/national-inquiry-sexual-harassment-australian-workplaces.

its effectiveness, and in the case of Australia's sexual harassment laws, there are strong counterforces. The existence of defamation laws that skew the balance of power toward public-figure harassers, legal structures that provide disincentives to bring complaints and cases, low damages payouts, the risks attached to speaking up, and punitive attitudes to those who do, all stop current sexual harassment laws and policies from being effective. There is much more work to be done to address sexual harassment in Australia. The Australian experience is evidence of how much we need the #MeToo movement: a collective recounting of the ubiquity and seriousness of sexual harassment until it can no longer be ignored.

Africa

CHAPTER 29

The #MeToo Movement in South Africa: A New Platform for an Old War

Debbie Collier[1]

"Maybe … [we] are searching among the branches, for what only appears in the roots."

—Rumi[2]

Introduction

Gender-based violence (GBV) and harassment are global phenomena, with exceedingly high prevalence rates in the various regions in Africa.[3] In South Africa, a country emerging from the complex trauma of an oppressive past shaped by patriarchal and racist ideologies, sex discrimination, sexual

---

1. Head of Department and Associate Professor, Institute of Development and Labour Law, Department of Commercial Law, University of Cape Town.

2. Jalāl ad-Dīn Muhammad Rūmī, known commonly as Rumi, was a thirteenth century Persian poet, scholar, and philosopher.

3. See, for example, KM Devries et al., "*The Global Prevalence of Intimate Partner Violence Against Women*," 340 SCIENCE, Issue 6140, pp. 1527-1528 (2013). Sexual violence is not only experienced by women, however. For an overview of the general absence of protection for LGBTI people in Africa, see *Mapping Anti-Gay Laws in Africa: Making Love a Crime*, AMNESTY INTERNATIONAL UK: LGBTI RIGHTS, May 31, 2018, https://www.amnesty.org .uk/lgbti-lgbt-gay-human-rights-law-africa-uganda-kenya-nigeria-cameroon.

offenses, and harassment occur at levels that significantly undermine human development and social relations.[4]

Most recently, the extent of the crisis in South Africa was highlighted by the brutal rape and murder of first-year University of Cape Town student, Uyinene Mrwetyana, at the Clarenreich Post Office in Cape Town. On August 24, 2019, Uyinene fell victim to the predilections of a post office teller when she visited the post office to collect a parcel.[5] This event—unfortunately, one of many—sparked outrage and mass action[6] that was visible both on the streets[7] and online in social media campaigns such as #RIPUyinene and #AmINext.

Although South Africa has a comprehensive legal framework to address the scourge of GBV and harassment, the effectiveness of the law has been limited. One area of progress at least has been in the context of the workplace and the world of work.[8]

With this as backdrop, perhaps the significance of the #MeToo movement is the sense of (global) solidarity and the momentum it has generated, nudging social and legal processes as a result. Although the #MeToo movement itself has had limited application in South Africa, and in African countries more generally,[9] it has shifted awareness, attitudes, and behavior toward GBV and

---

4. For an overview of the extent of the problem and recent statistics see Jackie Nagtegall, *The Cost of Rape: Seeking Justice in South Africa*, DAILY MAVERICK, Sep. 7, 2018, https://www .dailymaverick.co.za/opinionista/2018-09-07-the-cost-of-rape-seeking-justice-in-south-africa/.

5. The perpetrator, Luyanda Botha, received three life sentences for rape and murder and five years for defeating the ends of justice (he dumped her body and set her on fire to destroy the evidence). The perpetrator's account of the events (as he described these in court), is provided at Philane Nombembe, *In His Own Words/Luyanda Botha: "This is how I killed Uyinene"*, TIMES LIVE, Nov. 15, 2019, https://www.timeslive.co.za/news/south-africa/2019-11-15-in-his-own -words-luyanda-botha-this-is-how-i-killed-uyinene/.

6. For imagery of the protests see *Keeping "Enough is Enough" in Focus*, MAVERICK CITIZEN, Sep. 27, 2019, https://www.dailymaverick.co.za/article/2019-09-27-keeping -enough-is-enough-in-focus/, and Anso Thom, *One Voice at the Cape Town Protest: "No more, no f**king more!"*, DAILY MAVERICK, Sep. 5, 2019, https://www.dailymaverick.co.za /article/2019-09-05-one-voice-at-the-cape-town-protest-no-more-no-fking-more/.

7. Which included a petition and a march to parliament (see Jenna Etheridge, *Over 600,000 sign petitions over violence against women as SA prepares to march*, NEWS 24, Sep. 3, 2019, https://www.news24.com/SouthAfrica/News/over-600-000-sign-petitions-over -violence-against-women-as-sa-prepares-to-march-20190903); and protest action at a World Economic Forum event (see *South African anti-rape protests target business leaders in Cape Town*, BBC NEWS, Sep. 4, 2019, https://www.bbc.com/news/world-africa-49579682).

8. The *locus classicus* in terms of case law is Campbell Scientific Africa (Pty) Ltd v. Simmers & Others (2016) 37 ILJ 116 (LAC). On the applicable legal framework, see II. The legal framework in South Africa.

9. See Nina Bhalla and Inna Lazareva, *Why Africa's #MeToo is more murmur than an outcry*, REUTERS, Mar. 10, 2019, https://www.reuters.com/article/us-womens-day-africa -metoo-feature/why-africas-metoo-is-more-a-murmur-than-an-outcry-idUSKCN1QP1VO.

harassment, prompting more effective implementation of the law. This is apparent from a 2018 Labour Court judgment stating:

> In the face and growth of global movements such as '#MeToo'; 'The Silence Breakers'; '#NotInMyName', and '#BalanceTonPorc' or 'out your pig', there is an even greater need for more sensitisation to the scourge of sexual harassment in the workplace. Equally so, there is an even greater need for the … [labor dispute resolution tribunals] to place more emphasis on specialised training to deal with such cases.… [T]his case … [is] … a reminder of the need for the urgency and seriousness with which such training is necessary, and for it to be provided on an on-going basis.[10]

In the South African context, #MeToo builds on work that had already began to chip away at the heart of gender-based violence and harassment. In this regard, the life (and death) of Fezekile Ntsukela Kuzwayo, known to the public as *Khwezi*,[11] is worth recounting. Khwezi's experience draws attention to the power imbalance between perpetrators and victims, often securing the victim's silence. Khwezi, however, refused to remain silent.[12]

Remember Khwezi: The Backdrop to #MeToo in South Africa

Khwezi's trauma began at a young age: when, while exiled with her family during apartheid, she experienced sexual abuse at the age of five, and again at ages twelve and thirteen. These transgressions were dealt with by internal processes within the exiled community.[13] Subsequently, in 2006, she spoke out against one of South Africa's most powerful men when she accused Jacob Zuma of rape.

By the time Khwezi was thirty-one years old and Zuma was sixty-four; Khwezi's father had passed away when she was ten and Zuma, who knew her father, was a father figure to her. He would tell Khwezi stories of her father, and she would seek him out from time to time for his support and advice on her plans. She called Zuma "malume," meaning uncle, and on the evening in

---

10. Rustenburg Platinum Mines Ltd v. United Association of SA on behalf of Pietersen & Others (2018) 39 ILJ 1330 (LC) at para [3] (South Africa).

11. Published works include Mmatshilo Motsei, The Kanga and the Kangaroo Court, Reflection on the Rape Trial of Jacob Zuma (2007), Jacana and Redi Thlabi, Khwezi: The Remarkable Story of Fezekile Ntsukela Kuzwayo (2017).

12. Such injustices have fueled social movements against GBV and harassment; including, in 2016, "#EndRapeCulture," "#RememberKhwezi," and "#1in3."

13. State v. Zuma (WLD) 8/5/2006 at p. 52 (South Africa).

question, in November 2005, she visited Zuma at his home, upon receiving news that the son of her niece had been hospitalized in Swaziland. She sought his counsel, informing Zuma that she intended to travel to Swaziland. Notwithstanding her positive HIV status, Zuma had unprotected sex with Khwezi that evening which, Khwezi avowed, she would never have agreed to.

Of these events, and the subsequent trial, the judge hearing the matter took the view that:

> ... both of them are to be blamed for the fact that it [the trial] affected them [adding that] ... [t]he accused should not have had sexual intercourse with a person so many years younger than himself and furthermore being the child of an old comrade and a woman plus minus [half] his age.[14]

Notwithstanding condemnation of Zuma's conduct, he was acquitted (an outcome not supported by all legal commentators).[15] In the judge's view, what had happened between the two of them had been consensual; the judge rejected the argument that Khwezi's response had been to freeze and submit. In any event, the *mens rea* for rape is intention, and, to be found guilty, Zuma must have known that Khwezi did not consent. The judge was not convinced that it was shown, beyond reasonable doubt, that Zuma had the required *mens rea*.

According to the judge, the trial was "unfortunate" and "had a damaging effect on both."[16] The damage to Zuma could not have been extensive, however, as he would go on to become president of South Africa in 2009, just three years after the trial, while Khwezi, on the other hand, was vilified in the extreme by Zuma's supporters. She was confined to witness protection and her family house was burned down during the trial.[17] Immediately after the trial, she and her mother left South Africa for reasons of personal safety, remaining abroad for a period of five years before returning to South Africa.

In many respects, Khwezi was South Africa's #MeToo moment: she refused to be silenced, notwithstanding the backlash. She courageously owned and spoke her truth in the most hostile of environments and consequently, as

---

14. State v. Zuma (WLD) 8/5/2006 at p. 172 (South Africa).

15. There is an argument that the court admitted evidence that it should not have. Much more fundamental, however, is the argument that the legal system fails to adequately incorporate customary cultural interventions within the formal criminal justice processes. These interventions, it is argued, would "do more good than harm in South Africa's fight against sexual violence if they are properly regulated within the formal legal system." Bryant Greenbaum, "*An Elaboration of the Themes and Contentions in Mmatshilo Motsei's Book, The Kanga and the Kangaroo Court, Reflections on the Rape Trial of Jacob Zuma,*" 21 S. AFR. J. CRIM. JUST. 81 at p. 83 (2008).

16. State v. Zuma (WLD) 8/5/2006 at p. 172 (South Africa).

17. "Burn the bitch" was a common call by Zuma supporters during the rape trial.

Redi Tlhabi suggests, Khwezi opened the space "for us to have the conversation about male power, its entitlement and our complicity in aiding and abetting it."[18]

Perhaps the most salient feature of the #MeToo movement that resonates with Khwezi's story is the extent to which patriarchal values are shown to be so deeply embedded within our institutions and thought processes, shaping our realities and expectations and how we relate to each other and to ourselves. This is a state of being in which Khwezi refused to be complicit.

Khwezi's story was again animated a decade after Zuma's rape trial and just two months before Khwezi's passing. On this occasion, in August 2016, four young women, bearing placards with reference to Khwezi, stood in silent protest in front of a podium where Zuma was positioned to deliver the results of local government elections.[19] It was not long before the women were forcefully removed by security.

The #RememberKhwezi silent protest and the activities of young, primarily black, student activists on South African university campuses who, earlier in the year, mobilized under the banner of the #EndRapeCulture campaign, show a growing intolerance toward the normalization of sexual violence in South African, specifically in the context of South African universities.[20]

The #EndRapeCulture campaign draws attention to the role of culture as a factor in GBV and harassment, and how "individual men are socialised and groomed into the normalisation of sexual violence and … unless … [treated] as a systemic problem, we will only remove perpetrators one at a time and still not deal with cultures that promote sexual violence."[21] Consequently, the insensitive treatment of victims and the inadequate response to sexual violence on campuses prompted female students, black students in particular, to speak out, articulating from their position at the intersection of race, gender, and sexuality.[22] The response by Rhodes University students was to publish the "#RU Reference List," a list of the names of alleged rapists who were students at Rhodes

---

18. Redi Tlhabi, Khwezi: The Remarkable Story of Fezekile Ntsukela Kuzwayo, p. 76 (2017).

19. See Marianne Thamm, *Remember Khwezi: Zuma's rape accuser dies, never having known freedom*, THE DAILY MAVERICK, Oct. 9, 2016, https://www.dailymaverick.co.za /article/2016-10-09-rememberkhwezi-zumas-rape-accuser-dies-never-having-known-freedom/ and Zinhle Mapumulo, *#1 in 3: My Horror Story of Rape*, CITY PRESS, Aug. 17, 2016, https:// city-press.news24.com/News/1in3-my-horror-story-of-rape-20160813.

20. See Amanda Gouws, *Young Women Activists are Rewriting the Script*, DAILY DISPATCH, June 17, 2016, http://www.sun.ac.za/english/Documents/newsclips/AGouws _DailyDispatch_Jun2016.pdf.

21. Amanda Gouws, *Celebrity campaigns and rape culture: the pluses and the pitfalls*, MAIL & GUARDIAN, Nov 8, 2017, https://mg.co.za/article/2017-11-08-celebrity-campaigns -and-rape-culture-the-pluses-and-the-pitfalls.

22. See *supra*, note 11.

University, which was published on social media in April 2016, squarely advancing the struggle against sexual violence into cyberspace.[23]

Undoubtedly, emerging technologies, such as Twitter and other forms of social media, are an important platform for sharing experiences and organizing against sexual violence. The outcome is that, in the context of university campuses in South Africa, various task teams have been established to consider the institutional culture and the appropriate policy response, including a Ministerial task team.[24]

With these developments being shaped by the South African youth, it is perhaps not surprising that the #MeToo movement might catch the imagination of an older generation. In this case, including that of women freedom fighters who had, many years previously while in exile, experienced sexual violence at the hands of their male comrades alongside whom they received military training and fought against the apartheid government.[25] These are the women who planned to take their painful secrets to the grave and who, a decade earlier, would have put pressure on Khwezi to drop the rape charge against Zuma.

#MeToo has prompted women to shift out of the silence that society expected of, and imposed on, them. Their ability to speak out and to organize against sexual violence and harassment is supported, not only by access to technology and social media platforms, but also by a matrix of laws within a comprehensive legal framework. One of the virtues of the #MeToo movement has been the extent to which it has nudged this framework into action.[26]

The Legal Framework in South Africa

Pivotal legislation for the prevention of sexual violence in South Africa includes the 2007 "Sexual Offences Act (SOA),"[27] the enactment of which was long anticipated, with the legislation emerging after "a prolonged and iterative

---

23. See Gorata Chenleta, "*Challenging the Culture of Rape at Rhodes*," MAIL & GUARD-IAN, Apr. 25, 2017, https://mg.co.za/article/2017-04-25-00-challenging-the-culture-of-rape-at-rhodes.

24. On the Ministerial Task Team, see *Minister Pandor appoints a Ministerial Task Team to advise on Matters relating to Sexual Harassment and Gender-Based Violence in South African Universities*, May 27, 2019, http://www.dhet.gov.za/SiteAssets/Media%20Release%20and%20Statements%202019/27%20May%202019.pdf.

25. See Carl Collison, *Women Freedom Fighters Tell of Sexual Abuse in Camps*, MAIL & GUARDIAN, Oct. 27, 2017, https://mg.co.za/article/2017-10-27-00-our-women-freedom-fighters-tell-of-sexual-abuse-in-camps.

26. A good example of this is the Commission of Inquiry into Sexual Harassment at the public broadcaster (the SABC) discussed in IV Changes in the law or its enforcement.

27. Criminal Law (Sexual Offences and Related Matters) Amendment Act 32 of 2007.

reform process."[28] The Sexual Offences Act consolidated the law on sexual offences, providing a comprehensive criminal law framework for sexual offence prosecutions.

In the civil law context, the Promotion of Equity and Prevention of Unfair Discrimination Act[29] (PEPUDA) gives effect to the equality right, prohibits discrimination and harassment, and provides complainants with a civil law route to seek justice in the event of a transgression. The Employment Equity Act[30] (EEA) applies in the event of sexual harassment, or an act of discrimination more broadly, in the workplace. In addition, the EEA provides for affirmative action in the workplace for designated groups, including women, black people, and people with disabilities. The Protection From Harassment Act[31] provides a route to afford "victims of harassment an effective remedy against such behaviour."[32]

Criminal Law Framework

The objects of the Sexual Offences Act[33] include "criminalising all forms of sexual abuse or exploitation" and "enacting all matters relating to sexual offences in a single statute." Importantly, the legislation commits to an "effective, responsive and sensitive criminal justice system" tasked with "protecting complainants of sexual offences and their families from secondary victimisation and trauma," and "providing certain services to victims of sexual offences."

The offences created by the Sexual Offences Act include:

- Rape
- Compelled rape
- Sexual assault
- Compelled self-sexual assault; or compelling a person to witness sexual offences, self-masturbation, and flashing

---

28. The history is traced in Smythe et al., *Sexual Offences Commentary* (2014) who, in the preface, explains that "it began in 1996 when the South African Law Commission (SALC) announced the establishment of Project 107: Sexual Offences By and Against Children.... In May 1998 the Minister of Justice approved the extension of the project to all aspects of sexual offences committed against both adults and children, and a decade later, in December 2007, the Criminal Law (Sexual Offences and Related Matters) Amendment Act 32 of 2007 was passed."

29. Act 4 of 200.

30. Act 55 of 1998.

31. Act 17 of 2011.

32. Preamble.

33. Section 2.

- Exposure or display of child pornography, and pornography to children, and using children for or benefiting from child pornography
- Incest, bestiality, and a sexual act with a human corpse
- Consensual sexual acts with children who are under the age of sixteen
- Sexual offences against persons who are mentally disabled

The progressive nature of the Sexual Offences Act (SOA) is evident from the preamble text, which declares that "the prevalence of the commission of sexual offences in our society is primarily a social phenomenon, ... reflective of deep-seated, systemic dysfunctionality in our society, and that legal mechanisms to address this social phenomenon are limited and are reactive in nature, but nonetheless necessary." Regarding these legal mechanisms, the SOA expressly seeks "to afford complainants ... the maximum and least traumatising protection that the law can provide, [and] to provide measures ... to enable the relevant organs of state to give ... effect to the ... Act and ... ultimately eradicate the relatively high incidence of sexual offences committed in the Republic."

An initial stumbling block in the implementation of the Sexual Offences Act was the lack of specified penalties for certain sexual offences. In this regard, (ill-founded) objections were raised in defence of alleged perpetrators during prosecutions based on the principle of "legality," requiring legal certainty for an offence, including the terms of punishment.[34]

This gap was closed by amendments to the SOA in 2012,[35] which provide that if a court has convicted a person of an SOA offence and a penalty is not prescribed for that offence, then the court may impose a sentence as provided in the Criminal Procedure Act 1977, which that court considers appropriate and which is within that court's jurisdiction. The section elaborates on aggravating factors, such as if the accused committed the offence for financial gain, or to receive any benefit, reward, compensation or any other advantage.

A more fundamental concern raised against the SOA was its failure to prescribe a comprehensive and state-funded framework for the necessary medical and psychological care "essential to helping survivors of sexual assault who often experience extreme stress and trauma after an incident of sexual assault."[36]

---

34. See DPP v. Prins (Minister of Justice and Constitutional Development & two amici curiae intervening) (369/12) [2012] 106 ZASCA (June 15, 2012) (South Africa).

35. Section 56A was expressly included to address sentencing.

36. Smythe et al., *Sexual Offences Commentary* (2014), Chapter 15, at para. 3.4.

Although the South African Law Commission[37] endorsed a legal provision that would require medical care, treatment, and counseling to survivors (and, where appropriate to their families) to be provided at the state's expense, in the end result, the right to medical care in the SOA is limited to the right of access to postexposure prophylaxis, meaning access to treatment after potential exposure to HIV to prevent becoming infected.

Additional medical and psychological services, if made available as of right, would go a long way in assisting complainants dealing with the trauma and stress that sexual violence often evokes. For example, "[s]urvivors of sexual offences ... frequently ... ruminate about the role they played in 'provoking' a sexual assault (self-blame), experience anxiety about testifying (fear) and may even withdraw from the criminal justice process if it becomes too alienating (hopelessness)."[38] The experiences are a common theme in case law and other reports of sexual offences.

Finally, the SOA establishes a National Register for Sexual Offenders (NRSO), a database containing the details of persons convicted of any sexual offence against a child or mentally disabled person.[39] The SOA provides the framework for the appointment of a registrar to maintain the register and the process for applying for a certificate stating whether the particulars of a person mentioned in the application are recorded in the register,[40] in which case certain restrictions are applicable.

While the SOA entails the prosecution of an accused by the state, a complainant need not necessarily invoke the criminal law system. The additional opportunities for a complainant to seek protection and justice are considered next.

---

37. South African Law Commission, Sexual Offences (Project 107) Discussion Paper 102 (2001), available at http://www.justice.gov.za/salrc/dpapers/dp102.pdf.

38. Smythe et al., *Sexual Offences Commentary* (2014), Chapter 15, at para. 3.4.

39. The NRSO seeks to ensure that convicted offenders are prevented from working with these two vulnerable groups. A mechanism is provided for certain employers to check the register to verify an employee's suitability for fostering or adopting children or working with children or mentally disabled people. In addition, the Child Protection Register records people who are unsuitable for working with children in circumstances determined by the Children's Act 38 of 2005.

40. Section 44 indicates the persons who may apply for such a certificate, which includes employers, or prospective employers, any relevant authority, and an employee or a person themselves in respect of his or her own particulars.

Civil Law Protection

As mentioned, the Protection From Harassment Act provides victims with an effective remedy against harassment. It does so by providing complainants with an accessible route in the civil courts (the Magistrates' Courts) for the issuance of a protection order against a respondent. The act defines the terms "harassment" and "sexual harassment" and provides for the issuance of an interim protection order, outside ordinary court hours if necessary, and without notice to the respondent, which will then be served on the respondent by the clerk of the court, sheriff, or a peace officer identified by the court. In addition, when issuing a protection order or an interim protection order, the court must authorize the issuance of a warrant for the arrest of the respondent and suspend the execution of the warrant subject to compliance with the order. Details on accessing the protection provided by the Protection From Harassment Act and the relevant forms for doing so are readily available.[41]

The Protection From Harassment Act seeks to secure a level of physical security against harassment; complainants may seek compensation and additional remedies under the PEPUDA or, in the case of an employee, under the EEA.

PEPUDA provides a framework for procedures and remedies for complainants who allege discrimination, hate speech, or harassment. In addition, the act takes on responsibility to "raise public awareness on the importance of promoting equality and overcoming unfair discrimination, hate speech and harassment."[42]

The Equality Court, established by PEPUDA, has scope to "hold an enquiry" when proceedings are instituted and to refer matters to other appropriate fora. The Equality Court may make an appropriate order that includes payment of damages; an order restraining discriminatory practices; and any other "appropriate order of a deterrent nature." The court may also require the parties to provide regular progress reports to the court and may direct the clerk of the court to submit a matter to the Director of Public Prosecutions.[43]

Statistics on complaints before the Equality Court show a total of 844 and 558 cases in the years 2014/15 and 2015/16, respectively. The majority (40 percent) of these cases concerned hate speech, and most of the cases involved

---

41. See Forms: Protection from Harassment Act, 2011 (Act 17 of 2011), Dept. of Justice & Constitutional Development, Republic of South Africa, http://www.justice.gov.za /forms/form_pha.html; and see *Woman Know Your Rights: A Simplified Guide to the Protection from Harassment Act*, Women's Legal Centre, 2015, http://wlce.co.za/wp-content/uploads /2017/02/Protection-from-Harassment-Act-Booklet.pdf.

42. Section 2(e) of PEPUDA.

43. Section 21 of PEPUDA.

either hate speech or discrimination based on race.[44] Gender based violence, it would appear, has not taken center stage at the Equality Courts, notwithstanding the prevalence of gender and sex discrimination in South Africa.

Whereas PEPUDA applies outside of the employment relationship, the EEA deals with discrimination and harassment in the workplace. The EEA expressly prohibits sexual harassment (among other forms of harassment) and provides employees with an effective mechanism—access to the Commission for Conciliation, Mediation and Arbitration (CCMA) and the Labour and Labour Appeal Courts—to address harassment in the workplace. In addition, a Code of Good Practice on Sexual Harassment, interpreting the EEA, provides guidance on the handling of sexual harassment cases. Section 60 of the EEA provides a mechanism for holding employers, who fail to take the necessary steps to eliminate harassment in the workplace, directly liable in terms of the Act.[45]

Increasingly, dismissal is the likely sanction for employees whose behavior amounts to harassment. This is so, even in the event of once-off and seemingly "benign" incidents.

The Reality

The challenge is to move from "good laws on paper" to effective implementation of the law. As the 2017-18 Annual Report on the Implementation of the Criminal Law (Sexual Offences and Related Matters) Amendment Act explains:

> Since 1994 the South African Parliament has been passing progressive pieces of legislation to safeguard the rights of women and children against gender-based violence. Despite these globally-competitive laws, our homes and streets are still fraught with violence, particularly against women and children. Many are raped before they are killed, maimed, burned and buried in shallow graves. The need to strengthen the coordinated implementation of legislation has become more urgent than before. The country needs to explore ways of preventing violence from the family environment first and encourage community participation against gender-based violence.

---

44. Human Rights Commission, Research Brief on Gender and Equality in South Africa: 2013–2017 (2007) at p. 12.

45. Section 60 requires an employer, having been made aware of allegations of discrimination by the complainant, to "consult all relevant parties and must take the necessary steps to eliminate the alleged conduct and comply with the provisions of this Act," Failure to do so, or to "do all that was reasonably practicable" to prevent the discrimination, will mean that the employer may be held liable.

Importantly, in its formulation, implementation, and enforcement, the law must adequately accommodate the plurality of South African society and its legal system, reconciling the formal criminal law framework with customary practices. In this regard, after the Zuma rape trial, an argument was made for legislative reform to take account of African customary interventions that are traditionally invoked in the context of sexual violence.[46]

In his doctoral thesis, criminologist Bryant Greenbaum elaborates on the argument for the express reference in criminal law to the customary practices, ceremonies, and rituals ("living customary law") occurring within communities in the event of sexual violence or misconduct. For example, Greenbaum mentions the payment of damages after financial negotiations between the families involved, and cleansing ceremonies that may include compensatory elements (providing evidence of wrongdoing). Hence, Greenbaum argues for reform to "incorporat(e) ... [African customary] interventions into the formal criminal process,"[47] and "bridge the cultural divide that currently exists when women and children approach prosecutors and the courts for practical relief."[48] Importantly, the purpose is not to undermine the judicial process, but rather to encourage certainty and consistency. Without synergy between the plural systems, Greenbaum expresses concern that "a significant number of black women and children will continue to disregard, or withdraw from, the formal legal system and instead resort to customary interventions that better address their geographic, race, class and cultural concerns."[49] However, this is not a development that #MeToo is likely to impact.

Changes in the Law or Its Enforcement

Although it is too early to tell whether legislative reform will result from the #MeToo movement in South Africa, it seems unlikely that it will, primarily because of the extensive legal framework already in place. However, #MeToo has increased awareness of the pervasiveness of the problem, and of the need for

---

46. See in particular the discussion in Bryant Greenbaum, in Compensation for victims of sexual violence in South Africa: A human rights approach to remedial criminal compensation provisions, (2013) Doctorate in Criminal Justice, University of Cape Town, Faculty of Law; and see the discussion in Greenbaum, supra, note 14. In support of the argument, Greenbaum refers to the approach in Canada that requires a consideration of indigenous culture in cases of sexual violence involving First Nation offenders.

47. *Id.*, at pp. 82-83.

48. *Id.*, at p. 98.

49. Ibid.

effective enforcement and compliance with the laws already in place, particularly in the context of the workplace.

One example of the impact of #MeToo on compliance is an independent Commission of Inquiry into Sexual Harassment established by the South African public broadcaster (the "SABC") in June 2018.[50] The commission was established amid numerous complaints of sexual harassment, including allegations of sex-for-jobs and was intended to "change the tone" and the institutional culture of the organization. The SABC opened its inquiry, inviting a #MeToo moment by opening the space for:

> people … [to] be able to tell the SABC about sexual harassment and abuse they've experienced … [inviting] … both SABC staffers, as well as freelancers who've worked or are working for the SABC, as well as people who've never worked for the SABC but have had interaction with the public broadcaster and encountered sexual harassment or abuse.[51]

After gathering evidence, the Commission of Inquiry finalized its report, which resulted in the suspension of numerous alleged perpetrators, pending disciplinary inquiries into their conduct. The commission's findings stressed the vulnerability of the complainants and the impact on their well-being.[52] Measures were recommended to support the development of a culture of acceptance and respect for gender equality.

These and other developments in South Africa, some of them prompted by the #MeToo movement, are reason for cautious optimism. #MeToo has made it easier for victims to find their voice. However, there are still many obstacles and dangers in speaking out against violence and harassment; for many, these obstacles and dangers keep justice out of reach, just as it was for Khwezi.

Conclusion

Khwezi lived bravely, taking things "one fool at a time," as she would often say. She refused to remain silent, while others "turned a blind eye," and today

---

50. SABC Media Statement, Findings and Recommendations of the Commission of Inquiry into Sexual Harassment, November 2018 (Commission Report), http://www.sabc .co.za/sabc/findings-and-recommendations-of-the-commission-of-inquiry-into-sexual -harassment/.

51. Thinus Ferreira, "*SABC Joins #MeToo with Inquiry into Sexual Harassment*," CHANNEL 24, Jun. 1, 2018, https://www.channel24.co.za/TV/News/sabc-joins-metoo-with-inquiry -into-sexual-harassment-20180601.

52. Many were freelance workers who left the organization traumatized and without work, and therefore without medical insurance and access to counseling.

South Africa is paying the price for not standing up to a "fool" sooner. As former deputy chief justice, Dikgang Moseneke, confirms:

> [w]e went to sleep for 10 years (the duration of Zuma's presidency) and institutions were hollowed out.... We all lost the guts to tell a bumbling fool who was sitting out there, acting as a president, [to tell him that] he is a fool, [to] tell him he's incapable of doing the high ideals of our liberation struggle. As we failed to do that, we actually allowed so much devastation and poor people became poorer.[53]

Moseneke's words are a caution against the tyranny of silence and how easy it is to be complicit in a culture that enables abuse. In the context of sexual violence and harassment, #MeToo at least provides us with a countermeasure to this.

---

53. See News 24 Wire, "*Jacob Zuma is a 'bumbling fool'—former deputy chief justice Dikgang Moseneke*," POLITY, Nov. 30, 2018, https://www.polity.org.za/article/jacob-zuma -is-a-bumbling-fool-former-deputy-chief-justice-dikgang-moseneke-2018-11-30.

CHAPTER 30

Curbing Sexual Harassment of Students in Nigerian Academia: Place and Role of Legal Policies

Caroline Joelle Nwabueze[1]

Introduction

Women's rights are rights of equivalent worth to men's rights. The Convention on the Elimination of all Forms of Discrimination Against Women (CEDAW) addresses what is required for women's rights to approach equality with men's.[2] Article 5(a) specifically requires the modification of the "social and cultural patterns of conduct of men and women, with a view to achieving the elimination of prejudices and customary and all other practices which are based on the idea of the inferiority or the superiority of either of the sexes or on stereotyped roles for men and women." In Africa, some of the most serious violations of women's rights take place in the private sphere of the family. They are reinforced by traditional norms and cultural values.[3]

Sexual harassment in Nigeria is an example of a vice and crime that has lasted for decades. This chapter analyses the impact of legal policies combating sexual harassment on female academic groups in Nigeria. Several university lecturers have abused the fiduciary relationship between them and their female students to harass them sexually.

---

1. Department of Public Law, Faculty of Law, Enugu State University of Science and Technology (ESUT), Nigeria. Member of ESUT Ethics Committee.

2. Nicola Lacey, *Feminist legal theory and the rights of women*, in GENDER AND HUMAN RIGHTS 49 (Karen Knop, 2004).

3. Fitnat Naa-Adjeley Adjeley, *Reclaiming the African woman's individuality: the struggle between women's reproductive autonomy and African Society and Culture*, 44 AM. U. L. REV. 1353, 1351-1381 (1995).

First, this chapter defines sexual harassment in the Nigerian cultural context. It then examines the phenomenon of sexual harassment within various institutions, specifically academia. Several cases are reviewed, including penalties and disciplinary sanctions against lecturers caught in the legal net. The chapter then discusses the impact of the #MeToo movement and other international organizations in bringing structural changes to Nigeria. An examination of the obligations of Nigeria under international law follows, including the legal reform protecting women's rights. The paper ends with recommendations for the adoption of anti-discrimination laws in view of the total eradication of sexual harassment within the country.

Background

Claims of sexual harassment have become a daily feature of the news in Nigeria. Nearly half of Nigeria's 200 million citizens are female, of which only half are literate. The youth literacy level for females is put at 65.33 percent.[4]

In the Northern part of Nigeria, females in institutions of learning often fear being kidnapped by terrorists or gangs. It's no longer news that two famous kidnappings were carried out in the North East region of Nigeria (Dapchi and Chibok), which saw the kidnapping of over 300 schoolgirls. Kidnappings are not limited to schoolgirls; mothers who are peasant farmers and female traders have become major targets too. An additional difficulty for Northern Nigerian girls is that underage marriage is a common feature in the North, as girls under eighteen are forced into marriages.

In contrast, women and girls in the South enjoy greater freedom than their counterparts in the North. Southern Nigeria includes the country's big cities, like Lagos, Port-Harcourt, Enugu, and Calabar, and the population is more urban and exposed to technology and Western values. The South is largely Christian.

Percentage of Young Women Able to Attend School

One issue prevalent in the country is that of physical insecurity for female students' safety. It is most felt in the Nigerian North. According to a 2017 UNICEF report, states in the North East and North West have female primary school net attendance rates of 47.7 percent and 47.3 percent, respectively, meaning more than half of the girls are not in school. Educational deprivation

---

4. https://countrymeters.info/en/Nigeria.

in Northern Nigeria is driven by various factors, including economic barriers and socio-cultural norms and practices that discourage formal education of girls. Twenty-nine percent and 35 percent of Muslim children in the North East and North West, respectively, receive Qur'anic education, which does not include basic skills such as literacy and numeracy. Such children are considered by the Nigerian government to be officially out of school.[5]

Insecurity notwithstanding, parents still send their female wards to school—from primary school to secondary school and up to the university/ college (tertiary) level. There has been an increase in general female participation in tertiary institutions of learning, especially in Nigeria's South. In 2015, the number of females from Imo state (South East Nigeria) admitted to tertiary institutions was 15,501 against 13,382 for males. The rate of women in institutions of learning in Nigeria is on the increase. There is, however, less access to education in the North, but it is far from the Western picture painted by foreign media, which states that women are poorly represented in acquiring an education.[6] Despite insecurity in the North, you still have girls (who are most vulnerable) going to school.

Notwithstanding the above, many Nigerian women are highly educated. They are also well positioned in institutions of learning and in the corporate world. All these realities are happening amid incidents of discrimination and sexual harassment. A woman who avoids child marriage and manages to pursue a university degree may then be sexually harassed in the university context.

Perception of Sexual Harassment in Nigeria

Sexual harassment is widespread in Nigeria. The menace of sexual harassment is yet to be clearly understood by some sectors of Nigerian society. Some carry out acts without realizing they are violating the woman. Some women do not recognize when they are being sexually harassed, save for the now-growing acts of rape and sexual assault. Those who can identify when they've been sexually harassed are afraid to speak up for fear of their safety, stigma, and other social consequences that come with being a victim of sexual harassment. Sexual harassment has sadly been institutionalized in Nigeria, hence its pervasive nature. In various institutions, victims of sexual harassment are treated with disdain and disbelief and are sometimes threatened.

---

5. *UNICEF for Every Child: Nigeria/Education*, https://www.unicef.org/nigeria /education.

6. G. Bello, *Condition of Women in Nigeria: Issues and Challenges*, Arts Soc. Sci. J. (2017).

Sexual Quid Pro Quo in Nigerian Universities

A Nigerian newspaper reported the following dramatic statistic:

"In one survey of female graduates in Nigeria's higher institutions, at least 69.8 per cent said their lecturers and male classmates had sexually harassed them."[7]

The practice concerns lecturers toward students in their relations and relates to sexual advances in return for good grades.

Abuse of power plays a fundamental role in sexual harassment.[8] Lecturers are in a position of authority and the cornerstone in the grading system. In general, Nigeria academia is not equipped with the anonymous grading software for exams. In the absence of anonymity, the lecturer can easily track his or her prey and harm at will.[9] Grading without complete anonymity enables promotion at will when requested sexual favors have been obtained. This lust is fueled by cultural factors in some regions where the man is seen as the head or chief, and denial to sexual advances appears disrespectful or an open challenge.[10]

Sexual harassment as experienced by students frequently refers to fear and being hemmed in on every side by lecturers whose academic position can make refusal harmful.[11] In this context, the harassment faced by the student could manifest in threats to lose an academic benefit such as university admission. The University of Lagos for example has suspended a lecturer who solicited sex from an admission seeker.[12] The student in such case feels obliged to comply. Otherwise, she faces the risk of losing her admission. Protesting is difficult as the lecturer, an authority in position to tarnish or replenish the academic career of the student receiving the sexual advances, initiates the behavior. Unfortunately,

---

7. Iyabo Lawal, *Finding a lasting solution to sexual harassment in schools*, THE GUARDIAN, Apr. 26, 2018, https://guardian.ng/features/education/finding-a-lasting-solution-to-sexual-harassment-in-schools/.

8. Jennifer Berdahl, Vicki J. Magley & Craig R. Waldo, *The sexual harassment of men? Exploring the concept with theory and data*, PSYCHOL. WOMEN Q., 20(4): 527–47 (1996).

9. Anonymous grading forces students' names to be hidden and allows institutions to demonstrate their pledge to integrity in the assessment process. See https://www.law.berkeley.edu/wp-content/uploads/2015/04/Anonymous-Grading.jpg and J. Paul, *What is Anonymous Grading?*, D2L, Mar. 2, 2017, https://www.d2l.com/blog/what-is-anonymous-grading./.

10. T. Ajayi, *Cultural Explanations Of The Status Of Nigerian Women*, J. RES. NAT'L DEV., Vol. 6 (1) 2008: pp. 4-4, https://www.ajol.info//index.php/jorind/article/view/42397.

11. Billie Wright Dziech & Michael W. Hawkings, *Sexual Harassment in Higher Education*, GARLAND 1998, p. 4.

12. Bridget Edokwe, *UNILAB suspends lecturer who solicited sex from "admission seeker,"* BARRISTERNG, Oct. 7, 2019, http://www.barristerng.com/unilag-suspends-lecturer-who-solicited-sex-from-admission-seeker/.

students rarely denunciate this calamity and are powerlessly open to sexual advances.

The fear of retaliation is a fundamental deterrent to reporting. Also, collegiality protection could indefinitely harm the student's academics.[13] Remi Sonaiya, a retired Nigerian university professor, said:

> Unfortunately, many universities don't have strong deterrence or punishment for abusers. Students should be encouraged to speak out when such things happen. There must be at least someone in the institution who can be trusted and confided in. Justice must be done.[14]

Nationwide Campaign and #MeToo Movement

Fostering gender equality under law in Nigeria has been the fruit of NGO actions and international society pressure. There are organized movements in Nigeria to make structural changes to empower survivors of sexual assault. #MeToo is an example of a movement organized and structured in several regions. In Nigeria, there are few existing facilities to support victims of sexual harassment or sexual assault referral centers like Justice for All (J4A) programs.[15] Such facilities offer survivors a safe place where he/she can find protection and speak about the abuse. In addition, the use of international campaigns with global mobilization can captivate international attention on stereotypical practices hindering women's empowerment and awaken governments to the need for change.

Globalization includes internationalization, NGO activism, international cooperation, international openness, etc. Arjun Appadurai[16] defines globalization as the process by which global phenomena such as the #MeToo movement take a plethora of forms and have different impacts depending on local cultures.[17] Such globalization has led to a greater integration of women's rights in

---

13. Dziech, *supra*, note 11, p. 52.

14. Adejumo Kabir, *Three Nigerian universities face sexual harassment scandals*, PREMIUM TIMES, Jul. 30, 2018, at https://www.premiumtimesng.com/regional/ssouth-west/278213-feature-three-nigerian-universities-face-sexual-harassment-scandals.html.

15. The Justice For All (J4A) program supports Nigerian-led reform of the justice sector. The program works alongside counterparts from the entire justice community—the courts, the police, anti-corruption agencies, and civil society—to help develop the capacity, accountability and responsiveness of the sector in delivering Justice For All Nigerians. See https://www.britishcouncil.org.ng/justice-for-all-nigeria.

16. Arjun Appadurai, *Disjuncture and Difference in the Global Cultural Economy*, THEORY, CULTURE AND SOCIETY 7, 295-310 (1990).

17. *Ibid.*

society. An international perspective helps to expose national interests and local sexual practices as abusive and breaks the stranglehold these national interests and social customs have used to oppress women in their local environments.

The movement in Nigeria has exploded in a global discussion about sexual harassment.[18] In a social context where women suffer in silence, #MeToo is a platform for expression where women share their stories.[19] The movement has even reached the Muslim-majority Northern Nigeria.[20] Sometimes because sexual harassment is taboo, and some women cannot tell their stories, social media platforms like Twitter become the way out to raise awareness.[21] Several women have repeatedly taken a public stance on their abuse on social media. There have been several subsequent local movements. This includes "Market march," demonstrations by Nigerian women protesting harassment and groping in markets.[22]

According to Nigerian author and feminist Chimamanda Ngozi Adichie in her book, *We Should All Be Feminists*, gender equality is of great value for African nations. Oppressing a female because of her identity is a strangulation that hinders her empowerment.[23] When the victims of sexual harassment speak out on social media against the abuse, they face the risk of intimidation, retaliation, or even worse. In the Muslim North of Nigeria where women are still *invisible*, a young lady was unjustly charged for defamation and jailed by her assailant after speaking up on social media during a #MeToo campaign in the region.[24] The movement revealed grave accusations indicating how lecturers in the country use grades to coerce students, especially female ones, into sex. Failure to respond to lecturers' sexual advances led to lower or failing grades. The result was unreliable academic transcripts and emotionally traumatized young

---

18. Akinwale Akinyoade, *Watch—Chimamanda Adichie Speaks On the #MeToo Movement*, The Guardian, Oct. 12, 2018, https://guardian.ng/life/watch-chimamanda-adichie -speaks-on-the-metoo-movement/.

19. Stephanie Busari & Torera Idowu, *The #MeToo stories you haven't heard: Meet the women speaking out in Nigeria*, CNN, Mar. 2, 2018, https://edition.cnn.com/2018/03/02 /africa/nigeria-rape-survivors-metoo-asequals/index.html.

20. Linus Unah, *The #MeToo movement has reached Muslim-majority northern Nigeria*, Al Jazeera, Mar. 31, 2019, https://www.aljazeera.com/indepth/features/metoo-movement -reached-muslim-majority-northern-nigeria-190330231518587.html.

21. *Ibid.*

22. Linus Unah, *"Normalised but not normal": Nigerian women call out gropers and catcallers*, The Guardian, Feb. 4, 2019, https://www.theguardian.com/global-development /2019/feb/04/normalised-but-not-normal-nigerian-women-call-out-gropers-and-catcallers -market-march-movement-yaba-market-lagos.

23. Chimamanda Ngozi Adichie, The things around your neck (1st ed. 2010).

24. Unah, *supra*, note 20.

graduates, which disgraced the country's image and eroded trust in the educational system.

The practice of sex for grades has escalated in national shame when the whole nation heard the allegations of sexual harassment against lecturers in Nigerian Universities during the #MeToo movement. Parents, NGOs, and the international community mounted pressure for legal action. Testimonies revealed allegations of harassment by Nigerian academia coupled with downgrading during exams, refusal to supervise research projects, etc. Many women do not come forward with accusations for fear of society's rejection or retaliation by the professor.

It is against this background that the Sexual Harassment in Tertiary Educational Institutions Prohibition Bill was proposed in 2016. What was known as the "Sexual Harassment Act" was introduced by the Nigerian Senate to curb the spread of the practice of sex for grades, but ultimately was not enacted into law. The bill was the first legal instrument specifically addressing the issue of sexual harassment in Nigerian academia. The aim was to release students from their preying educators, set the proper sanctions, and restore sanity in the university system.

Without a proper legal framework, it has been difficult to curb sexual harassment in Nigeria. In the absence of discrimination laws in the country, or a specific law on sexual harassment in universities, the general law *mutatis mutandis* applies. Sexual harassment can be situated under the general rubric of sexual offenses against the person; legal actions are usually based on the common law of tort or criminal law.[25] The law of agency has sometimes been used to hold liable an administrative head, since sexual harassment affects both the academic institution represented by the lecturer and the student. According to the media reporting on the impact of sexual harassment on students' behavior, "for decades, female students in popular Nigerian universities have summoned up the courage to report randy male faculty members for sexual harassment."[26]

---

25. Section 252 Criminal Law: "A person who strikes, touches or moves or otherwise applies force of any kind to the person of another, either directly or indirectly, without consent, or with his consent, if the consent is obtained by fraud, or who by any bodily act or gesture attempts or threatens to apply force of any kind to the person of another without his consent, in such circumstances that the person making the attempt or threat has actually or apparently a present ability to effect his purpose, is said to assault that other person and the act is called an assault...." See also Section 262(1), Chapter 25, of the Criminal Law of Lagos States 2011, which provides that: "Any person who sexually harasses another is guilty of a felony and is liable to imprisonment for three years."

26. Ebiuwairo Uwagboe, *The culture of sexual harassment in Nigerian universities*, DAILY TRUST, Nov. 7, 2017, https://www.dailytrust.com.ng/the-culture-of-sexual-harassment-in-nigerian-universities.html.

In some cases, the victim had to rely on vague dispositions related to human rights protection such as Section 34 of the Constitution protecting human dignity ("Every individual is entitled to respect for the dignity of his person")[27] or on transnational human rights protections.

In 2016, for example, in *Abimbola Patricia Yakubu v. Financial Reporting of Nigeria & Anor*,[28] the claimant was fired after refusing sexual advances from the defendant. Delivering her judgment, Justice Oyewumi stated that the sexual harassment the claimant endured was "a violation of the claimant's human dignity and freedom from discrimination as protected by the African Charter on Human and People's Rights."[29]

Sexual harassment could also be censured under a university code of ethics. For this purpose, University of Ibandan has set up a committee to expose any sexual misconduct in the institution.[30] Also, the University of Lagos has set up a task force to handle sexual harassment issues.[31] The Nigerian Federal Competition and Consumer Protection Commission (FCCPC) collaborates with the Police and the National Universities Commission to fight sexual harassment in universities. A dedicated email address has been set to receive complaints about sexual harassment in the country's institutions of higher learning.[32]

Nigerian Duty to Eradicate Sexual Harassment: An Obligation Under International Law

Law has the power to deter and punish wrongdoing in a context where social and administrative controls have failed. Here, an efficient legal policy on sexual harassment in higher educational institutions should have an impact on various groups for institutions to avoid claims and create an environment free

---

27. Section 34(1) 1999 Constitution (as amended).

28. Suit No. NICN/LA/673/2013, judgment delivered Nov. 24, 2016.

29. *Ibid.*, African Charter on Human and Peoples' Rights (Ratification and Enforcement) Act, Chapter A9 (Chapter 10 LFN 1990) (No 2 of 1983). Laws of the Federation of Nigeria 1990.

30. *Sex For Grades: UI Sets Up Panel To Expose Lecturers Harassing Students*, INSIDE OYO, Oct. 17, 2019, https://www.insideoyo.com/sex-for-grades-ui-sets-up-panel-to-expose -lecturers-harassing-students/.

31. Bridget Edokwe, *Sex for marks: UNILAG gets sexual harassment task force*, BARRISTERNG.COM, Oct. 16, 2019, http://www.barristerng.com/sex-for-marks-unilag-gets-sexual -harassment-task-force/.

32. *FG Sets Up Dedicated Email Address for Sexual Harassment Complaints*, NIGERIA COMMUNICATIONS WEEK, Oct. 12, 2019, https://nigeriacommunicationsweek.com.ng /fg-sets-up-dedicated-email-address-for-sexual-harassment-complaints/.

of sexual harassment.[33] Though measures to combat workplace harassment have been increasingly legislated around the globe,[34] anti-harassment legislation tailored for universities is rare. There has nevertheless been advancement on the criminalization of sexual harassment in Lagos State. Under the Criminal Law of Lagos State,[35] harassment affecting educational opportunity is a crime. The same is true for harassment that unreasonably interferes with a person's educational performance or that creates an intimidating, hostile, or offensive learning environment. Unfortunately, this legal development is restricted to Lagos State and does not affect the Federal Republic of Nigeria as a whole.

Nigeria has adopted various international legal agreements in the field of gender equality and women's rights. Those include the Convention on the Elimination of all Forms of Discriminations Against Women (CEDAW) and the Protocol to the African Charter on the Rights of Women in Africa, 2003 (Maputo Protocol). Meanwhile, the practice of sexual harassment contributes to the continuation of sex differentiation of roles in society.[36] Sex difference in brain hemispheres is a stereotype,[37] and sexual harassment a form of sex discrimination. Sex discrimination in education could include the exclusion of any person from a course of instruction on the basis of his or her sex,[38] or the use of a sex-based admissions policy.[39] The question arises: Can the international women's rights contained in above treaties ratified by Nigeria be used to strengthen discrimination claims?

Upon signature in 1985 of CEDAW, Nigeria became a "state party" to the Convention, meaning that it agreed to abide by all provisions of the convention. No reservations were made. The country equally acceded to the Optional Protocol to the Convention on November 22, 2004. Nonetheless, according to Section 12 of the Nigerian Constitution, the adoption of an international treaty by the National Assembly is necessary for it to be applicable in Nigeria.[40]

---

33. Dziech, *supra*, note 11, p. xv.

34. ELLEN PINKOS COBB, WORKPLACE BULLYING AND HARASSMENT: NEW DEVELOPMENTS IN INTERNATIONAL LAW 396 (1st ed. 2017).

35. Section 262(1), *supra*, note 25.

36. Marlaine E. Lockheed et al., *Discrimination in Education: A Literature Review and Bibliography*, Educational Testing Service, Princeton, N.J. P. ii.

37. Patricia B. Campbell (1989), *The Hidden Discriminator: Sex and Race Bias in Educational Research*, Women's Educational Equity Act Program, U.S. Dept. of Ed., p.16.

38. N.Y. EDUC. Law § 3201-a (McKinney Supp. 1973).

39. Dinah L. Shelton and Dorothy Berndt, *Sex Discrimination in Vocational Education: Title IX and Other Remedies*, 62 CALIF. L.R. No. 4, 1121, 1137 (1974).

40. Section 12 of the Constitution of Federal Republic of Nigeria, 1999 provides: "(1) No treaty between the Federation and any other country shall have the force of law except to the extent to which any such treaty has been enacted into law by the National Assembly."

Unfortunately, due to the country's lengthy legislative processes, the CEDAW Convention has still not been adopted domestically.

The Protocol on the Rights of Women in Africa (Maputo Protocol)

Adopted July 11, 2003 during the 2nd Ordinary Session Assembly of the Union, the Maputo Protocol to the African Charter on Human and Peoples' Rights on the Rights of Women in Africa, entered into force, after being ratified by fifteen African governments. The African Union adopted this legal instrument to supplement the regional human rights charter, the African Charter on Human and Peoples' Rights (the African Charter). The Maputo Protocol provides broad protection for women's rights, including their sexual and reproductive rights.

Several provisions of CEDAW have been echoed in the African Maputo Protocol on the rights of women, emphasizing that African states should combat all forms of discrimination against women through appropriate legislative, institutional, and other means to promote gender equality. The Maputo Protocol also committed African states to commit themselves "to modify the social and cultural patterns of conduct of women and men through public education, information, education and communication strategies, with a view to achieving the elimination of harmful cultural and traditional practices and all other practices which are based on the idea of the inferiority or the superiority of either of the sexes, or on stereotyped roles for women and men."[41]

Article 17(1) of the Protocol extends its reach into the spheres of family, community, and tradition—the areas where women are most likely to experience violations of rights. Nevertheless, the Protocol failed to explicitly define discrimination against women. Article 1(5) of the Protocol restricts "discrimination" to "any distinction, exclusion or restriction or any differential treatment based on sex...." The Protocol additionally supports traditional values and practices impeding the recognition of women's rights in Africa.[42] Consequently, the Protocol has been criticized for "reproducing the essential tension that plagues the realization of the rights of women" in Africa, which has been criticized

---

41. Art. 2(f) Protocol.

42. Art. 17(1) and (2) Protocol to the African Charter state: "Women shall have the right to live in a positive cultural context and to participate at all levels in the determination of cultural policies. States Parties shall take all appropriate measures to enhance the participation of women in the formulation of cultural policies at all levels."

under the African Charter.[43] The Protocol seems to uphold the tradition, by protecting customary and religious laws that violate women's rights, such as the rights to equality and non-discrimination.[44]

Despite the ratification of these important treaties by Nigeria, obstacles remain in respect to the full enjoyment of rights by women. Those obstacles are resulting from:

- patriarchal cultural norms;
- dual legal system with respect to status, customs, and religious laws;[45]
- the lack of domestic application of regional and international standards; and
- national laws and administrative practices that reflect patriarchal attitudes and gender stereotypes.[46]

Nigerian Sexual Harassment Legal Regulatory Framework

In Africa, culture and tradition have been key strongholds of women's equality. Nigeria has adopted various laws and policies to deter sexual harassment in the country. Workplace policies are a determining factor in the prevention of sexual harassment within an institution.[47] The lack of policies or laws in

---

43. Articles 17(2) and (3) of the African Charter states that every individual "may freely take part in the cultural life of his community" and that "[t]he promotion and protection of morals and traditional values recognized by the community shall be the duty of the State." Article 27(1) of the African Charter further provides that "every individual shall have duties towards his family and society."

44. Center for Reproductive Rights, *The Protocol on the Rights of Women in Africa: An Instrument for Advancing Reproductive and Sexual Rights*, Feb. 2006, p. 11, https://reproductiverights.org/sites/default/files/documents/pub_bp_africa.pdf.

45. Some English laws made by the Nigerian colonial legislature before Nigeria's October 1, 1960 independence were not repealed and are now an integral part of the Nigerian legal system. This adds to the received English law as stipulated under Section 45(1) of the Interpretation Act comprising the common law, the doctrines of equity, and the statutes of general application in force on January 1, 1900.

46. Report of CEDAW Committee's Africa Regional Consultations on the Proposed General Recommendations on Women's Human Rights in Conflict and Post Conflict Situations, Addis Ababa, Ethiopia, Apr. 12-13, 2012, p. 10, https://www.ohchr.org/Documents/HRBodies/CEDAW/Womenconflictsituations/AddisAbabaApril2012_womeninconflict.pdf.

47. Tara C. Reich and M. Sandy Hershcovis, *Observing sexual harassment at work: a gendered extension of a gendered construct*, in GENDER AND THE DYSFUNCTIONAL WORKPLACE 120 (Suzy Fox and Terri R. Lituchy, eds., 2012).

the Nigerian context prior to 2017 caused the escalation of sexual harassment in general and of students' harassment by lecturers in particular.

Legal Turnaround Related to the Fight Against Sexual Harassment in Nigeria

Nigerian Academia is not the only sector experiencing the problem of sexual harassment. Other institutions in the country are also affected. Nevertheless, the days of impunity for sexual harassment in the country have been numbered since the amendment in 2017 of the Civil Procedure Rules of the National Industrial Court of Nigeria. This amendment introduced Order 14(1) which specifically refers to allegations of sexual harassment in the workplace.

Order 14(1) was a legal turnaround. For the first time in the history of the Nigerian national legal system, sexual harassment was specifically translated in legal terms. The legal provision refers to sexual harassment as: (1) a physical conduct of a sexual nature; (2) a verbal form of sexual harassment; (3) a non-verbal form of sexual harassment; or (4) a quid pro quo harassment.[48]

This order was a social breakthrough and also a victory over cultural and religious discrimination usually experienced toward the opposite sex. Nigerian courts have few cases of validating legal complaints by females' victims of sexual harassment. In *Ejike Maduka v. Microsoft*,[49] a female office worker alleged that her boss had consistently tickled and touched her in the office against her will. The office worker claimed that her subsequent termination could be traced to her refusal to succumb to her boss's sexual advances. After investigations, the National Industrial Court of Nigeria decided that there has been an infringement of her fundamental right to dignity and freedom from discrimination. The employer was therefore liable.

This legal protection has surely emboldened many women previously silenced by culture and religion, to come out and file a claim to seek justice regarding what they endured in silence: terrifying stories of sexual harassment.

To the contrary, LGBTQ community does not enjoy the same right to protest as women. With the passage of the Same Sex Marriage (Prohibition) Act, 2013,[50] LGBTQ Nigerians have been subjected to homophobic

---

48. Order 14(1) of the National Industrial Court of Nigeria Civil Procedure Rules 2017.

49. Unreported Suit NICN/LA/492/2012, Dec. 19, 2013 (Nigeria).

50. Nigerian law already prohibited same sex marriage. The 2013 Act added to this, "A person who registers, operates or participates in gay clubs, societies or organizations, or directly or indirectly makes public show of same-sex amorous relationship in Nigeria commits an offense and is liable on conviction to a term of 10 years."

persecution. Despite the protection granted under international human rights law and LGBTQ activism,[51] the community is oppressed by domestic social conditions in Nigeria.

Combating Sexual Harassment in Nigerian Academia

With the contribution of Order 14(1) NIC Rules in 2017, there has been a notable advancement of the jurisprudence on sexual harassment in Nigeria. However, the legal recognition of sexual harassment as an offence was only extended to the workplace, without specifically targeting academia. The proposed 2016 Sexual Harassment in Tertiary Educational Institutions Prohibition Bill ushers the protection granted under employment law to Nigerian academia. Teaching staff could face up to fourteen years in jail for having sexual relationships with their students. The backing of high officials and NGOs has shown the seriousness of the matter and prompted the vice-chancellors to act. Since then, several lecturers have been dismissed for sexual harassment. Examples are numerous: University of Abuja, for example, sacked two professors over a sex scandal,[52] while State University Ado-Ekiti sacked a lecturer over sexual harassment.[53] With the 2017 National Industrial Court Civil Procedure Rules and a re-submission of the Sexual Harassment draft bill in 2019, Nigeria has stopped being a safe haven for perpetrators.

There is now a clear understanding of what amounts to sexual harassment, and sexual harassment is now actionable, though not under the Sexual Harassment Bill (since it is not yet enacted into law).

---

51. Michelle Billies, *How Can Psychology Support Low-Income LGBTGNC Liberation?* in Women's Human Rights. A Social Psychological Perspective on resistance, Liberation, and Justice 44 (Shelly Grabe, 2018).

52. Chidimma C. Okeke, *UniAbuja sacks 2 professors, demotes others over sex scandal*, Daily Beast, Dec. 17, 2019, https://www.dailytrust.com.ng/uniabuja-sacks-2-professors -demotes-others-over-sex-scandal.html. See also Unini Chiome, *UPDATED: S*X-For-Marks: Uniabuja Dismisses Two Professors For Misconduct*, The Nigeria Lawyers, Dec. 6, 2019, https://thenigerialawyer.com/sx-for-marks-uniabuja-sacks-dean/.

53. Bridget Edokwe, *Ekiti varsity sacks lecturer over alleged sexual harassment*, BarristerNG, Dec. 6, 2019, http://www.barristerng.com/ekiti-varsity-sacks-lecturer -over-alleged-sexual-harassment/.

Toward Legal Reform?

The Sexual Harassment in Tertiary Educational Institutions Prohibition Bill proposed in 2016 did not pass Parliament.[54] In October 2019, BBC Africa Eye premiered an undercover exposé called *Sex for Grades*,[55] documenting claims made by multiple Ghanaian and Nigerian female university students that their male university lecturers had engaged in sexual misconduct and extortion. The Nigerian Senate has re-introduced the 2016 bill criminalizing any sexual advances made by lecturers toward students.[56] The bill is supported by the deputy president of the Nigerian Senate; the Nigerian First Lady, Hajia Aisha Buhari; and the Nigerian Academic Staff Union of Universities.[57] The entire nation, civil society, and academic union await to applaud the advent of new law curbing sexual harassment of students.

Nigeria is evenly divided among the three dominant tribes, Igbo, Yoruba, and Hausa/Fulani. Discrimination based on sex is significant in each of those tribes. For example, until a recent court decision, in the South East, Igbo women were unable to inherit property; hence they could not take part in the sharing of the estate of their deceased loved one. Islamic Law permits polygamy and the betrothal system.

Meanwhile, local courts have not remained silent. There have been several additional actions for the protection of women's rights in the country. Several courts' decisions have reformed the system. An example is the condemnation in 2012 by a Federal High Court in Ikeja, Lagos of the provisions of the Police Act, which prohibits a woman police officer from marrying a man of her choice without the permission of the Commissioner of Police.[58] The court declared the Police Act in violation of section 42 of the Nigerian Constitution,[59] and

---

54. Rufaro Samanga, *Nigeria Is Re-introducing a New Bill on Sexual Harassment*, OKAYAFRICA, Oct. 10, 2019, https://www.okayafrica.com/nigeria-is-re-introducing-a-new -bill-on-sexual-harassment/.

55. *Sex for Grades: Undercover in West African Universities*, BBC, Oct. 7, 2019, https:// www.bbc.com/news/av/world-africa-49907376/sex-for-grades-undercover-in-west-african -universities.

56. Samanga, *supra*, note 54.

57. *Ibid.*

58. Regulation 124 made pursuant to the Police Act (Cap P19), Laws of the Federation of Nigeria, states: "A woman Police Officer who is desirous of marrying must first apply in writing to the Commissioner of Police for the State Command in which she is serving, requesting permission to marry and giving name, address and occupation of the person she intends to marry. Permission will be granted for the marriage if the intended husband is of good character and the woman police officer has served in the force for a period of not less than three years."

59. Section 42(1)(a) states that "A citizen of Nigeria of a particular community, ethnic group, place of origin, sex, religion or political opinion shall not, by reason only that he is such

"inconsistent with article 2 of the African Charter on Human and Peoples' rights which prohibits discrimination on the basis of sex."[60]

Another example is the 2014 Nigerian Supreme Court decision in *Ukeje v. Ukeje*, which solemnly declared that "no matter the circumstances of the birth of a female child, such a child is entitled to an inheritance from her late fathers' estate."[61] The above Supreme Court verdict nullifies the age-old Igbo tradition prevalent in the old Eastern Region of Nigeria.

Conclusion

There must be a mental shift in Nigerian society. People need to be sensitized to understand that holding a woman without her consent and saying certain things and making certain remarks to her amount to sexual harassment on its own. This and many more facts are unknown to many Nigerians—hence the prevalence of conduct amounting to sexual harassment. The Nigerian constitution gives room for national adoption of the international rights contained in the CEDAW treaty and any treaty related to women's equality. Nigeria domestically must adopt these international requirements of equality. The issue of sexual harassment in Nigerian institutions of learning led to the enactment of the Sexual Harassment in Tertiary Educational Institutions Prohibition Bill 2016, now reintroduced in 2019. This bill is commendable but begs the question: why is the law limited to tertiary educational establishments and not all educational institutions? The government must adopt CEDAW and the African Maputo Protocol to protect women's rights in Nigeria.

---

a person:- (a) be subjected either expressly by, or in the practical application of, any law in force in Nigeria or any executive or administrative action of the government, to disabilities or restrictions to which citizens of Nigeria of other communities, ethnic groups, places of origin, sex, religions or political opinions are not made subject...."

60. *Women Empowerment and Legal Aid (WELA) v. Attorney General of the Federation*, unreported, Suit No. FHC/IKJ/CS/M128/2010 (Nigeria).

61. (2014) LPELR-22724 (SC) (Nigeria).

International Law

CHAPTER 31

Sexual Harassment at the United Nations: Changing the Standards and Changing the Practice

Purna Sen[1]

In 2017, the United Nations was hit with media stories of sexual harassment within several of its organizations.[2] The global MeToo movement reached into the United Nations with hashtags that addressed the UN system and the sector, including "#AIDTOO #MeTooUN." The journey from non-story to scandal has promoted a range of initiatives, as it has elsewhere, to show the seriousness with which this abuse is seen and, consequently, the many ways in which it is to be addressed.

Yet sexual harassment was neither new nor unknown; a number of factors made for a moment pregnant with possibilities for significant change. These included: interest among the international media (which was more than

---

1. Executive Coordinator and Spokesperson on Addressing Sexual Harassment and Other Forms of Discrimination, UN Women. This chapter was prepared by the author in her personal capacity. The opinions expressed in this article are the author's own and do not reflect the view of the United Nations or UN Women.

2. See, for example, *Sexual Harassment and Assault Rife at United Nations, Staff Claim*, THE GUARDIAN, Jan. 18, 2018, https://www.theguardian.com/global-development/2018 /jan/18/sexual-assault-and-harassment-rife-at-united-nations-staff-claim, Amy Lieberman, *#AidToo: Reporting Sexual Harassment at UN*, GIVING COMPASS, June 18, 2018, https:// www.givingcompass.org/article/aidtoo-reporting-sexual-harassment-at-un/, Tracy Lee, *United Nations Employees Claim They Faced Sexual Assault, Harassment Amid Culture of Silence: Report*, NEWSWEEK, Jan. 18, 2018, https://www.newsweek.com/united-nations-sexual-harass ment-abuse-784775, Rory Laverty and James LaPorta, *Eight Men Have Accused a Senior U.N. Adviser of Sexual Misconduct, Sources Say: Exclusive*, NEWSWEEK, Aug. 7, 2018, https://www .newsweek.com/2018/08/24/senior-un-official-investigated-sexually-harassing-male-subordi nates-1059209.html.

fleeting), shared understanding among survivors[3] that what had previously been tolerated need not continue to be so, and the reach of the global #MeToo movement into the UN. In addition, governments in various countries included members, mostly women, who had themselves experienced sexual harassment and there was growing public discussion of violence against women in politics (VAWP), including sexual harassment: these dynamics drove efforts to hasten change. These last two factors coincide with, and draw from, a growing sense among women across the world that intolerance and accountability could finally be in sight, that perpetrators might be held accountable and that their (that is, the targets of abuse) assumed sexual availability and acquiescence had an expiry date.

Efforts of the United Nations as an employer are briefly documented here as are those of UN member states, which have built upon prior decisions and standards to bring a focus on sexual harassment. The member states have also organized themselves into a group that seeks to sharpen the focus on sexual harassment and to act as champions of the needed changes.

2018 was an eventful year at the United Nations. The agitation and courage of victims of sexual harassment have been the indisputable engine behind the astonishing demand for change, for reckoning and for a new settlement. Survivors inside the United Nations and within their own countries, are the thread that runs from individual injuries to change at the highest international levels. Together, their efforts illustrate the systemic and structural nature of the discrimination that is sexual harassment.

The United Nations as an Employer

Public knowledge of sexual harassment at the UN goes back decades. The *New York Times* covered a case at the UN Secretariat in New York in 1994, involving sexual abuse against Catherine Claxton.[4] In December 1997,[5] a group

---

3. The terms victim and survivor are used in turn throughout this piece. This is to capture both that those who experience sexual harassment or any sexual violence cope with and manage their abuse so as to come through it, with their self-respect intact and are not reduced to the abuse they have experienced (survivors) and also acknowledging that a wrong, often a crime, has been perpetrated against them (victims), which necessitates recognition, redress, and accountability.

4. Ciceil L. Gross, *Catherine Claxton vs. the U.N.*, N.Y. TIMES, Sept. 15, 1994, https://www.nytimes.com/1994/09/15/opinion/catherine-claxton-vs-the-un.html?utm_source=PassBlue+List&utm_campaign=b1da34201b-PassBlue_CUNCR-CopyEditor&utm_medium=email&utm_term=0_4795f55662-b1da34201b-18607249.

5. Zehra Abid, *Book Launch: Fouzia Saeed Tells Every Woman's Story*, EXPRESS TRIBUNE, Dec. 24, 2011, https://tribune.com.pk/story/311146/book-launch-fouzia-saeed-tells-every-womans-story/?__cf_chl_jschl_tk__=a76d96b67f90320523718cbe7b916a2ac7389ab9

of eleven women employed by the UN in Pakistan[6] brought sexual harassment charges against their manager.[7] A review of historical, cultural, and contemporary concerns on sexual abuse associated with the UN are captured in a 2018 article[8] that also links sexual abuse of staff by staff (called sexual harassment, SH) and abuse by staff (or others operating on behalf of the UN) of those outside the UN—named sexual exploitation and abuse (SEA).

Recognition of SEA and efforts to address it have a longer institutional history than do those to end sexual harassment. Procedural distinctions between how protection of staff is to be managed and obligations owed to those being served by the UN have been the foundation of the separation of areas of sexual violence, defined by the (institutional or not) location of the victims. It has led to SEA and sexual harassment being understood as distinct, not as connected expressions of (predominantly) male sexual entitlement to (predominantly) female, less powerful colleagues, or non-colleagues. For many years the UN has used and promoted frameworks that recognize the continuum of violence against women[9] and that see it as a matter of gender inequality,[10] in a variety of contexts and forms. An understanding of the structural nature of sexual

---

-1577778523-0-AcvkWY315J3-hbe7r4AlwoVInVhg_k0fBHiJxy7FipA6jD2r_gXYS2YOxyv
Jv5viIO56b44t0PmZ3HS2AKTDhw0sOp80TT8H5koUup2lDnkdzfipuiCjkM-12k08Bn
FtV4JHnlH4wZXhIkqjGXdEhgBmp_6BoeCzDubnHOfmoKEPmAShbUWResHyoJ
-kppLviWNEGgpjQBlOdHR9tv8Ia5lBMKYdi8rUboLiqdZqD6W8PwYI1fsyU6DozzIPC
xw3CIRx6sIHqdNMhrLTL1LjguCdnouUpEaIrFWfBDQM67kLYoM0dW7IsMxxwBo0XL
-vA1cW7pzJQpq6g5cWmR5TSw4_oysehWzQFFBKYUm23Atg.

6. One of the women involved, Fauzia Saeed, wrote a book about this experience and went on to help shape the criminalization of sexual harassment in Pakistan. The book was titled: WORKING WITH SHARKS: A PAKISTANI WOMAN'S STORY OF COUNTERING SEXUAL HARASSMENT IN THE UNITED NATIONS—FROM PERSONAL GRIEVANCE TO PUBLIC LAW (1st ed. 2013).

7. *UN Embarrassed by Sacking of Pakistani Who Harassed Women*, THE GUARDIAN, Aug. 24, 1999, https://www.theguardian.com/world/1999/aug/24/unitednations.

8. Loraine Rickard-Martin, *The UN and #MeToo: The Saga of Abuse Must End, Once and for All*, THE GUARDIAN, May 10, 2018, http://www.ipsnews.net/2018/05/un-metoo-saga-abuse-must-end/.

9. In-depth study on all forms of violence against women: Report of the Secretary-General, Para 13 "An overview of forms and manifestations of violence against women and its consequences is provided in section IV. It shows the continuum of violence against women throughout their lives and in a variety of settings," https://documents-dds-ny.un.org/doc/UNDOC/GEN/N06/419/74/PDF/N0641974.pdf?OpenElement.

10. Resolution adopted by the General Assembly on 19 December 2006 on the report of the Third Committee (A/61/438)] 61/143. Intensification of efforts to eliminate all forms of violence against women, "Recognizing that violence against women is rooted in historically unequal power relations between men and women," https://documents-dds-ny.un.org/doc/UNDOC/GEN/N06/503/01/PDF/N0650301.pdf?OpenElement.

violence, expressed through claims to sexual entitlement, and its fundamentally discriminatory character, is at the core of this approach.

As #MeToo has reached inside the UN, this conceptual basis has been re-kindled and the links between SEA and SH are being re-asserted. Documents, guidelines, and normative developments on SEA define barred and discouraged behaviors, including:[11]

- Sexual activity with children (persons under the age of eighteen), which is prohibited regardless of the age of majority or age of consent locally. Mistaken belief in the age of a child is not a defense;
- Exchange of money, employment, goods, or services for sex, including sexual favors or other forms of humiliating, degrading, or exploitative behavior, is prohibited. This includes any exchange of assistance that is due to "beneficiaries";
- Sexual relationships between United Nations staff and "beneficiaries" of assistance, since they are based on inherently unequal power dynamics, undermine the credibility and integrity of the work of the United Nations and are strongly discouraged.

Two senior staff appointments were also made in 2017 to lead the work against SEA. Against this backdrop, the UN Secretary General (UNSG) and his chief executive team,[12] established a new, senior internal body[13] to review and upgrade work against sexual harassment: The Chief Executives Board Task Force on Addressing Sexual Harassment within the Organizations of the UN System. A statement issued in May 2018 outlined the problem thus, with gendered inequality of power at the center:

> Sexual harassment results from a culture of discrimination and privilege, based on unequal gender relations and power dynamics. It has no place in the United Nations system.
> Leaders of UN System organizations reiterate their firm commitment to uphold a zero-tolerance approach to sexual harassment;

---

11. Secretary-General's Bulletin Special measures for protection from sexual exploitation and sexual abuse, 2003, https://undocs.org/ST/SGB/2003/13.

12. These distinct entities include the Secretariat, Funds, Agencies and Programmes. In this chapter, they will all be referred to as UN organizations.

13. See the terms of reference and October 2018 progress report here: https://inter agencystandingcommittee.org/system/files/2018.hlcm_.14.add_.1_-_annexes_1-7_-_prog ress_report_by_the_ceb_task_force.pdf.

to strengthen victim-centered prevention and response efforts; and to foster a safe and inclusive working environment.[14]

The Task Force[15] oversaw many initiatives in 2018, including:

- a new model policy for the thirty-one member agencies
- a dedicated staff survey on the topic
- development of helplines
- a tracking database of those against whom allegations of sexual harassment have been upheld[16]
- guidance for managers
- improvement of investigation practices and
- a draft code of conduct for behavior at UN events

The model policy on sexual harassment recognizes the range of behaviors that can constitute sexual harassment, and opens a list of examples thus:[17]

Sexual harassment can take a variety of forms—from looks and words though to physical contact of a sexual nature. Examples of sexual harassment (non-exhaustive list) include:

- Attempted or actual sexual assault, including rape
- Sharing or displaying sexually inappropriate images or videos in any format;
- Sending sexually suggestive communications in any format
- Sharing sexual or lewd anecdotes or jokes

14. *Note to Correspondents and CEB Statement on Addressing Sexual Harassment within the Organizations of the UN System*, May 3, 2018, https://www.unsceb.org/CEBPublicFiles/Note%20and%20CEB%20statement_FINAL.pdf.

15. UN System Chief Executives Board for Coordination, *Addressing Sexual Harassment within the Organizations of the UN System*, https://www.unsceb.org/content/addressing-sexual-harassment-within-organizations-un-system.

16. The "clear check" database is populated with names of perpetrators of sexual exploitation, harassment, and abuse, to prohibit subsequent employment in the system. Access to it is limited.

17. UN System Chief Executives Board for Coordination, *UN System Model Policy on Sexual Harassment*, https://www.unsceb.org/CEBPublicFiles/UN%20System%20Model%20Policy%20on%20Sexual%20Harassment_FINAL.pdf.

A model Code of Conduct[18] to prevent harassment, including sexual harassment, at UN system events was drafted both by the Task Force and the Group of friends (see below) in response to allegations and incidents at UN-sponsored, -organized, or -hosted events. Behaviors listed to illustrate harassment and sexual harassment include derogatory comments, repeatedly asking for dates or sex, unwelcome touching, and attempted or actual sexual assault, including rape. Launched in June 2019, the Code is intended to be made available to all who participate in such events and provides for immediate responses, including fact-finding and termination of access by the perpetrator to that event.

There is a tangible overlap and commonality of behaviors recognized in SEA and sexual harassment. Both are steeped in myths and stereotypes that tend to minimize harm, deny credibility of victim voices, and (often implicitly) promote or reflect assumptions of male sexual entitlement—and, as a corollary, women's "obligation" to submit and not to challenge.

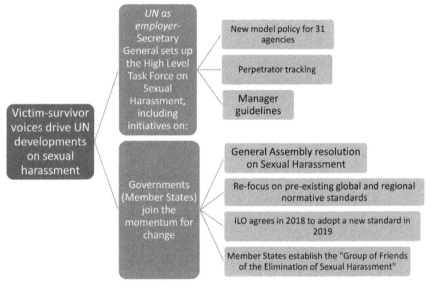

Figure 1. How sexual harassment impacted the UN in 2018.

---

18. UN System Code of Conduct, *Model Code of Conduct to Prevent Harassment, Including Sexual Harassment, at UN System Events*, https://www.un.org/en/content/codeof conduct/.

Member States and Normative Developments

Established and increasingly widely recognized as a form of sexual and gender discrimination, sexual harassment falls under the remit of the Convention on the Elimination of All Forms of Discrimination Against Women (CEDAW).[19] Although the treaty text does not make reference to sexual harassment or even violence against women (except for trafficking), interpretive advisory statements[20] by the Committee have clarified that violence against women is a form of sexual discrimination. Sexual harassment, as a form of gender-based discrimination, therefore, is a CEDAW concern, prohibited by it and thus States Parties[21] are duty-bearers that are obligated to end it. The Convention in its very title is concerned with the ending of all discrimination, and this intent was further reinforced in 2015, with a deadline, in Agenda 2030's[22] sustainable development goals (SDGs). In particular, Goal 5.2[23] commits to the elimination of all forms of violence against women and girls but others are also pertinent, such as: 8.8[24] (promoting safe and secure working environments), 10.3[25]

---

19. UN Human Rights, *Convention on the Elimination of All Forms of Discrimination against Women New York, 18 December 1979*, https://www.ohchr.org/EN/ProfessionalInterest/Pages/CEDAW.aspx.

20. In particular, General Recommendations 19 (1992): "The Convention in article 1 defines discrimination against women. The definition of discrimination includes gender-based violence, that is, violence that is directed against a woman because she is a woman or that affects women disproportionately. It includes acts that inflict physical, mental or sexual harm or suffering, threats of such acts, coercion and other deprivations of liberty. Gender-based violence may breach specific provisions of the Convention, regardless of whether those provisions expressly mention violence," https://tbinternet.ohchr.org/Treaties/CEDAW/Shared%20Documents/1_Global/INT_CEDAW_GEC_3731_E.pdf and 35 (2018) which updates it http://docstore.ohchr.org/SelfServices/FilesHandler.ashx?enc=6QkG1d%2fPPRiCAqhKb7yhsldCrOlUTvLRFDjh6%2fx1pWAeqJn4T68N1uqnZjLbtFua2OBKh3UEqlB%2fCyQIg86A6bUD6S2nt0Ii%2bndbh67tt1%2bO99yEEGWYpmnzM8vDxmwt.

21. These are States that have ratified the treaty, numbering 189 as of April 2019, http://indicators.ohchr.org/.

22. UN Sustainable Goals Knowledge Platform, *Transforming our world: the 2030 Agenda for Sustainable Development*, https://sustainabledevelopment.un.org/post2015/transformingourworld.

23. UN Sustainable Goals Knowledge Platform, *Sustainable Development Goal 5: Achieve gender equality and empower all women and girls*, https://sustainabledevelopment.un.org/sdg5.

24. UN Sustainable Goals Knowledge Platform, *Sustainable Development Goal 8: Promote sustained, inclusive and sustainable economic growth, full and productive employment and decent work for all*, https://sustainabledevelopment.un.org/sdg8.

25. UN Sustainable Goals Knowledge Platform, *Sustainable Development Goal 10: Reduce Inequality Within and Among Countries*, https://sustainabledevelopment.un.org/sdg10.

(eliminating discriminatory laws, practices, and policies), and 11.7[26] (access to safe, inclusive and accessible, green and public spaces), which has a monitoring indicator that explicitly mentions physical and sexual harassment.

There are several regional standards that are also pertinent to the legal framework on sexual harassment. These include:[27]

- Latin America—Belem do Para Convention (1994): "'Violence against women' shall be understood as any act or conduct, based on gender, which causes death or physical, sexual or psychological harm or suffering to women, whether in the public or the private sphere."[28]

- Africa—the Maputo Protocol (2003): "'Violence against women' means all acts perpetrated against women which cause or could cause them physical, sexual, psychological, and economic harm, including the threat to take such acts; or to undertake the imposition of arbitrary restrictions on or deprivation of fundamental freedoms in private or public life in peace time and during situations of armed conflicts or of war."[29]

- Europe—the Istanbul Convention (2011): "'Violence against women' is understood as a violation of human rights and a form of discrimination against women and shall mean all acts of gender-based violence that result in, or are likely to result in, physical, sexual, psychological or economic harm or suffering to women, including threats of such acts, coercion or arbitrary

---

26. UN Sustainable Goals Knowledge Platform, *Sustainable Development Goal 11: Make cities and human settlements inclusive, safe, resilient and sustainable*, https://sustainable development.un.org/sdg11.

27. Text here is taken from a recent UN Women publication: TOWARDS AN END TO SEXUAL HARASSMENT: THE NATURE AND URGENCY OF CHANGE IN THE ERA OF METOO, http://www.unwomen.org/-/media/headquarters/attachments/sections/library/publica tions/2018/towards-an-end-to-sexual-harassment-en.pdf?la=en&vs=4236.

28. Inter-American Convention on the Prevention, Punishment and Eradication of Violence Against Women "Convention of Belem do Para" adopted 1994 Organization of American States (entered into force March 5, 1995), http://www.oas.org/juridico/english/treaties/a-61 .html.

29. Protocol to the African Charter on Human and Peoples' Rights on the Rights of Women in Africa, adopted July 11, 2003 African Union (entered into force Nov. 25, 2005), http://www.achpr.org/instruments/women-protocol/.

deprivation of liberty, whether occurring in public or in private life."[30]

The African Commission on Human and Peoples' Rights developed Guidelines for Combating Sexual Violence and its Consequences that address the eradication of sexual violence, including sexual harassment.[31] The Organization of American States adopted a Model Law against violence against women in politics that directly addresses sexual harassment.[32]

Governments have adopted several resolutions on the elimination of violence against women through the UN General Assembly (UNGA), the Human Rights Council (HRC), and the Commission on the Status of Women (CSW). These include one on preventing and eliminating sexual harassment in the workplace, calling on member states to take a range of measures to prevent and respond to the issue.[33] Sexual harassment has also been addressed in the context of the online safety of women journalists,[34] violence against women in politics,[35] and action has been called for to end cyberbullying and cyberstalking.[36] A body of the UN that focuses on rights, the Human Rights Council, has adopted a resolution calling on member states to prevent and respond to

---

30. Council of Europe Convention on Preventing and Combating Violence against Women and Domestic Violence "Istanbul Convention" adopted May 11, 2011 (entered into force Aug. 1, 2014), https://rm.coe.int/168046031c.

31. Guidelines on Combating Sexual Violence and Its Consequences in Africa (the Guidelines), http://www.achpr.org/files/instruments/combating-sexual-violence/achpr_eng _guidelines_on_combating_sexual_violence_and_its_consequences.pdf.

32. Inter-American Model Law on the Prevention, Punishment and Eradication of Violence Against Women in Political Life, https://www.oas.org/en/mesecvi/docs/LeyModelo Femicidio-EN.pdf.

33. Commission on the Status of Women (CSW)—Report on the sixty-first session (24 March 2016 and 13-24 March 2017)—Resolution 61/1. Preventing and eliminating sexual harassment in the workplace, https://undocs.org/E/2017/27.

34. A/RES/72/290-278—Resolution adopted by the Human Rights Council on 22 May 2018 The promotion, protection, and enjoyment of human rights on the Internet, http:// undocs.org/A/HRC/32/L.20.

35. A/RES/72/278—Resolution adopted by the General Assembly on 22 May 2018 on Interaction between the United Nations, national parliaments, and the Inter-Parliamentary Union, https://undocs.org/A/RES/72/278.

36. "E/2018/27-E/CN.6/2018/20—Report of the Commission on the Status of Women—Report on the sixty-second session (24 March 2017 and 12–23 March 2018)— Chapter I—Matters calling for action by the Economic and Social Council or brought to its attention in A. Agreed conclusions of the sixty-second session of the Commission on the Status of Women/Strengthen normative, legal and policy frameworks: (i) Pursue, by effective means, programmes and strategies for preventing and eliminating sexual harassment against all women and girls, including harassment in the workplace and in schools, and cyberbullying and cyberstalking, including in rural areas, with an emphasis on effective legal, preventive and protective

violence against women and girls in digital contexts, much of which are forms of sexual harassment.[37]

In December 2018, the General Assembly passed a resolution on the "Intensification of efforts to prevent and eliminate all forms of violence against women and girls: sexual harassment."[38] This resolution notes the under-recognition and under-reporting of violence against women, that it reflects discriminatory norms, that impunity exists and that such violence impairs enjoyment of human rights. It recognizes that:

- "[S]exual harassment, is rooted in historical and structural inequality in power relations between men and women";
- It occurs in private and public spaces and digital contexts;
- It creates a hostile environment;
- Women and girls who know "multiple and intersecting forms of discrimination" are at particular risk. The resolution specifically names poor legal protections for domestic workers, including migrant domestic workers; and
- There exists risk of reprisals against victims.

The resolution calls for changes in social norms and for states to "address discrimination based on multiple and intersecting factors" and urges states to support the efforts of civil society for corrective action. Progress toward zero tolerance, criminalization (where appropriate), and provision of remedies including criminal sanctions are sought. Structural causes including discriminatory attitudes are noted and change among men and boys is deemed important. The resolution specifies a range of supports needed for victims, including legal protection, witness protection, adequately resourced services, and state cooperation with relevant parties including feminist groups, trade unions, and the private sector. States are asked to ensure the promotion and protection of sexual and reproductive health and rights.[39]

---

measures for victims of sexual harassment or those who are at risk of sexual harassment; (…)" https://undocs.org/E/2018/27.

37. "A/HRC/38/L.6—Human Rights Council—Thirty-eighth session (18 June–6 July 2018) Agenda item 3: Promotion and protection of all human rights, civil, political, economic, social and cultural rights, including the right to development—38/… Accelerating efforts to eliminate violence against women and girls: preventing and responding to violence against women and girls in digital contexts," http://undocs.org/A/HRC/38/L.6.

38. A/73/PV.55 17 December 2018 GA/12107 "Intensification of efforts to prevent and eliminate all forms of violence against women and girls: sexual harassment," https://undocs.org/en/A/RES/73/148.

39. In line with ICPD and BPfA and the review outcome documents.

In June 2019 the International Labour Organisation (ILO) adopted a new convention[40] on violence and harassment in the world of work. It recognizes "the right of everyone to a world of work free from violence and harassment, including gender-based violence and harassment," acknowledging that these can constitute violations of human rights. The convention addresses violence and harassment as a whole and addresses gender-based violence and harassment, under this definition:

> "gender-based violence and harassment" means violence and harassment directed at persons because of their sex or gender or affecting persons of a particular sex or gender disproportionately, and includes sexual harassment.

The convention defines the world of work to include travel to and from a workplace, places where workers take breaks and use sanitary facilities, official travel, and when it takes place through work-related communications including through technology. It covers those who are employed, volunteers, interns, apprentices, and job applicants.

For member states the relevance and reach of the #MeToo movement are significant. Perhaps driven by their national movements, as well as revelations from inside the UN, member states have established an interest group on the elimination of sexual harassment. Called the "Group of Friends to Eliminate Sexual Harassment," it was founded by France, Israel, the Netherlands, and Kenya. In the first year of its establishment, the group held five meetings, each with overflowing attendance and standing room only. The interest in, and sharing of, experiences within the group is powerful testimony to the effectiveness of victims and survivors speaking, making themselves heard and making space for others to speak. The close relationships between diplomats and politicians may also be a factor here. A growing public concern with violence against women in politics, including sexual harassment, has supported the emergence of a greater possibility for such discussion. Accounts of abuse in diplomatic circles have started to emerge. The possibility of common cause among politicians, diplomats, and UN staff is growing and this in turn will further strengthen the dynamic for urgent change.

---

40. International Labor Organization, *C190—Violence and Harassment Convention, 2019 (No. 190)*, https://www.ilo.org/dyn/normlex/en/f?p=NORMLEXPUB:12100:0::NO::P12100_ILO_CODE:C190.

October 2019: the State of Play

Victims and survivors continue to seek and demand change. They have made sufficient noise for even busy and important people to turn their attention to the long-ignored or downplayed issue of sexual harassment. The work remains very much in progress, with standards and procedures undergoing review and being strengthened. Cultural change remains a significant challenge, though resolutions, treaties, and platforms have called for such for several decades.

Results of the staff survey initiated by the Task Force on Sexual Harassment in 2018 found that[41] one in three UN staff reported sexual harassment in the previous two years and 38 percent across the entirety of their working lives at the UN. Junior staff and those on short contracts had higher than average reporting rates, as did LGBTI respondents, though no breakdown by disability or ethnicity was captured. Beyond these headlines, however, is the crucial figure that gives pause to interpretation of the data: the response rate was just 17 percent. In his statement accompanying the release of the survey results, the Secretary General notes that this indicates the difficulty of open discussion on sexual harassment as well as mistrust and poor expectations of accountability. Nevertheless, the practice of having a standalone effort to survey sexual harassment has established an important precedent for further work against sexual harassment inside the United Nations.

Though policies and standards are evolving fast, the cultural context[42] in which these operate adequately remains to be changed. This will be the major frontier of work in 2020 and beyond.

---

41. *United Nations of Harassment? 1-in-3 UN employees sexually harassed—report*, RT, Jan. 16, 2019, https://www.rt.com/news/448909-un-sexual-harassment-survey/.

42. This issue is addressed in a 2019 UN Women publication 'What will it take?' which is available for download at https://www.unwomen.org/en/digital-library/publica tions/2019/09/discussion-paper-what-will-it-take-promoting-cultural-change-to-end-sexual -harassment and complementing a previous publication framing work against sexual harassment in the era of MeToo, available at https://www.unwomen.org/en/digital-library/publications /2018/11/towards-an-end-to-sexual-harassment.

Intersectional Issues of Class, Gender, Disability, and Caste

CHAPTER 32

Not on the Menu: Sexual Harassment in the U.S. Restaurant Industry

Saru Jayaraman[1]

I grew up here in California but spent a lot of time on the East Coast for law school and graduate school. Right after law school and graduate school, I ended up working at an immigrant worker organizing center out in Long Island, New York. I was there representing immigrant workers when 9/11 happened. On 9/11 there was a restaurant at the top of the World Trade Center Tower 1 called "Windows on the World." On that morning, seventy-three workers died at the restaurant; they were almost all immigrants. They either jumped to their deaths or they were evaporated inside the restaurant because the plane hit below them, and the heat rose so quickly that they were literally evaporated. About 13,000 restaurant workers lost their jobs in the months and weeks following the tragedy. I was asked at the time as a young organizer and an attorney to start a relief center in the aftermath of the tragedy for the workers from Windows on the World and all of the restaurant workers that had been displaced as a result of the tragedy.

What had started as a relief center, post-9/11 has grown into a national organization. ROC grew to include 130,000 restaurant workers and restaurant owners, 770 restaurant companies working to promote better wages, working conditions, and an end to sexual violence in the restaurant industry, and 30,000 consumer members. All of these parties are working together for better wages and working conditions and, as I said, an end to segregation, harassment, and violence in our industry.

---

1. President, One Fair Wage; Co-Founder, Restaurant Opportunities Centers (ROC) United; Director, Social Movements, Organizing and Policy Institute at UC Berkeley. This chapter is based on the talk that Saru Jayaraman gave at the Berkeley Center on Comparative Equality and Anti-Discrimination Law at its May 14, 2019, Global Resistance to Sexual Harassment and Violence conference at University of California Berkeley Law School.

Our growth as an organization really has paralleled the explosion in the restaurant industry. We just surpassed the 13-million-worker mark in the restaurant industry in the United States, and we are getting close to the 14-million-worker mark. One in eleven, going on one in ten, a tenth of our workforce, works in one industry, the restaurant industry. It just continues to explode because we have made world history—for those of you from out of the United States and are wondering "why are we so crazy like this?"—in 2017, we became the first nation on Earth in which we now spend more money on eating food outside of the home than we do on food eaten inside of the home.

We eat out like crazy! We eat out in ever increasing numbers even during economic recessions and depressions and crises. This is the only industry that continues to grow, even when other industries stagnate or decline. It is like we eat out and we drink out even more, so when we are depressed, economically depressed, we just keep eating out. Restaurants in our country are not only the backbone of our economy as one-tenth of the American workforce, they are also a central location of our culture. It is where we, as Americans, are often proposed to; in terms of a wedding, it's where we have very special moments of our lives. We celebrate, as opposed to many other countries, at least that I have traveled to and experienced, our culture and important moments of our lives in restaurants more often than those in other parts of the world.

Thus, you would think that, restaurants, as a space of important moments of our lives, and ever incessant growth and importance in our culture, would not be the absolute bottom of the barrel, lowest paying employer in the United States. Every year, the United States Department of Labor lists the ten lowest paying jobs in America, and every year, seven of the ten lowest paid occupations in the United States are all in one industry. The restaurant industry.

So, before we even think about the implications of that, in terms of the restaurant industry, let's just talk about the implications of that for the United States. For the United States, you're talking about the largest and fastest growing industry in America, creating the absolute bottom of the barrel lowest paying jobs. All new entrants into the economy, these are the jobs that are available, for young people, formerly incarcerated individuals, or immigrants, or, frankly, for people actually being laid off from other sectors. This is the industry that is capturing everybody, and it is the absolute lowest paying industry in America, which is why we are just above one-in-three working Americans working full-time and living in poverty, and we are inching our way very soon to being a nation of one-in-two—one-in-two—working Americans working full-time and living in poverty; an absolute disgrace for what is supposed to be one of the wealthiest nations in the world. An absolute disgrace. That is mostly due to the growth of very low wage sectors of mostly women and that is epitomized by the restaurant industry.

How is it that we have gotten to the place where we have the largest and fastest growing industry with the absolute lowest paying jobs? Our research shows that it is due to the money, power, and influence of a trade lobby called the National Restaurant Association, or the "other NRA", and for people in other countries, please watch out because they have now developed the Multinational Hospitality and Restaurant Association, the MHRA—they're coming for you! The NRA, here in the United States, sadly, has been around for a long time. I thought before I first did research for my last book *Forked*, that they couldn't have been around more than thirty, forty, fifty years because they represent the restaurant chains in America—the IHOPs, the Applebee's, the Olive Gardens, the McDonald's—and these chains haven't been around very long. So, I thought that the trade association couldn't have around very long, but I was wrong. The restaurant trade lobby has been around in various forms since emancipation of slaves.

It turns out that tipping, a practice that is so embraced by us in America now, did not originate in the United States. It originated in feudal Europe. It was something that aristocrats and nobles gave to serfs and vassals but always on top of a wage. It was always an extra or bonus. It was never intended to be a wage. It was intended to be a gift. That idea of tipping as a bonus came to the United States around the 1850s, 1860s. At first, it was resoundingly rejected by Americans who said, "We're a democracy and we don't believe in this vestige of feudalism." In fact, Alexis de Tocqueville came from France hailing American democracy and wrote that one of the hallmarks of American democracy is that we didn't have tipping, a vestige of feudalism. That populist movement that rejected it spread to Europe. The labor movement picked it up in Europe and got rid of it in much of Europe with the rallying cry, "We are professionals and we don't rely on your tips!" and ended up getting rid of the practice for a while before Americans started visiting Europe in much greater numbers. But while we saw far greater wage emphasis than tip emphasis in the European hospitality industry, in the United States, we went in the exact opposite direction.

Because at Emancipation, two industries demanded the right to hire newly freed slaves, not pay them anything, and let them live entirely on tips. One was a mostly male industry and the other was a mostly female industry, both of Black workers. The male industry was the Pullman Train Car Co.—luxury liners that went across the country—this was how rich people used to travel from one coast to the other. You should see a wonderful movie called *10,000 Black Men Named George*.[2] The Black men who served as porters on those trains were asked to work without wages for tips alone, and as former slaves, they were all called George as a term of subservience. These men formed the first Black

---

2. Showtime, 2002, https://www.youtube.com/watch?v=_iiHhxHk64A.

union in the United States, the Brotherhood of Sleeping Car Porters, and won the right to an actual wage, rather than having to rely on tips alone. But the women were not so lucky.

The women in the restaurant industry were servers and at Emancipation, the restaurant lobby, the predecessor to the "other NRA," demanded the right to hire newly freed slaves, Black women, not pay them anything at all, have them live entirely on tips. That workforce of women did not have the Brotherhood of Sleeping Car Porters. The restaurant workers' waitress's union, at the time, was not open to Black women, and so they ended up with a zero-dollar wage. This was made law in 1938 as part of the New Deal, when everyone got the right to the minimum wage, except populations of Black workers, farmworkers, domestic workers, and tipped workers. Tipped workers were told, "You get a zero-dollar wage as long as tips bring you to the full minimum wage," and we went from zero in 1938 to the very whopping $2.13 an hour, which is the current federal minimum wage in the United States for tipped workers.

Now, you might think "Well, they are a sliver of the population, that's okay." I started this talk by telling you that this is the largest and fastest growing workforce in the United States. It is the largest workforce of women in the United States, and I might not need to continue my talk to just say that the largest workforce of women in the United States is allowed to be paid $2.13 an hour. What does that say about the value that America places on women? Not a whole lot. Even worse, when you are dealing with a population of millions of women who work largely at restaurants like IHOP and Denny's and Olive Garden, 40 percent of them are single mothers feeding their families on a $2 wage and tips. You're talking about forty-three states, the vast majority of states, with a sub-minimum wage with this legacy of slavery. You're talking about more than forty states that have a wage of less than $5 an hour and just over twenty states that are at that bottom of the barrel a $2 wage-to-$2.13 wage.

So, millions of women, millions of women, the largest and fastest growing workforce of women earns this wage, and half of America, one in two Americans, works in the restaurant industry at some point in their lifetime. This is generally the first job for a majority of Americans, and it is a job that people are being allowed to be paid $2. But beyond the first job for young people, maybe some of you who were in the industry in your youth, it is the job for the largest workforce of women, and this workforce of women struggles with three times the poverty rate of the rest of the United States workforce, double the usage of food stamps as the rest of the United States workforce, and worst of all, the absolute highest rates of sexual harassment of any comparable industry in the Unites States. Our research shows that 90 percent of workers in our industry report very regular consistent sexual harassment on a daily basis, but they do not call it that. Because we have done studies of tens of thousands of workers, we have found that if you ask them, "Have you experienced sexual harassment on the job?" one in five will say yes, but most will say no. But if you ask them, "Have you experienced sexual behavior in the restaurant that is scary or unwanted?" 90 percent of both men and women say it happens to them on a daily basis. That is because this experience of whatever you want to call it, frankly, that is sexual harassment, but that experience is so ingrained in the nature of the work and what is expected to be your job, that people do not view it as sexual harassment. This is because research shows, when you're paid a wage of $2.13 an hour, like you are in New Mexico or Texas or more than 20 states, or under $5 an hour, as you are in very blue states including Massachusetts and Pennsylvania and in Washington D.C., your wage is so low, it goes entirely to taxes, you're living completely off your tips, and you mostly tolerate whatever a customer does to you, however they touch you or treat you or talk to you, because "the customer is always right," the customer pays your bills, not your employer.

In my last book, I told a story of a young woman at an Olive Garden in Indiana, where the wage is $2.13 an hour. Her mother—by the way, it's been $2 for 28 years, so we have many members where we have two generations of women, mothers and daughters, who have worked for $2 their whole lives— the mother worked for $2, she worked for $2, and her mother actually worked at the Olive Garden when the daughter started working there, everybody had identified this extremely abusive harassing manager who would stick his hand down the women server's pants and repeatedly harass them, grab them from behind. Olive Garden is a part of a company called Darden, which has a "zero-tolerance-policy" for sexual harassment. Well, we call it a zero-tolerance policy for complaining about sexual harassment because every single woman who had complained was no longer there. Everybody knew that you just put up with the guy putting his hand down your pants or grabbing you from behind.

That is what you do all day, every day, to feed your child because this is the only income you receive is the tip income. How does it work? It works because the manager actually tells you, when your income comes from tips, not from a wage from your boss, to dress more sexy, show more cleavage, wear tighter clothing to make more money in tips, which, everybody has to understand, is not women told to tolerate harassment; no, it is women being told to go out and encourage harassment. Go and get as much as you can, that's what makes you a good worker. We have a member here in the Bay Area who moved from Utah, and she said, as a young person, she was consistently told when she complained about a customer grabbing her butt, "You're so lucky you can still get it while you're young. You're so lucky that you can get it, that's how you're going to make more money." Your value as a woman in our industry is based on how much breast you can show, how much you are willing to put up with the harassment because that makes you get more tips and that is the measure of how good of a worker you are.

We also know this because we have compared the forty-three states that have a subminimum wage for tipped workers to the seven states that don't. The seven states that have forsaken this legacy of slavery include California, Oregon, Washington, Nevada, Minnesota, Montana, and Alaska. These seven states have required the industry to have the same minimum wage for all workers, with tips on top, as they always were intended to be from feudal times. So we are in feudal times here, and the rest of the country is in pre-feudal times, but here in California, we have a higher restaurant sales per capita in the restaurant industry, higher job growth in the restaurant industry, higher rates of tipping, one-half the rate of sexual harassment in the restaurant industry, and one-third the rate of managers telling women "dress more sexy," "show more cleavage," "wear tighter clothing." I really hope this is not going to sound arrogant, but that is the most dramatic drop in sexual harassment I have seen in any sector with any intervention, and it reflects the fact that this is fundamentally about power. It's fundamentally about power because if a woman in New Mexico or Texas, where they are earning $2.13 an hour, knows that her only income comes from tips, she has no power to reject the harassment, not just from the customer but also from the co-workers who are male and the managers who are male.

If you have ever worked in an American restaurant, you know most of the dining floors are often women; that's where women are; they're the tipped workers. Men are in the kitchen; men are managers; and men are customers. So with the women being the only person in that space whose income is variable, entirely dependent on pleasing the customers, the power dynamic is problematic not just with customers but also with co-workers and management, because the woman is reliant, not just on the customer, but also on her co-workers in the kitchen to produce the meal that she needs to please the customer to get the tips, and she is reliant on the manager to give her the shift or the day or the table that will get her zero dollars in tips or $200 in tips. The variability of her income because of tipping, because of her entire reliance on tipping, means everybody but the female worker has power.

I was on NPR a few months ago and a woman called in. I'll never forget it, she said, "I didn't even understand this as sexual harassment until you came on the radio, but every day, I'm a server and I go into the kitchen, and I have to show my breasts to the kitchen staff to get them to make the meal just as I need it to please the customer." Or the many stories in the books I have written: I have to kiss the manager to make sure he gives me the best shift or the best table or the best customers. I have to kiss the kitchen staff. Or, I had one woman say, "I had to have sex with everybody in the kitchen in order to consistently get them to make the meals as I needed just to please the customers to get the tips." The variability of her income gives her no power, whereas in California, when she gets a full wage from her boss, it's so much better. I'm not saying that we're perfect here—in fact getting to half the rate of harassment as the rest of the country still makes us higher than every other industry in California because our rates of harassment in the restaurant industry are so high. But that dramatic drop of 50 percent in California is because if a woman in California gets a full wage from her boss, like every other worker in every other industry, she's not entirely reliant on the tips to feed her family.

When this is the first job—the first job—for half of American women and men, this is how they're introduced to the world of work, this is how they learn what is acceptable, normal, legal, and ethical in the workplace. So much so that we've been interviewing women later in their careers who worked in the industry in their youth and moved on to something else, who tell us, "I've been sexually harassed more recently in my career but I didn't do anything about it because it was never as bad as it was when I was a young woman working in restaurants." Which means our industry doesn't just have the highest rates of harassment, it sets the standard for what is normal, considered normal and acceptable for the rest of many women's lives in America.

That has dramatic impacts on women in every sector and has dramatic impacts on young women and has dramatic impacts on our country. After Trump was elected, we interviewed many of our members across the country, in places like Michigan and Pennsylvania, women servers. We asked them how can they support this man? He is clearly a predator. And they said, "We don't see him as a predator, he's the 'good tipper.' He's the guy that we have to please to get a good tip, and we've been trained to believe we're a better worker if we can please that guy. If we can make more money in tips." That is from our youth. This is how we are trained.

In fact, when the *Glass Floor* report[3] came out, a professor at UNLV, University of Nevada Las Vegas, wrote an op-ed in the *New York Times*, citing our report. She said, "I just read this report...." The title was, *Can you be a waitress and a feminist at the same time?*,[4] because as a professor at UNLV, a feminist academic, she was working in the restaurant industry on the side because she wasn't paid enough as a lecturer, a part-time professor at UNLV. So, she was also working as a waitress, and she said, "Here I am, a feminist academic and

3. *The Glass Floor: Sexual Harassment in the Restaurant Industry*, Restaurant Opportunities Center, United, Oct. 17, 2014, http://rocunited.org/wp2015b/wp-content/uploads/2014/10/REPORT_TheGlassFloor_Sexual-Harassment-in-the-Restaurant-Industry.pdf.

4. Brittany Bronson, *Can You Be a Waitress and a Feminist?* N.Y. TIMES, Apr. 17. 2015, https://www.nytimes.com/2015/04/19/opinion/sunday/can-you-be-a-waitress-and-a-feminist.html/.

until I read this report, even I didn't recognize what I was experiencing in the restaurant industry as sexual harassment." That is because there is such a fine line in our industry between doing what it takes to please the customer, doing your job well to please the customer, and what people call sexual harassment, which most of the women in our industry do not call it.

So, we realized very early on in doing this research that there was a fundamental structural problem. That it wasn't about the millions of individual bad-apple chefs and restaurant owners that are sexual harassers—no. It was about a structural problem of women in America being paid $2 and being asked to live on customer tips. So we launched a national campaign called "One Fair Wage" to say that if these seven states can do it, for God's sakes if feudal Europe can do it, every state in the United States can pay a full minimum wage to women and have tips be on top of that as they were always intended to be.

Thanks go to #MeToo and TimesUp, which very much elevated our research and our work. I was at the TimesUp action at the 2018 Golden Globes representing the restaurant industry together with many other women from many other sectors. That amazing act of women standing together across sectors resulted in 16 states introducing bills to fully eliminate the sub-minimum wage for tipped workers in 2019 and two bills moving in Congress this year to fully eliminate the sub-minimum wage for tipped workers. One of those is the "Raise the Wage Act," which, with the flipping of the House this year, has a good chance, let's knock on wood, to pass in the House. When it does, it will be the first time since Emancipation that either house of Congress moves to eliminate this legacy of slavery. It will be a very historic moment, but it is just the beginning. We need many more states to move in this direction. Governor Cuomo has said we will do this in New York, but he has not followed through. Many other states are considering it right now. We need this to happen if we are to address this core root of sexual harassment in our industry.

At the same time, while we are advancing in the rest of the country, here in California, where we already have one wage, we are taking it a step further. We are saying, cutting the harassment in half to 50 percent is still not enough, and so we have developed a whole program of actually working with what we call "high road" restaurant owners, about 700 of them around the country, to actually make dramatic changes in the way they hire, train, promote—the systems that they set up in their restaurants. We have created a whole course in partnership with Haas Business School here at UC Berkeley, to train employers on how to make these changes, and then we are working with the City of Oakland and many other cities and the state to create incentive programs for employers to work with us to make these shifts.

We have also created a consumer engagement program to engage consumers. We've created an app that you can download for free if you're in the states.

It's called the ROC National Diners' Guide. It tells you which restaurants are getting gold and silver awards on these issues. The idea was not to tell you where to eat, it was to give you a tool to speak to your favorite restaurant owner and say, "You really should be part of change; you should be working with this group to make change." So, we have created consumer programs and tax and other incentive programs for employers to move in this direction. We have even created a loan program to help employers make dramatic shifts.

We are thinking not just about how do we lift standards through something like "One Fair Wage" to get rid of the sub-minimum wage, but how do you actually create structures and systems and policy that incentivize more employers to go above and beyond as 700 companies have worked with us to do? I think fundamentally, we are at a fork in the road. We chose the title *Forked*[5] for my book not just because of the play on being really screwed, but also because we are also at a literal fork in the road in our industry and in America.

It isn't just that women are experiencing unprecedented levels of poverty, inequality, and sexual harassment. It isn't just that it's the wrong thing, and it shouldn't happen this way and our daughters are being impacted because this will be the first job for most of our daughters. It is also because the industry is cannibalizing itself. Because it is going through the worst labor shortage in the history of the industry and has the highest rates of employee turnover of any industry. We have documented the business case that you can cut your employee turnover in half by implementing better systems, higher wages, less dependence on tips, and better structures, such as the model anti-sexual violence policy we've created—all of that helps you cut down on turnover. But also, it will help you address the labor shortage because people will want to work for you if you actually create these systems and structures. Worst of all, the industry is cannibalizing itself because beyond the emotional impacts of sexual harassment, there are, as you know, incredible economic impacts for women of sexual harassment. Harassment and the incredibly low wages impact a women's ability to actually survive, thrive, feed her family, and consume and eat out herself, and the fact that she has to move from place to place to find a safe place to work. All of that impacts her ability and her family's ability to consume, and so we are seeing the restaurant industry itself, for all its dramatic growth, stagnate in certain segments because it is not paying its own workers, because it is not treating its own workers as the professionals that they are.

So ultimately this is about the health of the industry, this is about the health and welfare of our largest workforce of women in this country, and ultimately this is about, for all of us, having a much better dining experience.

---

5. *Forked: A New Standard for Restaurant Dining*, Restaurant Opportunities Centers United, Dec. 18, 2016, https://rocunited.org/publications/forked-the-book/.

For me, why I am so passionate about it, beyond everything that we've talked about, is that it's a fundamental issue of democracy. A 150 years ago there were two other industries that said what this industry is saying today, which is, "If you make us pay our own workers, we will go out of business; we can't afford it and we won't survive if you tell us we have to pay our own workers." We as a nation said at that time, "No, we don't care. It's immoral, it's inhuman. Find a different business model." And why are we here, a 150 years later, for the largest workforce of women, allowing an industry, because of a powerful trade lobby, to say that we shouldn't pay our own workers, other working people should pay our workers? That is fundamentally a question of democracy and how we view women in America, and collectively we can change that.

CHAPTER 33

Queering #MeToo? Making Room for LGBT Lives, Identities, and Experiences

Peter Dunne[1]

On August 13, 2018, approximately ten months after the (re)appearance[2] of the #MeToo movement, the *New York Times* published a high-profile report of alleged sexual harassment at an American graduate school.[3] The story appeared to mirror the (by then familiar) narratives of inappropriate conduct, which have been a constant feature of television, media, and online news since late 2017.[4] The allegations recounted requests for personal affection from a tenured professor, the assigned doctoral supervisor, when the student first arrived; they progressed into frequent demands for emotional and personal support; and they (purportedly) concluded with acts of retaliation, including subtle, yet effective attempts to stifle the student's access to the academic job market.[5]

In many ways, the accusations mapped neatly onto common understandings of sexual harassment and workplace power imbalances, both of which have gained prominence in the public's consciousness following the *Weinstein* and

---

1. Senior Lecturer, University of Bristol, and Associate Member of Garden Court Chambers.

2. Sandra E. Garcia, *The Woman Who Created #MeToo Long Before Hashtags*, N.Y. TIMES, Oct. 20, 2017, https://www.nytimes.com/2017/10/20/us/me-too-movement-tarana-burke.html.

3. Zoe Greenberg, *What Happens to #MeToo When a Feminist Is the Accused?*, N.Y. TIMES, Aug. 13, 2018, https://www.nytimes.com/2018/08/13/nyregion/sexual-harassment-nyu-female-professor.html.

4. #METOO AND THE POLITICS OF SOCIAL CHANGE (Biana Fileborn & Rachel Loney-Howes, eds., 2019); RONAN FARROW, CATCH AND KILL: LIES, SPIES AND A CONSPIRACY TO PROTECT PREDATORS (2019).

5. Garcia, *supra* note 2.

similar affairs.[6] Yet there were also key differences in this story—points of divergence that complicated the subsequent discussions (for reporters and academics alike) and that interrogated the core values of the #MeToo movement. First, the student raising the complaint, Nimrod Reitman, identified as male, and he was married to another man. Further complicating the narrative, the alleged perpetrator, Avita Ronell, was herself a queer woman and a globally recognized feminist philosopher. In the wake of the scandal, commentators struggled to easily digest the unusual fact scenario, and many observers were frequently too quick to draw assumptions and forced to express regret and contrition as the narrative later unfolded.[7]

The *Reitman/Ronell* story illustrates the difficulty that many gay, lesbian, bisexual, and transgender (LGBT) individuals have encountered in trying to locate their experiences in the discourse of #MeToo. In recent years, the Office of the UN High Commissioner for Human Rights has documented, in both the Global North and the Global South,[8] the high rates of discrimination and violence (often with extreme brutality and savagery) to which LGBT populations remain subject.[9] These findings are supported and reinforced by an emerging body of regional, domestic, and civil society research—showing that, despite limited progress on specific issues and in certain jurisdictions, lesbian, gay, bisexual, and transgender individuals remain disproportionately vulnerable to abuse in all parts of the world.[10] In many instances, this vulnerability stems explicitly

6. Ronan Farrow, *From Aggressive Overtures to Sexual Assault: Harvey Weinstein's Accusers Tell Their Stories*, THE NEW YORKER, Oct. 10, 2017, https://www.newyorker.com /news/news-desk/from-aggressive-overtures-to-sexual-assault-harvey-weinsteins-accusers -tell-their-stories.

7. Sara Schleede, *UT Austin professor clarifies defense of an NYU professor guilty of sexual misconduct*, THE DAILY TEXAN, Aug. 28, 2018, https://www.dailytexanonline.com /2018/08/28/ut-austin-professor-clarifies-defense-of-an-nyu-professor-guilty-of-sexual -misconduct; Judith Butler, *Judith Butler Explains Letter in Support of Avital Ronell*, THE CHRONICLE OF HIGHER EDUCATION (Aug. 20, 2018), https://www.chronicle.com/blogs /letters/judith-butler-explains-letter-in-support-of-avital-ronell/.

8. Countries, respectively, in the Northern and Southern hemispheres.

9. *See, e.g.*, U.N. High Commissioner for Human Rights, *Discriminatory laws and practices and acts of violence against individuals based on their sexual orientation and gender identity*, UN Doc No. A/HRC/19/41 (Nov. 17, 2011); and U.N. High Commissioner for Human Rights, *Discrimination and violence against individuals based on their sexual orientation and gender identity*, UN Doc No. A/HRC/29/23 (May 4, 2015).

10. *See, e.g.*, Inter-American Commission of Human Rights, *Recognition of the Rights of LGBTI Persons*, OEA/Ser.L/V/II.170 Doc. 184 (Dec. 7, 2018); African Commission on Human and People's Rights, Resolution on Protection against Violence and other Human Rights Violations against Persons on the basis of their real or imputed Sexual Orientation or Gender Identity (2014) Resolution 275; Fundamental Rights Agency of the European Union,

from the involuntary sexualization and objectification of LGBT bodies, harassment grounded in experiences and perceptions of both sex and gender.

Against this background, gay, lesbian, bisexual, and transgender persons appear ideally positioned, perhaps more so than other groups, to benefit from a #MeToo movement, which encourages society to tackle gender-based inequality and which seeks to confront gender-based norms. Yet two years after #MeToo captured the public's imagination, advocating an end to gendered abuse of power, the movement's relationship with LGBT populations remains complicated, characterized by feelings of suspicion, ambivalence and doubt.[11] This short chapter explores LGBT responses to #MeToo and suggests four (non-exhaustive) "dilemmas" that limit the extent to which the movement does (and can) resonate with LGBT lives. These are a:

(a)   Dilemma of Visibility;
(b)   Dilemma of Vulnerability;
(c)   Dilemma of Believability: and
(d)   Dilemma of Legality.

The chapter is not written from a place of hostility toward #MeToo, quite the contrary, nor does it seek to generalize a universal LGBT or queer experience. In writing how #MeToo can better accommodate LGBT persons, the chapter also should not be understood as downplaying a focus on the experiences and traumas of cisgender women.[12] Rather, understanding both the inherent potential of this #MeToo moment, and the complex, intersectional realities of LGBT lives, the chapter calls for a broader, more expansive movement, embracing and acknowledging all those who suffer discrimination, abuse, and violence.

EU LGBT Survey Technical Report (2013), https://fra.europa.eu/en/survey/2012/eu-lgbt -survey.

11.   Michael Segalov, *Why Hasn't the Gay Community Had a #MeToo Moment?*, THE GUARDIAN, Mar. 7, 2018, https://www.theguardian.com/commentisfree/2018/mar/07 /gay-community-metoo-moment-conversation-consent-sexual-assault; Kyli Rodriguez-Cayro; *Some Members Of The LGBTQ Community Feel Excluded By The Me Too Hashtag, & It's A Reminder Of How Important Inclusive Language Is*, BUSTLE, Oct. 19, 2017, https://www.bustle .com/p/some-members-of-the-lgbtq-community-feel-excluded-by-the-me-too-hashtag-its-a -reminder-of-how-important-inclusive-language-is-2953162.

12.   Cisgender refers to a person who does not feel a gender identity that conflicts with their assigned gender.

Dilemma of Invisibility

A potential critique of #MeToo, at least as it has been presented through the lens of televised and online media, is the absence of LGBT voices and experiences.[13] The typical narrative shared as part of the #MeToo movement foregrounds the experiences of cisgender female-identified individuals (usually white) who have been subject to physical, verbal, and/or emotional harassment by a cisgender male-identified person, who usually occupies a position of power (frequently in direct comparison to the individual whom he has abused).

Rarely are public stories that deviate from a heteronormative model incorporated into #MeToo dialogues,[14] the allegations directed toward Kevin Spacey, most notably by actor, Anthony Rapp, being a notable exception.[15] While #MeToo has been inspiring, and transformative, in its capacity to speak truth to power, it has been somewhat limited in shining a light on alternative harassment dynamics. In many respects, LGBT persons, particularly lesbian, bisexual, and transgender women, are the unseen faces and unheard voices of the movement. Although they experience harassment and violence at high rates,[16] their stories are comparatively absent from the narratives that shape #MeToo.

The absence of LGBT-focused reports within the public #MeToo discourse creates an obvious dilemma of visibility. If we understand a core achievement of the #MeToo movement as being affirmation through visibility, i.e., the idea of shared trauma encouraging others to confront and acknowledge their experiences of abuse, LGBT individuals clearly cannot share in that achievement if their experiences of harassment remain absent or hidden.[17] #MeToo has, of course, resulted in high-profile male individuals being publicly and professionally condemned; perhaps its more powerful legacy, however, will be creating

---

13. See: Gabriel Arkles, *Making Space for Trans People in the #MeToo Movement*, ACLU, Apr. 13, 2018, https://www.aclu.org/blog/womens-rights/violence-against-women/making-space-trans-people-metoo-movement.

14. Riley Villiers, *What Grinds My Gears: Why isn't the #MeToo movement more gay?*, THE DAILY FREE PRESS, Feb. 22, 2018, https://dailyfreepress.com/blog/2018/02/22/what-grinds-my-gears-why-isnt-the-metoo-movement-more-gay/.

15. *Kevin Spacey timeline: How the story unfolded*, BBC, July 18, 2019, https://www.bbc.co.uk/news/entertainment-arts-41884878.

16. Frances Perraudin, *Survey finds 70% of LGBT people sexually harassed at work*, THE GUARDIAN, May 17, 2019, https://www.theguardian.com/uk-news/2019/may/17/survey-finds-70-of-lgbt-people-sexually-harassed-at-work. A number of reports speak to the violence that LGBT individuals experience, e.g., National Center for Transgender Equality, The Report of the 2015 U.S. Transgender Survey (2016); Stonewall, LGBT in Britain—University Report (2018).

17. Villiers, *supra* note 14.

conversations around sexual harassment and creating space for survivors to publicly name their truth.

A key assumption within the idea of "empowerment through visibility" is that people can locate themselves within, and take strength from, the experiences of others. For LGBT populations, however, if #MeToo has prioritized heteronormative male-female power dynamics, what examples speak to their experiences of harassment?[18] Where can the female individual who experiences same-sex abuse locate her story and find her inspiration? What of the transgender man, whose abuse arises from the complex intersections of misogyny and transphobia, as well as the externalization of both toxic and fragile masculinity? For these individuals, just as there were for millions of cisgender women in recent decades, there are important and frightening questions as to whether, if they choose to disclose their survivor status, they will be believed and whether they will find supportive, affirmative communities. Failing to see their own narrative visibly reflected in existing #MeToo discourse, LGBT people have legitimate reasons to ask: #UsToo?

Dilemma of Vulnerability

A second dilemma raised by #MeToo is how to protect LGBT individuals who, because of additional and intersecting vulnerabilities, may face supplementary challenges when sharing their stories of harassment and abuse. A welcome feature of the #MeToo movement has been the extent to which, in various symbolic and practical ways, the past two years have created, or have begun to create, safety structures allowing individuals, who previously withheld stories of trauma because of apprehended retaliation, to publicly reveal and discuss their harassment. #MeToo has facilitated the emergence of space—both physical and virtual (e.g., online, etc.)—where there can be frank and open discussion of abuse, gender inequality, and strategies for empowerment.

It is important, however, to understand the full dimensions of public discourse, including unintended or unforeseen risks, so as to appreciate that, although public conversations can enhance both the healing processes and general life experiences of many individuals, they may actually increase the vulnerability of LGBT communities.

It is important to remember that when straight, cisgender persons reveal that they are a survivor of sexual harassment, that revelation, while

---

18. Tris Mamone, *The #MeToo Conversation Erases Trans People*, HUFFPOST, Feb. 21, 2018, https://www.huffpost.com/entry/opinion-mamone-trans-metoo_n_5a8c5c61e4b027 3053a539d1; Ebony Miranda, *Did #MeToo Forget About Me?*, N.Y. TIMES, Sept. 4, 2018, https://www.nytimes.com/2018/09/04/smarter-living/the-edit-me-too.html.

often extremely harrowing, is the only piece of information that the listener receives. In speaking about the experience of trauma, cisgender individuals are not required to expose other elements of personality or identity. Yet for LGBT individuals, such uni-dimensional revelations are frequently not possible, particularly where the harassment they suffer is linked to their sexual orientation or gender identity. For LGBT populations, declaring "Me Too" in the context of abuse often involves the additional statements "I am gay" and/or "I have a transgender history."

For gay men and transgender individuals, where sodomy and/or cross-dressing are criminal offenses, the inevitable revelation of identity, which attaches to public allegations of sexual harassment, places such individuals in an intolerable situation.[19] The need to protect oneself from an oppressive criminal justice system may override the oppression and trauma of harassment. Similarly, in countries where lesbians and trans men are subject to (possibly extreme) social sanctions, there may be little incentive to reveal abusive conduct that creates further re-victimization.[20] When one thinks about the power of saying "Me Too," there is benefit in reflecting upon the minimum levels of privilege which that act of speaking requires and to consider how LGBT communities may exist outside such zones of privilege.

Such considerations are particularly relevant to lesbian, gay, bisexual, and transgender youth, who are both disproportionately exposed to social discrimination and uniquely vulnerable to involuntary revelations of identity. For many LGBT young people, their capacity to reveal their own harassment is fundamentally bound up with experiences (or potential experiences) of familial and financial marginalization.[21] Where a child or adolescent is financially dependent upon parents, to whom they are not out and who they know would

---

19. U.N. High Commissioner for Human Rights, *supra*, note 9 [25]; Human Rights Watch, *India: Supreme Court Strikes Down Sodomy Law*, HRW, Sept. 6, 2018, https://www .hrw.org/news/2018/09/06/india-supreme-court-strikes-down-sodomy-law; UK Home Office, *Country Policy and Information Note Iran: Sexual orientation and gender identity or expression* (June 1, 2019) [5.1.6], https://assets.publishing.service.gov.uk/government/uploads/system /uploads/attachment_data/file/810845/CPIN_-_Iran_-_SOGI_-_v3.0__June_2019__EXT .PDF.

20. *See, e.g.*, Human Rights Watch, *"We'll Show You You're a Woman" Violence and Discrimination against Black Lesbians and Transgender Men in South Africa* (2011), https://www .hrw.org/sites/default/files/reports/southafrica1211.pdf. *See also*, U.N. High Commissioner for Human Rights (2015) *supra* note 9 [25].

21. Stephanie Ignatavicius, *Stress in Female-Identified Transgender Youth: A Review of the Literature on Effects and Interventions*, 10 J. OF LGBT YOUTH 267, 270 (2013); Lealah Pollock and Stephen Eyre, *Growth into manhood: identity development among female-to-male transgender youth*, 14 HEALTH AND SEXUALITY 209, 217 (2012); Jae Alexis Lee, *Why Do Parents Reject Their LGBT Children?* Huff Post (March 3, 2017), https://www.huffpost.com/entry/why-do -parents-reject-their-lgbtq-children_b_58b9a3f7e4b0fa65b844b26d.

disapprove of homosexuality or transgender identities, the child, like the gay man and transgender individual above, faces an unfathomable dilemma: silently tolerate LGBT-related harassment, with consequent negative impacts upon mental and physical well-being, or expose their harassment and possibly lose their home, emotional support, and financial stability.[22] Such a dilemma creates unique barriers for LGBT young people in accessing the discourse of #MeToo, and it should encourage greater reflection upon how existing vulnerabilities, beyond structures of support, impact the capacity to reveal experiences of abuse.

Dilemma of Believability

The third dilemma that LGBT individuals may encounter within the #MeToo movement is a deficit of belief. While refusals to accept the narratives of survivors is a common, and on-going, problem for all people who challenge gender-based abuse, it is, and historically has been, particularly prevalent where those raising complaints are lesbian, gay, bisexual, or transgender.

For lesbian and bisexual-identified women, difficulties in accessing #MeToo movements may be grounded in stereotypical understandings of femaleness, particularly where the survivor alleges that another woman has engaged in the abusive conduct. Tropes about femininity and gentleness can be raised to question the possibility of sexual abuse within such same-sex relationships.[23] There are still (surprisingly prevalent) assumptions that women are just *too nice to do that sort of thing*, undermining survivor narratives and raising an implicit presumption against female-perpetrated sexual harassment.[24] Such critiques of the way authorities (and society more generally) treat and receive lesbian narratives of abuse are not new, and they have long been raised in support of reforming domestic violence frameworks. Yet in the age of #MeToo, where increased numbers of women are sharing their experiences of abuse, one must be vigilant against a sole focus on male abuse and be open to the stories of lesbian survivors.

Historic tropes also act as a barrier to the way in which gay men approach #MeToo. While, in the context of gay harassment, the alleged conduct typically

---

22. *Id.*

23. Galop, *Myths and stereotypes about violence and abuse in same-sex relationships*, https://www.galop.org.uk/wp-content/uploads/For-Service-Providers-Myths.pdf; Catherine Donovan et al., *Comparing Domestic Abuse in Same Sex and Heterosexual Relationships* at 20 (Nov. 2006), http://www.equation.org.uk/wp-content/uploads/2012/12/Comparing-Domestic-Abuse-in-Same-Sex-and-Heterosexual-relationships.pdf.

24. Evashnee Naidu and Nonhlanhla Mkhize, *Gender-based violence: the lesbian and gay experience*, 1 DOMESTIC VIOLENCE 34, 35 (2005).

maps onto expected assumptions regarding male violence (i.e., there is a male perpetrating harassment), there are additional social expectations that discourage belief in survivor stories.

First, as with many men who experience abuse, there may be a general reluctance to accept the narrative of harassment because of social understandings that men are (or should be) capable of defending themselves.[25] As researchers within the sphere of family law have known for decades, male victims of domestic violence feel that they are less likely to be believed and more likely to be blamed for their own abuse.[26] Second, irrespective of official report structures, many gay men apprehend that they will be disbelieved or blamed for their harassment. These apprehensions are reinforced where public movements, such as #MeToo, fail to incorporate gay male narratives.

Finally, against a background where gay male identities have been (and continue to be) (mis)characterized as inherently sexual or hyper-sexualized,[27] there is an underlying assumption that gay men welcome all sexual attention and that harassing behavior is acceptable or even expected within gay male communities. These assumptions may dissuade gay men from sharing their stories, both because they fear that the involuntary nature of their abuse will be underplayed, and because they worry about validating harmful societal assumptions that have historically been used (and remain a primary justification) against LGBT equality.[28]

Dilemma of Legality

The final LGBT dilemma for #MeToo is a question of context, and whether a movement that calls out sexual harassment can substantively impact LGBT lives while more fundamental, legal barriers to equality remain.

As noted above, around the world, gay men and transgender women in almost 80 jurisdictions are criminally prohibited from engaging in consensual intercourse with a male individual. In certain jurisdictions, lesbian-identified persons are also subject to similar censures. Such laws are actively enforced in

---

25. *Id. See, e.g.*, Galop, *supra*, note 23.

26. Alyson Huntley et al., *Help-seeking by male victims of domestic violence and abuse (DVA): a systematic review and qualitative evidence synthesis*, BMJ Open 2019, pp. 7-8, https://bmjopen.bmj.com/content/bmjopen/9/6/e021960.full.pdf.

27. *See, e.g.*, John Finnis, *The Good of Marriage and the Morality of Sexual Relations: Some Philosophical and Historical Observations*, 42 AM. J. OF JURIS. 97, 127 (1998).

28. Natalie Hope McDonald, *LGBT Harassment in the Era of #MeToo*, THE PHILLY VOICE, Mar. 26, 2018, https://www.phillyvoice.com/lgbt-sexual-harassment-abuse-metoo-movement-philadelphia/.

a significant number of states and, even where that is not the case, they stand as a symbolic and practical impediment to rights for LGBT populations.[29] In many countries, anti-sodomy and cross-dressing laws may be used to blackmail or harass individuals, with the threat of exposure and criminal sanction coercing vulnerable persons into compliance with extortion and harassing demands.[30] For a modern #MeToo movement, determined to *de facto* reduce the extent to which LGBT communities experience gender-based abuse, a primary focus must be on confronting, challenging, and eradicating laws that facilitate and reproduce patterns of discrimination and violence.

In a growing number of jurisdictions, transgender persons are entitled to obtain legal gender recognition.[31] Domestic law validates individuals in their self-identified gender status. Yet a striking number of countries tie affirmation of gender to considerations of body.[32] A transgender man can obtain a male legal gender, but he may have to physically masculinize his body. Similarly, a transgender woman may have to forfeit her penis, testes, and submit to hormone-interventions. While key human rights actors increasingly critique the imposition of medical treatments as a pre-condition for legal gender recognition,[33] these procedures (resolutely) remain standard practice. In such circumstances, is it surprising that transgender individuals experience higher rates of sexual harassment and violence? Where national law legitimizes transgender bodies as a space of public discourse, is it not natural that private individuals will exhibit little respect for transgender dignity and physical integrity? Once again, such legal rules must be addressed if substantive progress on transgender experiences of sexual harassment is to be achieved.

Finally, in many countries, policy makers are grappling with the complex question of whether (and when) transgender women should be entitled to

---

29. *See generally* Lucas Ramos Mendos, *State-Sponsored Homophobia*, ILGA (2019), https://ilga.org/downloads/ILGA_State_Sponsored_Homophobia_2019.pdf.

30. Human Rights Watch, *India: Supreme Court Strikes Down Sodomy Law*, HRW, Sept. 6, 2018, https://www.hrw.org/news/2018/09/06/india-supreme-court-strikes-down -sodomy-law.

31. *See generally* Zhan Chiam, Sandra Duffy and Matilda González Gil, *Trans Legal Mapping Report* (ILGA 2017) who offer a global perspective on legal gender recognition.

32. *See, e.g.*, PETER DUNNE and MARJOLEIN VAN DEN BRINK, TRANS AND INTERSEX EQUALITY RIGHTS IN EUROPE: A COMPARATIVE ANALYSIS (European Commission) (2018), pp. 58-64. For a broader discussion of medico-legal gender recognition laws, see Zhan Chiam, *supra*, note 31.

33. *See, e.g.*, U.N. High Commissioner for Human Rights (2015), *supra*, note 9, [17]– [79(i)]; Report of the Independent Expert on protection against violence and discrimination based on sexual orientation and gender identity, UN Doc No. A/HRC/38/43 (12 May 2018), [44] and [98].

access women-only services and accommodations.[34] For such individuals, access to their preferred restroom or changing facilities is as much an issue of safety as it is about symbolic recognition of identity.[35] Research reveals that, when required to use male facilities, women with a transgender history face high rates of questioning and confrontation. As such, the movement toward adopting proportionate policies for transgender women to access their preferred services and accommodations is, fundamentally, a movement toward avoiding gender-based harassment. Yet, in recent times, much of the discourse on segregated space (at least in North America and Western Europe) has centered on allegations of potential abuse. Rather than considering either the existing harms to transgender women or the absence of evidence surrounding misuse of trans-focused equality laws, policy debates have prioritized potential abuse committed by non-transgender individuals, over whom transgender communities have no control.[36] While the question of segregated space is certainly not easy, and compromise may be required on all sides, surely the goals of the #MeToo movement cannot be achieved when LGBT persons are required to account for the potential misdeeds of cisgender men.

Conclusion

There is significant potential for LGBT populations within the discourse of #MeToo. As individuals who confront harassment and violence linked to their experience and performance of gender, LGBT communities are undoubtedly impacted by challenges to patriarchal norms and gender-motivated discrimination. Yet, despite their closeness to the issues, LGBT people continue to express frustration at the difficulty they experience in accessing the discourse of #MeToo. Underrepresentation and a detachment from the complexity of gay, lesbian, bisexual, and transgender lives have resulted in the perception that—two years later—the #MeToo movement remains (perhaps unintentionally) exclusive of LGBT survivors. Moving forward and seeking to overcome the four "dilemmas" identified in this short chapter, movement leaders (and policy makers who seeks substantive reform) must engage with LGBT populations and ensure that #WeToo matter in this important moment of change.

---

34. *See, e.g.*, SHEILA CAVANAGH, QUEERING BATHROOMS: GENDER, SEXUALITY AND THE HYGIENIC IMAGINATION (2010).

35. Jody Herman, *Gendered Restrooms and Minority Stress: The Public Regulation of Gender and its Impact on Transgender People's Lives*, J. OF PUB. MGMT. AND SOC. POL'Y 65, 72-74 (2013).

36. Peter Dunne, *(Trans)Forming Single-Gender Services and Communal Accommodations*, 26 SOC. AND LEGAL STUDIES 537, 547-551 (2017).

CHAPTER 34

Women with Disabilities: Forever on the Edge of #MeToo?

Lucy-Ann Buckley[1]

Introduction

In 2006, a seventeen-year-old deaf-mute girl, known only as RPB, was raped in the Philippines by a neighbor. Supported by her sister, she made a police complaint later that day. She was interviewed by a male police officer in breach of regulations. The police did not have a sign language interpreter, but RPB's sister was able to interpret for her. The police wrote out RPB's statement in Filipino, which she could not read because the education system for the deaf was almost exclusively based on written English. She underwent a medical examination; she then had to wait nearly five years for her case to be heard in court. During this time, she received no counseling or support services and lived in proximity to her rapist. Most of the delay was due to the lack of sign language interpreters in the court system. Eventually, some interpretative support was obtained from a non-governmental organization, but RPB was still left without interpretation for significant parts of the hearing.

On the day of the hearing, RPB had to wait long hours, in the presence of her rapist, for the case to be heard. The court then acquitted the defendant, holding that RPB was not a credible witness and had failed to prove that she had not consented to sex. Ironically, there was no interpreter in court at this point to explain the verdict to RPB. The court said that RPB had not acted reasonably; an ordinary Filipina would have summoned "every ounce of her strength and courage to thwart any attempt to besmirch her honour and blemish her purity." The court was particularly critical of RPB's failure to shout for help, saying that "her being a deaf mute does not render her incapable of creating

---

1. Senior Lecturer in Law, National University of Ireland Galway.

noise." Essentially, RPB's failure to act like the "ideal victim" undermined her credibility.

RPB subsequently brought a complaint to the CEDAW Committee (see below), which considered that the decision to acquit the accused was based on harmful gender myths and stereotypes, and that RPB had been denied the right to a fair trial. Although the verdict could not be overturned, the committee recommended that the Philippines should review its rape laws and interpretation policy, and that RPB should receive compensation and free counseling.[2]

RPB's story illustrates many of the problems facing women with disabilities in relation to gender-based violence. It seems likely that, as a neighbor, RPB's rapist targeted her specifically because he knew she had a disability. Research demonstrates that women and girls with disabilities are at a significantly increased risk of violence and sexual abuse compared to women without disabilities[3] and men with disabilities.[4] It has been estimated that the likelihood of rape or physical or sexual abuse is at least two[5] and possibly three times higher for women with disabilities than those without.[6] Within this broad figure, there are further intersections—for instance, while the risk of abuse is high for all children with disabilities (almost four times higher than for children without disabilities), the risks are even higher for girls with particular impairments—those who are deaf (like RPB), or who are blind or autistic, or who have intellectual, psychosocial, or multiple disabilities (again like RPB). Indigenous girls and women with disabilities face a higher risk of early marriage, sexual violence, and unwanted pregnancy. Other noteworthy intersections are based on race, sexuality, poverty, or involvement in humanitarian crises or conflict or post-conflict settings, where women with disabilities are particularly vulnerable.[7]

---

2. CEDAW Communication No. 34/2011, *R. P. B. v. the Philippines*.

3. Lisa Schur et al., People with Disabilities: Sidelined or Mainstreamed? 177 (2013).

4. Ingrid van der Heijden & Kristin Dunkle, *Preventing violence against women and girls with disabilities in lower- and middle-income countries (LMICs)*, What Works to Prevent Violence Against Women and Girls Evidence Review, Sept. 2017, https://www.what works.co.za/documents/publications/114-disability-evidence-brief-new-crop-3/file+&cd=1 &hl=en&ct=clnk&gl=ie&client=firefox-b-ab.

5. 57th Session of the Commission on the Status of Women, *Fact Sheet: Violence Against Women and Girls with Disabilities*, Feb. 2, 2013.

6. Rishi Iyengar, *Women with Disabilities are Three Times More Likely to Face Abuse: Report*, Time Health, Mar. 6, 2015, http://time.com/3734961/women-with-disabilities -three-times-as-likely-to-be-raped-human-rights-watch/.

7. For a detailed account of different disability intersections, see Catalina Devandas Aguilar, *Report of the Special Rapporteur on the Rights of Persons with Disabilities (theme: sexual and reproductive health and rights of girls and young women with disabilities)* (July 14, 2017) (A72/133) ('Report of the Special Rapporteur'), para 35.

However, RPB's story also illustrates many of the systemic barriers that severely limit the ability of women with disabilities to access justice. These include hostile, uninformed, and inaccessible courts and complaints procedures, the application of restrictive gender stereotypes, and the lack of effective remedies. The effect of harmful gender stereotypes can be even more pronounced in situations involving disability: in RPB's case, the stereotype of the "ordinary Filipina" who would struggle, shout, and make noise disadvantaged all female rape victims, but had a particularly harsh impact on RPB, given her greatly reduced capacity for noise-making.

International Human Rights Framework

Violence against women with disabilities has been increasingly recognized in international human rights law. The 1979 UN Convention on the Elimination of all Forms of Discrimination Against Women (CEDAW) does not expressly reference gender-based violence. However, the CEDAW Committee, which monitors implementation of the convention, has interpreted it to encompass gender-based violence as an aspect of discrimination, both in relation to individual complaints (as in RPB's case) and through a series of general recommendations (non-binding but highly persuasive treaty interpretations). General Recommendation No. 35 (2017) (updating General Recommendation No. 19, made in 1992)—defines gender-based violence as "violence which is directed against a woman because she is a woman or that affects women disproportionately." This expansive approach includes acts that inflict physical, mental, or sexual harm or suffering, deprivation of liberty, and related threats or coercion. Intersectional gender-based violence is explicitly recognized, including violence against women with disabilities. The UN Special Rapporteur on violence against women, its causes and consequences has also emphasized that violence particularly affects marginalized women, including women with disabilities, due to the effects of multiple layers of discrimination.[8]

Intersectional discrimination against women and girls with disabilities is explicitly recognized by Article 6 of the UN Convention on the Rights of Persons with Disabilities (CRPD), in force since 2008. Although Article 6 itself does not explicitly mention gender-based violence, the Preamble to the CRPD notes that women and girls with disabilities are often at greater risk of violence,

---

8. The UN Special Rapporteur on Violence Against Women, Its Causes and Consequences, *15 Years of the United Nations Special Rapporteur on Violence Against Women, Its Causes and Consequences (1994-2009); a Critical Review* (2009) Office of the UN High Commissioner on Human Rights, p. 42; Rashida Manjoo, *Report of the Special Rapporteur on Violence Against Women, its Causes and Consequences*, May 2, 2011 (A /HRC/17/26), p. 28.

exploitation and abuse. Furthermore, Article 6 must be taken into account in interpreting other provisions in the CRPD, including the rights to liberty, education, employment, health, and access to justice. Of specific relevance to harassment are the rights to integrity of the person (including bodily and mental integrity) in Article 17, and the right to freedom from violence, exploitation, and abuse contained in Article 16. Article 16 also explicitly references the gender-based aspects of such abuse.

Article 6 is amplified by General Comment No. 3, adopted by the CRPD Committee in 2016. This again provides an authoritative though non-binding interpretation of Article 6. General Comment No. 3 repeatedly highlights not only the intersection of gender and disability in general, but the importance of further intersections, such as those based on refugee or migrant status, sexual orientation, race or ethnicity, age and religion, or based on particular kinds of disability (for instance, multiple disabilities, albinism, intellectual, psychosocial or sensory conditions, or physical impairments). It outlines the scale of intersectional violence against women with disabilities, highlighting that they are often at greater risk of violence, injury, abuse, neglect, and exploitation than women without disabilities. It also recognizes that violence may be interpersonal or structural—in other words, violence is not just caused by individual perpetrators, but results from social attitudes, ideologies, practices, and institutions, including legal rules. This point has also been emphasized by the CEDAW Committee in General Recommendation No. 35.

The CRPD has been ratified (made legally binding) by 177 countries to date, though there are notable exceptions, such as the United States. Ratification obliges UN member States to take positive steps to promote equality and eliminate discrimination, so the CRPD has a significant impact on national legal systems. However, only ninety-three countries have ratified the Optional Protocol to the CRPD, which permits individuals to complain directly to the UN when their rights have been breached. The CRPD also has an effect at supra-national level: for instance, the European Union is a signatory and is therefore required to interpret relevant areas of its law in light of the treaty.

Other international measures also cover disability and sexual abuse or harassment, though not all recognize intersectionality. The UN Convention on the Rights of the Child, which applies to children up to the age of eighteen, requires States to protect children from sexual exploitation and abuse. It also specifies that all rights under the convention shall apply without discrimination, including discrimination based on sex or disability. Article 23 of the Protocol to the African Charter on Human and People's Rights on the Rights of Women in Africa (2003), ratified by thirty-six States to date, requires signatories to ensure that women with disabilities are protected from violence, including sexual abuse. By contrast, although the European Union has a legal framework to combat harassment based on gender, disability, race, and other grounds,[9] it does not yet provide a remedy for harassment based on a combination of these grounds. Furthermore, EU law accords different levels of protection to race, gender, and other protected characteristics, such as disability. Protection is broadest in relation to race and covers harassment in contexts other than employment (e.g., education, healthcare, and access to services). However, gender protection is narrower, and disability protection is narrower still, applying only to employment and vocational training. Therefore, even if EU law covered intersectional claims, harassment based on both gender and disability would not be covered outside of employment and vocational training.

Most recently (2019), the International Labour Conference adopted a new Convention and Recommendation on Violence and Harassment in work and related activities. The convention, which is not yet in force, recognizes that violence and harassment in the world of work can constitute a human rights violation or abuse. It then defines "violence and harassment" as behaviors, practices, or threats "that aim at, result in, or are likely to result in physical, psychological, sexual or economic harm." The convention is notable for its explicit recognition of the impact of "multiple and intersecting forms of discrimination," and the need to protect workers from "one or more vulnerable groups" or "groups in situations of vulnerability." The reference to vulnerable groups is amplified in the non-binding recommendation, which states that this should be interpreted by reference to international labor standards and human rights instruments.

On the Edge of #MeToo

Given the scale of the problem, and the level of international recognition, why have the experiences of women and girls with disabilities been so overlooked by #MeToo? It has been suggested the failure to gain traction, despite the best efforts of activists,[10] may partly be due to the emphasis of #MeToo on sexual

---

9. The EU legal framework includes the Racial Equality Directive (Directive 2000/43/EC), the Framework Employment Directive (Directive 2000/78/EC), dealing with disability, sexual orientation, and other grounds; the Recast Equal Treatment Directive (Directive 2006/54/EC), dealing with gender discrimination in relation to employment and social security; and Directive 2004/113, dealing with gender discrimination in relation to public goods and services (excluding education).

10. See, e.g., S.E. Smith, *Disability Should Be Integral to the #MeToo Conversation*, Rewire News, Nov. 1, 2017, https://rewire.news/article/2017/11/01/disability-integral -metoo-conversation/; Tamara Abueish, *The #MeToo Movement has a Serious Problem Addressing the Experiences of Women with Disabilities*, The Tempest, Mar. 5, 2018, https://thetempest .co/2018/03/05/culture-taste/women-disabilities-metoo-campaign/; Anne Wafula Strike, *Disabled Women See #MeToo and Think: What About Us?*, The Guardian, Mar. 8, 2018, https://

harassment in employment.[11] Since people with disabilities are much less likely to be employed, and women with disabilities are even less likely to be employed than men with disabilities,[12] an emphasis on workplace harassment is less likely to speak to their concerns. This, however, seems unlikely, given that there are still significant numbers of women with disabilities in the workforce and the figures for gender violence are so high for women with disabilities. A related possibility is that, since disabled people who are employed are more likely to be on low incomes and have precarious contracts,[13] they may be less likely to protest at mistreatment. This may certainly be a contributing factor, though it is also true of women generally,[14] so it is unlikely to be the full explanation. A further suggestion is that the emphasis of the disability movement on accessibility has contributed to a comparative neglect of disability-related harassment.[15] However, this does not explain its neglect by other feminists.

It seems more likely that the widespread exclusion of women with disabilities from #MeToo may be due to other factors. First, the situations in which disability-related abuse is likely to occur, the nature of certain impairments, and attitudes toward women with disabilities who complain about gender-based violence, are likely to prevent reporting. Second, social understandings of sexual harassment and other gender-based violence may exclude the experiences of women with disabilities from public consideration, particularly where the violence is state sanctioned. Each of these points will be examined in turn.

Contextual Barriers

Much of the violence against women with disabilities occurs in congregated settings (such as residential care homes) and affects women who are often

---

www.theguardian.com/commentisfree/2018/mar/08/disabled-people-metoo-womens-movement-inclusion-diversity; Nidhi Goyal, *Why Does the Women's Rights Movement Marginalise Women with Disabilities?*, The Guardian, Sept. 7, 2016, https://www.theguardian.com/global-development/2016/sep/07/why-does-womens-rights-movement-marginalise-women-with-disabilities-nidhi-goyal.

11. Shelley L. Tremain & Melinda C. Hall, *Is the #MeToo Movement Ableist?*, Discrimination and Disadvantage, Dec. 10, 2017, https://philosophycommons.typepad.com/disability_and_disadvanta/2017/12/is-the-metoo-movement-ableist.html.

12. See, e.g., David Pettinccchio & Michelle Maroto, Factors in Studying Employment for Persons with Disability 3-33 (Barbara M. Altman ed., 2017).

13. *Ibid.*

14. Caroline Criado Perez, Invisible Women: Exposing Data Bias in a World Designed for Men 133 (Chatto and Windus, 2019).

15. Theresia Degener, European Union Non-Discrimination Law and Intersectionality 32 (Dagmar Schiek and Anna Lawson, eds., 2011).

heavily institutionalized. In such environments, women who are vulnerable to begin with (for instance, women with intellectual or psychosocial disabilities) are often socialized to be compliant and to tolerate invasive procedures. They may also be over-medicated, heavily reliant on caregivers, or punished for perceived infractions. They are unlikely to have access to social media or legal representation, may not always be capable of self-advocacy, and their family members may be reluctant to interfere and jeopardize the provision of care. Although the CRPD requires facilities and programs for people with disabilities to be independently monitored, this does not always happen. Health care authorities may overlook physical signs of abuse on the assumption that a disabled woman is likely to have injured herself, either accidentally (in relation to mobility impairments or physical conditions such as brittle bones) or intentionally (in connection with psychosocial conditions such as schizophrenia).

In these circumstances, it is unsurprising that complaints are unlikely to be made or heard, and it is commonplace that sexual abuse is ignored or concealed, often for years. In a recent Irish example, a severely intellectually disabled and non-verbal woman known as "Grace" was left in the care of an abusive foster family for twenty years. Concerns were raised repeatedly over this period, with recurring observations of physical injuries and neglect. In 1996, serious allegations of sexual abuse were made against the foster father in respect of another foster child. These allegations were not properly investigated, but it was decided that no other children should be placed in the home. Arrangements were made to remove Grace but, inexplicably, this did not happen. Grace was finally removed in 2009, some thirteen years later. Investigation later disclosed that Grace had suffered both physical and sexual abuse of the worst kind, including repeated rape with implements, which was sustained over her twenty years of residence in the home. She was also defrauded of money. Even after an internal investigation was eventually completed, the responsible health care authority waited three years to inform the police.[16] Although Grace was later awarded compensation, no one in the responsible health authority was held accountable for her treatment.

Women with disabilities are also highly likely to be abused in intimate relationships, often by family members, partners, and caregivers.[17] This adds a particular layer of complexity, as complaining about abuse may entail the loss

---

16. Paul Hosford, *HSE "Took Three Years to Contact Gardai About Grace Report,"* THE-JOURNAL.IE, Mar. 5, 2017, https://www.thejournal.ie/hse-grace-report-gardai-3272046 -Mar2017/.

17. See, e.g., Joseph Shapiro, *The Sexual Assault Epidemic No One Talks About,* NATIONAL PUBLIC RADIO, INC. (US), Jan. 8, 2018, https://www.npr.org/2018/01/08 /570224090/the-sexual-assault-epidemic-no-one-talks-about, outlining the findings of a year-long investigation into U.S. Justice Department figures.

of support. It is not easy to complain about abuse if a caregiver's presence is essential for daily functioning, such as the ability to wash, dress, eat, travel, or care for children. It is therefore unsurprising that sexual assault is even less likely than usual to be reported where the victim has a disability.[18] The difficulty is increased by additional challenges that face those who do report abuse, such as the risk of being institutionalized.[19] There may also be a fear of retaliation in a context where it may be very difficult to escape.[20] Rape crisis centers and women's refuges are often inaccessible to women with mobility impairments, and are unsuitable for women with sensory impairments.[21] They may also lack interpreters for D/deaf women,[22] as may the police. Where, then, is the disabled woman to go for help? Although the CRPD requires states to provide protection services (including reporting mechanisms) that are age-, gender-, and disability-sensitive, this standard is by no means met in practice.

The widespread institutionalization of women with disabilities reflects a general pattern of exclusion, where disabled people are effectively barred from social participation, including public transport, employment, cultural participation, and mainstream education. This enforced invisibility may also contribute to broader legal and social barriers that prevent women with disabilities from having their voices heard, or from being considered worth protecting. This is particularly the case where other social power imbalances apply. Human Rights Watch highlights the case of Chandra, a twelve-year-old Indian girl with cerebral palsy, who was kidnapped, raped, and left bleeding in a field near her home in 2013. As she could not speak, sit, stand, or walk independently, she could not call for help or go home. She later died due to health complications. Her family came under significant pressure from local leaders not to pursue legal action against the perpetrator, who was politically well-connected.[23] In another Indian case, a man who raped and sexually abused his two disabled sisters because his father had left them some land was supported by the local villagers. The sisters ultimately had to go into hiding and could not make a legal complaint.[24]

---

18. See the Report of the Special Rapporteur, *supra* note 7, at para 36.

19. *Ibid.*

20. *Ibid.*

21. See, e.g., Frances Ryan, *"I'm tired and desperate"—a disabled victim of domestic violence on her struggle to survive*, THE GUARDIAN, Sept. 19, 2019, https://www.theguardian.com/lifeandstyle/2019/sep/19/disabled-victim-of-domestic-violence-on-her-struggle-to-survive.

22. "D/deaf" covers all people with some type of deafness.

23. Abhishek Kumar Mehan, *Invisible victims of sexual violence: access to justice for women and girls with disabilities in India*, HUMAN RIGHTS WATCH, Apr. 3, 2018, https://www.hrw.org/report/2018/04/03/invisible-victims-sexual-violence/access-justice-women-and-girls-disabilities.

24. *Ibid.*

Feminists have long highlighted institutional barriers to women making complaints of sexual violence, such as police hostility. However, the exclusion of women's voices from the legal process is magnified where a complainant is non-verbal or is unable to describe her experiences in a way that is considered to be legally sufficient. Complainants with intellectual disabilities are commonly deemed to lack sufficient legal capacity to initiate a complaint or give evidence.[25] In a well-known case in the Netherlands, a sixteen-year-old girl was raped in a residential care home. Under Dutch law, her father was unable to make a complaint on her behalf, as she was over sixteen. However, she was legally unable to make a complaint herself, as she had an intellectual disability. Her rapist was therefore not prosecuted. (The European Court of Human Rights eventually found that the girl's human rights had been breached).[26] In a Canadian case, an intellectually disabled young woman was repeatedly sexually assaulted by her mother's partner. The trial judge held that the victim could not testify because she had not shown she understood the duty to speak the truth. This decision was overturned by the Supreme Court of Canada on the grounds that it effectively permitted sexual abuse of the intellectually disabled with near impunity.[27] However, capacity issues may go beyond legal rules, as similar assumptions may undermine the complainant's credibility in complaints made to health and education professionals, social workers, or caregivers. For this reason, the CRPD requires states to implement "effective legislation and policies, including women- and child-focused legislation and policies, to ensure that instances of exploitation, violence and abuse against persons with disabilities is identified, investigated and, where appropriate, prosecuted."[28] Unfortunately, such measures are commonly either entirely lacking or inadequately implemented.

Feminists have also commonly critiqued "rape myths," such as assumptions that women who consume alcohol or wear revealing clothing are likely to consent to sex. These myths are exacerbated in the case of women with disabilities by what might be termed "disability myths." Examples include the belief that women with disabilities are asexual, or that they are hypersexual.[29] Neither myth has any basis in reality,[30] yet both serve to undermine complainants, either

---

25. *Ibid.* The General Comment on Article 6 of the CRPD classifies the refusal to recognize the testimony of women with intellectual or psychosocial disabilities in court proceedings as direct discrimination, which has the effect of denying women with disabilities access to justice.

26. *X and Y v. The Netherlands*, 8978/80, (1985) 8 EHRR 235, [1985] ECHR 4.

27. *R v. DAI*, 2012 S.C.C. 5.

28. Article 16 CRPD.

29. General Comment No. 3 on Article 6 CRPD, para 30; Report of the Special Rapporteur, *supra* note 7, para 18.

30. Report of the Special Rapporteur, *supra* note 7, para 18.

428 The Global #MeToo Movement

by suggesting that women with disabilities are unlikely to be sexually abused (notwithstanding all the evidence to the contrary), or that they are sexually voracious or desperate. When combined with the usual gender stereotypes that affect women's credibility (such as those discussed earlier in relation to RPB), the effect is often to fatally undermine any case. Further stereotypes may undermine the credibility of women with specific disabilities, e.g., a belief that women with psychosocial disabilities are confused or unlikely to recall events clearly, or that women with autism misinterpret social signals.[31] In another Indian example cited by Human Rights Watch, the police response to a reported gang rape of a woman with a psychosocial condition was, "She's mental. Why should I pay attention to her?"[32]

The myth of asexuality is particularly problematic as it contributes to other systemic issues. Girls with intellectual disabilities are often thought to have no need of education or information about sexuality and reproduction, particularly as they are commonly considered to lack the capacity to make decisions about sexual activity.[33] In practice, this denial of education is seriously disempowering, and further reduces the ability of women with intellectual disabilities to protest against inappropriate behavior, or to protect themselves from unwanted pregnancy or sexually transmitted infections.[34] The CRPD seeks to address this by requiring the provision of "information and education on how to avoid, recognize and report instances of exploitation, violence and abuse" to both carers and persons with disabilities,[35] but again, this may not often happen in practice.

Social Understandings of Gender-Based Violence

The broad failure of #MeToo to highlight the experiences of women with disabilities may also be attributable to the complex nature of gender-based violence, which is often different in the disability context. In this disability is not unique—gender-based violence may also look different for other intersectional

---

31. See, e.g., Alaina Leary, *Don't Use 'Functioning Labels' to Victim-Blame Me*, ROOTED IN RIGHTS, Apr. 19, 2018, https://www.rootedinrights.org/dont-use-functioning-labels-to -victim-blame-me/.

32. Abhishek Kumar Mehan for Human Rights Watch, "Invisible victims of sexual violence: access to justice for women and girls with disabilities in India" (Apr. 3, 2018), https:// www.hrw.org/report/2018/04/03/invisible-victims-sexual-violence/access-justice-women-and -girls-disabilities.

33. Report of the Special Rapporteur, *supra* note 7, para 19.

34. *Ibid.*, para 19.

35. Article 16 CRPD.

groups, such as Muslim women or lesbians. This is not to say there are no commonalities—rape and sexual assault are obvious examples—but rather that additional forms of abuse also exist, which are context-specific. In this sense, it can be useful to think of gender-based violence as comprising a wide array of controlling and coercive behaviors that may or may not have sexual aspects or overtones. Although this is recognized by the UN committees on CEDAW and the CRPD, it may not be generally understood, and persons outside a particular group may be unaware of nuances that would be appreciated within the group.

So, what does gender-based violence look like in the disability context? The UN Special Rapporteur on the Rights of Persons with Disabilities has highlighted multiple forms of gender-based violence experienced by women and girls with disabilities. Not all fall within common understandings of sexual harassment, the primary focus of #MeToo. For instance, women and girls with disabilities, particularly intellectual or psychosocial disabilities, are often subjected to forced sterilization, for reasons such as preventing pregnancy, controlling menstruation, and eugenics.[36] This form of gender-based violence is state sanctioned and happens globally, in countries as diverse as the United States, Australia, China, India, South Africa, and Norway, to name but a few.[37] Contraception is also frequently used for menstruation control, often without the woman's informed consent, but at the request of families and carers. The contraception methods used (such as injections, intrauterine devices, and even hysterectomies) are usually much more invasive than for women without disabilities, to make it easier for carers and service providers.[38] Women and girls with disabilities may also be subjected to forced abortions and gynecological checks (so-called "virgin testing"), again based on eugenic concerns.[39] Additionally, they may be treated with estrogen for so-called "growth attenuation," that is, to prevent entry into puberty and maintain a lower height or weight, again to make care easier.[40] In a well-known case in the United States that generated considerable ethical, medical, and legal debate, the parents of Ashley X, a severely disabled six-year-old girl, opted for a combination of estrogen therapy, hysterectomy, and breast bud removal to maintain a low body weight and improve her quality of life.[41] This has since become known as the "Ashley Treatment."

---

36. *Ibid.*, para 29.

37. Ashwin Roy et al., *The Human Rights of Women with Intellectual Disability* 105(9) J. OF THE ROYAL SOC. OF MEDICINE 384 (2012).

38. Report of the Special Rapporteur, *supra* note 7, paras 31-32.

39. *Ibid.*

40. *Ibid.*, para 32.

41. Steven D. Edwards, *The Case of Ashley X* 6(1) CLINICAL ETHICS 39-44 (2011).

The General Comment on Article 6 of the CRPD also highlights disability-specific forms of harm, such as: withholding or denying access to medication; removing or controlling communication aids; or refusing to assist with communication; refusal by caregivers to assist with hygiene or sanitation; withholding food or water; disability-specific verbal abuse; harming or threatening to harm pets or assistance animals; and controlling access to others or to social media. Other kinds of disability-specific harassment include: commenting about, removing, or touching mobility devices (e.g., grabbing a woman's wheelchair or forcibly moving her in a particular direction); barricading a disabled woman behind furniture so that she is unable to leave; and asking intrusive questions about whether and how she has sex, or about her body. Such harassment may or may not have sexualized overtones depending on the context and delivery.[42]

The General Comment also notes that women with disabilities who are institutionalized are exposed to additional forms of violence such as forcible undressing by male staff, forced administration of psychiatric medication, and overmedication (which can reduce the ability to resist, remember, or describe sexual violence—in effect, akin to a date rape drug). Such women are also less likely to be able to access helplines or reporting mechanisms, even if a complaints procedure exists. In a United Kingdom case, a severely disabled woman who was imprisoned for a number of days was left in inappropriate conditions, which included being forced to accept male assistance for toileting purposes. She alleged that on one occasion she was left sitting on a toilet for three hours until she agreed to let a male officer clean her. She also claimed that a female nurse removed her bedclothes in the presence of two male prison officers, exposing her naked lower body. The European Court of Human Rights later held that the claimant's treatment was humiliating and degrading, even though this was not intentional.[43]

Women with disabilities may also be subjected to specific harms due to endemic superstitions—for instance, that men with HIV/AIDS can be cured by having sexual intercourse with a disabled woman, particularly a virgin or a woman with albinism.[44] This cultural myth exposes women with albinism not only to violence but also to sexually transmitted infections and unwanted pregnancies. Women with albinism may also be subject to ritual killings to obtain their body parts for use in witchcraft.[45]

---

42. Smith, *supra* note 10.

43. *Price v. UK* [2001] ECHR 458 (UK).

44. Report of the Special Rapporteur, *supra* note 7, para 22.

45. CEDAW Committee, *Concluding Observations on the Report of the United Republic of Tanzania*, Mar. 9, 2016, para 18.

Women and girls with disabilities are disproportionately affected by a wide range of gender-based violence, including infanticide and trafficking, forced and child marriage, female genital mutilation, deprivation of liberty and domestic violence.[46] The UN Special Rapporteur on violence against women, its causes, and consequences has also noted that women from intersectional or marginal groups, including women with disabilities, are particularly affected by online violence.[47]

Finally, it should be noted that gender-based violence may in fact *cause* disability in many cases, due to physical or mental injuries (such as post-traumatic stress disorder and depression), pregnancy-related complications, and sexually transmitted infections.[48]

This wide range of harms suggests that the focus of #MeToo may often be too narrow to capture the kinds of abusive behavior experienced by women with disabilities. However, a further difficulty arises from the definition of sexual harassment as *non-consensual* behavior. This has proved problematic for women in general as failure to protest sufficiently may be legally construed as consent, regardless of the power dynamics at play or the woman's ability to protest. This is clearly illustrated by RPB's case, where the complainant's protests were deemed insufficient, even though she had struggled as much as she could against her much stronger attacker.

However, particular problems arise for women with disabilities, who commonly suffer violence in the context of medical treatment. This may go well beyond what was agreed, but the woman may not feel that she is in a position to protest, given the power imbalance and the fear of losing future medical care. A person without medical expertise may also be unable to say with certainty that a particular examination or treatment was unnecessary. These difficulties may be compounded by medical paternalism, which is particularly prevalent in relation to patients with disabilities. The jurist and former Chair of the CRPD Committee, Theresia Degener, describes an incident in which a woman was forced to use a tampon-shoot pistol (a medical device developed to assist women and girls with a weak arm function) to insert a tampon while sitting half-naked on a toilet in front of a number of male members of medical staff. When she initially refused to obey, she was told that if she did not do it herself, the men would do it for her. Eventually she complied, but was extremely upset.[49] In such

---

46. Report of the Special Rapporteur, *supra* note 7, para 34.

47. *Report of the Special Rapporteur on violence against women, its causes and consequences on online violence against women and girls from a human rights perspective*, June 18, 2018 (A/HRC/38/47), para 28.

48. Schur et al., 177, *supra* note 3.

49. Degener 29, *supra* note 15.

a context, where the woman consented to or participated in some of what was done, and remained silent in the face of the rest, or was uncertain as to whether it was necessary, how is non-consent to be determined, even in her own mind, and even if she suffered significant distress? Tellingly, in the tampon incident described above, Degener highlights that the woman in question was uncertain as to whether this counted as sexual violence.[50]

Similar difficulties may arise in relation to general personal care and relationships, arising from what the disability activist Mia Mingus has termed "forced intimacy."[51] Essentially, this means that people with disabilities are forced to bare themselves to others, both physically and emotionally, in order to access basic care and support, such as help with dressing or personal hygiene. In this context, how meaningful can consent be, given that disabled people may have to consent to particular intimacies just to function?

Forever on the Edge?

How can the omission of women with disabilities from #MeToo be addressed? Clearly, there is a strong need to educate, inform, and raise awareness, not just among the disability community, but among the public at large. This should be part of a broader public conversation about what sexual harassment and gender-based violence may look like for different groups, since so much of #MeToo has come to focus on a comparatively narrow understanding of sexual exploitation and the contexts in which it occurs. In this sense, #MeToo needs to return to its roots as a broad feminist movement targeting all kinds of gender-based violence and coercion. Achieving this shift cannot be left solely to disability activists but requires commitment from feminists generally. All feminists need to amplify the voices of women with disabilities and other intersectional groups, and highlight their experiences, and why they matter.

However, although it should be possible to raise awareness of the scale of the problem, it is clear that there is no easy solution to the problem of gender-based violence against women with disabilities.[52] The CRPD plays a vital role in addressing this, both in terms of the principles it sets out and in terms of the obligations it places on States to address the rights of disabled persons holistically, including positively supporting their recovery from experiences

---

50. *Ibid.*

51. Mia Mingus, *Forced Intimacy: an Ableist Norm*, Leaving Evidence (Aug. 6, 2017, 4:31 p.m.), https://leavingevidence.wordpress.com/2017/08/06/forced-intimacy-an-ableist -norm/.

52. Van der Heijden & Dunkle, *supra* note 4.

of exploitation and abuse. Greater compliance with the CRPD would help to uncover the scale of the problem (through the collection of specific data), address many of the barriers that currently prevent women with disabilities from making legal complaints, and greatly reduce the potential for sexual and other abuse by reducing the social exclusion of disabled people generally. Given what is involved, this remains a longer-term project.

CHAPTER 35

From Me to We: Locating Dalit Women in #MeToo

Shreya Atrey[1]

"As Dalit women, we write this statement at a difficult and a perplexing time. We have been wondering about the 'me' in #MeTooIndia and have not been able to locate ourselves in this current framework. Our points of assertion in dealing with violence of various forms have always been based on our collective consciousness. A caste-stratified society has denuded our personhood and often considered our lives as mere data or a story. We remain unnamed and our struggles unnoticed. Through this statement, we want to reiterate that we cannot even begin to imagine a gender just world in a society that is ridden by caste divisions."

—Anti-caste feminist statement on #MeTooIndia from
#DALITWOMENFIGHT (October 10, 2018)

Where are Dalit women[2] in #MeTooIndia? In order to answer that we need to go back in time to the postcolonial history of the Dalit women's resistance.

---

1. Shreya Atrey is an Associate Professor in International Human Rights Law at the Department for Continuing Education and Faculty of Law, based at the Bonavero Human Rights Institute at the University of Oxford.

2. "Dalit" means "broken." It is a term of assertive pride used by those who are outside of the four-tiered caste system in India (Brahmin, Kshatriya, Vaishya, Shudra) and have been subjected to the worst forms of discrimination and violence and in particular the practice of untouchability where contact with Dalits is deemed forbidden. Untouchability is formally banned by the Constitution of independent India which came into force in 1950. However, rampant mistreatment, extreme poverty, and degrading conditions of existence continue to characterize Dalit lives. The position of Dalit women is seen as "Dalits amongst Dalits" because they are considered "thrice alienated" on the basis of caste, class, and gender. Sexual harassment against them is not deemed inconsistent with untouchability and is in fact a way to reinforce

This chapter takes a cue from Anupama Rao's exceptional ethnography and in particular, the *Sirasgaon* incident as a tell-all account of casteist patriarchy.[3] This chapter makes four points about the nature of intersectional sexual harassment Dalit women suffer: the role of caste in the experience of sexual harassment, the extremity of violence involved in it, the duality of it being both public yet invisible, and the timelessness of it. With this historical account, one starts to exhume the reasons for longstanding invisibility of Dalit women's sexual harassment and understand why Dalit women remain marginalized in the current framework despite the solidarities engendered by #MeToo.

Sirasgaon

As Rao describes, the incident occurred at the end of 1963, sixteen years after India's independence from colonial rule and thirteen years into constitutional order, in the village of Sirasgaon, Aurangabad district of the State of Maharashtra. Sonabai, a Dalit woman, had carried lunch to her brother Kishan, who worked in the fields of a wealthy upper-caste landlord, Yedu Kale. Seeing her alone, Yedu had propositioned Sonabai, showing her money and touching her *sari*. Sonabai and her mother-in-law complained to Yedu's wife, Shevantibai, who had asked them to be discreet about it. But when Kishan left Yedu's service six months later, he visited Shevantibai to ask how she would have felt had he been immodest with her and touched her *sari*. The interaction was relayed to Yedu Kale.

On December 22, 1963, Yedu Kale and a group of men approached Kishan's hut armed with sticks. Not finding Kishan, the men started beating his father, Vithal Amrit. They then found Kishan's mother, Laxmibai, and later Sonabai, who were both beaten, stripped naked, dragged, paraded around the streets, and taken to the village entrance, *ves*, to be exhibited. Another group of men found Kishan's sisters-in-law, Kadubai and Sakrabai, who too were beaten, disrobed, and paraded to the *ves* while passing Yedu's house so Shevantibai could see them being punished for her ignomiry. The four women returned home that evening wrapped in a single *sari* someone had thrown at them.

While asked to settle the matter within the village, Kishan's family preferred legal recourse and against all odds, managed to lodge a complaint for crimes including rioting, intent to hurt, house trespass, and "outraging the

---

untouchability by disregarding their bodily integrity and sexual autonomy *because* they are Dalit women. See, for an account of Dalit women's position at the crossroads of caste, class, and patriarchy, Gopal Guru, *Dalit Women Talk Differently*, 30 ECON. & POL. WKLY. 2548 (1995).

3. ANUPAMA RAO, THE CASTE QUESTION: DALITS AND THE POLITICS OF MODERN INDIA 217-240 (2009).

modesty of a woman."[4] The act of stripping and parading naked was recorded only later, initially ignored by the police and downplayed by the Dalit women themselves due to humiliation. Despite a botched investigation, such was the evidence that the Magistrate found the men guilty and the District Judge upheld the conviction. The accused were sentenced to forty-three months' imprisonment and a fine of 300 rupees. Vithal Amrita received 1,000 rupees in damages.[5]

Casteist Patriarchy

The full story of Sirasgaon—the historical relations between Dalits and caste Hindus in Maharashtra, the way in which the incident unraveled legally and was covered by the media, and how it changed the lives of those involved and the entire village in fact—is a story of how class, caste, and patriarchy prevail in rural India. It is the story of casteist patriarchy that plays out in the theatre of everyday lives of Dalit women, whose rights and opportunities are dictated by the intersection of poverty, patriarchy, and the caste system, all of them at the same time. These factors' full intersectional force can be reckoned in four ways in which casteist patriarchy transpires.

First, Sirasgaon's story shows that sexual harassment of Dalit women is inseparable from casteism. Dalit women are targeted not only because of their sex or gender but because they are Dalit. Thus, the *form* of sexual harassment as unwelcome sexual behavior does not explain the *causality* of it. The four women in Sirasgaon were targeted in unequivocally "sexual" ways of being stripped and paraded naked, but the primary reason they were targeted was because they were women outside of the Hindu caste system. The exhibition of naked Dalit women is a form of sexual harassment specific to them alone. Dalit women's bodies serve as the site for caste lessons to be imparted, for Dalit men like Kishan to learn the cost of their transgressions like asking a landlord's upper-caste wife to empathize with his sister, a Dalit woman, being violated by the landlord. Kishan relied on his maleness to make a point that he too could violate a woman but did not factor in his caste. The cost of his behavior—which was also a form of sexual harassment against Shevantibai—was ultimately borne by his mother, sister, and sisters-in-law. The difference in the form of and reasons for sexual harassment of upper-caste women and Dalit women are apparent. While Shevantibai was improperly questioned by Kishan, it was Sonabai, Laxmibai, Kadubai, and Sakrabai who were dragged out of their homes, beaten, stripped, and paraded

---

4. An archaic phrase used to refer to sexual harassment in the Victorian-era legislation, the Indian Penal Code 1860, section 354 and section 509.

5. As narrated by Anupama Rao, *supra* note 3.

naked around the village for his infraction. Saying that both an upper-caste woman and Dalit women suffered sexual harassment would then be saying too little about the reason why sexual harassment came about: caste.

Second, the stark difference can also be recounted in terms of the sheer extremity of violence accompanying Dalit women's sexual harassment. Thus, the difference in the form of sexual harassment against Dalit women is both substantive and scalar. Sexual assault, rape, gang-rape, mutilation, stoning, pulling out of nails, forced prostitution, sexual slavery, bondage, and exploitation, are forms of sexual harassment visited upon Dalit women at a considerably higher rate than upper-caste women.[6] Sexual harassment of Dalit women far exceeds a mere infraction or transgression and can only be properly characterized as an "atrocity."[7]

Third, sexual harassment of Dalit women is uniquely accepted as a manifestation of caste relations that inhabits the public space. Take for example the practice of dedicating Dalit women to temples as *devdasis, joginis,* or *muralis,* who are essentially "temple prostitutes." The practice provides unfettered access to Dalit women dedicated to the sexual service of upper-caste men, sanctioned by religion and society. Although seemingly banned, the practice appears to be alive and well today.[8] There is unquestioned acceptance and hence invisibility of sexual harassment against Dalit women when it takes place openly and freely, often seen as necessitated in a caste society, like the Sirasgaon incident where Dalit women were made examples to Dalit men breaching caste codes. This is the ironic duality of public, yet invisible, sexual harassment suffered by Dalit women.

Finally, lest Sirasgaon seem like a distant memory, sexual harassment against Dalit women has continued unabated in postcolonial constitutional society in India. Identical incidents are recorded frequently; recently, in Mulgaon, Maharashtra, a Dalit woman was beaten and paraded naked by upper-caste women when her son eloped with an upper-caste girl in 2012. Similar incidents have occurred in Jalalabad, Punjab where a woman was stripped naked and beaten while tied to a tree when her son propositioned an upper-caste girl in 2013; in Shahjahanpur, Uttar Pradesh where five Dalit women were paraded naked and caned when a girl eloped with a Dalit boy in 2015; in Mudwara,

---

6. National Campaign on Dalit Human Rights (NCDHR), *Report: National Tribunal Violence Against Dalit Women in India (2013),* http://www.dalitweb.org/?p=2293.

7. In fact, that is the official term used in the Scheduled Caste and Scheduled Tribe (Prevention of Atrocities) Act 1989. See especially section 3 (xi)-(xii) concerning offenses against Dalit women.

8. *Devdasi System Continues to Exist Despite Ban,* OUTLOOK, May 29, 2016, https://www.outlookindia.com/newswire/story/devadasi-system-continues-to-exist-despite-ban-book/941639.

Madhya Pradesh where a Dalit woman was stripped and forced fed with urine by an upper-caste man and his wife when she tried to resist his acquisition of land that legally belonged to her in 2015; and in Kurara, Uttar Pradesh where a Dalit woman was thrashed, her private parts mutilated and paraded naked when she complained of being gang-raped by upper-caste men in 2018. But Sirasgaon is exceptional. Although it represents routine forms of sexual harassment and violence deployed against Dalit women, it is nonetheless a rare occasion where sexual harassment was acknowledged even if described as caste violence against Dalit men and families to assert community honor and pride rather than squarely as sexual harassment against Dalit women. In fact, it was Vithal Amrita, Kishan's father, who ended up receiving damages for all that happened in Sirasgaon in December 1963. Since then, while Dalit women have continued to resist and mobilize against sexual harassment and violence, the impunity for violations too has continued unencumbered, with less than 1 percent of Dalit women's complaints resulting in convictions compared to 25 percent of cases involving upper-caste women.[9] Compare this to the fact that nearly 50 percent of the Dalit women in India experience sexual harassment and violence on an everyday basis and 99 percent of the incidents go unreported.[10] Even the partial redress of the Sirasgaon atrocity appears like a staggering feat against this.

The Resistance

So where are Dalit women in #MeTooIndia? In October 2018, Google created a visualization of who was searching for "#MeToo" in India, and the entire map of the country lit up.[11] #MeToo was not merely a movement of the urban elite but meant something to everyone. Surely, one would think, Dalit women would have been part of everyone finally coming together in solidarity against sexual harassment.

9. International Dalit Solidarity Network, *Dalit Women—Facing Multiple Forms of Discrimination* (2014), http://idsn.org/wp-content/uploads/user_folder/pdf/New_files/Key_Issues/Dalit_Women/DALIT_WOMEN_-_IDSN_briefing_paper.pdf; Palak Nandil, *Dalit Women Cases: Crime Conviction Rate Poor*, TIMES OF INDIA (June 7, 2011), http://timesofindia.indiatimes.com/city/jaipur/Dalit-women-cases-Crime-convictionrate-poor/articleshow/9131045.cms?referral=PM.

10. Sujan Bandyopadhyay, *A Closer Look at Statistics on Sexual Violence in India*, THE WIRE, May 8, 2018, https://thewire.in/society/a-closer-look-at-statistics-on-sexual-violence-in-india.

11. Sruthi Radhakrishnan, *India Glows with #MeToo*, THE HINDU, Oct. 16, 2018, https://www.thehindu.com/sci-tech/technology/internet/india-glows-with-metoo/article25239194.ece.

This rendering obscures how Dalit women have engaged with movements and resisted sexual harassment in modern India. Long before middle-class, upper-caste women started resisting sexual harassment in homes, on the streets, and in workplaces, Dalit women's resistance to sexual harassment and violence defined the women's movement in India since the 1970s. The first notable nationwide agitation was because of the custodial rape of Mathura, a young tribal girl who had been gang-raped by two police men in 1972.[12] That led to significant amendments in Indian rape law in 1983,[13] though none recognized age, class, caste, or tribe as an aggravating factor that fundamentally changed the nature of sexual harassment in the ways described above. The second wave of agitation followed the gang-rape of Bhanwari Devi, a Dalit woman, who was punished by upper-caste men for having campaigned in her capacity as a government worker against child marriage in 1992. That led the Supreme Court of India to formulate the first ever Sexual Harassment at Workplace Guidelines in the case of *Vishaka v. State of Rajasthan* 1997 AIR 3011, which eventually became the Sexual Harassment of Women at Workplace (Prevention, Prohibition and Redressal) Act 2013. Once again, neither the guidelines nor the act acknowledged caste as what dictated the experience of women like Bhanwari Devi. Dimensions of caste, tribe, class, age, rurality, etc. were flattened into sex or gender, considered as the defining characteristic of sexual harassment. Thus, while Dalit women's experiences had furnished the basis for the organization of the women's movement against sexual harassment, the experiences themselves were sidelined as mere data or story, their implications failed to be understood and ultimately, redressed and reversed.[14]

That said, Dalit women have *always* protested sexual harassment meted out to them. They have spoken in loud and clear terms about their experiences of sexual harassment and violence, pointing out its intersectional nature and how it differs for women of caste. Yet their stories remain marginal. They may light up a whole map and continue to express solidarity with all women, but their experiences of sexual harassment, just like the Sirasgaon incident, get little

---

12. *Tuka Ram v. State of Maharashtra* 1979 AIR 185 (Supreme Court of India). See especially analysis in Kalpana Kannabiran and Ritu Menon, From Mathura to Manorama: 25 years of Resisting Violence against Women (2007).

13. The Criminal Law Amendment Act 1983 (No. 43), among other things, declared it an offence to reveal the identity of rape victims, shifted the burden of proof to the accused when the victim claimed that they had not consented, and deleted the provision allowing references to the character of the prosecutrix in rape cases.

14. Sharmila Rege, *"Real Feminism" and Dalit Women: Scripts of Denial and Accusation*, 35 Econ. & Pol. Wkly. 492 (2000); Sharmila Rege, *Dalit Women Talk Differently: A Critique of "Difference" and Towards a Dalit Feminist Standpoint Position*, 33 Econ. & Pol. Wkly. 39 (1998).

attention for what they are and are not generally considered to constitute "real" sexual harassment. Instead, their presence is co-opted as signifying shared experiences of sexual harassment rather than as diversifying what counts as women's experiences of sexual harassment in the first place. The result is that despite the awakening in #MeToo, few incidents like Sirasgaon have been brought forth, reckoned with, and made central to the case against sexual harassment of Indian women. In fact, we continue to lack a comprehensive understanding of the reasons for and forms of intersectional sexual harassment that occurs not only because of women's sex or gender, but because of their religion, race, color, caste, class, age, disability, sexual orientation, region, language, etc.

And that is why Dalit women, despite having led the resistance to sexual harassment in India, find themselves wondering about the "Me" in #MeToo-India. There is no doubt that the movement has engendered solidarity that has been unprecedented in going beyond the upper-caste middle-class urban masses. But solidarity without the full understanding of the nature of sexual harassment, especially intersectional sexual harassment, is liable to founder. There is no better time than now to issue a call for #MeToo to diversify and recognize the pain, struggle, and resilience of women who are Dalit, Adivasi, Muslim, disabled, queer, poor, rural, and non-English speaking, and whose accounts remain marginal in the mainstream discourse. This recognition rests on the full comprehension of the specific nature of intersectional sexual harassment running along the four dimensions described above, in terms of its causality, violence, public nature, and endurance. It is only in developing a collective consciousness of experiences dissimilar to our own that we may engender the stuff of true solidarity moving on from Me to We in #MeToo.

Techniques to Combat Harassment:
A Critical Review

CHAPTER 36

The #MeToo Movement, Symbolic Structures, and the Limits of the Law

Lauren B. Edelman[1]

In December 2017, *Time Magazine* gave its person of the year award to the "The Silence Breakers," commemorating a broad societal awakening about the pervasiveness of sexual harassment in the workplace. The #MeToo movement took off, and numerous prominent men were fired or resigned in the wake of allegations of sexual harassment.

The response of many organizations to the #MeToo movement was to create or update antiharassment policies, complaint procedures, and training programs. This response might, at first blush, seem like organizations were taking the necessary steps to eliminate workplace harassment. However, as I argue in *Working Law*,[2] these policies and procedures do more to shield companies from legal liability than they do to protect employees from sexual harassment. I refer to these types of policies, procedures, and training programs as *symbolic structures* because they symbolize compliance with law. Symbolic structures, however, do not guarantee substantive results.

The Decoupling of Symbolic Structures and Substantive Results

Antiharassment policies and complaint procedures, which proliferated in the latter part of the twentieth century, are now commonplace. Yet, as the

---

1. Agnes Roddy Robb Professor of Law and Professor of Sociology, University of California, Berkeley.

2. Lauren B. Edelman, Working Law: Courts, Corporations, and Symbolic Civil Rights (2016).

#MeToo movement made clear, sex-based harassment in the workplace is common. Social science research suggests that 60-75 percent of working women have experienced sexual harassment at work.[3] Harassment based on race, ethnicity, and disability is also common and women of color are disproportionately likely to experience harassment.[4] An important question, then, is why harassment remains so prevalent given that the majority of companies in the United States have implemented antiharassment policies and complaint procedures for those who believe that they have been subjected to harassment. As I discuss below, research suggests that antiharassment policies in organizations are often ineffective, employees are reluctant to complain about sexual harassment, and antiharassment training may in fact be counterproductive.

Sexual Harassment Policies Exist to Protect Organizations More Than to Protect Employees

My research—based on surveys of organizations, interviews with human resource (HR) professionals, and content analyses of both HR journals and federal court opinions—shows that antiharassment policies and complaint procedures can comfortably coexist with organizational cultures in which women are regularly subjected to demeaning commentary, unwanted physical contact, and even threats of or actual sexual assaults.[5] The coexistence of antiharassment policies and harassment can be explained by a concept in organizational theory called "decoupling," meaning that policies exist to demonstrate attention to legal ideals but that they are ignored at lower levels and leadership fails to demonstrate strong support for the policies.[6] High-value employees who often enjoy substantial power within an organization often feel immune from these policies and believe, often with good reason, that they are too valuable to be sanctioned.

---

3. U.S. Equal Employment Opportunity Commission, *Select Task Force on the Study of Harassment in the Workplace* ("EEOC Select Task Force") Report of Co-Chairs Chai R. Feldblum & Victoria A. Lipnic, June 2016, https://www.eeoc.gov/eeoc/task_force/harassment/report.cfm.

4. Patricia Hill Collins, *Intersectionality's Definitional Dilemmas*, ANN. REV. OF SOC. 41:1-20 (2015), Lilia M. Cortina, Kimberly A. Lonsway, Vicki J. Magley, Leslie V. Freeman, Linda. L. Collinsworth, Mary Hunter, and Louise F. Fitzgerald, *What's Gender Got to Do with It? Incivility in the Federal Courts*, LAW & SOC. INQUIRY 27(2): 235-270 (2002).

5. EDELMAN, WORKING LAW, *supra* note 2.

6. Karl E. Weick, 1976, *Educational Organizations as Loosely Coupled Systems*, ADMIN. SCI. Q. 21(1): 1-19.

Antiharassment policies, then, serve to symbolize the organization's commitment to legal ideals. In some organizations, moreover, leaders take harassment very seriously and genuinely work hard to develop or sustain a workplace culture in which all employees feel included and valued. Yet in many other organizations, leaders fail to set a strong example or to make clear that the antiharassment rules are to be taken seriously. In those organizations, rules banning harassment often exist alongside a culture in which harassment is common and where leaders look the other way to avoid losing power-players who they view as critical to the organization's profits or reputation. Such decoupling of policies and practices is especially common when organizations are decentralized and the day-to-day governance often relies on mid-level supervisors who may pay little attention to instructions from headquarters on how to behave. Where policies and practices are decoupled, policies serve as symbols of attention to law but fail to provide any substantive protection for employees. Substance is actually a continuum: all antiharassment policies are symbols of legality but those policies range from being both symbolic and substantive to being merely symbolic.[7]

Complaint Procedures Rarely Lead to Redress

Complaint procedures, moreover, are often of little value because people who experience harassment or other forms of discrimination are extremely reluctant to file complaints. Indeed, only about one in four women subjected to sex-based harassment report it using an internal complaint procedure and far fewer file an official complaint with the Equal Employment Opportunity Commission (EEOC).[8]

Why do so many employees choose not to report harassment? Common reasons include fear of retaliation or a belief that complaints will not be taken seriously. Often victims find the process of filing a formal complaint and enduring an investigation and hearing distasteful; they simply want the harassing behavior to stop.[9] Some employees report that filing a complaint would cast themselves as victims while they prefer to think of themselves as survivors.[10]

---

7. EDELMAN, WORKING LAW, *supra* note 2.

8. *Id.*

9. L.F. Fitzgerald, S. Swan and K. Fischer, *Why Didn't She Just Report Him? The Psychological and Legal Implications of Women's Responses to Sexual Harassment*, J. OF SOC. ISSUES 51(1): 117-138 (1995).

10. Kristin Bumiller, *Victims in the Shadow of the Law: A Critique of the Model of Legal Protection*, SIGNS 12(3): 421-439 (1987); KRISTIN BUMILLER, THE CIVIL RIGHTS SOCIETY: THE SOCIAL CONSTRUCTION OF VICTIMS (1988).

Women in particular are aware that success and promotion in organizations depends on being a team player, which often means putting up with unwanted sexual commentary, touching, or worse rather than complaining about it.[11]

When employees do use internal complaint procedures, they are often disappointed. Human Resource (HR) professionals frequently discourage women who inquire about filing a complaint from framing their complaints as sexual harassment, instead suggesting that the behavior is not sufficiently severe or pervasive to constitute compliance or that it is simply an instance of poor management or of interpersonal conflict.[12] Potential complainants, then, are easily discouraged from pursuing their complaints. Employees fail to achieve redress for their complaints and administrators may be denied important information about the abuses that are occurring.

Complaint handlers, moreover, rarely fit the ideal of a neutral decision-maker. Complaint handlers, who are often HR professionals, depend upon management for their paychecks, bonuses, and prospects for advancement. Complaint handlers who frequently challenge management are likely to be viewed skeptically by those in control of their future employment prospects. Thus, complaint handlers are often reluctant to label behavior as harassment. Anna-Maria Marshall, for example, found that complaint handlers frequently told those who sought their help that their experiences were not sufficiently severe or pervasive to be considered sexual harassment.[13]

Even when complaint handlers take complaints seriously, moreover, they are unlikely to characterize the events that led to the complaint as illegal sexual harassment. In a study of dispute resolution in organizations that I conducted with Howard Erlanger and John Lande, we found that complaint handlers rarely viewed complaints as legal issues, instead reframing complaints of discrimination or harassment as instances of poor management or as interpersonal difficulties. Complaint handlers, therefore, would resolve complaints by moving a complainant to a different manager or by requiring counseling. Even in egregious cases, complaint handlers were more likely to require a manager

11. Beth Quinn, *The Paradox of Complaining: Law, Humor, and Harassment in the Everyday Work World*, LAW & SOC. INQUIRY 25(4): 1151-1185; Anna-Maria Marshall, *Idle Rights: Employees' Rights Consciousness and the Construction of Sexual Harassment Policies* ("Idle Rights") LAW & SOC'Y REV. 39(1): 83-124 (2005).

12. Lauren B. Edelman, Howard S. Erlanger, and John Lande, *Internal Dispute Resolution: The Transformation of Civil Rights in the Workplace ("Internal Dispute Resolution")*, LAW & SOC. REV. 27(3): 497-534 (1993); Marshall, *supra* note 11, Edelman, *supra* note 2.

13. Edelman, Erlanger, and Lande, *Internal Dispute Resolution, supra* note 12, Anna-Maria Marshall, *Injustice Frames, Legality, and the Everyday Construction of Sexual Harassment ("Injustice Frames")*, LAW & SOC. INQUIRY 28: 659089 (2003), *Idle Rights, supra* note 11.

to apologize than they were to label the behavior as a violation of law or to impose serious sanctions.[14] Concerns about defamation lawsuits by the accused or about losing high-value employees often take precedence over efforts to end harassment.[15] The extreme reluctance to complain among victims of sexual harassment coupled with the fact that complaint handlers are part of the management structure together make complaint procedures more symbolic than substantive in many organizations.

Antiharassment Training Often Backfires

Antiharassment training is another organizational practice that symbolizes legal compliance, and one that has gained great traction among organizations. Sexual harassment training is now a multi-billion-dollar industry.[16] Indeed, in the wake of the #MeToo movement, bipartisan legislation was passed by both the House and Senate making sexual harassment training mandatory for all lawmakers and staffers. Many companies also instituted sexual harassment training. Yet the evidence that such training is effective is scant and is often based on attitudes rather than behavior. For example, an experimental study conducted by Kimberly A. Lonsway, Liliana M. Cortina, and Vicky J. Magley showed that students who underwent sexual harassment training were less likely to believe in classic myths about sexual harassment such as that women fabricate or invite sexual misconduct.[17] And a study by Shereen Bingham and Lisa Scherer showed that students randomly assigned to a sexual harassment training program were more knowledgeable about law prohibiting harassment and university policy than students who did not go through the training program.[18]

The Bingham and Scherer study, however, showed that the sexual harassment training had unanticipated counterproductive effects. Not only were students who had undergone training no more likely than those who had not to perceive sexually harassing situations but, contrary to the intent of the program,

---

14. Lauren B. Edelman, Howard S. Erlanger, and John Lande, *Internal Dispute Resolution, supra* note 12.

15. Edelman, Erlanger, and Lande, *Internal Dispute Resolution, supra* note 12, Edelman, WORKING LAW, *supra* note 2.

16. Susan Bisom-Rapp, *An Ounce of Prevention is a Poor Substitute for a Pound of Cure: Confronting the Developing Jurisprudence of Education and Prevention in Employment Discrimination Law*, BERK. J. OF EMPLOY. & LAB. LAW 221: 1-48 (2001).

17. Kimberly A. Lonsway, Liliana M. Cortina, and Vicki J. Magley, *Sexual Harassment Mythology: Definition, Conceptualization, and Measurement*, SEX ROLES 58:599-615 (2008).

18. Shereen G. Bingham and Lisa L. Scherer, *The Unexpected Effects of a Sexual Harassment Educational Program*, J. OF APPLIED BEHAV. SCI. 37(2): 125-153 (2001).

males who participated in the program were significantly less likely than non-participating males and all females to view coercion of a subordinate as sexual harassment. In addition, participating males were significantly less likely to report sexual harassment to authorities than nonparticipating males and all females. Further, participating males were also more likely to blame the victim than were other groups. In addition, all men, irrespective of participation in training, were more likely than women to believe that sexual behavior at work is harmless. In short, the only benefit of the program was to increase knowledge about the legal and policy aspects of harassment, but the training program seemed to have a backlash among participating males who became less likely to recognize and to report harassment and more likely to blame the victim.

Sexual harassment training programs, moreover, may reinforce stereotypical beliefs about gender. In an interview-based study, social psychologist Justine Tinkler found that antiharassment training sessions activate gendered stereotypes of women as passive, emotional, and duplicitous as well as gendered patterns of interactions. Men who underwent training became critical of women for being duplicitous and inviting attention or being overemotional whereas women expressed concern that strong rejection of sexual attention could jeopardize their positions in the workplace and tended to blame the university for failing to respond adequately to the problem of harassment.[19] Similarly, in an experimental study, Tinkler and colleagues found that exposure to a sexual harassment policy tended to activate beliefs about male superiority to women.[20]

Perhaps the most concerning finding about sexual harassment training is that mandatory training may provoke a backlash. Tinkler, for example, found that even when people expressed support for legal sanctions against sexual harassment, they showed widespread resistance toward antiharassment training programs.[21] Similarly, research conducted by Frank Dobbin and Alexandra Kalev shows that diversity training, which is closely related to sexual harassment training, is often ineffective, especially when mandatory.[22] Training may temporarily enable those who go through it to gain a better understanding of the situations that are legally impermissible, but they can evoke longer-term backlash against women (who, ironically, can be blamed for the burden of mandatory training).

19. Justine E. Tinkler, *Resisting the Enforcement of Sexual Harassment Law*, LAW & SOC. INQUIRY 37(1): 1-24 (2012).

20. Tinkler, Justine Eatenson, Yan E. Li, and Stefanie Mollborn, *Can Legal Interventions Change Beliefs? The Effect of Exposure to Sexual Harassment Policy on Men's Gender Beliefs*, SOC. PSYCHOL. Q. 70(4): 480-494 (2007).

21. Tinkler, *Resisting the Enforcement of Sexual Harassment Law*, supra note 19.

22. Frank Dobbin and Alexandra Kalev, *Why Diversity Programs Fail*, HARV. BUS. REV. Jul.-Aug. 2016.

A 2016 report by the EEOC concluded that there have been too few studies of sexual harassment training effectiveness to say definitively that it works, and there is clearly some evidence that it may be counterproductive.[23] The rush to antiharassment training programs in the wake of the #MeToo movement may be well-intentioned, but research suggests that it will not produce a dramatic reduction in workplace sexual harassment, and it may exacerbate the problem.

Judicial Deference to Symbolic Structures

Symbolic structures like antiharassment policies, complaint procedures, and training programs may be ineffective at curbing sexual harassment, but they are very effective at protecting employers from liability in lawsuits. That is because courts often fail to distinguish between symbolic structures that are effective in reducing harassment and discrimination and those that are not.

In *Working Law*, I present analyses of a half century of judicial opinions[24] that show that judges frequently defer to the mere presence of antiharassment policies and complaint procedures, either without scrutiny of whether those procedures are effective in reducing sexual harassment or, in some cases, with knowledge that the structures are *not* effective. By deference, I mean that judges infer nondiscrimination from the mere presence of these procedures without adequate scrutiny of whether they are effective.

Consider the case of *Leopold v. Baccarat, Inc.*, decided by a federal trial court in New York in 2000 and affirmed by a federal appeals court in 2001. Andree Leopold, a saleswoman, sued after her supervisor repeatedly threatened to replace her with someone "young and sexy" and referred to saleswomen using vulgar, dismissive language.[25] Baccarat, the employer, pointed to its policy against harassment and its grievance procedure as evidence of fair treatment. Leopold claimed that she did not use the grievance procedure because (like many procedures) it would have required her to report the harassment to her immediate supervisor, who in this case was the person she was accusing of harassment. The policy also lacked a guarantee that she would be protected from retaliation. The court ruled in favor of Baccarat anyway, recognizing that

---

23. EEOC Select Task Force, *supra* note 3.

24. The original analysis of judicial deference from 1965 through 1999 was designed with Linda Krieger and conducted with Linda Krieger, Scott Eliason, Catherine Albiston, and Virginia Mellema. The original results are reported in the AMERICAN JOURNAL OF SOCIOLOGY. This analysis was updated to include 2004, 2009, and 2014 with help from Brent Nakamura, and the full results are published in WORKING LAW, *supra* note 2.

25. *Leopold*, 2000 WL 174923 at *2.

the procedure was inadequate in some ways but nonetheless stating, "the law is very clear that any reasonable policy will do."[26]

This is just one case, but our aggregate data on federal judicial decisions tell a story of judges increasingly viewing the mere presence of antiharassment policies and complaint procedures as sufficient for employers to avoid liability, even where there is substantial evidence that harassment occurred. My colleagues and I coded a representative sample of 1,188 court decisions beginning in 1965 and continuing through 2014. We coded a judge as having deferred to the mere presence of symbolic structures when the judge found the structures legally relevant yet failed to consider the effectiveness of the structures at all, or (as in the Baccarat case above) declared that inadequate procedures were sufficient, or ignored substantial evidence of discrimination or harassment.[27] Our data included all types of organizational structures, a subset of which were antiharassment policies, complaint procedures, and training programs. In the early years, most structures were either explicitly antidiscrimination structures such as equal employment offices or they were general governance structures such as formal evaluation procedures. In later years, cases frequently referred to sexual harassment structures.

As shown in the figure below,[28] judicial deference to symbolic structures without adequate scrutiny of those structures increased steadily over time, especially in the circuit courts, and increased substantially after 2000 in both the district and circuit courts. By 2014, judges were deferring to symbolic structures in about 70 percent of district court cases and nearly 50 percent of circuit court cases without adequate scrutiny of these structures. The rise in judicial deference after 2000 is primarily due to two factors: (1) an increased tendency by judges to grant employers' motions for summary judgment, which means that the judge agrees with the employer's claim that the case need not proceed to a full trial; and (2) an increase in the number of sexual harassment cases coupled with a 1998 United States Supreme Court ruling that condoned deference to

---

26. *Leopold*, 2000 WL 174923 at *3.

27. We coded deference as occurring where the judge treated the organizational structure as relevant to the issue of whether the employer discriminated and, in addition, one of the following three conditions were met: (1) the judge gave no consideration at all to the quality or adequacy of the structure; (2) the judge explicitly stated that the organizational structure was inadequate but also stated that the inadequacy did not matter to the employer's liability; (3) the judge stated that the structure was adequate but the opinion included very clear evidence to the contrary.

28. This figure is based on two data sets, both of which are representative samples of federal EEO opinions. The total sample size (n) is 1,188. The original sample included data collected annually for all years for 1967-1999. A follow-up sample included data collected at five-year intervals after 1999, so includes the years 2004, 2009, 2014. Source WORKING LAW, *supra* note 2.

employer's antiharassment policies and complaint procedures in some types of sexual harassment cases.

The Role of the HR Profession in Establishing Symbolic Structures as Evidence of Legal Compliance

How did judges come to associate the mere presence of antiharassment policies and complaint procedures with compliance? As far back as the early 1970s, HR professionals (then called personnel professionals) began to suggest that the best way for employers to comply with complex and confusing civil rights laws was to formalize personnel practices. This statement, from a 1973 article in *Personnel Journal* entitled "Fair Employment Practices: the Compliance Jungle," was typical.

> It could be argued that the laws simply require the employer to do what he should be doing anyway in the interest of management. It is unquestionably sound business to design more effective personnel policies.[29]

The term "sexual harassment" gained attention with the publication of Catherine MacKinnon's book, *Sexual Harassment of Working Women*, in 1979,[30] and subsequent guidelines by the EEOC in 1980, which defined sexual harassment as a form of illegal sex discrimination. Just as the HR profession had argued that personnel policies were the solution to Title VII generally, they, along with management academics and management consultants, suggested that antiharassment policies and complaint procedures were the solution to the problem of sexual harassment.

The HR profession also played a critical role in framing the legal argument that antiharassment policies and complaint procedures should absolve employers of liability for sexual harassment by employees. Before that argument had gained traction in the courts and long before the Supreme Court weighed in on the issue, HR professionals were claiming that antiharassment policies and complaint procedures could protect employers from liability for sexual harassment. In a 1981 article in *Personnel*, the authors wrote:

---

29. Cary D. Thorp Jr., *Fair Employment Practices: The Compliance Jungle*, PERSONNEL J. 52(7) (1973): 642-649: 646.

30. See Catharine A. MacKinnon, *Global #MeToo, supra* chapter one.

If the employer has no knowledge of the harassment, liability may be avoided if two conditions have been met: (1) The employer has a policy discouraging sexual harassment, and the employee failed to use an existing grievance procedure and (2) the sexually harassing situations are rectified as soon as the employer becomes aware of them.[31]

In fact, this was not accepted law at the time, but it did foreshadow later legal developments. The Supreme Court formally recognized sexual harassment as a form of sex discrimination in *Meritor Saving Bank v. Vinson* in 1986.[32] Although the court found the employer's antiharassment policy and complaint procedure ineffective in that case, it did hint that an *effective* procedure *might* protect the employer from liability. The *Meritor* decision, in turn, led to a sharp increase in employers arguing that they should not be liable if they had an anti-harassment policy and complaint procedure in place.

It was not until 1998, a full seventeen years after the aforementioned article in *Personnel*, that the United States Supreme Court addressed the issue of personnel policies in a pair of cases: *Faragher v. City of Boca Raton*[33] and *Burlington Industries v. Ellerth*.[34] The Society for Human Resource Management (SHRM) filed an amicus brief in the *Faragher* case arguing that the Supreme Court should afford employers legal protection for creating antiharassment policies in part because employers expect legal protection when they create policies. SHRM also wrote that employers, rather than courts, were best suited to address sexual harassment. The EEOC also advocated a rule that antiharassment policies and complaint procedures should be a defense to allegations of sexual harassment but only for "hostile work environment harassment" in which a supervisor or a coworker engages in degrading or sexual commentary or unwanted physical contact in a manner sufficiently severe or pervasive to affect the employee's ability to perform her job. The EEOC brief would not apply the defense to "quid pro quo harassment" in which an employer conditions tangible job benefits on sexual favors.

The Supreme Court agreed and created the *Faragher-Ellerth* affirmative defense, which is nearly identical to the rule articulated in the 1981 *Personnel* article, with the distinction advanced by the EEOC. Although nothing in Title VII even mentions antiharassment policies or grievance procedures, Justice

---

31. Patricia Linenberger and Timothy J. Keaveny, *Sexual Harassment: The Employer's Legal Obligations*, Personnel Nov.-Dec. 1981: 60-68: 65.

32. *Meritor Savings Bank v. Vinson*, 477 U.S. 57 (1986).

33. *Faragher v. City of Boca Raton*, 524 U.S. 775 (1998).

34. *Burlington Industries, Inc. v. Ellerth*, 524 U.S. 742 (1998).

Anthony Kennedy, who wrote the *Ellerth* opinion, claimed that the rationale for the new affirmative defense was that "Title VII is designed to encourage the creation of antiharassment policies and effective grievance procedures."[35] Justice Kennedy's erroneous claim is not surprising, however, given that by 1998, antiharassment policies and complaint procedures had become the accepted form of compliance in sexual harassment cases. Studies by social psychologists Cheryl Kaiser and Brenda Major and their colleagues show that organizational diversity programs create an "illusion of fairness" that leads people to discount evidence of unfair treatment.[36]

Today, it is almost impossible for an employee to win a hostile work environment sexual harassment case where an employer has an antiharassment policy and complaint procedure in place, even if the policy is widely ignored and the employee justifiably fears retaliation were she to file a complaint. Nearly all these cases are disposed of at the summary judgment stage rather than proceeding to trial. In over half of these cases, district court judges defer to the presence of antiharassment policies and complaint procedures without adequate scrutiny of whether those symbolic structures are effective.

Implications for Employers and Human Resource Professionals

Given that judges too often rely on the mere presence of antiharassment policies and complaint procedures, we cannot look to the courts for a solution to the problem that the #MeToo movement has made so salient. Companies may be able to avoid liability with any symbolic structures but if HR professionals and other managers are serious about eliminating harassment, they should take steps to ensure that those structures are actively reducing discrimination and harassment.

Right now, there is too little research to know for sure the best way for HR professionals and organizational leaders to effect change, but the 2016 EEOC report[37] makes important recommendations based on social science research by prominent scholars. Perhaps the most important finding in the EEOC report is that workplace culture can have an enormous impact on the prevalence of harassment. Harassment is less likely where leaders make clear that they have a

---

35. *Ellerth*, 524 U.S. at 765 (1998); *Faragher*, 524 U.S. at 778 (1998).

36. Cheryl R. Kaiser, Brenda Major, Ines Jurcevic, Tessa L. Dover, Laura M. Brady, and Jenessa R. Shapiro, *Presumed Fair: Ironic Effects of Organizational Diversity Structures*, J. OF PERSONALITY & SOC. PSYCHOL. 104(2): 504-519 (2013).

37. EEOC Task Force, *supra* note 3.

strong commitment to a culture of inclusion and respect for all employees and where they hold managers and employees accountable for harassment. When a fair investigation leads to a finding of harassment, the harasser must be sanctioned in a manner that is proportionate to the offense, and this must apply to all harassers even if they are high-value employees.

Power differentials and gender representation, moreover, matter to the prevalence of sexual harassment.[38] A higher representation of women in management or in core organizational jobs can also lead to a culture in which harassment is not tolerated. By contrast, where management is dominated by men, it is more likely that an organizational culture will develop in which harassment is tolerated and complaints of harassment are not taken seriously. By contrast, more women in management is likely to lead to a culture in which harassment is not tolerated and complaints are taken seriously. Similarly, if professional jobs are dominated by men and most women are in subservient positions, the power differentials between men and women tend to lead to a culture where harassment is tolerated. Organizational leaders can reduce harassment by hiring more women in management and core professional jobs.[39]

HR professionals and managers should recognize the many obstacles that inhibit victims of harassment from using company complaint procedures. Managers who oversee the complaint process should make it as easy as possible for employees to report harassment, protect complainants from retaliation, respond to complaints seriously and swiftly, and take decisive action to sanction harassers. There should be multiple ways for employees to complain, such as a formal complaint procedure combined with a more informal system in which employees could confidentially seek assistance in dealing with harassment if they do not feel safe using a formal procedure. Protections against retaliation, of course, are critical. The EEOC report, moreover, recommends conducting confidential climate surveys of employees for a better sense of the prevalence of harassment.[40] Of course, survey feedback is useless unless organizations commit to making necessary changes based on the results.

HR professionals created the system of symbolic structures that the courts now treat as evidence of compliance with civil rights law. They now have the responsibility, alongside other managers and executives, to build a culture of respect and inclusion for all employees, and to ensure that antiharassment

---

38. Remus Ilies, Nancy Hauserman, Susan Schwochau, and John Stibal, *Reported Incidence Rates of Work-Related Sexual Harassment in the United States: Using Meta-Analysis to Explain Reported Rate Disparities*, PERSONNEL PSYCHOL. 56: 607-631 (2003).

39. Frank Dobbin and Alexandra Kalev, *Training Programs and Reporting Systems Won't End Sexual Harassment. Promoting More Women Will*, HARV. BUS. REV., Nov. 15, 2018.

40. EEOC Select Task Force, *supra* note 3.

policies are taken seriously and complaint procedures provide meaningful redress for harassment. The #MeToo movement has mobilized support for change, but symbolic structures will not curb harassment without strong efforts by corporate leaders.

The #MeToo movement has certainly raised public awareness of the prevalence of sexual harassment, but the actual impact of the movement may be very limited. The response of organizations to date has in many cases been more symbolic than substantive. Human resource professionals, employers, and judges alike must understand that symbolic compliance occurs with great frequency and is not, in and of itself, a solution to the harassment problem. Without strong efforts by organizational leaders to bring about a change in organizational cultures that too frequently condone harassment, the #MeToo movement will have been of little value.

CHAPTER 37

How the #MeToo Movement Is Transforming Corporate Governance

Amelia Miazad[1]

Introduction

As the preceding chapter reveals, companies and organizations have traditionally responded to sexual harassment by erecting "symbolic structures" that have proven ineffectual.[2] Relying on her empirical research, Professor Lauren Edelman cautions against these structures and demonstrates how they protect companies and executives at the expense of employees and sexual harassment victims.[3] Even the Equal Employment Opportunity Commission (EEOC), which long championed sexual harassment training and compliance programs, has conceded that "training programs from the past thirty years clearly have not worked because they focus on preventing legal liability instead of the actual sexual harassment."[4] But if sexual harassment training and compliance programs are anemic at best, and potentially counter-productive, what meaningful action *can* companies take to prevent sexual harassment?

---

1. Founding Director and Senior Research Fellow, Business in Society Institute, U.C. Berkeley School of Law. Danielle Santos, Research and Project Associate at Business in Society Institute, provided terrific research assistance and analysis for this chapter. For a more comprehensive account of the changes that companies have made in response to the #MeToo movement, see Amelia Miazad, *Sex, Power and Corporate Governance*, 54 U.C. Davis L. Rev. ___ (2020).

2. Lauren B. Edelman, *The #MeToo Movement, Symbolic Structures, and the Limits of the Law*, *supra* chapter 36.

3. *Id.*

4. Chai R. Feldblum & Victoria A. Lipnic, *Select Task Force on the Study of Harassment in the Workplace*, The EEOC Guidance (June 2016), https://www1.eeoc.gov//eeoc/task_force /harassment/report.cfm?renderforprint=1.

To answer that question we must first examine the root cause of sexual harassment, which social scientists have long identified as a gender-imbalanced culture that encourages men to exploit their power over women.[5] As Professor Dacher Keltner, an expert on the corrupting influence of power has explained, power leads to "empathy deficits and diminished moral sentiments."[6] Social psychologists have also found that "power encourages individuals to act on their own whims, desires, and impulses,"[7] and power-induced disinhibition[8] may lead to other bad behaviors including "sexual over-perception."[9] Numerous studies have corroborated that organizations that promote sexism[10] and sex segregation[11] are more likely to experience sexual harassment.[12] Importantly, as social scientist Vicki Schultz reminds us, "targeting only sexual misconduct without addressing related patterns of sexism and deeper institutional dynamics has serious shortcomings that risk undermining the broader quest for gender equality."[13] In summary, social science across disciplines is replete with examples of how an unequal distribution of power between men and women can lead to sexual harassment.

---

5. See, e.g., Frank Dobbin and Erin L. Kelley, *How to Stop Harassment: Professional Construction of Legal Compliance in Organizations*, 112:4 Am. J. Soc. 1203 (2007) [hereinafter Dobbin and Kelley, *How to Stop Harassment*].

6. Video: Gender, Power and Stemming Sexual Harassment (World Economic Forum Annual Meeting 2018) (available at https://www.weforum.org/events/world-economic-forum-annual-meeting-2018/sessions/gender-power-and-stemming-sexual-harassment).

7. Dacher Keltner, *The Power Paradox*, GREATER GOOD SCI. CTR. (Dec. 1, 2007), https://greatergood.berkeley.edu/article/item/power_paradox.

8. Joris Lammers, *Power and Morality*, 6 CURRENT OPINION PSYCHOL. 15 (2015).

9. Jonathan W. Kunstman & Jon K. Maner, *Sexual Overperception: Power, Mating Motives, and Biases in Social Judgment*, 100 J. PERSONALITY & SOC. PSYCHOL. 282, 282-294 (2011).

10. Vicki Schultz, *Open Statement on Sexual Harassment from Employment Discrimination Law Scholars*, 18, 20, 17- 48, FACULTY SCHOLARSHIP SERIES 5301(2018), https://digital commons.law.yale.edu/fss_papers/5301. Sexism may involve the pressure for men and women to adhere to stereotypical gender roles. This confinement to gender roles prevents women from benefiting from the privilege of exuding more socially valued characteristics. It also prevents men from compromising the hierarchy among values by embracing devalued norms. See Kathryn Abrams, *New jurisprudence of sexual harassment*, 83 Cornell L. Rev, 1209, 1169- 1230 (1997). See also Jennifer L. Berdahl et al., *Work as a masculinity contest*, 74(3) J. OF SOCIAL ISSUES, 428, 422-448. (2018).

11. Schultz, *supra* note 10, at 22, 23, 24, 17-48 (2018).

12. Chelsea R. Willness et al., *A Meta-Analysis of the Antecedents and Consequences of Workplace Sexual Harassment*, 60:1 PERSONNEL PSYCHOL. 127, 127-162 (2007).

13. Vicki Schultz, *Reconceptualizing Sexual Harassment, Again*, 33, 22- 66, FACULTY SCHOLARSHIP SERIES, 5366 (2018), https://digitalcommons.law.yale.edu/fss_papers/5366.

If the social scientists are correct, and gender power imbalances increase the risk of sexual harassment, then we ought not to wonder why the #MeToo movement brought its day of reckoning to corporate America.[14] U.S. companies are teeming with gender power imbalances, and they start at the very top, with the composition of the board of directors, the chief executive officer (CEO), and executive management. These power holders reinforce gender imbalances through unequal pay practices and pay secrecy policies. Contractual provisions in employment agreements, such as mandatory arbitration agreements and nondisclosure agreements, continue to reinforce these imbalances by silencing victims and masking the pervasiveness of sexual harassment. And multi-million-dollar golden parachutes in executive compensation agreements offer plush landings and insulate offenders from accountability.

After #MeToo, however, a chorus of influential stakeholders including investors, employees, customers, regulators, advisors, and NGOs are taking aim at these very power imbalances. This disquiet within the stakeholder community is beginning to cause executives and directors to institute meaningful reforms. While companies are still seeking comfort in training and compliance programs,[15] there is a novel focus on seismic corporate governance reforms, from increasing board gender diversity to tying executive compensation agreements to diversity targets. At this early juncture, it is rash to predict the eventual impact of these changes, and they are still far from widespread. Notwithstanding, as this chapter argues, these reforms are uniquely promising because they address gender power imbalances and may foreshadow a new era of corporate governance that is rooted in gender equity.

Influential Stakeholders Demand That Corporate Boards Address Gender Power Imbalances

Gone are the days when the board of directors was comfortably insulated from external voices. Today, a vocal chorus of stakeholders, which includes investors, employees, customers, regulators, advisors, and NGOs, are attempting to exert their influence on board strategy.[16] While gender equality had been

14. While gender power imbalances exist in companies globally, this chapter is focused on the United States.

15. Gerry Smith, *Demand for Anti-Harassment Training Videos Surges in #MeToo Era*, BLOOMBERG, Mar. 13, 2018, https://www.bloomberg.com/news/articles/2018-03-13/better-call-hr-demand-for-training-videos-surges-in-metoo-era.

16. Martin Lipton, *Stakeholder Governance—Issues and Answers*, HARVARD LAW SCHOOL FORUM ON CORPORATE GOVERNANCE, 2019, https://corpgov.law.harvard.edu/2019/10/25/stakeholder-governance-issues-and-answers/. See also *Business Roundtable*

brewing as a concern for many stakeholders by 2017, the #MeToo movement propelled it to the forefront of their agendas and united their disparate voices. As the examples below elucidate, these stakeholders are beginning to draw an explicit link between increasing gender diversity and equity and mitigating the risk of sexual harassment.

Investors

The Big Three

BlackRock, State Street, and Vanguard, referred to as "The Big Three," are the largest asset managers in the world. As the dominant shareholder in 40 percent of all U.S.-listed companies and 90 percent of companies in the S&P 500, their collective impact is massive,[17] and their growing focus on gender is palpable. One visible example is State Street's iconic "Fearless Girl" statue, which it erected in front of the charging bull on Wall Street when it launched its campaign for more board gender diversity.[18] While State Street's efforts began in January 2017, just before the #MeToo movement erupted, it has stepped up its efforts ever since. In 2018, State Street fearlessly voted against the chairs of the nominating committees of 500 companies with all-male boards.[19] State Street went further and announced that beginning in 2020, it would vote against the entire slate of board members on the nominating committee of any company not meeting its gender diversity criteria.[20] Also, in 2019 State Street made

---

Redefines the Purpose of a Corporation to Promote "An Economy That Serves All Americans, THE BUSINESS ROUNDTABLE, Aug. 19, 2019, https://www.businessroundtable.org/business-round table-redefines-the-purpose-of-a-corporation-to-promote-an-economy-that-serves-all-americans.

17. Jill E. Fisch, Asaf Hamdani & Steven Davidoff Solomon, *The New Titans of Wall Street: A Theoretical Framework for Passive Investors*, 168 U. PA. L. REV. 17 (Dec. 2019).

18. *State Street Global Advisors Calls on 3,500 Companies Representing More Than $30 Trillion in Market Capitalization to Increase Number of Women on Corporate Boards: On the Eve of International Women's Day, SSGA Issues Guidelines and Places Statue in New York City's Financial District as a Symbol of Need for Action*, STATE STREET, Mar. 7, 2017, https://news room.statestreet.com/press-release/corporate/state-street-global-advisors-calls-3500-companies -representing-more-30-tri-0.

19. *New York City Mayor and State Street Global Advisors Announce New Location for Fearless Girl Following her March 2017 Wall Street Debut, More Than 150 Publicly-Traded Companies Have Added Female Directors to their Boards*, STATE STREET, Apr. 19, 2018, https:// newsroom.statestreet.com/press-release/corporate/new-york-city-mayor-and-state-street -global-advisors-announce-new-location-f.

20. Andrea Vittorio and Jeff Green, *State Street to Vote Against More Directors at Male-Only Boards*, BLOOMBERG, Sept. 27, 2018, https://www.bloomberg.com/news/articles /2018-09-27/state-street-to-vote-against-more-directors-at-male-only-boards; Stewardship

"corporate culture" its chief engagement priority, arguing that a "flawed corporate culture has resulted in high-profile cases of excessive risk-taking or unethical behaviors that negatively impact long-term performance."[21]

State Street's efforts have perhaps been more visible, but BlackRock and Vanguard have also increased their advocacy for board gender diversity. In 2019, for example, BlackRock identified "governance, including your company's approach to board diversity," as its first engagement priority.[22] In its 2019 Investment Stewardship Annual Report, BlackRock confirmed that, during the 2019 proxy season, it voted against 52 directors at Russell 1000 companies that had fewer than two women on their boards.[23] For Vanguard, too, board diversity was one of its two engagement priorities in 2019, and Vanguard went even further to tie its own company's executive compensation metrics to improving diversity in its corporate hierarchy.[24]

Pension Funds

In direct response to #MeToo, the largest pension funds in California came together to launch the Trustees United Principles (the Principles) which explicitly link lack of diversity and "power imbalances" to an increased risk of sexual harassment.[25] On January 19, 2019, the Trustees announced that "Institutional Investor Trustees Representing $635 Billion in Assets Launch Principles Addressing Sexual Harassment and Workplace Misconduct."[26] The Trustees who drafted the Principles have emphasized that they are responding

Report 2018-2019, STATE STREET GLOBAL ADVISORS, https://www.ssga.com/investment-topics/environmental-social-governance/2019/09/annual-asset-stewardship-report-2018.pdf.

21. Cyrus Taraporevala, *2019 Proxy Letter—Aligning Corporate Culture with Long-Term Strategy*, STATE STREET GLOBAL ADVISORS, Jan. 15, 2019, https://corpgov.law.harvard.edu/2019/01/15/2019-proxy-letter-aligning-corporate-culture-with-long-term-strategy/.

22. Larry Fink, *Larry Fink's 2019 letter to CEOs*, BLACKROCK, 2019, https://www.blackrock.com/corporate/investor-relations/larry-fink-ceo-letter.

23. BlackRock, *2019 Investment Stewardship Annual Report 12* (2019), https://www.blackrock.com/corporate/literature/publication/blk-annual-stewardship-report-2019.pdf.

24. David Ricketts and Chris Newlands, *Vanguard and Fidelity link pay to gender diversity targets Industry titans bring in new measures as they implement Women in Finance Charter commitments*, FINANCIAL NEWS, Dec. 11, 2018, https://www.fnlondon.com/articles/vanguard-and-fidelity-tie-pay-to-female-representation-20181210.

25. *Trustees United Principles, Trustees United for Long Term Value*, TRUSTEESUNITED.COM (2020), https://www.trusteesunited.com/.

26. Trustees United, *Institutional Investor Trustees Representing $635 Billion in Assets Launch Principles Addressing Sexual Harassment and Workplace Misconduct Principles focus on promoting long-term value creation by advancing safe corporate cultures* (2019), https://www.trusteesunited.com/Home/News.

to the changing social norms on sexual harassment—"There's clearly an inflection point in our society where we're saying we're no longer going to tolerate this behavior, and that's an important signal to investors."[27]

The Principles are notable for their focus on engaging directors and top management on addressing power differentials. Principle 1 begins by asking directors to "publicly share due diligence processes used to respond to sexual harassment and violence complaints filed by all employees and contractors."[28] While this principle addresses compliance, the demand for board oversight of sexual harassment, which has traditionally been managed primarily by human resources (HR) departments, is a notable shift. Principle 2 blames contractual clauses, such as nondisclosure agreements and forced arbitration clauses, for perpetuating harassment and demands that companies put an end to those policies.[29] Principle 3 addresses diversity "at all levels" and correlates an increase in diversity to the ability "to be more attuned to the risks associated with harassment, misconduct, and discrimination."[30] By backing board diversity, in particular, these investors have staked their claim that "diverse boards which reflect the racial and gender composition of a company's workforce can help to create organizational cultures that prevent sexual harassment and related risks from materializing."[31] The most poignant example is Principle 4, which specifically asks companies to address "power imbalances" that lead to discrimination and abuse by implementing agreements, including collective bargaining agreements and responsible contractor policies.[32]

Shareholder Activists

The #MeToo movement has also triggered a rise in shareholder proposals addressing diversity and the gender pay gap.[33] Shareholder activist Arjuna

27. Bloomberg, *California pension trustees call for disclosures of #MeToo costs*, L.A. TIMES, Jan. 14, 2019, https://www.latimes.com/business/la-fi-calpers-calstrs-metoo-20190114-story .html.

28. *Id.*

29. *Id.*

30. *Id.*

31. *Id.*

32. *Id.*

33. David A. Katz, Corporate Governance Update: Shareholder Activism Is the Next Phase of #MeToo, HARVARD LAW SCHOOL FORUM ON CORPORATE GOVERNANCE, Sept. 28, 2018, https://corpgov.law.harvard.edu/2018/09/28/corporate-governance-update-share holder-activism-is-the-next-phase-of-metoo/.

Capital has been at the forefront of this movement.[34] Arjuna led a successful campaign to pressure seven technology giants, eBay, Intel, Apple, Amazon, Expedia, Microsoft, and Adobe, into upgrading their standards and transparency related to gender pay disparity.[35] On the heels of this success, Arjuna Capital next targeted nine financial services companies, resulting in Citi becoming the first U.S. bank to voluntarily disclose that its gender pay gap is 29 percent.[36] Six more followed Citi's lead, including American Express, Bank of America, Bank of New York Mellon, Citigroup, JPMorgan, Mastercard, and Wells Fargo, and disclosed their efforts to advance gender pay equity.[37] As Natasha Lamb, Arjuna's managing director has argued, "When women hold the lower-paying jobs and in turn have less power in the organization ... that *imbalance breeds an unhealthy culture.* The symptoms of that are *the power dynamics around sexual harassment*"[38] (emphasis added).

While Natasha Lamb has emphasized the link between gender inequity and sexual harassment, Trillium Asset Management has filed the first shareholder proposal to specifically mention this link.[39] That proposal was filed against Nike, Inc. (Nike) and asks Nike's Board Compensation Committee to improve its risk oversight concerning workplace sexual harassment by "preparing a report assessing the feasibility of integrating improvement of *culture or diversity metrics into the performance measures of senior executives* under the Company's compensation incentive plans."[40] There is reason to be optimistic about the outcome of this proposal, as Trillium has withdrawn it because Nike has committed to engage.[41]

---

34. *Press Release: 12 U.S. Banks and Tech Giants Targeted with "Median Gender Pay Gap" Shareholder Proposal*, ARJUNA CAPITAL, 2020, http://arjuna-capital.com/news/press-release-12-u-s-banks-and-tech-giants-targeted-with-median-gender-pay-gap-shareholder-proposal/.

35. *Showdown On Gender Pay Equity In Silicon Valley: Shareholders Press Seven Tech Giants To Follow Lead Of Intel, Apple On Fair Treatment Of Women*, ARJUNA CAPITAL, 2020, http://arjuna-capital.com/news/showdown-on-gender-pay-equity-in-silicon-valley-shareholders-press-seven-tech-giants-to-follow-lead-of-intel-apple-on-fair-treatment-of-women/.

36. Arjuna Capital, *supra* at 34.

37. *Id.*

38. *From Hollywood to Wall Street, investors confront sexual misconduct risk*, S&P GLOBAL, 2018, https://platform.mi.spglobal.com/web/client?auth=inherit#news/article?id=43771908&cdid=A-43771908-13093.

39. *Nike, Inc.—Sexual Misconduct Risk Management—(2018)*, TRILLIUM ASSET MANAGEMENT (2018), https://trilliuminvest.com/shareholder-proposal/nike-inc-sexual-misconduct-risk-management-2018/.

40. *Id.*

41. *Id.*

Shareholder Plaintiffs

With #MeToo revelations triggering double-digit stock price plunges, an increasing number of investors have turned to derivative suits against directors and officers of companies.[42] This increase in #MeToo derivative claims is igniting a discussion among corporate law scholars, D&O insurance experts, and board consultants and advisors on the present and future viability of these types of lawsuits under both state corporate law and federal securities law.[43] While those questions remain important and unresolved, an equally interesting phenomenon is playing out in the background. After the #MeToo movement, shareholder plaintiffs began to root their allegations in "corporate culture." Notably, the term "culture of sexual harassment" was rarely used prior to the #MeToo movement. In contrast, the very first shareholder derivative suit filed in the #MeToo era was filed against Twenty-First Century Fox and specifically faulted the board for failing to prevent the "culture of sexual harassment" perpetuated by Roger Ailes and Bill O'Reilly. The complaint in that case begins: "This case arises from the systematic, decades-long culture of sexual harassment, racial discrimination, and retaliation that led to a hostile work environment at Fox News Channel (Fox News)." The complaint goes on to refer to a "culture of sexual harassment" or "toxic culture" forty-four times.[44]

Following #MeToo, shareholders began to blame boards for failing to monitor, prevent, or disclose a "culture of sexual harassment" or "boys' club culture."[45] This marks a departure from the pre-#MeToo era where shareholders were focused on adequate compliance, training, and reporting systems. It would be a mistake to infer, as some have suggested, that these lawsuits have no impact because they have all been settled or dismissed. As illustrated below,

---

42. Daniel Hemel & Dorothy S. Lund, *Sexual Harassment and Corporate Law*, 118 Colum. L. Rev. 1583, 1583-1668 (2018).

43. There are two main ways for shareholders to hold individual directors personally liable. Shareholders can bring a claim under Delaware law, alleging that the directors breached their fiduciary duties of care or loyalty. Known as a "*Caremark* claim" these lawsuits are notoriously challenging for plaintiffs to prevail on. Shareholders of publicly listed companies can also bring a claim under the anti-fraud provisions of the Securities Exchange Act of 1934, alleging that the directors failed to disclose a material risk to shareholders. While these cases have either been settled or dismissed, there has been an increase in both kinds of claims since #MeToo. *See, e.g.*, Hemel & Lund, *supra*, at 42. *See also*, Kevin M. LaCroix, *Alphabet Board Hit With Derivative Suits Over Alleged Sexual Misconduct at Google*, The D&O Diary, Jan. 13, 2019, https://www.dandodiary.com/tags/metoo/.

44. See Verified Derivative Complaint at 1–2, City of Monroe Emps.' Ret. Sys. v. Murdoch, No. 2017-0833 (Del. Ch. filed Nov. 20, 2017).

45. *Id.* See also Verified Derivative Complaint at 24, Stein v. Knight, No. 18CV38553 (Or. Cir. Ct. filed Aug. 31, 2018).

irrespective of the actual *legal* risk, companies are responding to the reputational risk of #MeToo claims by increasing gender diversity and addressing other gender power imbalances.

Employees

The relationship between the employee and the employer is undergoing a transformative shift. As recent surveys confirm, employees' faith in their employers "to do what is right" eclipses their faith in government, the media, or even NGOs.[46] These newfound expectations are evident in the increasing amount of employee activism, with employees demanding that companies take positions on issues, from guns to immigration.[47] Thus, while worker wages are stagnant, workers' voices are getting louder. The #MeToo movement is playing out within this cultural context of employee activism. One dramatic example of this is the "Google Walk Out" in which 20,000 "Googlers" walked out from 65 percent of Google's offices around the world to protest the hero's farewell given to Google executives who were accused of harassment.[48] That walkout was accompanied by a demand for changes at Google, including corporate governance reforms. Specifically, the employees asked for: (1) an end to forced arbitration in cases of harassment and discrimination; (2) a commitment to end inequities in pay and opportunity; (3) a publicly disclosed sexual harassment transparency report; (4) a clear, uniform, globally inclusive process for reporting sexual misconduct; (5) a promotion of the Chief Diversity Officer to answer directly to the CEO and make recommendations directly to the board of directors; and (6) the appointment of an employee representative to the board.[49]

One week later Google's CEO agreed to, "make arbitration optional for individual sexual harassment and sexual assault claims"[50] and "recommit to our

---

46. Edelman, *Trust at Work Implications for Employers*, 1- 59, EDELMAN TRUST BAROMETER 2019, https://www.edelman.com/sites/g/files/aatuss191/files/2019-05/2019 _Edelman_Trust_Barometer_Implications_for_Employee_Experience.pdf?utm_source =downloads&utm_campaign=trust_barometer.

47. *Id.*, at 38. *See* Tom C.W. Lim, *Incorporating Social Activism*, 98 BOSTON UNIV. LAW REV. 1535, 1535–1605 (2018).

48. Daisuke Wakabayashi et al., *Google Walkout: Employees Stage Protest Over Handling of Sexual Harassment*, N.Y. TIMES, Nov. 1, 2018, https://www.nytimes.com/2018/11/01/tech nology/google-walkout-sexual-harassment.html.

49. Claire Stapleton et al., *We're the Organizers of the Google Walkout. Here Are Our Demands*, THE CUT, Nov. 1, 2018, https://www.thecut.com/2018/11/google-walkout-organiz ers-explain-demands.html.

50. Sundar Pichai, *A Note to Our Employees*, GOOGLE, Nov. 8, 2018, https://www.blog .google/inside-google/company-announcements/note-our-employees/.

company-wide OKR[51] around diversity, equity, and inclusion again in 2019, focused on improving representation—through hiring, progression, and retention—and creating a more inclusive culture for everyone."[52] Google has, predictably, ignored the key governance reforms. But the very same day that the CEO issued his statement, Google employees publicly doubled down on their demands.[53] As this story continues to unfold, some critics question the efficacy of this worker activism, pointing to the Google employees' relative lack of bargaining power. While it is true that many of these employees' demands remain unanswered, their advocacy continues and they are beginning to coordinate their efforts with shareholders and regulators, which could prove effective. This development is encouraging and could create an entirely new avenue for corporate accountability.

Boards Respond by Addressing Power Imbalances

The preceding section described how investors and employees are asking corporate boards to address the risk of sexual harassment by increasing gender diversity, addressing pay equality, and removing contractual provisions such as mandatory arbitration that have operated to silence women. The next obvious question is whether these pleas are falling on deaf ears. Cynics claim that corporate boards are merely paying lip service to quell the tide and that any reforms are either merely symbolic or too marginal to have any lasting impact. This section takes aim at that conclusion and argues that the changes we are seeing, while still not widespread, are potentially transformative because they address power differentials.

One stark example of this is Signet Jewelers, whose CEO Mark Light was alleged to have condoned and participated in a "culture of sexual harassment."[54]

---

51. *Id.* "OKR" refers to Objectives and Key Results.

52. Pichai, *supra* note 50.

53. Claire Stapleton et al., *#GoogleWalkout update: Collective action works, and we need to keep working. True equity depends on it*, MEDIUM, Nov. 8, 2018, https://medium.com /@GoogleWalkout/googlewalkout-update-collective-action-works-but-we-need-to-keep -working-b17f673ad513.

54. In re Signet Jewelers Ltd. Sec. Litig., No. 1:16-cv-06728-JMF (S.D.N.Y. filed Mar. 22, 2018), 61. For the most recent complaint in the case as of this writing, see Fifth Amended Class Action Complaint for Violations of the Federal Securities Laws, In re Signet Jewelers Ltd. Sec. Litig., No. 1:16-cv-06728-JMF (S.D.N.Y. filed Mar. 22, 2018) [hereinafter Signet Jewelers Complaint]. For earlier pleadings, see Second Amended Class Action Complaint for Violations of Federal Securities Law, Dube v. Signet Jewelers Ltd., No. 1:16-cv-06728-JMF (S.D.N.Y. filed Apr. 3, 2017); Complaint for Violation of the Federal Securities Laws, Irving Firemen's Relief & Ret. Sys. v. Signet Jewelers Ltd., No. 1:17-cv-02845 (S.D.N.Y. filed Mar. 28, 2017); Class Action

While Signet Jewelers chose to defend the allegations that shareholders made against the company in the shareholder derivative lawsuit, it also implemented significant governance reforms. First, Signet replaced Mark Light with its first female CEO, Virginia Drosos.[55] While a male-dominated board had tradition-ally led Signet, today it is one of the few boards to have achieved gender parity,[56] and Signet's C-suite is now women-led, which recently earned it accolades from the Bloomberg Gender-Equality Index.[57]

Also illustrative is 21st Century Fox (Fox), which settled a shareholder derivative claim against it the same day that it was filed for $90 million, one of the largest settlement amounts in a derivative lawsuit to date.[58] While the large settlement made headlines, the *non-monetary terms* of the settlement are far more powerful. Specifically, the settlement required Fox to establish a "Work-place Professionalism and Inclusion Council," which it formally announced on November 20, 2017:

> 21st Century Fox (21CF) announced today it has established the Fox News Workplace Professionalism and Inclusion Council (the Council), a committee comprising experts in workplace and *inclu-sion matters*, with a majority serving from outside the company. The Council will advise Fox News and its senior management in its ongoing efforts to ensure a proper workplace environment for all employees and guests, strengthen reporting practices for wrong-doing, enhance HR training on workplace behavior, and further *recruitment and advancement of women and minorities. Autho-rized by and reporting to the 21CF Board*, through its Nominating and Corporate Governance Committee, the Council will provide

---

Complaint for Violations of Federal Securities Laws, Mikolchak v. Signet Jewelers Ltd., No. 3:17-cv-00923 (N.D. Tex. filed Mar. 31, 2017) [hereinafter Mikolchak Complaint] (transferred to the Southern District of New York by Order Granting Agreed Motion to Transfer Venue, Mikolchak, No. 3:17-cv-00923-B (filed Apr. 17, 2017)).

55. Anthony DeMarco, *Signet Jewelers Appoints Virginia "Gina" C. Drosos as CEO*, FORBES, Jul. 17, 2017, https://www.forbes.com/sites/anthonydemarco/2017/07/17/signet-jewelers-appoints-virginia-gina-c-drosos-as-ceo/#3388b4673f0a.

56. Lucinda Shen, *Following Sexual Harassment Allegations, Signet Jewelers' Board Is Now 50% Female*, FORTUNE, Oct. 2, 2018, https://fortune.com/2018/10/02/following-sexual-harassment-allegations-signet-jewelers-board-is-now-50-female/.

57. Signet Jewelers, *Signet Jewelers Selected for 2019 Bloomberg Gender-Equality Index, Recognizing Commitment to Advancing Women in the Workplace*, SIGNETJEWELERS.COM, 2019, https://www.signetjewelers.com/investors/news-releases/news-release-details/2019/Signet-Jewelers-Selected-for-2019-Bloomberg-Gender-Equality-Index-Recognizing-Commitment-to-Advancing-Women-in-the-Workplace/.

58. Murdoch Complaint, *supra* at 44.

written reports to the 21CF Board, which will be posted on 21CF's website. (emphasis added)[59]

It is telling that all of the Council's members are women with expertise in creating a culture that supports the advancement of women, as opposed to expertise in sexual harassment compliance or training. Moreover, the Council's mandate includes recruiting and advancing women, again emphasizing that addressing power differentials and increasing diversity mitigates the risk of sexual harassment. Finally, the Council was authorized by and has the ear of the board of directors. As a result, the board can't deny knowledge of any "red flags" because the Council is required to provide written and public reports to the board's Nominating and Corporate Governance Committee. It is too early to predict the efficacy of the Council, but it has produced three reports to the board of directors, and each reveals that Fox News is increasing gender and racial diversity at different management levels throughout the organization.[60] Also, when Fox News CEO Paul Rittenberg retired and left a vacancy, the network opted to hire its first-ever woman CEO, Suzanne Scott.[61]

Wynn Resorts, formerly led by Steve Wynn, one of the most powerful men brought down by #MeToo, provides another example. On January 26, 2018, the *Wall Street Journal* published an article recounting allegations against Wynn of sexual misconduct and rape spanning decades, prompting an immediate 10 percent decline in Wynn's stock valuation.[62] By February 6, 2018, Wynn had resigned as chairman and CEO.[63] Investors began agitating for a shakeup on the board soon after. Before the allegations, Wynn's board was comprised of eight

---

59. *21st Century Fox Establishes the Fox News Workplace Professionalism and Inclusion Council,* BUSINESS WIRE, Nov. 20, 2017, https://www.businesswire.com/news/home/2017 1120006042/en/21st-Century-Fox-Establishes-Fox-News-Workplace.

60. *Report of the Fox News Workplace Professionalism and Inclusion Council,* FOX NEWS, June 6, 2018, 1-8, https://static.foxnews.com/pdf/Council_Report.pdf. See also, Fox News, Report of the FOX News Workplace Professionalism and Inclusion Council dated December 26, 2018 1-4 (2018), https://static.foxnews.com/pdf/Council_Second_Report_Final.pdf. See also, Fox News, Report of the FOX News Workplace Professionalism and Inclusion Council dated June 13, 2019 1-4 (2019), https://static.foxnews.com/pdf/Final_WPIC_June_2019 _Report.pdf.

61. Emily Steel and Michael M. Grynbaum, *Suzanne Scott Named First Female Chief Executive of Fox News,* N.Y. TIMES, May 17, 2018, https://www.nytimes.com/2018/05/17 /business/media/fox-news-suzanne-scott.html.

62. Alexandra Berzon and Micah Maidenberg, *Nevada: Wynn Resorts Executives Ignored Sexual Misconduct Claims Against Steve Wynn,* WALL ST. J., Jan. 26, 2018, https://www.wsj .com/articles/wynn-resorts-to-settle-nevada-regulators-probe-11548711027.

63. Maggie Astor and Julie Creswell, *Steve Wynn Resigns From Company Amid Sexual Misconduct Allegations,* N.Y. TIMES, Feb. 6, 2018, https://www.nytimes.com/2018/02/06 /business/steve-wynn-resigns.html.

directors, only one of whom was a woman. In a move that Wynn's new CEO called a "turning point" for the company, Wynn added three women as independent directors, which included Betsy Atkins, Dee Dee Myers, and Wendy Webb.[64] Today, Wynn's board has nine members, and four of them are women, achieving near gender parity.[65] Wynn also added an executive-level position and named Corrine Clement as vice president of a new Culture and Community Department that "supports diversity and inclusion, gender equality, fair treatment in the workplace, and employee charitable efforts in the communities Wynn Resorts serves."[66] This new department includes a Women's Leadership Forum, which is designed to close the gender gap in management and create equal pay.[67] Unlike the symbolic compliance of the past, which operated outside of the board, the Forum includes participation by the four Wynn female directors who hold "regular town halls, events, and fireside chats to promote engagement and advancement of the female employee base."[68]

Since the #MeToo movement, some boards have become more engaged in overseeing corporate culture and preventing male executives from abusing their positions of power. McDonald's Corp. CEO Steve Easterbrook's recent firing captured headlines in September 2019 and reflects how resolute some boards have become in holding executives accountable.[69] Easterbrook's removal is extraordinary because it was not done in response to any allegation of sexual harassment, but rather a consensual relationship with an employee that violated company policy. A far cry from the boards that allowed unscrupulous and illegal behavior by star executives to go unchecked for years, the McDonald's

---

64. Aaron Smith, *Wynn Resorts appoints 3 women to board in a 'turning point'*, CNN, Apr. 18, 2018, https://money.cnn.com/2018/04/18/news/companies/wynn-women-board-of -directors/index.html.

65. *Corporate Governance—Board Members, Wynn Resorts LTD.*, https://wynnresorts limited.gcs-web.com/corporate-governance/board-of-directors.

66. Maria Armental, *Wynn Resorts Creates "Culture and Community Department" in Wake of Sexual-Misconduct Scandal: Company veteran Corrine Clement leads new department that will also focus on diversity and gender equality*, WALL ST. J., Apr. 9, 2018, https://www.wsj .com/articles/wynn-resorts-creates-culture-and-community-department-in-wake-of-sexual -misconduct-scandal-1523307931.

67. Wynn Resorts, *Wynn Resorts Launches Women's Leadership Forum Series with Inaugural Event at Wynn Las Vegas*, 2018, https://press.wynnlasvegas.com/press-releases/wynn -resorts-launches-women-s-leadership-forum-series-with-inaugural--event-at-wynn-las-vegas /s/97d36392-e135-4bd3-be5b-bb373b772c12.

68. ValueEdge Blog Staff, *Betsy Atkins: The Aftermath of #MeToo Allegations Against Wynn Resorts*, CEOs #MeToo, BOARD DIVERSITY, BOARDS, https://valueedgeadvisors.com /2018/08/27/betsy-atkins-the-aftermath-of-metoo-allegations-against-wynn-resorts-ceos/.

69. Heather Haddon, *McDonald's Fires CEO Steve Easterbrook Over Relationship With Employee*, WALL ST. J., Nov. 4. 2019, https://www.wsj.com/articles/mcdonalds-fires-ceo-steve -easterbrook-over-relationship-with-employee-11572816660.

board removed Easterbrook *just three weeks* after learning about the relationship.[70] With quarterly profits as the traditional yardstick by which CEOs are measured, Easterbrook's ouster was even more surprising given McDonald's strong market position. Easterbrook's removal could very well have been a way for the McDonald's board to deflect the increasing scrutiny that the company is facing for sexual harassment in its franchises. From McDonald's employees who filed complaints with the U.S. Equal Employment Opportunity Commission to an employee walkout in thirteen states, the McDonald's board has been in the spotlight for allegedly tolerating a culture of sexual harassment.[71] Regardless of the board's motives, the firing of a CEO is perhaps the most drastic measure a board can take under any circumstances.

To be fair, we can expect that companies in the public eye for #MeToo scandals would attempt to rehabilitate their reputations by making, and broadcasting, visible changes. In many cases, these changes were in response to investor pressure, or even new regulations. Nonetheless, these reforms hold the promise for mitigating sexual harassment risk because they are rooted in addressing the corrupting influence of power. Moreover, given the crescendo of stakeholder demands, reforms are underway throughout the market. Take the identity of power holders, for example. As of 2019, there is no longer a company in the S&P 500 with an all-male board.[72] And in 2018 for the second consecutive year, women and minorities represent half of the new S&P 500 directors.[73] While the pace of change is far slower with respect to the identity of CEOs and executive management, as the McDonald's ouster demonstrated, there is more accountability for these leaders. One clear sign of this is that a boards are amending executive compensation agreements to change the definition of cause and eliminate the "golden parachutes" for perpetrators of sexual harassment.[74] With respect to pay equity, in response to both stakeholder pressure and investor pressure, companies are addressing the gender pay gap through pay equity audits and corrective measures.[75] Finally, as the next chapter details, contractual

---

70. *Id.*

71. *Id.*

72. Vanessa Fuhrmans, *The Last All-Male Board on the S&P 500 Is No Longer*, WALL ST. J., Jul. 24, 2019, https://www.wsj.com/articles/the-last-all-male-board-on-the-s-p-500-is-no-longer-11564003203.

73. Women on Boards—Gender, HARVARD BUSINESS SCHOOL HBS.EDU, https://www.hbs.edu/gender/Pages/women-on-boards.aspx.

74. Jena McGregor, *How #MeToo is reshaping employment contracts for executives*, WASH. POST, Oct. 31, 2018, https://www.washingtonpost.com/business/2018/10/31/how-metoo-is-reshaping-employment-contracts-executives/.

75. *Navigating the Growing Pay Equity Movement: What Employers Need to Know About What to Do*, HARVARD BUSINESS REVIEW ANALYTIC SERVICES, 2019, https://trusaic.com

terms such as mandatory arbitration and nondisclosure agreements that seek to silence victims and protect companies from the reputational risks of sexual harassment are slowly being eliminated.[76]

Conclusion

In summary, as a result to the #MeToo movement, the changes that companies are voluntarily making, or being forced to make by stakeholders or regulators, are focused on corporate culture as opposed to corporate compliance. Specifically, companies today are attempting to address the risk of sexual harassment by removing power imbalances between men and women. Since these reforms are tailored to what social scientists identify as the root cause of sexual harassment, they have the potential to be effective. Admittedly, the "old-boys' club" is still thriving in corporate America, but the #MeToo movement has shaken the gender power imbalances on which it is built.

/wp-content/uploads/2019/09/HBR_Trusaic_Navigating_the_Growing_Pay_Equity_Move ment.pdf.

76. Catherine Fisk, *Nondisclosure Agreements and Sexual Harassment: #MeToo and the Change in American Law of Hush Contracts, infra* chapter 38.

Nondisclosure Agreements and Sexual Harassment: #MeToo and the Change in American Law of Hush Contracts

Catherine L. Fisk[1]

In late 2017, the #MeToo moment began as one woman after another breached a contract requiring her to remain silent about sexual harassment, assault, or rape. The news reports began in October 2017, when numerous women said that Hollywood mogul Harvey Weinstein had sexually harassed, assaulted, or raped them over the course of many years.[2] As women began speaking out about experiencing harassment, assault, and rape in entertainment, journalism, politics, sports, and business, it became clear that many were victims of serial predators and their experiences followed a pattern. It also became clear that contractual settlements of harassment that required victims to keep silent were a part of the problem.

Weinstein would meet a young woman eager to launch her career in Hollywood. He would promise to help her and have his assistant arrange a meeting, ideally in a hotel suite. When, after the harassment, assault, or rape, the woman appeared likely to complain publicly about her experience, Weinstein's and his employer's lawyers would settle her claims by paying the victim a hundred thousand dollars or so in exchange for which she signed a contract promising not to reveal what happened or even to speak negatively about Weinstein. If the victim breached the contract, the contract stipulated she would pay a hefty penalty in

---

1. Barbara Nachtrieb Armstrong Professor of Law, University of California, Berkeley. This chapter draws on a superb unpublished research paper by Berkeley Law student Anika Holland, as well as on the scholarship cited infra notes 8-12, 18.

2. Jodi Kantor & Megan Twohey, *Harvey Weinstein Paid Off Sexual Harassment Accusers for Decades*, N.Y. TIMES, Oct. 5, 2017; Jacey Fortin, *The Women Who Have Accused Harvey Weinstein*, N.Y. TIMES, Oct. 10, 2017.

liquidated damages. The women did not breach the contract, and Weinstein continued to find new victims for at least two decades, until finally the women spoke out.[3]

One of the most shocking uses of nondisclosure agreements (NDAs) involved Larry Nassar, a doctor affiliated with the U.S. Olympic gymnastics program, who was accused of sexually assaulting over 150 young gymnasts over the course of many years. After several women came forward and reported (at least in some cases in violation of their NDAs) what he had done, he was convicted of several offenses and is serving a life sentence.[4] One of the women who spoke out, Olympic medalist McKayla Maroney, did so in violation of a December 2016 confidentiality agreement with USA Gymnastics which required her to remain silent about USA Gymnastics' arrangement with Nassar under penalty of a $100,000 liquidated damages provision.[5] When the existence of the agreement was reported, and wealthy women offered to pay the liquidated damages in order to allow Maroney to speak out, USA Gymnastics quickly abandoned it.[6] Unlike in the case of Weinstein, the USA Gymnastics agreement may not have been what enabled Nasser to get away with his serial predations. But in both cases, a contract that was once regarded by lawyers and public relations (PR) staff as essential to protect the reputation of a company by keeping harassment out of the news, suddenly came to be a PR liability in itself.

The #MeToo moment illuminated the prevalence of NDAs and their role in covering up serial predations. Zelda Perkins, one of Weinstein's former assistants, signed an NDA in 1998 when she left his employ, and as the stories of his decades of assaults spread, Perkins spoke out about how his use of NDAs had been crucial in enabling him to continue harassing women for decades.[7] As NDAs suddenly came to be seen as a public relations problem rather than a solution to a problem, and as news stories and legal scholars revealed the harms

---

3. James Rufus Koren, *Weinstein Scandal Puts Nondisclosure Agreements in the Spotlight*, L.A. TIMES, Oct. 23, 2017; Michelle Kaminsky, *The Harvey Weinstein Effect: The End of Non-disclosure Agreements in Sexual Assault Cases?*, FORBES, Oct. 26, 2017.

4. Scott Cacciola & Victor Mather, *Larry Nassar Sentencing: "I Just Signed Your Death Warrant,"* N.Y. TIMES, Jan. 24, 2018.

5. Victor Mather, *McKayla Maroney Says USA Gymnastics Forced Confidentiality in Sexual Abuse Settlement*, N.Y. TIMES, Dec. 20, 2017; Scott Gleeson, *Chrissy Teigen Offers to Pay $100,000 Fine for McKayla Maroney to Speak Out Against Nassar*, USA TODAY, Jan. 16, 2018.

6. Heather Tucker, *USA Gymnastics Says It Will Not Fine McKayla Maroney If She Speaks Out Against Larry Nassar*, USA TODAY, Jan. 16, 2018.

7. Holly Watt, *Harvey Weinstein Aide Tells of "Morally Lacking" Non-Disclosure Deal*, THE GUARDIAN, Mar. 28, 2018; Mark Townsend, *Ex-Weinstein Assistant Calls for Ban on Contracts to Silence Harassment Victims*, THE GUARDIAN, Aug. 26, 2018.

of silence, courts and legislatures began revising the law to restrict these "hush contracts."[8]

This chapter briefly surveys the developments in American law on the enforcement of NDAs in the wake of #MeToo. It first examines the reasons why confidentiality provisions are common in settlement agreements. It then explores the criticisms of them that the #MeToo moment has illuminated. Finally, the chapter briefly surveys the changes in law governing the enforceability of NDAs.

Confidentiality and Settlement

In the United States, most disputes are resolved by settlement. Most settlements are accomplished by a contract in which the plaintiff agrees to dismiss a suit (if one was filed) and not to bring any future claim arising out of the incidents in exchange for the defendant agreeing to pay money and/or otherwise to confer something of value (such as a favorable job reference). It is not uncommon for such contracts to include language in which the defendant denies any wrongdoing. And many such contracts include some kind of secrecy provision. Often both parties will agree that the terms of the agreement will remain secret and that neither will disparage the other. These are known as confidential settlements and nondisparagement agreements. Some, such as those involving Weinstein and USA Gymnastics, prohibit the plaintiff from speaking to anyone about her experiences that gave rise to the dispute. And some—known as noncooperation agreements—take the duty of silence so far as to prohibit the plaintiff from cooperating with law enforcement in a criminal investigation arising from the incidents.

Scholars of contracts have noted for some time that secrecy provisions in litigation settlements raise significant public policy problems, in employment cases and elsewhere. Secrecy provisions have long been criticized as enabling the continuation of unlawful employment practices.[9] Confidential settlements have been linked to the continued sale of dangerous products even though litigation had produced strong evidence of the dangers,[10] and to enabling the Catholic

---

8. David A. Hoffman & Erik Lampmann, *Hushing Contracts*, 97 Wash. Univ. L. Rev. 165-220 (2019); Elizabeth C. Tippett, *The Legal Implications of the MeToo Movement*, 103 Minn. L. Rev. 229 (2018).

9. Minna J. Kotkin, *Invisible Settlements, Invisible Discrimination*, 84 N.C. L. Rev. 927 (2006); Elizabeth Wilkins, Silent Workers, *Disappearing Rights: Confidential Settlements and the Fair Labor Standards Act*, 34 Berk. J. Emp. & Lab. L. 109 (2013).

10. Elizabeth E. Spainhour, *Unsealing Settlements: Recent Efforts to Expose Settlement Agreements that Conceal Public Hazards*, 82 N.C. L. Rev. 2155 (2004).

Church to delay dealing with priests who molested children.[11] For these reasons, some scholars of legal ethics have suggested that use of noncooperation agreements (confidentiality contracts employed for the purpose or with the effect of preventing crime victims or witnesses to cooperate with criminal investigations) violates a lawyer's professional duties and may even be obstruction of justice.[12]

Three kinds of laws are potentially relevant to the enforceability of these kinds of secrecy agreements. The first is the state common law of contracts. Contract law is generally established by states, not by the federal government. Moreover, most aspects of contract law are made by judges, as the United States is, for the most part, a common law system. In the wake of the #MeToo revelations, scholars have advocated that courts should exercise their traditional common law power to declare unenforceable as contrary to public policy non-disclosure provisions that would prevent revelation of alleged sexual harassment or assault.[13]

A second source of applicable law are state statutes that supplement or supplant common law to regulate the enforcement of contracts. Many states, and in a few narrow situations the federal government, have enacted statutes restricting the enforcement of particular types of contracts. Typically, legislatures have enacted these types of statutes when they determined that particular contracts or contract terms are used in ways that harm one party to the contract or the public. In California, for example, agreements restricting post-employment competition are unenforceable.[14] The federal government prohibits agreements that prevent workers from joining labor unions.[15]

A third source of law are the federal and state statutes prohibiting discrimination in employment on the basis of, among other statuses, sex. Title VII of the Civil Rights Act of 1964 prohibits employment discrimination, including harassment, on the basis of sex.[16] Many states have statutes that either duplicate Title VII or that go beyond what it prohibits.[17] It would not require a dramatic expansion of employment discrimination law to conclude that nondisclosure

---

11. Adam Liptak, *Price of Broken Vows of Silence*, N.Y. Times, May 26, 2002; see Christopher R. Drahozal & Laura J. Hines, *Secret Settlement Restrictions and Unintended Consequences*, 54 Kan. L. Rev. 1457 (2006); Ryan M. Philip, Note, *Silence At Our Expense: Balancing Safety and Secrecy in Non-Disclosure Agreements*, 33 Seton Hall L. Rev. 845 (2002).

12. Stephen Gillers, *Speak No Evil: Settlement Agreements Conditioned on Noncooperation Are Illegal and Unethical*, 31 Hofstra L. Rev. 2 (2002); Jon Bauer, *Buying Witness Silence: Evidence Suppressing Settlements and Lawyers' Ethics*, 87 Oregon L. Rev. 481 (2008).

13. Hoffman & Lampmann, *supra* note 8; Tippett, *supra* note 8.

14. Cal. Lab. Code 16600.

15. 29 U.S.C. 103.

16. 42 U.S.C. 2000e.

17. See, e.g., Cal. Govt. Code 12940(j).

agreements enable and perpetuate harassment. For that reason, as discussed below, some of the proposed reforms would amend Title VII or state fair employment law to prohibit NDAs or noncooperation agreements in settlements of employment discrimination cases alleging harassment or assault.

The Costs and Benefits of Confidentiality

The long debate in American law about the huge role that settlement agreements play in resolving disputes, as well as the more recent discussions of settlements in particular high-profile types of cases discussed above, have identified a number of benefits and costs of confidentiality provisions in settlement agreements generally and in harassment cases in particular.

The benefits of confidentiality in settlement are significant. First, there is money. To the extent that a company is willing to settle a doubtful case of harassment mainly because of concern about reputation, the confidentiality agreement provides more money to the victim than she would otherwise get.[18] That is an important consideration. Pressing a sexual harassment suit is grim. Hiring a lawyer to take a case requires the recovery to be large enough that the lawyer's share (typically one-third) is sufficient to compensate her time.

Second, there is the victim's desire to protect her privacy, her reputation, and her career. Relatedly, there is the interest of the wrongly accused harasser. Prohibiting NDAs, of course, will not necessarily prevent the parties from voluntarily declining to disclose information. A victim who does not wish to come forward need not. The harder question is the interest of the wrongly accused. While in theory a tort claim for defamation is available to prevent dissemination of false charges of harassment, in practice some individuals may not have the resources to hire a lawyer to bring suit and a company may not wish to sue.

The costs of confidentiality in settlement in harassment cases are considerable, as the Weinstein, Nassar, and other cases illustrate. The costs to the victim are obvious—she knows that the harasser is still working while her life has been upended and her career derailed. She also suffers the psychological costs of being unable to speak out about the experience, which is part of the process of coming to terms with being a survivor of sexual harassment or violence.

---

18. See Hoffman & Lampmann, *supra* note 8 at 182-1899 (exploring the benefits of confidentiality agreements); Scott A. Moss, *Illuminating Secrecy: A New Economic Analysis of Confidential Settlements*, 105 Mich. L. Rev. 867 (2007) (economic analysis of confidentiality provisions estimates that confidentiality increases the bargaining range and therefore increases likelihood of settlement). See also Saul Levmore & Frank Fagan, *Semi-Confidential Settlements in Civil, Criminal and Sexual Assault Cases*, 103 Cornell L. Rev. 311 (2018); Ian Ayres, *Essay, Targeting Repeat Offender NDAs*, 71 Stan. L. Rev. 76 (2018).

The costs to possible future victims are equally obvious—it was the secrecy that enabled Weinstein and Nassar to continue to harass and assault others for twenty years or more. Secrecy makes future victims less able to protect themselves by trying to avoid harassers. Of course, if those who negotiate confidentiality agreements believe that the harassment probably did not occur, they likely see little cost to future victims. But where it appears the harassment or assault did occur, or where too little investigation is done to determine what happened, or where a second, or fifth, or tenth claim of harassment involving the same accused is resolved with a confidential settlement, it is not wise to dismiss the costs to future victims of shielding the harasser and the organization that employs him.

The costs to the organization are less obvious, but scholars have shown that sexual harassment is an "organizational stressor" that increases conflict among work teams, reduces the willingness of team members to work for the benefit of the whole group, and reduces productivity of the victim and many others in her work team.[19] The U.S. Equal Employment Opportunity Commission has estimated that sexual harassment leads to increased job turnover and sick leave, as well as reduced productivity, which the EEOC estimates cost the government $327 million over two years.[20]

Changes in Law

Scholars have shown that in some states, courts have refused to enforce NDAs in settlement agreements in cases in which hushing up the assault seemed likely to risk future assaults.[21] In two cases involving teachers accused of sexually assaulting students, courts in California and Ohio concluded that the NDA was contrary to public policy because of the risk of harm to future students at the schools that employed the teachers after they were fired for sexual misconduct.[22]

---

19. Hoffman & Lampmann, *supra* note 8 at 177, citing Jana L. Raver & Michele J. Gelfand, *Beyond the Individual Victim: Linking Sexual Harassment, Team Processes, and Team Performance*, 48 ACADEMY OF MGT. J. 387, 400 (2005), and Leora F. Eisenstadt & Deanna Gaddes, *Suppressed Anger, Retaliation Doctrine, and Workplace Culture*, 20 U. PENN. J. BUSINESS LAW 147 (2018).

20. Chai R. Feldblum & Victoria A. Lipnic, *Select Task Force on the Study of Harassment in the Workplace* (2016).

21. Hoffman & Lampmann, *supra* note 8 at 187-190.

22. Picton v. Anderson Union High School Dist. [1996] 50 Cal. App. 4th 726 (USA); Bowman v. Parma Bd. of Ed. [Ohio App. 1988] 542 N.E.2d 663 (USA).

In other cases, however, courts have enforced the NDA and rejected the argument that it was contrary to public policy.[23]

The #MeToo moment spurred a number of states to enact laws restricting the enforceability of confidentiality agreements in settling sexual harassment or assault cases. Arizona,[24] California,[25] New Jersey,[26] New York,[27] Tennessee,[28] Vermont,[29] and Washington[30] enacted laws in 2018 or 2019 that restricted enforcement of nondisclosure or noncooperation agreements in harassment or

---

23. See Hoffman & Lampmann, *supra* note 8 at 193-194, citing Sanchez v. County of San Bernardino [2009] 176 Cal. App. 4th 516 (USA) (enforcing NDA in termination settlement agreement involving government official who had an affair with a sheriff's deputy); Giannecchini v. Hospital of St. Raphael [Conn. Super. Ct. 2000] 780 A.2d 1006 (USA) (enforcing NDA in termination settlement agreement involving nurse who made serious errors in administering medication).

24. H.B. 2020, signed into law April 25, 2018, prohibits noncooperation agreements (but not NDAs more broadly) and prohibits the expenditure of public money in exchange for an NDA. By prohibiting expenditure of public money in exchange for NDAs, the law prohibits public agencies from entering into them.

25. S.B. 820, signed into law September 30, 2018, prohibits NDAs in settlement agreements to the extent they would prevent disclosure of sexual harassment. An exception allows contracts to prohibit disclosure of the amount paid in settlement and also allows the victim to request anonymity in any case except where one of the parties is a government agency or a government official.

26. N.J.S.A. 10:5-12.7 (eff. Mar. 18, 2019) prohibits contracts that prospectively waive any rights under New Jersey's Law Against Discrimination. The legislative history states the following about the purpose of the prohibition of waivers: "The bill also provides that a provision in any employment contract or agreement which has the purpose or effect of concealing the details relating to a claim of discrimination, retaliation, or harassment, would be deemed against public policy and unenforceable. The bill applies to non-disclosure agreements; makes the non-disclosure provisions unenforceable against the employer if the employee publicly reveals sufficient details of the claim so that the employer is reasonably identifiable; and requires that every settlement agreement resolving a discrimination, retaliation, or harassment claim by an employee against an employer include a notice that although the parties may have agreed to keep the settlement and underlying facts confidential, such a provision is unenforceable against the employer if the employee publicly reveals sufficient details so that the employer is reasonably identifiable."

27. S.B. 7507-c, signed into law July 11, 2018, prohibits NDAs in settlements in sexual harassment cases, but it contains a huge exception that allows such provisions if the victim requests confidentiality.

28. H.B. 2613, signed into law May 15, 2018, prevents NDAs regarding harassment in any employment agreement. It is unclear whether it prohibits NDAs in settlement agreements.

29. H.B. 707, signed into law on May 28, 2018, prohibits NDAs relating to harassment in employment agreements.

30. S.B. 5996, signed into law March 21, 2018, prohibits employers from requiring new employees to agree to an NDA that prevents disclosing sexual harassment or assault. However, it allows confidentiality provisions in settlement agreements. S.B. 6068, signed into law March 21, 2018, prohibits noncooperation agreements.

assault cases. Legislation was introduced in at least a dozen other states but, as of this writing, it had not passed.[31] And note that the United Kingdom is similarly considering NDA restrictions in harassment cases.[32]

In the Republican-controlled Congress when the #MeToo stories broke, it was highly unlikely that any amendments to the federal civil rights law would pass, and of course none did. Nevertheless, Democrats introduced a bill that would prohibit nondisparagement and nondisclosure agreements, including settlement agreements, that cover workplace harassment.[33]

Although Congress is unlikely to enact legislation barring confidentiality provisions in harassment or assault settlements, some scholars[34] and a few courts have concluded that NDAs in settlements involving government enforcement of protective labor and employment laws are contrary to the statutory policy of providing workers knowledge of their rights.[35]

MeToo broke into the news at the time Congress was considering a tax law that the Republican majority was eager to enact. When the law was enacted, it contained a small provision that purported to address the issue of companies or individual harassers settling harassment claims and deducting from their taxable income the amount paid in settlement, and their attorneys fees incurred in defending against the claim, as a business expense. Critics insisted that this was a

---

31. Elizabeth A. Harris, *Despite #MeToo Glare, Efforts to Ban Secret Settlements Stop Short*, NY Times, June 14, 2019.

32. For example, see Aileen McColgan's chapter, *Silent Women? Non-Disclosure Agreements and the #Me Too Movement in the United Kingdom*, on sexual harassment in the United Kingdom, reporting that the UK Parliament's Women and Equalities Committee has recommended to Parliament that "a variety of legal changes to require that NDAs be clear, that they set out the disclosures which signatories are legally entitled to make, which disclosures should be wider than at present, and to make it an offence for employers and their professional advisers "to propose a confidentiality clause designed or intended to prevent or limit the making of a protected disclosure or disclosure of a criminal offence." Parliament has yet to make these changes.

33. EMPOWER Act, H.R. 6406, S. 2994. It would prohibit nondisparagement and nondisclosure clauses that cover workplace harassment and require public companies to disclose the number of settlements, judgments, and aggregate settlement amounts in connection with workplace harassment.

34. See Tippett, *supra* note 8 at 249, 253 (explaining that although "employees arguably have the right to publicly disclose harassment or discrimination under Title VII of the Civil Rights Act and the National Labor Relations Act, regardless of contrary language in a policy or contract," that right would not apply in the case of settlement agreement).

35. See Hoffman & Lampmann, *supra* note 8 at 195-196 (citing cases). Of particular note is EEOC v. Astra [1st Cir. 1996] 94 F.3d 788 (USA) (holding unenforceable a nondisclosure agreement that barred EEOC from disclosing facts of a case it had settled); Netter v. Barnes [4th Cir. 2018] 908 F.3d 932 (USA) (suggesting a court might find that Title VII protects the ability of a private party to reveal information in violation of an NDA in a settlement agreement with another private party).

federal subsidy for harassers. The law restricts the deductibility of such expenses only if the settlement contains a nondisclosure agreement.[36]

Conclusion

The nondisclosure agreement—once a standard term in an agreement settling employment (and other) litigation—has come to be seen (by some) as a legal tool that enables powerful men to get away with serial sexual predation. The #MeToo movement has been possible in part because of the willingness of women to breach such contracts and to speak out. As two scholars noted, the public "reaction to wrongdoing buried by a contract, and revealed by its breach" has been an important aspect of #MeToo.[37] Indeed, they say, "[p]ublic disclosures of contractual secrets are giving breach a good name."[38] The hostility and even disgust that people expressed to contracts requiring sexual harassment and assault victims to remain silent is evidence that the law may be changing to treat such contracts as contrary to public policy, or to violate protective labor statutes. As a crucial part of #MeToo came to be seen as breaking contractually enforced silence—what *Time* magazine declared in its 2017 Person of the Year story as "The Silence Breakers"[39]—legislatures in many states changed their law to restrict particularly problematic contract terms hushing up settlements of harassment cases.

---

36. 16 U.S.C. 162(q). See generally Ann Bauer, *We Can Do It? How the Tax Cuts and Jobs Act Perpetuates Implicit Gender Bias in the Code*, 43 HARV. J.L. & GENDER 1 (2019), available at https://ssrn.com/abstract=3353324. This is a new subsection to the provision making "ordinary and necessary business expenses" deductible. It prohibits deduction of "[a]ny settlement or payment related to sexual harassment or sexual abuse if such settlement or payment is subject to a nondisclosure agreement" and also "attorney's fees related to such settlement or payment." On account of poor drafting, the law appears to prohibit the deduction of attorney's fees for both the victim and the harasser regardless of the existence of a nondisclosure agreement, which may increase the tax liability for harassment victims as compared to prior law.

37. Hoffman & Lampmann, *supra* note 8 at 167.

38. Hoffman & Lampmann, *supra* note 8 at 167.

39. Stephanie Zacharek et al., *Time Person of the Year 2017: The Silence Breakers*, TIME, Dec. 18, 2017.

CHAPTER 39

Investigating Sexual Harassment

Amy Oppenheimer[1]

Sexual harassment and assault arise in a number of different contexts, including criminal assault by strangers, family members, and domestic partners (which is handled by the police), street harassment (for which there is rarely a legal remedy), harassment in housing (usually toward low-income renters) but, most commonly, at schools and in employment. Employers and educational institutions in the United States are tasked with preventing and responding to sexual harassment and assault and as a result there is both law and practice relating to how employers and educational institutions should investigate harassment. Inadequate institutional response to sexual harassment can lead to increased legal liability and is damaging both to the targets of the harassment and the institution in countless ways. When faced with a complaint of sexual harassment or assault, an institution cannot take appropriate action without determining what actually happened and given that the facts of what happened are often in dispute, a timely, fair and thorough investigation can help determine what occurred before action is taken.

In the United States, workplace discrimination and harassment come under one area of the federal law (Title VII of the 1964 Civil Rights Act) whereas gender discrimination at educational institutions comes under a different law (Title IX of the Education Amendments Act of 1972).

Title IX has developed separately from Title VII. It has only been over the last decade that sexual harassment and assault have come to be viewed as a violation of Title IX—prior to that, most Title IX cases focused on women having equal access to sports. During the Obama administration, robust policies were put into place relating to Title IX. Many of these policies have been rolled back under President Trump. Nevertheless, and although the law differs, the practice relating to how investigations are conducted is similar. For example,

---

1. Law Offices of Amy Oppenheimer, Berkeley, CA.

as is explained later in this chapter, the burden of proof used in workplace investigations is a preponderance of the evidence, which was also the standard articulated for Title IX investigations under the Obama administration. The rules relating to the burden of proof have been changed so that the educational institutions may now determine which burden of proof to use and while some will no doubt institute a higher burden (such as "clear and convincing"), many are staying with the preponderance of the evidence standard.

Certainly, practice regarding investigations at educational institutions is more in flux. But much of the law and practice is similar to and informed by the law and practice related to workplace investigations. Thus, this chapter will cover what is considered typical and appropriate practice in investigating sexual harassment in the workplace in the United States, including the legal basis for doing so, the practical approach taken based on the law, and what changes may be afoot as a result of the #MeToo movement.

The Law and Guidance Relating to Workplace Investigations

In 1986, the United States Supreme Court first defined sexual harassment in its decision *Vinson v. Meritor Savings Bank*.[2] Twelve years later, in 1998, the United States Supreme Court decided two sexual harassment cases, *Faragher* and *Ellerth*,[3] determining that under certain circumstances employers could avoid liability for sexual harassment if they took reasonable steps to prevent and respond to harassment. One upside of these decisions is that employers began to set policies prohibiting harassment and defining harassment more broadly than the law with the goal of addressing harassment before it met the legal threshold of being either severe or pervasive. Shortly after these decisions, the U.S. Equal Employment Opportunity Commission (EEOC), the federal agency charged with enforcing the law prohibiting employment discrimination (including sexual harassment), published guidelines for employers as to what actions to take to prevent and respond to sexual harassment.[4] These guidelines were probably the first official mention of an employer's duty to investigate complaints of

---

2. Meritor Savings Bank v. Vinson [1986] 477 U.S. 57 (USA). The Court held that for "sexual harassment to be actionable, it must be sufficiently severe or pervasive "to alter the conditions of [the victim's] employment and create an abusive working environment." 477 U.S. at 67.

3. Burlington Indus. v. Ellerth [1998] 524 U.S. 742 (USA); and Faragher v. City of Boca Raton [1998] 524 U.S. 775 (USA).

4. *Enforcement Guidance: Vicarious Employer Liability for Unlawful Harassment by Supervisors*, EEOC, June 1999, https://www.eeoc.gov/policy/docs/harassment.html.

sexual harassment, though certainly employers were conducting such investigations prior to 1998.

In the years since *Faragher/Ellerth*, United States appellate courts have commented favorably or unfavorably on specific workplace investigations, finding some of them fair and thorough[5] and others, essentially, a sham.[6] This case law helped form the basis for what was expected of an adequate investigation. In addition, many employment law firms and human resource organizations, such as the Society for Human Resource Management (SHRM), have provided guidance and published handbooks that focus on how to properly conduct an internal investigation of sexual harassment, and a number of books cover this material.[7] In 2012, the Association of Workplace Investigators (AWI), a professional organization for workplace investigators, published *Guiding Principles for Investigators Conducting Impartial Workplace Investigations.*[8]

The most current government guidelines relating to workplace investigations were published in 2017 by the Department of Fair Employment and Housing (DFEH), the state of California's enforcement agency.[9] The guidelines were developed by the DFEH Task Force on the Prevention of Sexual Harassment in the Workplace. Formed in 2016, this Task Force studies the problem of sexual harassment, the effects of ten years of harassment-prevention training in the state of California, and best practices to prevent harassment. The DFEH guidelines include some big-picture information, such as designing and implementing effective harassment-prevention programs, but also zeros in on how to conduct a prompt, thorough, and fair investigation.

Based on the EEOC guidance, DFEH guidance, case law, and various handbooks and articles, there is largely consensus in the United States for what meets the standard for an appropriate investigation of a complaint of workplace harassment. The remainder of this chapter will focus on those elements.

---

5. Mendoza v. Western Medical Center of Santa Ana [2014] 222 Cal. App. 4th 1334 (USA).

6. Cotran v. Rollings Hudig Hall Intl., Inc. [1998] 17 Cal. 4th 93(USA); and Silva v. Lucky Stores, Inc. [1998] 65 Cal. App. 4th 256 (USA).

7. *See* Amy Oppenheimer and Craig Pratt, Investigating Workplace Harassment: How to Be Fair, Thorough, and Legal (2003).

8. https://www.awi.org/page/Guiding_Principles.

9. Workplace Harassment Guide for California Employers (DFEH, 2017), https://www.dfeh.ca.gov/wp-content/uploads/sites/32/2017/06/DFEH-Workplace-Harassment-Guide.pdf.

Why and When to Do an Investigation

An investigation is needed when a complaint gives rise to contested facts that, if true, would violate the law or significant employer policies or expectations, and the employer is uncertain whether the actions complained of occurred (as opposed to conduct that was witnessed by a manager or conduct that was admitted by the respondent). At times, an investigation is not necessary. A complaint about conduct that would not violate the employer's rules does not call for an investigation, and if the conduct is admitted, the investigation can often stop there. At other times, a complaint (such as an anonymous complaint) is so general that it cannot be specifically investigated, and an employer may opt to do a "climate survey"[10] to help determine if there are issues that need to be addressed and where these issues are arising.

For example, if an employee went to human resources (HR) and said that she initiated giving her male co-worker a hug and now regrets it and fears he will expect more hugs from her, the employer need not investigate. Rather, the employer can help the complainant talk to the co-worker or otherwise set a limit with him. On the other hand, if the female employee says she did not initiate the hug and rather the male employee said, "Where is my morning hug?" an investigation would be in order. If the investigator (likely someone from HR) went to the respondent and he admitted saying what was alleged, the investigation could stop there. Armed with the information needed, the employer could then take whatever disciplinary or other measures were in order, consistent with its usual practice. But if the respondent denied the behavior, further investigation would be warranted.

Timeliness

One hallmark of an appropriate harassment investigation is timeliness. Harassment, as opposed to other types of discrimination, involves ongoing behavior that calls for immediate attention. A wage discrimination claim could take six months and, in the end, if discrimination was found, the complainant could be made financially whole. Not so with harassment. Thus the 1999 EEOC guidelines state that the investigation "should be launched immediately." The

---

10. Whereas an investigation takes place in response to a specific complaint, a "climate survey" may be used when an employer has some notice of concerns but does not have a specific complaint. A climate survey can be accomplished different ways and are often done confidentiality. For example, it could be done anonymously, by use of an electronic questionnaire sent out and evaluated by an outside company or it could involve in-person interviews with everyone in a given work group or company.

DFEH guidelines give parameters, including contacting the complainant at a minimum within a day or two of the complaint and striving to finish the investigation in a few weeks, depending on factors such as the availability of witnesses.

The timeliness factor is one reason why employers cannot sit back and wait for an enforcement agency to investigate the claim. Those investigations can take months or even years. In the meantime, the employer has a duty to act, and appropriate action is not possible without first determining what happened.

Timeliness is also a factor in deciding who should do the investigation. Even though external investigators may take more time to hire and schedule, an external investigator may be preferred, especially when the respondent is a high-level employee.

In many situations, the respondent is put on paid administrative leave pending the outcome of the investigation. This occurs when the allegations are relatively serious, in order to protect the complainant from the potential of further harm. It may also serve to protect evidence.

Fairness or Due Process

An essential element of a workplace investigation is that it is fair. Fairness dictates that when there is conflicting information, each viewpoint is considered without bias on the part of the investigator. This includes not allowing psychological biases such as confirmation bias and priming to influence the investigation process or the outcome. It is part of the investigator's job to be aware of implicit biases that could influence how members of certain groups are perceived.

Another term for fairness, in the United States, is "due process." The DFEH guidelines specifically use the term "due process" in relation to providing a fair investigation. Part of due process is making sure that both the complainant and respondent have an opportunity to tell his or her side of the story. Most practitioners agree that the investigation should start with a thorough interview of the complainant. The DFEH guidelines state that although the accused should be given an opportunity to tell his or her side of the story, the investigator does not have to give the accused the allegations prior to the interview or show the accused a written complaint. Rather, it is acceptable practice to reveal allegations during the interview, so long as the accused has an opportunity to fully respond.

However, the question of what is required to provide due process is one that can differ sharply. For example, in some countries, such as Canada, due process (referred to in Canada as "procedural fairness") includes providing information about the complaint to the respondent prior to the first interview.

A recent case in Ireland[11] went so far as to say that a respondent's right to a fair proceeding was violated by his not having the right to cross-examine his accuser—a right that has not been established in the United States in the employment context but does exist in some educational settings. That case also referenced a "right to the presumption of innocence." In the United States that term is used in the criminal context rather than the civil context, and the standard used in a sexual harassment investigation is a preponderance of the evidence (as is discussed below).

In the United States, some employees, including police officers, some unionized employees, and some public employees have greater rights associated with being a respondent in a complaint. This may include a right to pre-interview information regarding the complaint.

The DFEH guidelines set forth the need to interview relevant witnesses and collect relevant documents, but also state that the investigation need not include interviews with every potential witness. This is important as the investigator needs to exercise discretion as to what information might be relevant. Last, and most important, all guidelines and experts agree that the investigator should come to a "reasonable and fair conclusion."

Another aspect of fairness relates to what is being investigated. Workplace investigations focus on a specific complaint regarding something that happened at work or a work event. It may extend to non-work events if the behavior is impacting the workplace. However, the investigation should not be a general investigation of the complainant or the respondent such as looking at conduct outside of work that is not directly relevant to the allegations or attempting to investigate their overall character. Some complainants (and respondents) of harassment have found themselves subjected to general searches of their social media or surveillance. These types of heavy-handed tactics can be considered retaliatory and potentially violate laws and rules against retaliation.

Impartiality

Impartiality is key to a fair investigation. The EEOC refers to an "objective" investigation conducted by an "impartial" party, and DFEH uses the term "impartial" and speaks directly to the investigator addressing whether he or she has biases and how to assess those biases. AWI and the DFEH guidelines also state that the organization should check for any perception of bias on behalf of the chosen investigator. For example, if the investigator has less authority than

---

11. Lyons v. Longford Westmeath Education and Training Board [2017] IEHC 272 (Ireland).

either the complainant or respondent, a fair and unbiased investigation might appear less likely. Certainly, the alleged harasser should not have supervisory authority over the individual who conducts the investigation and should not have direct or indirect control over the investigation.

An internal investigation has some benefits such as lower costs, a faster schedule, and the investigator's knowledge of the company and perhaps history of the parties involved. However, when the investigator works for the employer, this may appear to indicate a lack of impartially. This has led to more employers retaining an outside investigator, especially in high-stakes cases. However, even when an external investigator is used, that individual is being paid by the employer, which has led some employee advocates to question whether that individual can truly be impartial.

The fact is that currently there is no mechanism to bring in an outside investigator, on a timely basis, who is not compensated by the employer. Certainly, the employee cannot and should not pay for the investigation, and government agency investigations are only done in certain cases and, as stated above, would not usually meet the timeliness test. Furthermore, it is the employer's duty to investigate, and a government investigation does not obviate the employer of that obligation. Thus, at this point, it is incumbent on those professionals who conduct investigations to commit to be truly impartial and to act accordingly so that employees and advocates for employees can have confidence in these investigations.

The Investigator's Qualifications

Internal investigations are usually performed by a human resource professional. These individuals, according to the 1999 EEOC guidelines, should be "well-trained in the skills that are required for interviewing witnesses and evaluating credibility." The DFEH guidelines state that the investigator should have knowledge of the laws, policies, investigative techniques, and documentation skills needed; have good communication skills; and have received training from a professional organization, such as SHRM or AWI.

Most outside investigators are attorneys with labor and employment experience. Indeed, under most state's laws, an outside investigator must be either a licensed private investigator (these are usually ex-law enforcement) or an attorney acting as an attorney—that is he or she has an attorney/client relationship with the employer.[12]

---

12. Cal. Bus. & Prof. Code §§ 7512-7573.

Confidentiality

The employer, and thus the investigator, is expected to keep the investigation as confidential as reasonably possible. However, requiring confidentiality of parties and witnesses is more problematic. In the wake of the #MeToo movement, confidentiality has come under scrutiny. While many parties and witnesses would like the complaint and what they have to say about it to remain confidential, the public increasingly feels a right to know about sexual harassment allegations and many complainants want to speak out about their experience.

Furthermore, there have been recent decisions, such as the *Banner* decision from the National Labor Relations Board (NLRB),[13] stating that employees cannot necessarily be asked to keep matters confidential because this could interfere with their rights to unionize, under Section 7 of the National Labor Relations Act. On the other hand, the *Banner* decision also states that there are exceptions when the employer can insist on confidentiality and *Banner* does not apply to management-level employees. Further, the *Banner* decision was recently reversed by the NLRB, throwing this whole area into question.[14]

Thus, confidentiality is an evolving area of the law that employers and investigators need to be aware of and evaluate on a case-by-case basis. While the employer and investigator should keep the complaint and information associated with it as confidential as possible, others may not be expected to do so, and employers must manage that.

The Burden of Proof and Types of Findings

An investigation is going to result in findings. When it comes to workplace investigations there is general agreement in the United States that the burden of proof is a preponderance of the evidence. The AWI guiding principles state that many workplace investigations should follow the preponderance of the evidence standard. The DFEH guidelines specifically say that findings should be based on a preponderance of the evidence standard, which is also referred to as "more likely than not" and that the standard is *not* "clear and convincing" or "beyond a reasonable doubt." This is important, in that employers sometimes mistakenly insist on a higher burden of proof, especially when the allegations are serious. As mentioned earlier, the issue of the applicable burden of proof in

---

13. Banner Health Sys., 362 NLRB No. 137 (2015), aff'd in relevant part, Banner Health Sys. v. NLRB [D.C. Cir. 2017] 851 F.3d 35 (USA).

14. Apogee Retail LLC d/b/a Unique Thrift Store, 368 N.L.R.B. No. 144 (2019).

Title IX investigations has become a hot issue in the United States. And some people mistakenly use the term "guilty until proven innocent" in connection with a non-criminal setting—as happened in the confirmation hearings for United States Supreme Court nominee Brett Kavanaugh. But workplace investigations are not criminal, and the term "guilt" is not really applicable.

There is also a question as to what type of findings the investigator should make. That is, there is a difference between making factual findings (e.g., witnesses saw Harry pat Sally's buttocks) as opposed to whether conduct violated an employer's policy (e.g., Harry violated the sexual harassment policy by patting Sally's buttocks) versus whether conduct violated the law (e.g., Harry subjected Sally to a hostile work environment when he patted her buttocks).

Most external investigators focus on making factual findings and are cautious about making findings about policy violations because they do not work for the employer and do not know how employer policies have been interpreted in the past. However, some external investigators will make such a finding if it is requested. Internal investigators more frequently will make a policy violation determination; however, this varies by employer. Some employers prefer to separate the function of the investigation (which makes factual findings) from the step of determining if there has been a violation of policy. Experts agree that making a legal finding is not a good idea.

Credibility Findings

In order to make factual findings, investigators often have to make credibility findings. This is exemplified in the classic "she said/he said situation." Contrary to what some people believe, independent corroboration is not necessary. In fact, the EEOC guidelines specifically state that an independent witness is not needed. This is a crucial concept, as many employers mistakenly believe that some independent evidence is necessary and therefore will not make a finding when a complaint consists of one employee's word against another's. Often there are no witnesses to harassment, especially sexual harassment. It is important for employers to know that the credibility of one individual's statement can be weighed against the other's in order to come up with a finding.

Thus, investigators need to understand how to assess credibility and to know which factors carry more weight. In some cases, a well-thought-out credibility analysis can be the foundation of an investigation's outcome.

The types of credibility factors that investigators use are the same or similar to those used by judges and juries in determining a witness's credibility. They are also set out in the EEOC and DFEH Guidelines. They include, among other things, the plausibility of the information, whether the party or witness has a motive to lie, whether there is corroboration for what is alleged, and the consistency or inconsistency of the information provided. While an investigator may include demeanor in determining credibility, experts encourage caution due to new empirical evidence that analysis of a witness's demeanor can lead to erroneous findings. Recent studies show that most people are not particularly good at determining truthfulness based on a witness's demeanor.

Documentation and Reports

Investigations should be carefully and objectively documented, including documenting the interviews (which could be via a recording or detailed notes), the findings made, and the steps taken to complete the investigation. While investigators use different methods to document, an investigator's documentation should be consistent throughout an investigation and employers should retain all documentation.

Most investigations include a report that, at a minimum, sets forth what the investigator did to investigate the matter, a summary of the information collected, and findings that include the basis for how the investigator reached his or her conclusions.

Investigations After #MeToo

The #MeToo movement has put a spotlight on investigations, causing organizations and professional investigators to reexamine how they respond to claims of sexual harassment. Due to this heightened awareness, investigators and organizations are under more intense scrutiny, which has led people to question further how we conduct investigations.

One issue under scrutiny is the impartiality of the investigator, which has led to an increased use of external investigators. Investigators also are discussing whether a government agency (such as DFEH) or a non-profit (such as the American Arbitration Association) could assist in the selection of an investigator.

Another way to work toward more impartial investigations is to have an independent review of the findings. For example, the California Legislature has instituted a Workplace Conduct Panel to review and evaluate investigative reports. The panel, modeled on a program currently in use in Los Angeles County, will do fact finding and make recommendations.

The #MeToo movement has also raised concerns regarding who has access to an investigative report. The California State Senate now makes public executive summaries of investigative reports of harassment. Some have been published in major newspapers. Even when the report is not disclosed to the public, increasingly the complainant and respondent are being given more detail about the findings of the investigation.

Another impact of the #MeToo movement is that more complaints are being investigated. Complaints involving allegations from as many as twenty years ago and complaints involving allegations of relatively innocuous behavior may be investigated when they would not have been investigated in the past. Employers are also being proactive by conducting more climate surveys so they can assess the work environment even in the absence of a specific complaint. Climate surveys give employees the opportunity to provide input and raise concerns while maintaining confidentiality and, if done well, can help an employer show that they care about the work environment.

Some of the impacts of #MeToo have had unintended consequences. Employers face practical issues that have not been thoroughly thought out and addressed by the law. One of these is the cost of investigating an increased number of complaints. Conducting a thorough investigation of every complaint, regardless of severity or how long ago the alleged behavior occurred, is an expensive process, not simply in the cost of the investigation itself, but in the time lost and the impact an investigation has on the workplace. The more formalized rights the parties have, the more expensive the process becomes. These unintended consequences tend to have a greater impact on small-business employers and may also create barriers for the targets of harassment—those whom the law is supposed to protect. For example, a woman who is a target of harassment may decide not to complain if it means subjecting herself to cross-examination by the respondent's attorney.

Last, some complaints arise when an employee has no outlet for a complaint other than the sexual harassment complaint process. This can lead to employees bringing harassment claims that stem from miscommunications rather than serious abuses of power. Investigations of this type of complaint can be time-consuming and often counterproductive because they can lack a satisfactory resolution. Alternative methods of addressing these complaints could take pressure off the system, leaving more time and resources to address serious incidents of sexual harassment. Although currently there are few good models for this type of alternative dispute resolution in the workplace, a system like this could actually help organizations prevent more egregious complaints by fostering a respectful environment for solving problems and letting employees know that their complaints—even small complaints—will be taken seriously.

CHAPTER 40

Defamation Law Is Being Weaponized to Destroy the Global #MeToo Movement: Can Free Speech Protections Help Counter the Impact?

David B. Oppenheimer[1]

On March 29, 1960, a full-page ad appeared in the *New York Times* seeking support for the civil rights movement. Signed by sixty-four well-known Americans, including Eleanor Roosevelt,[2] the ad also listed sixteen Southern civil rights leaders, most of them ministers, who endorsed the appeal and the request for financial help to continue their work. It appeared in the name of the "Committee to Defend Martin Luther King and the Struggle for Freedom in the South."

The ad, titled "Heed Their Rising Voices," described a "wave of terror" wrought by police and local governments to suppress the efforts of civil rights leaders in Orangeburg, South Carolina; Montgomery, Alabama; Tallahassee, Florida; Atlanta, Georgia; and several other Southern cities. The third paragraph of the ad read, "In Montgomery, Alabama, after students sang 'My Country, 'Tis of Thee' on the State Capitol steps, their leaders were expelled from school, and truckloads of police armed with shotguns and tear-gas ringed the Alabama State College Campus. When the entire student body protested to state authorities by refusing to re-register, their dining hall was padlocked in an attempt to starve them into submission." Each of these statements except the claim that the dining hall had been padlocked was partly true, yet in some

---

1. Clinical Professor of Law and Director of the Berkeley Center on Comparative Equality and Anti-Discrimination Law, University of California, Berkeley.

2. https://www.archives.gov/exhibits/documented-rights/exhibit/section4/detail/heed-rising-voices-transcript.html.

manner inaccurate. For example, the students sang the Star-Spangled Banner (the U.S. national anthem), not "My Country 'Tis of Thee."

Less than a month after the ad was published, L.B. Sullivan, an elected official in Montgomery charged with supervising the police and fire departments, filed a defamation action against the *New York Times* and four of the Alabama ministers who were listed in the ad.[3] Although Sullivan was not named in the ad, he claimed that the ad referred to him in describing the efforts of the police to suppress the civil rights movement. Within a month, Alabama Governor John Patterson brought an identical suit, and added Rev. Dr. Martin Luther King, Jr. as a defendant. Three other public officials, including the mayor of Montgomery, also brought cases.[4] Each sought $500,000 in damages.

Because the United States (along with the vast majority of the English-speaking world) had adopted the English common law, the plaintiffs would have to prove only that the advertisement described them and hurt their reputations. Beyond that, the burden of proof would be placed squarely on the defendants. Rather than requiring the plaintiffs to prove the statements were false, the defendants—Dr. King, the *New York Times*, and others—had to defend themselves by proving affirmatively that the statements were true.[5]

The case was tried in the state court in Montgomery before a judge famous for his opposition to civil rights. The courtroom was segregated, the jury all-white.[6] The jury found in favor of Sullivan and awarded him the $500,000 he sought.[7] It was the largest libel verdict in Alabama history,[8] roughly equivalent to $4 million today.[9] A few months later, in the case filed and won by the mayor, another $500,000 was awarded.[10]

Without the news coverage that galvanized support for the civil rights movement, it's hard to imagine the movement succeeding. Emotional narratives,

---

3. While the Supreme Court opinion referred to these men simply as "Negroes and Alabama clergymen," their names were Ralph D. Abernathy, Fred L. Shuttlesworth, S. S. Seay, Sr., and J. E. Lowery.

4. ANTHONY LEWIS, MAKE NO LAW: THE SULLIVAN CASE AND THE FIRST AMENDMENT 12-13 (1st ed. 1992).

5. "Where the words published tend to injure a person libeled by them in his reputation, profession, trade or business, or charge him with an indictable offense, or tends to bring the individual into public contempt [they] are libelous per se." White v. Birmingham Post Co., 233 Ala. 547, 172 So. 649 (1937) (USA); Iron Age Pub. Co. v. Crudup, 85 Ala. 519, 5 So. 332 (1889) (USA).

6. ANTHONY LEWIS, MAKE NO LAW, *supra* note 4, 25-27.

7. New York Times Co. v. Sullivan [1964] 376 U.S. 254, at 256.

8. ANTHONY LEWIS, MAKE NO LAW, *supra* note 4, 34-35.

9. See https://www.google.com/search?q=value+of+%24500+000+in+1960&ie=utf-8&oe=utf-8&client=ubuntu&channel=fs (last visited September 30, 2019).

10. ANTHONY LEWIS, MAKE NO LAW, *supra* note 4, 35.

shocking photographs, and horrific TV film helped bring the dehumanizing treatment of Black Americans into homes across the country. Now, suddenly, the ability of the nation's leading newspapers to report on the civil rights movement had been called into question, threatening the movement as a whole. If the verdicts against the *Times* were allowed to stand, none of the major newspapers or television networks in the United States could have risked continuing to cover civil rights. The potential of facing a lawsuit for any error, or alleged error, would have been too great. As a result, the *Sullivan* verdict, and those that followed, represented a grave threat to the success of the civil rights struggle of the 1960s.

The *Sullivan* verdict was appealed to the Supreme Court of Alabama, which affirmed the judgment.[11] But the U.S. Supreme Court agreed to hear the case, and it overturned the Alabama judgment based on the Free Press and Free Speech provisions of the U.S. Constitution. The Supreme Court held that, unless the plaintiff could prove that the defendant acted with "constitutional malice"—that is, with *knowledge* that the statement was false or *reckless disregard* for whether it was true or false[12]—states could not impose liability on those accused of defaming a public official.

In 1974, the Supreme Court further extended protections for defendants accused of defamation. It ruled that defamation liability could not be based merely on the publication of a false and injurious statement. Instead, the court held, the plaintiff must prove at least negligence.[13]

This rule was further extended in 1986 to shift the burden of proving falsehood in all defamation cases, even in cases of defamation between private persons on private matters, at least where the defamation concerned matters of public interest, like civil rights.[14]

These rules provide a vigorous constitutional free speech defense in defamation cases. As such, they are an important bulwark serving to protect against defamation suits brought to silence women reporting sexual harassment and assault. The weaponization of common law defamation claims in the United States has thus been restricted, protecting the #MeToo movement.

I first discovered the power of these constitutional free speech rules when I represented the defendant in a defamation case that was a precursor to the #MeToo movement. In 1984, the Santa Cruz Women Against Rape (SCWAR)

---

11. New York Times Co. v. Sullivan, 144 So. 2d 25 (Ala. 1962), rev'd, 376 U.S. 254 (1964) (USA).

12. New York Times Co. v. Sullivan, 376 U.S. 254 (1964) at 279-280; see also, Curtis Publishing Co. v. Butts, 388 U.S. 130 (1967) (USA).

13. Gertz v. Robert Welch, Inc., 418 U.S. 323 (1974) (USA).

14. Philadelphia Newspapers, Inc. v. Hepps, 475 U.S. 767 (1986) (USA).

received a phone call from a nineteen-year-old woman who reported that she'd been the target of an attempted rape and sexual assault by two co-employees.[15] She reported to SCWAR that she had voluntarily gone out with the two men and drank with them, but after she passed out from intoxication, they partially undressed her and touched her sexually. She believed they stopped because she woke up and stopped them from proceeding further. The SCWAR counselors, based on their training and experience, believed that her account was truthful. They discussed her options, including an offer to accompany her to make a police report, but the survivor decided not to go to the police.

From time-to-time, SCWAR published a newsletter and posted copies throughout the community. These newsletters reported sexual assaults in the region. SCWAR offered to publish the details of the woman's experience in the newsletter, and she accepted. So, in its next issue, the newsletter described what she had reported, and provided the names, descriptions, and contact information of the two men, under the heading "assault/attempted rape." One of the accused men brought a defamation lawsuit against SCWAR.[16] SCWAR retained Leslie Levy, a celebrated feminist lawyer in Oakland, California, to represent them. When it became clear that they case would not be settled, Levy invited me to join her in representing SCWAR at trial.

At trial, we lost. The jury awarded the plaintiff $7,500 in compensatory damages, and $25,000 in punitive damages. But the California Court of Appeal, relying on the constitutional free speech defense, overturned the jury's verdict. The Court of Appeal ruled that the trial court made two mistakes. First, the judge should have required the plaintiff to prove that SCWAR was at least *negligent* as to the truth of its report before it permitted the jury to consider compensatory damages. Second, the Court of Appeal said, the judge should have required the plaintiff to prove that SCWAR believed the statements in the newsletter were false, or that SCWAR was reckless regarding the statements' truth or falsity, before permitting the jury to consider punitive damages.[17]

Absent that constitutional free speech defense, SCWAR and other Women Against Rape groups would have been silenced by the threat of defamation suits—the suits would be frequent and costly, and SCWAR would be unlikely to be victorious. The Court of Appeal clarifying those two issues made all the difference. After that decision, what was at issue was whether SCWAR had been negligent or reckless in publishing the statements in its newsletter. As

---

15. Carney v. Santa Crus Women Against Rape, 221 Cal. App. 3d 1009 (1990) (USA).

16. See, Ann Japenga, *Rape Group Accused of 'Smear' List : Man Sues After Name Appears in Warnings*, L.A. TIMES, Dec. 10, 1987, https://www.latimes.com/archives/la-xpm -1987-12-10-vw-27980-story.html.

17. Carney v. Santa Cruz Women Against Rape, *supra* note 15.

long as it continued to do its research and listen carefully to survivors, it could continue to advocate and protect women in the community.

In countries without a constitutional free speech defense, women reporting sexual harassment and newspapers reporting on those allegations are finding themselves sued for defamation, losing in court, and thus silenced. The following examples, several of which are reported in detail in other chapters of this book, span the globe.

Australia

In Australia, the Academy Award-winning actor Geoffrey Rush recently won $2.9 million (Australian) in a defamation action against the Sydney newspaper *The Daily Telegraph*.[18] The newspaper reported that Rush had inappropriately touched his co-star Eryn Jean Norvill's breasts and back, followed her into a bathroom, and sent her an inappropriate text message. Norvill initially made the allegations in a private workplace complaint, but later agreed to testify for the paper in court. Though Rush denies the accusations, Norvill continues to maintain that her claims are true.[19] Another actress who worked with Rush has also spoken out about him sexually harassing her. She now describes herself as scared that she'll be sued, too.[20]

As Karen O'Connell reports in her chapter on Australia in this book, "Strikingly, then, in Australia, women alleging sexual harassment against men in public positions have been more likely to have cases brought *against them* than to claim unlawful harassment. The damages involved in each area of law also reflect a disturbing devaluing of the harm of sexual harassment.... [D]iscrimination law damages are notoriously low, with all but a small handful of successful federal sexual harassment cases involving payouts of less than $30,000 to women complainants (Australian Human Rights Commission, 2016). Australia has very strict defamation laws that explain why alleged harassers have brought actions rather than those harassed, and these are likely to fundamentally shape the way that #MeToo plays out in both law and in public conversation. There is no universal right to freedom of speech in Australian law, only pockets of limited protection of certain kinds of speech, and there is a very high chance of

---

18. Angus Watson, *Geoffrey Rush wins $1.9m payout on #MeToo defamation case*, CNN, May 23, 2019, https://www.cnn.com/2019/05/23/entertainment/geoffrey-rush-defamation-case-scli-intl/index.html.

19. *Ibid.*

20. Bari Weiss, *The Cost of Telling a #MeToo Story in Australia: Why Yael Stone Is Terrified to Talk About Geoffrey Rush*, N.Y. Times, Dec. 16, 2018, https://www.nytimes.com/2018/12/16/opinion/metoo-defamation-geoffrey-rush-yael-stone.html.

success when alleged harassers bring defamation actions in response to public statements about their inappropriate behavior. In Australian defamation law the publisher's primary defense is that the publication is true, and—crucially—the burden of proving truth lies with the publisher."[21]

A constitutional free speech defense would transform defamation law in Australia. Instead of women who speak out about sexual harassment losing lawsuits to those they have named as their harassers, a constitutional free speech defense would immunize women from defamation liability in most cases. It would shield—and in doing so, empower—the women on the front lines of the #MeToo movement.

Egypt

In Egypt, actor and human rights activist Amal Fathy was prosecuted for criminal defamation. She posted a video to her Facebook page describing the prevalence of sexual harassment in Egypt and criticizing the Egyptian government for its failure to act. In response, the government accused her of "spreading false news." Two days after her post, Egyptian security forces arrested her, her husband (also a well-known human rights activist), and her young son in their home in a pre-dawn raid. While her husband and son were later released, Fathy was put on trial for spreading false news with intent to harm the Egyptian state. She was convicted, sentenced to two years in prison, and fined 10,000 Egyptian pounds (about US$613). An appeals court upheld the verdict and sentence in late December 2018. Following an international outcry, with Amnesty International calling the decision an "outrageous injustice,"[22] Fathy was released from prison, but placed under house arrest.

In 2017, a Thomas Reuters Foundation poll described Cairo as the "most dangerous megacity in the world for women."[23] In a 2013 UN survey, 99 percent of Egyptian women reported that they had experienced some form of

---

21. Karen O'Connell, *The #MeToo Movement in Australia: Silenced by defamation and disbelief, supra* chapter 28.

22. *Egypt: Prison term for human rights defender who spoke out about sexual harassment an outrageous injustice,* AMNESTY INT'L, Dec. 30, 2018, https://www.amnesty.org/en/latest/news/2018/12/egypt-prison-term-for-human-rights-defender-who-spoke-out-about-sexual-harassment-an-outrageous-injustice/.

23. See *Thomson Reuters' Annual Poll: The world's most dangerous megacities for women 2017,* THOMSON REUTERS FOUNDATION, http://poll2017.trust.org/.

sexual harassment.[24] Would Fathy have been convicted if the prosecution were required to prove that her claims—that sexual harassment was prevalent and that the Egyptian government was failing to do something about it—were false?

Criminal defamation laws pose a risk in Turkey as well, as Kadriye Bakirci reports in her chapter,[25] in Italy, as Costanza Hermanin and Giorgia Serughetti report in theirs,[26] and in Russia, as Marianna Muravyeva reports in her chapter on Russia.[27]

France

In France, the #MeToo movement was translated into French by journalist Sandra Muller, who in October 2017 created the hashtag #balancetonporc (expose your pig) as a means of encouraging French women to speak out about sexual harassment. Within hours of creating it, she told her own story, tweeting about former television executive Eric Brion. She exposed Brion by name and position, revealing that he told her at a cocktail party, "You have big breasts. You are my type of woman. I will make you come all night."

Brion admitted making the comments and apologized. In a column in the French newspaper *Le Monde*, he wrote: "Effectively I did make misplaced comments to Sandra Muller during a drunken cocktail party very late one night, but only once. I liked her. I told her so, heavy-handedly. And only once, I must point out. I don't want to exonerate myself from my boorishness at the time. I reiterate my apologies."[28]

Nonetheless, Brion sued Muller for defamation, admitting the truth of her statement, but complaining that it was published out of context, because: (1) it was not made while at work; as implied; (2) he was not her direct supervisor; (3) the statement was only made once, and under the influence of alcohol;, (4) he apologized; (5) she was taking a private conversation and making it

---

24. See Colin Schultz, *In Egypt, 99 Percent of Women Have Been Sexually Harassed*, Smithsonian.com, June 13, 2014, https://www.smithsonianmag.com/smart-news/egypt-99-women-have-been-sexually-harassed-180951726/.

25. Kadriye Bakirci, *Public Campaigns, the Reception of #MeToo and the Law Concerning Sexual Harassment in Turkey, supra* chapter 18.

26. Costanza Hermanin and Giorgia Serughetti, *The #MeToo Movement in Italy: Chronicle of a Death Foretold?, supra* chapter 11.

27. Marianna Muravyeva, *I Am Not Afraid To Tell: The #MeToo Movement in the Russian Federation, supra* chapter 17.

28. Translated and quoted in *Woman Behind French #MeToo Found Guilty of Defaming Media Executive*, The Guardian, Sep. 25, 2019, https://www.theguardian.com/world/2019/sep/25/woman-behind-french-metoo-sandra-muller-guilty-defaming-media-boss.

public; (6) she was unfairly suggesting he was comparable to Harvey Weinstein; (7) it did not constitute harassment; and (8) her tweet interfered with what his lawyer Marie Burguburu described as his "right to flirt."[29]

The court agreed, ordering Muller to delete the tweets and pay Brion €15,000 in damages and €5,500 in legal fees. "She surpassed the acceptable limits of freedom of expression, as her comments descended into a personal attack," the court said in its ruling.[30]

As Marie Mercat-Bruns reports in her chapter on France, the *Brion v. Muller* case has revealed a second French paradox, as many French feminists have denounced the #balancetonporc hashtag, and women who expose their harassers are compared with collaborators who turned over their Jewish neighbors to the police during the occupation. She tells us that even President Emmanuel Macron has warned against a "culture of informers."[31]

It may be difficult to picture a court awarding damages to Muller after a one-off conversation, no matter how distressing or crude it was. But remember that Muller was not the one to bring this conversation to court. In this case, the court is ruling not only that Muller has no legal recourse against Brion for humiliating and harassing her, but also that she must keep her experience a secret. In ruling this way, the court revealed that it was more concerned with Brion's humiliation and reputational harm than it was with Muller as a person, journalist, or activist. Brion's embarrassment at his own actions got him €20,000 and his day in court, but Muller's humiliation, degradation, and interest in protecting other women from a similar experience required that she pay a steep price. She, and in essence all other French women, were directed to keep their mouths shut when men objectify them. Brion's right to "flirt" (a bizarre description of Brion's statement and behavior) was so much more important than Muller's right to be treated with dignity, that she was ordered to pay him damages for truthfully publicizing what he said to her.

United Kingdom

As Aileen McColgan reports in her chapter on the United Kingdom, there, too, the survivor of sexual assault who reports it publicly may find herself

---

29. See *Sandra Muller, France's #MeToo creator, fined for defamation*, BBC NEWS, Sep. 25, 2019, https://www.bbc.com/news/world-europe-49824683; Aurelien Breeden, *French #MeToo Movement's Founder Loses Defamation Case*, N.Y. TIMES, Sep. 25, 2019, https://www.nytimes.com/2019/09/25/world/europe/france-sandra-muller-verdict.html.

30. Breeden, N.Y. TIMES, *supra* note 29.

31. Marie Mercat Bruns, *The #MeToo Movement in France: A Wave of Ambivalence*, *supra* chapter 8.

on the wrong side of a defamation case. And if she does, the burden will be on her to prove the truth of her assault, rather than requiring that her assailant prove its falsehood. McColgan's report on the *Stocker v. Stocker* case is especially speech chilling. There, a woman who complained about her ex-husband having tried to strangle her was found liable for an award of £5,000, with £200,000 costs, despite considerable evidence that he did try to strangle her (including bruises on her neck), and that he had a history of violence.[32]

Israel

In the Israel chapter, by Israeli Supreme Court Justice Daphne Barak-Erez, defamation is again identified as a weapon used to silence women. Justice Barak-Erez explains that in Israel, "the defendant to a defamation suit bears the burden of proving that her statement was truthful and convincing the court that a public interest rationale supported its publication." As an example of how survivors are silenced, she points to the *Uri Daniel* case (in which she filed a dissenting opinion in the Supreme Court). Four women reported being raped by the same man. The police wouldn't investigate because too much time had elapsed, so the women brought a civil action against him; he counter-claimed for defamation. Their claims against him were dismissed as untimely, but his defamation claims against them was permitted to move forward.[33]

China

In Puja Kapai's chapter on Hong Kong, she describes women in Hong Kong and elsewhere in China as fearing that if they report being harassed, they would be "blamed as troublemakers and sued for defamation." She recounts that in China, "Only two cases on the public record have ever been pursued against perpetrators of sexual harassment in the workplace as compared with hundreds of countersuits that have been brought by men accused of sexual harassment against their accusers.[34] This demonstrates clearly the power of the

---

32. Aileen McColgan, *Silent Women? Non-Disclosure Agreements and the #MeToo Movement in the United Kingdom, supra* chapter 12.

33. Daphne Barak-Erez, *Sexual Harassment Law in Israel and the #MeToo Challenge, supra* chapter 19.

34. See also, Sui-Lee Wee and Li Yuan, *They Said #MeToo. Now They Are Being Sued*, Dec. 26, 2019, https://www.nytimes.com/2019/12/26/business/china-sexual-harassment-metoo.html.

law but also, how male perpetrators feel empowered to use the full force of the law to threaten and muzzle their accusers, rare as it is to have them speak out."[35]

Berkeley, California, United States

A final example, from the United States again, and my own home institution of the University of California at Berkeley, illustrates the strength of the United States' free speech protections. Here in California, as in many states, we have given further effect to the free speech defense by passing a law that permits early dismissal of defamation cases when they are being used as "strategic litigation against public participation (SLAPP)."[36]

In 2012, the University of California at Berkeley hired Blake Wentworth as an assistant professor. Nicole Hemenway, an undergraduate, asked him to be her thesis advisor in 2014. By 2016, Hemenway had come forward with a formal complaint to the university. Hemenway complained that Wentworth overshared details about his personal life, told Hemenway that she was "a gorgeous young woman" who would be an "obvious target" for sexual harassment, called her "honey" and implied they could have a sexual relationship after she graduated, and put his hands on her while complimenting her and staring intensely into her eyes. An investigation conducted by the University determined that Wentworth had sexually harassed four students, including Hemenway.

Hemenway made a total of nine statements to two newspapers in 2016 as issues like hers were covered in mainstream media. In response to Hemenway's statements to the press, Wentworth filed a defamation suit.[37] In response to Wentworth's defamation action, Hemenway filed an anti-SLAPP motion. The court determined that Wentworth was unlikely to be able to prove constitutional malice, and that his lawsuit was brought to silence Hemenway, thus unduly interfering with her free speech rights on an important issue of public concern. The court thus dismissed Wentworth's action, entering a judgment in favor of Hemenway.

This and the other cases in this chapter serve to illustrate a number of important points. First, defamation law has been weaponized to silence women who complain about sexual harassment, and others who report misconduct. Whether be they whistle-blowers, investigative reporters, activists seeking

---

35. Puja Kapai, *#MeToo as Catharsis for Hong Kong's Child Sexual Abuse Victims: Confronting Cultures of Silence and Shame and Creating Conditions for Substantive Change, supra* chapter 26.

36. California Code of Civil Procedure Section 425.16.

37. Wentworth v. Hemenway, 2019 WL 2368520 (2019).

support, or #MeToo tweeters, the law should shield them, not silence them. Second, if the law fails to protect the right to speak out about abuses like sexual harassment and violence, those who benefit from unequal power will use that power to sustain inequality, including gender inequality. Third, if we truly value free speech and recognize the importance of speaking truth to power, we can create free speech defenses to defamation laws. We can adopt these protections by interpreting existing free speech rights in international conventions and national constitutions and by legislative code reform. The path is clear; the cost of inaction is intolerable.